http://www.hbschool.com

http://www.hbschool.com

PREPARATION FOR ALGEBRA

MATH

ADVANTAGE

Harcourt Brace & Company

Orlando • Atlanta • Austin • Boston • San Francisco • Chicago • Dallas • New York • Toronto • London

http://www.hbschool.com

ISBN 0-15-305676-2

2 3 4 5 6 7 8 9 10 032 2000 99 98 97

▼▼ Senior Authors ▼▼

Grace M. Burton
Chair, Department of Curricular Studies
Professor, School of Education
University of North Carolina at Wilmington
Wilmington, North Carolina

Evan M. Maletsky
Professor of Mathematics
Montclair State University
Upper Montclair, New Jersey

▼▼ Authors ▼▼

George W. Bright
Professor of Mathematics Education
The University of North Carolina at Greensboro
Greensboro, North Carolina

Sonia M. Helton
Professor of Childhood Education
Coordinator, College of Education
University of South Florida
St. Petersburg, Florida

Loye Y. (Mickey) Hollis
Professor of Mathematics Education
Director of Teacher Education and Undergradu-
  ate Programs
University of Houston
Houston, Texas

Howard C. Johnson
Dean of the Graduate School
Associate Vice Chancellor for Academic Affairs
Professor, Mathematics and Mathematics
  Education
Syracuse University
Syracuse, New York

Joyce C. McLeod
Visiting Professor
Rollins College
Winter Park, Florida

Evelyn M. Neufeld
Professor, College of Education
San Jose State University
San Jose, California

Vicki Newman
Classroom Teacher
McGaugh Elementary School
Los Alamitos Unified School District
Seal Beach, California

Terence H. Perciante
Professor of Mathematics
Wheaton College
Wheaton, Illinois

Karen A. Schultz
Associate Dean and Director of Graduate Studies
  and Research
Research Professor, Mathematics Education
College of Education
Georgia State University
Atlanta, Georgia

Muriel Burger Thatcher
Independent Mathematics Consultant
Mathematical Encounters
Pine Knoll Shores, North Carolina

▼▼▼▼▼▼▼▼▼▼▼▼

Advisors

Anne R. Biggins
Speech-Language Pathologist
Fairfax County Public Schools
Fairfax, Virginia

Carolyn Gambrel
Learning Disabilities Teacher
Fairfax County Public Schools
Fairfax, Virginia

Asa G. Hilliard, III
Fuller E. Callaway Professor of
  Urban Education
Georgia State University
Atlanta, Georgia

Marsha W. Lilly
Secondary Mathematics
  Coordinator
Alief Independent School
  District
Alief, Texas

Clementine Sherman
Director, Division of USI
  Mathematics and Science
Dade County Public Schools
Miami, Florida

Judith Mayne Wallis
Elementary Language Arts/So-
  cial Studies/Gifted Coordinator
Alief Independent School
  District
Houston, Texas

CONTENTS

NUMBER SENSE AND OPERATIONS — CHAPTERS 1–4

Key Skills

Key Skills

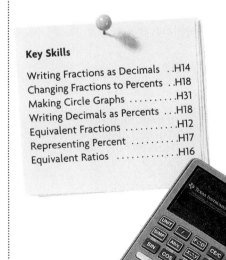

v

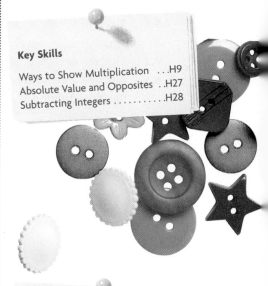

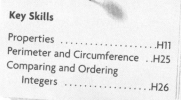

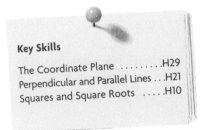

Key Skills

The Coordinate Plane H29
Perpendicular and Parallel Lines ...H21
Squares and Square Roots H10

PATTERNS   CHAPTERS 9–11

Key Skills

Types of Polygons H22
Transformations H23
Types of Solid Figures H23
Identifying Points, Planes, Lines,
    Rays, and Segments H20
Measuring Angles H21

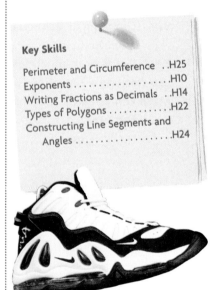

Key Skills

Terminating and Repeating
   Decimals H9
Simplest Form of Fractions H12
Place Value H5
Writing Decimals as Fractions . . .H8
Prime Factorization H3
Divisibility Rules H2
Area and Volume H25
Perimeter and Circumference . . .H25

Key Skills

Perimeter and Circumference . .H25
Exponents H10
Writing Fractions as Decimals . .H14
Types of Polygons H22
Constructing Line Segments and
   Angles H24

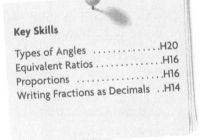

PROPORTIONAL REASONING   CHAPTERS 12–15

Key Skills

Types of Angles H20
Equivalent Ratios H16
Proportions H16
Writing Fractions as Decimals . .H14

Key Skills

Equivalent Ratios H16
Proportions H16
Solving a Proportion H17
Types of Solid Figures H23
Perimeter and Circumference . .H25
Area and Volume H25

Key Skills

Benchmark Fractions and
     Decimals H13
Representing Percent H17
Changing Fractions to Percents . .H18
Writing Percents as Fractions
     and Decimals H19
Percent of a Number H19
Solving a Proportion H17

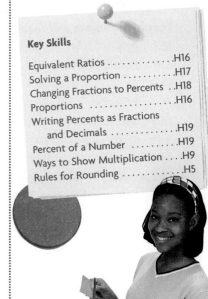

Key Skills

Equivalent Ratios H16
Solving a Proportion H17
Changing Fractions to Percents . .H18
Proportions H16
Writing Percents as Fractions
     and Decimals H19
Percent of a Number H19
Ways to Show Multiplication H9
Rules for Rounding H5

STATISTICS, GRAPHING, AND PROBABILITY — CHAPTERS 16–19

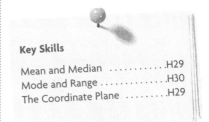

GEOMETRY   CHAPTERS 20–22

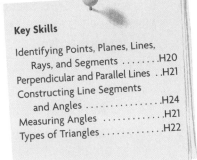

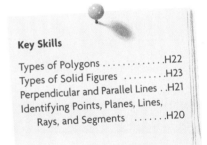

ALGEBRA: RELATIONS AND FUNCTIONS   CHAPTERS 23–25

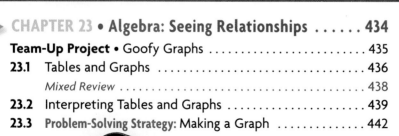

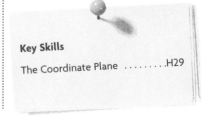

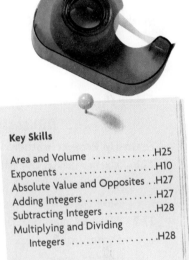

Key Skills

The Coordinate Plane H29
Sample Space H31
Area and Volume H25

Key Skills

Area and Volume H25
Exponents H10
Absolute Value and Opposites . .H27
Adding Integers H27
Subtracting Integers H28
Multiplying and Dividing
   Integers H28

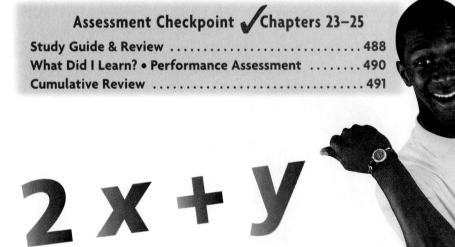

$2x + y$

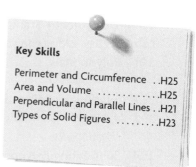

Key Skills

Precision and Greatest Possible Error H26
Perimeter and Circumference ..H25
Area and Volume H25
Types of Solid Figures H23
Types of Polygons H22

Key Skills

Perimeter and Circumference ..H25
Area and Volume H25
Perpendicular and Parallel Lines ..H21
Types of Solid Figures H23

STUDENT HANDBOOK

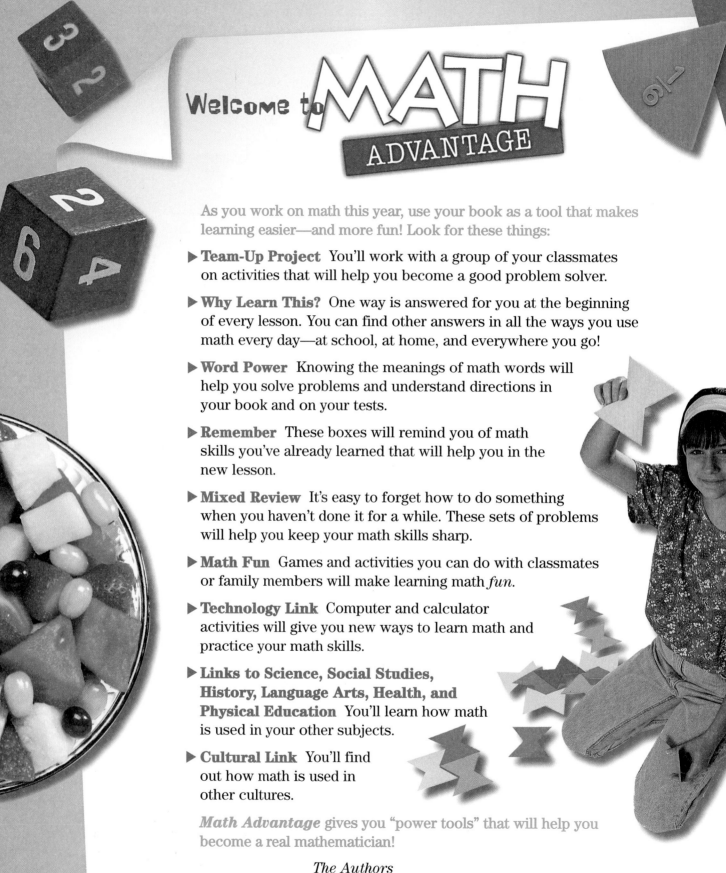

Welcome to MATH ADVANTAGE

As you work on math this year, use your book as a tool that makes learning easier—and more fun! Look for these things:

▶ **Team-Up Project** You'll work with a group of your classmates on activities that will help you become a good problem solver.

▶ **Why Learn This?** One way is answered for you at the beginning of every lesson. You can find other answers in all the ways you use math every day—at school, at home, and everywhere you go!

▶ **Word Power** Knowing the meanings of math words will help you solve problems and understand directions in your book and on your tests.

▶ **Remember** These boxes will remind you of math skills you've already learned that will help you in the new lesson.

▶ **Mixed Review** It's easy to forget how to do something when you haven't done it for a while. These sets of problems will help you keep your math skills sharp.

▶ **Math Fun** Games and activities you can do with classmates or family members will make learning math *fun*.

▶ **Technology Link** Computer and calculator activities will give you new ways to learn math and practice your math skills.

▶ **Links to Science, Social Studies, History, Language Arts, Health, and Physical Education** You'll learn how math is used in your other subjects.

▶ **Cultural Link** You'll find out how math is used in other cultures.

Math Advantage gives you "power tools" that will help you become a real mathematician!

The Authors

FOCUS ON PROBLEM SOLVING

Good problem solvers need to be good thinkers. They also need to know these strategies.

- Draw a Diagram
- Act It Out
- Make a Model
- Use a Formula
- Work Backward
- Find a Pattern
- Guess and Check
- Solve a Simpler Problem
- Make a Table or Graph
- Write an Equation
- Account for All Possibilities

This plan can help you think through a problem.

☑ **Understand** the problem.

Ask yourself...	Then try this.
What is the problem about?	Retell the problem in your own words.
What is the question?	Say the question as a fill-in-the-blank sentence.
What information is given?	List the information given in the problem.

☑ **Plan** how to solve it.

Ask yourself...	Then try this.
What strategies might I use?	List some strategies you can use.
About what will the answer be?	Predict what your answer will be. Make an estimate if it will help.

☑ **Solve** the problem.

Ask yourself...	Then try this.
How can I solve the problem?	Follow your plan and show your solution.
How can I write my answer?	Write your answer in a complete sentence.

☑ **Look Back** and check your answer.

Ask yourself...	Then try this.
How can I tell if my answer is reasonable?	Compare your answer to your estimate. Check your answer by redoing your work. Match your answer to the question.
How else might I have solved the problem?	Try using another strategy to solve the problem.

On the following pages, you can practice being a good problem solver. Each page reviews a different strategy that you can use throughout the year. These pages will help you recognize the kinds of problems that can be solved with each strategy. Think through each problem you work on and ask yourself questions as you **Understand, Plan, Solve, and Look Back.** Then be proud of your success!

Draw a Diagram

Problem Solving
....
• Understand
• Plan
• Solve
• Look Back

Erica has 36 ft of fencing for a dog kennel. Her friend, Sam, suggests that she make the kennel circular instead of rectangular. Which shape will give the greater area?

✓ **UNDERSTAND** You know the total length of fencing. You need to find a rectangle with a perimeter of 36 ft that has the greatest area. You need to find the area of a circle with a circumference of 36 ft. You need to decide which shape will provide Erica's dog with more area.

✓ **PLAN** Draw sketches of all the rectangles with perimeters of 36 ft. Find the area of each rectangle and identify the rectangle with the greatest area.

✓ **SOLVE** List the possible dimensions of rectangles with a perimeter of 36 ft:

Dimensions	Area	Dimensions	Area
1 ft × 17 ft	17 ft^2	6 ft × 12 ft	72 ft^2
2 ft × 16 ft	32 ft^2	7 ft × 11 ft	77 ft^2
3 ft × 15 ft	45 ft^2	8 ft × 10 ft	80 ft^2
4 ft × 14 ft	56 ft^2	9 ft × 9 ft	81 ft^2 ← greatest area
5 ft × 13 ft	65 ft^2		

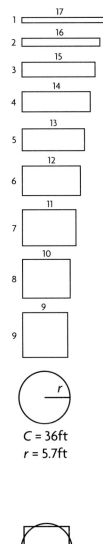

Calculate the area of a circle with a circumference of 36 ft. Use 3.14 for π. Compare the area to 81 ft^2.

$$C = \pi d$$
$$36 = 3.14d$$
$$11.5 = d$$

$$A = \pi r^2$$
$$A = 3.14(5.75)^2 \quad \textit{If } d = 11.5, \text{ then } r = 5.75.$$
$$A = 103.82$$

$C = 36\text{ft}$
$r = 5.7\text{ft}$

$$103.82 \text{ ft}^2 > 81 \text{ ft}^2 \leftarrow \text{ Circle gives the greater area.}$$

✓ **LOOK BACK** Since the diameter of the circle is greater than the width of the 9-ft × 9-ft rectangle, it is reasonable that the area of the circle is greater.

Try These

1. Eight flags are evenly spaced around a circular track. It takes Lisa 15 sec to run from the first flag to the third flag. At this pace how long will it take her to run twice around the track?

2. A right triangle has an area of 30 ft^2. One of the legs is 5 ft long. What is the length of the other leg? What is the perimeter of the triangle?

Act It Out

An art gallery has reserved four display locations for a show. The artist has 4 paintings but is uncertain about how to display them. She plans on trying every possible arrangement before making her decision. If she takes 10 min to set up and view each arrangement, how long will it take her to view all the arrangements?

☑ **UNDERSTAND** You need to determine the total number of display arrangements.

☑ **PLAN** Set up 4 display locations and 4 paintings. Determine the number of possible arrangements for each painting and the amount of time involved in viewing the arrangements.

☑ **SOLVE** The first painting can be placed in location A. The other 3 paintings can be moved into and among the remaining three locations. There are 6 possibilities with the first painting in position A:

ABCD, ABDC, ACBD, ACDB, ADBC, ADCB

The same type of arrangement can be made with each of the other paintings in the first location:

BACD, BADC, BCAD, BCDA, BDAC, BDCA
CABD, CADB, CBAD, CBDA, CDAB, CDBA
DABC, DACB, DBAC, DBCA, DCAB, DCBA

There are a total of 24 possible arrangements.
Time to set up and view: 24×10 min = 240 min or 4 hr

☑ **LOOK BACK** You can also use 4! to find the total number of arrangements. $4! = 4 \times 3 \times 2 \times 1 = 24$

Try These

1. The five starting basketball players came onto the floor as each of their names were called. As they did, each one slapped a high-five to the other team members on the floor. How many high-fives were exchanged?

2. How can you cut the board into 2 equal pieces to cover the hole completely?

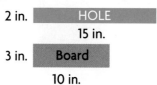

2 in. | HOLE
15 in.

3 in. | Board
10 in.

Make a Model

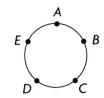

How many triangles can you make by connecting any three of the five points on the circle?

✓ **UNDERSTAND** You need to find the total number of triangles. You know that a triangle such as △ABC has several different names (△ACB, △BCA, △BAC, △CAB, △CBA) and can be listed only once.

✓ **PLAN** Use toothpicks or uncooked spaghetti to make different triangles. Record each triangle.

✓ **SOLVE** Begin with point A. Model and record all possible triangles:

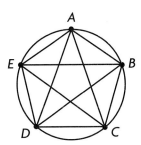

△ABC	△ACD
△ABD	△ACE
△ABE	△ADE

Likewise for Point B:

△BCD
△BCE
△BDE

and for Point C:

△CDE

All other triangles are different names for those listed. So, you can make a total of 10 triangles.

✓ **LOOK BACK** Have all possible triangles been recorded? Check that no triangles have been listed twice.

Try These

1. The figure below shows the faces of a cube. If the six faces of the cube are numbered consecutively, what is the sum of the numbers on all six faces?

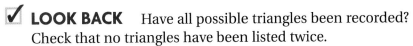

2. Arrange four congruent squares on graph paper. Each square should touch another square along a side. How many *different* arrangements can you make?

Guess and Check

Problem Solving
. . . .
- Understand
- Plan
- Solve
- Look Back

During practice for the math contest, you are asked to add two numbers. By mistake you subtract the numbers and get 10. Another member of your team multiplies the numbers and gets 551. What are the numbers? What is the sum?

✓ **UNDERSTAND**   You know the difference and the product of the two numbers. You need to find the numbers and the sum.

$$\boxed{}\boxed{} \times \boxed{}\boxed{} = 551$$
$$\boxed{}\boxed{} - \boxed{}\boxed{} = 10$$

✓ **PLAN**   Since the numbers have a difference of 10, the unit digits must be the same. The product is 551. What digit gives a product with a 1 in the units' digit when squared? Guess and check the products.

$$\begin{array}{r} \boxed{}\boxed{1} \\ \times \boxed{}\boxed{1} \\ \hline 1 \end{array} \quad \text{or} \quad \begin{array}{r} \boxed{}\boxed{9} \\ \times \boxed{}\boxed{9} \\ \hline 1 \end{array}$$

✓ **SOLVE**   Since $\sqrt{551}$ is about 23.5, look for numbers ending in 1 or 9, less than 23 and greater than 23. Try 21 and 31, or 19 and 29.

$21 \times 31 = 651$
$19 \times 29 = 551 \leftarrow$ The numbers are 19 and 29.

Find the sum: $19 + 29 = 48$

✓ **LOOK BACK**   Check all conditions: The *difference* of 29 and 19 is 10 and the *product* of 29 and 19 is 551.

Try These

1. The difference of 2 numbers is 37. Their sum is 213. What are the numbers?

2. A package of 4 pens cost $3.00 and a package of 7 pens cost $5.00. What is the greatest number of pens that can be purchased for $33.00?

3. Shana threw 5 darts. All of them hit the target. Her score was 43. How is this possible?

Work Backward

Becca is directing the school play on Saturday. The play starts at 8:15 P.M. She wants the cast ready to "call places" 10 minutes before the play starts. The make-up people need 45 min to do their jobs. The costume people need 35 min to get the cast ready before make-up. Becca needs a 10-min meeting with the cast when they arrive at school. What time should the cast arrive at school?

✓ **UNDERSTAND**   You must find the time that the cast needs to arrive at school. You know when the play begins and the time needed for backstage activities.

✓ **PLAN**   Find the sum of the times for each activity. Subtract the sum from the play's starting time.

✓ **SOLVE**   List each backstage activity and time:

Director's Meeting	10 min
Costumes	35 min
Make-up	45 min
Call Places	+ 10 min
	100 min = 1 hr 40 min

Subtract this time from the starting time:

$$8:15 \text{ P.M.}$$
$$-1:40$$
$$6:35 \text{ P.M.}$$

So, the cast should arrive at school at 6:35 P.M.

✓ **LOOK BACK**   Check the original problem using 6:35 P.M. as the starting time.

Add: 10 min for the meeting → 6:45 P.M.
       35 min for costumes   → 7:20 P.M.
       45 min for make-up   → 8:05 P.M.
       10 min for "call places" → 8:15 P.M.

Try These

1. A couple who won the lottery gave their children half of the money. They gave their grandchildren half of the remaining money and kept $5.2 million. How much did the couple win?

2. Ted is 4 years younger than Roger. Roger is 2 years older than Mary. Mary is 14 years old. How old is Ted?

Account for All Possibilities

The Drum Roll Band wants to change its name. The band members will fill in each blank with one of the words below it. How many different names are possible?

The			
	Artistic	Sound	Notes
	Cool	Blues	Trio
	Incredible	Tune	
	Musical		

☑ **UNDERSTAND** You must find all the possible combinations of names that can be made.

☑ **PLAN** Account for all possibilities by making a list.

☑ **SOLVE** List all the possible combinations.

The Artistic Sound Notes
The Artistic Sound Trio
The Artistic Blues Notes
The Artistic Blues Trio
The Artistic Tune Notes
The Artistic Tune Trio

The Incredible Sound Notes
The Incredible Sound Trio
The Incredible Blues Notes
The Incredible Blues Trio
The Incredible Tune Notes
The Incredible Tune Trio

The Cool Sound Notes
The Cool Sound Trio
The Cool Blues Notes
The Cool Blues Trio
The Cool Tune Notes
The Cool Tune Trio

The Musical Sound Notes
The Musical Sound Trio
The Musical Blues Notes
The Musical Blues Trio
The Musical Tune Notes
The Musical Tune Trio

So, there are 24 possible combinations of names.

☑ **LOOK BACK** There are 4 choices for the first word, 3 choices for the second word, and 2 choices for the third word.

$$4 \times 3 \times 2 = 24 \text{ combinations}$$

Try These

1. The four tiles at the right are placed in a box and are drawn out 2 at a time. If a score is the sum of the numbers on the tiles, how many different scores are possible?

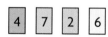

2. In the range of numbers between 1 and 192, how many times will the digits of each number add to 8?

3. How many different ways can you make change for a 50¢ piece without using pennies?

Find a Pattern

Problem Solving
....
• **Understand**
• **Plan**
• **Solve**
• **Look Back**

A PIN, or personal identification number, is a 4-digit code you enter at an automatic teller machine (ATM). A customer was selecting her first PIN. She wanted to remember only the first two numbers and use them to find the last two. She tried 1334, then 2365, then 3396 but they all belonged to other people. How many more numbers fit this pattern?

☑ **UNDERSTAND**   You need to find the pattern used in 1334, 2365, and 3396, and you need to find out how many numbers fit the same pattern.

☑ **PLAN**   Find the pattern. Then use the pattern to find other numbers.

☑ **SOLVE**   Pattern: Multiply the first 2 digits to get the third digit. Add the first 2 digits to get the fourth digit.

1334 → $1 \times 3 = 3$ and $1 + 3 = 4$ 2365 → $2 \times 3 = 6$ and $2 + 3 = 5$
3396 → $3 \times 3 = 9$ and $3 + 3 = 6$

Other 4-digit numbers with the same pattern:

1001	2002	3003	4004	5005	6006	7007	8008	9009
1112	2123	3134	4145	5156	6167	7178	8189	
1223	2244	3265	4286					
1334	2365	3396						
1445	2486							
1556								
1667								
1778								
1889								

There are 30 possible 4-digit numbers that fit this pattern. The customer already tried 3 of these numbers, so there are 27 more number choices.

☑ **LOOK BACK**   Check each number in the list to make sure that the sum and product of the first 2 digits is 9 or less.

Try These

1. Without finding the value of 2^{20}, tell what digit is in ones place.

2. The utility bills for the Music Shop for the past four months were $230, $244, $258, and $272. If the utility bills continue to increase at the same rate, what will be the utility bill this month?

Make a Table or Graph

Problem Solving
- Understand
- Plan
- Solve
- Look Back

Your class is planning to raise $1,200 by sponsoring a car wash.

The Student Council decided to charge $4 for each car and $8 for each minivan. How many cars and minivans would have to be washed to raise $1,200?

✓ **UNDERSTAND** You must determine the number of cars and the number of minivans that need to be washed. You know the charge for each vehicle.

✓ **PLAN** Draw a graph to show all the possible combinations of cars and minivans.

✓ **SOLVE** Let x represent the number of cars and let y represent the number of minivans. Then $4x$ represents the amount in dollars earned from cars and $8y$ represents the amount in dollars earned from minivans. Make sure that the total is always 1,200.

Cars, x	$4x$	Minivans, y	$8y$	Total
300	1,200	0	0	1,200
200	800	50	400	1,200
100	400	100	800	1,200

There are many ways to raise $1,200. The table of values identifies some of the pairs of numbers that satisfy the conditions of the problem. The graph shows all of the number pairs.

✓ **LOOK BACK** Check some of the values shown in the graph.

50 cars and 125 minivans:
$50 \times \$4 + 125 \times \$8 = \$200 + \$1,000 = \$1,200$

150 cars and 75 minivans:
$150 \times \$4 + 75 \times \$8 = \$600 + \$600 = \$1,200$

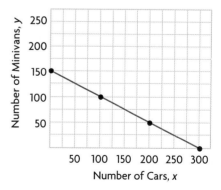

Try These

1. In how many different ways can three people divide 10 cookies so that each person receives at least one cookie?

2. Two cars are being driven around a 1-mi track. One car makes a lap every 80 sec, the other, every 60 sec. At these rates, how long will it take the faster car to gain a lap on the slower car?

Solve a Simpler Problem

Problem Solving
- **Understand**
- **Plan**
- **Solve**
- **Look Back**

LaToya and her family plan to fence a square lot using 44 posts. They plan to place the posts 5 ft apart. What is the area of the lot?

✓ **UNDERSTAND**   You know that there are 44 posts to form the square. You also know the distance between each post. You need to find the area of the lot.

✓ **PLAN**   Solve simpler problems by making smaller squares with fewer posts. Calculate the areas of each square. Collect and record the data in a table.

✓ **SOLVE**   Sketch each square. Find the number of posts needed for each. Calculate the areas. Analyze the number patterns in the table.

The number of posts increases by 4 from square to square. The area increases by squares of multiples of 5.

Size	Number of Posts	Area
	4	25 ft^2
	8	100 ft^2
	12	225 ft^2
	16	400 ft^2
	20	625 ft^2

$$4 \rightarrow 5^2 = 25 \qquad 16 \rightarrow 20^2 = 400$$
$$8 \rightarrow 10^2 = 100 \qquad 20 \rightarrow 25^2 = 625$$
$$12 \rightarrow 15^2 = 225$$

Continuing the pattern:

$$24 \rightarrow 1,225 \text{ ft}^2$$
$$28 \rightarrow 1,600 \text{ ft}^2$$
$$32 \rightarrow 2,025 \text{ ft}^2$$
$$36 \rightarrow 2,500 \text{ ft}^2$$
$$40 \rightarrow 3,025 \text{ ft}^2$$
$$44 \rightarrow 3,600 \text{ ft}^2 \qquad \text{So, the area of the lot is 3600 ft}^2.$$

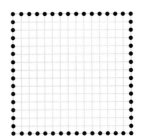

✓ **LOOK BACK**   A square lot with an area of 3,600 ft^2 would have sides 60 ft long. There are 44 posts.

Try These

1. What is the ones digit of the product when one hundred 9s are multiplied? when one hundred 2s are multiplied?

2. Find the next three numbers in this pattern.

   4, 12, 36, 108, . . .

Use a Formula

Problem Solving

• Understand

• Plan

• Solve

• Look Back

The maximum safe heart rate for a person exercising can be found using the formula

$$m = 220 - a$$

where m = maximum heart beats per minute and a = person's age. What is the maximum safe heart rate for a 14 year old?

☑ **UNDERSTAND**   You are asked to find maximum safe heart rate for a 14 year old. You know the formula for finding the maximum heart rate.

☑ **PLAN**   Use the formula $m = 220 - a$ to find the maximum exercise heart rate.

☑ **SOLVE**   Write the formula. Replace a with 14 since the age is 14.

$$m = 220 - a \leftarrow a = 14$$
$$m = 220 - 14$$
$$m = 206$$

So, the maximum exercise heart rate for a 14 year old is 206 beats per minute.

☑ **LOOK BACK**   You can check your answer by replacing m with 206 and a with 14 in the formula.

$$m = 220 - a$$
$$206 = 220 - 14$$
$$206 = 206 \checkmark$$

Try These

1. The isosceles triangle is cut in half and reassembled as the rectangle shown. What is the perimeter of the rectangle?

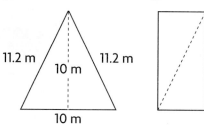

11.2 m   11.2 m
10 m
10 m

2. The length of a rectangular parking lot is 6 times the width. The width is 20 ft. What is the area of the parking lot?

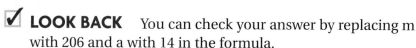

20 ft

Write an Equation

Problem Solving
....
- **Understand**
- **Plan**
- **Solve**
- **Look Back**

The SouthAir Commuter flight has seats for 111 people. On one flight to Phoenix, there was 1 empty seat for every 2 passengers. How many passengers were on the flight?

✓ **UNDERSTAND** You know the total number of seats on the airplane. You also know that for every 2 passengers, there was 1 empty seat. You need to find the number of passengers on board.

✓ **PLAN** Set up a ratio of the number of empty seats to total seats. Then subtract.

✓ **SOLVE** For every 3 seats, 1 is empty. Use a proportion to compare like ratios. Let x = the total number of empty seats.

$$\frac{\text{empty seats}}{\text{total seats}} = \frac{\text{empty seats}}{\text{total seats}}$$

$$\frac{1 \text{ empty}}{3 \text{ seats}} = \frac{x}{111 \text{ seats}}$$

Occupied Seat	Empty Seat	Occupied Seat

Solve the proportion by finding the cross products.

$$\frac{1}{3} = \frac{x}{111}$$

$$3 \cdot x = 111 \cdot 1$$

$$\frac{3x}{3} = \frac{111}{3}$$

$$x = 37 \leftarrow \text{37 empty seats}$$

So, the number of passengers on board is $111 - 37 = 74$.

✓ **LOOK BACK** If 1 out of 3 seats is empty, that means that 2 are occupied. You could use this proportion to find the number of passengers, y.

$$\frac{\text{occupied seats}}{\text{total seats}} = \frac{y}{\text{total seats}}$$

$$\frac{2}{3} = \frac{y}{111}$$

$$3y = 222$$

$$y = 74 \checkmark$$

Try These

1. The ratio of the number of students who bought lunch today to the number of students who bought lunch yesterday is 5 to 6. Today 250 students bought lunch. How many students bought lunch yesterday?

2. A stack of 3 quarters is 5 mm high. What is the value of a stack of quarters 25 mm high?

Use the strategy of your choice to solve.

1. A rectangular tile has a width of 2 in. and a length of 3 in. What is the least number of tiles needed to completely cover a square region 3 ft on a side?

2. An example of five consecutive numbers is 61, 62, 63, 64, 65. The sum of five consecutive numbers is 750. What is the greatest of these five numbers?

3. A solid pyramid-like stack is made from a number of identical blocks. A top and side view of the stack are shown below. How many blocks were used for the entire stack?

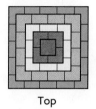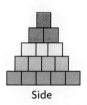

Top   Side

4. These five tins contain a total of 225 pieces of candy. How many pieces of candy are in each tin if each tin contains ten more pieces than the previous one?

5. Mark enlarged a 5-in. × 7-in. photo so that the short side was 12.5 in. long. If the ratio of the length to the width stayed the same, how long was the longer side of the enlargement?

6. Rita can wash a car in 12 min. It takes Sam 9 min to wash a car. They begin at the same time. How much time will they spend washing cars if they finish at the same time?

7. A cardboard strip is 1 in. wide and 48 in. long. It is cut with scissors at 1-in. intervals, making 48 square inches. If each cut takes 1 sec, how long will it take to make all the cuts?

8. The numbers 123, 235, and 347 use the first two digits to find the third. What number follows the same pattern and has 9 as the digit in the ones place?

9. Wendy is going to put a fence around her circular garden. The diameter of the garden is 12 ft. Use the formula $C = \pi d$ and 3.14 for π to find the length of fence she will need.

10. Elmer has 12 pieces of wooden fencing each 3 ft long. What are the dimensions of the greatest rectangular area he can enclose using all 12 pieces? What is the area?

11. If you multiply my age by 2, add 16, then divide by 3, the result is 20. How old am I?

12. A building has 6 doors. Find the number of ways a person can enter the building by one door and leave by another.

CHAPTER 1

REAL NUMBERS

LOOK AHEAD

In this chapter you will solve problems that involve

- classifying numbers
- using exponents and scientific notation

- finding products and quotients of powers
- finding squares and square roots and modeling cubes and cube roots

Launch Time

Astronomers use scientific notation to describe the distances of planets from our sun. They also use it to describe the distance to stars and galaxies.

Plan
- Work with a partner. Convert the data on large distances using scientific notation.

Act
- Convert the distances to scientific notation.
- Calculate the differences in distances between adjacent planets and stars.
- Make a chart of your results.

Share
- Share and compare your data with the class.

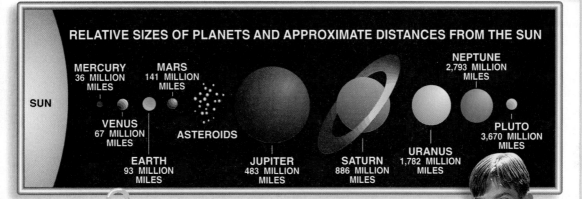

RELATIVE SIZES OF PLANETS AND APPROXIMATE DISTANCES FROM THE SUN

SUN

MERCURY
36 MILLION
MILES

VENUS
67 MILLION
MILES

EARTH
93 MILLION
MILES

MARS
141 MILLION
MILES

ASTEROIDS

JUPITER
483 MILLION
MILES

SATURN
886 MILLION
MILES

URANUS
1,782 MILLION
MILES

NEPTUNE
2,793 MILLION
MILES

PLUTO
3,670 MILLION
MILES

DID YOU

☑ Convert the numbers to scientific notation?

☑ Calculate the differences in distances?

☑ Make a chart of your results?

ALGEBRA CONNECTION

Sets of Numbers

REMEMBER:

An even number is divisible by 2. An odd number is not divisible by 2. A prime number is a whole number greater than 1 that has exactly two factors, itself and 1. A composite number is a whole number that has more than two whole-number factors.
See page H2.

When was the last time you chose an appropriate kitchen utensil to complete a task, or an appropriate tool to complete a repair? Just as we use a variety of utensils and tools in daily tasks, we also use many sets of numbers.

- Identify each set of numbers.

$\{0, 1, 2, 3, 4, 5, \ldots\}$ $\{1, 2, 3, 4, 5, 6, \ldots\}$

$\{2, 4, 6, 8, 10, 12, \ldots\}$ $\{1, 3, 5, 7, 9, 11, \ldots\}$

$\{2, 3, 5, 7, 11, 13, \ldots\}$ $\{4, 6, 8, 9, 10, 12, \ldots\}$

You can use Venn diagrams to describe the relationships among sets of numbers.

EXAMPLE 1   Start with the whole numbers 25 or less. Use a Venn diagram to show which are even and which are composite.

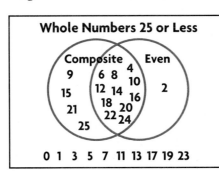

Use a rectangle for the set of whole numbers 25 or less.

Use overlapping circles for the sets of even numbers and composite numbers 25 or less.

Then sort the numbers into the diagram.

So, the even numbers are 2, 4, 6, 8, 10, 12, 14, 16, 18, 20, 22, and 24. The composite numbers are 4, 6, 8, 9, 10, 12, 14, 15, 16, 18, 20, 21, 22, 24, and 25.

- Which whole numbers 25 or less are both even and composite? neither even nor composite?

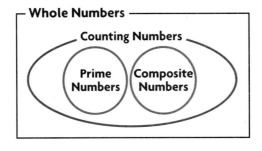

Many sets of numbers are parts of other sets of numbers. This Venn diagram shows that all prime numbers and all composite numbers are counting numbers and that all counting numbers are whole numbers.

GUIDED PRACTICE

For Exercises 1–3, use the first Venn diagram below.

1. Which counting numbers 15 or less are even? Which are prime? Which are odd?

2. Which counting numbers 15 or less are both even and prime? both prime and odd?

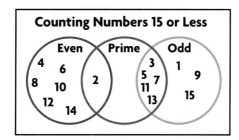

3. Are any counting numbers 15 or less both even and odd? Explain.

4. Copy and complete the Venn diagram shown at the right. Sort the whole numbers 20 or less into the diagram. Which numbers are both composite and odd? neither composite nor odd?

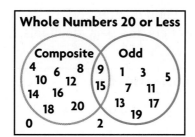

5. In a Venn diagram, what does it mean when a number is in the area where two circles overlap? when it is outside both circles?

Rational Numbers

You have used other sets of numbers, including integers and rational numbers. An **integer** is one of the set of whole numbers and their opposites. Examples of integers are shown on the number line.

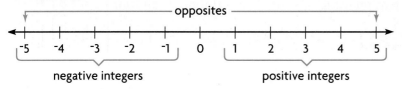

• What is the opposite of 7? of ⁻13?

Integers belong to the set of rational numbers. A **rational number** is any number that can be expressed as a ratio in the fraction form $\frac{a}{b}$, where a and b are integers and $b \neq 0$.

These are examples of rational numbers:

973   0 $\frac{1}{5}$ $\frac{-4}{7}$ ⁻8   5.8   ⁻0.63

Computer Link

Most large prime numbers are discovered to be prime by using multimillion-dollar supercomputers. But the largest known prime number ($2^{1,398,269} - 1$), which has 420,921 digits, was recently discovered by using a group of PCs (personal computers). If a PC could print 1,500 digits per page, how many pages would it take to print this number of digits?

REMEMBER:

A ratio is a comparison of two numbers. There are three ways to write the ratio of triangles to squares. **See page H16.**

3 to 4   3:4 $\frac{3}{4}$

17

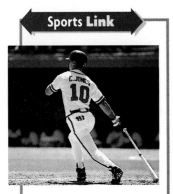
In baseball a player's batting average (hits per times at bat) is written as a decimal to the thousandths place. Suppose a player's batting average is 0.250, which is read as "250." Write that average in fraction form, and then write it in another ratio form.

You can write a rational number in fraction form.

EXAMPLE 2 Are each of the following numbers rational numbers? 6, ⁻8, and 0.4

Think: Try to write each number in fraction form.

Write each as a fraction where a and b are integers and b ≠ 0.

$$6 = \frac{6}{1} \qquad ^{-}8 = \frac{^{-}8}{1} \qquad 0.4 = \frac{2}{5}$$

Each can be written in fraction form using integers. So, 6, ⁻8, and 0.4 are rational numbers.

• Are whole numbers, integers, and decimals rational numbers? Explain.

The Venn diagram below shows how counting numbers, whole numbers, integers, decimals, fractions, and rational numbers are related.

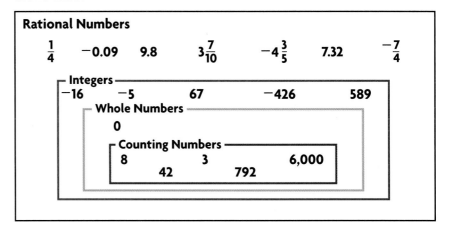

You can classify a number as a counting number, a whole number, an integer, a rational number, or all four.

EXAMPLE 3 Classify the following numbers as counting numbers, whole numbers, integers, or rational numbers: 4, 0, ⁻8, $5\frac{3}{4}$, 9.5. Make a table to show your results.

	Counting Number	Whole Number	Integer	Rational Number
4	✓	✓	✓	✓
0		✓	✓	✓
⁻8			✓	✓
$5\frac{3}{4}$				✓
9.5				✓

INDEPENDENT PRACTICE

Copy and complete the Venn diagram by placing each number in the correct set.

1.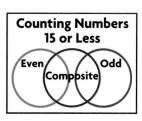

2.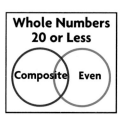

3.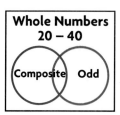

For Exercises 4–5, use the Venn diagram you completed in Exercise 3.

4. Which whole numbers 20–40 are both odd and composite?

5. Which whole numbers 20–40 are not both odd and composite?

Classify each number as a counting number, whole number, integer, or rational number. Make a table to show your work.

6. $^-10$, 5.5, 139, $\frac{^-1}{2}$

7. $^-0.25$, $\frac{3}{4}$, 900, 0

8. 1.9, $^-45$, 67, $2\frac{3}{4}$

Problem-Solving Applications

For Problems 9–12, write *true* or *false* for each statement. Give an example to explain your answer.

9. Every whole number is a rational number.

10. Some rational numbers are negative numbers.

11. Every integer is a counting number.

12. All whole numbers are counting numbers.

13. **✏️ WRITE ABOUT IT** Explain how you can determine if a number is a rational number.

Mixed Review

Find the product.

14. 18×18

15. $4 \times 4 \times 4$

16. $7 \times 7 \times 7$

17. $3 \times 3 \times 3 \times 3$

Evaluate for $n = 3$.

18. $n + 15$

19. $42 - n$

20. $63 \div n$

21. $14 \times n$

22. $n - 40$

23. **TAXES** Ana has saved $82.00 for the purchase of a CD player. If the CD player costs $79.00 and the sales tax rate is $0.06 per dollar, has she saved enough money? Explain.

24. **COLLECTING** Vic has 4,402 stamps in his stamp collection. He wants to give each grandchild an equal number of stamps. He has 31 grandchildren. How many will each receive?

ALGEBRA CONNECTION

Exponents and Scientific Notation

REMEMBER:

In the expression 7^4, 7 is the base and 4 is the exponent.

$7^4 \leftarrow$ exponent
$^{\llcorner}$ base

The zero power of any number (except zero) equals 1. $8^0 = 1$

The first power of any number equals that number. $8^1 = 8$

See page H10.

Did you ever take a shortcut in walking from one place to another?

You can also use shortcuts in mathematics. When you use an exponent, you are writing a multiplication problem in a shortened form.

Exponent Form	Read	Meaning
3^2	the second power of 3, or 3 squared	3×3, or 9
$(8.1)^3$	the third power of 8.1, or 8.1 cubed	$8.1 \times 8.1 \times 8.1$, or 531.441
5^4	the fourth power of 5	$5 \times 5 \times 5 \times 5$, or 625

Talk About It

• How do you read 6^4?

• How do you write $9 \times 9 \times 9 \times 9$ in exponent form?

• What multiplication problem does 2^5 represent?

You can find the value of a power by using pencil and paper or a calculator.

EXAMPLE 1 Ali has a job that pays $2 on the first day of work. On each day after the first, he receives double the preceding day's wages. How much will he receive on the seventh day?

Think: Find the value of 2^7.

Method 1: Use pencil and paper.

$2 \times 2 \times 2 \times 2 \times 2 \times 2 \times 2 = 128$ *Multiply the factors.*

Method 2: Use a scientific calculator that has an x^y key.

2 [x^y] 7 [=] [128.]   *Use this key sequence.*

So, Ali will receive $128 on the seventh day.

• How do you find the value of $(\frac{1}{2})^4$?

You can use exponents to write prime factorizations.

EXAMPLE 2 Find the prime factorization of 200, and write it using exponents.

Think: Divide by the smallest possible prime factors until the quotient is 1.

$2\overline{)200}$ *200 ÷ 2 = 100*

$2\overline{)100}$ *100 ÷ 2 = 50*

$2\overline{)50}$ *50 ÷ 2 = 25*

$5\overline{)25}$ *25 ÷ 5 = 5*

$5\overline{)5}$ *5 ÷ 5 = 1*

1

$2 \times 2 \times 2 \times 5 \times 5$ *Write the product of the prime factors you divided by. This is the prime factorization.*

$2^3 \times 5^2$ *Write the prime factorization, using exponents.*

> **REMEMBER:**
> A composite number can be expressed as the product of prime numbers. This product is called the prime factorization of the number.
>
>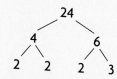
>
> The prime factorization of 24 is $2 \times 2 \times 2 \times 3$, or $2^3 \times 3$. **See page H3.**

GUIDED PRACTICE

Tell how you would read the number.

1. 2^8 **2.** $(6.3)^5$ **3.** $(\frac{1}{3})^4$

Write in exponent form.

4. $4 \times 4 \times 4$ **5.** 3.2×3.2 **6.** $7 \times 7 \times 7 \times 7 \times 7$

Find the value.

7. 5^2 **8.** 8^1 **9.** 4^0 **10.** $(\frac{1}{4})^3$ **11.** $(1.5)^2$

Write the prime factorization, using exponents.

12. 81   **13.** 125   **14.** 64   **15.** 100   **16.** 124

Scientific Notation

On average, the Earth is 92,900,000 mi from the sun. It is convenient to write large numbers like this in scientific notation. **Scientific notation** expresses a number as the product of a number between 1 and 10, and a power of 10.

standard form   scientific notation

$92,900,000 = 9.29 \times 10^7$ ← power of 10

REMEMBER:
....
When dividing decimal numbers by powers of 10, move the decimal point one place to the left for each power of 10. **See page H7.**

$387.4 \div 10 = 38.74$

$387.4 \div 100 = 3.874$

$387.4 \div 1,000 = 0.3874$

To change a large number from standard form to scientific notation, divide.

EXAMPLE 3 The area of the Earth's surface is estimated to be 296,938,800 sq mi. Write this number in scientific notation.

Think: Divide to get a number between 1 and 10.

296,938,800

To divide, move the decimal point 8 places to the left.

$296,938,800 = 2.969388 \times 10^8$

Use the exponent 8.

So, the area is about 2.969388×10^8 sq mi.

- What number of places was the decimal point moved to get a number between 1 and 10? How does this number compare with the exponent of the power of 10?

- What shortcut can you use to divide by a power of 10 when changing from standard form to scientific notation?

To change a large number from scientific notation to standard form, multiply.

EXAMPLE 4 The maximum distance from Pluto to the sun is about 4.5514×10^9 mi. Write this number in standard form.

$4.5514 \times 10^9 = 4.551400000 \times 10^9$

To multiply, move the decimal point 9 places to the right.

$= 4,551,400,000$

So, the maximum distance of Pluto to the sun is about 4,551,400,000 mi.

- What shortcut can you use to multiply by a power of 10 when changing from scientific notation to standard form?

- The estimated weight of the Earth's atmosphere is about 5.7×10^{15} tons. What would you do to write the number in standard form?

History Link

In 1978 a satellite, or moon, of Pluto was discovered. The satellite, named Charon, is 750 mi in diameter and is 1.2×10^4 mi from Pluto. Express the distance from Charon to Pluto in standard form.

INDEPENDENT PRACTICE

Write in exponent form.

1. 6×6

2. $8 \times 8 \times 8 \times 8 \times 8$

3. $7 \times 7 \times 7$

4. $10 \times 10 \times 10 \times 10 \times 10 \times 10$

5. 4

6. $5.4 \times 5.4 \times 5.4$

7. 2×2

8. $12 \times 12 \times 12 \times 12$

9. $6 \times 6 \times 6 \times 6 \times 6$

10. $\frac{3}{4} \times \frac{3}{4} \times \frac{3}{4} \times \frac{3}{4} \times \frac{3}{4} \times \frac{3}{4}$

Find the value.

11. 8^1 | **12.** 3^6 | **13.** 11^0 | **14.** 12^2
15. 6^3 | **16.** 9^4 | **17.** 2^5 | **18.** 8^2
19. 7^3 | **20.** 4^6 | **21.** 5^4 | **22.** 9^3
23. $(1.4)^2$ | **24.** $(2.4)^2$ | **25.** $(\frac{1}{2})^3$ | **26.** $(\frac{2}{3})^2$

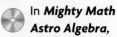

In *Mighty Math Astro Algebra,* take what you know about using exponents into the *Cargo Bay* and complete the mission *The Strange Cloud of Machine Parts III.*

Write the prime factorization, using exponents.

27. 25 | **28.** 36 | **29.** 54 | **30.** 16
31. 24 | **32.** 98 | **33.** 68 | **34.** 72
35. 75 | **36.** 144 | **37.** 44 | **38.** 48
39. 325 | **40.** 99 | **41.** 120 | **42.** 288

Write in scientific notation.

43. 678 | **44.** 89,765 | **45.** 987,000,000
46. 44,783,400 | **47.** 123,400 | **48.** 3,457,070,000
49. 108,980,000,000 | **50.** 1,124,100,000,000
51. 23,478,090,000,000,000 | **52.** 5,279,000,000,000,000

Write in standard form.

53. 1.092×10^4 | **54.** 5.656×10^6 | **55.** 9.2×10^7 | **56.** 8.09123×10^5
57. 6×10^8 | **58.** 8.89×10^{10} | **59.** 1.278555×10^{13} | **60.** 2.34×10^{10}
61. 4.892×10^{12} | **62.** 2.2569×10^9 | **63.** 8.9785×10^9 | **64.** 5.5545×10^{14}

Problem-Solving Applications

65. The formula for the volume of a cube is $V = e^3$, where V is the volume and e is the length of each edge. Find the volume of a cube when the length of each edge is 12 cm. Write the answer in cubic centimeters.

66. Joey saved 2 nickels today. If he doubles the number of nickels he saves each day, how many days, including today, will it take him to save more than 500 nickels?

67. In January 1997, demographers estimated the population of the world to be 5,818,429,000 people. Write this number in scientific notation.

68. Every day in the United States, chickens lay an average of 2.02×10^8 eggs. Write this number in standard form.

69. ▬▶ **WRITE ABOUT IT** You may have noticed that $2^4 = 4^2$. Does $2^3 = 3^2$? Explain.

ALGEBRA CONNECTION
Products and Quotients of Powers

In the study of algebra, you will find the products and quotients of two powers with the same base.

You can find the product of powers by writing all the factors of each number. Look for a pattern in these products:

$$8^4 \cdot 8^2 = 8 \cdot 8 \cdot 8 \cdot 8 \cdot (8 \cdot 8) \qquad 3^2 \cdot 3^3 = 3 \cdot 3 \cdot (3 \cdot 3 \cdot 3)$$
$$8^4 \cdot 8^2 = 8^6 \qquad\qquad\qquad\qquad 3^2 \cdot 3^3 = 3^5$$

$$5^3 \cdot 5^4 = 5 \cdot 5 \cdot 5 \cdot (5 \cdot 5 \cdot 5 \cdot 5) \qquad 7^2 \cdot 7^2 = 7 \cdot 7 \cdot (7 \cdot 7)$$
$$5^3 \cdot 5^4 = 5^7 \qquad\qquad\qquad\qquad 7^2 \cdot 7^2 = 7^4$$

- In each of the examples above, how is the exponent of the product related to the exponents of the factors?

- What rule can you write for finding the exponent of the product of any two powers with the same base?

You can find the product of any two powers with the same base.

EXAMPLE 1   Write the product as one power. $2^3 \cdot 2^4$

$$2^3 \cdot 2^4 = 2^{3\,+\,4} = 2^7 \qquad \textit{Add the exponents.}$$

You can find the quotient of two powers with the same base.

EXAMPLE 2   Write the quotient as one power. $4^5 \div 4^2$

$$4^5 \div 4^2 = \frac{4^5}{4^2} = \frac{\overset{1}{\cancel{4}} \cdot \overset{1}{\cancel{4}} \cdot 4 \cdot 4 \cdot 4}{\underset{1}{\cancel{4}} \cdot \underset{1}{\cancel{4}}} = 4^3$$

Write the division as a fraction, and write all the factors of each number. Divide by common factors.

REMEMBER:
Multiplication can be shown in different ways.

$7 \times 8 \qquad 7 \cdot 8$

See page H9.

A division problem can be expressed as a fraction.

$8 \div 2 = \frac{8}{2}$

See page H9.

A common factor is a number that is a factor of two or more numbers. **See page H4.**

Talk About It

- How is the exponent of the quotient related to the exponents of 4^5 and 4^2?

- 💡 **CRITICAL THINKING**   What rule can you use for finding the exponent of the quotient of two powers with the same base?

- How can you use this rule to find $9^6 \div 9^4$?

GUIDED PRACTICE

Write the addition or subtraction expression that will give you
the exponent of the product or quotient.

1. $2^3 \cdot 2^4$ **2.** $3^4 \cdot 3^4$ **3.** $6^5 \cdot 6^1$ **4.** $7^7 \cdot 7^2$ **5.** $5^5 \cdot 5^4$

6. $4^3 \div 4^1$ **7.** $8^5 \div 8^4$ **8.** $2^4 \div 2^2$ **9.** $10^6 \div 10^5$ **10.** $3^8 \div 3^3$

Write the product as one power.

11. $6^2 \cdot 6^2$ **12.** $5^4 \cdot 5^1$ **13.** $4^3 \cdot 4^5$ **14.** $2^8 \cdot 2^1$ **15.** $12^2 \cdot 12^5$

Write the quotient as one power.

16. $2^4 \div 2^2$ **17.** $8^8 \div 8^2$ **18.** $3^9 \div 3^5$ **19.** $9^6 \div 9^4$ **20.** $10^7 \div 10^4$

INDEPENDENT PRACTICE

Write the product as one power.

1. $3^4 \cdot 3^6$ **2.** $5^3 \cdot 5^2$ **3.** $7^2 \cdot 7^4$ **4.** $10^4 \cdot 10^9$ **5.** $6^1 \cdot 6^6$

6. $2^3 \cdot 2^3$ **7.** $9^2 \cdot 9^6$ **8.** $8^7 \cdot 8^2$ **9.** $12^6 \cdot 12^5$ **10.** $4^4 \cdot 4^2 \cdot 4^3$

Write the quotient as one power.

11. $6^4 \div 6^1$ **12.** $3^6 \div 3^2$ **13.** $5^7 \div 5^5$ **14.** $9^3 \div 9^2$ **15.** $4^8 \div 4^4$

16. $2^9 \div 2^6$ **17.** $7^{10} \div 7^5$ **18.** $8^5 \div 8^3$ **19.** $12^{10} \div 12^3$ **20.** $10^3 \div 10^3$

Write the product or quotient as one power.

21. $5^5 \cdot 5^5$ **22.** $6^8 \cdot 6^4$ **23.** $4^3 \cdot 4^6$ **24.** $2^6 \div 2^4$ **25.** $3^8 \div 3^6$

26. $9^5 \div 9^2$ **27.** $7^9 \div 7^1$ **28.** $5^4 \cdot 5^4$ **29.** $10^8 \cdot 10^2$ **30.** $11^7 \div 11^3$

31. $4^8 \div 4^4$ **32.** $8^{12} \div 8^6$ **33.** $6^7 \div 6^2$ **34.** $2^{12} \cdot 2^{16}$ **35.** $10^{10} \cdot 10^7$

Problem-Solving Applications

36. Suppose a researcher tests a new method of pasteurization on a strain of bacteria in his laboratory. If the bacteria are killed at a rate of 8^9 per sec, how many bacteria would be killed after 8^2 sec?

37. A scientist estimates that a certain plant produces 10^7 grains of pollen. If there are 10^4 plants, how many grains of pollen do they produce?

38. Suppose a satellite orbits the earth at about 13^4 km per hour. How long would it take to complete 24 orbits, which is a distance of about 13^5 km?

39. ▭▶ **WRITE ABOUT IT** Explain how to find the product and the quotient of powers with the same base.

MORE PRACTICE Lesson 1.3, page H45

ALGEBRA CONNECTION

Squares and Square Roots

WORD POWER
perfect square

REMEMBER:

When you square a number, you multiply the number by itself. The square root of a number is one of two identical factors of the number. **See page H10.**

$3^2 = 9$ $\sqrt{9} = 3$

History Link

Colonists made quilts from scraps of fabric that were squares, rectangles, hexagons, and other shapes. If a square quilt is made from 400 squares, how many squares are on a side?

How are squares and square roots related?

Think about the relationship between the area of the square at the right and the length of its side. The area is 36 square units. The length of a side is $\sqrt{36}$, or 6 units, since $6^2 = 6 \times 6 = 36$. Taking the square root of a number is the inverse of squaring the number.

Every positive rational number has two square roots, one positive and one negative. The radical symbol, $\sqrt{\ }$, represents the positive square root, and $^-\sqrt{\ }$ represents the negative square root.

$\sqrt{16} = 4$, since $4 \times 4 = 16$. $^-\sqrt{49} = ^-7$, since $^-7 \times ^-7 = 49$.

$\sqrt{16} = 4$ ← **Read:** The positive $^-\sqrt{49} = ^-7$ ← **Read:** The negative
square root of 16   square root of 49
equals 4.   equals $^-7$.

The numbers 36, 16, and 49 are examples of perfect squares. A **perfect square** is a number that has integers as its square roots. Other perfect squares include 1, 4, 9, 25, 64, and 81.

• Find $\sqrt{100}$. Explain your thinking.

You can estimate the square root of a number that isn't a perfect square.

EXAMPLE 1   Estimate $\sqrt{20}$.

Think: Since 20 is not a perfect square, $\sqrt{20}$ is not an integer.

Locate 20 between two   *Locate $\sqrt{20}$ between*
perfect squares.   *two integers.*

$16 < 20 < 25$ $\sqrt{16} < \sqrt{20} < \sqrt{25}$

$4^2 < 20 < 5^2$ $4 < \sqrt{20} < 5$

So, $\sqrt{20}$ is between 4 and 5.

You can also use a calculator to find square roots.

EXAMPLE 2   Find $^-\sqrt{1.44}$.

1.44 SHIFT $\sqrt{\ }$ +/−   [-1.2]

$^-\sqrt{1.44} = ^-1.2$

Calculator Activities, page H39

GUIDED PRACTICE

Find the length of each side of the square.

1.

$A = 49 \text{ m}^2$

2.

$A = 25 \text{ m}^2$

3.

$A = 9 \text{ m}^2$

4.

$A = 64 \text{ m}^2$

5.

$A = 16 \text{ m}^2$

Write *SR* if the first number is the square root of the second number,
S if it is the square of the second number, or *N* if it is neither.

6. 9, 81   **7.** 4, 2   **8.** 3, 27   **9.** 8, 56   **10.** 36, 6

INDEPENDENT PRACTICE

Find the square.

1. 5^2 **2.** 12^2 **3.** $(^-6)^2$ **4.** $(^-9)^2$ **5.** 15^2

6. $(0.3)^2$ **7.** $(\frac{1}{4})^2$ **8.** $(^-2.2)^2$ **9.** $(\frac{2}{5})^2$ **10.** $(\frac{^-7}{8})^2$

Find the two square roots of the number.

11. 36   **12.** 100   **13.** 196   **14.** 81   **15.** 400

Find the square root.

16. $\sqrt{4}$ **17.** $^-\sqrt{64}$ **18.** $\sqrt{169}$ **19.** $\sqrt{256}$ **20.** $^-\sqrt{25}$

21. $^-\sqrt{900}$ **22.** $\sqrt{0.01}$ **23.** $^-\sqrt{0.09}$ **24.** $\sqrt{\frac{4}{9}}$ **25.** $^-\sqrt{\frac{25}{49}}$

Name the two integers the square root is between.

26. $\sqrt{12}$ **27.** $\sqrt{32}$ **28.** $\sqrt{72}$ **29.** $\sqrt{101}$ **30.** $\sqrt{150}$

Find the square root to the nearest hundredth.

31. $^-\sqrt{50}$ **32.** $\sqrt{27}$ **33.** $^-\sqrt{45}$ **34.** $\sqrt{106}$ **35.** $\sqrt{136}$

Problem-Solving Applications

36. The length of each side of Caitlin's square room is 14 ft. Find the number of square feet of carpet needed to cover the floor.

37. The area of a square field is 324 m². Find the length of each side of the field.

38. The formula for the length of the diagonal of a square is $d = s\sqrt{2}$. Suppose $s = 14$ cm. Use the formula to find d to the nearest tenth.

39. ⬛➤ **WRITE ABOUT IT** Explain how squaring a number is related to finding a square root.

Exploring Cubes and Cube Roots

LAB Activity

WHAT YOU'LL EXPLORE
How to model cubes and cube roots

WHAT YOU'LL NEED
centimeter cubes

REMEMBER:

A cube is a square prism with edges of equal lengths. **See page H23.**

Volume is the number of cubic units that can fit inside a solid figure. **See page H25.**

Is there a relationship between the volume of a cube and the length of an edge?

Explore

Work together to find out about the volumes of cubes and the lengths of their edges. Record your results.

- Start with one centimeter cube. What is the length of an edge? What is the volume?

- Use centimeter cubes to make a model of a cube with a length of 2 cm. What is the volume?

- Make a model of a cube with a length of 3 cm. What is the volume?

- Make a model of a cube, using 64 centimeter cubes. What is the volume? What is the length of an edge?

- Make a model of a cube, using 125 centimeter cubes. What is the volume? What is the length of an edge?

Think and Discuss 💡 CRITICAL THINKING

- How is the number of centimeter cubes used to build a model of a cube related to the volume of the cube?

- What is the relationship between the length of an edge of a cube and the volume of the cube?

- Suppose you know the volume of a cube. How do you find the length of an edge?

Try This

Find the number of centimeter cubes needed to make a cube with the given length.

1. 2 cm   **2.** 4 cm   **3.** 5 cm   **4.** 9 cm   **5.** 7 cm

Find the length of an edge of a cube with the given volume.

6. 8 cm^3 **7.** 64 cm^3 **8.** 27 cm^3 **9.** 125 cm^3

 **Link**
E–Lab • Activity 1 Available on CD-ROM and the Internet at http://www.hbschool.com/elab

Real Numbers on the Number Line

1.5

WHAT YOU'LL LEARN
How to explore real numbers

WHY LEARN THIS?
To understand why every point on the number line represents a real number

WORD POWER
irrational number
real numbers
Density Property

All rational numbers can be written in a decimal form that is either terminating or repeating.

$$3\frac{4}{5} = \frac{19}{5} = 3.8 \qquad \frac{2}{3} = 0.\overline{6} \qquad \sqrt{9} = 3 = \frac{3}{1} \qquad \frac{2}{9} = 0.\overline{2}$$

- Which of the rational numbers shown above are written as terminating decimals? as repeating decimals?

Complete the following activity to find out whether there are numbers that are not rational.

ACTIVITY

WHAT YOU'LL NEED: a calculator with a $\sqrt{}$ key

- What is $\sqrt{1.21}$? How can you check this result?

- Is the square root of 1.21 a terminating or a repeating decimal? Is $\sqrt{1.21}$ a rational number? Explain.

- What is $\sqrt{2}$? Check this result by multiplying it by itself. What is the product? Is $\sqrt{2}$ a rational number? Explain.

- Repeat the steps above for $\sqrt{3}$, $\sqrt{4}$, $\sqrt{5}$, and $\sqrt{6}$. Are any of these numbers rational numbers? Explain.

The numbers $\sqrt{2}$, $\sqrt{3}$, $\sqrt{5}$, and $\sqrt{6}$ are not rational numbers. Calculators give approximate rational values for them.

$$\sqrt{2} \approx 1.414213562\ldots \qquad \sqrt{3} \approx 1.732050808\ldots$$

$$\sqrt{5} \approx 2.236067978\ldots \qquad \sqrt{6} \approx 2.449489743\ldots$$

Each is an irrational number. An **irrational number** can be written as a nonterminating and nonrepeating decimal. The set of **real numbers** is formed by combining the set of rational numbers and the set of irrational numbers.

REMEMBER:

You can change a fraction to a decimal by dividing the numerator by the denominator. When the division produces a remainder of zero, the resulting decimal is a terminating decimal. When the division produces a quotient in which one or more digits repeat, the resulting decimal is a repeating decimal. **See page H9.**

The Venn diagram at the right shows how whole numbers, integers, rational numbers, irrational numbers, and real numbers are related.

Real Numbers

Rational Numbers
$\sqrt{\frac{1}{4}}$ $0.\overline{6}$
$\frac{4}{5}$ Integers
      $-\sqrt{9}$ -122 -81
-4 Whole Numbers
    0   2 $\sqrt{100}$ 57

Irrational Numbers
$\sqrt{2}$ π
    $\sqrt{6}$ $\sqrt{3}$
$\sqrt{5}$

Talk About It

- Is the number 1.87 a rational number or an irrational number? Is it a real number? Explain.

- Is the number $\sqrt{7}$ a rational number or an irrational number? Is it a real number? Explain.

The graph of all real numbers is the entire number line.

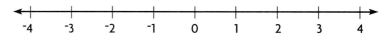

Every point on the number line corresponds to a real number, either a rational number or an irrational number. Between every two real numbers, rational or irrational, there is always another real number. This is called the **Density Property** for the real numbers.

One way to find an approximate value of an irrational number is to locate it between two rational numbers on the number line.

EXAMPLE   Locate $\sqrt{2}$ on the number line.

Think: 2 is between the perfect squares 1 and 4, so $\sqrt{2}$ is between $\sqrt{1}$ and $\sqrt{4}$, or between 1 and 2.

Find other pairs of rational numbers that $\sqrt{2}$ is between.

$\sqrt{2}$ is between

  1.4 and 1.5, since $1.4^2 = 1.96$ and $1.5^2 = 2.25$.

  1.41 and 1.42, since $1.41^2 = 1.9881$ and $1.42^2 = 2.0164$.

  1.414 and 1.415, since $1.414^2 = 1.999396$ and $1.415^2 = 2.002225$.

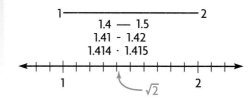

As shown on page 26, you can also use a calculator to find an approximate value of an irrational number.

$\sqrt{2} \rightarrow 2$ [SHIFT] [$\sqrt{\ }$] [1.414213562]

  $1.414213562 \approx 1.41$

- Find the value of $\sqrt{5}$ to the nearest tenth.

GUIDED PRACTICE

Write an *R* or an *I* to classify the real number as rational or irrational.

1. $\frac{11}{13}$ **2.** 6.25 **3.** $\sqrt{196}$ **4.** $\sqrt{17}$ **5.** $^-\sqrt{13}$ **6.** $\sqrt{\frac{1}{9}}$

Write the letter that identifies the position of the irrational number.

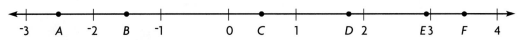

7. $^-\sqrt{2}$ **8.** $\sqrt{3}$ **9.** $\sqrt{8}$ **10.** $^-\sqrt{6}$ **11.** $\sqrt{12}$ **12.** $\sqrt{0.25}$

INDEPENDENT PRACTICE

Write an *R* or an *I* to classify the real number as rational or irrational.

1. $\sqrt{144}$ **2.** $\frac{5}{6}$ **3.** 10.2 **4.** $^-\sqrt{20}$ **5.** $\sqrt{14}$ **6.** $\sqrt{\frac{1}{9}}$

Name two rational numbers the irrational number is between.

7. $\sqrt{7}$ **8.** $^-\sqrt{5}$ **9.** $\sqrt{15}$ **10.** $\sqrt{24}$ **11.** $\sqrt{0.72}$ **12.** $^-\sqrt{47}$

13. $\sqrt{135}$ **14.** $^-\sqrt{32}$ **15.** $\sqrt{\frac{11}{23}}$ **16.** $\sqrt{0.82}$ **17.** $^-\sqrt{0.57}$ **18.** $\sqrt{\frac{5}{34}}$

Find the value of the irrational number to the nearest tenth.

19. $\sqrt{11}$ **20.** $\sqrt{41}$ **21.** $^-\sqrt{8}$ **22.** $^-\sqrt{22}$ **23.** $\sqrt{\frac{7}{19}}$ **24.** $\sqrt{163}$

Problem-Solving Applications

25. Alan says that $\sqrt{48}$ is a rational number. Is he correct? Explain.

26. The area of a square rug for a dollhouse is 12 cm². Find the length of each side to the nearest tenth.

27. ✏️ **WRITE ABOUT IT** Explain how the sets of rational numbers, irrational numbers, and real numbers are related.

Mixed Review

Find the quotient.

28. $15 \div 30$ **29.** $10 \div 100$ **30.** $12 \div 16$ **31.** $10 \div 40$ **32.** $4 \div 20$

Name the property shown.

33. $5 + (4 + 9) = (5 + 4) + 9$ **34.** $3 \times 2 \times 3 = 3 \times 3 \times 2$ **35.** $8 \times (4 + 1) = (8 \times 4) + (8 \times 1)$

36. **MONEY** How does the value of a hundred $1,000 bills compare with the value of a thousand $100 bills?

37. **LOGICAL REASONING** It took Tina 6 min to saw a board into 3 pieces. How long would she have taken to saw it into 9 pieces? Explain.

CULTURAL CONNECTION

The Space Station Mir

On February 20, 1986, the first stage of the Soviet Mir space station was launched. Since then, Mir has orbited the earth over 63,000 times at an altitude of 242 mi or 1,277,760 ft.

The space station has hosted many space explorers from different countries. Recently, the United States's Space Shuttle has docked with Mir several times. American astronauts and Russian cosmonauts have spent months together in space performing experiments. Many of the experiments being conducted are in preparation for the construction of the International Space Station. The International Space Station is an important step towards a manned mission to Mars.

Write the altitude in feet of Mir using scientific notation.

$$1{,}277{,}760 \text{ ft} \rightarrow 1.277760 \times 10^6 \text{ ft}$$

WORK TOGETHER

1. The Mir space station orbits the earth at an altitude of 15,333,120 in. Write the altitude using scientific notation.

2. Use a calculator to decide if 5^8 ft or 5^9 ft is closer to the altitude of the Mir space station.

3. Use a calculator to decide if 4^{12} in. or 4^{13} in. is closer to the altitude of the Mir space station.

4. Write your answer to Exercise 2 as the product of powers.

5. Write your answer to Exercise 3 as the quotient of powers.

6. While conducting an experiment on Mir, a cosmonaut recorded the data 2.3, ‾7.9, 0, 4.6, and ‾3.1. Draw a number line and plot points that correspond to the data.

CULTURAL LINK

The docking of Mir and the Space Shuttle is not the first time cosmonauts and astronauts have met in space. On July 17, 1975, two cosmonauts docked a Soyuz spacecraft with three astronauts in an Apollo spacecraft. It was the first meeting in space between cosmonauts and astronauts. This meeting paved the way for the Space Shuttle dockings with Mir.

EXAMPLES

EXERCISES

- **Classify and compare sets of numbers.**
  (pages 16–19)

  ┌─**Rational Numbers**─────────────┐
  │ ┌─**Integers**──────────────┐ │
  │ │ ┌─**Whole Numbers**──────┐ │ │
  │ │ │ ┌─**Counting Numbers**─┐ │ │ │
  │ │ │ │   │ │ │ │
  │ │ │ └──────────────────────┘ │ │ │
  │ │ └──────────────────────────┘ │ │
  │ └──────────────────────────────┘ │
  └──────────────────────────────────┘

1. VOCABULARY A _?_ number is any number that can be expressed as a ratio in the fraction form $\frac{a}{b}$, where a and b are integers and $b \neq 0$.

Classify each number as a counting number, whole number, integer, or rational number.

2. $6, \,^-7, \, 0, \, \frac{-1}{3}, \, 3\frac{3}{4}$ **3.** $\frac{1}{3}, \, 4, \, ^-2\frac{5}{9}, \, ^-8, \, 4.5$

4. $0.5, \, 156, \, ^-4.3, \, ^-6$ **5.** $10, \, ^-32, \, 2.78, \, 17$

- **Use exponents, and write large numbers in scientific notation and standard form.**
  (pages 20–23)

Write 6.457×10^7 in standard form.

To multiply, move the decimal point 7 places to the right.

$6.457 \times 10^7 = 6.4570000$

Write in scientific notation.

6. 34,500,450,000,000

7. 8,989,623,400,000,000,000,000

Write in standard form.

8. 8.989×10^8 **9.** 1.62345×10^{11}

10. 3.26×10^{14} **11.** 2.7895×10^9

- **Find the products and quotients of powers.**
  (pages 24–25)

Write as one power.

$10^3 \cdot 10^4 = 10^{3+4} = 10^7$ *Add exponents.*

$5^8 \div 5^3 = 5^{8-3} = 5^5$ *Subtract exponents.*

Write the product or quotient as one power.

12. $7^5 \cdot 7^7$ **13.** $10^{11} \div 10^8$

14. $2^{12} \div 2^6$ **15.** $15^8 \cdot 15^6$

16. $4^6 \cdot 4^5$ **17.** $9^8 \div 9^3$

18. $6^{12} \div 6^4$ **19.** $5^{13} \div 5^7$

- **Find the square root of a number.** (pages 26–27)

Find $^-\sqrt{16}$.

$^-\sqrt{16} = ^-4$ *Think:* $^-4 \times ^-4 = 16$

Find the square root.

20. $\sqrt{169}$ **21.** $^-\sqrt{49}$

22. $^-\sqrt{0.81}$ **23.** $\sqrt{\frac{36}{49}}$

- **Explore real numbers.** (pages 29–31)

Locate $\sqrt{5}$ on the number line.

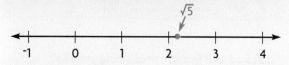

5 is between 4 and 9, so $\sqrt{5}$ is between $\sqrt{4}$ and $\sqrt{9}$, or between 2 and 3.

24. VOCABULARY An _?_ number can be written as a nonterminating or a nonrepeating decimal.

Name two rational numbers the irrational number is between.

25. $\sqrt{10}$ **26.** $\sqrt{20}$

27. $\sqrt{0.67}$ **28.** $^-\sqrt{115}$

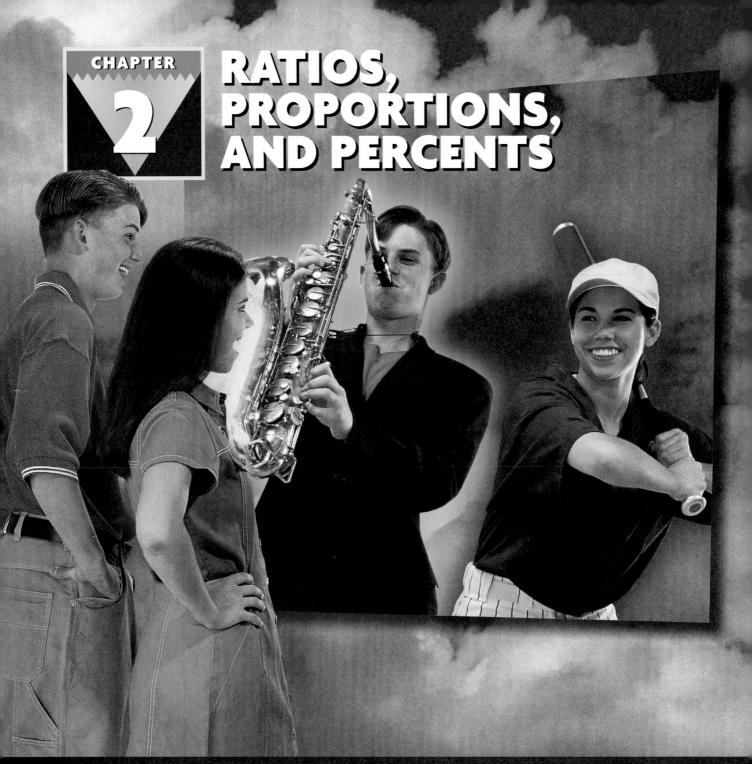

2

RATIOS, PROPORTIONS, AND PERCENTS

LOOK AHEAD

In this chapter you will solve problems that involve

- relationships among decimals, fractions, and percents
- ratios, rates, proportions, and percents

- stacked bar graphs and circle graphs
- estimating with percents

Gauge Yourself

How do people see themselves? What percent of the people in your class believe they are funny? What is the ratio of class members who think they are creative to those who do not? What fraction of your class feels they are healthy?

Make a list of at least five traits. Then take a survey to find out if people think they possess those traits. Write an article for the school paper describing your findings.

Plan
- Work with a small group. Decide on survey questions. Ask each person whether or not specific traits describe him or her. Then write a newspaper article describing the results of the survey.

Act
- Write a list of five or more characteristics you wish to survey.
- Decide how you will record the results of your survey.
- Survey at least 15 people.
- Use ratios, fractions, and percents in a newspaper article describing the results of your survey.

Share
- Share your survey results and newspaper articles with the rest of the class.

Personality Traits

Survey   Results
1. Are you funny?   funny   ꟼꟼꟼꟼ
2. Are you creative?   creative ꟼꟼꟼꟼ ꟼꟼꟼꟼ llll
3. Are you shy?   shy   ꟼꟼꟼꟼꟼꟼ
4. Are you athletic?   athletic ꟼꟼꟼꟼꟼꟼ
5. Are you outgoing?   outgoing ꟼꟼꟼꟼꟼ

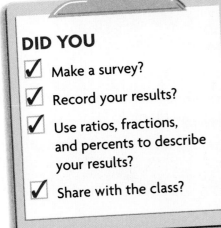

DID YOU

- ✓ Make a survey?
- ✓ Record your results?
- ✓ Use ratios, fractions, and percents to describe your results?
- ✓ Share with the class?

The Best Class Ever

Can you guess which math period fits this description? About $\frac{1}{3}$ ($\frac{5}{15}$ or $\frac{33}{100}$ or 33%) of us consider ourselves funny. We are highly creative, or so $\frac{14}{15}$ ($\frac{99}{100}$ or 99%) of us think. Exactly $\frac{2}{3}$ ($\frac{10}{15}$ or $\frac{66}{100}$ or 66%) of us are shy, and the other $\frac{1}{3}$ ($\frac{5}{15}$ or $\frac{33}{100}$ or 33%) of us are outgoing. When we are not studying math (creatively), you will find $\frac{2}{3}$ ($\frac{10}{15}$ or $\frac{66}{100}$ or 66%) of us following our athletic interests. Drop by and visit us during third period in room 16.

GEOMETRY CONNECTION
Relating Decimals, Fractions, and Percents

You have learned that there are many names for the same number. For example, one quarter can also be named as $\frac{1}{4}$, $\frac{2}{8}$, 0.25, and 25%. Since there are different ways to write a number, how do you know which form to use?

Names for numbers are like names for people. The name that is used depends on the situation. Your father's friends at his class reunion may call him Chip, but at work he is called Mr. Richardson.

When you tell time, you might say "It is a quarter after 7," but you wouldn't say "It is 25% after 7" or "It is 0.25 after 7" or "It is $\frac{1}{4}$ after 7."

• When might you use 25%? 0.25? $\frac{1}{4}$?

In some situations it makes sense to use fractions, as in measurement of distance in customary units: inches, feet, and yards. The measuring tools are usually marked in intervals of $\frac{1}{8}$ in., $\frac{1}{4}$ in., and $\frac{1}{2}$ in.

Talk About It

• When measuring with metric units, such as meters, would you use decimals or fractions? Give an example.

• When writing amounts of money, do you use decimals or fractions? Give an example.

• What is another way of saying you have a 50-50 chance of being selected?

• Would you think of fractions or decimals when getting gasoline for a car? Explain.

You can compare geometric figures by using fractions, decimals, and percents.

ACTIVITY

WHAT YOU'LL NEED: pattern blocks or paper replicas of pattern blocks

• Compare the triangle with the parallelogram, trapezoid, and hexagon. Find how many triangles it takes to cover each of the other figures.

• In area, a triangle is $\frac{1}{2}$ of the parallelogram. A triangle is what fraction of the trapezoid? of the hexagon?

• A triangle is 50% of the area of the parallelogram. A triangle is what percent of the trapezoid? of the hexagon?

• Copy and complete this table. Round decimals to the nearest thousandth.

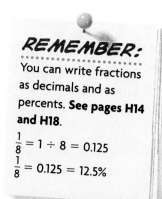

Figure	Number of Triangles	Fraction	Decimal	Percent
Parallelogram	2	$\frac{1}{2}$	?	50%
Trapezoid	3	?	?	?
Hexagon	6	?	?	?

• Use the pattern blocks to draw new figures that are related by the common fractions $\frac{1}{4}$ and $\frac{3}{4}$. Then express the relationships as decimals and percents.

GUIDED PRACTICE

Copy and complete the table to describe the shaded part of each figure.

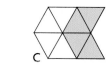

A   B   C

	Figure	Fraction	Decimal	Percent
1.	A	$\frac{1}{4}$	?	?
2.	B	?	0.75	?
3.	C	?	?	50%

Fractions, Decimals, and Percents in Data

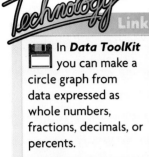

In **Data ToolKit** you can make a circle graph from data expressed as whole numbers, fractions, decimals, or percents.

For a project, Tory and Nicole recorded the number of minutes they saw of different types of television content during a 2-hr period. They put their data in a table and then made three circle graphs.

Television Content from 7 P.M. to 9 P.M.	
Regular programs	60 min
Commercials	36 min
Station promotions	12 min
Public service	12 min

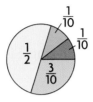 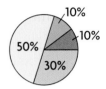

• How did Tory and Nicole get the decimal 0.3 that represents 36 min?

Often it is a matter of preference whether to use fractions, decimals, or percents—it is your choice.

EXAMPLE Suppose you collect data about television content for 2 hr. How can you make a circle graph to display your data?

Television Content from 9 A.M. to 11 A.M.	
Regular programs	78 min
Commercials	35 min
Station promotions	3 min
Public service	4 min

To find the size of the central angle for each part of the graph, divide the number of minutes by the total number of minutes and then multiply that decimal by 360.

78 ÷ 120 × 360 = ⌐234.⌐

35 ÷ 120 × 360 = ⌐105.⌐

3 ÷ 120 × 360 = ⌐9.⌐

4 ÷ 120 × 360 = ⌐12.⌐

So, the circle graph has central angles of 234°, 105°, 9°, and 12°.

• Why do you divide by 120 and then multiply that decimal by 360?

REMEMBER:

The sum of the percents in a circle graph is 100%.
See page H31.

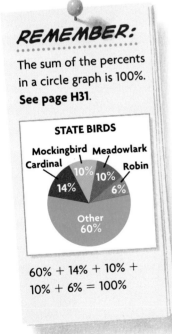

STATE BIRDS
Mockingbird Meadowlark
Cardinal   Robin
10% 10%
14%   6%
Other
60%

60% + 14% + 10% + 10% + 6% = 100%

Copy and complete the table.

$200 TOTAL BUDGET FOR SCHOOL CLOTHING			Fraction	Decimal	Percent
1.	Dresses	$70	?	?	?
2.	Shirts	$60	?	?	?
3.	Skirts	$40	?	?	?
4.	Shoes	$30	?	?	?

Copy the circle graph, and express the labels as percents.

5.   **6.**   **7.** 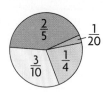 **8.**

9. Make a circle graph to display the data from Exercises 1–4.

Problem-Solving Applications

10. On the stock market, the price of a stock is listed as $18\frac{3}{8}$. How would you write this price with a dollar sign?

11. A dime is 10% of a dollar. In what other ways can you write the value of a dime?

12. **WRITE ABOUT IT** Tell whether you would use decimals, fractions, or percents to write numbers for customary units of measure, for money, and for analysis of data.

Mixed Review

Write an addition equation for each subtraction equation.

13. $6 - 7 = {}^-1$ **14.** $8 - {}^-3 = 11$ **15.** ${}^-5 - 2 = {}^-7$ **16.** ${}^-9 - {}^-6 = {}^-3$

Find the value.

17. 3^3 **18.** 5^3 **19.** 4^4 **20.** 9^2 **21.** 2^5 **22.** 10^5

23. **DATA** In 1996 the U.S. Postal Service handled an average of four hundred ninety-five million pieces of mail a day. Write the number in standard form.

24. **COMPARE AND ORDER** For every 1,000 people in the United States, there were 9.8 marriages in 1990 and 9.1 marriages in 1994. Which year had more marriages?

Stacked Bar Graphs

You can use a stacked bar graph to show how parts of a data set are related to one another and to the whole.

Explore

• Work with a partner. Copy and complete the table of data. Write fractions that compare the number of students voting for each sport to the total number of students who voted. Then write each fraction as a decimal and a percent.

Favorite Sport	Number of Students	Fraction	Decimal	Percent
Baseball	8	$\frac{8}{40}$	0.2	20%
Flag Football	10	?	?	?
Softball	20	?	?	?
Volleyball	2	?	?	?

• Label a decimal square pattern as shown. Select one color to represent each sport in the table. Let each horizontal bar on the decimal square pattern represent 10%.

• Starting at the bottom of the decimal square pattern, use the color selected for baseball and color 2 bars. Color bars to represent each percent.

Think and Discuss 💡 CRITICAL THINKING

• Why do you have just the right number of bars to represent all of the percents in the table?

Try This

Take a survey in your class to find out about favorite sports, music, or movies. Make a stacked bar graph with the data.

Technology Link ▶
E–Lab • Activity 2 Available on CD-ROM
and the Internet at http://www.hbschool.com/elab

Ratios and Percents

Fractions are called ratios when they are used to compare numbers. Percents are ratios also. However, they are special ratios. They compare a number with 100 and are written with a percent sign rather than as fractions or in other forms used for ratios.

WHAT YOU'LL LEARN
How ratios and percents are related

WHY LEARN THIS?
To find patterns and trends in data such as sports scores

EXAMPLE 1   What percent of each figure is represented by the single red cube?

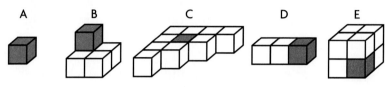

A   B   C   D   E

Step 1   Write as a fraction the ratio of the number of red cubes to the total number of cubes.

Step 2   Multiply to find an equivalent fraction with a denominator of 100.

Step 3   Write the numerator of the equivalent fraction with a % symbol.

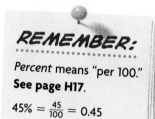

REMEMBER:

Percent means "per 100."
See page H17.

$45\% = \frac{45}{100} = 0.45$

Figure	Ratio of Red Cubes to Total Cubes	Equivalent Fraction with Denominator of 100	Percent
A	$\frac{1}{1}$	$\frac{1}{1} = \frac{1 \times 100}{1 \times 100} = \frac{100}{100}$	100%
B	$\frac{1}{5}$	$\frac{1}{5} = \frac{1 \times 20}{5 \times 20} = \frac{20}{100}$	20%
C	$\frac{1}{10}$	$\frac{1}{10} = \frac{1 \times 10}{10 \times 10} = \frac{10}{100}$	10%
D	$\frac{1}{3}$	$\frac{1}{3} = \frac{1 \times 33\frac{1}{3}}{3 \times 33\frac{1}{3}} = \frac{33\frac{1}{3}}{100}$	$33\frac{1}{3}\%$
E	$\frac{1}{8}$	$\frac{1}{8} = \frac{1 \times 12\frac{1}{2}}{8 \times 12\frac{1}{2}} = \frac{12\frac{1}{2}}{100}$	$12\frac{1}{2}\%$

- Look at the percents. In which two figures does the red cube represent the greatest percent?

- Would your answer change if Figure A had 1 red block and 3 white blocks? Explain.

Consumer Link

Suppose you see an ad that claims that 7 out of 10 dentists recommend Whiter Than White toothpaste to their patients. If the claim is based on a survey of 30 dentists, how many of them recommended Whiter Than White?

41

As statistician for the basketball team, Patty wants to analyze the scoring results for the coach. What comparisons can she make with the data from the last home game, shown below?

SCORES AT THE END OF EACH QUARTER				
Team	First Quarter	Second Quarter	Third Quarter	Fourth Quarter
Home	11	30	54	95
Visitor	22	50	72	100

Comparisons can be differences, or they can be ratios and percents. There are many possible comparisons. Before you decide what comparison to make, you need to know how the comparison will be used.

EXAMPLE 2 What comparisons would help the coach make encouraging comments to the team about the game?

Compare the final scores.
The difference in the two scores is $100 - 95$, or 5.
So, the team lost by only 5 points.

Compare the home team's score with the visitor's score at the end of each quarter.

$\frac{11}{22} = \frac{1}{2} = 50\%$ $\frac{30}{50} = \frac{60}{100} = 60\%$ *Write a ratio and a percent for each quarter.*

$\frac{54}{72} = \frac{3}{4} = 75\%$ $\frac{95}{100} = 95\%$

So each quarter, the team improved its score relative to the other team's score.

• What is another comparison that could be used to encourage the team?

EXAMPLE 3 What comparisons can be made that would help the coach point out some areas that need improvement?

Find how many points each team scored after the first quarter.

home team: $95 - 11 = 84$ *Subtract number of points scored in first quarter from total number of points.*

opponent: $100 - 22 = 78$

The home team actually outscored the opponent after the first quarter. So, the home team should try to do better at the start.

• What is another comparison that can be used to identify an area that needs improvement?

Find an equivalent fraction that has 100 as its denominator. Then write the percent.

1. $\frac{1}{4}$ **2.** $\frac{2}{5}$ **3.** $\frac{3}{4}$ **4.** $\frac{9}{10}$ **5.** $\frac{4}{5}$ **6.** $\frac{1}{20}$

Express the area of the shaded region as a percent of the area of the circle.

7.   **8.**   **9.**   **10.**

INDEPENDENT PRACTICE

Find an equivalent fraction that has 100 as its denominator. Then write the percent.

1. $\frac{1}{2}$ **2.** $\frac{1}{25}$ **3.** $\frac{3}{5}$ **4.** $\frac{16}{25}$ **5.** $\frac{7}{10}$ **6.** $\frac{7}{20}$

7. $\frac{26}{50}$ **8.** $\frac{3}{10}$ **9.** $\frac{12}{25}$ **10.** $\frac{24}{25}$ **11.** $\frac{11}{20}$ **12.** $\frac{3}{50}$

Express the area of the shaded region of the given polygon as a percent.

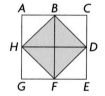

13. rectangle *ABFG* **14.** square *ACEG*

15. triangle *HDF* **16.** rectangle *HDEG*

17. pentagon *BCDFH* **18.** pentagon *BDEFH*

Problem-Solving Applications

19. The owner of a T-shirt shop calculated that 37 of the 50 T-shirts he sold on Monday had sports themes. What percent is this?

20. David scored 2 of the 3 goals in the soccer game. What percent of the goals did he make?

21. Kenny scored 17 of the 50 points in the first half of the game. What percent of the points did he make?

22. The TV weather forecaster has correctly predicted the weather for the games about $\frac{17}{20}$ of the time. Write this as a percent.

23. ✏️ **WRITE ABOUT IT** Explain how to find the percent for the ratio 1:50.

In *Mighty Math Astro Algebra*, you can have fun with ratios when you go to *VariaBLOX* and complete the mission *A Chotchkee Holiday.*

Ratios and Proportions

WORD POWER

odds
proportion

In a fraction that names a ratio, the numerator is the first term of the ratio, and the denominator is the second term.

In Cassie's school, the ratio of teachers to students is 1 to 35. You can write ratios in three ways.

1 to 35   1:35 $\frac{1}{35}$ $\leftarrow$ first term
                                        $\leftarrow$ second term

When you express a ratio as a fraction, you can use equivalent fractions to write the ratio in simplest form.

EXAMPLE 1   There are 324 eighth graders and 36 chaperones on the field trip. Express in simplest form the ratio of chaperones to students.

$\frac{36}{324}$ 36 [/] 324 [SIMP] [=] [18/162]

[SIMP] [=] [9/81]

[SIMP] [=] [3/27]

[SIMP] [=] [1/9]

So, the ratio is $\frac{1}{9}$, or 1 chaperone to 9 students.

• What if you cannot enter a fraction on your calculator? How can you simplify the fraction?

_____

Ratios are important when you want to know the chance of an event happening. A ratio that compares the number of favorable outcomes and the number of unfavorable outcomes is called the **odds**.

Look at the spinner shown at the left. All sections of the spinner are congruent. Recall that congruent means having the same size and shape. One section is red, and 5 sections are not red.

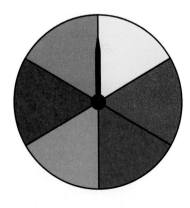

Suppose you are playing a game in which you get to go first if the pointer lands on red when you spin it. To find the odds in favor of your going first, compare the number of sections that are red to the number of sections that are not red.

odds in favor $= \dfrac{\text{number of red sections}}{\text{number of sections not red}} = \dfrac{1}{5}$

So, the odds in favor of your spinning red and going first in the game are 1 to 5.

EXAMPLE 2 Suppose the spinner has 12 congruent sections as shown. Does this change the odds of your spinning red and going first in the game?

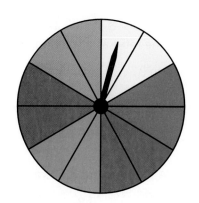

The 12 sections are all congruent, and there are 2 red sections and 10 nonred sections. So, the odds are 2 to 10.

Since odds are ratios, you can test to see if the ratio 1 to 5 is equivalent to the ratio 2 to 10.

$$\frac{1}{5} = \frac{1 \times 2}{5 \times 2} = \frac{2}{10} \quad \textit{Multiply.}$$

Since the ratios are equivalent, the odds of your spinning red and going first are the same and do not change.

• What are the odds against your going first when you use the 12-section spinner?

Remember that a **proportion** is an equation which states that two ratios are equivalent. To determine whether two ratios are equivalent, you can multiply or divide to show that the fractions are equivalent. Or, you can show that the cross products are equal.

EXAMPLE 3 Show that $\frac{90}{240} = \frac{3}{8}$ is a proportion.

Equivalent Fractions

$$\frac{90}{240} = \frac{90 \div 30}{240 \div 30} = \frac{3}{8} \quad \textit{Divide.}$$

Cross Products

$$\frac{90}{240} \overset{?}{=} \frac{3}{8}$$

$$3 \times 240 \overset{?}{=} 90 \times 8$$

$$720 = 720$$

Since the cross products are equal, $\frac{3}{8}$ and $\frac{90}{240}$ are equivalent ratios. So, $\frac{90}{240} = \frac{3}{8}$ is a proportion.

• Is $\frac{5}{9} = \frac{60}{108}$ a proportion? Explain.

You can make a ratio table to find ratios that form proportions.

EXAMPLE 4 What are some ratios that form a proportion with $\frac{3}{5}$?

Use multiplication to make a table of equivalent ratios.

First term	3	6	9	12	15
Second term	5	10	15	20	25

So, you can write proportions with $\frac{3}{5}$ and $\frac{6}{10}$, $\frac{9}{15}$, $\frac{12}{20}$, and $\frac{15}{25}$.

• What are two other fractions that form a proportion with $\frac{3}{5}$?

Sports Link

This year the Alachua State University football team won 8 games out of 10. For the university's basketball team to have the same ratio of wins to losses, how many of the 35 scheduled games must it win?

Write the ratio as a fraction.

1. 4 to 37   **2.** 5:49   **3.** 7 out of 99   **4.** 10 to 249   **5.** 12:247

Write the ratio in simplest form.

6. $\frac{15}{20}$ **7.** $\frac{8}{64}$ **8.** $\frac{10}{100}$ **9.** $\frac{4}{36}$ **10.** $\frac{14}{35}$ **11.** $\frac{11}{66}$

Decide whether the ratios are equivalent. Write = or ≠.

12. $\frac{4}{5} \bullet \frac{16}{20}$ **13.** $\frac{5}{7} \bullet \frac{15}{28}$ **14.** $\frac{7}{8} \bullet \frac{21}{32}$ **15.** $\frac{12}{42} \bullet \frac{2}{7}$ **16.** $\frac{33}{66} \bullet \frac{11}{21}$

Write the ratio as a fraction in simplest form.

1. 6 to 48   **2.** 5 to 100   **3.** 12:32   **4.** 25 out of 75   **5.** 36:927

6. 7 to 42   **7.** 12 out of 54   **8.** 14:56   **9.** 45 to 72   **10.** 52:624

Decide whether the ratios form a proportion. Write = or ≠.

11. $\frac{7}{14} \bullet \frac{13}{28}$ **12.** $\frac{22}{33} \bullet \frac{2}{3}$ **13.** $\frac{27}{36} \bullet \frac{15}{20}$ **14.** $\frac{8}{14} \bullet \frac{6}{21}$ **15.** $\frac{5}{8} \bullet \frac{75}{160}$

16. $\frac{80}{100} \bullet \frac{4}{5}$ **17.** $\frac{12}{49} \bullet \frac{4}{7}$ **18.** $\frac{1}{3} \bullet \frac{15}{45}$ **19.** $\frac{7}{9} \bullet \frac{140}{180}$ **20.** $\frac{30}{36} \bullet \frac{15}{16}$

Copy and complete the ratio table.

21.

First term	2	4	6	?	10	?
Second term	?	14	21	28	?	42

Problem-Solving Applications

For Problems 22–25, express each ratio in simplest form.

22. There are 675 students and 30 teachers in the middle school. What is the ratio of teachers to students?

23. There are 540 students that ride the bus, and 20 buses. What is the ratio of students to buses?

24. Lea and Beth are playing a game. The spinner is divided into 15 congruent sections, and 3 of the sections are blue. What are the odds that Lea will spin blue?

25. The weather forecast indicates a 25% chance of rain. What are the odds in favor of rain? What are the odds against rain?

26. ◖▬▬ **WRITE ABOUT IT** Explain how you determine if two ratios form a proportion.

    MORE PRACTICE Lesson 2.3, page H47

Rates

WHAT YOU'LL LEARN
How ratios and rates are related

WHY LEARN THIS?
To find unit prices for comparison shopping

WORD POWER
rate
unit rate
unit price

Ratios that compare quantities of different units are called **rates**. Some examples are:

rate of speed: 35 mph
cost of gasoline: $1.51 per gallon
rate of pay: $6.50 per hour

It took 3 hr for Pascal to drive 129 mi to visit her parents. What was Pascal's average rate of speed?

$$\frac{129}{3} = \frac{129 \div 3}{3 \div 3} = \frac{43}{1}$$ *Divide to form an equivalent ratio with 1 as the second term.*

So, Pascal's average rate of speed was 43 mph.

When the second term of the ratio is 1, the rate is a **unit rate**. A unit rate for prices is often called a **unit price**.

EXAMPLE 1   Derrick sells firewood in bundles of 8 small logs for $10. Mrs. Strong wants to buy only 5 logs. If she pays the same rate, how much should she pay?

Find the unit price.

$$\frac{\$10}{8 \text{ logs}} \rightarrow$$ 10 ÷ 8 = 1.25   *Divide to find the price of 1 log.*

5 × $1.25 = $6.25   *Multiply the unit price by 5.*

So, Mrs. Strong should pay Derrick $6.25.

To find the best buys, often you need to find the unit prices.

EXAMPLE 2   A 64-oz bottle of apple juice costs $2.39, and a 20-oz bottle costs $0.79. Which is the better buy?

2.39 ÷ 64 = 0.03734375   *Find unit price for 64-oz bottle.*

.79 ÷ 20 = 0.0395   *Find unit price for 20-oz bottle.*

Since the unit price for the 64-oz bottle is less than the unit price for the 20-oz bottle, the 64-oz bottle is the better buy.

• **CRITICAL THINKING**   You can use a 25-cents-off coupon if you buy four 20-oz bottles. Is the better buy still the 64-oz bottle? Explain.

GUIDED PRACTICE

Write an equivalent ratio that has 1 as its second term.

1. $\dfrac{\$2.40}{4 \text{ candy bars}}$ 2. $\dfrac{100 \text{ mi}}{4 \text{ hr}}$ 3. $\dfrac{\$2.00}{20 \text{ min}}$ 4. $\dfrac{\$1.89}{10 \text{ lb of potatoes}}$

Find the unit rates. Then solve.

5. A 2-lb package of hamburger costs $3.98; a 3-lb package of hamburger costs $5.67. Which is the better buy?

6. A compact car gets 135 mi per 5 gal of gas; a midsize car gets 210 mi per 10 gal of gas. Which car gets better gas mileage?

INDEPENDENT PRACTICE

Find the unit rate.

1. $\dfrac{\$1.00}{5 \text{ lb of bananas}}$ 2. $\dfrac{\$3.20}{20 \text{ oz of cereal}}$ 3. $\dfrac{176 \text{ mi}}{8 \text{ gal of gasoline}}$ 4. $\dfrac{3{,}600 \text{ calories}}{10 \text{ slices of cake}}$

5. 64 beats in 4 measures of music

6. 96 chairs in 8 rows

7. $525.00 for 40 hr of work

8. $7.47 for 3 yd of fabric

Find the unit rates. Then solve.

9. A long-distance phone company charges $1.70 for 10 min; a competitor charges $4.50 for 45 min. Which has the better rate?

10. A 30-oz can of beans costs $1.29; a 16-oz can costs $0.89. Which is the better buy?

11. Wireless service A charges $6.00 for 30 min of cellular airtime; wireless service B charges $9.99 for 55 min of airtime. Which has the better rate?

12. A 1-qt container of milk costs $0.98; a 1-gal container costs $2.39. Which is the better buy?

Problem-Solving Applications

13. John is selling his comic book collection. His asking price is 5 comic books for $6.00. Ernie wants to buy 14 comic books. Using John's rate, how much will Ernie pay?

14. Pam reads 5 pages of a mystery book in 3 min. If she continues to read at the same rate, how long will it take her to read a 225-page mystery book?

15. A national cereal company pays $59,969 to have its new cereal placed in a display area at the head of an aisle in a grocery store for one week. Find the daily rate.

16. Rocky's dog loves to chew socks. Rocky wants to find the best price he can for new socks. He found 6 pairs for $19.50 and 12 pairs for $30.00. Which is the better buy?

17. A fast-food restaurant charges a total of $17.45 for five identical value meals. What is the cost of one value meal? What is the cost of 8 value meals?

18. ✏️ **WRITE ABOUT IT** Explain how to find a unit rate. Give an example.

MORE PRACTICE Lesson 2.4, page H47

Estimating with Ratios and Percents

WHAT YOU'LL LEARN
How to estimate with ratios and percents

WHY LEARN THIS?
To estimate your grade on a test

WORD POWER
Golden Ratio

To be eligible to play sports this week, Larry needs to score at least 70% on his language test. His score is 91 out of 120 questions. Is this high enough?

You can quickly estimate his percent by using a familiar, nearly equivalent fraction. Use compatible numbers to write a fraction that is easy to simplify. It should be about the same as the ratio of Larry's score to the number of questions.

$\frac{91}{120} \approx \frac{90}{120}$ *Estimate with compatible numbers.*

$\frac{90}{120} = \frac{9}{12} = \frac{3}{4}$ *Write in simplest form.*

Since $\frac{3}{4} = 75\%$, Larry's score is greater than 70%. He is eligible.

• What if Larry's score were 79 out of 120? Would he be eligible? Explain.

EXAMPLE 1 The students in the science class have earned $62 of the $188 they need for their project. About what percent of the money do they still need to earn?

$\frac{62}{188} \approx \frac{60}{200}$ *Estimate with compatible numbers.*

$\frac{60}{200} = \frac{6}{20} = \frac{3}{10}$ *Write in simplest form.*

Since $\frac{3}{10} = 30\%$, they have earned about 30%. They still need to earn about 100% − 30%, or about 70% of the money.

• What if you use $\frac{60}{180}$ to estimate? Does your estimate change? Explain.

GUIDED PRACTICE

Use mental math and compatible numbers to estimate an equivalent ratio. Then write your ratio in simplest form.

1. $\frac{55}{185}$ **2.** $\frac{110}{214}$ **3.** $\frac{42}{435}$ **4.** $\frac{83}{99}$

Estimate the percent. Choose 1%, 10%, or 100%.

5. 36 out of 40   **6.** 4:400   **7.** 72 of 663

8. 5:46   **9.** 236 of 256   **10.** 77 of 8,234

Sometimes estimates of ratios are made with calculators.

ACTIVITY

In this activity you will estimate the value of a famous ratio, the Golden Ratio. This ratio has been used by artists and architects over the centuries because it is very pleasing visually.

WHAT YOU'LL NEED: metric rulers, calculator

• Measure the lengths of segments *a, b, c, d,* and *e,* and draw a copy of each on your paper. Record each measure.

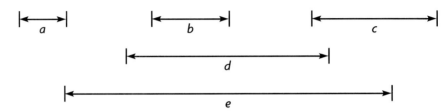

• Use the measures of the segments to write these ratios: $\frac{b}{a}, \frac{c}{b}, \frac{d}{c}, \frac{e}{d}$.

• Use a calculator to change each ratio to an equivalent decimal. Compare the decimals. How are they alike? How are they different?

• Record the calculator display of each decimal, to the hundredths place.

These decimals are estimates of the **Golden Ratio**, which is exactly $\frac{1 + \sqrt{5}}{2}$.

You can use your calculator to find an approximate decimal value for the Golden Ratio.

Talk About It

• Look at the measures of the line segments in order from least to greatest. What pattern do you see? HINT: Look at the sums of adjacent measures.

• If this pattern continues, how long will the next two line segments be?

• Look at your two predicted measures. What decimal value do you predict will result from the ratio of the greater measure to the lesser measure? How can you check your prediction?

INDEPENDENT PRACTICE

Use mental math and compatible numbers to estimate an equivalent ratio. Then write your ratio in simplest form.

1. $\frac{94}{368}$ 2. $\frac{23}{122}$ 3. $\frac{247}{536}$ 4. $\frac{62}{415}$ 5. $\frac{88}{133}$ 6. $\frac{51}{629}$

Estimate the percent.

7. $\frac{76}{144}$ 8. $\frac{47}{256}$ 9. 34:104   10. 82 of 326   11. 189 of 197

12. 48 of 495   13. 36:189   14. 3:291   15. 120:205   16. 1,291:2,500

17. 67:98   18. 48 of 124   19. 89 of 921   20. 123:162   21. 98 of 11,380

22. 236 out of 250 is about what percent?   23. 67 is about what percent of 98?

Problem-Solving Applications

24. Victor's father told him that if he brought up his next math test score to at least 83%, he could try out for the track team. Victor answered 183 out of 200 math questions correctly. Was his score high enough for him to try out for the track team? Explain.

25. A video rental company will open a new store only if 75% of the households in the area have an income of $25,000 or more. Of the 1,031 households in one area, 830 have that much income. Should the company open a store here? Explain.

26. Wendy ordered a CD from a mail-order company. The total cost was $19.98, which included a $3.95 charge for shipping and handling. About what percent of the total cost was the charge for shipping and handling?

27. Mrs. Davis has collected $115 out of the $195 needed for the class trip. About what percent of the money is still needed?

28. ✏️ **WRITE ABOUT IT** Explain how you estimate the percent 345 is of 511.

Mixed Review

Write the absolute value.

29. $|{}^-16|$ 30. $|5|$ 31. $|145|$ 32. $|{}^-9|$ 33. $|{}^-57|$ 34. $|{}^-89|$

Find the two square roots of the number.

35. 9   36. 49   37. 64   38. 25   39. 81   40. 144

41. **MEASUREMENT** Jim's father asked the butcher for a 12-oz steak. The meat scale measures pounds. What did the scale show in decimals?

42. **RATES** Charlie worked 15 hr in his father's store and earned $71.25. Find the hourly rate.

MATH FUN!

PARTS OF A WHOLE

PURPOSE To practice relating fractions, decimals, and percents to each other (pages 36–39)

YOU WILL NEED tangram pattern, scissors

One of the most popular puzzles of the 19th century was a Chinese puzzle called a tangram. Work with a partner. Cut out and label the tangram pieces as shown. Express each piece as a fraction, a decimal, and a percent of the whole pattern. Make a table like the one shown to keep a record.

Piece	Fraction	Decimal	Percent
A	$\frac{1}{4}$	0.25	25%

CUBICAL QUANDARY

PURPOSE To practice relating ratios and percents (page 41–43)

YOU WILL NEED 100 centimeter cubes

Work with a partner. Build the solid figure using all 100 cubes. Write a ratio and find the percent of the cubes that form each part.

1. the top layer

2. front and back sides

3. all the outside surfaces

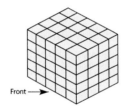

Front →

Write a ratio for 30% of the cubes.

Make a different solid figure with the 100 cubes. Find the ratios and percents of the same parts as the first figure.

BOUNCING BALLS

PURPOSE To practice finding rates (pages 47–48)

YOU WILL NEED basketball, timepiece with a second hand

Work with a partner. One partner bounces the basketball. The other partner counts the number of times his or her partner bounces the basketball in 2 minutes. Then partners trade roles and repeat the activity. Find each partner's rate per minute. Compare your rates. Who has the fastest rate?

Try this with other activities such as jumping rope and sharpening pencils.

CHAPTER 2 REVIEW

EXAMPLES

EXERCISES

- **Relate decimals, fractions, and percents.**
  (pages 36–39)

 The shaded area is $\frac{2}{5}$, 0.4, or 40% of the area of the rectangle.

Copy and complete the table.

	Fraction	Decimal	Percent
1.	?	?	75%
2.	$\frac{6}{20}$	?	?
3.	?	0.6	?

- **Relate ratios and percents.** (pages 41–43)

Write $\frac{1}{5}$ as a percent.

$\frac{1}{5} = \frac{1 \times 20}{5 \times 20} = \frac{20}{100}$ *Find an equivalent fraction with a denominator of 100.*

20%   *Write the numerator and a % symbol.*

Write as a percent.

4. $\frac{1}{4}$ **5.** $\frac{12}{25}$ **6.** $\frac{47}{50}$

7. $\frac{7}{10}$ **8.** $\frac{11}{20}$ **9.** $\frac{4}{5}$

10. $\frac{15}{30}$ **11.** $\frac{7}{25}$ **12.** $\frac{17}{68}$

- **Relate fractions, ratios, and proportions.**
  (pages 44–46)

Decide whether $\frac{2}{3}$ and $\frac{10}{15}$ form a proportion.

$\frac{2}{3} = \frac{10}{15}$ *Use cross products.*

$2 \times 15 = 3 \times 10$ *Decide if cross products are equal.*

$30 = 30$

So, $\frac{2}{3}$ and $\frac{10}{15}$ do form a proportion.

13. VOCABULARY An equation which states that two ratios are equivalent is a __?__ .

Decide whether the ratios form a proportion. Write = or ≠ .

14. $\frac{1}{4}$ ● $\frac{4}{16}$ **15.** $\frac{3}{4}$ ● $\frac{5}{12}$

16. $\frac{7}{8}$ ● $\frac{42}{56}$ **17.** $\frac{5}{10}$ ● $\frac{20}{40}$

- **Relate ratios and rates.** (pages 47–48)

Divide to find the unit rate.

$\frac{\$1.89}{32 \text{ oz}} \rightarrow 1.89 \div 32 = 0.0590625$

The unit rate is about \$0.06 per ounce.

Find the unit rate.

18. \$4.00 for 8 pens   **19.** 300 mi in 6 hr

20. 4,015,000 babies born in 365 days

21. \$6.75 for 5 gal of gasoline

- **Estimate ratios and percents.** (pages 49–51)

Estimate the percent.

$\frac{71}{284} \approx \frac{70}{280}$ *Estimate the ratio.*

$\frac{70}{280} = \frac{7}{28} = \frac{1}{4}$ *Write in simplest form.*

$\frac{1}{4} = 25\%$ *Write as a percent.*

Estimate the percent.

22. 37 to 103   **23.** 438 to 789

24. 96:478   **25.** 312 to 1,235

26. 48 to 204   **27.** 495 to 508

CHAPTER 3

OPERATIONS WITH INTEGERS

LOOK AHEAD

In this chapter you will solve problems that involve

- addition and subtraction of integers
- finding patterns with integers
- multiplication and division of integers
- integers as exponents

Where in the World?

What location experienced the greatest range of temperatures in the past year? Find the range of temperatures for various places. Try to find the place with the greatest temperature range.

Plan
- Work with a small group. Find a place that had the greatest difference between its highest and lowest temperature.

Act
- Select some locations that you think have a large range of temperatures.
- Find their highest and lowest temperatures for the past year.
- Find which location had the greatest range of temperatures.
- Compare your greatest range with the greatest range of other groups.
- Try to find another place with an even greater range of temperatures.

Share
- Share your list of locations and temperature ranges with the class.

DID YOU

- ✓ Find different locations?
- ✓ Find their temperature ranges?
- ✓ Compare ranges with other groups?
- ✓ Present your findings to the class?

Yearly Highs and Lows

City / State	High	Low	Range
Albany, NY	99°F	–18°F	
Barrow, AK	64°F	–51°F	
Bismarck, ND	98°F	–28°F	
Burlington, VT	100°F	–13°F	
Caribou, ME	93°F	–33°F	
Duluth, MN	94°F	–22°F	
Fairbanks, AK	88°F	–48°F	
Rapid City, SD	102°F	–15°F	

Adding Integers

REMEMBER:
. . . .
The sum of opposite integers is always 0. **See page H27.**

$^-1 + 1 = 0$

Positive and negative integers are used to solve problems involving temperatures above and below 0°F, yards gained and lost in a football game, or money earned and spent.

• What problem have you solved using integers?

To solve such problems, you often have to perform operations with integers. To add integers, you can choose from several different methods. It doesn't matter which method you choose; all result in the same sum.

ACTIVITY

WHAT YOU'LL NEED: two-color counters or squares of paper

Work in a small group to practice solving integer addition problems with models.

In this model each yellow counter represents 1 and each red counter represents $^-1$.

• Write an addition equation with integers to match the model.

• Write a real-life problem that can be solved with your equation. Share your problem with the class.

• Make two different models that show a sum of $^-5$. For each model, write an addition equation with integers.

• Now make two different models that have a sum of 5. Write an integer addition equation for each.

You can use number lines to show addition of integers.

EXAMPLE 1 Use a number line to find the sum. $5 + {}^-8$

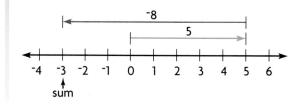

Start at 0.

Move 5 spaces to the right. From that point, move 8 spaces to the left.

You finish at $^-3$, so $5 + {}^-8 = {}^-3$.

EXAMPLE 2 Use a number line to find the sum. ⁻2 + 6

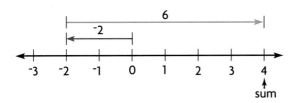

Start at 0. Move 2 spaces to the left. From that point, move 6 spaces to the right. You finish at 4. You can write the addition equation ⁻2 + 6 = 4.

Another Method When adding integers, you can use their absolute values to find the sum.

> When adding integers with the same sign, add the absolute values of the integers. Then use the sign of the addends.

EXAMPLE 3 Find the sum. ⁻4 + ⁻3

$|{}^-4| + |{}^-3| = 4 + 3 = 7$ *Add the absolute values.*

$^-4 + {}^-3 = {}^-7$ *Use the sign of the addends.*

• The sum of two negative integers is *sometimes, always,* or *never* negative?

> When adding integers with unlike signs, find the difference of their absolute values. Then use the sign of the addend with the greater absolute value.

EXAMPLE 4 Find the sum. ⁻6 + 2

$|{}^-6| - |2| = 6 - 2 = 4$ *Subtract the absolute values.*

Think: $|{}^-6| > |2|$ *Compare the absolute values.*

So, ⁻6 + 2 = ⁻4. *Use the sign of the addend with the greater absolute value.*

GUIDED PRACTICE

Find each sum by using a model or drawing a number line. Write the addition equation that shows the sum.

1. ⁻6 + ⁻5 **2.** ⁻6 + 5 **3.** 6 + ⁻5 **4.** ⁻5 + 6

5. ⁻4 + 6 **6.** ⁻5 + ⁻3 **7.** 7 + ⁻5 **8.** ⁻1 + ⁻4

REMEMBER:

The absolute value of a number is its distance from 0. **See page H27.**

$|{}^-4| = 4$

Read: "The absolute value of negative four is four."

$|4| = 4$

Read: "The absolute value of positive four is four."

Career **Link**

Corporations may report losses with brackets around the numbers instead of negative signs.

[$34,000] shows a loss of $34,000.

Big Mack Computers received $39,233,892 for the products it sold and paid out $39,365,494 for labor, parts, and other expenses. Show the loss using brackets.

Draw a model. Write an addition equation that shows the sum.

1. ⁻1 + 3   **2.** 5 + ⁻7   **3.** ⁻3 + ⁻3   **4.** ⁻2 + ⁻4   **5.** ⁻2 + 6

Draw a number line to find the sum. Write an addition equation.

6. 1 + ⁻3   **7.** ⁻2 + ⁻2   **8.** ⁻3 + 6   **9.** 2 + ⁻6   **10.** 6 + ⁻2

11. ⁻3 + ⁻2   **12.** ⁻3 + 2   **13.** 3 + ⁻2   **14.** 5 + ⁻4   **15.** ⁻5 + ⁻4

Find the sum.

16. 5 + ⁻4   **17.** ⁻3 + 7   **18.** ⁻3 + ⁻7   **19.** 10 + ⁻5   **20.** ⁻8 + ⁻2

21. ⁻17 + 14   **22.** ⁻38 + 14   **23.** 100 + ⁻100   **24.** ⁻12 + 32   **25.** ⁻53 + ⁻33

26. 57 + ⁻59   **27.** ⁻88 + 88   **28.** ⁻25 + 21   **29.** ⁻42 + ⁻7   **30.** ⁻100 + ⁻42

31. ⁻48 + ⁻17   **32.** ⁻93 + 47   **33.** 36 + ⁻19   **34.** ⁻9 + 52   **35.** ⁻259 + 27

Problem-Solving Applications

36. In an offensive drive in the football game, Rick's team lost 3 yd and then gained 10 yd. Write an addition equation to show how many yards were gained or lost.

37. On Monday the temperature was ⁻5°F. A warm front moved through the area during the night. It increased the temperature by 15°. What is the new temperature?

38. A submarine is cruising at 40 m below sea level, or ⁻40 m. The submarine ascends 18 m. What is the submarine's new location?

39. **WRITE ABOUT IT** Explain how you would find the sum of a negative integer and a positive integer.

Mixed Review

Tell which addition expression is equivalent to the subtraction expression.

40. 5 − 3
5 + ⁻3 or 5 + 3

41. 6 − 2
6 + 2 or 6 + ⁻2

42. 8 − 7
8 + 7 or 8 + ⁻7

Write as a decimal.

43. 30%   **44.** 150%   **45.** 75%   **46.** 200%   **47.** $45\frac{1}{2}\%$

48. **RATIOS AND PROPORTIONS** If you can address 20 envelopes in $\frac{1}{2}$ hr, how many envelopes can you address in 3 hr?

49. **NUMBER SENSE** The sum of 6 and a number is equal to 7 minus the number. What is the number?

Subtracting Integers

Did you ever hear someone say, "You can't subtract a larger number from a smaller number"? Is that true?

Try it with a calculator. Find the difference. $2 - 8$

2 ⊟ 8 ⊟ [$^-6.$]

You can subtract a greater number from a lesser number. However, the answer is not a positive number. When you subtract integers, the difference is sometimes negative and sometimes positive.

ACTIVITY

WHAT YOU'LL NEED: two-color counters or squares of paper

With your group, make a model like the one shown. Let a yellow counter represent 1 and a red counter represent $^-1$.

- What number is modeled with these counters?

- Take away 8 yellow counters. What remains in the model? What number does this represent?

- Write a subtraction equation to match your model.

Addition and subtraction of integers are related operations. Compare these addition and subtraction problems.

Subtraction	Addition
$^-1 - ^-3 = 2$	$^-1 + 3 = 2$
$^-4 - 3 = ^-7$	$^-4 + ^-3 = ^-7$
$7 - 12 = ^-5$	$7 + ^-12 = ^-5$
$6 - ^-4 = 10$	$6 + 4 = 10$

- How are the numbers in the addition and subtraction equations related?

- Write a rule that tells how to change an integer subtraction equation to an integer addition equation.

Geography Link

Not all dry land is above sea level. There are places on earth where the land is actually below sea level. The lowest elevation in North America, $^-282$ ft, is at Death Valley, in California. The highest elevation in North America, 20,320 ft, is at Mount McKinley, in Alaska. What is the difference between the highest and the lowest elevations in North America?

EXAMPLE 1 Change the subtraction equation to an addition equation and then solve. $^-7 - ^-9 = n$

$^-7 - ^-9 = n$ *To subtract $^-9$, add its opposite.*

$^-7 + 9 = n$

$2 = n$

So, $^-7 - ^-9 = 2$.

- Change to an addition equation and then solve. $^-8 - ^-5 = n$.

EXAMPLE 2 When Ollie read the thermometer Thursday evening, the temperature was 14°F. On Friday morning, he heard on the radio that the temperature had dropped 31 degrees overnight. What was the temperature Friday morning?

14 [−] 31 [=] [⁻17.]

So, the temperature Friday morning was $^-17$°F.

Integers can also be used to describe measurements of altitude.

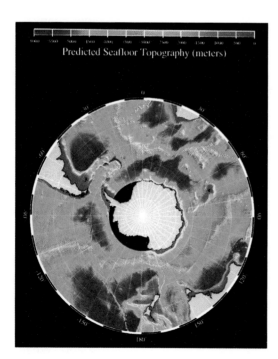

Predicted Seafloor Topography (meters)

On the Internet, Jillian found this map of predicted altitudes (below sea level) of ocean floors of the southern oceans. Estimate the differences in altitudes between the oceans off the southern tip of South America at $^-70$° and off the coast of Antarctica at $^-150$°.

Compare the colors on the map at the two locations with the given scale. The red color off the tip of South America represents an altitude of about $^-500$ m, and the black color off the coast of Antarctica represents an altitude of about $^-8,000$ m.

$^-500 - ^-8,000 =$

$^-500 + 8,000 = 7,500$

So, the difference in altitudes is about 7,500 m.

- Compare the altitudes of the ocean floors off the southern tip of Africa at 20° and off the southern tip of Australia at 145°. Estimate the difference.

Use a model to find each difference. Draw your model. Write an addition equation for each subtraction equation.

1. $8 - 15 = {}^-7$ **2.** ${}^-5 - {}^-6 = 1$ **3.** $4 - {}^-2 = 6$ **4.** $9 - {}^-11 = 20$

Change each subtraction equation to an addition equation. Then solve for *n*.

5. ${}^-2 - {}^-3 = n$ **6.** $5 - {}^-4 = n$ **7.** $6 - 19 = n$ **8.** ${}^-8 - {}^-6 = n$

INDEPENDENT PRACTICE

Write an addition equation for each subtraction equation.

1. $7 - 8 = {}^-1$ **2.** $10 - {}^-2 = 12$ **3.** $8 - {}^-10 = 18$ **4.** ${}^-5 - {}^-8 = 3$

5. $9 - 14 = {}^-5$ **6.** $6 - {}^-10 = 16$ **7.** ${}^-10 - 2 = {}^-12$ **8.** ${}^-8 - {}^-5 = {}^-3$

9. ${}^-15 - 11 = {}^-26$ **10.** ${}^-20 - {}^-10 = {}^-10$ **11.** $12 - {}^-8 = 20$ **12.** $3 - {}^-7 = 10$

Find the difference.

13. $3 - {}^-2$ **14.** $11 - 16$ **15.** $10 - {}^-4$ **16.** ${}^-7 - 2$

17. $6 - {}^-6$ **18.** ${}^-15 - 15$ **19.** ${}^-9 - {}^-8$ **20.** ${}^-4 - {}^-4$

21. ${}^-12 - {}^-8$ **22.** $20 - {}^-2$ **23.** $34 - 45$ **24.** $18 - {}^-11$

25. $18 - {}^-10$ **26.** $24 - 38$ **27.** $60 - {}^-35$ **28.** $46 - {}^-10$

29. $57 - {}^-24$ **30.** ${}^-32 - 53$ **31.** ${}^-94 - 99$ **32.** ${}^-40 - {}^-24$

33. $89 - 99$ **34.** ${}^-50 - 66$ **35.** ${}^-347 - {}^-25$ **36.** ${}^-456 - 2$

37. $978 - 36$ **38.** $832 - {}^-32$ **39.** ${}^-56 - {}^-247$ **40.** ${}^-124 - 478$

41. $462 - {}^-198$ **42.** ${}^-903 - 651$ **43.** ${}^-267 - {}^-392$ **44.** ${}^-758 - 439$

Problem-Solving Applications

45. Wind chill makes the temperature feel colder. One day in December, the temperature outside is 15°F. With the wind chill the temperature feels like ${}^-22$°F. Find the difference between the two temperatures.

46. Special sonars are used to map the ocean floor. While at ${}^-215$ ft in the Atlantic Ocean, one of the sonars indicated that the ocean floor was at ${}^-19{,}345$ ft. How far was the sonar from the ocean floor?

47. The highest point on the Atlantic coast is 1,530 ft. The lowest point in the United States is ${}^-282$ ft. Find the difference between the two points.

48. ✏️ **WRITE ABOUT IT** Explain how subtraction of integers is related to addition.

Integer Games

REMEMBER:

Locations on the coordinate plane are named with ordered pairs, (x,y). The first number in the pair, the x-coordinate, tells how to move horizontally (left or right) from the origin, and the y-coordinate tells how to move vertically (up or down). **See page H29.**

You can make games that will help you practice skills such as adding and subtracting integers. Samantha and John made the game described in the box below.

Explore

• Work in pairs. Copy the gameboard shown on the next page and the spinner shown below.

• Play the game, using the rules given.

Race Across the Grid

1. The objects of the game are to
   • move all of your markers to your opponent's baseline.
   • capture as many of your opponent's markers as you can.

2. Each player chooses a color. Place three counters on your baseline as shown, with your color facing up. Decide who will go first, and then alternate turns.

3. Spin the pointer. Write an addition or subtraction equation, using the number from the spinner and the y-coordinate of the marker you choose to move. You can add or subtract the numbers in any order.

4. The sum or difference in your equation is the y-coordinate of the point to which you'll move the marker. The x-coordinate always remains the same for any marker.

   Example: Samantha spins and gets $^-6$. To move her marker from $(0,^-4)$ toward John's baseline, she writes the equation $^-4 - ^-6 = 2$. The new location for her marker is $(0,2)$.

5. Move your marker to the new location. If the new location is occupied by your opponent's marker, you capture the marker and occupy the location. Players can move their markers up or down when it is their turn.

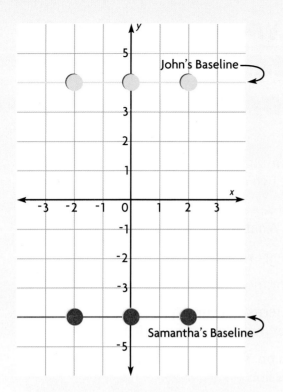

John's Baseline

Samantha's Baseline

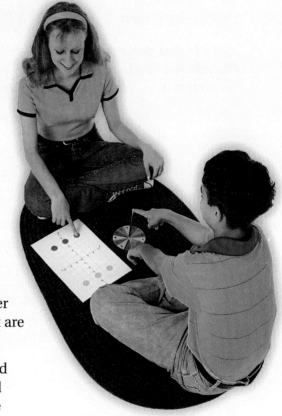

Think and Discuss 💡 CRITICAL THINKING

• What if Samantha spins a ⁻6 and wants to move the marker that is at (2,⁻4)? If she uses the equation ⁻6 − ⁻4 = ▓, what are the new coordinates for the marker?

• Suppose John wants to move his marker from (⁻2,4) toward Samantha's baseline. If he spins a 3, what equation should he use to move his marker as close to Samantha's baseline as possible? What are the new coordinates for the marker?

• Suppose John has a marker at (⁻2,1) and Samantha has a marker at (⁻2,⁻4). If Samantha spins a ⁻5, what equation can she write to capture John's marker? What if she spins a ⁻3? What equation can she write to capture the marker?

Try This

• Work with your partner to make a new game, also on a coordinate plane, that can be used to practice adding and subtracting integers. Explain your game to two classmates, and ask them to play the game. Revise your game rules if necessary.

Technology Link ▸
E–Lab • Activity 3 Available on CD-ROM
and the Internet at http://www.hbschool.com/elab

PROBLEM-SOLVING STRATEGY

Using Patterns to Find Products

Problem Solving
....
• **Understand**
• **Plan**
• **Solve**
• **Look Back**

What are the rules for multiplying integers? What is the product of two positive integers? two negative integers? a positive integer and a negative integer?

☑ **UNDERSTAND**   What are you asked to do?

☑ **PLAN**   What strategy will you use?

You can *find a pattern* for the rules for multiplying integers.

☑ **SOLVE**   What patterns can you explore to help you remember the rules for multiplying integers?

A multiplication expression, such as $4 \times {}^-2$, can be written as a repeated addition expression.

$$4 \times {}^-2 = {}^-2 + {}^-2 + {}^-2 + {}^-2 = {}^-8$$

So, a positive integer times a negative integer equals a negative integer. Use that idea to make a pattern that will help you find the product of two negative integers.

$$4 \times {}^-2 = {}^-8$$
$$3 \times {}^-2 = {}^-6$$
$$2 \times {}^-2 = {}^-4 \quad \text{\textit{In this pattern, as the first factor decreases}}$$
$$1 \times {}^-2 = {}^-2 \quad \text{\textit{by 1, the product increases by 2.}}$$
$$0 \times {}^-2 = 0$$
$${}^-1 \times {}^-2 = 2 \quad \text{\textit{Continue the pattern to find the product of}}$$
$${}^-2 \times {}^-2 = 4 \quad \text{\textit{two negative integers.}}$$
$${}^-3 \times {}^-2 = 6$$
$${}^-4 \times {}^-2 = 8$$

So, the product of two negative integers is a positive integer.

☑ **LOOK BACK**   What pattern can you make to show that the product of a negative integer and a positive integer is negative?

What if . . . you forget the rules for dividing integers? What patterns can you use?

PRACTICE

Find and extend a pattern to complete.

1. $^-2 \times ^-4 = 8$

$^-2 \times ^-3 = 6$

$^-2 \times ^-2 = \blacksquare$

$^-2 \times ^-1 = \blacksquare$

$^-2 \times 0 = \blacksquare$

$^-2 \times 1 = \blacksquare$

2. $^-4 \times ^-3 = 12$

$^-4 \times ^-2 = 8$

$^-4 \times ^-1 = 4$

$^-4 \times 0 = \blacksquare$

$^-4 \times 1 = \blacksquare$

$^-4 \times 2 = \blacksquare$

3.

$^-1$	0	1	2	3	4
5	0	$^-5$	?	?	?

4. George has a credit card balance of $3,467. He makes payments of $10, $30, $90, and $270. If his payments continue this same pattern, how much will his next amount be? What will be his remaining balance?

5. Sally is a sporting-goods buyer. In the past four years, her stores sold 160, 320, 640, and 1,280 soccer balls. If sales this year follow this pattern, how many soccer balls should she buy this year?

MIXED APPLICATIONS

CHOOSE

Choose a strategy and solve.

Problem-Solving Strategies
- **Find a Pattern**
- **Guess and Check**
- **Work Backward**
- **Draw a Diagram**
- **Make a Model**
- **Write an Equation**

6. Stephen's dad wants to fence in the family's yard. The yard, which is square, has an area of 6,400 ft². How much fencing is needed?

7. At 5 A.M. the temperature was $^-15.4°F$. At 7 A.M. the next day, the temperature was $^-10.3°F$. At which time was the temperature warmer?

8. The corner vegetable stand is selling tomatoes at $1.85 for 5 lb. The local grocery store is selling them at $0.79 for 2 lb. Which is the better buy?

9. Of the 240 hot dogs sold at the concession stand, 10% were corn dogs, 25% were chili dogs, and the rest were plain hot dogs. How many plain hot dogs were sold?

10. A new sports car costs $30,599. Each year the car depreciates in value. After 1 year, the car is worth $26,399; after 2 years, $22,199; after 3 years, $17,999. If the car continues to depreciate in the same pattern, how much will the car be worth after four years?

11. Mr. Griffiths told his history class that the ratio of the number of people in town who voted to the number of people who did not vote was 3:5. If the town has a population of 16,000 people, how many people voted?

12. ✏️ **WRITE ABOUT IT** Write a problem that can be solved with a pattern. Exchange with a classmate and solve.

ALGEBRA CONNECTION

Multiplying and Dividing Integers

WHAT YOU'LL LEARN
How to multiply and divide integers

WHY LEARN THIS?
To solve problems such as finding an average temperature

Amal made this study guide to help him remember how to multiply integers.

$$+ \times + = +$$
$$+ \times - = -$$
$$- \times + = -$$
$$- \times - = +$$

• What do you think each row of Amal's guide means?

• Give an example for each row of his study guide.

To make a study guide for remembering the rules for dividing integers, Missy suggested they change each multiplication sign in Amal's guide to a division sign.

$$+ \div + = +$$
$$+ \div - = -$$
$$- \div + = -$$
$$- \div - = +$$

Missy supported her idea with the rules for multiplying integers and the relationship between multiplication and division. She used this reasoning.

Since $8 \times 3 = 24$, $24 \div 8 = 3$. $+ \div + = +$

Since $^-8 \times ^-3 = 24$, $24 \div ^-8 = ^-3$. $+ \div - = -$

Since $8 \times ^-3 = ^-24$, $^-24 \div 8 = ^-3$. $- \div + = -$

Talk About It

• What do you think each row of Missy's guide means?

• What example would you use to show $- \div - = +$?

• Write a different example to show $- \div + = -$.

You can use a calculator to multiply and divide integers.

EXAMPLE 1   Find the product or quotient.

A. $12 \times {}^-8$

12 [×] 8 [+/−] [=] [⁻96.   ]   *Use the change of sign key to change 8 to ⁻8.*

$12 \times {}^-8 = {}^-96$

B. ${}^-168 \div {}^-14$

168 [+/−] [÷] 14 [+/−] [=] [12.   ]

${}^-168 \div {}^-14 = 12$

Use the correct order of operations and mental math to evaluate an integer expression.

EXAMPLE 2   Find the value of $(3 - 8) - ({}^-3)^3 \div 9$.

$$\begin{aligned}
(3 - 8) - ({}^-3)^3 \div 9 = \qquad &\textit{Operate inside parentheses.}\\
{}^-5 - ({}^-3)^3 \div 9 = \qquad &\textit{Multiply as indicated by exponents.}\\
{}^-5 - {}^-27 \div 9 = \qquad &\textit{Divide.}\\
{}^-5 - {}^-3 = {}^-2 \qquad &\textit{Subtract.}
\end{aligned}$$

So, $(3 - 8) - ({}^-3)^3 \div 9 = {}^-2$.

EXAMPLE 3   The temperatures last week were 16°F, ⁻2°F, ⁻5°F, ⁻12°F, ⁻7°F, 4°F, and 13°F. What was the average temperature?

First, find the sum of the daily temperatures.

16 [+] 2 [+/−] [+] 5 [+/−] [+] 12 [+/−] [+] 7 [+/−] [+]

4 [+] 13 [=] [7.   ]

Then, divide the sum by the number of days. $7 \div 7 = 1$

So, the average temperature last week was 1°F.

• 💡**CRITICAL THINKING** What if the temperature on the first day had been 9°F instead of 16°F and the temperature on the last day had been 20°F instead of 13°F? Would the average be higher, lower, or the same? Explain.

GUIDED PRACTICE

Tell whether the product or quotient is positive or negative.

1. 7×5 **2.** ${}^-6 \times 3$ **3.** ${}^-4 \div {}^-2$ **4.** ${}^-3 \times {}^-2$ **5.** $8 \div {}^-2$

REMEMBER:

The order of operations tells you the order in which to do the operations in an expression:
1. Operate inside parentheses.
2. Multiply as indicated by exponents.
3. Multiply and divide from left to right.
4. Add and subtract from left to right.

See page H11.

Science Link

The thermometers used most in the U.S.A. show temperatures in degrees Fahrenheit (°F). In most other countries the thermometers used show temperatures in degrees Celsius (°C). Room temperature is about 21°C, and normal body temperature is about 37°C. Check the weather report. How are temperatures reported?

Tell whether the product or quotient is positive or negative.

1. $2 \times {}^-5$ **2.** $^-6 \times {}^-3$ **3.** $^-16 \div {}^-2$ **4.** $^-3 \times 2$ **5.** $^-15 \div 3$

Find the product or quotient.

6. $20 \div 4$ **7.** $^-16 \div 4$ **8.** $^-6 \times {}^-3$ **9.** $^-18 \div {}^-6$ **10.** $5 \times {}^-4$

11. $15 \div 5$ **12.** $^-18 \div 9$ **13.** $^-3 \times {}^-2$ **14.** $^-9 \div {}^-3$ **15.** $3 \times {}^-4$

16. $12 \div {}^-4$ **17.** $^-6 \times {}^-3$ **18.** $^-14 \div {}^-2$ **19.** $^-5 \times 9$ **20.** $^-6 \div 3$

21. $^-8 \times {}^-2$ **22.** $^-24 \div {}^-4$ **23.** $7 \times {}^-4$ **24.** $81 \div 9$ **25.** $20 \div {}^-5$

26. $^-10 \times {}^-3$ **27.** $^-36 \div {}^-6$ **28.** $^-8 \times 4$ **29.** $^-64 \div {}^-8$ **30.** $^-33 \div 11$

31. $32 \div {}^-8$ **32.** $^-6 \times {}^-10$ **33.** $^-28 \div 2$ **34.** $9 \times {}^-8$ **35.** $45 \div {}^-15$

36. $52 \div {}^-26$ **37.** $^-40 \div 8$ **38.** $^-3 \times {}^-16$ **39.** $64 \div {}^-8$ **40.** $^-141 \div {}^-47$

Find the value.

41. $(^-4 \times {}^-2) + 3$ **42.** $(3 \times 5) + 27 \div 3$ **43.** $2 \times {}^-4 \times {}^-6$

44. $(4 - 6) - (^-2)^2 + 2$ **45.** $(^-2 \times 3) \div (^-3 \times {}^-1)$ **46.** $(9 \div {}^-3) - 4 \times {}^-3$

47. $(12 \div {}^-2) - (2 \times {}^-3)$ **48.** $3 \times (^-10 \div {}^-2) \times {}^-1$ **49.** $^-5 \times {}^-6 \times {}^-6$

50. $^-5 \times (^-2 + 5)$ **51.** $2 - 12 + (27 \div 3)$ **52.** $4 - 6 + (^-2)^3$

Problem-Solving Applications

53. A water tank has a leak. The amount of water changes by $^-6$ gal a day. When the total change is $^-192$ gal, the water pump will stop working. In how many days will this happen?

54. For the first week in January, the daily high temperatures in Bismarck, North Dakota, were 7°F, $^-10$°F, $^-10$°F, $^-7$°F, 8°F, 12°F, and 14°F. What was the average temperature for the week?

55. Last month Tom Davidson went scuba diving in the Atlantic Ocean. He moved to the ocean floor at a rate of $^-4$ m per minute. It took him 8 min to reach the ocean floor. Write an integer multiplication problem to find his position.

56. The ocean floor is at $^-96$ m. Tom has reached $^-15$ m. If he continues to move at $^-3$ m per minute, how far will he be from the ocean floor after 7 min?

57. ✏️ **WRITE ABOUT IT** Explain how multiplying or dividing integers is different from multiplying or dividing whole numbers.

MORE PRACTICE Lesson 3.4, page H49

Patterns with Integer Exponents

WHAT YOU'LL LEARN
How to find the value of expressions with negative exponents

WHY LEARN THIS?
To write very small numbers

What happens if you use a negative integer as an exponent?

ACTIVITY

Work with a partner to copy and complete the following pattern.

$10^4 = 10 \times 10 \times 10 \times 10 = 10{,}000$

$10^3 = ■ \times ■ \times ■ = ■$

$10^2 = ■ \times ■ = ■$

$10^1 = ■$

$10^0 = 1$

$10^{-1} = ■$

$10^{-2} = ■$

$10^{-3} = ■$

- As the exponents of 10 decrease by 1, what happens to the products?
- What do you think the value of 10^{-4} would be? 10^{-5}?
- How many places are there to the right of the decimal point in 0.1? in 0.01? in 0.001?
- How is the negative exponent related to the number of decimal places when the base is 10?

REMEMBER:
Any number, except 0, with an exponent of 0 has a value of 1. **See page H10.**

$4^0 = 1$

$2^0 = 1$

$9^0 = 1$

$(20)^0 = 1$

There is another way to show the pattern. You can write fractions.

$$10^{-1} = \frac{1}{10^1} = \frac{1}{10}$$

$$10^{-2} = \frac{1}{10^2} = \frac{1}{10 \times 10} = \frac{1}{100}$$

$$10^{-3} = \frac{1}{10^3} = \frac{1}{10 \times 10 \times 10} = \frac{1}{1{,}000}$$

EXAMPLE 1 Write each expression as a fraction.

A. $5^{-2} = \frac{1}{5^2} = \frac{1}{25}$

B. $4^{-3} = \frac{1}{4^3} = \frac{1}{64}$

C. $10^{-4} = \frac{1}{10^4} = \frac{1}{10{,}000}$

D. $2^{-5} = \frac{1}{2^5} = \frac{1}{32}$

When a whole number greater than 0 has a negative integer exponent, the value of the expression is greater than 0 but less than 1.

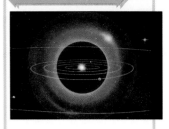

There are many instances in science where very large or very small measurements must be made. The numbers involved with these measurements can be hard to work with, unless scientific notation is used. For example, the distance from Earth to the Sun is about 150,000,000 km. How would this distance be written in scientific notation?

GUIDED PRACTICE

Write as a fraction.

1. 4^{-2} **2.** 10^{-3} **3.** 5^{-3} **4.** 2^{-4} **5.** 3^{-2}

6. 7^{-2} **7.** 4^{-3} **8.** 2^{-5} **9.** 9^{-3} **10.** 3^{-4}

Scientific Notation

You know that scientific notation shows the product of a power of 10 and a number. And you know you can change a number from scientific notation to standard form.

$$2.9 \times 10^3 = 2.9 \times 1,000 = 2,900$$
$$\uparrow \qquad\qquad\qquad\qquad \uparrow$$
scientific notation   standard form

You can also write very small numbers in scientific notation.

EXAMPLE 2   Write 0.000028 in scientific notation.

$$0.000028 = 2.8 \times 0.00001 \quad \textit{Move the decimal 5 places to the right.}$$
$$= 2.8 \times 10^{-5}$$
$$\uparrow \qquad \uparrow \text{a power of 10}$$
number from 1 to 10

So, 0.000028 written in scientific notation is 2.8×10^{-5}.

• Write 0.00053 in scientific notation.

EXAMPLE 3   Write 9.154×10^{-2} in standard form.

$$9.154 \times 10^{-2} = 9.154 \times 0.01 \quad \textit{Another name for } 10^{-2} \textit{ is 0.01.}$$
$$= 0.09154 \quad \textit{Multiply.}$$

So, 9.154×10^{-2} written in standard form is 0.09154.

• Explain why 91.54×10^{-3} is not in scientific notation.

REMEMBER:

A number is in scientific notation when it is written as the product of a number from 1 up to, but not including, 10 and a power of 10. **See page H7.**

$4,500,000 = 4.5 \times 10^6$

INDEPENDENT PRACTICE

Write as a fraction.

1. 10^{-2} **2.** 3^{-3} **3.** 6^{-2} **4.** 2^{-6} **5.** 10^{-5} **6.** 8^{-3}

7. 2^{-3} **8.** 9^{-2} **9.** 5^{-2} **10.** 3^{-5} **11.** 4^{-4} **12.** 10^{-6}

Write in scientific notation.

13. 34,000   **14.** 0.0467   **15.** 0.00000059

16. 0.000005399   **17.** 0.000068   **18.** 0.00885

19. 0.000000042   **20.** 0.00000000915   **21.** 0.0008666

22. 0.0076   **23.** 0.000000879   **24.** 0.0000000104

Write in standard form.

25. 3.5×10^3 **26.** 1.3×10^{-3} **27.** 4.45×10^{-2}

28. 8.58×10^{-5} **29.** 5.3×10^{-3} **30.** 2.5×10^2

31. 7.9×10^{-5} **32.** 9.112×10^{-4} **33.** 2.9×10^{-4}

34. 5.6×10^4 **35.** 3.4×10^{-6} **36.** 9.567×10^{-7}

In *Mighty Math Astro Algebra,* you can apply what you know about integer exponents when you enter the *Cargo Bay* and complete the mission *The Expired Warranty IV.*

Problem-Solving Applications

37. The diameter of a hydrogen atom is 0.0000000106 cm. Write the diameter in scientific notation.

38. The weight of a dust particle is 10^{-7} g. Write the weight in standard form.

39. Atomic clocks measure time in microseconds. A microsecond is 0.000001 second. Write this number in scientific notation.

40. The world's smallest cut diamond is 9×10^{-5} in. in diameter. Write the diameter in standard form.

41. ✐ **WRITE ABOUT IT** Is the value of a positive integer with a negative exponent greater than 1, greater than 0 but less than 1, or less than 0? Explain.

Mixed Review

Find the sum or difference.

42. $12.5 + 3.6$ **43.** $\frac{3}{4} - \frac{1}{3}$ **44.** $5.4 - 3.2$ **45.** $\frac{2}{3} - \frac{1}{9}$

Write as a percent.

46. $\frac{39}{100}$ **47.** $\frac{1}{1}$ **48.** $\frac{1}{5}$ **49.** $\frac{5}{4}$ **50.** $\frac{3}{4}$

51. **PERCENTS** A pizzeria sold 125 pizzas. Of those pizzas, 50 were delivered. What percent were delivered? Of the 125 pizzas, 60 were cheese pizzas. What percent were cheese pizzas?

52. **ART** When 3 friends divide 2 sets of colored pastels evenly, each gets 32 pastels. How many pastels are in each set?

CULTURAL CONNECTION

COOPERATIVE LEARNING

Magic Squares

Magic squares, square arrays of numbers in which the rows, columns, and diagonals have the same sums, appeared in Chinese writings as early as 2200 B.C. What is the sum for the magic square at the right?

13	3	17
15	11	7
5	19	9

Kim learned to solve magic squares while he was growing up in China. He likes to make magic squares for his classmates in America to solve.

Work Together

Cut nine pieces of paper. Write each of the integers below on one of the pieces of paper.

$^-1, ^-2, ^-3, ^-4, ^-5, ^-6, ^-7, ^-8, ^-9$

1. Arrange the nine pieces of paper to make a 3 × 3 magic square with three rows and three columns.

2. What is the sum of each row, column, and diagonal of the magic square you made?

3. Compare the magic square you made with those of your classmates. Is the sum of each row, column, and diagonal the same?

4. Use the same nine pieces of paper to make a different magic square. How many different magic squares can be made using the same nine negative integers?

5. Make a 3 × 3 magic square using this set of integers.

$0, ^-1, ^-2, ^-3, ^-4, ^-5, ^-6, ^-7, ^-8$

6. Kim made the magic square at the right for his classmates to solve. Correctly place the missing integers $^-8, 0, 5, 6,$ and $^-6$ in the magic square so each diagonal, row, and column have the same sum.

3	$^-2$	2	$^-9$
	1	$^-3$	4
$^-7$		$^-4$	
	$^-5$	$^-1$	

CULTURAL LINK

The magic square had its origin in China. The earliest record of a magic square is seen in a Chinese myth. According to the story, about 2200 B.C. the emperor Yu stood by the Yellow River and saw a magic square called *lo-shu* appear on the back of a tortoise in the river. The lo-shu, the oldest known magic square, was later represented as knots on strings. Black knots stood for even numbers, and white knots stood for odd numbers.

EXAMPLES

EXERCISES

• **Add integers.** (pages 56–58)

$^-5 + 4$

$|^-5| - |4| =$ *When addends have unlike signs, subtract the absolute values.*

$5 - 4 = 1$

Think: $|^-5| > |4|$ *Compare the absolute values of the addends.*

So, $^-5 + 4 = ^-1$.   *Use the sign of the addend with the greater absolute value.*

Find the sum.

1. $^-7 + 3$	**2.** $9 + ^-4$	**3.** $^-4 + ^-5$
4. $6 + ^-8$	**5.** $^-8 + 4$	**6.** $^-3 + ^-6$
7. $6 + ^-7$	**8.** $^-9 + 2$	**9.** $^-6 + ^-4$
10. $8 + ^-3$	**11.** $^-5 + ^-1$	**12.** $7 + ^-9$

• **Subtract integers.** (pages 59–63)

$^-8 - ^-4 = ^-8 + 4$ *To subtract $^-4$, add its opposite.*

$ = ^-4$

Find the difference.

13. $^-6 - ^-3$	**14.** $8 - ^-4$	**15.** $^-10 - ^-8$
16. $^-4 - 7$	**17.** $6 - 10$	**18.** $18 - ^-6$
19. $20 - ^-6$	**20.** $^-12 - ^-7$	**21.** $^-11 - 4$

• **Use the strategy of using patterns to find products.** (pages 64–65)

PROBLEM-SOLVING TIP: For help in solving problems by using patterns to find products, see pages 8 and 64.

Find a pattern and solve.

22.

$^-2$	$^-1$	0	1	2	3
6	3	0	?	?	?

23. Mr. Herman is a department store coat buyer. In the last three years, the coat department sold 60, 120, and 240 navy coats. If sales continue this pattern, how many navy coats will be sold this year?

• **Multiply and divide integers.** (pages 66–68)

$^-3 \times ^-4 = 12$ $- \times - = +$

$12 \div ^-3 = ^-4$ $+ \div - = -$

Find the product or quotient.

24. $^-6 \times ^-5$	**25.** $8 \div ^-2$	**26.** $^-2 \times 10$
27. $^-12 \div ^-3$	**28.** $^-8 \times 12$	**29.** $18 \div ^-2$
30. $^-15 \div 5$	**31.** $12 \div ^-4$	**32.** $^-8 \times ^-6$

• **Find the value of expressions with negative exponents.** (pages 69–71)

$10^{-5} = \dfrac{1}{10^5}$ *Write as a fraction.*

$\phantom{10^{-5}} = \dfrac{1}{100,000}$ *Find the value of 10^5.*

Write as a fraction.

33. 10^{-3}	**34.** 8^{-2}	**35.** 3^{-4}
36. 2^{-5}	**37.** 4^{-3}	**38.** 20^{-2}
39. 6^{-1}	**40.** 3^{-3}	**41.** 5^{-4}

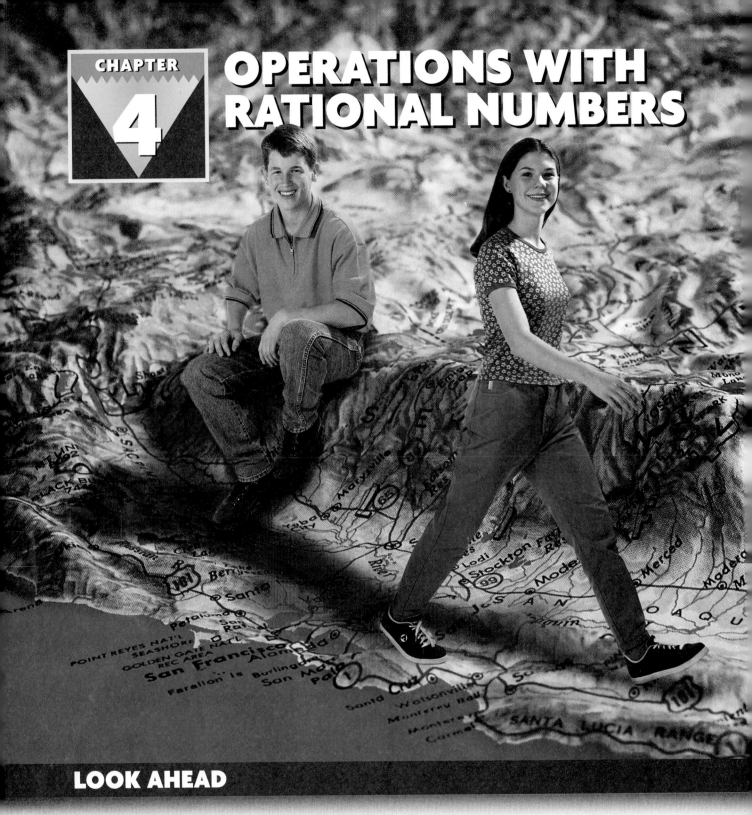

CHAPTER 4

OPERATIONS WITH RATIONAL NUMBERS

LOOK AHEAD

In this chapter you will solve problems that involve

- adding and subtracting rational numbers
- multiplying and dividing rational numbers
- using the order of operations
- making magic squares

Team-Up Project

To the Heights and Depths of the Earth

A survey of the Earth's surface shows the highest and lowest points relative to sea level.

Plan
- Analyze the data for each continent. Find the difference in height between the highest and lowest points.

Act
- Compute the difference for each continent.
- Record the highest and lowest points. Also record the greatest difference between high and low points.
- Make a chart to display your results.
- Try to find the highest and lowest points on the moon.

Share
- Share your chart with the class.

	A	B	C	D	E	F	G	H
1	Continent	Africa	North America	South America	Antarctica	Asia	Europa	Oceania
2	Location	Kilimanjaro	Mt. McKinley	Cerro Aconcagna	Vinson Massif	Mt. Everest	Mt. Elbrus	Puncak Jaya
3	Above Sea Level	+19,340 ft	+20,320 ft	+22,831 ft	+16,864 ft	+29,028 ft	+18,510 ft	+16,500 ft
4	Sea Level							
5	Below Sea Level	-512 ft	-282 ft	-131 ft	-8,327 ft	-1,312 ft	-94 ft	-52 ft
6	Location	Lake Assal	Death Valley	Peninsula Valdez	Bentley	Dead Sea	Caspian Sea	Lake Eyre
7					Subglacial			
8					Trench			

DID YOU

☑ Compute the differences?

☑ Record the highest and lowest points?

☑ Record the greatest difference?

☑ Make a chart of your data?

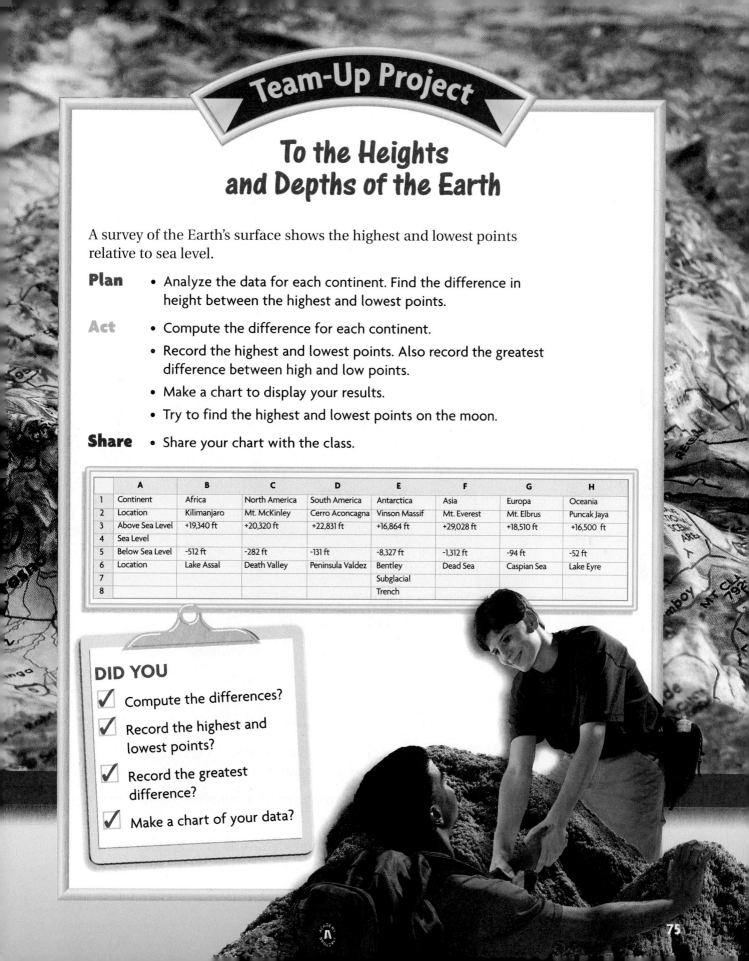

ALGEBRA CONNECTION
Adding Rational Numbers

You have learned how to add integers with like signs, as in $^-5 + {}^-7 = {}^-12$, and integers with unlike signs, as in $5 + {}^-7 = {}^-2$. What if you want to add fractions or decimals with like signs, as in $\frac{-3}{4} + \frac{-5}{4}$, and unlike signs, as in $^-0.6 + 1.5$?

You can use number lines to add rational numbers like these.

EXAMPLE 1 Find the sum. $\frac{-3}{4} + \frac{-5}{4}$

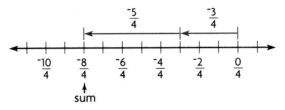

So, $\frac{-3}{4} + \frac{-5}{4} = \frac{-8}{4}$, or $^-2$. *The sum of two negative numbers is negative.*

• How can you use a number line to find the sum? $\frac{-5}{4} + \frac{-5}{4}$

You can also use this rule:

> When adding rational numbers with the same sign, add the absolute values of the rational numbers. Use the sign of the original addends.

Talk About It

• What is the absolute value of $\frac{-3}{4}$? of $\frac{-5}{4}$?

• What is the sum of these absolute values?

• What is the common sign of $\frac{-3}{4}$ and $\frac{-5}{4}$?

• When you use the absolute value rule, do you get the same sum for $\frac{-3}{4} + \frac{-5}{4}$ as you do using a number line? Explain.

• Is the sum of two positive rational numbers positive or negative? Support your answer with an example.

• Is the sum of two negative rational numbers positive or negative? Give an example.

• How can you find the sum of $^-5.8$ and $^-1.3$? What is the sum?

EXAMPLE 2 Find the sum. ⁻0.6 + 1.5

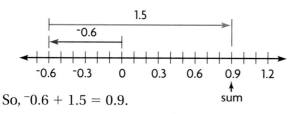

So, ⁻0.6 + 1.5 = 0.9.

> When adding rational numbers with unlike signs, find the difference of the absolute values of the addends. Use the same sign as the original addend with the greater absolute value.

You can use this rule to find the sum of rational numbers with unlike signs.

Find the sum. 14.9 + ⁻23.5

|⁻23.5| − |14.9| =   *Find the difference of the*
                            absolute values of the addends.
    23.5 − 14.9 = 8.6

⁻23.5 has the greater absolute   *Use the same sign as the addend*
value. Use a negative sign.   *with the greater absolute value.*

So, 14.9 + ⁻23.5 = ⁻8.6.

EXAMPLE 3 Find the sum. ⁻3.2 + 7.1

|7.1| − |⁻3.2| = 7.1 − 3.2 = 3.9

Since 7.1 has the greater absolute value, the sum is positive.

So, ⁻3.2 + 7.1 = 3.9.

You can use a calculator to find the sum of rational numbers.

EXAMPLE 4 Find the sum. $^-1\frac{3}{4} + 4\frac{5}{8}$

1 UNIT 3 / 4 +⟳− + 4 UNIT 5 / 8

= ⌈ 2U 7/8. ⌉

So, $^-1\frac{3}{4} + 4\frac{5}{8} = 2\frac{7}{8}$.

GUIDED PRACTICE

Tell whether the sum will be *positive, zero,* or *negative.* Use the method of your choice to find the sum.

1. $\frac{5}{12} + \frac{-1}{12}$ **2.** $\frac{-4}{5} + \frac{4}{5}$ **3.** $\frac{-1}{6} + \frac{5}{12}$

4. 10.7 + ⁻9.3   **5.** 9.2 + ⁻12.5   **6.** ⁻4.5 + ⁻5.6

Tell whether the sum will be *positive*, *zero*, or *negative*.

1. $15.4 + {}^{-}6.9$ **2.** ${}^{-}4.5 + 11$ **3.** $\frac{{}^{-}4}{9} + \frac{2}{9}$ **4.** ${}^{-}2 + \frac{7}{8}$ **5.** $\frac{9}{15} + \frac{{}^{-}3}{5}$

Use a number line to find the sum. Write the sum in simplest form.

6. ${}^{-}3.2 + {}^{-}6$ **7.** $\frac{{}^{-}7}{12} + \frac{7}{12}$ **8.** $3.8 + {}^{-}5.9$ **9.** ${}^{-}5 + 8.9$ **10.** $\frac{3}{4} + \frac{{}^{-}1}{4}$

Find the sum. Write it in simplest form.

11. $\frac{{}^{-}3}{8} + \frac{7}{8}$ **12.** $\frac{{}^{-}1}{6} + \frac{1}{4}$ **13.** $\frac{{}^{-}4}{25} + \frac{11}{5}$ **14.** $\frac{{}^{-}12}{25} + 1$ **15.** ${}^{-}0.9 + {}^{-}0.7$

16. $\frac{5}{6} + \frac{{}^{-}7}{12}$ **17.** $\frac{{}^{-}10}{13} + \frac{5}{26}$ **18.** ${}^{-}7\frac{3}{4} + {}^{-}6\frac{5}{12}$ **19.** ${}^{-}13 + 5\frac{1}{3}$ **20.** $6 + {}^{-}4\frac{5}{16}$

21. $0.8 + {}^{-}0.5$ **22.** ${}^{-}10.8 + 9.3$ **23.** ${}^{-}0.98 + {}^{-}0.02$ **24.** $10 + {}^{-}3.7$ **25.** ${}^{-}15.1 + 12.9$

26. $14.2 + {}^{-}5.9$ **27.** ${}^{-}16.4 + 12.5$ **28.** $0.15 + {}^{-}0.5$ **29.** $16 + {}^{-}17.9$ **30.** ${}^{-}20.2 + {}^{-}2.9$

Problem-Solving Applications

31. One of the goals Paco set for his new exercise program is running three times a week for a total of at least 15 mi. On Monday, Paco ran 4.2 mi. On Wednesday, he ran 4.6 mi, and on Friday, 5.9 mi. Did Paco meet his goal this week? Explain.

32. A national grocery chain was adding up the profits and losses for the year. The totals for the four quarters were $46.3 million, $37.5 million, [$23.3 million], and [$7.5 million]. What was the total profit or loss for the year? ([ ] indicates a loss.)

33. Mark's home in New Orleans is 7.5 ft below sea level, or ${}^{-}7.5$ ft. His friend's home in Michigan is 1,845.9 ft above sea level. What is the vertical distance between the two levels?

34. ✏️ **WRITE ABOUT IT** When adding rational numbers with unlike signs, how do you determine if the sum is positive or negative?

Mixed Review

Find the difference.

35. $16 - 37$ **36.** ${}^{-}5 - 4$ **37.** ${}^{-}20 - {}^{-}3$ **38.** ${}^{-}17 - 9$ **39.** ${}^{-}6 - 28$

Find the product or quotient.

40. ${}^{-}3 \times 12$ **41.** ${}^{-}13 \times {}^{-}9$ **42.** ${}^{-}990 \div {}^{-}30$ **43.** ${}^{-}4,800 \div 80$ **44.** ${}^{-}5,680 \div {}^{-}8$

45. **ART** In 1996, Grove's new *The Dictionary of Art* was published. It contains 263,000,000 words and 15,000 illustrations. Write these numbers in scientific notation.

46. **HEALTH** In the United States, more than 5 million children have asthma. In 1993, that amounted to 1 in 13 children. About what percent of the children have asthma?

MORE PRACTICE Lesson 4.1, page H50

ALGEBRA CONNECTION

Subtracting Rational Numbers

4.2

WHAT YOU'LL LEARN
How to subtract rational numbers

WHY LEARN THIS?
To find the difference of positive and negative fractions and decimals

Howcan you find the difference of two negative rational numbers such as ⁻63.85 − ⁻20?

The subtraction expression ⁻63.85 − ⁻20 can represent a real-life situation.

Tessie borrowed $63.85 from her parents to buy an outfit for her recital. After she did some chores for her parents, they reduced her debt by $20.00. How much does Tessie still owe?

Let ⁻63.85 represent the amount she borrowed and ⁻20.00 represent the amount of the debt her parents took away.

To find ⁻63.85 − ⁻20.00, draw a diagram.

$$^-63.85 - {}^-20.00 = {}^-43.85.$$

If you subtract $20.00 of Tessie's debt, she still owes $43.85.

• Which number is greater, ⁻43.85 or ⁻63.85? Explain.

You don't have to draw a diagram to subtract rational numbers.

> To subtract a rational number, add its opposite.

EXAMPLE 1 Find the difference. $^-1\frac{1}{2} - 4\frac{2}{3}$

$^-1\frac{1}{2} - 4\frac{2}{3} = {}^-1\frac{1}{2} + {}^-4\frac{2}{3}$ *Use a common denominator, and add the opposite of $4\frac{2}{3}$.*

$= {}^-1\frac{3}{6} + {}^-4\frac{4}{6}$

$= {}^-5\frac{7}{6}$, or $^-6\frac{1}{6}$ *The sum of two negative numbers is negative.*

EXAMPLE 2 Find the difference. $^-17.3 - {}^-32.1$

$^-17.3 - {}^-32.1 = {}^-17.3 + 32.1 = 14.8$

Sports Link

Golf is probably the only sport in which a negative score, a score below par, is good. Par is usually 36 shots for nine holes. A golfer with ⁻4 on the first nine holes has shot 4 strokes below par and so has a score of 32. If this golfer shoots a 31 on the last nine holes, what will be the score for all 18 holes, expressed as a negative number?

79

Write as an addition problem.

1. $^-6.3 - ^-2.7$ **2.** $^-3.5 - ^-4.5$ **3.** $6 - ^-2\frac{3}{4}$ **4.** $^-4\frac{1}{3} - 1\frac{3}{4}$ **5.** $5\frac{11}{12} - ^-5\frac{5}{12}$

Tell whether the difference will be *positive* or *negative*. Then find the difference.

6. $5.1 - ^-1.36$ **7.** $^-4.6 - ^-11.8$ **8.** $^-9.6 - 8.7$ **9.** $\frac{2}{5} - \frac{^-1}{5}$ **10.** $\frac{^-3}{7} - \frac{^-5}{7}$

11. $^-7.2 - 3.9$ **12.** $^-83.5 - ^-61.7$ **13.** $\frac{5}{9} - \frac{^-3}{9}$ **14.** $^-3\frac{5}{12} - 1\frac{7}{12}$ **15.** $7\frac{3}{10} - ^-5\frac{1}{5}$

INDEPENDENT PRACTICE

Find the difference. Write it in simplest form.

1. $10.3 - ^-5.2$ **2.** $^-4.1 - 12.7$ **3.** $^-3.3 - ^-8.9$ **4.** $^-14.8 - ^-9.2$ **5.** $2.01 - ^-9.43$

6. $^-8.4 - 7.7$ **7.** $9.7 - ^-9.1$ **8.** $^-4.7 - ^-15.2$ **9.** $^-23.3 - ^-5.7$ **10.** $0.56 - ^-4.02$

11. $^-25.9 - ^-1.2$ **12.** $96.3 - ^-10.9$ **13.** $^-5.8 - 58.7$ **14.** $87.8 - ^-0.99$ **15.** $^-92.3 - ^-2.8$

16. $\frac{^-1}{5} - \frac{^-4}{5}$ **17.** $\frac{^-7}{8} - 1\frac{3}{8}$ **18.** $9\frac{5}{16} - ^-3\frac{1}{4}$ **19.** $^-20 - 8\frac{7}{10}$ **20.** $15\frac{5}{16} - ^-7\frac{3}{16}$

21. $\frac{^-3}{14} - \frac{^-5}{14}$ **22.** $3\frac{1}{6} - ^-2\frac{5}{6}$ **23.** $^-10\frac{1}{5} - 8\frac{3}{10}$ **24.** $^-8\frac{5}{12} - ^-4\frac{5}{12}$ **25.** $7 - ^-6\frac{7}{8}$

26. $^-9\frac{7}{12} - ^-6\frac{1}{12}$ **27.** $^-4\frac{1}{7} - 6\frac{3}{14}$ **28.** $11\frac{1}{4} - ^-2\frac{1}{4}$ **29.** $^-3\frac{2}{15} - ^-10\frac{7}{15}$ **30.** $14\frac{5}{8} - ^-7$

Problem-Solving Applications

31. Jerry kept a record of the daily low temperatures during February for Barrow, Alaska. The average low temperatures for the four weeks were $^-5°F$, $^-16.3°F$, $^-20.6°F$, and $^-3.7°F$. What was the difference between the highest and lowest average temperatures?

32. The world's record high temperature of 136°F was recorded at Azizia, Tripolitania, in northern Africa in 1922. The record low temperature was $^-128.6°F$, recorded at the Soviet Antarctic station Vostock in 1983. What is the difference between the highest and lowest temperatures?

33. George owes $225.87 on his gas credit card. He made a payment of $68.25. Use the expression $^-\$225.87 - ^-\$68.25$ to find his new balance before finance charges.

34. ✏️ **WRITE ABOUT IT** When a negative rational number is subtracted from a positive rational number, is the difference positive or negative? Give an example.

Link

In *Mighty Math Astro Algebra,* you can enter the *Cargo Bay* and use your knowledge of adding and subtracting rational numbers to complete *The Strange Cloud of Machine Parts* mission.

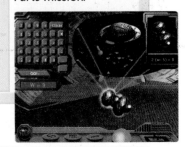

MORE PRACTICE Lesson 4.2, page H50

Multiplying and Dividing Rational Numbers

WHAT YOU'LL LEARN
How to multiply and divide rational numbers

WHY LEARN THIS?
To find averages of positive and negative fractions and decimals

The rules for multiplying positive and negative integers also apply to fractions and decimals.

> The product of rational numbers with like signs is positive.
>
> The product of rational numbers with unlike signs is negative.

You can use a calculator to find a product such as $^-2.8 \times {}^-14$.

2.8   14 | 39.2 |

So, $^-2.8 \times {}^-14 = 39.2$.   *The product of two negative rational numbers is positive.*

REMEMBER:

The product of two negative integers is positive.

$^-2 \times {}^-3 = 6$

The product of a negative and a positive integer is negative.

$^-4 \times 8 = {}^-32$

$4 \times {}^-8 = {}^-32$

See page H28.

EXAMPLE 1 Find the product. $^-4\frac{1}{2} \times 12$

$^-4\frac{1}{2} \times 12 = \frac{^-9}{2} \times \frac{12}{1}$ *Rewrite $^-4\frac{1}{2}$ as $\frac{^-9}{2}$.*

$= \frac{^-9}{2} \times \frac{\overset{6}{12}}{\underset{1}{1}} = \frac{^-9 \times 6}{1 \times 1}$ *Multiply numerators and denominators.*

$= \frac{^-54}{1} = {}^-54$ *The product of a negative and a positive rational number is negative.*

So, $^-4\frac{1}{2} \times 12 = {}^-54$.

• How are the products $4\frac{1}{2} \times {}^-12$ and $^-4\frac{1}{2} \times 12$ related?

• Predict the sign of the product $^-5.9 \times {}^-3.4$.

To find a product mentally, you can use the Distributive Property.

EXAMPLE 2 Find the product. $6 \times {}^-2.9$

$6 \times {}^-2.9 = 6(^-2 + {}^-0.9)$ *Rewrite $^-2.9$ as $(^-2 + {}^-0.9)$.*

$= (6 \times {}^-2) + (6 \times {}^-0.9)$ *Multiply $^-2$ and $^-0.9$ by 6.*

$= {}^-12 + {}^-5.4$ *Find the sum of $^-12$ and $^-5.4$.*

$= {}^-17.4$

• How are the products $2.9 \times {}^-6$ and $6 \times {}^-2.9$ related?

• Predict the sign of the product $^-3.5 \times 47.1$

EXAMPLE 3 With scuba gear, Jo went to ⁻12 ft and then to 5 times ⁻12 ft. What was her final position?

$5 \times {}^-12 = {}^-60$ *Multiply.*

So, Jo's final postion was ⁻60 ft.

To multiply more than two rational numbers, you can use reasoning and patterns to predict the sign of the product.

EXAMPLE 4 Find the products.

A. $2.75 \times {}^-3.4 \times {}^-2.1 \leftarrow$ even number of negative factors

2.75 ▨ X ▨ 3.4 ▨+↻−▨ ▨ X ▨ 2.1 ▨+↻−▨ ▨ = ▨

▭ 19.635 ▭

So, the product is positive.

B. $^-2.75 \times {}^-3.4 \times {}^-2.1 \leftarrow$ odd number of negative factors

2.75 ▨+↻−▨ ▨ X ▨ 3.4 ▨+↻−▨ ▨ X ▨ 2.1 ▨+↻−▨ ▨ = ▨

▭ ⁻19.635 ▭

So, the product is negative.

C. $^-4 \times 2.75 \times {}^-3.4 \times {}^-2.1 \leftarrow$ odd number of negative factors

4 ▨+↻−▨ ▨ X ▨ 2.75 ▨ X ▨ 3.4 ▨+↻−▨ ▨ X ▨ 2.1 ▨+↻−▨

▨ = ▨ ▭ ⁻78.54 ▭

So, the product is negative.

D. $^-4 \times {}^-2.75 \times {}^-3.4 \times {}^-2.1 \leftarrow$ even number of negative factors

4 ▨+↻−▨ ▨ X ▨ 2.75 ▨+↻−▨ ▨ X ▨ 3.4 ▨+↻−▨ ▨ X ▨ 2.1

▨+↻−▨ ▨ = ▨ ▭ 78.54 ▭

So, the product is positive.

- 💡**CRITICAL THINKING** Is the product positive or negative when there is an even number of negative factors? when there is an odd number of negative factors?

Science Link

NASA's Mission to Planet Earth is a 15-year program to learn how the Earth is changing. Scientists collect satellite data about the atmosphere, land, and water. What if the data show that the size of a glacier is changing at an average rate of ⁻13.7 cm per year? How can you find the total change in size for 5 years?

GUIDED PRACTICE

Tell whether the product will be *positive, zero,* or *negative.* Then find the product, and write it in simplest form.

1. $4 \times {}^-3\frac{1}{4}$ **2.** $^-5\frac{1}{6} \times {}^-2$ **3.** $^-2\frac{1}{3} \times {}^-3\frac{1}{4}$ **4.** $^-2.5 \times 9.2 \times 0$

Dividing Rational Numbers

Because multiplication and division are inverse operations, once you know the rules for multiplying rational numbers, you also know the rules for dividing rational numbers.

Multiplication   **Division**

$6 \times {}^-2.9 = {}^-17.4 \quad \leftrightarrow \quad {}^-17.4 \div {}^-2.9 = 6$

${}^-2.8 \times {}^-14 = 39.2 \quad \leftrightarrow \quad 39.2 \div {}^-14 = {}^-2.8$

- What are two division sentences related to the multiplication sentence ${}^-4.25 \times 3 = {}^-12.75$?

- What are two multiplication sentences related to the division sentence $8.25 \div {}^-0.75 = {}^-11$?

_____

Gloria and Al are experimenting with the diameters of parachutes to see effects on the rate of descent. Their first parachute took 12.4 sec to fall a distance of 8 ft. What was the average rate of descent in inches per second?

The parachute fell $8 \times 12 = 96$ in. To find the average rate of descent, use this formula:

$\text{rate} = \dfrac{\text{distance}}{\text{time}}$, or $r = \dfrac{d}{t}$.

$r = \dfrac{96}{12.4}$

96 12.4 $\boxed{7.741935484}$ ← about 7.75, or $7\frac{3}{4}$

So, the average rate of descent was about $7\frac{3}{4}$ in. per second.

- **CRITICAL THINKING** Suppose a second parachute took 18.3 sec to fall the 96 in. Did the average rate of descent increase or decrease? Explain.

EXAMPLE 5 Find the quotients.

A. $8.4 \div {}^-0.21 =$

8.4 .21 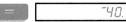 $\boxed{{}^-40.}$

$8.4 \div {}^-0.21 = {}^-40$

B. ${}^-3\frac{1}{8} \div \dfrac{{}^-5}{16} =$

$\dfrac{{}^-\overset{5}{\cancel{25}}}{\underset{1}{\cancel{8}}} \times \dfrac{{}^-\overset{2}{\cancel{16}}}{\underset{1}{\cancel{5}}} = \dfrac{10}{1} = 10$ *Multiply by the reciprocal of the divisor.*

So, ${}^-3\frac{1}{8} \div \dfrac{{}^-5}{16} = 10$.   *A negative divided by a negative is positive.*

Tell whether the product or quotient will be *positive, zero,* or *negative.*

1. $12.2 \times {}^-6.8$ **2.** ${}^-7\frac{3}{4} \times {}^-4\frac{7}{12}$ **3.** $18\frac{1}{6} \div {}^-3\frac{5}{6}$ **4.** ${}^-10.5 \div {}^-3.5$ **5.** $25.3 \times {}^-3.6$

6. ${}^-6.4 \times {}^-5.32 \times {}^-4.4$ **7.** ${}^-6.4 \times 5.32 \times {}^-4.4 \times 10.7$ **8.** ${}^-7.9 \times {}^-10 \times {}^-5.8 \times {}^-9.7$

9. $4.2 \times {}^-2.3$ **10.** $3.1 \times {}^-5.2 \times 0$ **11.** ${}^-1.5 \times {}^-9.3 \times 5$

Find the product or quotient. Write it in simplest form.

12. ${}^-5.5 \times 7.2$ **13.** 0.12×6.8 **14.** ${}^-11.3 \times {}^-2.6$ **15.** ${}^-0.99 \times {}^-8.1$ **16.** 15.6×3.4

17. $6\frac{2}{5} \times {}^-2\frac{5}{8}$ **18.** ${}^-2\frac{2}{5} \times {}^-5\frac{3}{4}$ **19.** ${}^-2\frac{1}{4} \times {}^-12\frac{1}{9}$ **20.** $9\frac{6}{11} \times {}^-3\frac{2}{3}$ **21.** ${}^-10\frac{5}{6} \times 4\frac{1}{5}$

22. ${}^-9.9 \div 3$ **23.** ${}^-6.72 \div {}^-1.2$ **24.** ${}^-67.67 \div 6.7$ **25.** $724.5 \div {}^-3.5$ **26.** ${}^-40.94 \div {}^-5$

27. ${}^-8\frac{1}{4} \div {}^-4\frac{5}{7}$ **28.** $8\frac{7}{9} \div \frac{{}^-4}{9}$ **29.** ${}^-10\frac{2}{3} \div 4$ **30.** ${}^-11\frac{5}{6} \div {}^-5\frac{1}{6}$ **31.** $9\frac{5}{13} \div {}^-4\frac{2}{3}$

32. $3\frac{1}{5} \div {}^-1\frac{2}{5}$ **33.** ${}^-8\frac{3}{4} \times 3\frac{3}{7}$ **34.** ${}^-7\frac{3}{5} \times 4\frac{1}{2}$ **35.** ${}^-9\frac{3}{4} \div {}^-3\frac{1}{4}$ **36.** $16 \div {}^-2\frac{2}{3}$

37. ${}^-52.4 \times 3.6$ **38.** ${}^-48.6 \div {}^-0.6$ **39.** $37.9 \times {}^-1.4$ **40.** ${}^-236.64 \div 2.4$ **41.** ${}^-8.8 \times {}^-3.9$

Problem-Solving Applications

42. Ana needs $\frac{3}{4}$ cup of blueberries to make 12 muffins. How many blueberries does she need to make 36 muffins?

43. A coastline is changing at a rate of ${}^-2\frac{1}{4}$ in. per year. At that rate, by how many inches will the coastline have changed in 75 years? What is the meaning of this change?

44. A Midwest city's low temperatures for one week were 4.5°F, ${}^-6.7$°F, ${}^-7.8$°F, ${}^-7$°F, ${}^-3.2$°F, 5.5°F, and 6.7°F. Find the average low temperature for the week, rounded to the nearest tenth.

45. ✏️ **WRITE ABOUT IT** Suppose two rational numbers have the same sign. When does their product or quotient have the opposite sign?

Mixed Review

Find the value of the expression.

46. $71 - 45 + 10$ **47.** $34 + 33 - 23$ **48.** $60 \times 35 \times 10$ **49.** $55 \times 3 \times 44$

Write in scientific notation.

50. $365,000,000$ **51.** 0.0000000089 **52.** 0.00047 **53.** 0.00000000078

54. **NUMBER SENSE** If you add ${}^-7$ to an integer and then subtract ${}^-4$ from the sum, is the result less than or greater than the original number?

55. **CONSUMER MATH** A 16-oz box of cereal costs $3.20. A 24-oz box of the same cereal costs $3.60. Find each unit price. Which box is the better buy?

MORE PRACTICE Lesson 4.3, page H50

Making Magic Squares with Rational Numbers

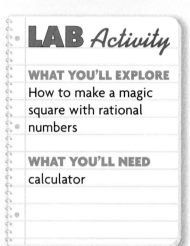
In a magic square, the sums of the numbers in each row, diagonal, and column equal the same number, the magic sum. In this activity you will change magic squares of integers into magic squares of positive and negative fractions and decimals.

Explore

• How are the corresponding cells of Squares A and B related?

• Find the magic sum for Square A and for Square B.

Square A

6	1	8
7	5	3
2	9	4

Square B

⁻6	⁻1	⁻8
⁻7	⁻5	⁻3
⁻2	⁻9	⁻4

• Make a new square, C, with the number in each cell equal to half the number in the corresponding cell of Square A. Write each number as a whole number or decimal. Is C a magic square? Explain.

• Make a new square, D, with the number in each cell equal to $\frac{3}{4}$ the number in the corresponding cell of Square B. Write each number as an integer, a fraction, or a mixed number. Is D a magic square? Explain.

Think and Discuss

• How are the magic sums of Squares A and C related? the magic sums of Squares B and D?

Try This

• Make a new square, E, by dividing the number in each cell of Square B by 1.5. Is Square E a magic square? Explain.

• Make a new magic square, F, by altering Square A or Square B with the operation or operations of your choice. Share your magic square with your classmates, and challenge them to find the magic sum.

Technology Link ►

E–Lab • Activity 4 Available on CD-ROM and the Internet at http://www.hbschool.com/elab

ALGEBRA CONNECTION
Order of Operations

You must follow the correct order of operations when solving problems that use more than one operation. Recall these rules:

> 1. Do the operations inside parentheses or above and below a fraction bar.
> 2. Find the value of any numbers in exponent form.
> 3. Multiply and divide from left to right.
> 4. Add and subtract from left to right.

Use the correct order of operations when computing with rational numbers.

EXAMPLE 1 Find the value. Name the operations in the correct order.

$(6\frac{1}{2} + \frac{1}{4}) \times 5 - 3^4$ *Add inside parentheses.*

$6\frac{3}{4} \times 5 - 3^4$ *Find the value of 3^4.*

$6\frac{3}{4} \times 5 - 81$ *Multiply.*

$33\frac{3}{4} - 81 = {}^{-}47\frac{1}{4}$ *Subtract.*

• What would you do first to find the value of the expression? What would you do second? $5\frac{7}{10} + 4\frac{1}{2} - (1\frac{3}{10})^2$

EXAMPLE 2 Find the value. Name the operations in the correct order.

$7.3 + 10.5 \div 1.5 - \dfrac{0.5 \times 10}{2}$ *Multiply above the fraction bar.*

$7.3 + 10.5 \div 1.5 - \dfrac{5}{2}$ *Divide from left to right.*

$7.3 + 7 - 2.5$ *Add.*

$14.3 - 2.5 = 11.8$ *Subtract.*

• What expression is represented by this sequence of calculator keys? What is the value of the expression?

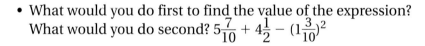

REMEMBER:
....
A calculator with an algebraic operating system (AOS) automatically uses the order of operations.
See page H11.

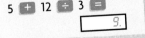

Tell what you would do first to find the value of each expression.

1. $6.2 - 5.4 \times 3 + {}^-4.5$

2. $(99.1 - 3.4) \times 10 + {}^-7.2$

3. ${}^-12.1 + 3.4 \div 10^2 + 7.2$

4. $8.2 \div 4.1 \times 4.3 + {}^-16.5$

5. $12.4 + 6.2 \times ({}^-9 + {}^-3.4)$

6. ${}^-34.1 - 3.78 + 8.5 - 8.9$

Give the order of operations. Then find the value.

7. $6.2 - 5.4 \times (3 + {}^-4.5) + 3.2$

8. $4.3 - 9.3 \div 3.1 - (2 \times 3.1)^2$

9. $\frac{3}{4} + \frac{{}^-2}{3} + 9^2$

10. $8\frac{1}{3} \div \frac{1}{2} \times (\frac{{}^-4}{5} + \frac{{}^-1}{10})$

Tell what you would do first to find the value of each expression.

1. $11.1 - 6.4 + 12 + {}^-4.7$

2. $6.2 + 12.9 \times 6.4 - 5.6$

3. $16.2 + 3.6 \div 2 + {}^-13.5$

4. ${}^-12.1 \times 3.4^3 \div 5.6 + 7.8$

5. $45.5 - 3.55 + 13.5 - 7.5$

6. $(5.64 + 2.2) \div ({}^-6 + {}^-2.7)$

Find the value.

7. $11.1 - (6.4 + 12)$

8. $4 + 13.4 \times {}^-6.4 - 5.6$

9. ${}^-8.2 \times 2^3 \div 4 - 2.3$

10. $(4\frac{5}{8} + 7\frac{3}{8}) \div ({}^-6.1 + 2.1)$

11. $16\frac{1}{2} + 4\frac{4}{5} \div 2^2 + {}^-10$

12. $11 \times (10\frac{3}{4} + 12\frac{1}{2}) - 6$

13. $14.4 + {}^-6.4 \times {}^-2.4 + {}^-6.5 \times 5.6$

14. $54.2 - 12.3 \div (7.1 - 4.1) \times 3^2$

15. $4^2 \times 6.2 - 14.8 \div ({}^-7.9 + 3.9)$

16. $8.3 \times {}^-4.4 \times ({}^-2.4 + {}^-6.5) + 5.6$

Write the expression represented by the sequence of calculator keys.
Then give the value of the expression.

17. 6.5 9.6 4 +⟳− (2.5 × 3.2 +⟳−) =

18. 9 + 5.4 +⟳− × (6.2 +⟳− + 4.5) =

Problem-Solving Applications

For Problems 19–21, write the expression. Then solve.

19. Multiply fifteen and the sum of three squared and forty-five.

20. Subtract thirty from the product of four squared and negative sixty.

21. Joey's father borrowed $325,000 to start his own business. If he pays back $10,800 per year, how much will he owe after 5 years? Write negative numbers for the money owed.

22. ✏ **WRITE ABOUT IT** Tony said the value of the expression $4^2 \times 5.5 + 4.5 \div 2$ is 80. Explain what he did wrong. Then find the correct value.

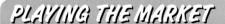

MATH FUN!

PLAYING THE MARKET

PURPOSE To practice adding and subtracting rational numbers (pages 76–80)

YOU WILL NEED page from the financial section of a newspaper, colored pencils or markers

Work with a partner. Each partner chooses a letter from the alphabet and examines the stocks in that section of the newspaper. In one color, circle every amount of money that is "gained" or "earned." In a second color, circle every amount of money that is "lost" or "spent." How much did you gain in a day? Lose in a day? Compare your earnings and losses with your partner.

ORDER UP

PURPOSE To practice using the order of operations with rational numbers (pages 86–87)

The order of operations is important in preparing a meal and in finding a value.

Work with a small group. Place the given signs and symbols in the correct order of operation to make each statement true. The person with the correct order first earns 1 point. The person with the most points wins.

+	12.1	6.4	12	$^-$4.5 = 11
$-$	24	$^-$7	$^-$3.2	$^-$6.2 = 52.6
$\times$	4	3.5	(10.6	$^-$2) = 8.7
$\div$	(6.5	2.5)	($^-$8	$^-$6) = $^-$18
( )	52.8	12	$^-$3	$^-$6 = 2.2

ABRACADABRA: IT'S COLOR-PERFECT MAGIC

PURPOSE To practice making magic squares (page 85)

YOU WILL NEED graph paper, colored pencils

Copy the magic square. Color the center number. Use a second color for the inner square, and a third color for the numbers in the outer square. Add any 2 numbers of the same color and on opposite sides of the center either horizontally, vertically, or diagonally.

1.2	28.8	20.4	18	9.6
16.8	8.4	6	27.6	19.2
26.4	24	15.6	7.2	4.8
12	3.6	25.2	22.8	14.4
21.6	13.2	10.8	2.4	30

Examples
6 + 25.2 = □
12 + 19.2 = □
8.4 + 22.8 = □

HOME NOTE Create a magic square by multiplying the number in each cell by 2.4. Find the magic sum.

REVIEW

EXAMPLES

• **Add rational numbers.** (pages 76–78)

Find the sum. $24.6 + {}^-3.5$

$$\left|24.6\right| - \left|{}^-3.5\right| =$$
$$24.6 - 3.5 = 21.1$$
$$24.6 + {}^-3.5 = 21.1$$

Subtract absolute values of addends. Use the same sign as the addend with the greater absolute value.

• **Subtract rational numbers.** (pages 79–80)

Find the difference. $^-3\frac{1}{2} - 2\frac{1}{4}$

$$^-3\frac{1}{2} - 2\frac{1}{4} = {}^-3\frac{1}{2} + {}^-2\frac{1}{4}$$
$$= {}^-3\frac{2}{4} + {}^-2\frac{1}{4}$$
$$= {}^-5\frac{3}{4}$$

Add the opposite of $2\frac{1}{4}$, and use a common denominator.

• **Multiply and divide rational numbers.** (pages 81–84)

Multiplication and division are inverse operations.

Multiplication		Division
$3.8 \times 4.3 = 16.34$	$\leftrightarrow$	$16.34 \div 4.3 = 3.8$
$9 \times {}^-5.4 = {}^-48.6$	$\leftrightarrow$	$^-48.6 \div {}^-5.4 = 9$
$^-6.3 \times {}^-3.7 = 23.31$	$\leftrightarrow$	$23.31 \div {}^-6.3 = {}^-3.7$

• **Use the order of operations.** (pages 86–87)

$7.3 + 4.4 \div 2^2 \times (4.5 - 3.2)$ *Subtract in parentheses.*

$7.3 + 4.4 \div 2^2 \times 1.3$ *Clear exponent.*
$7.3 + 4.4 \div 4 \times 1.3$ *Divide.*
$7.3 + 1.1 \times 1.3$ *Multiply.*
$7.3 + 1.43$ *Add.*
8.73

EXERCISES

Find the sum. Write it in simplest form.

1. $\frac{7}{12} + {}^-1\frac{11}{12}$ **2.** $^-3\frac{1}{9} + {}^-3\frac{2}{9}$

3. $^-4.8 + 10.7$ **4.** $^-6.2 + {}^-12.8$

5. $^-12.3 + {}^-5.28$ **6.** $^-11.5 + 8.17$

7. $\frac{^-5}{9} + 1\frac{1}{9}$ **8.** $^-4\frac{3}{7} + {}^-5\frac{6}{7}$

Find the difference. Write it in simplest form.

9. $^-6\frac{1}{4} - 8\frac{1}{4}$ **10.** $6\frac{2}{3} - {}^-3\frac{1}{9}$

11. $8.9 - {}^-3.5$ **12.** $^-13.4 - 2.5$

13. $^-88.3 - {}^-16.5$ **14.** $^-39.7 - {}^-54.3$

15. $^-9\frac{3}{5} - 2\frac{1}{2}$ **16.** $^-4\frac{2}{3} - {}^-7\frac{3}{4}$

Find the product or quotient. Write it in simplest form.

17. $^-22.4 \times {}^-6.6$ **18.** $34.1 \times {}^-2.9$

19. $^-5\frac{1}{5} \times 7\frac{1}{4}$ **20.** $^-4\frac{1}{4} \times {}^-9\frac{1}{3}$

21. $^-114.4 \div 2.2$ **22.** $^-15.12 \div {}^-4.2$

23. $^-12\frac{1}{4} \div {}^-4\frac{1}{4}$ **24.** $^-8\frac{4}{5} \div 2\frac{2}{5}$

25. $^-25.7 \times 8.5$ **26.** $^-404.8 \div {}^-0.8$

Find the value.

27. $^-1.3 + 81.9 \div 3^2$ **28.** $^-3.6 \times (4.5 - 6.2)$

29. $6.2 \times (1.5 - 4.2)^2$ **30.** $3.7 + 1.3 \times {}^-4.5$

31. $7\frac{1}{2} \div 3\frac{1}{3} + 4\frac{1}{4}$ **32.** $^-8\frac{2}{5} \times 4\frac{1}{3} - 3\frac{3}{5}$

33. $7.4 \times {}^-2.2 \div 2 + (6.5 - 3.5)^2$

34. $^-3.5^2 - 3.2 \times {}^-4.2 \div 3 + 8.8$

35. $^-3\frac{2}{3} - 2\frac{1}{2} \div (1\frac{1}{4})^2$

VOCABULARY CHECK

1. A number that has an integer as its square root is a _?_ square. (page 26)
2. An equation that states that two ratios are equivalent is a _?_ . (page 45)

EXAMPLES

EXERCISES

- **Classify and compare sets of numbers.**

(pages 16–19)

The Venn diagram shows that 2 is the only even whole number less than 20 that is not a composite number.

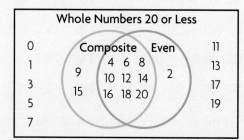

For Exercises 3–4, use the Venn diagram below.

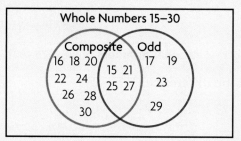

3. Which whole numbers between 15 and 30 are odd but not composite numbers?

4. Which whole numbers between 15 and 30 are both odd and composite?

- **Find the products and quotients of powers.**

(pages 24–25)

Write the product or quotient as one power.

$7^3 \cdot 7^5 = 7^{3+5} = 7^8$ *Add the exponents.*

$4^6 \div 4^2 = 4^{6-2} = 4^4$ *Subtract the exponents.*

Write the product or quotient as one power.

5. $9^5 \cdot 9^{11}$

6. $17^3 \cdot 17^{10}$

7. $24^9 \cdot 24^{20}$

8. $12^{10} \div 12^8$

9. $15^9 \div 15^6$

10. $35^{21} \div 35^{12}$

- **Find the square root of a number.**

(pages 26–27)

Find $^-\sqrt{36}$.

$^-\sqrt{36} = {^-6}$ *Think: $^-6 \times {^-6} = 36$*

Find the square root.

11. $\sqrt{100}$

12. $^-\sqrt{144}$

13. $^-\sqrt{256}$

14. $\sqrt{\dfrac{4}{9}}$

- **Relate ratios and proportions.** (pages 44–46)

Decide whether $\frac{3}{5}$ and $\frac{18}{30}$ form a proportion.

$\frac{3}{5} \overset{?}{=} \frac{18}{30}$ *Find cross products.*

$3 \times 30 \overset{?}{=} 5 \times 18$

$\quad 90 = 90$ *Compare.*

So, $\frac{3}{5}$ and $\frac{18}{30}$ do form a proportion.

Decide whether the ratios form a proportion. Write = or ≠.

15. $\frac{6}{12}$ ● $\frac{24}{36}$ **16.** $\frac{8}{24}$ ● $\frac{16}{48}$

17. $\frac{5}{12}$ ● $\frac{40}{96}$ **18.** $\frac{3}{4}$ ● $\frac{27}{40}$

19. $\frac{21}{49}$ ● $\frac{45}{105}$ **20.** $\frac{12}{20}$ ● $\frac{72}{100}$

- **Add and subtract integers.** (pages 56–61)

$^-9 + 3 \rightarrow \lceil^-9\rceil - |3|$ *Addends have unlike signs:*
$\qquad\qquad 9 - 3$ *subtract absolute values.*
$\qquad\qquad\quad 6$

Think: $|^-9| > |3|$ *Compare absolute values.*

So, $^-9 + 3 = {}^-6$.   *Use sign of addend with greater absolute value.*

Find the sum or the difference.

21. $^-11 + 15$ **22.** $^-8 + {}^-6$

23. $24 + {}^-41$ **24.** $^-19 - 18$

25. $80 - {}^-30$ **26.** $^-95 - {}^-20$

- **Multiply and divide integers.** (pages 66–68)

$^-6 \times 4 = {}^-24$ *The product or quotient of a negative integer and a positive integer is a negative integer.*

$^-56 \div {}^-8 = 7$ *The product or quotient of two negative integers is a positive integer.*

Find the product or quotient.

27. $^-2 \times {}^-7$ **28.** $6 \times {}^-11$

29. $^-20 \times 10$ **30.** $^-81 \div {}^-9$

31. $^-48 \div 4$ **32.** $108 \div {}^-12$

- **Use the order of operations.** (pages 86–87)

$2.8 - 1.5 \times 3^2 \div (0.7 + 2.3)$ *Add inside parentheses.*
$2.8 - 1.5 \times 3^2 \div 3$ *Clear exponent.*
$2.8 - 1.5 \times 9 \div 3$ *Multiply.*
$2.8 - 13.5 \div 3$ *Divide.*
$2.8 - 4.5$ *Subtract.*
$^-1.7$

Find the value.

33. $2.4 \times (3.6 + {}^-8) + 5^2$ **34.** $^-10 - 5\frac{1}{3} \times {}^-2\frac{1}{2}$

35. $^-4\frac{3}{4} \div 3\frac{1}{8} + 1\frac{3}{5}$ **36.** $(9 \div {}^-1.5) - 4^2$

37. $40.3 - 25.2 \div (8.8 - 4.6) \times 9^2$

PROBLEM SOLVING

Solve. Explain your method.

38. Through a microscope, Tao observed bacteria that were 4.03072×10^{-3} cm. Write the length of the bacteria in standard form. (pages 69–71)

39. At noon the water temperature was 70°. By nightfall it had changed by $^-24$°. What was the water temperature at night? (pages 76–78)

Write About It

1. Show how to write 62,500,000 in scientific notation. Explain your method. (pages 20–23)

2. Estimate what percent 146 is of 300. Explain your method. (pages 36–39)

3. Subtract these integers: $^-8 - 7 = n$. Explain your method. (pages 49–51)

4. Show how to find the quotient for $^-3\frac{3}{4} \div 3\frac{1}{3}$. Explain your method. (pages 81–84)

✔ Performance Assessment

Choose a strategy and solve. Explain your method.

> ### Problem-Solving Strategies
> - **Find a Pattern**
> - **Act It Out**
> - **Make a Model**
> - **Make a Table**
> - **Write an Equation**

5. A fast food restaurant is building a playground for children. The area of the square playground is 650 ft². What is the length of each side of the playground to the nearest tenth of a foot? (pages 26–27)

6. Band members conducted a survey of 200 residents to see if they would contribute to the band fund. Of the first 50 people asked, 36 agreed to contribute and 14 declined. Predict the results of the total survey. (pages 44–46)

7. Find the missing numbers. What is the pattern? (pages 64–65)

$^-4$	$^-3$	$^-2$	$^-1$	0	1	2	3	4
8	6			0		$^-4$		

8. On Monday the value of stock was $10\frac{1}{2}$. The price dropped $1\frac{1}{2}$ each day. On Friday, the value increased by $5\frac{1}{2}$. What was the value at the end of the week? (pages 76–80)

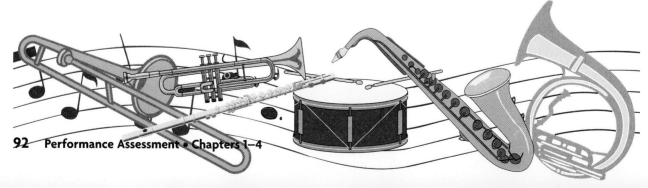

CUMULATIVE REVIEW

Solve the problem. Then write the letter of the correct answer.

1. Write the quotient of $9^{12} \div 9^3$ as one power. (pages 24–25)

   A. 9^4 B. 9^9
   C. 9^{15} D. 9^{36}

2. Find $\sqrt{121}$. (pages 26–27)

   A. 0.1   B. 0.11
   C. 10   D. 11

3. Choose the pair of rational numbers that the irrational number $\sqrt{38}$ is between. (pages 29–31)

   A. 3 and 4   B. 4 and 5
   C. 5 and 6   D. 6 and 7

For Exercises 4–5, use the table.

Points Scored in Each Round				
Round	1	2	3	4
Points	12	18	20	10

4. In which round were $\frac{1}{3}$ of the points scored? (pages 36–39)

   A. round 1   B. round 2
   C. round 3   D. round 4

5. What percent of the total points were scored in round 2? (pages 41–43)

   A. 20%   B. 30%
   C. 40%   D. 50%

6. Which pair of ratios forms a proportion? (pages 44–46)

   A. $\frac{9}{17}, \frac{27}{51}$ B. $\frac{12}{25}, \frac{3}{5}$
   C. $\frac{4}{32}, \frac{25}{100}$ D. $\frac{12}{120}, \frac{6}{54}$

7. The last four weeks, Lucas has spent 15, 45, 135, and 405 min building a model train. If this pattern continues, how many minutes will he spend next week? (pages 64–65)

   A. 540 min   B. 600 min
   C. 810 min   D. 1,215 min

8. Write 0.00000458 in scientific notation. (pages 69–71)

   A. 4.58×10^{-5} B. 4.58×10^{-6}
   C. 4.58×10^{-7} D. 4.58×10^{-8}

9. $\frac{^-3}{12} + \frac{5}{8}$ (pages 76–78)

   A. $\frac{3}{8}$ B. $\frac{1}{6}$
   C. $\frac{^-9}{24}$ D. $\frac{^-3}{7}$

10. $^-13.1 - {}^-4.8$ (pages 79–80)

    A. $^-17.9$ B. $^-8.3$
    C. 8.3 D. 17.9

11. Stock A changed $\frac{^-1}{4}$ in value today. Stock B changed $5\frac{1}{2}$ times as much as Stock A. What was the change in Stock B? (pages 81–84)

    A. $5\frac{1}{4}$ B. $2\frac{3}{4}$
    C. $^-1\frac{3}{8}$ D. $^-5\frac{1}{8}$

12. Find the value.

    $5 \times (12 + {}^-7) - (^-2)^3$
    (pages 86–87)

    A. $^-59$ B. $^-33$
    C. $^-17$ D. 33

NUMBERS, EXPRESSIONS, AND EQUATIONS

There is more to this than meets the eye.

$t > e$

LOOK AHEAD

In this chapter you will solve problems that involve

- identifying expressions, equations, and inequalities
- evaluating and writing expressions
- modeling and combining like terms

Equations For Expressions

Sometimes a quotation written in words can be expressed as an equation or inequality written with symbols. The symbols used are letters, or variables.

Plan
- Write symbolic equations or inequalities for quotations or expressions.

Act
- Work with a small group. List quotations or expressions that can be written symbolically. Make up your own expressions if necessary.
- Discuss the meaning of each quotation with your group. Write an explanation of each quotation.
- Write an inequality or equation for each quotation.

Share
- Combine your quotations, explanations, and equations with those of other groups to create a display.

A bird in hand is worth two in the bush.
$$h = 2b$$

A rose is a rose is a rose.
$$r = r = r$$

Two wrongs don't make a right.
$$2w \neq r$$

Television? The word is half Latin and half Greek. No good can come of it. — *C.P. Scott*
$$t = \frac{1}{2}l + \frac{1}{2}g$$

DID YOU

- ✓ List quotations or expressions?
- ✓ Explain their meanings?
- ✓ Write an equation or inequality for each?
- ✓ Create a display?

WORD POWER

numerical
   expression
algebraic
   expression
variable
equation
inequality

REMEMBER:

Multiplication can be shown in several ways.

7×8 $7 \cdot 8$ $7(8)$ $(7)(8)$

In an algebraic expression, the multiplication symbol is usually left out. $5n$ means $5 \times n$. y means $1y$, or $1 \times y$. **See page H9**.

Expressions, Equations, and Inequalities

$$n + 5$$
$$7y \quad x^2$$
$$= \geq$$

Do you speak the language of algebra? Learning the vocabulary and symbols of algebra will help you translate an everyday problem into a mathematical sentence so that it can be solved.

A **numerical expression** includes numbers and at least one of the operations of addition, subtraction, multiplication, and division. These are examples of numerical expressions:

$$6 + 8.1 \qquad 57 - 48 \qquad 21.6 - 18.6 \qquad 3\frac{1}{2} \times 4$$

An **algebraic expression** is an expression that is written using at least one variable. A **variable** is a letter that represents one or more numbers. These are examples of algebraic expressions:

$$n + 4 \qquad t - \frac{4}{5} \qquad 7.6 - y \qquad 4.3c + 2d$$

- What is the difference between a numerical expression and an algebraic expression?

An **equation** is a mathematical sentence that uses an equals sign to show that two expressions are equal. These are examples of equations:

$$9 + 8 = 17 \qquad 8.5 - 0.5 = 8 \qquad \frac{h}{2} + 4 = 5 \qquad y = x + 11$$

Some equations contain one or more variables.

- Which of the equations shown above contain one or more variables?

An **inequality** is a mathematical sentence that compares expressions that are not equal, using the symbol $<$, $>$, $\leq$, $\geq$, or $\neq$. These are examples of inequalities:

$$x + 13 < 16 \qquad h > 8 \qquad 9 + 8 \leq 18 \qquad n - 9 \geq 28 \qquad b - 80 \neq 3$$

Talk About It

- How do you read $<$? $>$? $\leq$? $\geq$? $\neq$?

- How would you decide whether to use $<$ or $>$ to complete the inequality $8^2 - 9 \bullet 9 \times 6$?

Tell whether each is a *numerical expression*, an *algebraic expression*, an *equation*, or an *inequality*.

1. $r - 2 > 35$ **2.** $x + 5$ **3.** $4 + h^2 = 68$ **4.** $5^2 - 3$ **5.** $25 \leq n + 30$

6. $30 + 4 = 34$ **7.** $3y + 4 \leq 34$ **8.** $45.5x$ **9.** $50 - 16$ **10.** $30a - 6$

INDEPENDENT PRACTICE

Write *expression*, *equation*, or *inequality* for each.

1. $16 + 5 = 21$ **2.** $h + 36$ **3.** $32 + 11 \geq 42$ **4.** $x + 15 < 26$ **5.** 12×150

6. $4f - 3 = 29$ **7.** $13 - y = 5$ **8.** $50 - 34$ **9.** $90.5y$ **10.** $4x > 20$

11. $40 - 3k$ **12.** $14 + 8 = 22$ **13.** $8 \div 4 \leq 2$ **14.** $20 - 3x > 7$ **15.** $4s + 4 = 24$

Write an example of each.

16. equation **17.** algebraic expression **18.** inequality **19.** numerical expression

Complete. Write $<$, $>$, or $=$.

20. $5 \times 3 \bullet 15$ **21.** $8 + 4 \bullet 6$ **22.** $36 \div 3 \bullet 20$ **23.** $88 - 81 \bullet 7$ **24.** $16 + 5 \bullet 8$

25. $97 - 9 \bullet 89$ **26.** $64 \div 16 \bullet \frac{24}{6}$ **27.** $\frac{84}{2} \bullet 41$ **28.** $4.5 \bullet 1.5 \times 3$ **29.** $49 + 13 \bullet 62$

Use the expression to write an equation.

30. $115 - 5$ **31.** $52 + 6$ **32.** $88 - 44$ **33.** 12×6 **34.** $125 \div 5$

35. $4y + 8$ **36.** $12 - 4k$ **37.** $5s \div 3$ **38.** $10 - 2x$ **39.** $7 + 7s$

Use the expression to write an inequality.

40. $30 \div 6$ **41.** $4x - 3$ **42.** $17 + 5$ **43.** $6y$ **44.** $5s + 2$

Problem-Solving Applications

45. Leah's teacher asked her to write an equation that shows the sum of 12 and 15. This is what she wrote: $12 + 15 = 28$. Did she write an equation? Explain.

46. Write a numerical equation that uses multiplication and shows the number of days in 4 weeks.

47. Write a numerical expression that uses addition and shows the number of boys and the number of girls in your class.

48. Write an equation that represents the sum of the ages of all of the people who live with you.

49. ✏ **WRITE ABOUT IT** Explain the difference between an expression and an equation.

Evaluating Expressions

REMEMBER:

Use the correct order of operations.

1. Do the operations inside parentheses or above and below a fraction bar.
2. Find the value of any numbers in exponent form.
3. Multiply and divide from left to right.
4. Add and subtract from left to right.

See page 67.

Have you ever tried to operate a VCR or set up a stereo system without understanding the directions?

In mathematics, you use directions called the order of operations. They tell you in what order to add, subtract, multiply, and divide in an expression having more than one operation.

You can find the value of, or **evaluate**, a numerical expression by completing the operations in the correct order.

EXAMPLE 1   Evaluate the expression. $48 - 18 \div 3 \times 5$

$48 - 18 \div 3 \times 5$ *Divide.*

$48 - 6 \times 5$ *Multiply.*

$48 - 30$ *Subtract.*

18

EXAMPLE 2   Find the value of the expression. $3 \times 4 - \dfrac{8 \times 3}{6} + 7^2$

Think: A fraction bar means division: $(8 \times 3) \div 6$.

$3 \times 4 - \dfrac{8 \times 3}{6} + 7^2$ *Do the operation above the fraction bar, and find the value of the fraction.*

$3 \times 4 - 4 + 7^2$ *Find the value of 7^2.*

$3 \times 4 - 4 + 49$ *Multiply.*

$12 - 4 + 49$ *Add and subtract from left to right.*

57

Numerical expressions are **equivalent** when they have the same value. The following expressions are equivalent:

$5 - 1$ $3.5 + 0.5$ $2 \div \dfrac{1}{2}$ $4^2 - 12$ $\dfrac{^-8}{^-2}$ $^-5 + 9$

• What is the value of each expression?

You may have to evaluate expressions to tell whether they are equivalent.

• Are $\dfrac{^-16}{^-8}$ and $^-2 \times 1$ equivalent? Explain.

You can write equivalent numerical expressions.

EXAMPLE 3   Write three numerical expressions equivalent to $(25 + 5) \div 3 - 4 \times 2$.

Think: Find the value of the expression.

$(25 + 5) \div 3 - 4 \times 2$	*Do the operation inside the parentheses.*
$30 \div 3 - 4 \times 2$	*Divide and multiply from left to right.*
$10 - 8$	*Subtract.*
2	

$3 - 1 \leftarrow$ value is 2	*Write three expressions with a value of 2.*
$8 \div 4 \leftarrow$ value is 2	
$2 \times 1 \leftarrow$ value is 2	*Compare values: 2 = 2 = 2 = 2.*

So, $3 - 1$, $8 \div 4$, and 2×1 are equivalent to $(25 + 5) \div 3 - 4 \times 2$.

- Write three numerical expressions equivalent to $9 - (48 \div 3) \div 8 \times 3$.

GUIDED PRACTICE

Give the order in which you would do the operations.

1. $8 + 15 \div 3 - 1$ **2.** $4^2 + (7 - 5)$

3. $6 - 9.7 \times 2$ **4.** $\frac{^-2}{^-6} + 10$ **5.** $(4 + 3) \times 6$

Evaluate the expression.

6. $6 - 9.7$ **7.** $^-6 \times 5 - 3$ **8.** $(4 + 3) \times 6 - 2$

9. $^-6 \times (5 - 3)$ **10.** $\frac{^-8}{^-2} - 9$ **11.** $9 + 2^3 \times 4$

Write *yes* or *no* to tell whether the expressions are equivalent.

12. $8^2 - 5, 7 \times 8 + 3$ **13.** $\frac{2 \times 5}{1 + 4}, 2^2 - 1$ **14.** $8 - 3, 4 \times 3 - 7$

Write an equivalent expression.

15. $20 - 5 \times 4$ **16.** $8 \div {^-4} + 4$ **17.** $3^2 + 1$

18. $96 \div 6 - 5^2$ **19.** $\frac{8 \times 4}{3 + 5} + 9^2$ **20.** $(8^2 + 2) \div 11$

21. How can you tell whether two numerical expressions are equivalent?

Career Link

Many careers involve evaluating things. Property appraisers, for example, determine the value of a house and lot before the property is sold or taxed. The appraiser first examines the property and then compares it with similar properties in the area. Suppose a property is valued at $100,000 and the taxes are 7.5% of the value. How much are the taxes?

REMEMBER:

You can write the product of a number and a variable in many ways. These are ways to write the product of 8 and *c*:

$8c$ $8 \times c$ $8 \cdot c$ $8(c)$

See page H9.

Algebraic Expressions

To evaluate an algebraic expression, you need to translate the meaning of its symbols. An algebraic expression such as $5b$ is the product of a number and a variable. The number that is multiplied by the variable is the **coefficient**. A coefficient can be positive or negative.

• Identify the coefficient of each expression.

$2y$ $\qquad\qquad$ ^-7a $\qquad\qquad$ $9.8x$ $\qquad\qquad$ $3\frac{2}{5}k$

You can evaluate an algebraic expression for given values of one or more variables. Replace each variable with its value. Then evaluate the expression.

EXAMPLE 4 Evaluate $2x^2 - y$ for $x = 4$ and $y = {}^-3$.

$2x^2 + y$ $\qquad$ *Replace x with 4, and replace y with $^-3$.*

$2 \cdot (4)^2 + (^-3)$ $\qquad$ *Find the value of $(4)^2$.*

$2 \cdot 16 + (^-3)$ $\qquad$ *Multiply.*

$32 + (^-3)$ $\qquad$ *Add.*

29

• How can you evaluate $b^2 + c$ for $b = {}^-5$ and $c = 2$?

• Evaluate $9x + 4y^3$ for $x = {}^-2$ and $y = 5$.

You evaluate an algebraic expression every time you use a formula to solve a problem.

EXAMPLE 5 The length of a side of Ernesto's square living room is s. The algebraic expression $4s$ represents the perimeter of the room. If $s = 12$ ft, what is the perimeter of the room?

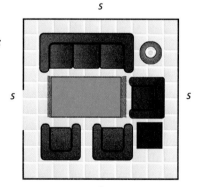

$4s$ $\qquad$ *Write the expression.*

$4 \cdot 12$ $\qquad$ *Replace s with 12.*

48 $\qquad$ *Multiply.*

So, the perimeter of the room is 48 ft.

• Suppose $s = 15$ ft. What is the perimeter?

• Write an algebraic expression that represents the perimeter of a regular pentagon.

REMEMBER:

Perimeter is the distance around a polygon. Use the formula $P = s + s + s + s$ or $P = 4s$ to find the perimeter of a square. **See page H25.**

Evaluate the expression.

1. $4 + 5 \times 3 - 4$ **2.** $(6 + 2) \times 5 + 4$ **3.** $10 - 3^2 \times 4 + 3$ **4.** $\dfrac{4}{8} \times 16 - 4 \div 2$

5. $9^2 - 10 \div 5$ **6.** $\dfrac{9 \times 7}{4 + 17}$ **7.** $(1.5 + 3.75) \times 9$ **8.** $\dfrac{4 + 4 \times 8}{8^2 + 8}$

Write *yes* or *no* to tell whether the expressions are equivalent.

9. $8 \div 4 + 2;\ 2 \times 2$ **10.** $12 \div 6 + 4;\ 36 \div (2 \times 3)$ **11.** $9 + 9 \div 3;\ (9 + 9) \div 3$

Write the variable and the coefficient of each expression.

12. $3.5x$ **13.** $14s^3$ **14.** $\dfrac{1}{2}k$ **15.** $\dfrac{x}{3}$ **16.** ^-23h **17.** $^-6.7y$

Evaluate for $x = 3$ and $y = {^-2}$.

18. $16x + 2$ **19.** $x + (1 - 4y)$ **20.** $4x + 4 - 5y$ **21.** $5y^2$

22. $(x - 5) \times y^3$ **23.** $2x - 3 \times 3y^2$ **24.** $\dfrac{x + 1}{2} + 3y$ **25.** $\dfrac{4x + 2}{7} - 4y$

Problem-Solving Applications

26. The average number of people who visit the Statue of Liberty daily can be represented by c. The expression $2c + 5$ represents the number who visited on July 1. If $c = 300$, how many people visited the Statue of Liberty on July 1?

27. The width of a kitchen can be represented by w. The length can be represented by l. The algebraic expression $2w + 2l$ represents the perimeter of the room. If $w = 6$ ft and $l = 10$ ft, what is the perimeter?

28. Abraham Lincoln's Gettysburg Address begins, "Four score and seven years ago." A score is a group of 20 things. How many are four score and seven years?

29. **WRITE ABOUT IT** Todd says the expressions $3n + 3$ and $3 + 3n$ are equivalent. Is he correct? Explain.

Mixed Review

Write in words.

30. $6 + 8$ **31.** 4×9 **32.** $10 \div 5$ **33.** $5 - 4$ **34.** $\dfrac{4 + 2}{3}$

Find the sum or difference.

35. $14.5 - 13.2$ **36.** $23.6 - {^-24.5}$ **37.** $^-4.3 + 15.9$ **38.** $^-16.3 + 13.4$ **39.** $^-4.3 + {^-16.5}$

40. **CHOOSE A STRATEGY** Vincent bought two suits. The total cost for both was $420. The difference of the costs of the two suits was $30. What did he pay for each suit?

41. **HEALTH** There are 8.5 calories and 0.6 grams of sugar per ounce of broccoli. How many calories and grams of sugar are in a 5.3-oz serving?

Writing Expressions

WHAT YOU'LL LEARN
How to translate and write algebraic expressions

WHY LEARN THIS?
To represent and solve real-life problems such as finding the cost of a trip

Have you ever translated the word expressions of a young child into adult language?

Some real-life word expressions can be translated into algebraic symbols. This table shows some word expressions and the corresponding algebraic expressions.

Word Expression	Algebraic Expression
3 more than the number of horses, h The sum of a number, n, and 8 The cost of the order, c, increased by $4	$h + 3$ $n + 8$ $c + 4$
4 meters less than the distance, d The difference between the weight, w, and 20 pounds The amount of the award, a, decreased by $10	$d - 4$ $w - 20$ $a - 10$
5 times the number of baseball cards, b The number of hours, x, multiplied by 4.8 The product of 9 and the price, p	$5b$ $4.8x$ $9p$
The area, a, divided by 12 The quotient of a number, n, and 5.8 480 mi divided by the time, t	$a \div 12$, or $\frac{a}{12}$ $n \div 5.8$, or $\frac{n}{5.8}$ $480 \div t$, or $\frac{480}{t}$

You can translate a word expression into an algebraic expression.

EXAMPLE 1 Write an algebraic expression for this word expression: half the distance to the goal.

Let d = the distance to the goal.   *Choose a variable.*

operation: division   *Identify the operation.*

$$\frac{d}{2}$$ *Write an algebraic expression.*

Talk About It 💡 CRITICAL THINKING

• How is $\frac{d}{2}$ related to $\frac{1}{2}d$?

• Is dividing a number by 3 the same as multiplying the number by $\frac{1}{3}$? Give an example to support your answer.

• Identify an algebraic expression for this word expression: the time, t, increased by 7 days.

Sports Link

Most sports have a language of their own. Expressions such as *home run* in baseball and *first down* in football have special meanings. Suppose that you watch a basketball game and see Penny Hardaway shooting from beyond the *3-point line*. Write an algebraic expression that represents his team's score after he makes the shot. Let s = the team's current score.

Sometimes one algebraic expression can represent two different word expressions.

EXAMPLE 2 Write an algebraic expression for these two word expressions:

a. $70 less than the regular price

b. a 70°F drop in temperature

Let n = the regular price in dollars.   *Choose a variable.*

Let n = the original temperature in °F.   *Use the same variable.*

operation: subtraction   *Identify the operation.*

$n - 70$ *Write an algebraic expression.*

Some real-life situations can be represented by an algebraic expression with more than one operation.

EXAMPLE 3 The cost of the trip to the state fair is $5 more than twice the amount of Andrea's savings. Write an algebraic expression that represents the cost of the trip.

Let s = the amount of Andrea's savings in dollars.   *Choose a variable.*

operations: addition and multiplication   *Identify the operations.*

$2s + 5$ *Write an algebraic expression.*

- Suppose Andrea's savings total $100. How would you find the actual cost of the trip to the state fair?

GUIDED PRACTICE

Choose from the box the algebraic expression that represents the word expression.

1. 7 more than a number, n

2. a number, n, divided by 7

3. 7 less than a number, n

4. the product of 7 and a number, n

5. Write a word expression for the algebraic expression $10n$.

$$7n$$
$$n - 7$$
$$n + 7$$
$$\frac{n}{7}$$

INDEPENDENT PRACTICE

Choose from the box the algebraic expression that represents the word expression.

1. ten less than a number, n

2. a number, n, times 10

3. a number, n, divided by ten

4. ten more than a number, n

$$10n$$
$$n + 10$$
$$n - 10$$
$$\frac{n}{10}$$

In **Mighty Math Astro Algebra,** be ready to translate words to algebraic expressions when you report to the *Number Line* and complete the *Running the Energy Gauntlet II* mission.

Write an algebraic expression for the word expression.

5. 16 times the distance, d

6. $15 off the total cost of the bike, t

7. the quotient of the number of days, d, and 30

8. the number of horses, h, increased by 17

9. the number of students, s, decreased by 25

10. the product of the cost of the shirt, s, and 3

11. the number of players, p, divided by 2

12. 5 less than the number of trumpets, t

13. the difference between 15 and the number of fish, f

14. the sum of 14 home runs and the total number of home runs, r

15. twice the number of sports fans, f

16. 10 more than the number of trains, t

Write two word expressions for the algebraic expression.

17. $16 - p$

18. $44 + d$

19. $\frac{x}{10}$

20. $a \div 4$

21. $65m$

Problem-Solving Applications

22. Petra bought a video game on sale at $7 off the regular price, r. Write an expression that represents the sale price of the video.

23. Stella bought t books that cost $3.75 each. Write an expression that represents the total cost of the books.

24. John's dog had 5 more puppies in her second litter than the number in her first litter, p. Write an expression that represents the number of puppies in her second litter.

25. The gym teacher is dividing the class members, c, into 4 teams. Write an expression that represents the number of members on each team.

26. ✏️ **WRITE ABOUT IT** Reggie says that the algebraic expression for "a number, n, divided by 4" is $\frac{4}{n}$. Is he correct? Explain.

MORE PRACTICE Lesson 5.3, page H52

Modeling Like Terms

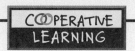

A **term** is a real number, a variable, or the product of real numbers and variables. In the expression $5x + 4$, the terms are $5x$ and 4. Some expressions have terms that are similar. When two or more terms have the same variables and the same powers of these variables, they are called **like terms**.

like terms: $8y$, ^-4y, $9.1y$ unlike terms: $7c$, $3.4x$, ^-y

Explore

You can use algebra tiles of the same size and shape to represent like terms. Let a green rectangle represent x; a red rectangle, ^-x; a yellow square, 1; and a red square, $^-1$.

• Make the model of $6x + 5 + {}^-2x$ shown below.

• Which tiles represent $6x$? 5? ^-2x? Which are like terms?

• Rearrange the tiles so that the like terms are side by side. Combine, or add, the like terms by removing all pairs of opposite tiles (green and red). What tiles remain in the model? What expression describes these tiles?

Think and Discuss  CRITICAL THINKING

• Suppose you evaluate $6x + 5 + {}^-2x$ and $4x + 5$ for $x = 2$. Predict the result. Try it.

• Are the two expressions equivalent? Explain.

Try This

Model the expression with algebra tiles or a drawing. Combine like terms, and write the new expression.

1. $5x + 4x$ **2.** $^-4x + 5 + {}^-2x$ **3.** $7x + {}^-3x + 9$

Technology Link →
E–Lab • Activity 5 Available on CD-ROM
and the Internet at http://www.hbschool.com/elab

WORD POWER

term
like terms

REMEMBER:

The sum of a number and its opposite is zero.

$^-5 + 5 = 0$

$a + {}^-a = 0$

See page 56.

Combining Like Terms

WHAT YOU'LL LEARN
How to combine like terms in an expression

WHY LEARN THIS?
To represent and solve real-life problems such as sorting coins

WORD POWER
combine like terms
simplify
simplest form

REMEMBER:
Commutative Property
$3 + 9 + 7 = 3 + 7 + 9$
Associative Property
$(5 + 2) + 8 = 5 + (2 + 8)$
Distributive Property
$6 \cdot 52 = 6(50 + 2)$
See page H11.

Consumer Link
Have you ever used a mechanical coin sorter to separate mixed coins? How is sorting coins similar to combining like terms?

Have you ever sorted your change into groups of like coins—quarters, dimes, nickels, and pennies?

In mathematics, the process of sorting and collecting like terms is called combining like terms. To **combine like terms** means to add or subtract them.

To add or subtract like terms, add or subtract the coefficients.

EXAMPLE 1 Combine like terms. $^-2x + 6x + {}^-8x + 7$

$^-2x + 6x + {}^-8x + 7$	
$6x + {}^-2x + {}^-8x + 7$	*Use Commutative Property.*
$6x + ({}^-2x + {}^-8x) + 7$	*Use Associative Property.*
$6x + {}^-10x + 7$	
$^-4x + 7$	*Add like terms.*

You **simplify** an algebraic expression by combining like terms. The expression that results is described as the **simplest form** of the expression. In Example 1, $^-4x + 7$ is the simplest form of $^-2x + 6x + {}^-8x + 7$.

You may have to use the Distributive Property before you can combine like terms.

EXAMPLE 2 Simplify. $4(y + 9) + {}^-3y$

$4(y + 9) + {}^-3y$	
$4 \cdot y + 4 \cdot 9 + {}^-3y$	*Use Distributive Property.*
$4y + 36 + {}^-3y$	
$4y + {}^-3y + 36$	*Use Commutative Property.*
$y + 36$	*Add like terms.*

• Simplify. $^-6n + 7(5n + 3)$

Sometimes an expression has more than one variable.

• How can you simplify $^-4n + {}^-9w + 11n + 3w$?

GUIDED PRACTICE

Write the like terms.

1. $5n, 6n, 7, 4x$ **2.** $^-2y, 6, 2.5y, y$ **3.** $2n, 8y, 4x, 15$ **4.** $3a, ^-6b, 7b, 4a, 8$

Simplify by combining like terms.

5. $4a + 3a + ^-4 + ^-2a$ **6.** $9x + ^-6x + 4 + ^-11$ **7.** $10a + 3 + 4b + ^-4 + ^-2a$

8. $12n + ^-n + 7(n + 8)$ **9.** $k + 5(7 + 2k) + ^-6k$ **10.** $8c + 3(c + ^-4) + ^-4c + 10$

INDEPENDENT PRACTICE

Simplify.

1. $12 + 5b + 2b + ^-6 + ^-2b$ **2.** $6x + ^-8 + ^-5x + ^-8 + ^-8x$ **3.** $^-4 + 4x + ^-3x + x + 6$

4. $2.5h + ^-6 + ^-h + 2.1h$ **5.** $5(x + 1) + ^-3$ **6.** $^-9 + 3(n + 1) + 3n$

7. $^-7s + 4(s + 4) + 5s + ^-6$ **8.** $6(2 + 2n) + 3n + 4$ **9.** $^-14x + 4y + ^-3y + 5x + 6$

10. $9 + ^-4a + 3b + 5a + 7b$ **11.** $7x + ^-3y + ^-9 + 2(x + 2)$ **12.** $9a + 4(a + b) + ^-5a + ^-6$

Problem-Solving Applications

13. Suppose the three lengths of the sides of a triangle are represented by the expressions $2m$, $m + 5$, and $4m + 2$. Write the sum of the lengths (the perimeter), and then simplify. Find the perimeter for $m = 3$ in.

14. Bob has n nickels and d dimes. His sister has 3 times as many nickels and 5 times as many dimes as Bob has. Write the sum of the numbers of coins they have, and then combine like terms.

15. ✏️ **WRITE ABOUT IT** Explain how you would simplify $4x + 3(x + 4)$.

Mixed Review

Write in words.

16. $12 + 4 = 16$ **17.** $10 \times 3 = 30$ **18.** $12 \div 6 = 2$ **19.** $16 - 5 = 11$

Find the product or quotient. Write in simplest form.

20. $4.5 \div 5$ **21.** $^-2.5 \times ^-2.3$ **22.** $2\frac{1}{4} \times ^-3\frac{5}{8}$ **23.** $10\frac{2}{5} \div ^-5\frac{1}{5}$ **24.** $^-4\frac{2}{3} \div ^-2\frac{1}{3}$

25. **ESTIMATION** The shortest Presidential inaugural speech was about 133 words, and the longest was about 8,400 words. If it takes 1 min to say 90 words, about how long did each speech last?

26. **RATES** An athlete's heart beats about 115,200 times per day. About how many beats is this per hour? per minute? per second?

CULTURAL CONNECTION

COOPERATIVE LEARNING

Ethiopian Equations

Ruth's uncle lives in New York City and works for the United Nations. When he travels to Ethiopia, where he and Ruth's mother were born, he sends pictures and letters to Ruth. She shares the information with her classmates in Dallas, Texas.

Ruth's uncle wrote that Ras Dashen, the tallest peak in Ethiopia, is 15,539 ft higher than the lowest place in the country, the Denakil Depression. Ruth found that the Denakil Depression is 381 ft below sea level. Write a word sentence and an algebraic equation to show the altitude of Ras Dashen.

Work Together

1. Ruth's uncle wrote about the animals he saw in Ethiopia when he traveled to preserves where the wildlife is protected. He saw about 48 elephants in four small herds. If there were the same number of elephants in each herd, how many elephants did he see each time? Use algebra tiles or paper rectangles to find the number of elephants in each herd. Write the equation and solution.

2. Part of Ruth's uncle's job with the United Nations is to show farmers new ways to grow their crops. With better seed, a farmer should be able to produce 10 more bushels each year than the year before. Write an algebraic expression that represents how many more bushels a farmer will be producing after y years. If a farmer is producing 80 bushels per year now, how many will he produce the fifth year from now if he uses better seed?

3. Ruth's uncle met with representatives from other African nations. The representatives from the following countries asked the following numbers of questions: Somalia, q questions; Kenya, $2q$ questions; Niger, $q + 4$ questions; Djibouti, $q - 3$ questions. Write an expression that describes how many questions Ruth's uncle answered. Simplify the expression by combining like terms.

> **CULTURAL LINK**
>
> Ethiopia is the home of a great Olympic runner, Abebe Bikila, who grew up in an Ethiopian village about 100 mi from Addis Ababa. In 1960, he competed barefoot in the marathon race in Rome. He set a new world record of 2 hr, 15 min, and 16 sec. In 1964, he ran the Olympic marathon in Tokyo, Japan. He won again with a time of 2 hr, 12 min, and 11 sec, setting another world record.

EXAMPLES

EXERCISES

- **Identify expressions, equations, and inequalities.** (pages 96–97)

25.6×4 $\rightarrow$ *numerical expression*

$14y - 35$ $\rightarrow$ *algebraic expression*

$26 \div 2k = 6.5$ $\rightarrow$ *equation*

$4a + 15 > {}^-3$ $\rightarrow$ *inequality*

1. VOCABULARY An expression that is written using at least one variable is an **?** expression.

Write *expression, equation,* or *inequality* for each.

2. $2x - 15$ **3.** $16 + 20 \leq 36$

4. $30 \div 6 = 5$ **5.** $365 + 40$

- **Evaluate expressions.** (pages 98–101)

Evaluate $7c^3 + 6d$ for $c = {}^-2$ and $d = 5$.

$7c^3 + 6d$

$7 \cdot ({}^-2)^3 + 6(5)$ *Replace c with $^-2$ and replace d with 5.*

$7 \cdot {}^-8 + 6(5)$ *Find the value of $({}^-2)^3$.*

$^-56 + 30$ *Multiply.*

$^-26$ *Add.*

Evaluate the expression.

6. $3 + 12 \div 4$ **7.** $^-4 - (2 + 5) \times 4$

8. $(12 - 6) \div 2 + 1$ **9.** $24 + 3 \times 2 - 12$

10. VOCABULARY Numerical expressions are **?** when they have the same value.

Evaluate the expression for $x = {}^-3$ and $y = 4$.

11. $^-9x + 2y$ **12.** $^-5x - 6y$

13. $\dfrac{24}{x} - y$ **14.** $2.5x + y^2$

- **Translate and write algebraic expressions.** (pages 102–104)

Write an algebraic expression for this word expression: the number of touchdowns, *t*, increased by 3.

   Identify the operation: addition.

$t + 3$ *Write an algebraic expression.*

Write an algebraic expression for the word expression.

15. 65 times the distance, *m*

16. 10 more than the number of birds, *b*

17. the number of flowers, *f*, divided by 5

18. the number of points, *p*, less 10

19. 25 decreased by the number of coins, *c*

- **Combine like terms.** (pages 106–107)

Simplify $^-3n + 8(3n + 4)$.

$^-3n + 8(3n + 4)$

$^-3n + 8 \cdot 3n + 8 \cdot 4$ *Use the Distributive Property.*

$^-3n + 24n + 32$

$21n + 32$ *Add like terms.*

20. VOCABULARY To **?** an algebraic expression means to combine like terms.

Simplify.

21. $4 + 14b + {}^-5b + {}^-8 + {}^-4b + 10$

22. $6s + {}^-3(s + 7) + {}^-7s + {}^-12$

23. $^-9 + 4n + 2(3 + {}^-n) + 4n$

24. $12a + {}^-4a + 4 + 3b + 6a + 5b + 12$

25. $9x + 5 - 3x + 4y + 2x + y + {}^-8$

CHAPTER 6
SOLVING EQUATIONS

LOOK AHEAD

In this chapter you will solve problems that involve

- writing equations and checking solutions
- solving addition, subtraction, multiplication, and division equations

- solving two-step equations
- using the problem-solving strategy *work backward*

Rainbow Formulas

You can paint a rainbow using just red, yellow, and blue paint. Figure out how to do it. Let y = yellow, r = red, and b = blue. Write the formulas for the colors you use in your rainbow.

YOU WILL NEED: red, yellow, and blue paint, paper plates, paint brush, eyedropper

Plan
- Work with a partner. Mix drops of paint on a paper plate to make a rainbow of colors. Write formulas for the colors.

Act
- To make different colors, try different combinations of red, yellow, and blue paint.
- Measure the paint in drops. Mix the colors with a paint brush.
- Write a formula for each mixed color.
- Record your formulas.

Share
- Have another group try to reproduce your colors using your formulas.

DID YOU
- ✓ Make different colors?
- ✓ Measure the paint in drops?
- ✓ Write a formula for each color?
- ✓ Share formulas with another group?

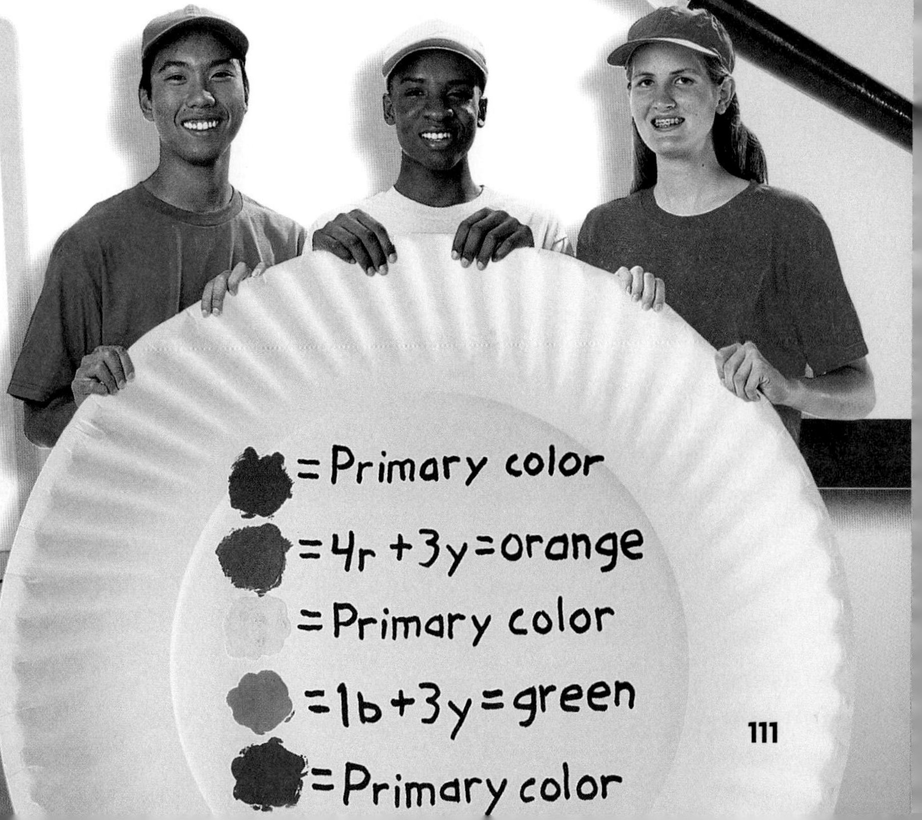

= Primary color

$= 4r + 3y =$ orange

= Primary color

$= 1b + 3y =$ green

= Primary color

111

CULTURAL LINK

Many English words used in the United States are the same in other languages. The word *algebra* has the same spelling and meaning in English, French, Spanish, and Italian. What other words do you know that are the same in English and other languages?

REMEMBER:

When a variable is used in a multiplication equation, the multiplication sign is usually omitted. An equation such as $5 \times n = 40$ is written as $5n = 40$. **See page H9.**

Relating Words to Equations

How is an equation like a word sentence? A word sentence uses letters and words to express ideas. An equation is a mathematical sentence that uses symbols such as numbers, an equals sign, and operations signs to express mathematical ideas.

You can translate a word sentence into a numerical equation.

Word Sentence	Numerical Equation
3 more than 24 is 27.	$24 + 3 = 27$
The difference between 10 and 6 is 4.	$10 - 6 = 4$
The product of 5 and 9 is 45.	$5 \times 9 = 45$
63 divided by 7 equals 9.	$63 \div 7 = 9$

A numerical equation can represent a real-life situation.

EXAMPLE 1 The cost of a $40 sweatshirt minus a discount of $8 is $32. Write a numerical equation for the word sentence.

$$
\begin{array}{cc}
\text{minus} & \text{is} \\
\downarrow & \downarrow
\end{array}
$$
$$40 - 8 = 32 \leftarrow \text{numerical equation}$$

• Write a numerical equation for the word sentence "7 less than 25 is 18." Which word or words help you identify the operation?

You can also translate a word sentence involving an unknown value into an algebraic equation containing a variable.

Word Sentence	Algebraic Equation
The sum of 15 and a distance, *d*, is 27.	$15 + d = 27$
$54 decreased by the cost, *c*, is $20.	$54 - c = 20$
Three times the number of hours, *h*, is 120.	$3h = 120$
The quotient of a number, *n*, and 5.9 is 4.	$n \div 5.9 = 4,$ or $\frac{n}{5.9} = 4$

You can write an algebraic equation to represent a real-life problem involving an unknown value.

EXAMPLE 2 LaVon and Ammad bought tickets for a concert. LaVon's ticket cost $10 more than Ammad's ticket. LaVon paid $16 for her ticket. How much did Ammad's ticket cost? Write an algebraic equation that represents the problem.

Think: You don't know the cost of Ammad's ticket, so that is the unknown.

Let a = the cost of Ammad's ticket. *Choose a variable to represent the unknown.*

Then $a + 10$ = the cost of LaVon's ticket. *Write an expression.*

You know that LaVon's ticket cost $16, so

$a + 10 = 16$ *Write an equation.*

- A plane with 250 seats has a number of seated passengers, p, plus six empty seats. Tell what the variable represents. Then write an algebraic equation that represents the word sentence.

History Link

The use of symbols in mathematics is relatively new. The first symbol for equality was probably α. It may have come from the abbreviation æ, which stood for the Latin word *aequalis,* meaning "level" or "equal." The modern symbol for equality (=) wasn't used until the fifteenth century. Write an equation using the symbol α.

GUIDED PRACTICE

Choose the numerical equation that represents the word sentence. Write the word or words that help you identify the operation.

1. 9 less than 27 equals 18.

2. The quotient of 27 and 9 is 3.

3. The product of 3 and 9 is 27.

$27 \div 9 = 3$

$3 \times 9 = 27$

$27 - 9 = 18$

Choose the algebraic equation that represents the word sentence. Write the word or words that help you identify the operation.

4. 9 times the number of cats, c, equals 18.

5. 9 more than the number of cats, c, is 18.

6. 9 less than the number of cats, c, is 18.

7. 18 divided by the number of cats, c, equals 9.

$c - 9 = 18$

$9c = 18$

$18 \div c = 9$

$c + 9 = 18$

Write an algebraic equation for the word sentence.

8. The quotient of the number of students, n, and 2 is 41.

9. The difference between a number, n, and 8 is 3.

INDEPENDENT PRACTICE

Write an algebraic equation that represents the word sentence. Write the word or words that help you identify the operation.

1. 34 decreased by a number, n, is 12.

2. 4 times a number, n, equals 24.

3. The sum of a number, n, and 5 is 300.

4. The quotient of 36 and a number, n, equals 9.

Choose the equation that represents the word problem.

5. Ned has saved $14. He wants to buy a video game that costs $35. How much more does Ned need to save?

    a. $s + 14 = 35$

    b. $s - 14 = 35$

6. Mrs. Adkins is 42 years old. This is 3 times Sally's age. How old is Sally?

    a. $a + 3 = 42$

    b. $3a = 42$

Problem-Solving Applications

Choose a variable to represent the unknown. Write an algebraic equation that represents the word problem.

7. Joey's savings account balance was $120.23. He made a deposit. His new balance is $180.00. How much money did Joey deposit?

8. The class was divided into 4 teams. Each team has 7 students. How many students are in the class?

9. You can make purple food coloring by mixing red food coloring with 3 times as much blue. How many drops of blue should be mixed with 5 drops of red?

10. Juan's uncle travels 335 mi to get to Juan's house. This is twice the distance his aunt travels. How far does his aunt travel?

11. ➡ **WRITE ABOUT IT** Write a word problem that can be represented by the algebraic equation $n - 70 = 34$.

Mixed Review

Evaluate the expression for the given values of the variables.

12. $4n + 2$ for $n = 3$

13. $5a - 3b + 3$ for $a = 5$, $b = 2$

14. $x^2 + x + 3$ for $x = 3$

Write an algebraic expression for the word expression.

15. 12 more than 6 times the distance, d

16. 15 less than the number of pens, p

17. **SIMILAR FIGURES** A rectangle measures 4 in. wide and 6 in. long. If the width and length are doubled, what are the new measurements?

18. **LOGICAL REASONING** If the value of $2x - 10$ is 45, what is the value of $2x - 15$?

MORE PRACTICE Lesson 6.1, page H52

Solving Addition and Subtraction Equations

WHAT YOU'LL LEARN
How to find out whether a value is a solution of an equation and how to solve addition and subtraction equations

WHY LEARN THIS?
To solve real-life problems such as finding the age of a person when given the relationship with another person's age

What is a solution of an equation?

If a value of a variable makes an equation true, that value is a **solution** of the equation. To find out whether a value is a solution, first **substitute** the value for the variable—that is, put the value in place of the variable. Then perform the indicated operation or operations.

EXAMPLE 1   Which of the values 12, 20, and 21 are solutions of $x - 4 = 16$?

Substitute each of the values for x in the equation.

Use x = 12.	*Use x = 20.*	*Use x = 21.*
$x - 4 = 16$	$x - 4 = 16$	$x - 4 = 16$
$12 - 4 = 16$	$20 - 4 = 16$	$21 - 4 = 16$
$8 \neq 16$	$16 = 16$	$17 \neq 16$
not a solution	*solution*	*not a solution*

• Is $y = 5$ a solution of $y + 8 = 15$? Why or why not?

You can also decide whether a value is a solution of an equation with two operations by substituting the value for the variable.

EXAMPLE 2   Which of the values 6, 7, and 8 are solutions of $6m + 9 = 57$?

Substitute each of the values for m in the equation.

$6m + 9 = 57$	$6m + 9 = 57$	$6m + 9 = 57$
$6 \cdot 6 + 9 = 57$	$6 \cdot 7 + 9 = 57$	$6 \cdot 8 + 9 = 57$
$36 + 9 = 57$	$42 + 9 = 57$	$48 + 9 = 57$
$45 \neq 57$	$51 \neq 57$	$57 = 57$
not a solution	*not a solution*	*solution*

Talk About It

• Is $b = 25$ a solution of $b - 9 = 16$? Why or why not?

• Is $e = 27$ a solution of $3e + 9 = 81$? Explain.

• How can you find out whether $d = 6$, $d = 5$, or $d = 4$ is a solution of $\frac{d}{4} + 6 = 7$?

• Is $n = 30$ a solution of $\frac{n}{3} - 4 = 7$? Explain.

WORD POWER

solution
substitute

Language Link

How is sending in a substitute in a game like substituting a value for a variable? A *substitute* is "one that takes the place of another." How can you use substitution to find out whether $x = 6$ is a solution of $3x + 2 = 20$?

115

You can solve an addition equation by using algebra tiles.

ACTIVITY

WHAT YOU'LL NEED: algebra tiles or paper rectangles and squares

• Copy the model for $x + 4 = 9$ shown below.

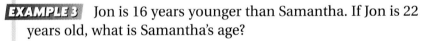

• What is represented by the rectangle? by the squares on the left side? by the squares on the right side?

• What kind of equation is $x + 4 = 9$? What operation is the inverse of addition?

• Subtract enough squares from each side of the equation to get the rectangle (variable) by itself. How many squares did you subtract from each side? What tiles remain on the left side? on the right side?

• What is the solution of $x + 4 = 9$? How can you show that the value is the solution?

Since addition and subtraction are inverse operations, you can subtract to solve an addition equation and add to solve a subtraction equation.

You can translate an everyday problem into an equation that can be solved.

EXAMPLE 3   Jon is 16 years younger than Samantha. If Jon is 22 years old, what is Samantha's age?

Let s = Samantha's age in years.   *Choose a variable.*
Then $s - 16$ = Jon's age.
$\qquad s - 16 = 22$ *Write an equation.*
$\quad s - 16 + 16 = 22 + 16$ *Add 16 to each side.*
$\qquad\qquad s = 38 \leftarrow$ solution

$\qquad s - 16 = 22$ *Check the solution.*
$\quad 38 - 16 = 22$ *Substitute 38 for s.*
$\qquad\qquad 22 = 22$ ✓   *The solution checks.*

So, Samantha is 38 years old.

• **CRITICAL THINKING**   What kind of equation is $s - 16 = 42$? Why was addition used to solve the equation?

You can solve addition and subtraction equations that contain rational numbers.

REMEMBER:

A rational number is any number that can be written in the form $\frac{a}{b}$, where a and b are integers and b is not equal to zero. **See page 17.**

EXAMPLE 4   Alexei Nemov of Russia placed first in the men's vaulting event at the 1996 Summer Olympics by earning 0.031 more points than Hong-Chul Yeo of South Korea. Alexei Nemov earned 9.787 points. How many points did Hong-Chul Yeo earn?

Let h = the number of points   *Choose a variable.*
earned by Hong-Chul Yeo.
Then $h + 0.031$ = the number
of points earned by Alexei Nemov.

$h + 0.031 = 9.787$	*Write an equation.*
$h + 0.031 - 0.031 = 9.787 - 0.031$	*Subtract 0.031 from each side.*
$h = 9.756 \leftarrow$ **solution**	

$h + 0.031 = 9.787$	*Check the solution.*
$9.756 + 0.031 = 9.787$	*Substitute 9.756 for h.*
$9.787 = 9.787$ ✓	*The solution checks.*

So, Hong-Chul Yeo earned 9.756 points.

• Solve the equation and check the solution. $t - \frac{1}{2} = \frac{5}{8}$

EXAMPLE 5   Solve and check. $k + 8 = {}^-9$

$k + 8 = {}^-9$	
$k + 8 - 8 = {}^-9 - 8$	*Subtract 8 from each side.*
$k + 8 - 8 = {}^-9 + {}^-8$	*Add ${}^-8$, the opposite of 8.*
$k = {}^-17 \leftarrow$ **solution**	

$k + 8 = {}^-9$	*Check the solution.*
${}^-17 + 8 = {}^-9$	*Substitute ${}^-17$ for k.*
${}^-9 = {}^-9$ ✓	*The solution checks.*

REMEMBER:

To subtract an integer, add the opposite of the integer.

$9 - 6 = 9 + {}^-6 = 3$

See page H28.

GUIDED PRACTICE

Write *yes* or *no* to tell whether the given value is a solution of the equation.

1. $0.6 = 0.15 + d, d = 0.45$

2. $y - 13 = 72, y = 59$

3. ${}^-5.4 + x = 2.8, x = 8.2$

4. $3b - 2.5 = {}^-7.5, b = 5$

Tell whether you would add or subtract to solve.

5. $2.9 + d = 6.4$

6. $x - 8.8 = 15.9$

7. $t - \frac{5}{8} = \frac{{}^-3}{8}$

8. $p + 7.99 = 14$

9. $m - \frac{3}{4} = 5\frac{1}{4}$

10. $b + 0.6 = 2.4$

INDEPENDENT PRACTICE

Determine which value is a solution of the given equation.

1. $x - 7 = 12$;
$x = 18, 19$, or 20

2. $k - 15 = 32$;
$k = 45, 46$, or 47

3. $b + 6 = 14$;
$b = 8, 9$, or 10

4. $a + 17 = 43$;
$a = 25$ or 26

5. $c + 2.94 = 8.1$;
$c = 5.15$ or 5.16

6. $4k + 7 = {}^-45$;
$k = {}^-12$ or ${}^-13$

7. $2m - 2.1 = {}^-4.5$;
$m = {}^-1.1$ or ${}^-1.2$

8. ${}^-1.2q + 4 = 1.24$;
$q = 2.1$ or 2.3

Solve the equation and check the solution.

9. $x + 7 = 12$

10. $8 + z = 20$

11. $m - 9 = 15$

12. $n - 14 = 31$

13. $h + 52 = 21$

14. $z + \frac{1}{4} = \frac{3}{4}$

15. $m - 2.34 = 8.19$

16. $k - 7 = {}^-3$

17. $y + 3.5 = 17.2$

18. $w - \frac{4}{5} = \frac{2}{5}$

19. ${}^-13 + p = 8$

20. $t + 14 = {}^-15$

21. $k - 2.4 = {}^-7.8$

22. $d + \frac{3}{4} = {}^-2$

23. $c - 9.87 = {}^-10.97$

24. ${}^-7 + b = {}^-7$

Problem-Solving Applications

Choose a variable and tell what it represents. Then write an equation for the problem.

25. Sam has 5 fewer markers than Ned. If Sam has 13 markers, how many does Ned have?

26. Penny scored 3 more points than Nick. If Penny scored 24 points, how many did Nick score?

27. Maria's batting average is 0.024 points higher than Rick's. If Maria's batting average is 0.315, what is Rick's?

28. Todd has $3.27 less than Shannon. If Todd has $15.75, how much does Shannon have?

Write and solve an equation that represents the problem.

29. Andre had $3.46 when he left the movie theater. This is $12.34 less than he had when he entered the theater. How much did Andre have when he entered the theater?

30. On Wednesday 140 pizza slices were sold in the cafeteria. This was 32 more than were sold on Thursday. How many slices were sold on Thursday?

31. Amy jogged 4.75 mi more on Tuesday than she did on Monday. She jogged 8.4 mi on Tuesday. How many miles did Amy jog on Monday?

32. Four students were absent. Twenty-five students attended class. How many students are on the class roll?

33. ✏️ **WRITE ABOUT IT** Write a set of rules to use when solving addition and subtraction equations. Then write an addition equation or a subtraction equation, exchange equations with a classmate, and use the rules to solve the equation.

MORE PRACTICE Lesson 6.2, page H53

Solving Multiplication and Division Equations

You can use algebra tiles to solve a multiplication equation.

ACTIVITY

WHAT YOU'LL NEED: algebra tiles or paper rectangles and squares

• Look at the model for $3x = 15$ shown below. What is represented by the rectangles? by the squares?

• Copy the model.

• Divide each side of the model into 3 equal groups. Look at 1 group on each side. What's on the left? What's on the right? What equation does this model?

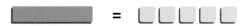

Multiplication and division are inverse operations. You can divide to solve a multiplication equation and multiply to solve a division equation.

EXAMPLE 1   Including interest, Rosita will pay a total of $2,280 on her auto loan. Her monthly payment on the loan is $190. How many more months must Rosita pay?

Let m = the number of monthly payments.   *Choose a variable.*

Then $190m$ = her balance.

$$190m = 2,280$$ *Write an equation.*

$$\frac{190m}{190} = \frac{2,280}{190}$$ *Divide each side by 190.*

$$m = 12 \leftarrow \text{solution}$$

$$190m = 2,280$$ *Check the solution.*

$$190 \cdot 12 = 2,280$$ *Substitute 12 for m.*

$$2,280 = 2,280 \checkmark$$ *The solution checks.*

So, Rosita must pay for 12 more months.

119

GUIDED PRACTICE

Use algebra tiles to model and solve the equation.

1. $2x = 12$ **2.** $3p = 15$ **3.** $4y = 12$

Tell what you would do to solve the equation.

4. $7x = 42$ **5.** $6.3 = 9b$ **6.** $3.5n = 21$

Tell whether the given value is a solution of the equation. Write *yes* or *no*. If the value is not a solution, solve the equation.

7. $3c = 4.8; c = 12$ **8.** $4.7m = 42.3; m = 9$ **9.** $18k = 432; k = 34$

You can use multiplication to solve a division equation.

EXAMPLE 2 Ivan has saved $21.40. This is $\frac{1}{3}$ of what he needs to save to buy a new piece of software. What is the total amount that Ivan needs to save?

Let s = the total amount Ivan needs to save.   *Choose a variable.*

Then $\frac{1}{3}s$ or $\frac{s}{3}$ = the amount he has saved.

$\frac{s}{3} = 21.40$ *Write an equation.*

$(3)\frac{s}{3} = 21.40(3)$ *Multiply each side by 3.*

$s = 64.20 \leftarrow$ solution

$\frac{s}{3} = 21.40$ *Check the solution.*

$\frac{64.20}{3} = 21.40$ *Substitute 64.20 for s.*

$21.40 = 21.40 \checkmark$ *The solution checks.*

So, Ivan needs to save a total of $64.20.

• Solve and check. $\frac{a}{11} = 23$

EXAMPLE 3 Solve and check. $\frac{z}{5} = {}^-7$

$\frac{z}{5} = {}^-7$ $\frac{z}{5} = {}^-7$ *Check the solution.*

$(5)\frac{z}{5} = {}^-7(5)$ *Multiply.* $\frac{{}^-35}{5} = {}^-7$ *Substitute $^-35$ for x.*

$z = {}^-35$ ${}^-7 = {}^-7 \checkmark$ *The solution checks.*

INDEPENDENT PRACTICE

Solve and check.

1. $6x = 24$

2. $\frac{x}{4} = 12$

3. $1{,}188 = 54b$

4. $\frac{y}{246} = 27$

5. $7y = 63$

6. $5 = \frac{s}{2.4}$

7. $26 = 5.2d$

8. $\frac{z}{10.7} = 4$

9. $2.5m = {}^{-}17.5$

10. $9.3p = 29.76$

11. $\frac{b}{3.12} = 8.05$

12. $\frac{a}{32} = {}^{-}192$

13. $\frac{t}{1.9} = {}^{-}14.7$

14. $^{-}15 = \frac{y}{7}$

15. $\frac{x}{345} = {}^{-}12.6$

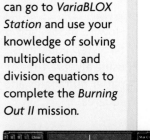

In *Mighty Math Astro Algebra* you can go to *VariaBLOX Station* and use your knowledge of solving multiplication and division equations to complete the *Burning Out II* mission.

Problem-Solving Applications

Choose a variable and tell what it represents. Then write an equation for the problem.

16. A company manufactures 3,216 tennis balls a day. Each container holds 3 balls. How many containers are needed daily?

17. Jerry spent $29 on clothes. This is $\frac{1}{4}$ of his weekly income. What is Jerry's weekly income?

Write and solve an equation that represents the problem.

18. The Torres family drove 235 mi toward its destination. This was $\frac{2}{3}$ of the total distance. What is the total distance?

19. Sally's Sub Shop made a 6-ft sub. Tim cut it into 18 equal pieces. How long was each piece?

20. ✏️ **WRITE ABOUT IT** How do you get a variable alone on one side of a multiplication equation? on one side of a division equation?

Mixed Review

Write an algebraic expression for each word expression.

21. the difference between the total hits, t, and 26 hits

22. the number of miles, m, increased by 365.4 miles

Combine like terms.

23. $4r + 6r + 10 - 6$

24. $6b - 4b + 2c - 5c$

25. $16 - 4ab + 20ab$

26. NUMBER SENSE Lisa travels many miles for her job. Her employer pays her $0.31 for each mile. If she receives a total of $75.95, how many miles did she travel?

27. GEOMETRY A rectangle with a perimeter of 18 in. and a width of 3 in. was cut into two congruent squares. What was the length of the rectangle?

Two-Step Equations

You can use algebra tiles to model and solve a two-step equation. A **two-step equation** represents two different operations.

Explore

• Model $2x + 3 = 9$.

• Take away, or subtract, 3 squares from each side.

• What remains on the left side? on the right side? Write the equation that represents the remaining tiles.

• Divide each side of the model into 2 equal groups. Look at 1 group on each side. What's on the left? What's on the right? What equation does this model?

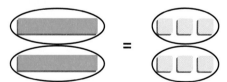

Think and Discuss 💡 CRITICAL THINKING

• What did you do to the model to undo the addition so that the rectangles were by themselves? to undo the multiplication so that a single rectangle was by itself?

Try This

Use algebra tiles to model and solve. Record each step.

$3x + 4 = 10$

$5y + 6 = 11$

Technology Link
E–Lab • Activity 6 Available on CD-ROM and the Internet at http://www.hbschool.com/elab

Solving Two-Step Equations

When you send a letter, you fold it, put it in an envelope, and seal the envelope. When you receive a letter, one by one you undo the steps that were completed earlier.

Likewise, you can undo the two operations represented in a two-step equation, by using two different inverse operations. First undo the addition or subtraction by subtracting or adding; then undo the multiplication or division by dividing or multiplying.

You can represent and solve a real-life problem by writing and solving a two-step equation.

EXAMPLE 1 A Clydesdale colt weighed 125 lb at birth. In each of its first 12 months, it gained the same amount of weight. At the end of its first year, it weighed 1,325 lb. How much weight did it gain each month?

Let w = weight (in lb) gained each month.

$$12w = \text{total weight gained}$$
$$12w + 125 = \text{total weight}$$

$$12w + 125 = 1,325 \qquad \textit{Write an equation.}$$
$$12w + 125 - 125 = 1,325 - 125 \qquad \textit{Subtract 125 from each side.}$$
$$12w = 1,200$$
$$\frac{12w}{12} = \frac{1,200}{12} \qquad \textit{Divide each side by 12.}$$
$$w = 100 \leftarrow \textbf{solution}$$

$$12w + 125 = 1,325 \qquad \textit{Check the solution.}$$
$$12 \cdot 100 + 125 = 1,325 \qquad \textit{Substitute 100 for w.}$$
$$1,325 = 1,325 \checkmark \qquad \textit{The solution checks.}$$

So, the colt gained 100 lb each month.

- What operation did you undo first? What operation did you use?

- What operation did you undo second? What operation did you use?

History Link

Draft horses, such as Clydesdales, weigh 1,200 to 1,500 lb. They are descendants of horses that carried knights in armor into battle. Write a problem about a horse or another four-legged animal. Then solve the problem by writing and solving an equation.

EXAMPLE 2   Solve and check. $3p - 10 = {}^-4$

$$3p - 10 = {}^-4$$
$$3p - 10 + 10 = {}^-4 + 10 \qquad \textit{Add 10 to each side.}$$
$$\frac{3p}{3} = \frac{6}{3} \qquad \textit{Divide each side by 3.}$$
$$p = 2 \leftarrow \text{solution}$$

$$3p - 10 = {}^-4 \qquad \textit{Check the solution.}$$
$$3 \cdot 2 - 10 = {}^-4 \qquad \textit{Substitute 2 for p.}$$
$$6 - 10 = {}^-4$$
$$6 + {}^-10 = {}^-4 \qquad \textit{Add the opposite.}$$
$${}^-4 = {}^-4 \checkmark \qquad \textit{The solution checks.}$$

- In the correct order, name the two steps you would use to solve the equation. $9u + 4 = 22$

You can also use inverse operations to solve two-step equations that involve both subtraction and division.

EXAMPLE 3   Solve. $\frac{m}{5} - 7.1 = 2.9$

$$\frac{m}{5} - 7.1 = 2.9$$
$$\frac{m}{5} - 7.1 + 7.1 = 2.9 + 7.1 \qquad \textit{Add 7.1 to each side.}$$
$$\frac{m}{5}(5) = 10.0(5) \qquad \textit{Multiply each side by 5.}$$
$$m = 50.0 \leftarrow \text{solution}$$

- How can you check the solution?

GUIDED PRACTICE

Tell whether the given value is a solution of the equation. Write *yes* or *no*.

1. $73u + 2 = 75$ $\qquad$ **2.** $9.2 = 4b - 2.8$ $\qquad$ **3.** $\frac{t}{0.5} + 7 = 19$

$\quad u = 2$ $\qquad\qquad\qquad b = 4$ $\qquad\qquad\qquad t = 6$

In the correct order, name the operations you would use to solve the equation.

4. $6c + 5 = 47$ $\qquad$ **5.** $\frac{y}{8} - 4 = 2$ $\qquad$ **6.** $3x - 6 = {}^-30$

Solve the equation, and check the solution.

7. $4x - 2 = 10$ $\qquad$ **8.** $5t + 1 = {}^-4$ $\qquad$ **9.** $\frac{d}{3} - 2 = 2$

10. $\frac{x}{6} + 2 = 5$ $\qquad$ **11.** $8m - 9 = 15$ $\qquad$ **12.** $\frac{k}{10} - 4 = 5$

INDEPENDENT PRACTICE

Solve and check.

1. $5x + 6 = 31$ **2.** $\frac{x}{6} - 2 = 4$ **3.** $8z - 3 = 45$ **4.** $\frac{t}{7} + 4 = 9$

5. $7y + 5 = 40$ **6.** $3a - 4 = {}^-16$ **7.** $\frac{d}{2} + 7 = 18$ **8.** $\frac{n}{3} + 6 = 22$

9. $5m - 3 = 17$ **10.** $4p + 5 = 25$ **11.** $\frac{k}{3} - 4 = 17$ **12.** $16n + 2 = {}^-46$

13. $\frac{a}{9} + 2 = 3.5$ **14.** $\frac{t}{7} - 5 = {}^-10$ **15.** ${}^-6m + 12 = 18$ **16.** $7 = \frac{y}{8} + {}^-9$

17. $105 = 2p + 5$ **18.** $2 + \frac{k}{5} = 10$ **19.** $2k - 7 = {}^-29$ **20.** $\frac{a}{2} - 14 = {}^-27$

21. ${}^-12b + 10 = 154$ **22.** $\frac{y}{7} - 2 = {}^-3$ **23.** ${}^-48 = 3k - 3$ **24.** $8 + \frac{p}{13} = {}^-18$

25. ${}^-4c + 5 = 1$ **26.** $\frac{u}{2.5} - 8 = {}^-4$ **27.** ${}^-3b - 8 = {}^-47$ **28.** $7 + \frac{r}{12.8} = {}^-9.4$

One mistake was made in solving each equation. Describe the mistake and find the correct solution.

29. $2x + 4 = 8$
$2x = 12$
$x = 6$

30. $\frac{n}{3} - 2 = 4$
$\frac{n}{3} = 2$
$n = 6$

31. $\frac{y}{2} - 3 = 7$
$\frac{y}{2} = 10$
$y = 5$

32. $3a - 2 = {}^-11$
$3a = {}^-9$
$a = {}^-27$

Problem-Solving Applications

Write and solve an equation that represents the problem.

33. Ruby's Rent-a-Car offers car rentals for $29.99 a day plus $0.15 per mile. Jim rented a car for one day and paid $35.54. How many miles did Jim drive?

34. Junior made a $500 payment on his automobile loan. This payment was $10 less than $\frac{1}{4}$ of the total amount he borrowed. How much did he borrow?

35. If you make a deposit in Tri-City Bank and leave the money there for two years, your balance will be $1,000 plus $\frac{1}{4}$ of your original investment. At the end of two years, Jane's balance is $1,200. What was her original investment?

36. Joanna makes a $50 deposit on a $275 bicycle. The store owner agrees to let Joanna pay the balance in 12 equal monthly payments. How much will each monthly payment be?

37. David finished a 32-mi bicycle race. This distance is 4 mi less than twice the distance that he rode during last year's race. How far did he ride last year?

38. ✏️➡ **WRITE ABOUT IT** In the correct order, describe the operations you would use to solve $\frac{a}{2} - 4 = 8$.

Work Backward to Solve a Two-Step Problem

WHAT YOU'LL LEARN
How to solve a
two-step problem
using the strategy
work backward

WHY LEARN THIS?
To be able to find out
how you have spent
your money

Problem Solving
• **Understand**
• **Plan**
• **Solve**
• **Look Back**

**Many teenagers
communicate by
E-mail. You can use**
smileys **to express
emotions in your
E-mail messages.
These groups of
typed characters,
when looked at
sideways, resemble
faces. Here are some
common smileys:**

:-)   smile

;-)   wink

:-(frown

You can use the strategy *work backward* to
solve real-life two-step problems.

Lilia called a friend in a nearby city. The
long-distance rate is $0.10 for the first
minute and $0.06 for each additional
minute. The phone call cost $3.28. How
long was the phone call?

✓ **UNDERSTAND**   What are you asked
to find?

What facts are given?

✓ **PLAN**   What strategy will you use?

You can use inverse operations and the strategy *work backward*
to solve the problem.

✓ **SOLVE**   How will you solve the problem?

The cost of the phone call was calculated in this way:

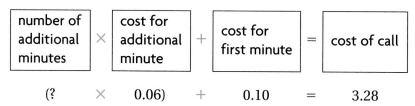

number of additional minutes	×	cost for additional minute	+	cost for first minute	=	cost of call
(?	×	0.06)	+	0.10	=	3.28

You can work backward by reversing the operations.

(3.28   −   0.10)   ÷   0.06   =   53

first minute + additional minutes = total time

1 min + 53 min = 54 min

So, the phone call was 54 min long.

✓ **LOOK BACK**   What other strategy could you use to solve
the problem?

What if ... the long-distance rate is $0.25 for the first minute
and $0.12 for each additional minute, and a phone call cost
$7.09. How long was the phone call?

PRACTICE

Work backward to solve.

1. Felipe has a total of 18 trophies on his trophy shelf. When he was ten years old, he added 2 trophies to his original collection. He now has 3 times as many as he had when he was ten. How many trophies did he have originally?

2. The Jones family went on vacation and rented a minivan for one week. The total rental charge was $142.00. A weekly rental costs $99.00 plus $0.20 per mile. How many miles did they drive the minivan?

3. Ingrid and her friends have a lawn-mowing business. Ingrid mowed 10 lawns, Rosie mowed 8 lawns, and Mindy mowed the remaining lawns. They earned $10 per lawn. After spending $45.87 of their earnings for fuel, they had $204.13 left. How many lawns did Mindy mow?

4. Lori spent $6.99 on tennis balls, $8.00 on sport socks, and $42.00 on a tennis racket. Then she bought a pair of hand weights for $9.99. She had $3.02 when she arrived home. How much did she have when she started shopping?

MIXED APPLICATIONS

CHOOSE

Choose a strategy and solve.

> **Problem-Solving Strategies**
> - **Guess and Check**
> - **Draw a Diagram**
> - **Use a Formula**
> - **Make a Table**
> - **Work Backward**
> - **Find a Pattern**

5. A closet holds a stack of 5 identical boxes. The bottom of the top box is 4.5 ft from the ceiling. The bottom of the next box is 6 ft from the ceiling. How high is the ceiling?

6. Mrs. Ruiz bought pencils and rulers. Pencils cost $0.25 each, and rulers cost $0.65 each. She spent $4.50. How many of each did she buy?

7. Sophie's sock drawer holds 32 single socks. There are 20 white socks, 8 green socks, and 4 blue socks. Suppose the electricity went out as Sophie was getting ready for school. What is the least number of socks she would have to take out of the drawer to make sure she had a matching pair?

8. Charla Davis withdrew money from the bank before going to the mall. She paid back the $3.00 she owed her friend. She bought 3 T-shirts for $6.49 each and lunch for $7.85. When she arrived home, she had $4.68 left. How much did she withdraw from the bank?

9. On Monday, Sammy ate 1 apple. On Tuesday he also ate 1, on Wednesday he ate 2, on Thursday he ate 3, and on Friday he ate 5. If Sammy continues this pattern, how many apples will he eat on Saturday? on Sunday? on Monday?

10. Mr. Thomas wants to lay sod on a rectangular section of his yard that is 80 ft long and 60 ft wide. One pallet of sod covers 400 ft². How many pallets of sod will he need?

MATH FUN!

AN ANCIENT GREEK CHALLENGE

PURPOSE To practice writing algebraic equations for word problems (pages 112–114)

Diophantus of Alexandria (c. 275 A.D.) was a mathematician who catalogued everything the Greeks knew about algebra. Diophantus had a puzzle etched on his tombstone. Write an equation to determine how old he was when he died, then solve. Let y represent Diophantus's total age.

Diophantus passed $\frac{1}{6}$ of his life in childhood, $\frac{1}{12}$ in youth and $\frac{1}{7}$ more as a bachelor. 5 years after his marriage was born a son who died 4 years before his father at $\frac{1}{2}$ the age at which his father died.

HOME NOTE Explain the puzzle to a family member

EQUATION IMAGINATION

PURPOSE To practice modeling and solving two-step equations (pages 122–125)

YOU WILL NEED black, red, and yellow markers or colored pencils

How many turtles does the zoo have? Write the equation shown by the drawing. Then solve.

Work with a partner. Write any equation that has 1 variable, involves addition or subtraction and multiplication, and has no numbers

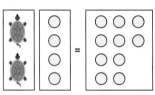

greater than 10. Use red to draw negative numbers or show subtraction. Use yellow to draw positive numbers or show addition. Draw a diagram to represent the variable. Trade drawings. Write the equation shown by your partner's drawing and solve.

INVERSE OPERATIONS

PURPOSE To practice solving two-step equations (pages 123–125)

YOU WILL NEED 1-in. graph paper, 8-section spinner, two-color counters

Play with a partner. Copy the gameboard. Label equal sections of the spinner ⁻13, ⁻7, ⁻1, 11, 17, 23, 29, 35. Each player places a counter at the start line. In turn, spin the spinner. Substitute the number on the spinner for the variable y in the equation $y = 6x + 5$. Solve for x. Move the counter the number of spaces given by the solution. Move forward for a positive solution and backward for a negative solution.

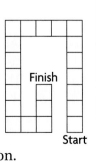

Finish

Start

EXAMPLES

- **Write numerical equations and algebraic equations.** (pages 112–114)

8 less than a number, *n*, equals 12.

$n - 8 = 12$ *Write as an algebraic equation.*

- **Solve addition and subtraction equations.** (pages 115–118)

$$x + 7 = 19$$
$$x + 7 - 7 = 19 - 7 \qquad \text{Subtract 7.}$$
$$x = 12 \leftarrow \text{solution}$$

- **Solve multiplication and division equations.** (pages 119–121)

$$\frac{x}{3} = 5$$

$$(3)\frac{x}{3} = 5\,(3) \qquad \text{Multiply by 3.}$$

$$x = 15 \leftarrow \text{solution}$$

- **Solve two-step equations.** (pages 123–125)

$$4b - 3 = 5$$
$$4b - 3 + 3 = 5 + 3 \qquad \text{Add 3.}$$
$$\frac{4b}{4} = \frac{8}{4} \qquad \text{Divide by 4.}$$
$$b = 2 \leftarrow \text{solution}$$

- **Use the strategy *work backward* to solve a two-step problem.** (pages 126–127)

PROBLEM-SOLVING TIP: For help in solving problems by working backward, see pages 6 and 126.

EXERCISES

Write an algebraic equation for the word sentence.

1. 17 decreased by a number, *n*, is 6.
2. 3 times a number, *n*, equals 21.
3. The quotient of 8 and a number, *n*, equals 2.

4. VOCABULARY If a value of a variable makes an equation true, that value is a ___?___ of the equation.

Solve and check.

5. $x + 9 = 32$ **6.** $c + 19 = 4$
7. $y + 4 = {}^-9$ **8.** $a - 7 = {}^-8$

Solve and check.

9. $3x = 33$ **10.** $\frac{c}{6} = {}^-12$

11. $\frac{b}{2.5} = 17$ **12.** ${}^-8z = {}^-56$

Solve and check.

13. $3x + 2 = 8$ **14.** $\frac{a}{3} + 2 = 8$

15. $2z + 9 = 5$ **16.** $\frac{c}{6} + 9 = {}^-4$

17. Morgan's mom ordered custom color 8-in. by 10-in. prints from a photo lab. The first print cost $5.00, and each additional print of the same image cost $3.50. She spent a total of $33.00. How many prints did she order?

18. Tina thought of a number. She multiplied it by 10, subtracted 25, and added 12. The result was 27. What was Tina's number?

When the moon is light   5s

We are asleep in our beds.   7s

The world is at peace.   5s

Let s = syllables and h = haiku.

$$5s + 7s + 5s = h$$

LOOK AHEAD

In this chapter you will solve problems that involve

- solving equations with like terms
- using the problem-solving strategy *write an equation*

- graphing and solving inequalities
- modeling and solving equations with variables on both sides

Poetry Equations

Poems are built on patterns of sounds, syllables and lines. Do you hear the meter of a poem like "Stopping by the Woods on a Snowy Evening" by Robert Frost? Try counting syllables per line.

Write an equation for a poem or a song. Be sure to define your variables. Then write your own poem or song and its equation.

Plan
- Work with a small group. Find a favorite poem or song and write an equation for it. Write your own poem or song and its equation.

Act
- Copy the words of a poem or song.
- Look at the syllables, patterns, and rhymes.
- Identify the variables and write an equation that describes a pattern.
- Write a poem of your own and an equation that describes your poem.

Share
- Share your poem and equation with the class.

DID YOU

- ✓ Find a poem or song?
- ✓ Write an equation for it?
- ✓ Write your own poem and equation?
- ✓ Share your poem with the class?

Dances with Dad

It was dark and wet,
a horrible night.
My dad was digging,
with no one in sight.

This messy night work,
was his summer job,
to dig worms out of
the squishy black bog.

He did this gross job
so that fish would bite,
so fishers could fish;
only worms felt fright.

This was my father,
and a surprising event,
that helped me to make
create and invent,
this wonderful poem,
a poem of truth,
in the days of my father,
in the days of his youth.

Solving Equations with Like Terms

REMEMBER:

Like terms have the same variable or combination of variables. In like terms, corresponding variables have the same exponents. In the expression $x^2 + 3x + 2y + x - z + 7$, $3x$ and x are like terms.
See page 105.

How is identifying like terms similar to matching things such as buttons?

You can model and solve an equation that has like terms.

ACTIVITY

WHAT YOU'LL NEED: algebra tiles or paper rectangles and squares

• The algebra tiles shown below model the equation $3x + 4 + x = 12$.

• How is this equation different from the equations that you have solved in the past?

• What are the like terms? What is the total number of green rectangles on the left side?

• Regroup the green rectangles so that they are together. Write an equation that represents this new grouping.

• Use algebra tiles and inverse operations to solve the new equation. What is the solution?

To solve an equation that has like terms, first simplify by combining those terms.

EXAMPLE 1   Solve. $5d - 7 + 3d = 17$

$$5d - 7 + 3d = 17$$
$$5d + 3d - 7 = 17 \qquad \textit{Use the Commutative Property.}$$
$$8d - 7 = 17 \qquad \textit{Combine like terms: } 5d + 3d = 8d.$$
$$8d - 7 + 7 = 17 + 7 \qquad \textit{Add 7 to each side.}$$
$$8d = 24$$
$$\frac{8d}{8} = \frac{24}{8} \qquad \textit{Divide each side by 8.}$$
$$d = 3 \leftarrow \text{solution}$$

Like terms may appear on the right, on the left, or on both sides of an equation.

EXAMPLE 2 Solve and check. $^-48 + ^-2 = 10k + 6 - 3k$

$^-48 + ^-2 = 10k + 6 - 3k$	*Use the Commutative*
$^-48 + ^-2 = 10k - 3k + 6$	*Property.*
$^-50 = 7k + 6$	*Combine like terms.*
$^-50 - 6 = 7k + 6 - 6$	*Subtract 6 from each side.*
$^-56 = 7k$	
$\dfrac{^-56}{7} = \dfrac{7k}{7}$	*Divide each side by 7.*
$^-8 = k \leftarrow$ solution	
$^-48 + ^-2 = 10k + 6 - 3k$	*Check the solution.*
$^-50 = (10 \cdot {}^-8) + 6 - (3 \cdot {}^-8)$	*Substitute $^-8$ for k.*
$^-50 = {}^-80 + 6 - (^-24)$	
$^-50 = {}^-50$ ✓	*The solution checks.*

REMEMBER:
The Commutative Property can be used with addition or with multiplication. **See page H11.**

$a + b = b + a$
$12 + 6 = 6 + 12$

$a \times b = b \times a$
$8.2 \times 5 = 5 \times 8.2$

Talk About It

- What are the like terms?

- How would you solve $^-40 = 7c + 5 - 2c$?

- How would you solve $^-18 + ^-7 = 8y - 3y - 10$?

GUIDED PRACTICE

For Exercises 1–4, use the model shown below.

1. What equation is modeled? Explain.

2. What are the like terms on the left side?

3. What equation represents the result of combining these like terms?

4. What is the solution? How can you check the solution?

Identify the like terms. Then solve and check.

5. $2y + 5y + 4 = 25$

6. $89 = 4h + 8 + 7h - 2h$

7. $6m + 4m - m + 5 = 23$

8. $53 = 3c - 7 + 12c$

9. $8d - 3d + 2 = {}^-33$

10. $10e - 2e - 9 = 39$

11. $^-83 = 6k + 17 + 4k$

12. $56n + 21 - 8n + 3n = {}^-81$

To solve an equation with parentheses, first use the Distributive Property and then combine like terms.

EXAMPLE 3   Solve and check. $4(n - 3) + 2n = 12$

$$4(n - 3) + 2n = 12$$
$$(4 \cdot n) - (4 \cdot 3) + 2n = 12 \qquad \textit{Use the Distributive Property.}$$
$$4n - 12 + 2n = 12 \qquad \textit{Use the Commutative}$$
$$4n + 2n - 12 = 12 \qquad \textit{Property.}$$
$$6n - 12 = 12 \qquad \textit{Combine like terms.}$$
$$6n - 12 + 12 = 12 + 12 \qquad \textit{Add 12 to each side.}$$
$$6n = 24$$
$$\frac{6n}{6} = \frac{24}{6} \qquad \textit{Divide each side by 6.}$$
$$n = 4 \leftarrow \text{solution}$$

$$4(n - 3) + 2n = 12 \qquad \textit{Check the solution.}$$
$$4(4 - 3) + 2 \cdot 4 = 12 \qquad \textit{Substitute 4 for n.}$$
$$4 + 8 = 12$$
$$12 = 12 \checkmark \qquad \textit{The solution checks.}$$

• Identify the like terms. Then solve and check.
  $2(3y + 5) + y = 38$

You can use the Distributive Property and combine like terms on the left side, the right side, or both sides of an equation.

EXAMPLE 4   Solve. $18 = \frac{1}{2}(p + 8) - 3$

$$18 = \frac{1}{2}(p + 8) - 3$$

$$18 = \frac{1}{2}p + \frac{1}{2}(8) - 3 \qquad \textit{Use the Distributive Property.}$$

$$18 = \frac{1}{2}p + 4 - 3$$

$$18 = \frac{1}{2}p + 1$$

$$18 - 1 = \frac{1}{2}p + 1 - 1 \qquad \textit{Subtract 1 from each side.}$$

$$17 = \frac{1}{2}p$$

$$17 \cdot 2 = \frac{1}{2}p \cdot 2 \qquad \textit{To divide each side by } \frac{1}{2}, \textit{multiply by 2.}$$

$$34 = p \leftarrow \text{solution}$$

• How can you check the solution?

• Suppose $\frac{1}{3}y = 21$. How can you find the value of y?

INDEPENDENT PRACTICE

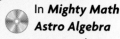

In *Mighty Math Astro Algebra* you can enter the *VariaBLOX Station* and practice combining like terms as you complete the *Disk Trouble* mission.

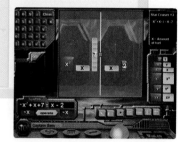

Identify the like terms. Then solve and check.

1. $3x + 2x + 5 = 15$

2. $10 + 4d - 3d = 13$

3. $28 = 10a - 5a - 2$

4. $36 - 4c - 3c = 22$

Use the Distributive Property to solve. Then check.

5. $4(x - 3) + 2x = 12$

6. $30 = 7(y - 5) + 6y$

7. $5(x - 1) - 2x = 4$

8. $3y + 6(y - 2) + 2 = 26$

9. $\frac{1}{2}(x + 6) - x = 1$

10. $5y - 2(y + 8) = 5$

11. $3 = 3(d + 7) - 6d$

12. $6k + 5(k - 2) = 78$

13. $4c + 8(2c + 4) = {}^-18$

14. $^-9 = 6(d + 2) - 2d + 1$

Problem-Solving Applications

15. Mark and Jane each solved the equation $3(x + 1) + 2x = 28$. Mark got $x = 5.4$ and Jane got $x = 5$. Who solved the equation correctly? Explain how you know.

16. A friend has a total of 9 syllables in her full name. The numbers of syllables in her first name, middle name, and last name can be represented by s, $s + 1$, and $s + 2$. Use the equation $s + s + 1 + s + 2 = 9$ to find the number of syllables in each of her names.

17. Karen's age is $2x$. Nancy's age is x. The sum of their ages is 24. Use the equation $2x + x = 24$ to find Nancy's age in years.

18. **WRITE ABOUT IT** Explain how to solve equations that have like terms.

Mixed Review

Write an algebraic equation that represents the word sentence.

19. 5 times a number, n, is 55.

20. A number, n, decreased by 15 is 42.

21. $10 more than a number, n, is $20.

22. $54 divided by the total cost, n, is $9.

Solve and check.

23. $10x - 4 = 26$

24. $5x + 5 = {}^-10$

25. $\frac{x}{4} - 4 = 0$

26. $5x - 4 = 21$

27. **CRITICAL THINKING** A calculator that did not follow the rules for order of operations gave the value 36 for the expression $8 + n \times 3$. What is the value of n and the value for the expression using that value of n?

28. **MENTAL MATH** Donald's cat is 9 years older than his dog. His dog is 4 years old. How old is his cat?

PROBLEM-SOLVING STRATEGY

Write an Equation with Like Terms

You can use the strategy *write an equation* to solve real-life problems.

Abe is one year older than Thai. The sum of their ages is 27. How old is Thai? How old is Abe?

✓ **UNDERSTAND**   What are you asked to find?

What facts are given?

✓ **PLAN**   What strategy will you use?

You can translate each of the ages into an algebraic expression and use the strategy *write an equation* to solve the problem.

✓ **SOLVE**   How will you solve the problem?

Write an equation to represent the problem.
Let t = the age of Thai in years.
Let $t + 1$ = the age of Abe in years.
Then, $t + t + 1$ = the sum of Thai's and Abe's ages.

You know that the sum of Thai's and Abe's ages is 27.
So, the equation is $t + t + 1 = 27$.

Solve the equation by combining like terms.

$$t + t + 1 = 27$$ *Write the equation.*
$$2t + 1 = 27$$ *Combine like terms.*
$$2t + 1 - 1 = 27 - 1$$ *Subtract 1 from each side.*
$$\frac{2t}{2} = \frac{26}{2}$$ *Divide each side by 2.*
$$t = 13 \leftarrow \text{Thai's age}$$

$$t + 1 = 13 + 1 = 14$$ *Find Abe's age by substituting 13 for t.*

So, Thai is 13 years old and Abe is 14 years old.

✓ **LOOK BACK**   How can you check the solution?

What if . . . Abe is 3 years older than Thai and the sum of their ages is 53? What equation could you write to find the ages? How old is Thai? How old is Abe?

Use the strategy *write an equation* to solve.

1. The Blue Sox and the Generals scored a total of 12 runs. The Blue Sox scored 4 more runs than the Generals. How many runs did each softball team score?

2. The perimeter of a rectangle is 70 ft. The length is 5 ft more than the width. Find the length and width.

3. Sue Peck and Sally Jenkins joined a book club. A book-club member is required to buy a minimum number of books each year. Sally Jenkins bought 3 times the minimum. Sue Peck bought 5 more than the minimum. Together, they bought 17 books. What is the minimum?

4. Brad needs to fence in a rectangular space for his dog. He has 36 ft of chain-link fencing. He wants the length of the space to be 6 ft less than twice its width. Find the length and width of the rectangular space.

MIXED APPLICATIONS

CHOOSE

Choose a strategy and solve.

> **Problem-Solving Strategies**
> - **Write an Equation**
> - **Guess and Check**
> - **Work Backward**
> - **Draw a Diagram**
> - **Make a Model**
> - **Find a Pattern**

5. The perimeter of a triangle is 23 in. The longest side is 5 in. longer than the shortest side. The third side is 3 in. longer than the shortest side. Find the length of each side.

6. The first term in a sequence is 4. Each of the next terms in the sequence is 3 more than 2 times the term before. What are the third and fourth terms in the sequence?

7. The ratio of the number of boys to the number of girls in a school is 2:3. There are 600 boys. How many girls are there?

8. A student answers 160 of 200 questions on an exam correctly. What percent of the questions did he answer correctly?

9. Diana bought a jewelry bead kit for $4.20. She used the same number of quarters as dimes to pay for the kit. How many of each did she use?

10. Anna is 4 years older than Marcy. The sum of their ages is 30. How old is Anna? How old is Marcy?

11. Dave designed a color brochure on his computer. The cost for color output is $10.00 for the first copy and $0.95 for each additional copy. Dave paid $17.60 for color copies. How many copies did he have made?

12. **WRITE ABOUT IT** Write a problem that can be solved with the strategy *write an equation*. Exchange with a classmate and solve.

Modeling Equations with Variables on Both Sides

You can use algebra tiles to solve equations that have variables on both sides of the equals sign.

Explore

• Model $2x + 4 = x + 6$.

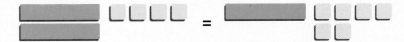

• Subtract one rectangle from each side so that these green rectangles representing variables are all on one side.

• What remains on the left side? on the right side? Write an equation that represents the remaining tiles.

• Subtract 4 squares from each side so that the green rectangle (variable) is by itself. What remains on the left? on the right? What equation does this represent?

Think and Discuss

• What did you do to the model to have all the green rectangles (variables) on one side? to undo the addition?

• What is the solution? How can you check your solution?

Try This

Model and solve the equation. Record each step.

$$3y + 1 = 2y + 4 \qquad 2n + 10 = 6n + 2 \qquad 3 + 5y = y + 7$$

 **Link**

Solving Equations with Variables on Both Sides

What equation does the diagram represent?

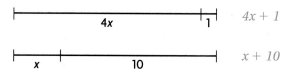

$4x + 1$

$x + 10$

The diagram represents the equation $4x + 1 = x + 10$. The like terms $4x$ and x appear on opposite sides of the equation. It's easy to solve such equations by collecting the like terms on the side with the term that has the greater coefficient.

REMEMBER:

In a term such as $7h$, the number 7 is called the coefficient. **See page 100.**

EXAMPLE 1   Solve. $4x + 1 = x + 10$

$$4x + 1 = x + 10$$
$$4x + 1 - x = x + 10 - x \qquad \textit{Subtract x from each side.}$$
$$4x - x + 1 = x - x + 10 \qquad \textit{Use the Commutative Property.}$$
$$3x + 1 = 10 \qquad \textit{Combine like terms.}$$
$$3x + 1 - 1 = 10 - 1 \qquad \textit{Subtract 1 from each side.}$$
$$3x = 9$$
$$\frac{3x}{3} = \frac{9}{3} \qquad \textit{Divide each side by 3.}$$
$$x = 3 \leftarrow \textbf{solution}$$

• Why are the terms $4x$ and x collected on the left side?

Some equations involve the Distributive Property.

EXAMPLE 2   Solve. $3n - 6 = 7(n + 2)$

$$3n - 6 = 7(n + 2)$$
$$3n - 6 = 7n + 14 \qquad \textit{Use the Distributive Property.}$$
$$3n - 6 - 3n = 7n + 14 - 3n \qquad \textit{Subtract 3n from each side.}$$
$$3n - 3n - 6 = 7n - 3n + 14 \qquad \textit{Use the Commutative Property.}$$
$$^-6 = 4n + 14 \qquad \textit{Combine like terms.}$$
$$^-6 - 14 = 4n + 14 - 14 \qquad \textit{Subtract 14 from each side.}$$
$$^-20 = 4n$$
$$\frac{^-20}{4} = \frac{4n}{4} \qquad \textit{Divide each side by 4.}$$
$$^-5 = n \leftarrow \textbf{solution}$$

• How can you check the solution?

You can also solve equations that have variables on both sides when the equations contain rational numbers.

EXAMPLE 3 Solve. $4(y + \frac{1}{2}) = 6(y - \frac{2}{3})$

$$4(y + \tfrac{1}{2}) = 6(y - \tfrac{2}{3})$$

$$4y + 4(\tfrac{1}{2}) = 6y - 6(\tfrac{2}{3}) \qquad \textit{Use the Distributive Property.}$$

$$4y + \tfrac{4}{2} = 6y - \tfrac{12}{3}$$

$$4y + 2 = 6y - 4 \qquad \textit{Simplify the fractions.}$$

$$4y + 2 - 4y = 6y - 4 - 4y \qquad \textit{Subtract 4y from each side.}$$

$$2 = 2y - 4$$

$$2 + 4 = 2y - 4 + 4 \qquad \textit{Add 4 to each side.}$$

$$6 = 2y$$

$$\tfrac{6}{2} = \tfrac{2y}{2} \qquad \textit{Divide each side by 2.}$$

$$3 = y \leftarrow \text{solution}$$

- How can you check the solution?

You can solve real-life problems by writing and solving equations with variables on both sides.

EXAMPLE 4 Mr. Smith's rectangular yard has the same perimeter as Ms. Meyer's triangular yard. Let $x =$ the width of Mr. Smith's yard in feet. What is the perimeter of each yard?

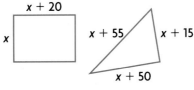

perimeter of Mr. Smith's yard = $2(x) + 2(x + 20)$
perimeter of Ms. Meyer's yard = $(x + 50) + (x + 15) + (x + 55)$

Think: Write an equation showing equal perimeters.

$$2(x) + 2(x + 20) = (x + 50) + (x + 15) + (x + 55)$$

$$2x + 2x + 40 = x + 50 + x + 15 + x + 55$$

$$4x + 40 = 3x + 120 \qquad \textit{Combine like terms.}$$

$$4x + 40 - 3x = 3x + 120 - 3x \qquad \textit{Subtract 3x from each side.}$$

$$x + 40 = 120$$

$$x + 40 - 40 = 120 - 40 \qquad \textit{Subtract 40 from each side.}$$

$$x = 80 \leftarrow \text{solution}$$

$$2(80) + 2(80 + 20) = 360 \qquad \textit{To find the perimeter,}$$
$$(80 + 50) + (80 + 15) + (80 + 55) = 360 \qquad \textit{substitute 80 for x.}$$

So, the perimeter of each yard is 360 ft.

REMEMBER:

The perimeter is the distance around a polygon. **See page H25.**

GUIDED PRACTICE

Tell which side of the equation has the term with the greater coefficient.

1. $5x + 2 = x + 6$ **2.** $6a - 6 = 8 + 4a$ **3.** $3x + 9 = 10x - 5$ **4.** $4y - 2 = 6y + 6$

Tell what you would add to or subtract from each side of the equation to collect like variable terms on one side.

5. $8y - 3 = 17 - 2y$ **6.** $2n + 6 = 7n - 9$ **7.** $9x - 2 = 10 - 3x$

8. $5n + 3 = 14 - 6n$ **9.** $9y - 6 = 7y + 8$ **10.** $5x + 2 = x + 6$

INDEPENDENT PRACTICE

Solve and check.

1. $2n + 12 = 5n$ **2.** $x + 40 = 6x$ **3.** $4x + 15 = 8x + 3$

4. $5x - 2 = 9x + 10$ **5.** $4n - 6 = 2(n + 3)$ **6.** $3y + 9 = 8(y - 2)$

7. $5(y - 1) = 3(y - 3)$ **8.** $8n - 4 = 4(n + 5)$ **9.** $2(n + 10) = 4(n - 5)$

10. $2y - 12 = 6(y - 1)$ **11.** $4(x - 5) + 2 = x + 3$ **12.** $3(x - 4) - 4 = 2x + 6.9$

13. $6(x + \frac{1}{2}) = x + 8$ **14.** $2x + 6 = 5(x + \frac{3}{5})$ **15.** $\frac{1}{2}(2n + 6) = 4(n - 3)$

16. $7(x - 1) = 3(x + \frac{1}{3})$ **17.** $12(x - \frac{1}{2}) = 8(x + \frac{3}{4})$ **18.** $4(y - \frac{2}{4}) = 9(y + \frac{1}{3})$

Problem-Solving Applications

19. The two triangles below have the same perimeter. Find the length of each side of each triangle. All measurements are in meters.

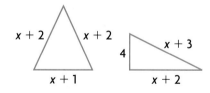

20. The rectangle and the triangle shown below have the same perimeter. Find the length of each side of the triangle. All measurements are in feet.

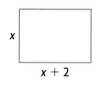 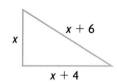

21. Bob is 3 times as old as Jim. Let x = Jim's age. Let Bob's age = $3x$. In 5 years Bob's age will be twice Jim's age. Use the equation $3x + 5 = 2(x + 5)$ to find out Jim's age now.

22. Cathi is 4 times as old as Erv. Let x = Erv's age. Let Cathi's age = $4x$. In 4 years Cathi's age will be 3 times Erv's age. Use the equation $4x + 4 = 3(x + 4)$ to find out how old Cathi is now.

23. ✏️ **WRITE ABOUT IT** Make up an equation that has like variable terms on both sides. Exchange with a classmate and solve.

Inequalities

WHAT YOU'LL LEARN
How to graph the solutions of an inequality on a number line

WHY LEARN THIS?
To represent a real-life situation such as temperature

WORD POWER
algebraic inequality

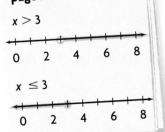

REMEMBER:

An open circle means that the circled value is not a solution. A closed circle means that the value is a solution. **See page H26.**

$x > 3$

$x \leq 3$

Marco has more than $2 in his pocket. Which of the following graphs represents this situation?

a. 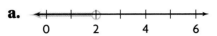   **b.**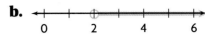

An inequality that contains a variable is an **algebraic inequality**.

If a value of a variable makes an inequality true, that value is a solution of the inequality. An inequality can have many solutions. You can graph the solutions of an inequality.

EXAMPLE 1 Graph $4 > y$ and describe the solutions in words.

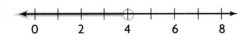

solutions: all real numbers less than 4

Sometimes you are given an inequality and a set of values. To find out whether a value is a solution, substitute the value for the variable. Then do the operation or operations.

EXAMPLE 2 Which of the values, 3, 4, and 5 are solutions of $2m - 3 \leq 5$?

Replace m with each value.

$2m - 3 \leq 5$	$2m - 3 \leq 5$	$2m - 3 \leq 5$
$2 \cdot 3 - 3 \leq 5$	$2 \cdot 4 - 3 \leq 5$	$2 \cdot 5 - 3 \leq 5$
$6 - 3 \leq 5$	$8 - 3 \leq 5$	$10 - 3 \leq 5$
$3 \leq 5$	$5 \leq 5$	$7 \leq 5$
a solution	a solution	not a solution

• Which of the values ⁻1, 0, 1, and 2 are solutions of $h + 2 < 3$?

You can represent a real-life situation by writing and graphing an inequality.

EXAMPLE 3 Today the high temperature, h, in Miami, Florida, will be at least 80°F. Write and graph an algebraic inequality to represent this situation.

Think: *At least* means "greater than or equal to."

$h \geq 80$ *Translate the words into an inequality symbol.*

Graph the inequality on a number line.

GUIDED PRACTICE

For Exercises 1–4, write the letter of the matching graph.

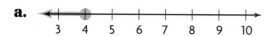

a. (number line 3 to 10, filled circle at 4)

b. (number line -1 to 6, open circle at 4)

c. (number line -1 to 6, open circle at 4)

d. (number line 2 to 9, filled circle at 4)

1. $x < 4$ **2.** $4 \leq x$ **3.** $4 \geq x$ **4.** $x > 4$

For Exercises 5–8, write the letter of the matching graph.

a. (number line 3 to 10, filled circle at 5)

b. (number line -2 to 4, filled circle at 2)

c. (number line -2 to 4, open circle at 2)

d. (number line 3 to 10, open circle at 5)

5. all real numbers less than 5

6. all real numbers greater than or equal to 2

7. all real numbers greater than 2

8. all real numbers less than or equal to 5

INDEPENDENT PRACTICE

Graph the inequality on a number line.

1. $x < 8$ **2.** $10 \leq p$ **3.** $3 \geq y$ **4.** $x > 5$ **5.** $^-3 < n$

6. $m \leq ^-4$ **7.** $x \geq 6$ **8.** $12 > h$ **9.** $15 \geq p$ **10.** $x > 20$

Tell whether the value is *a solution* or *not a solution* of the inequality.

11. $x - 6 \leq 3; x = 9$ **12.** $9 \leq 2p + 1; p = 3$ **13.** $3 \geq 3y - 5; y = 5$ **14.** $x + 3 > 8; x = 6$

15. $^-2 < 3n; n = 1$ **16.** $m - 9 \leq 4; m = 9$ **17.** $3x + 2 \geq 9; x = 2$ **18.** $2 > h + 9; h = 3$

For Exercises 19–20, write an inequality to match the graph.

19. 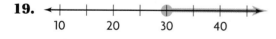 (number line 10 to 40, filled circle at 30)

20. 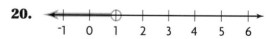 (number line -1 to 6, open circle at 1)

Problem-Solving Applications

21. The number of hours, h, it will take to complete the project will be at least 4 hr. Write and graph an algebraic inequality to represent the situation.

22. According to the weather forecast, the high temperature, t, will be less than 85°F. Write and graph an algebraic inequality to represent the situation.

23. ✏️ **WRITE ABOUT IT** Explain why the graph of $x \geq 10$ is different from the graph of $x > 10$.

Solving Inequalities

Nancy buys a CD on sale. After subtracting a $5 discount from the regular price, she pays more than $11. What was the regular price?

You can represent this problem by writing an inequality. Then you can solve the inequality by using inverse operations.

Think: regular price − discount > $11

Let r = the regular price of the CD. *Choose a variable to represent the unknown.*

$$r - 5 > 11$$ *Write an inequality to represent the problem.*
$$r - 5 + 5 > 11 + 5$$ *Solve by adding 5 to each side.*
$$r > 16$$ *solutions: all real numbers greater than 16*

So, the regular price was more than $16.

You can graph the solutions on a number line.

Talk About It

• Why was 5 added to both sides of the inequality shown above?

• What operation would you use to solve an inequality involving addition? multiplication? division?

• **CRITICAL THINKING** How is solving an inequality like solving an equation?

You can solve inequalities that contain rational numbers.

EXAMPLE 1 Solve and graph. $y + 9.4 < {}^-3.2$

$$y + 9.4 < {}^-3.2$$
$$y + 9.4 - 9.4 < {}^-3.2 - 9.4$$ *Subtract 9.4 from each side.*
$$y < {}^-3.2 + {}^-9.4$$
$$y < {}^-12.6$$ *solutions: all real numbers less than ${}^-12.6$*

Graph the solutions on a number line.

You can also solve inequalities involving multiplication and division.

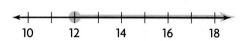 **EXAMPLE 2** Solve and graph. $4m \geq 48$

$$4m \geq 48$$

$$\frac{4m}{4} \geq \frac{48}{4}$$ *Divide each side by 4.*

$$m \geq 12$$ *solutions: all real numbers greater than or equal to 12*

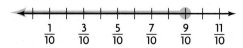

- How would you solve $\frac{g}{2} \leq 5$?

GUIDED PRACTICE

Name the operation you would use to solve the inequality.

1. $x + 9 \leq 10$ **2.** $y - 24 \leq 11$ **3.** $9m > {}^-2{,}700$

4. $\frac{n}{7} \leq 100$ **5.** $x + 2 \geq {}^-1.5$ **6.** $b - 4.9 < 8.9$

Solve and graph.

7. $k - 16 \geq 21$ **8.** $r + 4.5 > 10.5$ **9.** $16b < {}^-64$

Be careful. When you multiply or divide by a negative number, you reverse the inequality symbol.

$3 < 5$ If you multiply 3 and 5 by $^-1$, you get $^-3$ and $^-5$. You know that $^-3 > {}^-5$, so the inequality symbol is reversed.

EXAMPLE 3 Solve and graph. $\frac{k}{^-3} \geq \frac{^-3}{10}$

$$\frac{k}{^-3} \geq \frac{^-3}{10}$$

$${}^-3 \cdot \frac{k}{^-3} \leq \frac{^-3}{10} \cdot {}^-3$$ *Multiply each side by $^-3$. Reverse the inequality symbol.*

$$k \leq \frac{9}{10}$$ *solutions: all real numbers less than or equal to $\frac{9}{10}$*

Graph the solutions on a number line.

- Suppose $k = 2$. Does the solution check? Explain.

- How would you solve $\frac{c}{^-8} < {}^-5$?

Career Link

Before the use of computers, letters to be printed were cast individually from molten lead. Then, the printer coated the letters with ink and pressed them onto paper. The inked type and the letters on the paper were mirror images of each other. Therefore, the letters had to be cast in reverse and set in reverse order from the way they would appear on the printed page. Write the following inequality as it would look to the typographer who cast the letters and symbols.

$2c - 4 < 8$

145

To solve inequalities that involve two operations, use the inverse operations. First undo the addition or subtraction, and then undo the multiplication or division.

EXAMPLE 4   Solve and graph. $^-8c - 2 < 1.2$

$$^-8c - 2 < 1.2$$
$$^-8c - 2 + 2 < 1.2 + 2 \quad \textit{Add 2 to each side.}$$
$$^-8c < 3.2$$
$$\frac{^-8c}{^-8} > \frac{3.2}{^-8} \quad \begin{array}{l}\textit{Divide each side by}\ ^-8.\\ \textit{Reverse the inequality symbol.}\end{array}$$
$$c > ^-0.4 \quad \begin{array}{l}\textit{solutions: all real numbers}\\ \textit{greater than}\ ^-0.4\end{array}$$

Graph the solutions on a number line.

(number line marked: $^-0.6$, $^-0.4$, $^-0.2$, 0, 0.2, 0.4 with open circle at $^-0.4$)

- In the correct order, name the operations that were used to solve the inequality in Example 4.

- In the correct order, name the operations you would use to solve the inequality $\frac{x}{2} + 7 < 9$.

You can solve some real-life problems by writing and solving inequalities.

EXAMPLE 5   A concert takes place in an auditorium that can hold no more than 550 people. There are 25 rows with 20 seats in each row. Every seat is occupied. How many more people can the auditorium hold?

Think: number of people in seats + number of additional people ≤ 550

Let p = the number of additional people.   *Choose a variable.*

$$25 \times 20 = 500 \quad \begin{array}{l}\textit{Multiply to find the total number}\\ \textit{of seats.}\end{array}$$
$$500 + p \le 550 \quad \textit{Write an inequality.}$$
$$500 + p - 500 \le 550 - 500 \quad \textit{Subtract 500 from each side.}$$
$$p \le 50 \quad \begin{array}{l}\textit{solutions: all whole numbers less}\\ \textit{than or equal to 50}\end{array}$$

So, the auditorium can hold 0 to 50 more people.

- **CRITICAL THINKING** Why is the solution whole numbers instead of all real numbers?

- Suppose the auditorium could hold no more than 600 people. How many more people can it hold?

INDEPENDENT PRACTICE

Write *yes* or *no* to tell whether the inequality symbol would be reversed in the solution.

1. $^-7h < 49$ **2.** $3x > ^-15$ **3.** $3p \leq 45$ **4.** $^-2y + 1 \geq 8$ **5.** $^-8x - 3 < 4$

In the correct order, name the operations you would use to solve the inequality.

6. $10x + 2 > 42$ **7.** $\frac{c}{8} - 3 \leq 4$ **8.** $\frac{d}{10} + 3 \geq ^-4$ **9.** $5y - 5 > 35$

Solve and graph.

10. $k + 4 > 10$ **11.** $z - 5.5 \leq 6.4$ **12.** $5y < ^-25$ **13.** $\frac{k}{6} \geq 7$

14. $^-10x \leq 150$ **15.** $\frac{b}{^-4} < 6$ **16.** $\frac{k}{^-8} \geq 4$ **17.** $^-8x > 64$

18. $3k - 2 > 13$ **19.** $4y + 1.5 \geq 13.5$ **20.** $\frac{k}{6} + 4 \geq 6.4$ **21.** $\frac{b}{^-4} - 2 < 5$

Problem-Solving Applications

For Problems 22–24, write an inequality and solve.

22. Mr. Garcia is opening a restaurant. The fire code states that the restaurant can seat no more than 124 people at a time. If Mr. Garcia buys tables that seat 4 people each, what is the maximum number of tables he should buy?

23. Alex used a $10 discount coupon to buy a sweatshirt. After subtracting the discount, he paid less than $15 for the sweatshirt. What was the regular price of the sweatshirt?

24. Sue has 2 more shirts than sweaters. The total number of shirts and sweaters she has is less than 14. How many shirts does she have?

25. 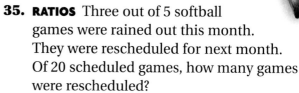 **WRITE ABOUT IT** When do you reverse the inequality symbol in an inequality problem?

Mixed Review

Find the value of *y* for *x* = 5.

26. $y = x + 3$ **27.** $y = x - 2$ **28.** $y = 4x$ **29.** $y = \frac{x}{5}$

Solve and check.

30. $8 = 2k + 2$ **31.** $2y - 6 = ^-10$ **32.** $\frac{k}{4} - 2 = 6$ **33.** $\frac{b}{7} - 6 = ^-8$

34. SPORTS In this week's soccer game, David scored 2 more than twice the number of goals that he scored in last week's game. He scored 6 goals this week. How many goals did he score last week?

35. RATIOS Three out of 5 softball games were rained out this month. They were rescheduled for next month. Of 20 scheduled games, how many games were rescheduled?

CULTURAL CONNECTION

Crafts From Ecuador

Eduardo learned to make Panama hats by hand when he lived in Ecuador. When he moved to the United States he wanted to teach his new friend, Sam, how to make the hats. Sam learned quickly and soon could make hats as fast as Eduardo. When Sam was first learning, though, it took him twice as long as Eduardo to make a hat. If Eduardo took 1.5 hr to make one hat, how long would it take Sam to make a hat?

Write the equation to find the time Sam spends making one hat.

Let x = Sam's time
Let y = Eduardo's time

$x = 2y$
$x = 2(1.5)$
$x = 3$

It would take Sam 3 hours to make a hat.

Work Together

Write an equation or inequality to solve.

1. Each Saturday Eduardo helps his parents in a booth at a flea market where they sell crafts. Wool blankets, jackets, and rugs woven by Eduardo's uncles in Ecuador are popular items. Eduardo's parents usually sell a jacket for $125 more than a blanket. They usually sell a rug for $400 more than a blanket. The cost of all three items together is $675. How much does the blanket cost?

2. Eduardo helps his parents keep track of what they sell. A picture of the Andes mountains costs $2 more than a doll. Ten dolls sell for the same price as eight pictures. How much does a doll cost? a picture?

3. Eduardo receives $10 a week for helping his parents on Saturday. He saves $3 of this money. In addition, he saves at least $5 from his weekly allowance. Make a number line to show the inequality that describes the money he saves every week from both his allowance and his parents.

CULTURAL LINK

The Otavaleños, South American Indians who farm in the Andes Mountains in Ecuador, are expert weavers and salespeople. Their wool products are sold all over the world. They often travel to distant markets in South America and other countries to sell their products. Tourists flock to the market in the town of Otavalo to buy rugs, sweaters, and ponchos.

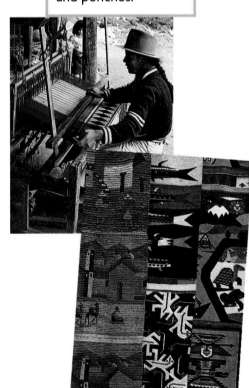

EXAMPLES

EXERCISES

- **Solve an equation with like terms.**

  (pages 132–135)

  $3(x + 3) + 2x = 29$
  $3x + 9 + 2x = 29$ *Distributive Property*
  $5x + 9 = 29$ *Combine like terms.*
  $5x + 9 - 9 = 29 - 9$ *Subtract 9 from each*
  $5x = 20$ *side.*
  $\dfrac{5x}{5} = \dfrac{20}{5}$ *Divide each side by 5.*
  $x = 4 \leftarrow$ solution

Solve and check.

1. $4x + 2x + 4 = 10$ **2.** $15 + 7y - y = 51$

3. $3b + b + 2 = 18$ **4.** $9 + 7a - a = {}^-3$

5. $5(a + 3) - a = 23$ **6.** $b + 3(b + 3) = 5$

7. $4(x - 2) - x = 4$ **8.** $7 = 3(y - 3) + y$

9. $3(d + 5) + 2d = 0$ **10.** $21 = 3(y - 1) + y$

11. $33 = m + 4(m + 2)$

12. ${}^-51 = 9(x - 1) + 2x$

- **Use the strategy *write an equation* to solve a problem.** (pages 136–137)

  PROBLEM-SOLVING TIP: For help in solving problems by writing an equation, see pages 12 and 136.

13. Patti and Rick deliver a total of 72 newspapers each morning before school. Patti delivers 6 more than twice the number Rick delivers. How many newspapers does Rick deliver?

- **Solve an equation with variables on both sides.** (pages 139–141)

  $5x = x + 30$
  $5x - x = x + 30 - x$ *Subtract x from each side.*
  $4x = 30$ *Combine like terms.*
  $\dfrac{4x}{4} = \dfrac{30}{4}$ *Divide each side by 4.*
  $x = 7.5 \leftarrow$ solution

Solve and check.

14. $6a = 8 + 4a$ **15.** $4y + 3 = y - 6$

16. $3x = 8(x - 5)$ **17.** $\frac{1}{2}(b - 3) = 2b + 6$

18. $5y = 2(y + 3)$ **19.** $2.5(x + 1) = 1.5x$

20. $\frac{1}{3}(d - 6) = \frac{{}^-2}{3}d + 27$

- **Graph the solutions of an inequality on a number line.** (pages 142–143)

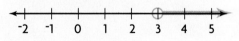

  Graph the inequality $y > 3$.

21. **VOCABULARY** An inequality that contains a variable is an __?__ .

Graph the inequality on a number line.

22. $y \leq {}^-3$ **23.** $x > 8$ **24.** $4 \geq x$

25. ${}^-2 > a$ **26.** $5 \leq p$ **27.** $b < 3$

- **Solve an inequality.** (pages 144–147)

  ${}^-8x \leq 64$

  $\dfrac{{}^-8x}{{}^-8} \geq \dfrac{64}{{}^-8}$ *Divide each side by ${}^-8$. Reverse the inequality symbol.*

  $x \geq {}^-8 \leftarrow$ solution

Solve and graph.

28. $3a > 16 - a$ **29.** $\frac{{}^-x}{5} \geq 4$

30. $5y - 5 < 35$ **31.** $3b + 4.3 \leq {}^-2$

8

GRAPHING EQUATIONS AND INEQUALITIES

LOOK AHEAD

In this chapter you will solve problems that involve

- solving equations with two variables
- using the problem-solving strategy *guess and check*
- graphing ordered pairs, linear equations, inequalities, and nonlinear equations

Team-Up Project

Eating at a Steady Rate

Do you eat at a steady rate? Make a table to show the amount you eat over a period of time. Then graph your data and decide if your eating rate is steady.

YOU WILL NEED: graph paper, foods, stopwatch

Plan
- Work in a small group. Make data tables showing the amount eaten over time. Then graph the data and use the graph to determine if your eating rate is steady.

Act
- Choose something to eat.
- Record the time and the amount you eat. Make a table to show the amount you eat over a period of time.
- Graph the data.
- Decide if your eating rate is steady.

Share
- Compare your tables and graphs with other groups. Discuss how you can determine if a rate is steady.

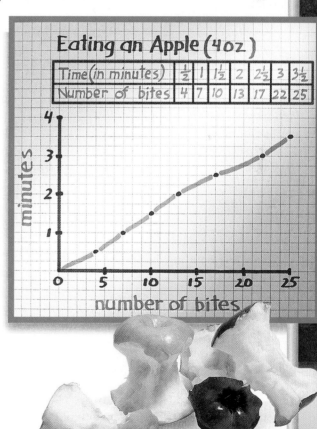

Eating an Apple (4 oz)

Time (in minutes)	$\frac{1}{2}$	1	$1\frac{1}{2}$	2	$2\frac{1}{2}$	3	$3\frac{1}{2}$
Number of bites	4	7	10	13	17	22	25

DID YOU
- ✓ Choose something to eat?
- ✓ Make a table?
- ✓ Graph the data?
- ✓ Determine if your eating rate is steady?

WORD POWER

solution of an equation with two variables

REMEMBER:
You can organize data in a table of values that includes the values for x, values for y, and the ordered pairs. **See page H29.**

Equations with Two Variables

Emil and his family are driving to the Grand Canyon National Park. If they travel at an average speed of 60 mph, how far will they travel in 8 hr? in 12 hr? in 16 hr?

The equation $y = 60x$ shows the relationship between the total distance in miles, y, and the number of hours, x. The equation has two variables. To solve an equation with two variables, choose a replacement value for one variable and then find the value of the other variable. An equation with two variables usually has many solutions.

Find solutions of $y = 60x$, and make a table of values.

x (in hr)	$60x$	y (in mi)	(x,y)	
8	$60 \cdot 8$	480	(8,480)	← *The ordered pairs are solutions of the equation.*
12	$60 \cdot 12$	720	(12,720)	
16	$60 \cdot 16$	960	(16,960)	

An ordered pair is a **solution of an equation with two variables** if the equation is a true statement when the values of x and y are substituted in the equation.

You can check ordered pairs to see if they are solutions.

EXAMPLE 1   Which of the following are solutions of $y = 3x + 2$? (1,3), (2,8), or (⁻3,⁻7)

Substitute the values in the equation.

$y = 3x + 2$	$y = 3x + 2$	$y = 3x + 2$
$3 = 3 \cdot 1 + 2$	$8 = 3 \cdot 2 + 2$	$⁻7 = 3 \cdot ⁻3 + 2$
$3 \neq 5$	$8 = 8$	$⁻7 = ⁻7$
not a solution	solution	solution

So, (2,8) and (⁻3,⁻7) are solutions.

• Are there other solutions of $y = 3x + 2$? Explain.

Copy and complete the table of values for $y = 4x - 1$.

	x	$4x - 1$	y	(x,y)
1.	1	$4 \cdot 1 - 1$	3	$(1,?)$
2.	3	$4 \cdot 3 - 1$	11	?
3.	7	?	27	?

Write *yes* or *no* to tell whether the ordered pair is a solution of the equation $y = \frac{x}{2} + 5$.

4. $(2,6)$ **5.** $(0,5)$ **6.** $(^-2,3)$ **7.** $(^-6,2)$

You can use equations with two variables to solve problems.

EXAMPLE 2 The bank thermometer reads 40°C. The equation $F = \frac{9}{5}C + 32$ describes the relation between Celsius and Fahrenheit temperatures. What is the temperature in °F?

Think: Substitute the Celsius value for C in the equation.

$F = \frac{9}{5}C + 32$

$F = \frac{9}{5} \cdot 40 + 32$ *Replace C with 40.*

$F = \frac{360}{5} + 32$

$F = 72 + 32$ *Simplify the fraction.*

$F = 104$ *solution: (40,104)*

So, 40°C is equivalent to 104°F.

Sometimes an equation with two variables has both variables on one side. You can rewrite an equation of this kind so that y is on one side of the equation and expressed in terms of x.

EXAMPLE 3 Rewrite the equation $y + x = 8$ to express y in terms of x.

$y + x = 8$
$y + x - x = 8 - x$ *Subtract x from each side.*
$y = 8 - x$ *Now y is expressed in terms of x.*

• What would you do to the equation $y - x = 5$ to express y in terms of x?

Science Link

Water boils at 212° on the Fahrenheit scale (F) and at 100° on the Celsius scale (C). Water freezes at 32°F and at 0°C. In the equation in Example 2, let $F = C$. At what temperature are the two scales the same? (HINT: Find the value of C.)

REMEMBER:

To solve an addition equation, subtract the same quantity from each side of the equation.
See page 116.

Rewriting an equation to express y in terms of x sometimes makes it easier to find solutions of the equation.

EXAMPLE 4 Rewrite the equation $8x + 4y = 5$ to express y in terms of x. Find three solutions of the equation.

$$8x + 4y = 5$$
$$8x + 4y - 8x = 5 - 8x \qquad \textit{Subtract 8x from each side.}$$
$$4y = 5 - 8x$$
$$\frac{4y}{4} = \frac{5}{4} - \frac{8x}{4} \qquad \textit{Divide each side by 4.}$$
$$y = 1.25 - 2x \qquad \textit{Simplify the fractions.}$$

Think: Find solutions by choosing three values for x and substituting them for x in the equation $y = 1.25 - 2x$.

Let $x = {}^-1, 0, 1$.

x	$1.25 - 2x$	y	(x,y)
$^-1$	$1.25 - 2 \cdot {}^-1$	3.25	$(^-1, 3.25)$
0	$1.25 - 2 \cdot 0$	1.25	$(0, 1.25)$
1	$1.25 - 2 \cdot 1$	$^-0.75$	$(1, ^-0.75)$

Make a table of values.

So, $(^-1, 3.25)$, $(0, 1.25)$, and $(1, ^-0.75)$ are three solutions of the equation $8x + 4y = 5$.

• Do the choices for the values of x matter? Explain.

• Rewrite the equation $y - 5x = 2$ to express y in terms of x.

INDEPENDENT PRACTICE

Copy and complete the table of values.

$y = 5 + x$

	x	$5 + x$	y	(x,y)
1.	4	$5 + 4$	$?$	$?$
2.	$^-4$	$5 + {}^-4$	$?$	$?$
3.	6	$5 + 6$	$?$	$?$
4.	2.5	$5 + 2.5$	$?$	$?$

$y = 3x - 10$

	x	$3x - 10$	y	(x,y)
5.	2	$3 \cdot 2 - 10$	$?$	$?$
6.	4	$3 \cdot 4 - 10$	$?$	$?$
7.	7	$3 \cdot 7 - 10$	$?$	$?$
8.	$^-2$	$3 \cdot {}^-2 - 10$	$?$	$?$

Write *yes* or *no* to tell whether the ordered pair is a solution of the equation $y = 8 - 3x$.

9. $(2,2)$ **10.** $(^-4,20)$ **11.** $(^-2,12)$ **12.** $(0,7)$ **13.** $(6,^-10)$

14. $(4,^-4)$ **15.** $(8,^-24)$ **16.** $(^-6,26)$ **17.** $(4,0)$ **18.** $(8,^-16)$

Rewrite the equation to express *y* in terms of *x*.

19. $y + 3x = 15$ **20.** $y - 6x = 3$ **21.** $y - 10x = 5$ **22.** $y + 7x = 8$

23. $2y - 4x = 6$ **24.** $3y + 6x = 24$ **25.** $5y + 20x = 15$ **26.** $2y - 9x = 10$

Make a table of values to find three solutions of the equation.
Let $x = {}^-2, 0, 2$.

27. $y + 4x = 17$ **28.** $y - 4x = 7$ **29.** $y - 3x = 9$ **30.** $y + \frac{x}{2} = 6$

31. $2y - 6x = 12$ **32.** $3y + 3x = 27$ **33.** $4y + 6x = 8$ **34.** $2y - 11x = 6$

35. $5y - 10x = 15$ **36.** $y + 3x = 2$ **37.** $y + 2x = 0$ **38.** $y - 3x = 1$

Problem-Solving Applications

39. Kelly spends 5 hr more a week reading than watching television. Write an equation to show the relationship between television time, *x*, and reading time, *y*. Find the number of hours she spends reading if she spends 5 hr watching television.

40. Adam takes care of a large dog and a small dog. The amount of food that the large dog eats daily, *y*, is 3 times the amount for the small dog, *x*. Write an equation to show the relationship between the two amounts of food.

41. David is $9\frac{1}{2}$ years older than his sister Merry Lynn. Write an equation to show the relationship between David's age, *y*, and Merry Lynn's age, *x*.

42. The almanac says the average high temperature in Paris this month is about 5°C. Use the formula $F = \frac{9}{5}C + 32$ to find the temperature in °F.

43. ✏️ **WRITE ABOUT IT** Explain how you can find an ordered pair that is a solution of an equation with two variables.

Mixed Review

Compare the two expressions for $x = 4$. Write $=$ or $\neq$.

44. $2x + 1 \bullet x + 5$ **45.** $3x - 6 \bullet 20 + x$ **46.** $14 - 2x \bullet 3x + 5$ **47.** $5x - 4 \bullet 3x + 4$

Solve and check.

48. $3(x + 4) = 4x - 1$ **49.** $6(x - 5) = 4x + 4$ **50.** $6(x + 3) = 4(x - 1)$

51. **PATTERNS** The planning committee wants to order food for the fourth annual school picnic. The attendance in the past three years was 344, 394, and 444. If this pattern continues, how many people will attend this year? How many will attend next year?

52. **DATA** The population near a miniature golf course is 2,949. About 9% of the population is 10–14 years old. About how many people are 10–14 years old?

Use *Guess and Check* to Solve an Equation with Two Variables

WHAT YOU'LL LEARN
How to guess and check to solve equations with two variables

WHY LEARN THIS?
To solve everyday problems such as finding the numbers of stamps you can purchase

Problem Solving
....
- **Understand**
- **Plan**
- **Solve**
- **Look Back**

Most music stores charge more for CDs than they do for tapes of the same music. However, it actually costs less to make a CD than it does to make a tape.

You can use the strategy *guess and check* to solve problems.

You own a music store that sells CDs for $13 and cassette tapes for $10. Yesterday you sold a total of 19 CDs and tapes for $232. How many CDs did you sell? How many tapes did you sell?

✓ UNDERSTAND   What are you asked to find?

What facts are given?

✓ PLAN   What strategy will you use?

You can write an equation with two variables and use the *guess-and-check* strategy to find the solution.

✓ SOLVE   How will you represent the number of CDs and the number of tapes?

Let x = the number of CDs, with a price of $13 each.
Let y = the number of tapes, with a price of $10 each.

$$\text{sales of CDs} + \text{sales of tapes} = \$232$$

$$\$13x \quad + \quad \$10y \quad = \$232$$

Think: x and y must be whole numbers, and their sum must equal 19.

Guess 1: Let x = 10 and y = 9, or (10,9).
Check 1: $13(10) + 10(9) = 220$ ← *too small; use different values*

Guess 2: Let x = 12 and y = 7, or (12,7).
Check 2: $13(12) + 10(7) = 226$ ← *too small; use different values*

Guess 3: Let x = 14 and y = 5, or (14,5).
Check 3: $13(14) + 10(5) = 232$ ← *correct; solution is (14,5)*

So, you sold 14 CDs and 5 tapes.

✓ LOOK BACK   What other strategy could you use?

What if . . . the total sales a week ago were $238? How many CDs and tapes were sold?

Use the strategy *guess and check* to solve.

1. Karen and Sally made 11 batches of cookies for their class party. They made a total of 137 cookies. Each of Karen's batches was a baker's dozen and each of Sally's batches was a dozen. How many batches did each girl make? (HINT: A baker's dozen is 13.)

2. For extra-credit points, Matt read a total of 10 books. He received 3 points for each nonfiction book he read and 2 points for each fiction book. He received a total of 26 points. How many nonfiction books and how many fiction books did he read?

3. During a vacation, Maria's father spent $178 on 8 tickets for a theme park: $36 each for adults' tickets and $14 each for children's tickets. How many of each type of ticket did he buy?

4. Sue spent $3.76 for a total of 14 postcards and letters. It cost $0.20 to mail each postcard and $0.32 to mail each letter. How many postcards and how many letters did she mail?

MIXED APPLICATIONS   CHOOSE

Choose a strategy and solve.

> ### Problem-Solving Strategies
> - **Guess and Check**
> - **Find a Pattern**
> - **Work Backward**
> - **Draw a Diagram**
> - **Make a Table**
> - **Write an Equation**

5. Members of the booster club will mail 10,000 newsletters. They plan to mail $\frac{1}{2}$ on Monday and $\frac{2}{5}$ of the rest on Tuesday. How many newsletters will they need to mail on Monday? on Tuesday?

6. The concession stand sold 26 hot dogs and hamburgers for a total of $29.50. The hot dogs cost $0.95 and the hamburgers cost $1.25. How many hot dogs and how many hamburgers were sold?

7. The first banner Diana made took her 3 hr. The second banner took half that time. If she makes each additional banner in the same amount of time as the second, how long will it take her to make 6 more banners?

8. The doughnut shop is having a special on doughnuts. The first dozen is $3.60, and each additional dozen is $1.00 off. The breakfast club paid $21.80. How many dozen doughnuts did the club buy?

9. Kyle checked out 14 books from the library in July. This was $\frac{1}{3}$ the number of books he checked out in June. How many books did he check out in June?

10. The park ranger is fencing in an area that is 24 ft wide and 36 ft long. The fence posts will be 3 ft apart. How many fence posts will he need?

11. ✏️ **WRITE ABOUT IT** Write a problem that can be solved with the strategy *guess and check*. Exchange with a classmate and solve.

Graphing in the Coordinate Plane

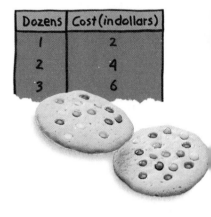

Dozens	Cost (in dollars)
1	2
2	4
3	6

Kelly is selling baked goods at a school bazaar. A dozen cookies sell for $2. Kelly made a table of values to show the cost for different quantities of cookies. For a presentation, she represented this information in a graph. Identify one set of values as x and the other as y.

Let $x =$ the number of dozens.
Let $y =$ the total cost in dollars.

Form an ordered pair from each x-coordinate and its corresponding y-coordinate.

x	y	(x,y)
1	2	(1,2)
2	4	(2,4)
3	6	(3,6)

• How do you graph (1,2)?

Then graph the ordered pairs in the coordinate plane.

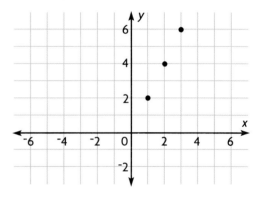

EXAMPLE Graph the ordered pairs.

x	y	(x,y)
⁻1	⁻3	(⁻1,⁻3)
0	⁻1	(0,⁻1)
1	1	(1,1)
2	3	(2,3)

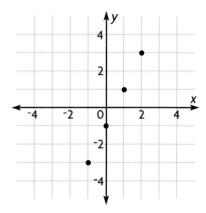

• In an ordered pair, which value comes first? second?

• Suppose the value of x is ⁻2 and the value of y is ⁻4. What ordered pair represents these values?

GUIDED PRACTICE

Use a separate coordinate plane to graph the ordered pairs shown in each table.

1.

x	y	(x,y)
¯1	¯2	(¯1,¯2)
0	0	(0,0)
1	2	(1,2)
2	4	(2,4)

2.

x	y	(x,y)
¯1	3	(¯1,3)
0	4	(0,4)
1	5	(1,5)
2	6	(2,6)

3.

x	y	(x,y)
¯1	¯1	(¯1,¯1)
0	1	(0,1)
1	3	(1,3)
2	5	(2,5)

INDEPENDENT PRACTICE

Draw a coordinate plane. Graph and label these points.

1. (4,5) **2.** (0,0) **3.** (¯1,3) **4.** (2,¯2) **5.** (¯3,¯2)

For Exercises 6–11, use a separate coordinate plane to graph the ordered pairs shown in each table.

6.

x	y	(x,y)
¯1	¯3	(¯1,¯3)
0	0	(0,0)
1	3	(1,3)

7.

x	y	(x,y)
¯1	¯4	(¯1,¯4)
0	0	(0,0)
1	4	(1,4)

8.

x	y	(x,y)
¯1	¯4	(¯1,¯4)
0	1	(0,1)
1	6	(1,6)

9.

x	y	(x,y)
¯2	¯5	(¯2,¯5)
1	1	(1,1)
2	3	(2,3)

10.

x	y	(x,y)
¯2	¯7	(¯2,¯7)
¯1	¯4	(¯1,¯4)
2	5	(2,5)

11.

x	y	(x,y)
1	3	(1,3)
2	5	(2,5)
3	7	(3,7)

Problem-Solving Applications

12. Paula wants to earn money for her class trip. For each plant hanger she completes and sells, she makes $3. She made a table of values to show how much she could earn. Graph the ordered pairs.

x	y
4	12
6	18
8	24

13. Paula realized that she might not earn enough to pay for her class trip. Her mother promised to give her $2 extra for every plant hanger she sold. Paula made a new table of values to show how much she could earn. Graph the ordered pairs.

x	y
4	20
6	30
8	40

14. David walked 5 blocks east, 2 blocks north, 7 blocks west, 4 blocks south, and 2 blocks east. How many blocks north does he need to walk to get back to his starting point?

15. ▭➤ **WRITE ABOUT IT** Do the ordered pairs (2,3) and (3,2) name the same point? Explain.

Graphing Linear Equations

Real-Life Link

Many teens charge more than one rate for baby-sitting. Suppose Marta charges $4 per hour for the first child and $1 per hour more for each additional child. Marta will baby-sit two children. Let x equal the number of hours and y the amount charged. Write an equation to represent the relationship between the number of hours and the earnings.

Marta baby-sits. Her rate is $4 per hour. How can you represent the relationship between the number of hours and the charge?

You can write and graph an equation that shows the relationship between the number of hours and the charge.

Let x = the number of hours.
Let y = the charge.

$y = 4x$

To graph $y = 4x$, make a table of values using at least three ordered pairs. Then graph the ordered pairs and join them with a line.

x	$4x$	y	(x,y)
0	$4 \cdot 0$	0	(0,0)
1	$4 \cdot 1$	4	(1,4)
2	$4 \cdot 2$	8	(2,8)

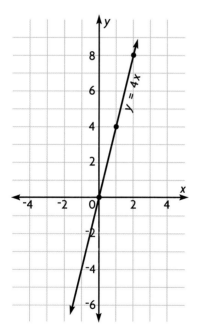

A **graph of an equation** is the graph of all its solutions. The ordered pairs from the table above lie in a straight line on the graph. Other solutions of $y = 4x$ can also be found on the line. Any equation whose graph is a straight line is a **linear equation**.

Talk About It

- What does the ordered pair (2.5,10) tell you about the amount charged?

- **CRITICAL THINKING** Is the ordered pair $(^-1,^-4)$ a solution of the equation $y = 4x$? Would you include this point on a graph that showed the number of hours of baby-sitting? Why or why not?

- Look at the graph. Identify another ordered pair that is a solution.

Write *yes* or *no* to tell whether the ordered pair is a solution of $y = 5x - 3$.

1. (2,7)　　　**2.** (5,28)　　　**3.** (⁻3,⁻12)　　　**4.** (1.5,4.5)

5. (0,3)　　　**6.** (3,12)　　　**7.** (⁻2,⁻13)　　　**8.** (4,⁻23)

Let $x = {}^{-}1$, 0, and 1. Name the ordered pairs you would use to graph the equation. Then graph the equation.

9. $y = 5x$　　　**10.** $y = 3x + 2$　　　**11.** $y = 5x - 1$

You can graph a linear equation that has both variables on one side. Solve the equation for y.

EXAMPLE 1　　Graph $6x + 2y = 9$.

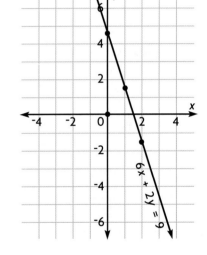

$$6x + 2y = 9$$
$$6x + 2y - 6x = 9 - 6x \quad \textit{Subtract 6x from each side.}$$
$$2y = 9 - 6x$$
$$\frac{2y}{2} = \frac{9}{2} - \frac{6x}{2} \quad \textit{Divide each side by 2.}$$
$$y = 4.5 - 3x \quad \textit{Solve the equation for y.}$$

Think: Make a table of values for $y = 4.5 - 3x$. Substitute the values in the equation, and solve for y. Then graph the ordered pairs.

x	$4.5 - 3x$	y	(x,y)
0	$4.5 - 3 \cdot 0$	4.5	(0,4.5)
1	$4.5 - 3 \cdot 1$	1.5	(1,1.5)
2	$4.5 - 3 \cdot 2$	⁻1.5	(2,⁻1.5)

- The graph of $6x + 2y = 9$ is a straight line. How many solutions of the equation do you think there are?

- You can graph a linear equation by using two ordered pairs. How does using a third ordered pair act as a check?

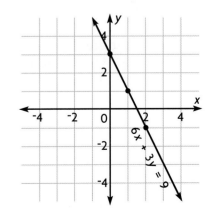

x	$3 - 2x$	y	(x,y)
0	$3 - 2 \cdot 0$	3	(0,3)
1	$3 - 2 \cdot 1$	1	(1,1)
2	$3 - 2 \cdot 2$	⁻1	(2,⁻1)

- The graph of $6x + 3y = 9$ is a straight line. How many solutions of the equation do you think there are?

Linear Equations with One Variable

Some linear equations, such as $y = 2$, have only one variable.

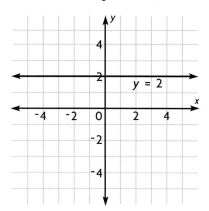

The graph of $y = 2$ is a horizontal line 2 units above the x-axis and parallel to it.

- Look at the graph of $y = 2$. What is the value of y for any value of x?

- Name three ordered pairs that lie on the graph.

You can graph a linear equation that has one variable.

EXAMPLE 2   Graph $x = {}^-3$. Describe the graph.

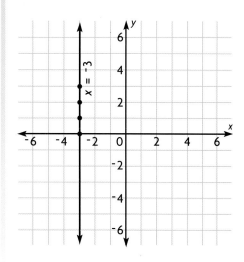

x	y
$^-3$	0
$^-3$	1
$^-3$	2
$^-3$	3

The graph of $x = {}^-3$ is a vertical line 3 units to the left of the y-axis and parallel to it.

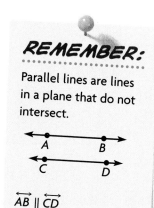

REMEMBER:

Parallel lines are lines in a plane that do not intersect.

$\overleftrightarrow{AB} \parallel \overleftrightarrow{CD}$

$\overleftrightarrow{AB}$ is parallel to $\overleftrightarrow{CD}$. **See page H21.**

- Look at the graph of $x = {}^-3$. What is the value of x for any value of y? What are three ordered pairs with $y < 0$ that represent solutions of the equation?

INDEPENDENT PRACTICE

Write *yes* or *no* to tell whether the ordered pair is a solution of $y = 4 + 6x$.

1. (3,22)   **2.** (1,10)   **3.** (4,20)   **4.** (5,32)   **5.** ($^-2$,8)   **6.** ($^-1$,$^-2$)

Let $x = {}^-1, 0, 1$. Name the ordered pairs you would use to graph the equation. Then graph the equation.

7. $y = 4x$ **8.** $y = 2x + 5$ **9.** $y = 6x - 3$

10. $y = x - 10$ **11.** $y = 4x - 2$ **12.** $y = 5x$

13. $y = 4x + 3$ **14.** $y = 2x - 4$ **15.** $y = x + 7$

16. $y = 7x - 2$ **17.** $y = 3x + 2.5$ **18.** $y = \frac{3}{2}x + 1$

Graph the equation.

19. $y = 3$ **20.** $y = {}^-4$ **21.** $x = {}^-3$

Solve for y. Then graph the equation. Use at least three ordered pairs.

22. $y - x = 5$ **23.** $y + 5x = 20$ **24.** $y + 7x = 8$

25. $3y + 6x = 24$ **26.** $2y + 4x = 12$ **27.** $y - 4x = {}^-5$

Problem-Solving Applications

28. The difference between Margo's age, y, and Kristen's age, x, is 9 years. Margo is older. Write an equation to show the relationship. Then graph the equation. How old will Margo be when Kristen is 12 years old?

29. Chris studies twice as long as his brother. Write an equation to find the number of hours Chris studies, y, when his brother studies x hr. Graph the equation.

30. Use the graph in Problem 29 to find how many hours Chris studies when his brother studies $3\frac{1}{2}$ hr. How can you check your answer?

31. ✏️ **WRITE ABOUT IT** Explain how you can show that $y = 5x$ is a linear equation.

Mixed Review

Solve each inequality.

32. $y + 6 \geq 10$ **33.** $y + 2 \leq 7$ **34.** $y - 8 \leq 10$ **35.** $y - 10 > 15$

Solve and check.

36. $7n = 21$ **37.** $p + 9 = 4p$ **38.** $5x - 2 = 13$ **39.** $6 = 2(h + 3)$

40. **AVERAGES** The low temperatures each day in Syracuse, New York, for the first week in January were $9°$, $5°$, $^-6°$, $^-10°$, $^-16°$, $^-6°$, and $3°$. Find the average low temperature for the week.

41. **PERCENTS** Joe intercepted 3 out of the 20 passes in the game. What percent of the passes did he intercept?

Technology **Link**

In *Mighty Math Astro Algebra*, you can enter *Grapher Station* and practice graphing linear equations in the *Sparky Takes Off* mission.

Graphing Inequalities with Two Variables

A center line divides a road into three parts—the line itself, a lane on one side, and a lane on the other side.

In the same way, a graph of a linear equation separates the coordinate plane into three parts—the points on the line, the points on one side of the line, and the points on the other side of the line. The coordinates of every point in the coordinate plane at the right make one of the following statements true:

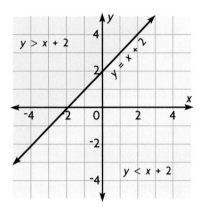

$y = x + 2 \quad y > x + 2 \quad y < x + 2$

Talk About It

- Name an ordered pair that describes a point on line $y = x + 2$. Is the statement true when you substitute the x- and y-coordinates into $y > x + 2$? into $y < x + 2$?

- Is line $y = x + 2$ included in the graph of inequality $y > x + 2$? in the graph of inequality $y < x + 2$? Explain.

You can graph an inequality with two variables such as $y > 3x$.

Graph equation $y = 3x$. Since the inequality symbol $>$ indicates that the points on line $y = 3x$ are not solutions of $y > 3x$, do not include line $y = 3x$ in the graph of $y > 3x$. So, represent $y = 3x$ with a dashed line rather than a solid line.

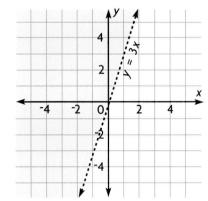

$(^-4,1)$ *To decide which side to shade, choose any point that is not on the line.*

$y > 3x$

$1 > 3 \cdot ^-4$ *Replace x with $^-4$ and y with 1 in $y > 3x$.*

$1 > ^-12$

Since $1 > ^-12$ is true, shade the graph on the side of the line where $(^-4,1)$ is located.

Calculator Activities, page H43

EXAMPLE 1 Graph $y \geq 2x - 2$.

Graph the equation $y = 2x - 2$. Use a solid line to show that points on the line $y = 2x - 2$ are solutions of the inequality.

Think: Pick a point such as (3,2) which is not on the line $y = 2x - 2$.

$y \geq 2x - 2$
$2 \geq 2 \cdot 3 - 2$ *Replace x with 3 and y with 2.*
$2 \geq 4$

Since $2 \geq 4$ is not true, shade the graph on the side of the line that does not contain (3,2).

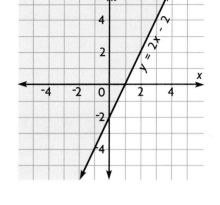

You can solve some real-life problems by graphing inequalities.

EXAMPLE 2 Hamburgers cost $3 each, and soft drinks cost $1 each. Make a graph to find three different ways that Shameika can get both hamburgers and soft drinks for $10. Then find the nine ordered pairs that describe the different ways she can get both hamburgers and soft drinks for less than $10.

Think: Write an inequality to represent the situation.

Let x = the number of hamburgers.
Let y = the number of soft drinks.

cost of hamburgers + cost of soft drinks up to $10

$$3x \qquad + \qquad 1y \qquad \leq \qquad 10$$

$3x + y \leq 10$ *Write 1y as y.*
$3x + y - 3x \leq 10 - 3x$ *Subtract 3x from each side.*
$y \leq 10 - 3x$ *Express y in terms of x.*

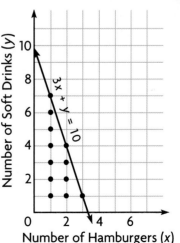

Graph the line $y = 10 - 3x$. Choose the point (0,5), which is not on the line.

$y \leq 10 - 3x$
$5 \leq 10 - 3 \cdot 0$ *Replace x with 0 and y with 5.*
$5 \leq 10$

Since the inequality is true, the solutions of the inequality are represented by points on the same side of the line as (0,5).

So, for exactly $10 Shameika can buy 1 hamburger and 7 soft drinks (1,7), 2 hamburgers and 4 soft drinks (2,4), or 3 hamburgers and 1 soft drink (3,1). The following ordered pairs describe what she can get for less than $10: (1,1), (1,2), (1,3), (1,4), (1,5), (1,6), (2,1), (2,2), (2,3).

Graph the inequality $y \leq 2x + 4$. Write *yes* or *no* to tell whether the ordered pair is a solution of the inequality.

1. (1,2) **2.** (5,16) **3.** (2,1) **4.** (2,8) **5.** (4,20)

6. (5,15) **7.** (3,10) **8.** ($^-$2,3) **9.** ($^-$7,$^-$1) **10.** (3,7)

Graph the inequality $y > 3x - 3$. Write *yes* or *no* to tell whether the ordered pair is a solution of the inequality.

1. (3,1) **2.** (4,6) **3.** (5,14) **4.** (2,3) **5.** (6,19)

6. (1,3) **7.** ($^-$3,$^-$12) **8.** ($^-$1,$^-$9) **9.** (0,$^-$1) **10.** (0,$^-$2)

Graph the inequality.

11. $y > x + 4$ **12.** $y < 2x - 5$ **13.** $y \geq 5x$ **14.** $y \leq x - 3$

15. $y \leq 2x - 9$ **16.** $y > 8 - x$ **17.** $y - 3x \geq 4$ **18.** $y - 9x < 24$

Problem-Solving Applications

Use the graph to solve Problems 19–23.

Tony is shopping for video games and books. The video games cost $15 each, and the books cost $5 each. Tony can spend up to $60.

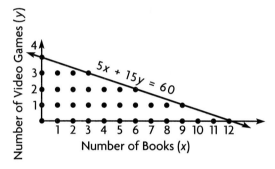

19. x books cost $5x$. How much do y video games cost?

20. Can Tony buy 2 books and 6 video games? Is (2,6) on the graph?

21. Can Tony buy 8 books and 1 video game? Is (8,1) on the graph?

22. In what five ways can Tony spend exactly $60? Write the answers as ordered pairs.

23. Write ordered pairs to describe 5 different ways that Tony can buy both books and video games for less than $60.

For Problems 24–28, graph the inequality $y > x + 5$.

24. Name an ordered pair that is a solution of the inequality.

25. Is (3,5) a solution of $y > x + 5$? Explain how to check your answer.

26. Which side of the graph of $y = x + 5$ do you shade?

27. Name an ordered pair that is a solution of $y \leq x + 5$.

28. ⬛▷ **WRITE ABOUT IT** When do you use a dashed line rather than a solid line to graph an inequality?

MORE PRACTICE Lesson 8.5, page H57

Exploring Graphs of Nonlinear Equations

COOPERATIVE LEARNING

Are all the streets and roads in your town straight? Or do some have turns and curves?

Like roads, the graphs of equations are not always straight lines.

Explore

- Find solutions of the equation $y = x^2$. Let $x = {}^-2, {}^-1, 0, 1,$ and 2. Record the ordered pairs in a table of values.

- Graph the points for the ordered pairs by placing the counters in the coordinate plane. Connect the points. What is the shape of the graph?

- Graph $y = {}^-x^2$. Let $x = {}^-2, {}^-1, 0, 1,$ and 2. Record the equation, and describe the shape of the graph.

- Graph $y = 2x^2$. Let $x = {}^-2, {}^-1, 0, 1,$ and 2. Record the equation, and describe the shape of the graph.

- Graph $y = {}^-3x^2$. Record the equation, and describe the shape of the graph.

Think and Discuss 💡 CRITICAL THINKING

- How are the graphs alike? How are they different?

- The U-shaped curve on each graph in this activity is called a **parabola**. For which equations does the parabola open upward? downward?

- Look at the equations. How are they alike? How are they different?

- How is the sign of the x^2 term related to the way the parabola opens?

Try This

- Write *upward* or *downward* to predict the appearance of the graph of the equation. Check your prediction by graphing.

  $y = 3x^2$ $\qquad$ $y = {}^-4x^2$ $\qquad$ $y = 6x^2$ $\qquad$ $y = {}^-5x^2$

LAB *Activity*

WHAT YOU'LL EXPLORE
How to graph one type of nonlinear equation

WHAT YOU'LL NEED
large-grid coordinate plane, straightedge, counters

WORD POWER
parabola

167

MATH FUN!

SEARCH AND RESCUE

PURPOSE To practice graphing ordered pairs in a coordinate plane (pages 158–159)

YOU WILL NEED coordinate planes, colored pencils or markers

Play with a partner. On the coordinate plane, secretly draw a plane figure by shading at least 6 squares. Each square should touch at least one other square. In turn, each player tries to locate his or her partner's figure by calling out ordered pairs. Respond "found" for each correct guess, and "not found" for each incorrect guess. Plot your guesses on a blank coordinate graph with a different color to mark "found" ordered pairs. The first player to rescue his or her partner's figure wins.

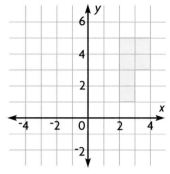

HOME NOTE Play this game with a member of your family.

GRAPHIC ART

PURPOSE To practice graphing inequalities (pages 164–166)

YOU WILL NEED coordinate plane, straightedge, colored pencils

On one coordinate plane, graph the following inequalities. Lightly shade each of your graphs with a different color.

$$y \leq 6 - x \qquad x \geq {}^-2$$
$$y \geq 0 \qquad y \leq 6 + x \qquad x \leq 2$$

What shape does the area included by all the inequalities make?

PAPER FOLDING

PURPOSE To practice predicting the appearance of a nonlinear equation (page 167)

YOU WILL NEED a big sheet of paper, coordinate plane

Fold a sheet of paper in half, then open it. Into how many sections is the paper divided? Fold the paper in half twice, then open it. Always fold in the same direction. How many sections are there now?

Make a table with two columns, labeled "Number of Folds, x" and "Sections Formed, y." Find the values for up to five folds, then graph your ordered pairs. From the pattern in your table, what is the equation? How many sections will six folds produce? Test your answer.

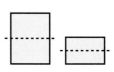

EXAMPLES

- **Solve equations with two variables.**
  (pages 152–155)

Find three solutions of $y = 55x$.

Make a table of values for x, 55x, y, and (x,y). The ordered pairs are solutions.

- **Use *guess and check* to solve equations with two variables.** (pages 156–157)

PROBLEM-SOLVING TIP: For help in solving problems using *guess and check*, see pages 5 and 156.

- **Graph ordered pairs in the coordinate plane.**
  (pages 158–159)

x	y	(x,y)
⁻1	⁻1	(⁻1,⁻1)
1	1	(1,1)
3	3	(3,3)

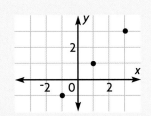

- **Graph linear equations.** (pages 160–163)

Graph the linear equation $y = 3x - 2$.

Make a table of values of at least 3 ordered pairs. Graph the ordered pairs and join them with a line. Label the line y = 3x − 2.

- **Graph inequalities with two variables.**
  (pages 164–166)

Graph $y > 2x - 1$.

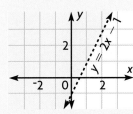

Represent y = 2x − 1 with a dashed line. Shade the graph on the same side of the line as a point that makes the inequality true.

EXERCISES

Make a table of values to find three solutions of the equation. Let $x = {}^-3, 0, 2$.

1. $y = 10x$ **2.** $y = 6 + x$
3. $y + 2x = 10$ **4.** $2y - 2x = 8$

5. Tom sold some baseball cards for $0.25 each and some football cards for $0.35 each. He received $3.60 for 12 cards. How many of each type did he sell?

Use a separate coordinate plane to graph the ordered pairs shown in each table.

6.

x	y	(x,y)
⁻2	1	(⁻2,1)
1	0	(1,0)
2	3	(2,3)

7.

x	y	(x,y)
⁻2	⁻3	(⁻2,⁻3)
1	3	(1,3)
3	7	(3,7)

Graph the equation by using at least three ordered pairs.

8. $y = x + 4$ **9.** $y = 2 + 3x$
10. $y = 4$ **11.** $y = 4 + 2x$
12. $y + 4x = 4$ **13.** $3y - 3x = 9$
14. VOCABULARY Any equation whose graph is a straight line is a _?_ equation.

Graph the inequality.

15. $y \geq 4x$ **16.** $y < 7 - x$
17. $y > 6 - 3x$ **18.** $y \leq 1 + 2x$
19. $y - 4x < 4$ **20.** $y + 5x \leq 10$

VOCABULARY CHECK

1. An expression that is written using at least one variable is an __?__ expression. (page 96)

2. Expressions are __?__ when they have the same value. (page 98)

3. If a value of a variable makes an equation true, that value is a __?__ of the equation. (page 115)

4. Any equation whose graph is a straight line is a __?__ equation. (page 160)

EXAMPLES

EXERCISES

- **Write an algebraic equation.** (pages 112–114)

  5 less than a number, n, equals 9.

  $n - 5 = 9$ *Write as an algebraic equation.*

Write an algebraic equation for the word sentence.

5. 12 more than a number, n, equals 20.

6. A number, b, divided by 4 equals 16.

- **Solve two-step equations.** (pages 123–125)

  $9x + 6 = {}^-12$

  $9x + 6 - 6 = {}^-12 - 6$ *Subtract 6 from each side.*

  $\dfrac{9x}{9} = \dfrac{{}^-18}{9}$ *Divide each side by 9.*

  $x = {}^-2$

Solve and check.

7. $2r + 8 = {}^-16$

8. $4w - 15 = 21$

9. $\dfrac{b}{7} + 2 = {}^-4$

10. $\dfrac{x}{12} - 11 = {}^-5$

- **Solve an equation with like terms.** (pages 132–135)

  $4(k - 5) + 6k = 30$

  $4k - 20 + 6k = 30$ *Distributive Property*

  $10k - 20 = 30$ *Combine like terms.*

  $10k - 20 + 20 = 30 + 20$ *Add 20 to each side.*

  $10k = 50$

  $\dfrac{10k}{10} = \dfrac{50}{10}$ *Divide each side by 10.*

  $k = 5$

Solve and check.

11. $4d + 8(2 + d) = 76$

12. $82 = 3(x + 6) + 5x$

13. $6n + 7(n + 3) = {}^-63$

14. $\dfrac{3}{2}(y + 4) - y = 9$

15. $3z + 5(4 - z) = 11$

16. ${}^-14 = 6(f + 2) - 2f$

- **Solve an inequality.** (pages 144–147)

$^-6y \le 42$

$\dfrac{y}{^-6} \ge \dfrac{42}{^-6}$ *Divide by $^-6$. Reverse the*
                                      inequality symbol.

$y \ge {}^-7$

Solve and graph.

17. $11g - 26 > 29$ **18.** $^-5j + 28 < {}^-17$

19. $\dfrac{c}{3} \ge {}^-13$ **20.** $\dfrac{d}{2} + 9 \le {}^-12$

- **Graph linear equations.** (pages 160–163)

Graph the linear equation $y = 2x + 1$.

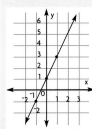

List the values of at least three ordered pairs.

Graph the ordered pairs, and connect them with a line.

Graph the equation. Use at least three ordered pairs.

21. $y = x + 3$ **22.** $y = 4x$

23. $y = 2x - 1$ **24.** $y = {}^-3x + 2$

25. $y + x = {}^-4$ **26.** $y = 2$

- **Graph inequalities with two variables.** (pages 164–166)

Graph $y \le 3x + 2$.

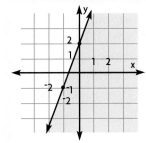

Graph $y = 3x + 2$.

A solid line shows $y = 3x + 2$ is in the solution.

Shade graph on same side of the line as a point that makes the inequality true.

Graph the inequality.

27. $y < x + 5$ **28.** $y \ge 3x$

29. $y < 1 - x$ **30.** $y \le {}^-3x$

31. $y + 4x \ge 5$ **32.** $y - 2x > 6$

PROBLEM SOLVING

Solve. Explain your method.

33. Siegfried called a friend in another city. The long-distance rate is $0.20 for the first three minutes and $0.05 for each additional minute. The phone call cost $4.45. How long was the phone call?

(pages 126–127)

34. Mr. Chen sells banners. Small banners cost $4 and large banners cost $6. Yesterday he sold 15 banners for a total of $80. How many of each size did he sell? (pages 156–157)

Write About It

1. Explain how to combine the like terms in the following expression.
   $^-3x + 4x + {}^-8 + {}^-2x + {}^-6 = n$ (pages 106–107)

2. Show the steps involved in solving $\frac{y}{3} - 5 = 10$. (pages 123–125)

3. Show how to solve and check the equation $3n - 8 = n - 10$.
   (pages 139–141)

4. Graph the equation $y = 2x - 1$. Explain your method. (pages 164–166)

✔ Performance Assessment

Choose a strategy and solve. Explain your method.

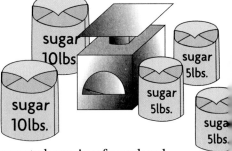

Problem-Solving Strategies
- **Find a Pattern**
- **Make a Model**
- **Work Backward**
- **Make a Graph**
- **Write an Equation**
- **Guess and Check**

5. Lian has $3.60 in nickels and dimes. The number of dimes is 1 more than 3 times the number of nickels. How many dimes and nickels does she have? (pages 123–125)

6. Lori and Martin went shopping for school clothes. Lori spent $30, which is $\frac{1}{4}$ of her monthly allowance. Martin spent $\frac{2}{5}$ of his monthly allowance. His monthly allowance is $10 more than Lori's. How much did Martin spend on clothes?
   (pages 126–127)

7. Josh and Lian read a total of 24 books. Josh read 3 more than $\frac{1}{2}$ the number of books that Lian read. How many books did each student read? Show your solution.
   (pages 132–135)

8. Sugar is sold in 5-lb bags and 10-lb bags. Earl bought 14 bags of sugar with a total weight of 125 lb. How many 5-lb bags and 10-lb bags did he buy? (pages 156–157)

CUMULATIVE REVIEW

Solve the problem. Then write the letter of the correct answer.

1. Find the prime factorization of 168.
(pages 20–23)

   A. $2^3 \times 42$ **B.** $2 \times 3 \times 7$

   C. $2^3 \times 3 \times 7$ **D.** $2 \times 3^2 \times 7$

2. Which is equivalent to $\frac{13}{20}$?
(pages 41–43)

   A. 13%   **B.** 20%

   C. 52%   **D.** 65%

3. Find the sum. $^-9 + {}^-17$
(pages 56–58)

   A. $^-26$ **B.** $^-8$

   C. 8   **D.** 26

4. Find the difference. $6 - {}^-15$
(pages 59–61)

   A. $^-21$ **B.** $^-9$

   C. 9   **D.** 21

5. Find the value. $^-9 \div (3.8 - 5.3)^2$
(pages 86–87)

   A. $^-30.458$ **B.** $^-25.72$

   C. $^-4.00$ **D.** $^-0.108$

6. Which is an inequality?
(pages 96–97)

   A. $45.3 - 21.7$ **B.** $x = 3y + 4$

   C. $\frac{a}{8} - 16b$ **D.** $10 + w > 35$

7. Simplify. $4(2x + {}^-3) + 2y + 9 + {}^-2x + {}^-5y$
(pages 106–107)

   A. $10 - 3y$ **B.** $6x + {}^-3y + {}^-3$

   C. $6x + 7y + 21$ **D.** $10x + 3y + 3$

8. Solve for d. $d - 12 = {}^-5$
(pages 115–118)

   A. $d = {}^-17$ **B.** $d = {}^-7$

   C. $d = 7$ **D.** $d = 17$

9. Solve for z. $2z + 18 = {}^-54$
(pages 123–125)

   A. $z = {}^-36$ **B.** $z = {}^-6$

   C. $z = 6$ **D.** $z = 12$

10. The perimeter of a rectangular field is 140 yd. The width is 20 yd less than the length. What is the width of the field?
(pages 136–137)

   A. 25 yd   **B.** 45 yd

   C. 50 yd   **D.** 70 yd

11. Choose the inequality that represents the graph. (pages 142–143)

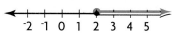

   A. $x > 2$ **B.** $x \geq 2$

   C. $x < 2$ **D.** $x \leq 2$

12. Mr. Turner bought hot dogs and ice-cream cones for the team. Each hot dog cost $1.25, and each ice-cream cone cost $0.75. He bought 12 snacks in all and spent $12.50. How many hot dogs did he buy?
(pages 156–157)

   A. 3 hot dogs   **B.** 5 hot dogs

   C. 7 hot dogs   **D.** 9 hot dogs

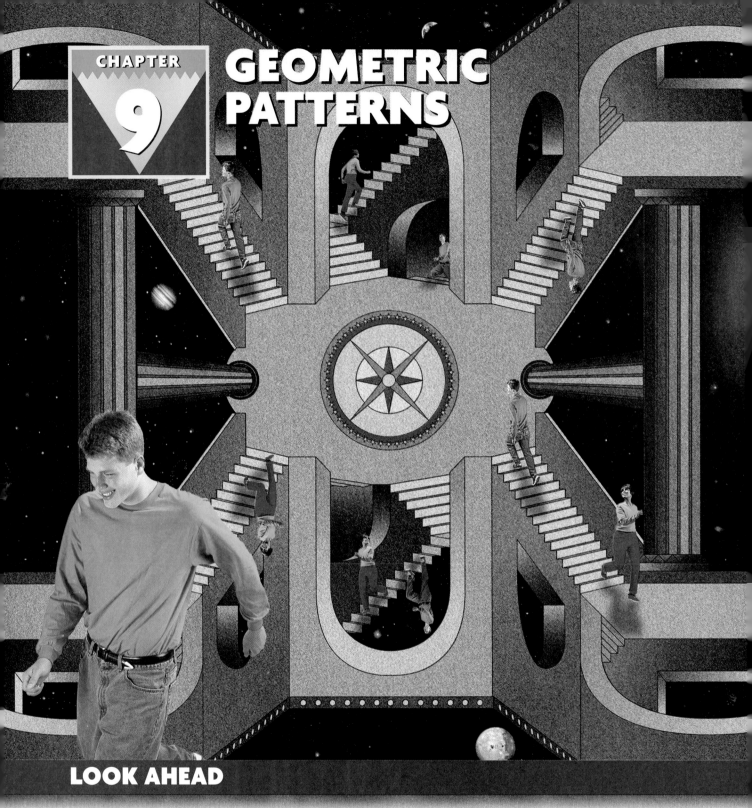

CHAPTER 9
GEOMETRIC PATTERNS

LOOK AHEAD

In this chapter you will solve problems that involve

- constructing tessellations
- making models of solid figures
- identifying spirals
- generating fractals

Delightful Dissections

Look at the patterns. Some patterns repeat while others contain multiple pattern repetitions. Some seem to spiral.

Plan
- Identify the shapes that repeat to make a pattern. Look at both printed and blank areas. Design a pattern of your own.

Act
- List each component of each pattern.
- Choose a set of similar geometric shapes.
- Make a pattern of your own.

Share
- Display your pattern. How is your pattern like those of other students? How is your pattern different?

DID YOU

- ✓ Identify the components?
- ✓ Choose a set of your own?
- ✓ Make your own pattern?

Tessellation Patterns

WHAT YOU'LL LEARN
How to construct polygonal and Escher-like tessellation patterns

WHY LEARN THIS?
To identify tessellation patterns that you see every day

WORD POWER
tessellation
basic unit

REMEMBER:

A hexagon is one regular polygon that will tessellate a plane.

A regular hexagon has six congruent sides and six congruent angles.
See page H22.

What kind of geometric patterns are used by artists, bricklayers, quilters, and fabric designers?

They all use tessellation patterns. A **tessellation** is a repeating pattern of plane figures that completely covers a plane with no gaps or overlapping.

Designs on tile floors and ceilings and on quilts and wrapping paper are often tessellation patterns. These patterns can be made from one or more kinds of regular congruent polygons, such as squares, equilateral triangles, or regular hexagons. Throughout history, tessellations have been used by architects, tile layers, and designers.

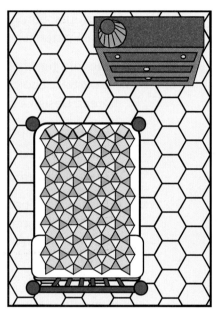

• What kinds of regular polygons appear in the tessellations shown above?

The Dutch artist M. C. Escher (1898–1972) is well known for his use of tessellations. Escher was fascinated with the challenge of filling a plane with repeating patterns. He produced more than 150 artistic tessellations by starting with a polygon and skillfully modifying, repeating, and decorating it. Escher made tessellation patterns from basic units in the shapes of birds, reptiles, and fish.

A **basic unit** is the shape that is repeated in a tessellation.

Talk About It

• What plane figure was modified to create the basic unit for the Escher-like tessellation on the left?

• How was the plane figure modified?

• How many times was the basic unit repeated?

• Describe how the basic unit was decorated.

• In what different way could the basic unit be decorated?

Escher changed polygons into basic units for tessellations by using transformations.

A square can be modified by using a translation.

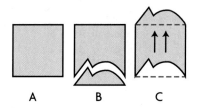

A   B   C

REMEMBER:

A transformation changes the shape or position of a geometric figure. Three types of transformations are translations, reflections, and rotations.

See page H23.

• How do the areas of Figures A, B, and C compare?

EXAMPLE 1   Modify a hexagon by using two translations.

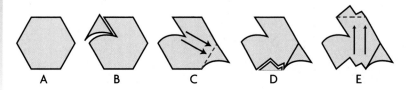

A   B   C   D   E

• How do the areas of Figures A, C, and E compare?

EXAMPLE 2   Modify an equilateral triangle by using a rotation.

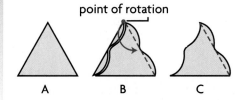

A   B   C

GUIDED PRACTICE

Write *translation* or *rotation* to describe how the figure is modified.

1. before   after   **2.** before   after

          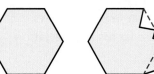

Trace each figure, and see if you can use it as a basic unit for a tessellation pattern of at least two rows. Write *yes* or *no* to tell whether the figure forms a tessellation.

3.    **4.** 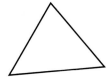   **5.**

You can create a basic unit from a polygon by using translations and rotations.

ACTIVITY

WHAT YOU'LL NEED: drawing paper; patterns for squares, hexagons, triangles; colored pencils or markers; scissors; tape

You will create Escher-like basic units by modifying polygons with translations. Then you will use your basic units to construct original tessellation patterns.

- Start with a square. Modify one of the sides by cutting out an irregular shape.

- Translate the cutout shape to the opposite side of the square, and tape it in place. Be sure to attach the shape directly opposite the cutout side.

- Construct a tessellation pattern by tracing around your basic unit on a sheet of paper. Carefully line up your basic unit with the shapes you have already traced. Use translations, reflections, and rotations to arrange the shapes side by side without any overlapping and without any gaps. Repeat until you have constructed at least three rows of a tessellation pattern.

- Carefully add detail and color to each basic unit in your tessellation pattern. Use your imagination!

- Now start with a square, equilateral triangle, or regular hexagon. Create a different basic unit and then use it to construct a tessellation pattern of at least two rows.

Computer Link

How are tessellations related to computers? The backgrounds of some computer screens are tessellations formed by simple plane figures. With some computers, you can modify the basic unit and then observe the new tessellation. Suppose the basic unit of a screen pattern is a square with a length of 1 in. How many times will the square appear on a screen that is 12 in. × 9 in.?

INDEPENDENT PRACTICE

Trace each figure, and see if you can use it as a basic unit for constructing a tessellation pattern of at least two rows. Write *yes* or *no* to tell whether the figure forms a tessellation.

1.

2.

3.

4.

5.

6.

Write *translation* or *rotation* to describe how the figure is modified. Then construct a tessellation pattern of at least two rows, by using the after shape.

7. before   after

 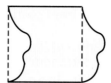

8. before   after

Technology Link

In *Mighty Math Cosmic Geometry* go to *Tessellation Creation Station*. Be ready to have fun making tessellations!

Problem-Solving Applications

9. Create a basic unit by using one or more translations or rotations to modify a square, equilateral triangle, or regular hexagon. Use the basic unit to construct a tessellation pattern of at least three rows. Add details and color.

10. Think of tessellation patterns in your school, home, or neighborhood. Draw at least two of these patterns, describe them, and give their locations.

11. **WRITE ABOUT IT** What is a tessellation?

Mixed Review

Describe the polyhedron formed by the net. Tell the shape of the base or bases and the shape of the other faces.

12.   **13.** 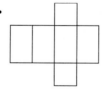   **14.**

Make a table of values to find three solutions of the equation. Let $x = {}^-1, 0, 1$.

15. $y = 5x$ **16.** $y = 4 - x$ **17.** $x - y = 3$ **18.** $y - 2x = 6$

19. **INSURANCE** At age 50, Betty buys a 20-year insurance policy that costs $310 a year. At age 60, Ed buys a 10-year insurance policy that costs $660 a year. Who will spend less in all? Explain.

20. **WEATHER** In January the average temperature in Miami, Florida, is 67°F. If the average temperature in Fairbanks, Alaska, is lower by 80°F, what is the average temperature there?

Patterns of Solid Figures

You have created tessellation patterns by using polygons. Now you will make models of solids from patterns of polygons.

About 2,600 years ago, Greek mathematicians identified five regular polyhedrons: the tetrahedron, cube, octahedron, dodecahedron, and icosahedron. Later, Plato (427?–347? B.C.), a Greek philosopher and educator, gave detailed directions for making models of these solids. So, these regular polyhedrons became known as the **Platonic solids**.

Today scientists recognize that the shapes of regular polyhedrons exist in rock crystals and in the skeletons of some sea creatures.

These are the five regular polyhedrons.

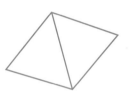 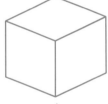  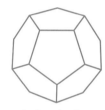 

tetrahedron   cube   octahedron   dodecahedron   icosahedron

Talk About It

• Look at the faces of the regular polyhedrons shown above. What kinds of regular polygons appear as faces?

• Which regular polyhedrons can be formed by using faces that are congruent squares? triangles? pentagons?

• How are Platonic solids used in everyday life?

You can make models of the five regular polyhedrons by using nets, or patterns of polygons, like those shown below.

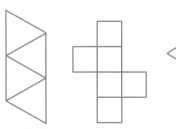   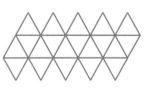

tetrahedron   cube   octahedron   dodecahedron   icosahedron

Work with other students to discover relationships among the five regular solids.

ACTIVITY

WHAT YOU'LL NEED: nets for solids, scissors, transparent tape

- Make models of the five regular polyhedrons, using the nets. Join common edges by using transparent tape.

- On the cube, three squares meet at each vertex. Look for a pattern in the number of polygons that meet at each vertex of the other solids. What is the pattern for each regular solid?

- Look at your models of the regular polyhedrons shown in the table. Count the numbers of vertices, faces, and edges. Copy the following table, and record your data.

	Vertices (v)	Faces (f)	Edges (e)
Tetrahedron	?	?	?
Cube	?	?	?
Octahedron	?	?	?
Dodecahedron	?	?	?

- Look for patterns in the numbers of vertices, faces, and edges in your table. What is the relationship between the number of edges and the numbers of faces and vertices?

- There is a formula that relates the numbers of vertices, faces, and edges of a polyhedron. Look at the relationship you found above. Express the relationship by writing a formula.

- Suppose you know that an icosahedron has 20 faces. Use your formula to predict the numbers of vertices and edges. Then check your prediction by looking at your model of an icosahedron.

Science Link

Are there organisms shaped like regular polyhedrons? Many viruses have such shapes. Their faces consist of individual proteins that give the virus its shape. Suppose a virus has 20 congruent triangular faces. What regular polyhedron does it resemble?

GUIDED PRACTICE

Identify the regular polyhedron that will be formed by each net.

1. 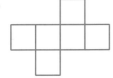   **2.**    **3.**

181

History Link

Archimedes identified
polyhedrons by the
number of sides in
the regular polygons
that meet at each
vertex. The cut
cube in the example
is described as
3.8.8. How would
you describe
the semiregular
polyhedron shown
below? Explain.

Semiregular Polyhedrons

You have seen that the five regular polyhedrons are formed from
patterns of regular polygons. Now you will learn about another
special group of solid figures, called the Archimedean solids.
Mathematicians have known about these figures since about
200 B.C., when Archimedes first described them. They are also
known as semiregular polyhedrons.

A **semiregular polyhedron** is a solid formed from patterns of
more than one kind of regular polygon. The polygons meet in
the same arrangement at each vertex.

A soccer ball has the shape of a semiregular
polyhedron. Look at the pattern made by
the polygons. The figure consists of
regular pentagons and regular hexagons.

- Which plane figures meet at each vertex
  of the soccer ball?

Some semiregular polyhedrons can be created
by modifying regular polyhedrons.

EXAMPLE A cube can be changed into a semiregular polyhedron
by cutting off each vertex at the same angle to form regular
polygons as faces. How many cuts have to be made?

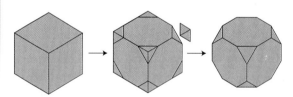

*Cut off a triangular
pyramid at each
vertex.*

So, eight cuts
are made.

Talk About It

- Compare the faces of the cube with the faces of the new figure.
  What regular polygon replaces each square face?

- What new face replaces each vertex of the original cube?

- Describe the kinds of polygons and the number of each that
  meet at each new vertex.

- How many vertices are on the cube? How many vertices are on
  the semiregular polyhedron?

- How many faces are on the cube? How many faces are on the
  semiregular polyhedron?

Identify the regular polyhedron formed by each pattern of polygons.

1.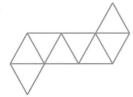

2.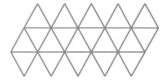

3.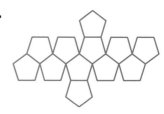

Use a copy of the net to make a three-dimensional model of the polyhedron. Identify the solid as *regular* or *semiregular*. Describe the regular polygons that meet at each vertex.

4.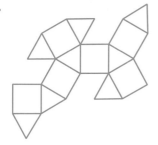

5.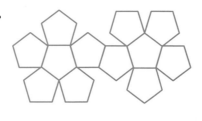

6.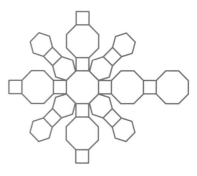

For the named polyhedron, create a pattern of polygons by using the given polygon as a unit for your pattern. Make a model from your pattern.

7.
cube

8.
tetrahedron

9.
octahedron

Problem-Solving Applications

10. Samantha has played many games with a number cube. Suppose she designs a game that requires rolling a regular polyhedron with four congruent faces. What kind of figure should she choose? Explain.

11. Tremayne was asked to draw a net for a cube. He drew the net shown at the right. Will his net form a cube? Why or why not? Copy and fold the net to check your prediction.

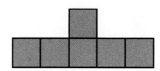

12. 💡 **CRITICAL THINKING** Which of the regular polyhedrons would be best suited for packaging? Explain your thinking.

13. ✏️ **WRITE ABOUT IT** How are a regular polyhedron and a semiregular polyhedron alike? How are they different?

Spiral Patterns

WORD POWER

spiral
Archimedean spiral
equiangular spiral
helix

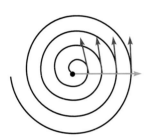

Archimedean spiral

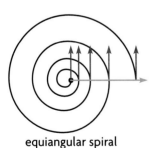

equiangular spiral

A **spiral** is a curve traced by a point rotating around and away from a fixed point.

Spiral patterns, such as the one you see in the shell of the chambered nautilus at the right, can be found in many things. They can be seen in growth patterns of plants and animals, in galaxies, and in the architecture and art of many different cultures.

There are several types of spirals.

An **Archimedean spiral** is a spiral in which the loops are evenly spaced. A ray drawn from the center, or pole, intersects the spiral at decreasing angles. The measures of these angles get closer to 90° as the distance from the pole increases.

• For the Archimedean spiral at the left, estimate the measure of the angle at which the ray intersects the innermost loop. How do the angles change as you move to the outermost loop?

In an equiangular spiral, the loops are not evenly spaced. An **equiangular spiral** is one in which a ray drawn from the center intersects the loops at a constant angle. The distances between the loops increase as you move outward from the pole.

• For the spiral shown at the left, how can you show that the measures of the angles at which the ray intersects the loops are the same?

Talk About It

• Which type of spiral do you see in the shell of the chambered nautilus, shown above?

• 💡**CRITICAL THINKING** Compare the two spiral patterns shown at the left by measuring the distances of the loops from the poles. What patterns do you see? How are the spirals different?

• How are the spirals alike?

• Look for spirals in your classroom. Describe each spiral you find. Then identify as an Archimedean spiral or an equiangular spiral.

Write *Archimedean* or *equiangular* to classify each spiral.

1. **2.** **3.**

The Helix: A Spiral-Like Pattern

When studying health and science, you probably learned about DNA, deoxyribonucleic acid. DNA molecules are sometimes called the building blocks of life. They are in the form of an intertwined spiral-like pattern called a double helix. A **helix** is a spiral-shaped curve in space that goes around an axis. A helix lies on the surface of a cylinder or a cone.

You can make a helix on a cylinder.

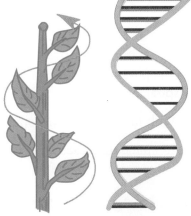

single helix   double helix

ACTIVITY

WHAT YOU'LL NEED: copies of the pattern for a rectangle, tape, scissors, ruler

- With your ruler, draw a diagonal on the rectangle on one of the patterns as shown.

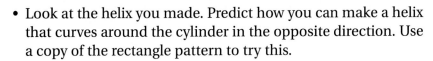

- Cut out the rectangle, curl it up, and tape it together to form an open cylinder, with the diagonal showing on the outside.

- Look at the helix you made. Predict how you can make a helix that curves around the cylinder in the opposite direction. Use a copy of the rectangle pattern to try this.

- Suppose you want to make a double helix like the form of the DNA molecule, pictured above. How should you change your rectangle pattern to make a double helix? Try it.

You can see spiral and helix patterns in seashells; on horns of animals; on bolts, nuts, screws, springs, and ropes; in vines, leaves, and flowers; in water draining out of a sink; in spiral staircases; and on candy canes.

- Look for spiral and helix patterns in your school, home, or neighborhood. Draw at least two of these patterns, describe them, and give their locations.

Science Link

The Milky Way Galaxy, the galaxy to which the sun belongs, is a spiral galaxy about 100,000 light-years across. A light-year is the distance light travels in a year—about 1.0×10^{13} km. Does the Milky Way Galaxy form an Archimedean or an equiangular spiral?

185

Write *Archimedean spiral, equiangular spiral,* or *helix* to classify each pattern.

1.

2.

3.

Tell whether the phrase describes an Archimedean spiral, an equiangular spiral, or a helix.

4. a spiral with loops not evenly spaced

5. a spiral with loops evenly spaced

6. a curve in space that goes around an axis

7. equal angles of intersection between loops and ray from the pole

Problem-Solving Applications

Use copies of polar graph paper for Problems 8–10.

8. Make a spiral like the one at the right. Mark point *A* on the pole of your polar graph paper. Turn your graph 45° clockwise, and mark point *B* one unit from the pole. Turn the graph 45° clockwise, and mark point *C* one unit farther from the pole. Continue until point *J* is marked. Connect the points to complete your spiral.

9. Compare the locations of the successive points in Problem 8.

10. Make another spiral pattern, but use 30° turns instead of 45° turns. Will this spiral be more open than the one in Problem 8, or will it be tighter?

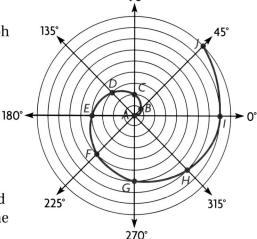

11. Copy this equiangular spiral by repeating these steps, starting with the largest square.
   a. Draw a square inside by locating and connecting the midpoints of the sides.
   b. Turn the figure 45° counterclockwise, and shade the triangles at the top and bottom.

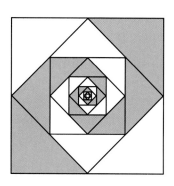

12. ✏️ **WRITE ABOUT IT** In what ways are a candy cane, the Milky Way Galaxy, and a spiral staircase alike?

MORE PRACTICE Lesson 9.3, page H58

Making Spirolaterals

A **spirolateral** is a geometric design that is generated from a sequence of numbers. You can construct spirolaterals on dot paper by using sequences of consecutive integers. Recall that a sequence is an ordered list of numbers.

Consecutive integers are integers that are next to one another in counting order, such as 3 and 4, or 8, 9, and 10.

Explore

- Make a spirolateral by using the number sequence (1, 2). Mark the starting point. Move 1 space to the right, based on the first digit. Make a 90° turn in a clockwise direction. Move 2 spaces, based on the second digit. Let the parentheses mean that you repeat the sequence over and over. How many cycles does it take to close, or reach the starting point? What figure results?

- Use the same process to make spirolaterals for (1, 2, 3), (1, 2, 3, 4), (1, 2, 3, 4, 5), and (1, 2, 3, 4, 5, 6).

- Which sequences repeat after two cycles? after four cycles? Which sequence never closes?

- Make spirolaterals for the sequences (2, 3), (2, 3, 4), (2, 3, 4, 5), (2, 3, 4, 5, 6), and (2, 3, 4, 5, 6, 7). Which sequences repeat after two cycles? after four cycles? Which never closes?

Think and Discuss 💡 CRITICAL THINKING

- Which types of number sequences generate spirolaterals that repeat after two cycles? after four cycles?

- Which type of number sequence generates spirolaterals that never close?

Try This

Write *yes* or *no* to predict whether the spirolateral closes. Write *2* or *4* to tell the number of cycles needed to close.

1. (3, 4) **2.** (3, 4, 5) **3.** (3, 4, 5, 6)

Technology Link ▶
E–Lab • Activity 9 Available on CD-ROM and the Internet at http://www.hbschool.com/elab

Fractal Patterns

WHAT YOU'LL LEARN
How to generate
fractal patterns

WHY LEARN THIS?
To understand some
of the patterns that
appear in nature

WORD POWER
fractal
diverge
converge
scale factor
Sierpinski triangle

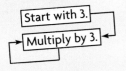

REMEMBER:

You can write an
iteration rule to describe
the repetition of a
process or a set of
instructions.

Start with 3.
Multiply by 3.

3, 9, 27, 81, 243, . . .

What kind of repeating
pattern can be seen in natural
things, such as ferns, broccoli,
and cauliflower?

This kind of repeating pattern
can be found in a very special
geometric figure called a fractal.
A **fractal** is a structure with
repeating patterns containing
shapes that are like the whole
but of different sizes throughout.

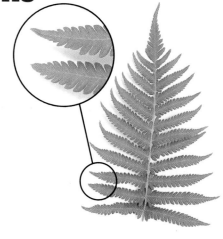

• Does the frond of a fern look like the whole plant? Explain.

You can generate a fractal pattern by using an iteration rule.

EXAMPLE 1 What figure will this iteration rule generate?

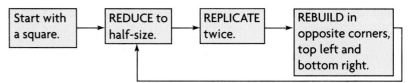

| Start with a square. | REDUCE to half-size. | REPLICATE twice. | REBUILD in opposite corners, top left and bottom right. |

Think: Follow three steps of the iteration process at each stage.

REDUCE: *Reduce the length of each side to half the original length.*

REPLICATE: *Make two copies to go to the next stage.*

REBUILD: *Position the new images in the top left and bottom right corners of the square being rebuilt.*

The iteration rule generates the following figure:

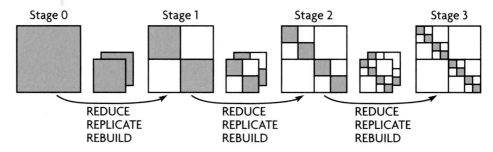

Stage 0   Stage 1   Stage 2   Stage 3

REDUCE
REPLICATE
REBUILD

REDUCE
REPLICATE
REBUILD

REDUCE
REPLICATE
REBUILD

• At each stage, how is the pattern of shaded figures built from
the preceding stage?

The following table shows how the shaded figure in Example 1 changes from Stage 0 to Stage 5. The geometric patterns correspond to numerical patterns. Look for these patterns.

Stage	0	1	2	3	4	5
Number of shaded squares	1	2	4	8	16	32
Total shaded area	1	$\frac{1}{2}$	$\frac{1}{4}$	$\frac{1}{8}$	$\frac{1}{16}$	$\frac{1}{32}$

At successive stages, some of the values **diverge**, or get large without bound. Other values **converge**, approaching some fixed value. In this case they become small, approaching 0.

- In the table, as the stage increases, does the number of shaded squares diverge or converge?

- Is the total shaded area converging or diverging? What value does it approach?

- How does the number of shaded squares change from one stage to the next?

The shaded squares in the fractal pattern in Example 1 are similar figures. You can use scale factors to compare them. A **scale factor** is the ratio for pairs of corresponding sides of similar figures. In Example 1 the scale factor for the dimensions of one square compared to the next is 2 to 1. At each successive stage, each dimension of the square is $\frac{1}{2}$ that of the preceding stage. You can use the ratio of 1 to 2 to compare the number of shaded squares from one stage and the next.

- What ratio describes the change in total shaded area from one stage to the next?

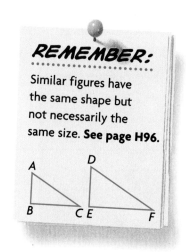

REMEMBER:
Similar figures have the same shape but not necessarily the same size. **See page H96.**

GUIDED PRACTICE

Write *diverging* or *converging* to describe the pattern.

1. ———————— ——————— —— — -

2. - — —— ——————— ————————

3. 1, 3, 9, 27, 81, . . .   **4.** 800; 400; 200; 100; 50; . . .

Identify the ratio that describes the changing pattern.

5. _   1 cm   **6.** _____ 64 in.
     __   2 cm   _____   32 in.
     ____   4 cm   ___   16 in.
     _____   8 cm   _   8 in.

189

Where have scientists discovered fractals? Geologists have detected fractal patterns in ragged mountains and valleys. In addition, they describe faults in the Earth's surface, such as California's San Andreas fault, as fractal-like. Why do you think geologists classify irregular shorelines as fractals?

By generating fractal patterns, you can create fantastic geometric images that imitate nature. The pattern shown below leads to a fractal called the **Sierpinski triangle**.

Stage 0

Stage 1

Stage 2

Stage 3

You can determine the iteration rule for a fractal pattern.

EXAMPLE 2 What is the iteration rule for the Sierpinski triangle?

Think: At each stage, the side of the triangle is $\frac{1}{2}$ that of the side of the triangle at the preceding stage.

scale factor: $\frac{1}{2}$ — *Reduce to half size.*

number of replications: 3 — *Make 3 copies.*

directions for rebuilding: Place the new images at the top, bottom left, and bottom right corners. — *Rebuild in the corners.*

So, the iteration rule is reduce length to half size, replicate 3 times, and rebuild in the corners.

• How would you build Stage 4 from Stage 3?

You can use ratios to make predictions.

EXAMPLE 3 How can you use ratios to predict the number of shaded triangles and the total shaded area for Stage 4 and Stage 5 of the Sierpinski triangle?

Think: The number of shaded triangles changes by a ratio of 1 to 3, and the shaded area changes by a ratio of 4 to 3.

Stage	0	1	2	3	4	5	
Number of shaded triangles	1	3	9	27	81	243	*Multiply by 3.*
Total shaded area	1	$\frac{3}{4}$	$\frac{9}{16}$	$\frac{27}{64}$	$\frac{81}{256}$	$\frac{243}{1,024}$	*Multiply by $\frac{3}{4}$.*

Stage 4: shaded triangles, $3 \times 27 = 81$; shaded area, $\frac{3}{4} \times \frac{27}{64} = \frac{81}{256}$

Stage 5: shaded triangles, $3 \times 81 = 243$; shaded area, $\frac{3}{4} \times \frac{81}{256} = \frac{243}{1,024}$

Write *diverging* or *converging* to describe the pattern, and give the ratio.

1.
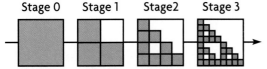
1m 2m 4m   8m

2.
8m   4m 2m 1m

3. 27, 9, 3, 1, . . .

4. 1, 4, 16, 64, . . .

Problem Solving Applications

For Problems 5–11, use the following iteration process.

Stage 0   Stage 1   Stage 2   Stage 3

REDUCE to half size.

REPLICATE three times.

REBUILD in three corners.

5. How does the length of a figure change from one stage to the next?

6. How many replications are needed for each new stage?

7. How is the new stage rebuilt?

8. What is the iteration rule?

9. Copy and complete the table to describe the iteration.

Stage	0	1	2	3	4	5	n
Number of shaded squares	1	3	9	?	?	?	?
Total shaded area	1	$\frac{3}{4}$	$\frac{9}{16}$	?	?	?	?

10. As the iteration continues, does the number of squares converge or diverge? What is the ratio?

11. Does the shaded area of the changing figure converge or diverge? What is the ratio?

12. ✏️ **WRITE ABOUT IT** How do repeating patterns occur in fractals?

Mixed Review

Find the product by using mental math.

13. 12×200

14. 40×22

15. 25×15

16. 36×8

Graph the inequality in the coordinate plane.

17. $y \geq 3x$

18. $y < x + 3$

19. $2x + y > 4$

20. $x - y > 2$

21. MENTAL MATH Suppose there are about 266,800,000 people in the United States. If one person is born every 8 sec and one person dies every 12 sec, about what will the population be 1 hr from now?

22. SQUARE ROOTS The area of a square restaurant is 8,100 ft². Find the length and width of the restaurant.

CULTURAL CONNECTION

Norwegian Sweaters

Geometric designs and patterns have been used to make clothing for centuries. Norway is famous for the gorgeous sweaters produced there. Tessellations, transformations, spiral patterns, and fractal patterns can be found in many designs used for Norwegian sweaters. Norwegian designers can use computer programs to design sweater patterns. The design can then be downloaded to a sewing machine. The machine will then sew the sweater using the design created using the computer program.

To prepare for winter, Sven went shopping for a Norwegian sweater. He liked the design of the sweater shown at the right. Describe the sweater design using the term tessellation, transformation, spiral pattern, or fractal pattern.

The diamond patterns could have been formed using transformations.

WORK TOGETHER

1. Sven saw the pattern shown below on part of another Norwegian sweater. Draw the pattern on a sheet of graph paper. Use the pattern to tessellate half of the sheet.

2. Sven saw the pattern shown below along the bottom of a Norwegian sweater. Describe the pattern using as many geometric terms as you can.

3. On a half sheet of graph paper, design a pattern for your own Norwegian sweater. Use tessellations, transformations, spiral patterns, or fractal patterns.

REVIEW

EXAMPLES

- **Construct polygonal and Escher-like tessellation patterns.** (pages 176–179)

Modify a square by using a translation.

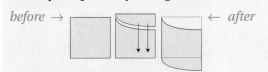

before →   ← *after*

- **Make models of regular solids and explore semiregular solids.** (pages 180–183)

Identify the regular polyhedron that can be formed by the pattern of polygons.

 A tetrahedron is made up of 4 triangles. It has 4 vertices, 4 faces, and 6 edges.

- **Identify Archimedean and equiangular spiral patterns and helix patterns.** (pages 184–186)

Identify the spirals and spiral-like pattern.

Archimedean spiral   equiangular spiral   helix

- **Generate fractal patterns.** (pages 188–191)

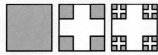 What is the iteration rule?

Stage 0   Stage 1   Stage 2

REDUCE sides to one-third size.

REPLICATE four times.

REBUILD in the four corners.

EXERCISES

1. VOCABULARY A __?__ is a repeating pattern of plane figures that completely covers a plane with no gaps or overlapping.

Write *translation* or *rotation* to describe how the figure is modified.

2.    **3.**

Identify the regular polyhedron that can be formed by the pattern of polygons. Describe the polygon that forms each face.

4.    **5.**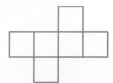

Write *Archimedean spiral, equiangular spiral,* or *helix* to classify each pattern.

6.   **7.**

8.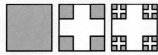

9. VOCABULARY The ratio for pairs of corresponding sides of similar figures is the __?__ .

Copy and complete the table to describe the iteration at the left.

Stage	0	1	2	3	4	5
10. Number of shaded squares	1	4	16	?	?	?
11. Shaded area	1	$\frac{4}{9}$	$\frac{16}{81}$	?	?	?

CHAPTER 10

NUMBER PATTERNS

LOOK AHEAD

In this chapter you will solve problems that involve

- patterns with calculators
- decimal and divisibility patterns

- patterns in Pascal's Triangle
- discovering relationships with patterns

Team-Up Project

Stacking Patterns

There are many ways to stack objects. For example, think of how items are stacked in a supermarket. The way the items are arranged makes a particular pattern. How many items can be stacked in a given pattern?

YOU WILL NEED: centimeter cubes, marbles, cards

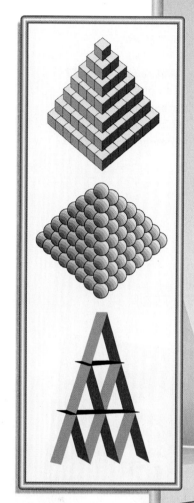

Plan
- Work with a partner. Design stacking patterns. Figure out how many items can be stacked in each pattern.

Act
- Design different ways to stack various items. Each arrangement should make a different pattern.
- For each pattern, record the number of layers and the number of items per layer.
- Find the total number of items that can be stacked in each pattern.

Share
- Share your patterns with another group. Challenge them to make your patterns.

DID YOU
- ✓ Design stacking patterns?
- ✓ Record the number of layers and items?
- ✓ Share your patterns with another group?

Patterns in Measurement Systems

WHAT YOU'LL LEARN
How to represent measurement patterns by using equations and tables

WHY LEARN THIS?
To convert measurements within a system and between systems

There are many different patterns in measurement systems.

• What patterns do you remember in the metric system?

You can use patterns in tables to convert measurements from one system to another. For example, to convert kilograms to pounds or vice versa, you can make tables that show the basic relationships. Start with 1 kg ≈ 2.2 lb and 1 lb ≈ 0.45 kg.

EXAMPLE 1 Andrea, Josh's pen pal in France, writes that her dog weighs 14 kg. Josh's dog weighs 26 lb. Whose dog is heavier?

You can make tables to help you estimate the dogs' weights. Either table can be used to solve the problem.

Kilograms	Pounds
1	2.2
2	4.4
3	6.6
4	8.8
5	11
10	22

Pounds	Kilograms
1	0.45
2	0.90
3	1.35
4	1.80
5	2.25
10	4.50

Andrea's dog is 14 kg.

$$14 \text{ kg} = 10 \text{ kg} + 4 \text{ kg}$$
$$\approx 22 \text{ lb} + 8.8 \text{ lb}$$
$$\approx 30.8 \text{ lb}$$

Josh's dog is 26 lb.

$$26 \text{ lb} = 13 \times 2 \text{ lb}$$
$$\approx 13 \times 0.9 \text{ kg}$$
$$\approx 11.7 \text{ kg}$$

Andrea's dog is heavier than Josh's dog.

The patterns and relations in a measurement system are often expressed with equations or formulas.

$$1 \text{ ft} = 12 \text{ in.} \quad 3 \text{ ft} = 1 \text{ yd} \quad 5{,}280 \text{ ft} = 1 \text{ mi}$$

To convert yards to inches or inches to yards, you can express the relationship 1 yd = 36 in. with the formula $i = 36y$. Let y = the number of yards, and let i = the number of inches.

Andrea et Fifi

EXAMPLE 2 Each award for the science fair uses 30 in. of ribbon. The ribbon is sold by the yard. How many yards of ribbon are needed to make 100 awards?

100×30 in. $= 3{,}000$ in.   *Multiply to find the total number of inches.*

$i = 36y$ ← formula that relates inches to yards

$3{,}000 = 36y$ *Substitute 3,000 for i.*

$\dfrac{3000}{36} = \dfrac{36y}{36}$ *Divide each side by 36.*

$83.\overline{3} = y$

So, $83.\overline{3}$ yd of ribbon are needed.

• What if each award took only 24 in. of ribbon? How many yards would be needed to make 100 awards?

Suppose you have a metric ruler, but you need a measurement expressed in customary units. To convert from one system to the other, you can use the relationships 1 in. ≈ 2.5 cm and 1 cm ≈ 0.4 in.

EXAMPLE 3 Convert from centimeters to inches or from inches to centimeters.

A. 25 cm ≈ __?__ in.

1 cm ≈ 0.4 in.

25×1 cm ≈ 25×0.4 in.

≈ 10 in.

So, 25 cm ≈ 10 in.

B. $8\frac{1}{2}$ in. ≈ __?__ cm

1 in. ≈ 2.5 cm

8.5×1 in. ≈ 8.5×2.5 cm

≈ 21.25 cm.

So, $8\frac{1}{2}$ in. ≈ 21 cm

GUIDED PRACTICE

Copy and complete the tables.

1.

Liters	1	2	3	4	5	10
Gallons	0.26	0.52	?	?	?	?

2.

Gallons	1	2	3	4	5	10
Liters	3.79	7.58	?	?	?	?

Use the patterns from Exercises 1–2 to convert each measurement.

3. 15 L ≈ ▉ gal

4. 8 gal ≈ ▉ L

5. 24 gal ≈ ▉ L

6. 16 gal ≈ ▉ L

7. 20 L ≈ ▉ gal

8. 9 L ≈ ▉ gal

Science Link

In science, temperatures are measured in degrees Celsius instead of degrees Fahrenheit. A table can be used for converting between the two scales. Make a table that shows temperature equivalents starting at ⁻40°, where the two scales are the same. Every increase of 10°C is equal to 18°F. Show the temperatures at every interval of 10°C through 30°C.

INDEPENDENT PRACTICE

Convert the given measurement.

1. 17 kg ≈ ▦ lb   **2.** 105 lb ≈ ▦ kg   **3.** 38 lb ≈ ▦ kg   **4.** 45 kg ≈ ▦ lb

5. 36 yd = ▦ ft   **6.** 127 ft = ▦ yd   **7.** 105 ft = ▦ in.   **8.** 71 in. = ▦ ft

9. 42 mi = ▦ ft   **10.** 138 ft = ▦ mi   **11.** 315 in. = ▦ yd   **12.** 56 yd = ▦ in.

13. 95 cm ≈ ▦ in.   **14.** 84 in. ≈ ▦ cm   **15.** 4 gal ≈ ▦ L   **16.** 12 L ≈ ▦ gal

Compare. Write <, >, or ≈.

17. 5 kg ⬤ 6 lb   **18.** 24 L ⬤ 10 gal   **19.** 34 in. ⬤ 50 cm   **20.** 78 in. ⬤ 195 cm

21. 5 kg ⬤ 9 lb   **22.** 7 gal ⬤ 27 L   **23.** 57 in. ⬤ 140 cm   **24.** 48 cm ⬤ 20 in.

Problem-Solving Applications

25. It is 235 mi from New York City to Washington D.C. Hans, from Germany, would like to know how far this is in kilometers. Convert the distance, using 1 km ≈ 0.62 mi.

26. Lynn's uncle lives in Japan. He sent her a Japanese recipe that calls for 30g of tofu. Convert the grams to ounces, using 1g ≈ 0.035 oz.

27. Jordan is a stock person at Norman's Supermarket. He is stacking canned food in a shelf space with a height of 5 ft. How many 5-in. cans will stack in this space? 4-in. cans? 3-in. cans?

28. Erin's pen pal, Niki, said she weighs 56.25 kg and is 160 cm tall. Convert these measurements to customary units.

29. ✏️ **WRITE ABOUT IT** Explain how you can convert 7 cm to inches.

Mixed Review

Complete the prime factorization.

30. 36 = 2 × 2 × 3 × ▦   **31.** 90 = 2 × 3 × 3 × ▦   **32.** 54 = 2 × 3 × 3 × ▦

Give the number of vertices, faces, and edges of each polyhedron.

33. cube   **34.** tetrahedron   **35.** octahedron   **36.** dodecahedron

37. **DIMENSIONS** Last year, Sam's garden was 24 ft by 18 ft. This year he would like to double its dimensions. If he divides this larger garden into 4 congruent plots, what will be the area of each plot? What will be the perimeter of the enlarged garden?

38. **GEOMETRY** Alan's fish tank is a prism with a hexagonal base, each side measuring 9 in. What is the perimeter of the base of his fish tank?

MORE PRACTICE Lesson 10.1, page H59

Rational Number Patterns

WHAT YOU'LL LEARN
How to use fraction and decimal patterns; how to predict whether a fraction will be a terminating or a repeating decimal

WHY LEARN THIS?
To convert decimals to fractions when interpreting weights

Rational numbers can be written as fractions or as decimals. Sometimes the decimals are easier to use than the fractions.

By remembering a few patterns, you can do some computations faster mentally than with a calculator.

$\frac{1}{8} = \frac{1}{4} \div 2 = \frac{0.25}{2}$, or 0.125

$\frac{2}{8} = \frac{1}{4} = 0.25$

$\frac{3}{8} = 3 \times \frac{1}{8} = 3 \times 0.125 = 0.375$

$\frac{4}{8} = 4 \times \frac{1}{8} = 4 \times 0.125 = 0.500$

$\frac{5}{8} = \frac{4}{8} + \frac{1}{8} = 0.500 + 0.125 = 0.625$

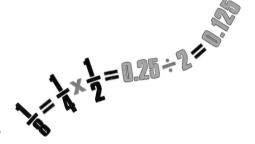

EXAMPLE 1 Use mental math to change each fraction to a decimal.

A. Since $\frac{7}{8} = \frac{3}{8} + \frac{4}{8}$,

$\frac{7}{8} = 0.375 + 0.500$

$= 0.875.$

B. Since $\frac{1}{6} = \frac{1}{3} \times \frac{1}{2}$ or $\frac{1}{3} \div 2$,

$\frac{1}{6} = \frac{0.\overline{3}}{2}$

$= 0.1\overline{6}.$

• How can you mentally find the decimal equivalent for $\frac{1}{12}$?

To predict whether a fraction is equivalent to a terminating or a repeating decimal, look for a pattern. When a fraction is written in simplest form and the prime factors of the denominator are 2's or 5's, the decimal terminates. Otherwise, the decimal repeats.

EXAMPLE 2 Predict whether $\frac{7}{20}$ is equivalent to a terminating or a repeating decimal. Verify your prediction.

Write the fractions in simplest form with the denominators as products of prime factors.

$\frac{7}{20} = \frac{7}{2 \times 2 \times 5}$

Prime factors are 2 and 5. The decimal will terminate.

7 20 | 0.35 | *Check the prediction.*

• Is $\frac{3}{40}$ equivalent to a terminating or a repeating decimal?

REMEMBER:
Some common fractions terminate, but others repeat. **See page H9.**

$\frac{1}{2} = 0.5$ $\frac{1}{3} = 0.\overline{3}$

$\frac{1}{4} = 0.25$ $\frac{1}{5} = 0.2$

$\frac{1}{6} = 0.1\overline{6}$ $\frac{1}{8} = 0.125$

$\frac{1}{10} = 0.1$ $\frac{1}{100} = 0.01$

EXAMPLE 3 Predict whether $\frac{6}{36}$ is equivalent to a terminating or a repeating decimal. Verify your prediction.

$$\frac{6}{36} = \frac{1}{6} = \frac{1}{2 \times 3}$$

Prime factors are 2 and 3.
The decimal will repeat.

6 ÷ 36 = [0.166666667]   *Check the prediction.*

- Is $\frac{9}{36}$ equivalent to a terminating or a repeating decimal? Explain.

To write a repeating decimal as a fraction or a mixed number, look for a pattern in the repeating digits.

EXAMPLE 4 Write the decimal as a fraction.

A. $0.\overline{6}$

Let $n = 0.\overline{6}$.   *One digit repeats.*

$$\begin{aligned} 10n &= 6.\overline{6} \quad \text{\textit{Multiply each side by 10.}} \\ -\ n &= 0.\overline{6} \quad \text{\textit{Subtract the original equation.}} \\ \hline 9n &= 6.\overline{0} \quad \leftarrow 6.\overline{0} = 6 \end{aligned}$$

$$\frac{9n}{9} = \frac{6}{9} \quad \text{\textit{Solve the equation.}}$$

$$n = \frac{6}{9}, \text{ or } \frac{2}{3}$$

- Since $0.\overline{6} = \frac{6}{9}$, what fraction do you think is equivalent to $0.\overline{5}$? to $0.\overline{7}$?

B. $0.\overline{54}$

Let $n = 0.\overline{54}$.   *Two digits repeat. Multiply each side by 100.*

$$\begin{aligned} 100n &= 54.\overline{54} \\ -\ n &= \ \ 0.\overline{54} \quad \text{\textit{Subtract the original equation.}} \\ \hline 99n &= 54.00 \quad \leftarrow 54.\overline{00} = 54 \end{aligned}$$

$$\frac{99n}{99} = \frac{54}{99} \quad \text{\textit{Solve the equation.}}$$

$$n = \frac{6}{11}$$

Talk About It 💡 **CRITICAL THINKING**

- Since $0.\overline{09} = \frac{1}{11}$ and $0.\overline{18} = \frac{2}{11}$, what fraction is equivalent to $0.\overline{45}$? to $0.\overline{63}$?

- How can you change $0.\overline{36}$ into a fraction?

- What fraction is equivalent to $0.\overline{81}$? to $0.\overline{90}$?

GUIDED PRACTICE

Complete by writing decimals. Use mental math.

1. Since $\frac{3}{8} = \frac{2}{8} + \frac{1}{8}$, $\frac{3}{8} = 0.25 +$ ▓ = ▓.

2. Since $\frac{3}{4} = \frac{3}{1} \times \frac{1}{4}$, $\frac{3}{4} = 3 \times$ ▓ = ▓.

3. Since $\frac{7}{12} = \frac{6}{12} + \frac{1}{12}$, $\frac{7}{12} = 0.5 +$ ▓ = ▓.

4. Since $\frac{1}{15} = \frac{1}{3} \times \frac{1}{5}$ or $\frac{1}{3} \div 5$, $\frac{0.\overline{3}}{5} =$ ▓.

Write each fraction in simplest form. Write the prime factorization of the denominator. Predict whether each fraction is equivalent to a *terminating* or a *repeating* decimal.

5. $\frac{8}{32}$　　6. $\frac{4}{24}$　　7. $\frac{22}{72}$　　8. $\frac{35}{125}$

9. $\frac{12}{80}$　　10. $\frac{25}{110}$　　11. $\frac{24}{54}$　　12. $\frac{25}{40}$

In *Mighty Math Astro Algebra*, you can practice changing fractions to decimals and decimals to fractions as you enter the *Number Line* and complete the mission *The Wonky Controls*.

INDEPENDENT PRACTICE

Predict whether each fraction is equivalent to a *terminating* or a *repeating* decimal. Then write each fraction as a decimal.

1. $\frac{5}{16}$　　2. $\frac{3}{20}$　　3. $\frac{7}{8}$　　4. $\frac{7}{12}$　　5. $\frac{5}{6}$

6. $\frac{5}{12}$　　7. $\frac{3}{2}$　　8. $\frac{9}{4}$　　9. $\frac{10}{3}$　　10. $\frac{13}{6}$

Write the equivalent fraction or mixed number in simplest form.

11. 1.25　　12. 0.0625　　13. 4.125　　14. 5.375　　15. 0.1875

16. 3.2　　17. 0.55　　18. $0.\overline{6}$　　19. $4.\overline{18}$　　20. $0.\overline{8}$

21. $0.\overline{5}$　　22. $0.\overline{45}$　　23. $0.\overline{27}$　　24. $0.\overline{7}$　　25. $0.\overline{72}$

Problem-Solving Applications

26. Since one nickel is $\frac{1}{20}$ of a dollar, 27 nickels equal $\frac{27}{20}$. You know that $\frac{27}{20} = \frac{20}{20} + \frac{7}{20}$, or $1 + \frac{7}{20}$. So, 27 nickels equal $1.00 + 7 \times \$0.05$, or $1.35. Use this pattern to mentally compute the value of 47 nickels, of 63 nickels, and of 115 nickels.

27. Since 1 ft = $\frac{1}{3}$ of a yard, 28 ft = $\frac{28}{3}$. You know that $\frac{28}{3} = \frac{27}{3} + \frac{1}{3}$, or $9 + 0.\overline{3}$. So, 28 ft = $9.\overline{3}$ yd. Use this pattern to mentally compute the number of yards equivalent to 33 ft, to 61 ft, and to 80 ft.

28. Elise collected 24.3 lb of newspapers. Joe collected $24\frac{1}{3}$ lb of newspapers. Who collected more newspapers? Explain.

29. ◁▭▷ **WRITE ABOUT IT** Name a situation in which changing a fraction to a decimal would be helpful. Explain.

REMEMBER:

Divisibility rules help you decide whether one number divides into another number evenly. **See page H2.**

Nearly 65% of American teens work outside their homes. High school seniors who work spend an average of 20 hr per week at their jobs—the equivalent of half a full-time job. They earn an average of $225 per month.

Extending Divisibility Patterns

Some patterns in division with whole numbers are summarized as divisibility rules. Do you think these division patterns or rules can be extended to decimals?

Suppose you have $21.60. Can you divide the money to have the same amount (expressed as a terminating decimal) to spend each week for 3 weeks? for 4 weeks? for 5 weeks? for 6 weeks?

Talk About It

• What is the whole-number divisibility rule for 3?

• Disregarding place values, what is the sum of the digits for 21.60? Is $21.60 divisible by 3? Support your answer.

• What is the whole-number divisibility rule for 4?

• Does the divisibility rule for 4 work on $21.60? Explain.

• What are the whole-number divisibility rules for 5 and 6?

• Do the divisibility rules for 5 and 6 work on $21.60? Explain.

• A whole number is divisible by 9 if the sum of the digits is divisible by 9. Is $21.60 divisible by 9? Explain.

EXAMPLE 1   How can you show that 528.24 is divisible by 8?

Begin with the whole-number divisibility rule for 8: A number is divisible by 8 if the number formed by the last three digits is divisible by 8.

Extend the rule to see if it works with decimals.

528.24   *Divide the last three digits by 8.*

$8.24 \div 8 = 1.03$

So, 528.24 should be divisible by 8.

528.24 ÷ 8 = *66.03*   *Check with a calculator.*

• 💡**CRITICAL THINKING** Is 528.24 divisible by 0.8? by 0.08? Explain.

GUIDED PRACTICE

Solve. Explain your reasoning.

1. Can 154 basketballs be divided equally into 2 groups? into 4 groups? into 8 groups?

2. Can $154 be divided equally between 2 people? among 4 people? among 8 people?

3. Can 154 1-ft lengths of rope be divided equally into 2 groups? into 4 groups? into 8 groups?

4. Can 154 ft of rope be divided equally into 2 lengths? into 4 lengths? into 8 lengths?

Use your divisibility rules to answer each question.

5. Is 41.32 divisible by 2? by 3? by 6?

6. Is 0.45 divisible by 2? by 5? by 10?

7. Is 2.48 divisible by 3? by 4? by 8?

8. Is 53.22 divisible by 2? by 4? by 8?

9. Is 40.5 divisible by 2? by 3? by 6?

10. Is 92.16 divisible by 2? by 4? by 8?

INDEPENDENT PRACTICE

Tell whether each is divisible by 2, 3, or 6.

1. 28 batteries
2. $267.87
3. $44,000.10
4. 21 pans
5. $21.00

Tell whether each is divisible by 4 or 8.

6. $34.40
7. $7.23
8. 524 flowers
9. 56 watches
10. 292 pencils

Tell whether each is divisible by 5, 9, or 10.

11. 21 quarters
12. $5.25
13. 45 nickels
14. 1,170 books
15. 360 birds

Problem-Solving Applications

16. The cheerleaders raised $355.50 for charity. Can they divide the money equally among 3 charities? among 4 charities? among 6 charities?

17. Robin has 22.4 yd of custom fabric at her store. She can sell it by measuring to 0.2 yd. Can she sell equal amounts to 2 people? 3 people? 4 people?

18. Nine friends have dinner at Jerry's Restaurant. Including tax and tip, the total bill is $105.75. Can nine people divide the bill equally? How much will each person pay?

19. Can 75 fishing lines be divided equally among 3 people? among 5 people? among 9 people?

20. WRITE ABOUT IT If a number is divisible by 10, it is also divisible by 2 and 5. Is this rule correct? Explain.

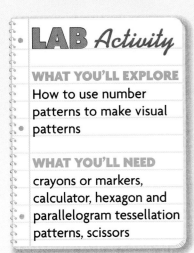

LAB *Activity*

WHAT YOU'LL EXPLORE
How to use number patterns to make visual patterns

WHAT YOU'LL NEED
crayons or markers, calculator, hexagon and parallelogram tessellation patterns, scissors

Patterns in Pascal's Triangle

You have probably seen the triangular pattern of numbers shown at the right. It is called Pascal's triangle.

Work with a partner or small group to find patterns in the array of numbers.

```
              1          1
            1   1        2
          1   2   1      3
        1   3   3   1    4
      1   4   6   4   1    5
    1   5  10  10   5   1   6
  1   6  15  20  15   6   1   7
1   7  21  35  35  21   7   1   8
1   8  28  56  70  56  28   8   1   9
1   9  36  84 126 126  84  36   9   1   10
1  10  45 120 210 252 210 120  45  10   1   11
```

Explore

• What pattern is used to write the numbers in each row?

• What other number patterns do you see in the array of numbers?

• Copy the 11 rows of the array onto a hexagon tessellation pattern. Then extend the array until there are 15 completed rows. Cut out your array.

• Shade the odd numbers in your array.

Think and Discuss

• Describe the visual pattern created by your shading.

• Describe the visual pattern for the even numbers.

Try This

• Make a new triangular array by using the parallelogram tessellation pattern. Copy the numbers for the first 15 rows of Pascal's triangle into your new array. Cut out your array.

• Shade each parallelogram containing a number whose remainder is 1 when the number is divided by 3.

• Describe the visual pattern in your array.

• Design a triangular array by using a different geometric figure.

Patterns with Calculators

$\mathbf{Y}$ou can use patterns of calculator keys to help you perform the same operation repeatedly.

WHAT YOU'LL LEARN
How to recognize and use patterns on a calculator

EXAMPLE 1 Use the formula $A = \pi r^2$ to find the areas of circles with the given radii:

	Circle 1	Circle 2	Circle 3	Circle 4	Circle 5
Radius	3.5 cm	5.7 cm	8.9 cm	10.2 cm	18.3 cm
Area	?	?	?	?	?

WHY LEARN THIS?
To use a calculator more efficiently

You can use keys like the following to find the areas:

| × | | π | | OP1 |

Set operation key to multiply by π.

↓ Square the radius.

3.5 x^2 OP1 38.48451001 *area ≈ 38.5 cm²*

5.7 x^2 OP1 102.0703453 *area ≈ 102.1 cm²*

8.9 x^2 OP1 248.8455541 *area ≈ 248.8 cm²*

10.2 x^2 OP1 326.8512997 *area ≈ 326.9 cm²*

18.3 x^2 OP1 1052.087964 *area ≈ 1,052.1 cm²*

• What if you aren't sure whether you entered the correct keys when finding the area of a circle with radius 10.2 cm? What is a reasonable estimate of the area?

To fix decimals automatically to the tenths place, you can use the   2nd   key and the   FIX   key and enter a 1 before you begin the sequence of keys given above.

EXAMPLE 2 The Playhouse Theater pays its entry-level employees $5.45 per hour and subtracts $3.75 each week for laundry of uniforms. Use the formula Pay = $5.45h − $3.75 to find the before-taxes pay for the following employees:

	Employee 1	Employee 2	Employee 3	Employee 4
Hours worked, h	7	13.5	19.25	8.5
Pay	?	?	?	?

Computers help us by quickly calculating complex formulas, such as those in spreadsheet programs. Spreadsheets can also recalculate formulas quickly when data entries are changed.

How is a computer better than a calculator? How might a calculator be better?

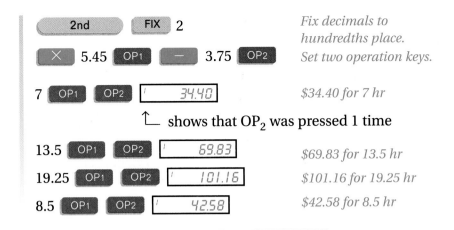

| 2nd | FIX | 2 | *Fix decimals to hundredths place.* |

| × | 5.45 | OP1 | − | 3.75 | OP2 | *Set two operation keys.* |

7 OP1 OP2 ' 34.40 *$34.40 for 7 hr*

↰ shows that OP₂ was pressed 1 time

13.5 OP1 OP2 ' 69.83 *$69.83 for 13.5 hr*

19.25 OP1 OP2 ' 101.16 *$101.16 for 19.25 hr*

8.5 OP1 OP2 ' 42.58 *$42.58 for 8.5 hr*

Some keys on calculators "undo" one another.

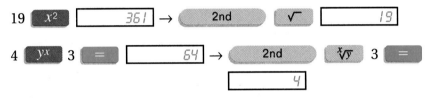

19 x^2 361 → 2nd $\sqrt{\ }$ 19

4 y^x 3 = 64 → 2nd $\sqrt[x]{y}$ 3 = 4

Talk About It

- What does the x^2 key do?

- What does the $\sqrt{\ }$ key do?

- What multiplication equation shows what happens with the sequence of keys 4 y^x 3 = ?

- What is the final display for the following sequence of keys?

  2 y^x 3 =   2nd $\sqrt[x]{y}$ 3 =

- What other "undoing" patterns of keys can you find?

GUIDED PRACTICE

Copy and complete the table. Use the formula $C = 2\pi r$ and a calculator. Round to the nearest tenth. Write the sequence of calculator keys.

	Circle 1	Circle 2	Circle 3
Radius (r)	2.6 cm	3.7 cm	17.4 cm
Circumference (C)	?	?	?

Calculator Activities, page H33

INDEPENDENT PRACTICE

For Exercises 1–2, copy and complete each table. Use the given formula to solve. Write the sequence of calculator keys used.

1. An insurance company pays a food allowance plus mileage for one-day business trips. Use *Expenses* = $65.00 + 0.32*m*.

	Trip 1	Trip 2	Trip 3	Trip 4	Trip 5
Miles (m)	93	150	234	335	423.5
Expenses	?	?	?	?	?

2. A photographer charges $125 per hour plus film expenses. Use *Fee* = $125 × *h* + $25 × *f*.

	Shoot 1	Shoot 2	Shoot 3	Shoot 4	Shoot 5
Hours (h)	2.5	4	8	12.5	16
Rolls of film (f)	4	8	14	24	30
Fee	?	?	?	?	?

Problem-Solving Applications

For Problems 3–4, write a formula and solve using your calculator.

3. The hospital pays orderlies $10.25 an hour and deducts $6.28 each week for insurance. Find the pay for an orderly who works 30 hr, 37.5 hr, and 40 hr during three different weeks.

4. A clothing store is having a storewide sale. Everything is $\frac{1}{3}$ off. Find the sale price of a $15.99 T-shirt, a $12 belt, and a $36.72 pair of shorts.

5. ✏️ **WRITE ABOUT IT** Write a problem that can be solved using a repeated pattern of calculator keys. Exchange with a classmate and solve.

Mixed Review

Evaluate.

6. 1 + 2 + 4 + 6 + 8 + 10

7. 100 − 90 + 80 − 70

8. 5 × 10 × 15 × 20

For Exercises 9–10, find the number of tiles required to complete each project.

9. tiles: 5-in. square; project: 60-in. square

10. tiles: 3-in. square; project: 54-in. square

11. **NUTRITION** Some nutritionists believe that only 30% of your total daily calories should come from fat. Suppose 450 out of your daily 2,500 calories come from fat. Estimate the percent from fat.

12. **PLACE VALUE** About 304.7 million pairs of jeans are made in one year. On average, about how many are made in a day? in an hour?

MATH FUN!

DECIMAL CHALLENGE

PURPOSE To practice finding patterns in rational numbers (pages 199–201)

YOU WILL NEED a set of number cards numbered 1–10.

Work with a small group. Take turns drawing two cards to represent a fraction. Turn the cards face up. The first card drawn represents the numerator of the fraction and the second card, the denominator. Each player writes the fraction as a decimal or whole number.

The player who writes the correct answer first earns 10 points. The player who writes the correct answer second earns 5 points. A player who writes a wrong answer loses 5 points. The first player to reach 100 points wins.

ADDING WITH PASCAL'S TRIANGLE

PURPOSE To practice finding patterns in Pascal's Triangle (page 204)

YOU WILL NEED completed hexagonal pattern of Pascal's Triangle (at least 11 rows)

Start with the second row of Pascal's triangle. Look at the first 5 numbers, 1, 2, 3, 4, and 5, that run diagonally down the right side of the triangle. Find their sum by looking down and to the left of the last number in the line, 5. So their sum is 15. This will work for any line of numbers.

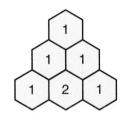

 Show your family how to find a sum.

Use Pascal's Triangle to find the sum.

1. $1 + 3 + 6 + 10$ **2.** $1 + 8 + 36 + 120$

MEASURE UP

PURPOSE To practice converting between measurements (pages 196–198)

YOU WILL NEED a yardstick, string, scissors, and a bag

Work with a partner or a small group. Cut strings of length 12 in., 18 in., 24 in., 30 in., 36 in., 42 in., 48 in., 54 in., and 60 in. Put the strings in a bag. Draw one string from the bag and lay it on the floor. Estimate the length of the string in cm. Measure the length in inches and convert to centimeters. The player with the estimate closest to the length earns 5 points. The first player to reach 25 points wins.

CHAPTER 10 REVIEW

EXAMPLES

EXERCISES

• **Use patterns to convert measurements.**
  (pages 196–198)

Find how many pounds are equal to 4 kg.

1 kg ≈ 2.2 lb

4 kg ≈ 4 × 2.2 lb   *Multiply by 4.*

  ≈ 8.8 lb ← So, 4 kg ≈ 8.8 lb.

Convert the given measurement.

1. 45 in. = ■ ft   **2.** 8.5 ft = ■ in.

3. 15 yd = ■ ft   **4.** 237 ft = ■ yd

5. 20 lb = ■ kg   **6.** 23 kg = ■ lb

7. 88 cm = ■ in.   **8.** 37 in. = ■ cm

• **Use patterns to change fractions and decimals.** (pages 199–201)

Write $0.\overline{18}$ as a fraction.

Let $n = 0.\overline{18}.$ *Two digits repeat.*

$100n = 18.\overline{18}$ *Multiply each side by 100.*

$\underline{- n = 0.\overline{18}}$ *Subtract the original equation.*

$99n = 18.\overline{00}$ ← $18.\overline{00} = 18$

$\dfrac{99n}{99} = \dfrac{18}{99}$ *Solve the equation.*

$n = \dfrac{2}{11}$

Predict whether each fraction is equivalent to a *terminating* or a *repeating* decimal. Then write as a decimal.

9. $\dfrac{9}{16}$ **10.** $\dfrac{7}{20}$

11. $\dfrac{11}{12}$ **12.** $\dfrac{4}{9}$

Write as a fraction in simplest form.

13. 0.3125   **14.** 0.375

15. $0.\overline{4}$ **16.** $0.8\overline{1}$

• **Extend divisibility patterns to decimals.**
  (pages 202–203)

Is 124.4 divisible by 4?

$4.4 \div 4 = 1.1$ ← The number formed by the last 2 digits is divisible by 4.

124.4 is divisible by 4.

Tell whether each is divisible by 3, 6, or 9.

17. $48.90   **18.** 33 markers

19. $87.00   **20.** 136 cans

21. 60 nickels   **22.** $3.06

23. $34.50   **24.** 347 buttons

• **Use patterns of calculator operations.**
  (pages 205–207)

Find the areas of triangle 1 and triangle 2, using $A = \frac{1}{2}bh$ and a calculator with an
OP1 key.

triangle 1: $b = 3$ cm; $h = 4$ cm
triangle 2: $b = 4.5$ cm; $h = 3$ cm

For help, see pages 205–206.

Copy and complete the table. For every dollar donated to charity, the company contributes $0.20. Use Total Donation = $0.20g + g$ to solve. Write the sequence of calculator keys.

25.

	Gift 1	Gift 2	Gift 3
Gift (*g*) in dollars	35.75	125.00	500.00
Total Donation	?	?	?

CHAPTER 11

PATTERNS IN SEQUENCES

Traditional

LOOK AHEAD

In this chapter you will solve problems that involve

- finding patterns in arithmetic and geometric sequences
- predicting terms for arithmetic and geometric sequences
- finding patterns in Fibonacci sequences

Team-Up Project

Sum It Up

The language of music is recorded in notes which are grouped in measures. Each note has a time value. A quarter note will be held twice as long as an eighth note, no matter how fast or slow the music is. Each measure must have the same total time value.

Plan
- Work with a small group. Describe the patterns of fraction equations in a piece of music.

Act
- Look at the music piece shown at the left. Write the value of each note as a fraction.
- Write a fraction equation for each measure.
- Label each type of measure pattern with a letter.
- Write a final equation using the letters to show the pattern sequences in the entire piece.

Share
- Compare your results with another group.

NOTE VALUES FOR $\frac{4}{4}$ TIME:

♪ $= \frac{1}{8}$

two $\frac{1}{8}$ notes tied together

$\frac{1}{8} + \frac{1}{8} = \frac{1}{4}$

♩ $= \frac{1}{4}$

♩. $= \frac{3}{8}$

quarter note rest

𝅗𝅥 $= \frac{1}{2}$

In $\frac{4}{4}$ time all notes and rests in a measure must have a sum of $\frac{4}{4}$.

𝅗𝅥. $= \frac{3}{4}$

DID YOU

☑ Write each note as a fraction?

☑ Write each measure's fraction equation?

☑ Write a final equation?

☑ Compare results with another group?

Sequences

Business Link

One of the best examples of an arithmetic sequence is the Holiday-Club account. An account holder deposits a set amount each week. Since the account pays no interest, its growth is arithmetic. If a person deposits $10 a week, how much will be in the account in 50 weeks?

Todd Jones started the payroll savings plan with a balance of $16. Each week $5 of his earnings was deposited in his account.

Week	0	1	2	3	4
Total Amount (in dollars)	16	21	26	31	36

The amounts in the table form a sequence. Recall that a sequence is an ordered list of numbers. A **term** of the sequence is a number in the sequence.

16, 21, 26, 31, 36, . . .

16, 21, 26, 31, 36, . . .
    5   5   5   5
              — common difference

The sequence above is an arithmetic sequence. When new terms of a sequence are formed by adding a fixed number, called the **common difference**, the sequence is an **arithmetic sequence**. In this sequence the common difference is 5.

Suppose Todd wants to double the amount in his account each week. The sequence 16, 32, 64, 128, 256, . . . shows the amounts that would be in his account.

When new terms of a sequence are formed by multiplying by a constant factor, called the **common ratio**, the sequence is a **geometric sequence**. You can find the common ratio by comparing a term to the preceding term.

The common ratio in this sequence is $\frac{32}{16}$, or $\frac{2}{1}$, or 2.

16, 32, 64, 128, 256, . . .
   2   2   2   2 ◀—— common ratio

You can classify a sequence as arithmetic, geometric, or neither.

EXAMPLE Decide if the sequence is arithmetic, geometric, or neither. Then find the next three terms.

A. 8, 5, 2, ⁻1, ⁻4, . . .

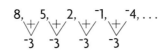

There is a common difference, ⁻3. So, the sequence is arithmetic.

next terms: ⁻7, ⁻10, ⁻13

B. 2, ⁻4, 8, ⁻16, 32, . . .

There is a common ratio, ⁻2. So, the sequence is geometric.

next terms: ⁻64, 128, ⁻256

Look for a pattern. Write *arithmetic, geometric,* or *neither*. If the sequence is arithmetic or geometric, name the common difference or the common ratio.

1. $^-4, ^-2, 0, 2 , \ldots$

2. $2.2, 2.02, 2.002, 2.0002, \ldots$

3. $4, 12, 36, 108, \ldots$

4. $5, ^-5, 5, ^-5, \ldots$

5. $5\frac{1}{2}, 7, 8\frac{1}{2}, 10, \ldots$

6. $10, 6, 2, ^-2, \ldots$

7. $30, 28, 25, 21, \ldots$

8. $10, 5, 2.5, 1.25, 0.625, \ldots$

9. $2, 3, 10, 12, \ldots$

INDEPENDENT PRACTICE

For Exercises 1–8, write *arithmetic, geometric,* or *neither*. Write the next three terms in the sequence.

1. $11, 14, 17, 20, \ldots$

2. $\frac{3}{16}, \frac{3}{8}, \frac{3}{4}, \frac{3}{2}, \ldots$

3. $^-2, ^-4, ^-6, ^-8, \ldots$

4. $^-2, ^-4, ^-8, ^-16, \ldots$

5. $^-0.1, 0.4, ^-1.6, 6.4, \ldots$

6. $^-7, ^-6, ^-4, ^-1, \ldots$

7. $1, 2\frac{1}{3}, 3\frac{2}{3}, 5, \ldots$

8. $48,000; 24,000; 12,000; 6,000; \ldots$

9. Write the first four terms of an arithmetic sequence that begins with 2.5 and has a common difference of 1.5.

10. Write the first four terms of a geometric sequence that begins with $^-12$ and has a common ratio of $^-0.5$.

11. The fifth term of a geometric sequence is 48. The common ratio is $^-2$. What are the first four terms of the sequence?

12. Is the sequence 200, 195, 190, 185, . . . arithmetic, geometric, or neither? Explain.

Problem-Solving Applications

For Problems 13–16, look for a pattern in each sequence. Write *arithmetic, geometric,* or *neither*.

13. A puppy gains 3 lb each month.

14. A watch loses 5 min each day.

15. The number of hours a student studies in a week goes from 20 to 10 to 5 to 0.

16. The population of a town doubles every five years.

17. Jon studied for 10 min on Monday and then doubled his study time on each of the next five days. How long did he study on Friday?

18. Mailing a letter costs $0.32 for the first ounce and $0.23 for each additional ounce. How much does it cost to mail a 6-oz letter?

19. Jay bought a sport utility vehicle for $24,400. If it loses $\frac{1}{4}$ of its value every year, what will be its value at the end of 2 years? at the end of 3 years?

20. **WRITE ABOUT IT** What are the first five terms of an arithmetic sequence with a common difference of 3? of a geometric sequence with a common ratio of 3?

ALGEBRA CONNECTION

Patterns in Arithmetic Sequences

WHAT YOU'LL LEARN
How to write an expression for the terms in an arithmetic sequence

WHY LEARN THIS?
To solve problems that involve patterns or trends that are arithmetic sequences

Look at the pattern created by the perimeters of these figures formed from regular hexagons.

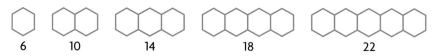

6   10   14   18   22

You can write the sequence 6, 10, 14, 18, 22, . . . to describe how the perimeters of the figures change.

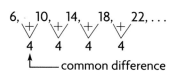

6, 10, 14, 18, 22, . . .

4   4   4   4

common difference

• Explain the process of going from one term to the next in the sequence.

• **CRITICAL THINKING** How do you know that this is an arithmetic sequence?

You can use an iteration diagram to describe a sequence.

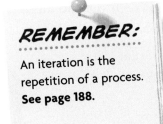

REMEMBER:
An iteration is the repetition of a process.
See page 188.

EXAMPLE 1 Name the first four terms in the sequence.

Start with 8. ⟶ Add 5.

first term: 8

Add 5 to the last term. **next 3 terms:** $8 + 5 = 13$

$13 + 5 = 18$

$18 + 5 = 23$

So, the sequence is 8, 13, 18, 23, . . .

GUIDED PRACTICE

Describe how to find the next three terms in the sequence. Then, name the next three terms.

1. Start with 2. ⟶ Add 3.

2. Start with 10. ⟶ Add ⁻5.

Draw an iteration diagram for the sequence described. Then name the first five terms in the sequence.

3. Sequence starts with ⁻4. Common difference is 3.

4. Sequence starts with 11.6. Common difference is ⁻2.1.

If you want to find the 25th term in the sequence 6, 10, 14, 18, 22, . . . , you can continue to add 4 to each term until you have 25 terms: 6, 10, 14, 18, 22, 26, 30, 34, 38, 42, 46, 50, 54, 58, 62, 66, 70, 74, 78, 82, 86, 90, 94, 98, 102.

Or you can write an algebraic expression that will help you find any term in the sequence. You can use it to find the 25th term.

You can write an algebraic expression for the nth term in the sequence 6, 10, 14, 18, 22, ... Use the expression to find the 25th term. Let n = the number of the term.

Think: The sequence starts with 6, and $n - 1$ terms follow this first term. The common difference is 4.

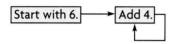

Draw an iteration diagram for the sequence.

$6 + 4(n - 1)$ *Write an expression for the nth term. In the nth term, 4 is added (n − 1) times.*

$6 + 4n - 4$ *Simplify the expression.*

$4n + 2$

$4(25) + 2$ *Substitute 25 for n in the expression.*

102

So, the algebraic expression is $4n + 2$, and the 25th term is 102.

- Write an expression for the nth term in the sequence described by the diagram at the right.

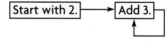

EXAMPLE 2   Write an expression for the nth term in the sequence 10, 7, 4, 1, ⁻2. Use the expression to find the 50th term.

Think: The first term is 10, and the common difference is ⁻3.

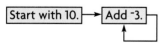

Draw an iteration diagram for the sequence.

$10 + {}^-3(n - 1)$ *Write an expression for the nth term.*

$10 + {}^-3n + 3$ *In the nth term, ⁻3 is added (n − 1) times.*

$^-3n + 13$ *Simplify the expression.*

$^-3(50) + 13$ *Substitute 50 for n.*

$^-137$ ← **The expression is ⁻3n + 13, and the 50th term is ⁻137.**

- Why would you write an expression to find the nth term rather than list all the terms?

Science Link

Just as you can predict the nth term in an arithmetic sequence, you can also predict the height of some plants. Several species of bamboo plants grow about the same amount every day. Suppose a bamboo plant is 40 cm tall and it grows 20 cm a day. How tall will it be in 7 days?

215

Draw an iteration diagram for the described sequence. Then name the first five terms in the sequence.

1. Sequence starts with 3. Common difference is 6.

2. Sequence starts with ⁻8. Common difference is 2.

3. Sequence starts with 9.2. Common difference is ⁻4.

Draw an iteration diagram for the sequence. Then name the next three terms in the sequence.

4. ⁻4, ⁻2, 0, 2, 4, . . .

5. 1.4, 1.0, 0.6, 0.2, . . .

6. 20, 13, 6, ⁻1, . . .

7. $4\frac{1}{2}$, 6, $7\frac{1}{2}$, 9, . . .

Write an expression for the *n*th term of the sequence. Find the 25th term.

8. Start with 3.5. → Add 4.

9. Start with 2. → Add 3.

Draw an iteration diagram for the sequence. Write an expression for the *n*th term. Find the 50th term.

10. 100, 102, 104, 106, . . .

11. ⁻8, ⁻4, 0, 4, . . .

12. ⁻2.2, ⁻2.0, ⁻1.8, ⁻1.6, . . .

Problem-Solving Applications

For Problems 13–14, look at the pattern created by the perimeters of the figures formed from regular octagons.

13. Find the perimeter of each figure. Write the first four terms of a sequence.

14. Write an expression for the *n*th term.

15. ✏️ **WRITE ABOUT IT** How can you find the *n*th term of an arithmetic sequence that starts with 7 and has a common difference of 6?

Mixed Review

Find the value for *n* = 5.

16. 2^{n-1}

17. 4^{n-1}

18. 3^{n-1}

19. $(0.5)^{n-1}$

20. $(0.3)^{n-1}$

Convert the given measurement.

21. 78 in. = ▦ ft

22. 31 yd = ▦ ft

23. 65 kg = ▦ lb

24. 120 lb = ▦ kg

25. **RATES** A T-shirt company sells T-shirts by the dozen or by the case. One dozen T-shirts costs $50.76. One case of 72 T-shirts costs $281.52. Which is the better buy?

26. **PATTERNS** Kintha designed this tile for a tessellation. How many tiles must she use to cover a 12-in. × 16-in. rectangle?

1 in.

3 in.

3 in.

MORE PRACTICE Lesson 11.2, page H60

Patterns in Geometric Sequences

11.3

WHAT YOU'LL LEARN
How to write an expression for the terms in a geometric sequence

WHY LEARN THIS?
To solve problems that involve patterns or trends that are geometric sequences

W hat pattern do you see in the areas of these figures?

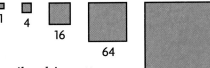

You can write a sequence to describe this pattern.

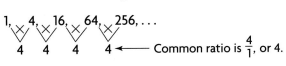

1, 4, 16, 64, 256, . . .

Common ratio is $\frac{4}{1}$, or 4.

You can draw an iteration diagram to describe this pattern.

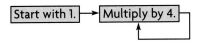

The numbers in this sequence continue to grow beyond any given number. This sequence does not approach a single value. The sequence diverges. You can see this on a number line.

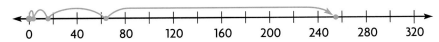

• How can you find the sixth term in the sequence?

If a sequence starts with 3 and has a common ratio of $\frac{1}{2}$, the iteration diagram looks like this:

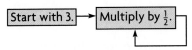

The first five terms of the sequence are 3, $\frac{3}{2}$, $\frac{3}{4}$, $\frac{3}{8}$, $\frac{3}{16}$.

• What is the common ratio?

The numbers in this sequence continue to shrink. This sequence approaches a single value, 0. The sequence converges. You can see this on a number line.

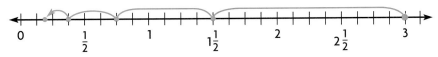

• How can you find the 6th term in the sequence? What is the 6th term?

Science Link

Microorganisms grow geometrically. One paramecium divides to become 2. The 2 divide to become 4, the 4 become 8, and so on. Starting with one paramecium, how many would there be in ten generations?

Does your school have a math club? Math clubs offer an informal way to learn more about patterns in math. One of the first math "clubs" in history was a secret society formed by the loyal followers of the Greek mathematician Pythagoras of Samos. The Pythagoreans studied number patterns and also discovered irrational numbers.

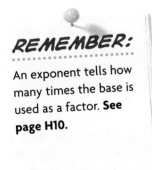

REMEMBER:

An exponent tells how many times the base is used as a factor. **See page H10.**

GUIDED PRACTICE

Name the common ratio for the geometric sequence. Then, draw an iteration diagram for the sequence.

1. 5, 10, 20, 40, . . .

2. 297, 99, 33, 11, . . .

Draw the sequence on a number line. Write *converge* or *diverge* to describe the sequence.

3. $54, 18, 6, 2, \frac{2}{3}, \ldots$

4. $\frac{1}{4}, \frac{1}{2}, 1, 2, 4, \ldots$

To find the *n*th term of a geometric sequence, use the same steps you used to find the *n*th term of an arithmetic sequence. You can write an expression for the *n*th term in the sequence 3, 6, 12, 24, 48, ... Then you can use the expression to find the 10th term.

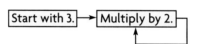

3, 6, 12, 24, 48, . . .

2   2   2   2 ←—— Common ratio is $\frac{6}{3}$, or $\frac{2}{1}$, or 2.

| Start with 3. | → | Multiply by 2. |

Draw an iteration diagram for the sequence.

$3 \times 2^{n-1}$ *Write an expression for the nth term. In the nth term, 2 is multiplied (n − 1) times.*

$3 \times 2^{10-1}$ *Substitute 10 for n in the expression.*

$3 \times 2^9 = 1{,}536$ *Find the value.*

So, the expression is $3 \times 2^{n-1}$ and the 10th term is 1,536.

• Find the 7th term in the sequence.

You can find the *n*th term of a geometric sequence when the common ratio is a rational number.

EXAMPLE Find the 12th term in the sequence 192, 96, 48, 24, 12, ...

Think: The sequence starts with 192; the common ratio is $\frac{96}{192}$, or $\frac{1}{2}$, or 0.5.

$192 \times (0.5)^{n-1}$ *Write an expression for the nth term. In the nth term, 0.5 is multiplied (n − 1) times.*

$192 \times (0.5)^{12-1}$ *Substitute 12 for n.*

192   0.5   11 | 0.09375 |

So, the 12th term is 0.09375.

218 Chapter 11

Calculator Activities, page H36

Name the common ratio for the geometric sequence. Then draw an iteration diagram for the sequence.

1. 3, 12, 48, 192, . . . **2.** 800, 200, 50, 12.5, . . . **3.** 4, 20, 100, 500, . . .

4. 1, 3, 9, 27, 81, . . . **5.** 24, 12, 6, 3, 1.5, . . . **6.** 1,000, 100, 10, 1, $\frac{1}{10}$, . . .

Draw the sequence on a number line. Write *converge* or *diverge* to describe the sequence.

7. 1, 2, 4, 8, 16, . . . **8.** 100, 50, 25, 12.5, 6.25, . . . **9.** 2, 6, 18, 54, 162, . . .

10. 4, 12, 36, 108, . . . **11.** 64, 16, 4, 1, . . . **12.** 25, 5, 1, $\frac{1}{5}$, . . .

Write the first four terms of the sequence described by the iteration diagram. Draw the sequence on a number line. Write *converge* or *diverge* to describe it.

13. Start with 24. → Multiply by $\frac{1}{2}$.

14. Start with 4. → Multiply by 2.

Write an algebraic expression for the *n*th term. Find the 10th term.

15. Start with 1. → Multiply by 7.

16. Start with 3. → Multiply by 2.5.

17. Start with 0.5. → Multiply by 4.

18. Start with 500. → Multiply by 0.2.

Write an algebraic expression for the *n*th term. Find the 8th term.

19. 1, 3, 9, 27, 81, . . . **20.** 250, 50, 10, 2, 0.4, . . . **21.** 0.5, 2, 8, 32, 64, . . .

22. 100, 10, 1, 0.1, 0.01, . . . **23.** 2, 4, 8, 16, 32, . . . **24.** 48, 24, 12, 6, 3, . . .

Problem-Solving Applications

25. The sequence 4, 12, 36, 108 shows the number of members of the ecology club in each of its first 4 years. If this rate of growth continues, how many members will there be in year 5? in year 6?

26. In an experiment a population of insects doubles every month. The experiment starts with 100 insects. How many insects will there be by month 7? by month 12?

27. Suppose you can double your money every day. If you have 1¢ on the first day, how much will you have on the 10th day? on the 20th day?

28. ◄▬▶ **WRITE ABOUT IT** How can you find the *n*th term of a geometric sequence that starts with 100 and has a common ratio of 2?

ALGEBRA CONNECTION

Patterns in the Fibonacci Sequence

Science Link

The Fibonacci sequence is related to the growth of lobsters. To grow, a lobster must shed its shell. In the first year, this happens 8 times; in the second year, 5 times; in the third year, 3 times. After the third year, a male sheds only 2 times per year and a female sheds only 1 time. How is the Fibonacci sequence related to this growth pattern?

For centuries, people have studied a fascinating sequence that appears in mathematics, nature, art, architecture, science, music, and poetry.

The sequence can occur in the growth pattern of a plant.

This plant began with one stem. It grew for one month and added a new stem in the second month. One month later it added another stem. After six months the plant had all the stems shown at the right.

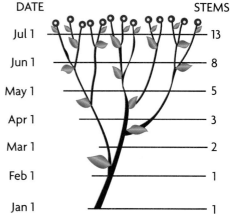

DATE		STEMS
Jul 1		13
Jun 1		8
May 1		5
Apr 1		3
Mar 1		2
Feb 1		1
Jan 1		1

The branching pattern of this plant illustrates the first seven terms of the **Fibonacci sequence**.

$$1, 1, 2, 3, 5, 8, 13, \ldots$$

- **CRITICAL THINKING** How is each term of this sequence related to the two terms before it?

- If the plant continued this pattern, how many stems did it have on August 1? September 1? October 1?

Consecutive terms of the Fibonacci sequence form patterns. Look at these four consecutive terms.

2, 3, 5, 8   *Multiply the first and last terms.*
$2 \times 8 = 16; \ 3 \times 5 = 15$ *Multiply the two middle terms.*

- Compare the products.

Look at these four consecutive terms.

3, 5, 8, 13   *Multiply the first and last terms.*
$3 \times 13 = 39; \ 5 \times 8 = 40$ *Multiply the two middle terms.*

- What is the result?

- Write other sequences of four consecutive terms. Multiply the numbers as shown. What pattern do you see in the products?

1. Write the first 12 terms in the Fibonacci sequence.

Multiply the first and last terms. Tell whether this product is 1 more or 1 less than the product of the two middle terms.

2. 1, 1, 2, 3   **3.** 1, 2, 3, 5   **4.** 5, 8, 13, 21

5. 8, 13, 21, 34   **6.** 13, 21, 34, 55   **7.** 21, 34, 55, 89

Golden Ratios and Golden Rectangles

A special relationship exists between the length and the width of a rectangle whose dimensions are two consecutive terms of the Fibonacci sequence.

EXAMPLE 1   What is the length-to-width ratio of these rectangles?

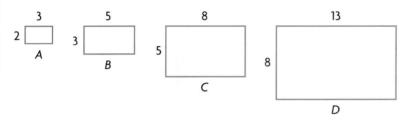

rectangle A: $\frac{3}{2} = 1.5$ rectangle B: $\frac{5}{3} \approx 1.67$

rectangle C: $\frac{8}{5} = 1.6$ rectangle D: $\frac{13}{8} \approx 1.63$

So, the length-to-width ratios are about 1.6 to 1.

The **Golden Ratio** is any ratio that has a value of $\frac{1 + \sqrt{5}}{2}$ and a decimal value of about 1.6. A **Golden Rectangle** is a rectangle that has a length-to-width ratio of about 1.6 to 1. You can identify golden rectangles by using this ratio.

EXAMPLE 2   Are rectangles E and F Golden Rectangles?

Rectangle	Length	Width	Length-to-Width Ratio	Golden Rectangle?
E	9.7 m	6 m	1.6 to 1	yes
F	6 cm	3 cm	2 to 1	no

- How can you find out whether the rectangle shown at the right is a Golden Rectangle?

8 in.

11 in.

History Link

Leonardo Fibonacci (1170–1250) was the first great mathematician of medieval Europe. In addition to identifying the now famous sequence, he did work in number theory, geometry, and trigonometry. Find or draw a Golden Rectangle and another rectangle of about the same size that is not a Golden Rectangle. Ask a friend or relative which is more pleasing to the eye.

INDEPENDENT PRACTICE

Multiply the first and last terms. Then tell whether this product is 1 more or 1 less than the product of the two middle terms.

1. 34, 55, 89, 144

2. 55, 89, 144, 233

3. 89, 144, 233, 377

The first 14 terms of the Fibonacci sequence are 1, 1, 2, 3, 5, 8, 13, 21, 34, 55, 89, 144, 233, and 377. Use these terms for Exercises 4–7.

4. Where in the sequence are the multiples of 2?

5. Where do you think the next four multiples of 2 will occur?

6. Where in the sequence are the multiples of 3?

7. Where do you think the next four multiples of 3 will occur?

The length and width of a rectangle are given in inches. Write *yes* or *no* to tell whether the rectangle is a Golden Rectangle.

8. $l = 13$
$w = 5$

9. $l = 24$
$w = 15$

10. $l = 63$
$w = 29$

11. $l = 16$
$w = 9$

12. $l = 8$
$w = 5$

13. $l = 39$
$w = 24$

Problem-Solving Applications

14. This section of a piano keyboard shows the 13 keys in one octave. Look for patterns of the Fibonacci sequence on the keyboard. How is the keyboard related to the terms of the Fibonacci sequence?

15. Nancy wants a canvas that is a Golden Rectangle. The following sizes are available: 18 in. × 24 in., 9 in. × 12 in., and 5 in. × 8 in. Which is the best choice?

16. ✏ **WRITE ABOUT IT** Is the Fibonacci sequence an arithmetic sequence, a geometric sequence, or neither? Explain.

Mixed Review

Solve the proportion.

17. $\frac{x}{5} = \frac{3}{15}$

18. $\frac{x}{24} = \frac{5}{6}$

19. $\frac{3}{x} = \frac{4}{12}$

20. $\frac{26}{x} = \frac{39}{120}$

Write *T* or *R* to predict whether the fraction is equivalent to a terminating or a repeating decimal. Then write as a decimal.

21. $\frac{5}{8}$

22. $\frac{3}{16}$

23. $\frac{5}{6}$

24. $\frac{7}{3}$

25. $\frac{9}{20}$

26. INEQUALITIES At the Old Post Apartments, a renter's monthly income, p, must be at least 3 times the rental rate, r. Write an algebraic inequality to represent this situation.

27. RATIONAL NUMBERS Yesterday the low temperature was ⁻7°F and the high temperature was 12°F. What was the difference between the high and the low?

MORE PRACTICE Lesson 11.4, page H61

Constructing a Golden Rectangle

You can construct a Golden Rectangle by completing a few steps.

Explore

- On graph paper, draw and label square *ABCD* with a length of 4 units.

- Mark the midpoint of $\overline{DC}$, and label it *M*. Place the compass point on *M*. Open the compass so that *MB* is the radius. Construct an arc intersecting the extended side $\overline{DC}$ at *E*.

- Mark the midpoint of $\overline{AB}$, and label it *N*. Without changing the compass opening from the previous step, place the compass point on point *N*. Construct an arc intersecting the extended side $\overline{AB}$ at *F*. Draw $\overline{FE}$.

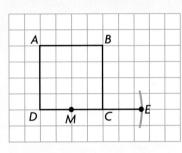

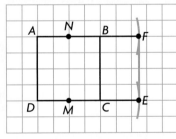

Think and Discuss

- Record the lengths of $\overline{AD}$ and $\overline{DE}$. Use a calculator to find $\frac{DE}{AD}$.

- How does this ratio show that *AFED* is a Golden Rectangle?

Try This

- Construct a Golden Rectangle by starting with a square with a length of 6 units and completing the steps shown above.

- Use a ruler to measure the lengths and widths of several rectangular objects. Record the dimensions in a table.

- Find the length-to-width ratios of the rectangles you measured. Which are Golden Rectangles?

223

LAB *Activity*

WHAT YOU'LL EXPLORE
How to construct a Golden Rectangle

WHAT YOU'LL NEED
graph paper, compass, ruler

CULTURAL CONNECTION

Patterns in New Zealand

The people of New Zealand enjoy outdoor activities. The mild climate makes camping, hiking, and mountain climbing possible year-round. Katherine and her parents plan to hike along the trails to see the mountains and waterfalls. To prepare themselves, they walk every Saturday in October and November. They walk 3 mi the first Saturday. They want to increase their distance by 2 mi each week.

Copy and complete the chart below showing the number of miles they will walk each week.

	October				November				
Date	4	11	18	25	1	8	15	22	29
Miles	3	5	7						

Work Together

1. What type of sequence is used to find the missing numbers in the table above?

2. Katherine wants to save extra money for a trip to the United States. She multiplies the amount she saves the first week by 3. She makes a chart for what she hopes to save over 5 weeks. Complete the sequence she uses and then tell the type of sequence. What is the total amount she hopes to save?

Week	1	2	3	4	5
Savings	$1	$3			

3. Sheep are raised for wool. The first day Katherine's father shears 30 sheep. The second day he shears 36 sheep, and the third day he shears 42. Write an algebraic expression to find the number of sheep he will shear on the tenth day.

4. A farmer had 384 kg of kiwis to sell to tourists. On Monday a group of tourists bought half of the kiwis. On Tuesday another group of tourists bought half of the remaining kiwis. This pattern continued until the farmer decided to keep the last 12 kg of kiwis. How many groups of tourists bought kiwis?

EXAMPLES

EXERCISES

• **Identify arithmetic and geometric sequences.**

(pages 212–213)

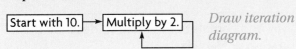

3, 6, 12, 24, 48, . . .

2   2   2   2 ← common ratio = $\frac{6}{3}$ = $\frac{2}{1}$, or 2

geometric sequence

For help with identifying arithmetic sequences, see page 212.

Write *arithmetic, geometric,* or *neither* to identify the sequence. Name the next three terms.

1. 4, 12, 20, 28, . . .   **2.** 1, 4, 9, 16, . . .

3. 1, 2, 4, 8, . . .   **4.** 96, 48, 24, 12, . . .

• **Write an expression for the *n*th term in an arithmetic sequence.** (pages 214–216)

Write an expression for the *n*th term in the sequence 2, 5, 8, 11, ... Find the 25th term.

| Start with 2. | → | Add 3. | *Draw iteration diagram.*

$2 + 3(n - 1)$ *Write expression for nth term.*

$3n - 1$ ← expression

$3(25) - 1 = 74$ ← 25th term: 74

Draw an iteration diagram for the sequence. Name the next three terms in the sequence.

5. 16, 26, 36, 46, . . .   **6.** 0, ⁻2, ⁻4, ⁻6, . . .

Write an expression for the *n*th term of the arithmetic sequence. Then find the 12th term.

7. 3.5, 6, 8.5, 11, . . .

8. 12.5, 12, 11.5, 11, . . .

9. $2\frac{1}{5}, 3\frac{2}{5}, 4\frac{3}{5}, 5\frac{4}{5}, \ldots$

10. ⁻20, ⁻17, ⁻14, ⁻11, . . .

• **Write an expression for the *n*th term in a geometric sequence.** (pages 217–219)

Write an expression for the *n*th term in the sequence 10, 20, 40, 80, ... Find 8th term.

| Start with 10. | → | Multiply by 2. | *Draw iteration diagram.*

$10 \times 2^{n-1}$ *Write expression.*

$10 \times 2^{8-1}$ *Substitute 8 for n.*

$10 \times 2^7 = 1{,}280$ ← 8th term: 1,280

Draw the sequence on a number line. Write *diverge* or *converge* to describe it.

11. 24, 12, 6, 3, . . .   **12.** 2, 6, 18, 54, . . .

Write an expression for the *n*th term of the geometric sequence. Then find the 8th term.

13. 192, 96, 48, 24, . . .   **14.** 2, ⁻2, 2, ⁻2, . . .

• **Find patterns in the Fibonacci sequence.**

(pages 220–222)

13 m

8 m

Tell if the figure is a Golden Rectangle.

$\frac{13}{8} = 1.625$ ← length-to-width ratio ≈ 1.6 to 1

So, this is a Golden Rectangle.

Find the length-to-width ratio expressed as a decimal. The dimensions are given in inches.

15. $l = 40; w = 25$ **16.** $l = 24; w = 17$

Write *yes* or *no* to tell whether the figure is a Golden Rectangle.

17. $l = 89; w = 55$ **18.** $l = 100; w = 75$

19. $l = 25; w = 13$ **20.** $l = 34; w = 21$

VOCABULARY CHECK

1. An arrangement of plane figures that covers a plane with no gaps or overlapping is a ___?___. (page 176)

2. A curve traced by a point rotating around and away from a fixed point is a ___?___. (page 184)

3. Any ratio that has a decimal value of about 1.6 is a ___?___. (page 221)

EXAMPLES

- **Make models of regular solids, and explore semiregular solids.** (pages 180–183)

Identify the regular polyhedron that can be formed by the pattern of polygons.

A cube can be formed.

- **Identify Archimedean and equiangular spiral patterns and helices.** (pages 184–186)

Identify the spiral pattern.

Archimedean spiral   equiangular spiral

- **Generate fractal patterns.** (pages 188–191)

Stage 0   Stage 1   Stage 2

What is the iteration rule?
REDUCE to one-half size.
REPLICATE two times.
REBUILD in bottom left and upper right corners.

EXERCISES

Identify the regular polyhedron that can be formed by the pattern of polygons. Tell how many vertices, faces, and edges in each.

4.   5.

Write *Archimedean spiral, equiangular spiral,* or *helix* to classify each pattern.

6.   7.

Copy and complete the table to describe the iteration at the left.

8.
9.

Stage	0	1	2	3	4	5
Number of Shaded Squares	1	2	4	?	?	?
Shaded Area	1	$\frac{1}{2}$	$\frac{1}{4}$	?	?	?

- **Use patterns to convert measurements.**
  (pages 196–198)

  Find how many centimeters are equal to 8 in.

  1 in. ≈ 2.5 cm
  8 in. ≈ 8 × 2.5 cm
        ≈ 20 cm
  So, 8 in. ≈ 20 cm.

Convert the given measurement.

10. 62 yd = ■ ft   **11.** 102 in. = ■ ft

12. 5 lb = ■ kg   **13.** 10 L = ■ gal
[1 lb = 0.45 kg]   [1 L = 0.26 gal]

14. 32 in. = ■ cm   **15.** 20 yd = ■ in.

- **Write an expression for the nth term in a geometric sequence.** (pages 217–219)

  Write an expression for the nth term in the sequence 4, 12, 36, 108, ... Find the 7th term.

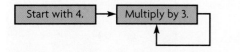

  Draw an iteration diagram.

  $4 \times 3^{n-1}$ *Write the expression.*
  $4 \times 3^{7-1}$ *Substitute 7 for n.*
  $4 \times 729 = 2{,}916$ The 7th term is 2,916.

Write an expression for the nth term of the geometric sequence.

16. 240, 120, 60, 30, . . .   **17.** 3, ⁻12, 48, ⁻192, . . .

Find the 10th term.

18. ⁻1, ⁻3, ⁻9, ⁻27, . . .   **19.** $\frac{1}{2}$, ⁻1, 2, ⁻4, . . .

20. 2, 10, 50, 250, . . .   **21.** ⁻5, 5, ⁻5, 5, . . .

- **Find patterns in the Fibonacci sequence.**
  (pages 220–222)

  Tell if the figure is a Golden Rectangle.

  | 34 ft | 21 ft |

  $\frac{34}{21} = 1.619$ The ratio is about 1.6 to 1.

  So, the figure is a Golden Rectangle.

Find the length-to-width ratio expressed as a decimal to the nearest tenth. Write yes or no to tell whether the figure is a Golden Rectangle.

22. $l = 144$; $w = 89$ **23.** $l = 240$; $w = 190$

24. $l = 55$; $w = 9$ **25.** $l = 13$; $w = 8$

PROBLEM SOLVING

Solve. Explain your method.

26. At the carnival it costs $8.50 for ten tickets. Every ticket after that costs $0.75. How much does it cost to buy 15 tickets?
(pages 214–216)

27. A bacterial colony 0.5 mm in diameter quadruples in size every week. What will be the diameter of the colony in 6 weeks?
(pages 217–219)

✏️ Write About It

1. Show how you can use a square, an equilateral triangle, or a regular hexagon to create a tessellation pattern of at least 3 rows. Explain how you do this including rotations and translations. **(pages 176–179)**

2. Change $0.\overline{63}$ to a fraction. Explain your method. **(pages 199–201)**

3. Show how you would write an expression for the nth term of the sequence 8, 11, 14, 17, 20, . . . where 8 is the first term. Use the expression to find the 50th term. **(pages 214–216)**

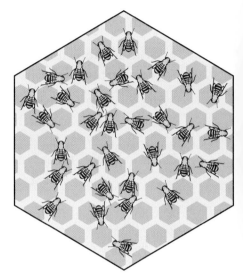

✔️ Performance Assessment

Choose a strategy and solve. Explain your method.

Problem-Solving Strategies
- **Find a Pattern** • **Act It Out** • **Make a Model**
- **Make a Graph** • **Write an Equation**

4. Modify a square by making a translation. Then use this new shape as a basic unit to construct at least 3 rows of a tessellation pattern. **(pages 176–179)**

5. An Internet service charges a base fee of $5.95 per month plus $1.95 per hour. Find the total fee for 5 hr, 10 hr, and 15 hr. **(pages 214–216)**

6. Some insects can multiply in number at an amazing rate. Suppose you start in Week 1 with 2 insects that can double their number every week. How many insects will there be at the end of 4 weeks? 10 weeks? **(pages 217–219)**

Solve the problem. Then write the letter of the correct answer.

1. Which number is not an integer?
(pages 16–19)

A. ⁻84   **B.** 0
C. 7.3   **D.** 4,136

2. Computer programs cost $38.25 for 3. What do 10 computer programs cost?
(pages 47–48)

A. $12.75   **B.** $114.75
C. $127.50   **D.** $382.50

3. Which expression represents the cost of the tickets, t, plus 6? (pages 102–104)

A. $6t$ **B.** $6 - t$
C. $\frac{t}{6}$ **D.** $t + 6$

4. Which inequality is represented by the graph? (pages 142–143)

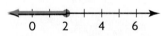

A. $x \geq 2$ **B.** $x \leq 2$
C. $x > 2$ **D.** $x < 2$

5. Which ordered pair is a solution of $2y = 4 - 2x$? (pages 152–155)

A. $(2, ⁻4)$ **B.** $(⁻4, ⁻2)$
C. $(⁻2, 0)$ **D.** $(⁻2, 4)$

6. Which figure was modified by using a rotation? (pages 176–179)

A. 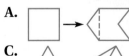   **B.**

C.    **D.**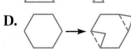

7. Which regular polyhedron will be formed by the pattern of polygons below?
(pages 180–183)

A. tetrahedron   **B.** octahedron
C. dodecahedron   **D.** icosahedron

8. Convert 72 ft into yards. (pages 196-198)

A. 6 yd   **B.** 24 yd
C. 69 yd   **D.** 216 yd

9. Which fraction is equivalent to a repeating decimal? (pages 199–201)

A. $\frac{2}{9}$ **B.** $\frac{7}{16}$
C. $\frac{11}{20}$ **D.** $\frac{13}{4}$

10. Which number is divisible by 2, 3, and 6?
(pages 202–203)

A. 27.5   **B.** 63
C. 84   **D.** 256

11. Use the iteration diagram to find the 20th term. (pages 214–216)

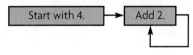

A. 26   **B.** 42
C. 44   **D.** 120

12. Which rectangle is a Golden Rectangle?
(pages 220–222)

A. $l = 8, w = 4$ **B.** $l = 12, w = 10$
C. $l = 18, w = 3$ **D.** $l = 21, w = 13$

SIMILAR FIGURES

LOOK AHEAD

In this chapter you will solve problems that involve

- properties of similar figures
- proportions and scale factors
- scale drawings
- self-similarity

Team-Up Project

Define Similar

What does similar mean? What are examples of things that are similar? What are some synonyms for similar?

Plan
- Work with a small group. Find examples of things that are similar. Record and present your information.

Act
- Find examples of similar objects, images, sounds, and ideas.
- Describe the similarity of the items.
- Make a chart about similarity. Include examples, definitions, synonyms, and drawings. Does similar have a different meaning in different situations?

Share
- Present your chart to the class.

DID YOU

- ✓ Find examples of similar items?
- ✓ Describe the similarity of the items?
- ✓ Make a chart about similarity?
- ✓ Present your chart to the class?

ALGEBRA CONNECTION
Similar Figures

Size and shape are two key ideas in geometry. Congruent figures have the same size and shape. **Similar figures** have the same shape but not necessarily the same size.

For two polygons to be similar,

• corresponding angles must be congruent, and

• corresponding sides must have lengths that form equal ratios.

EXAMPLE 1 Is rectangle *A* similar to rectangles *B* and *C*?

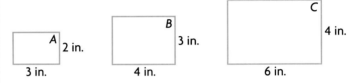

A 2 in. 3 in.

B 3 in. 4 in.

C 4 in. 6 in.

Since the three figures are all rectangles, all angles are right angles. So, the corresponding angles are congruent.

Compare the ratios of corresponding sides to see if they are equal.

$$\frac{\text{length of rectangle } A}{\text{length of rectangle } B} \rightarrow \frac{3}{4} \neq \frac{2}{3} \leftarrow \frac{\text{width of rectangle } A}{\text{width of rectangle } B}$$

Ratios are not equal.

$$\frac{\text{length of rectangle } A}{\text{length of rectangle } C} \rightarrow \frac{3}{6} = \frac{2}{4} \leftarrow \frac{\text{width of rectangle } A}{\text{width of rectangle } C}$$

Ratios are equal.

So, rectangle *A* is not similar to rectangle *B*, but is similar to rectangle *C*.

• **CRITICAL THINKING** Are all rectangles similar? Explain.

• Is rectangle *B* similar to rectangle *C*? Explain.

An equation stating that two ratios are equal is a proportion. Since corresponding sides of similar figures have lengths that form equal ratios, you can say the sides are **proportional**, or in proportion.

The scale factor of two similar figures is the common ratio of the lengths of pairs of corresponding sides. Another name for the scale factor is the **similarity ratio**. You can write a proportion with the scale factor to find an unknown length of a similar figure.

REMEMBER:

Proportions have equal cross products. **See page H16.**

$8 \times 12 = 3 \times 32$

$96 = 96$

EXAMPLE 2 Use a proportion to find the length, x, that will make rectangle D similar to rectangle A.

The scale factor $\frac{2}{5}$ is the ratio of corresponding sides.

$\frac{3}{x} = \frac{2}{5}$ *Write the proportion.*

$2x = 3 \times 5$ *Find the cross products.*

$\frac{2x}{2} = \frac{15}{2}$ *Solve for x.*

$x = 7\frac{1}{2}$

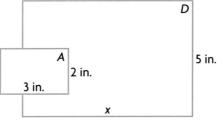

So, when the length of rectangle D is $7\frac{1}{2}$ in., the corresponding sides are proportional and the two rectangles are similar.

- Suppose the length of rectangle D is 5 in. and the width is x. Find the width that will make rectangle D similar to rectangle A.

———————————————————

You can use the similarity ratio to find the unknown measurements of similar figures such as trapezoids.

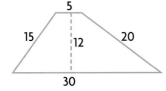 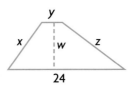

A ratio that compares the smaller trapezoid to the larger trapezoid is the ratio of corresponding sides $\frac{24}{30}$.

Since $\frac{24}{30} = \frac{24 \div 6}{30 \div 6} = \frac{4}{5}$, the scale factor, or similarity ratio, is $\frac{4}{5}$.

You can find the other measurements of the smaller trapezoid by using the similarity ratio.

$x = \frac{4}{5} \times 15 = 12$ $y = \frac{4}{5} \times 5 = 4$

$z = \frac{4}{5} \times 20 = 16$ $w = \frac{4}{5} \times 12 = \frac{48}{5} = 9\frac{3}{5}$

Computer Link

With a computer drawing program, it is easy to make similar figures like the trapezoids at the left. A drawing program uses percents for scale factors. Would a trapezoid with a scale factor of 120% be larger or smaller than the original trapezoid?

Tell whether the figures in each pair are similar. Write *yes* or *no*. If the answer is *no*, explain.

1.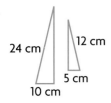

2.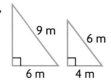

3.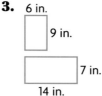

4.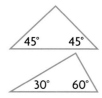

INDEPENDENT PRACTICE

Tell whether the figures in each pair are similar. Write *yes* or *no*.

1.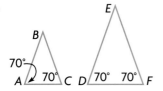

2.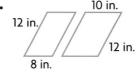

3.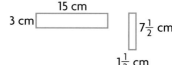

The figures in each pair are similar. Find the scale factor. Then solve for *x*.

4.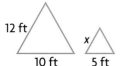

5.

6.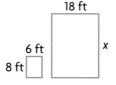

7.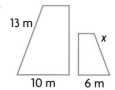

For Exercises 8–9, use the figure at the right. A rectangular piece of paper has been cut into four rectangular parts.

8. Which parts, if any, are similar to the original rectangle?

9. Which parts are similar? Find the similarity ratio.

Problem-Solving Applications

10. Ann's room is 10 ft × 12 ft 6 in. Her sketch of the room is 8 in. × 10 in. Is Ann's sketch a scale drawing? What scale factor did she use? (HINT: 10 ft = ? in.)

11. Owen has a 3-in. × 5-in. photograph. He wants to make it as large as he can for a 10-in. × 12.5-in. ad. What scale factor will he use? What will be the new size?

12. Bill is 6 ft tall. He casts a 4-ft shadow at the same time a tree casts a 16-ft shadow. Use similar triangles to find the height of the tree.

13. ✏️ **WRITE ABOUT IT** All similar figures are congruent. Is this statement true or false? Explain.

MORE PRACTICE Lesson 12.1, page H61

Cutting Similar Figures

In this activity you will cut index cards according to directions and look for similar figures.

Explore

• Work in a group. Cut one 4-in. × 6-in. index card in half on its longer side.

• Are the two halves similar to each other? to another 4-in. × 6-in. card? Explain.

• Cut one of the half cards in half on its longer side.

• Are the two halves of the half card similar to each other? to the other half card? to the remaining 4-in. × 6-in. card? Explain.

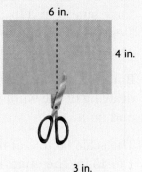

6 in.

4 in.

3 in.

4 in.

LAB Activity

WHAT YOU'LL EXPLORE

How to cut similar figures from index cards

WHAT YOU'LL NEED

two 4-in. × 6-in. index cards and a pair of scissors for each group

Think and Discuss

You should now have a 4-in. × 6-in. card, a 3-in. × 4-in. card, and two 2-in. × 3-in. cards. **Think but do not cut.**

• Where would you cut the shorter dimension of the 3-in. × 4-in. card to make it similar to the 4-in. × 6-in. card?

• Where would you cut the longer dimension of a 2-in. × 3-in. card to make it similar to the 3-in. × 4-in. card?

Try This

• Cut along a diagonal of the 4-in. × 6-in. card, the 3-in. × 4-in. card, and a 2-in. × 3-in. card.

• Are the two triangles formed from each card congruent to each other? similar to each other? Explain.

• Compare the triangles of different sizes. Can you find two that are similar? If so, find their similarity ratio.

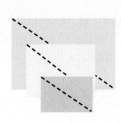

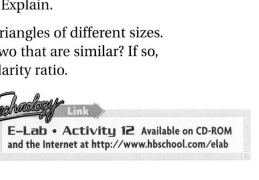

Technology Link

E–Lab • Activity 12 Available on CD-ROM and the Internet at http://www.hbschool.com/elab

235

Scale Drawings

A **scale drawing** represents a real object or place. The figure shown in the drawing is similar to a real object. It has the same shape, and its dimensions are related by a ratio, or scale. Depending on the ratio selected, a scale drawing can be larger or smaller than the original object.

Both the drawing of the quilt block, on the left below, and the drawing of the whole quilt are reduced versions of the real block and quilt.

The scale factors of these drawings are 1 to 3 for the block and 1 to 15 for the quilt. This means the drawing on the left is $\frac{1}{3}$ the length of the actual quilt block. The drawing on the right is $\frac{1}{15}$ the length of the actual quilt.

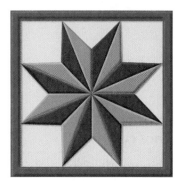

The outline scale drawing at the right can be used to make a full-size drawing of the star-pattern quilt block.

The star is drawn to $\frac{1}{8}$ scale. A length of 1 in. on the drawing equals 8 in. on the actual fabric.

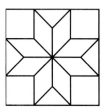

scale: $\frac{1}{8}$ in. = 1 in.

ACTIVITY

Working in a group, use the scale drawing to make a full-size drawing of the star-pattern quilt block.

WHAT YOU'LL NEED: three 3-in. × 5-in. index cards, a ruler marked in sixteenths of an inch, scissors, drawing paper, markers or crayons

• Measure the sides of the corner squares in the scale drawing. What is the length?

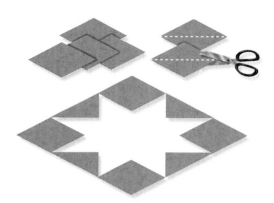

- Since the scale is $\frac{1}{8}$ in. = 1 in., multiply your measurement by 8 to find out how long the sides of the corner squares should be in your drawing.

- Using the length you calculated for the sides of the corner squares, cut six squares from the index cards. Cut two of the squares on their diagonals to form right isosceles triangles.

- On a sheet of paper, arrange the four squares and four triangles into the large square shown. Trace the squares and triangles. Draw the four remaining line segments to complete the full-size drawing. Color your drawing.

- How long is the outside edge of the quilt back in your full-size drawing?

EXAMPLE The actual measurements for the media center are shown on the drawing below. How long should each measurement be on a scale drawing that uses a scale of 1 in. = 20 ft?

A length of 20 ft in the actual media center will be represented by 1 in. on the scale drawing.

Divide each given measurement by 20 to find the corresponding measurement in inches for the scale drawing.

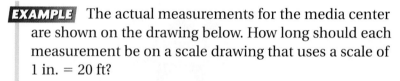

$65 \div 20 = 3.25$	$45 \div 20 = 2.25$	$35 \div 20 = 1.75$
65 ft ↔ $3\frac{1}{4}$ in.	*45 ft ↔ $2\frac{1}{4}$ in.*	*35 ft ↔ $1\frac{3}{4}$ in.*
$20 \div 20 = 1$	$30 \div 20 = 1.5$	$25 \div 20 = 1.25$
20 ft ↔ 1 in.	*30 ft ↔ $1\frac{1}{2}$ in.*	*25 ft ↔ $1\frac{1}{4}$ in.*

- 💡 **CRITICAL THINKING** Suppose the scale drawing is too large for your sheet of paper and you want to reduce the size by one-half. What will be the new scale?

GUIDED PRACTICE

The scale of a drawing is 1 in. = 10 ft. Find the length each measurement would be in the drawing.

1. 75 ft   **2.** 55 ft   **3.** 35 ft

4. 20 ft   **5.** 30 ft   **6.** 90 ft

Art Link

Each quilt is a unique work of art. One name for the star pattern shown on page 236 is the Lemoyne Star. However, often quilts that look alike have different names. Many quilts have one name in one region and a different name in another. Contact a local historical society or quilters guild to learn about common quilt patterns in your region. Are any of them similar to the Lemoyne Star pattern?

The scale of a scale drawing is $\frac{1}{2}$ in. = 10 ft. Find the actual measurement.

1. 3 in.   **2.** 2 in.   **3.** 1 in.   **4.** 5 in.   **5.** 6.5 in.   **6.** 7.25 in.

The scale is 1 in. = 15 mi. Find the length each distance would be on a scale drawing.

7. 30 mi   **8.** 45 mi   **9.** 90 mi   **10.** 7.5 mi   **11.** 142.5 mi   **12.** 153.75 mi

Use the given scale to make a scale drawing.

13. square with a 15-in. side; scale 1 in. = 5 in.   **14.** rectangle 12 ft × 44 ft; scale $\frac{1}{4}$ in. = 1 ft

For Exercises 15–16, use the figure at the right.

15. Make an enlargement of this design. Use a scale of 1 in. = $\frac{1}{4}$ in.

16. Find the lengths of the sides of the triangles in the enlargement. Find the dimensions of the two sizes of squares in the enlargement.

Problem-Solving Applications

17. A mapmaker uses a scale of 1 in. = 13 mi. If a state is actually 585 mi wide, how wide is the state on the map? Suppose the state is 400 mi long. How long is it on the map?

18. Cathi is designing a billboard. The billboard is 12 ft × 40 ft. Use a scale of $\frac{3}{8}$ in. = 1 ft to find the size of her design.

19. ✏️ **WRITE ABOUT IT** An architect made two drawings of a building. In the first, he used a scale of 1 in. = 25 ft. In the second, he used a scale of 1 in. = 30 ft. In which drawing did the building appear larger? Explain.

Mixed Review

Find the product.

20. $\frac{1}{2} \times \frac{1}{2} \times \frac{1}{2}$ **21.** $\frac{1}{2} \times \frac{1}{2} \times \frac{1}{2} \times \frac{1}{2}$ **22.** $\frac{1}{4} \times \frac{1}{4} \times \frac{1}{4} \times \frac{1}{4}$ **23.** $\frac{1}{10} \times \frac{1}{10} \times \frac{1}{10} \times \frac{1}{10}$

Identify each sequence. Write *arithmetic, geometric,* or *neither.*

24. 1, 6, 11, 16, 21, . . .   **25.** 1, ⁻3, 9, ⁻27, 81, . . .   **26.** 1, 2, 5, 6, 9, . . .   **27.** 1, 0, 2, 1, 3, . . .

28. **AVERAGES** Chris received 11 points for an A, 9 points for each of two B's, and 6 points for a C. What is Chris's grade point average?

29. **NUMBER SENSE** The product of two numbers is 240, and their sum is 31. What are the numbers?

MORE PRACTICE Lesson 12.2, page H62

Self-Similarity

Similarity can be found in many places. It often appears in nature.

These balsam fir trees, though different in size, have similar shapes.

The graduated marks on a metric ruler show a special type of similarity. In a one-dimensional metric scale, units are repeatedly divided into tenths to form smaller units.

WHAT YOU'LL LEARN
How to recognize self-similarity

WHY LEARN THIS?
To make self-similar drawings

WORD POWER
self-similarity

1 decimeter

10 centimeters

100 millimeters

The 1-mm divisions of each 1-cm unit are similar to the 1-cm divisions of each 1-dm unit. The similarity ratio is $\frac{1}{10}$.

1 decimeter

1 centimeter

1 millimeter

Such a scale has a special property called **self-similarity**. When a figure is self-similar, it contains a repeating pattern where small parts of the figure are scale drawings of the whole figure at different scales.

EXAMPLE Imagine a 4-in. square divided into 1-in. squares, each of which is divided into $\frac{1}{4}$-in. squares, and those into $\frac{1}{16}$-in. squares, and so on. Will the resulting figure show self-similarity? What is the similarity ratio?

Yes, the figure will show self-similarity everywhere. Each smaller square is similar to a larger square by a similarity ratio of $\frac{1}{4}$.

teen times

Has anyone ever told you, "You look just like your sister"? Similarities between brothers and sisters are common, but the greatest similarities are between identical twins. Identical twins have the same genetic makeup. Fraternal twins look no more alike than other brothers and sisters.

GUIDED PRACTICE

Tell whether the figure shows self-similarity. Write *yes* or *no*.

1.

2.

3.

4.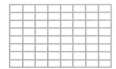

INDEPENDENT PRACTICE

For Exercises 1–2, use two 3-in. × 5-in. cards.

1. Leave one of the 3-in. × 5-in. cards uncut. Cut the other card in half both vertically and horizontally. Cut one of the quarters in half again both vertically and horizontally. Repeat.

2. Stack the rectangles as shown at the right. If the process continued, would the resulting figure show self-similarity around that corner? What is the similarity ratio?

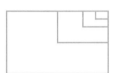

For Exercises 3–5, use a right triangle cut from paper. The base should be 8 in. long.

3. Repeatedly cut the base of the triangle in half to form a smaller right triangle.

4. Watch how the triangle you form changes as the cut gets closer and closer to vertex *A*. Is each triangle similar to the one before? If so, what is the similarity ratio? If not, explain.

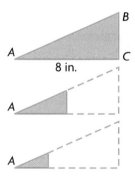

5. Draw a model of the different-size triangles, stacked as the rectangles were in Exercise 2. Is a self-similarity pattern emerging? Explain.

Problem-Solving Applications

6. Make a list of self-similar structures you have seen in your school, home, or neighborhood. Describe the appearance and location of at least two of these.

7. Make a model to describe self-similarity. Use a square or a rectangle. Tell what similarity ratio you used.

8. ✏️ **WRITE ABOUT IT** Explain what is meant when a figure is described as having self-similarity.

Similar Solid Figures

WHAT YOU'LL LEARN
How to recognize similar solid figures

WHY LEARN THIS?
To compare solid figures

Katie and Rachel are shopping for shoes for their cheerleading uniforms. Katie wears size 6, and Rachel wears size 8.

• Are the right shoes in the two sizes similar, congruent, both, or neither? Explain your choice.

• What about the right and left shoes of one size? Explain.

> Two solid objects are similar when they have exactly the same shape. The corresponding sides are proportional, and the corresponding angles are congruent.

EXAMPLE 1 A shoe box measures 4 in. × $5\frac{1}{2}$ in. × 11 in. Another shoe box measures 5 in. × $6\frac{7}{8}$ in. × 12 in. Are the boxes similar?

Since all angles on the two boxes are right angles, corresponding angles are congruent.

Check to see whether corresponding sides are proportional.

$$\frac{4}{5} \stackrel{?}{=} \frac{5.5}{6.875} \qquad \textit{Write fractions as decimals in a proportion.}$$

$$4 \times 6.875 \stackrel{?}{=} 5.5 \times 5 \qquad \textit{Find the cross products.}$$

$$27.5 = 27.5 \qquad \textit{Heights and widths are proportional.}$$

$$\frac{4}{5} \stackrel{?}{=} \frac{11}{12} \qquad \textit{Write another proportion.}$$

$$4 \times 12 \stackrel{?}{=} 11 \times 5 \qquad \textit{Find the cross products.}$$

$$48 \neq 55 \qquad \textit{Heights and lengths are not proportional.}$$

Since not all pairs of corresponding sides are proportional, the two boxes are not similar.

• Suppose the larger box were $13\frac{3}{4}$ in.-long. Would the boxes be similar? Explain.

Visiting Las Vegas, Nevada, is like taking a world tour. There are buildings like a huge English castle, the ancient Roman forum, a $\frac{1}{3}$-scale copy of the New York City skyline, and a 30-story Egyptian pyramid with a copy of the Great Sphinx that is bigger than the original. The Great Sphinx, a lion-human statue at Giza, Egypt, is 66 ft high and 240 ft long. The Las Vegas sphinx is 110 ft high. If it is similar to the Great Sphinx in Egypt, how long must this enlargement be?

EXAMPLE 2 A toy maker is cutting wood to carve into toy trains of different sizes. All measurements are given in inches. Are these two pieces of wood similar?

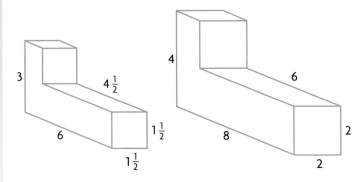

Since all angles are right angles, corresponding angles are congruent.

Check to see that the ratios of corresponding sides are all equal.

To compare the ratios, write each one as a decimal.

$$\frac{3}{4} = 0.75 \qquad \frac{6}{8} = 0.75 \qquad \frac{1.5}{2} = 0.75 \qquad \frac{4.5}{6} = 0.75$$

The ratios of corresponding sides are all equal to 0.75. So, the pieces of wood are similar.

GUIDED PRACTICE

Use the visual clues to decide whether the objects in each pair are *similar, congruent, both,* or *neither.*

1.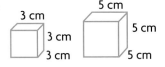

2.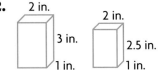

Write the ratios of corresponding sides as decimals. Then tell whether the objects in each pair are similar. Write *yes* or *no.*

3.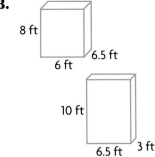

4.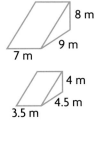

INDEPENDENT PRACTICE

Tell whether the objects in each pair are *similar, congruent, both,* or *neither.*

1.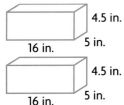

2.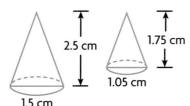

3.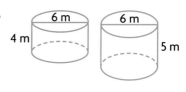

The objects in each pair are similar. Find the ratios of corresponding sides. Write each as a decimal.

4.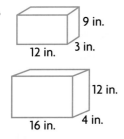

5.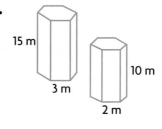

6.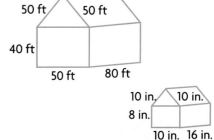

Problem-Solving Applications

7. A stone carver's final design needs to fit in a rectangular space 12 ft × 8 ft × 4 ft. His model fits in a space 3 ft × 2 ft × 1 ft. Are the spaces similar? Explain.

8. ✏️ **WRITE ABOUT IT** All spheres and all cubes are similar regardless of their dimension. Is this statement *true* or *false*? Explain.

Mixed Review

Solve for *x.*

9. $\dfrac{3}{12} = \dfrac{x}{20}$ **10.** $\dfrac{8}{3} = \dfrac{16}{x}$ **11.** $\dfrac{2}{10} = \dfrac{x}{5}$ **12.** $\dfrac{3}{4} = \dfrac{x}{12}$ **13.** $\dfrac{x}{14} = \dfrac{3}{4}$ **14.** $\dfrac{x}{5} = \dfrac{30}{15}$

Write a rule for each sequence. Then find the next term.

15. 7, 13, 19, 25, . . .   **16.** 2, 6, 18, 54, . . .   **17.** 1, 1, 2, 4, 7, . . .   **18.** 10, 7, 4, 1, . . .

19. **MENTAL MATH** The retired astronaut Charles "Pete" Conrad receives $11,000 per guest appearance. If he makes 2 guest appearances a month for one year, how much money will he receive? Suppose he makes 3 appearances a month for one year. How much money will he receive?

20. **PATTERNS** Sue is organizing her box of buttons. All the buttons in the first section are $\frac{1}{4}$ in.; the second, $\frac{3}{8}$ in.; and the third, $\frac{1}{2}$ in. If she continues this pattern, what size will go in the fifth section?

MORE PRACTICE Lesson 12.4, page H62

PERPLEXING POLYGON

PURPOSE To practice determining if one figure is similar to another (pages 232–234)

Work with a partner. There are five groups of similar rectangles in the figure at the right. One group has three similar rectangles and four groups have two similar rectangles. There is one rectangle left over.

At the same time, you and your partner try to find the groups of similar rectangles. The first one to find all five groups is the winner.

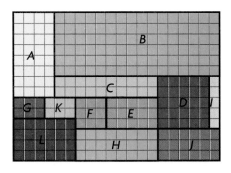

SHARK SIGHTING

PURPOSE To practice making scale drawings (pages 236–238)

YOU WILL NEED tangram pattern, ruler

Use the tangram pieces to make the shark shown at the right. Then use the scale 2 in. = 1 in. to make an enlarged scale drawing of the shark.

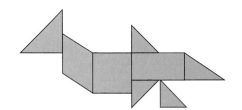

 Make different tangram animals with your family. Show your family how to make a scale drawing of the animals.

BUILDING BLOCKS

PURPOSE To practice recognizing similar solid figures (pages 241–243)

YOU WILL NEED centimeter cubes, isometric dot paper

Use the indicated number of centimeter cubes to make a figure similar to the given figure. Check all corresponding sides to make sure they are proportional. Draw the similar figure on isometric dot paper.

1. 27 cubes   **2.** 16 cubes   **3.** 24 cubes

CHAPTER 12 REVIEW

EXAMPLES

EXERCISES

- **Identify similar figures and scale factors.**
  (pages 232–234)

Is rectangle *A* similar to rectangle *B*?

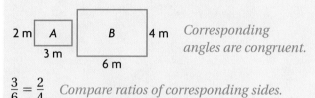

Corresponding angles are congruent.

$\frac{3}{6} = \frac{2}{4}$ *Compare ratios of corresponding sides.*

Rectangle *A* is similar to rectangle *B*.

1. **VOCABULARY** The ? for similar figures is the common ratio of the pairs of corresponding sides.

Tell whether the figures in each pair are similar. Write *yes* or *no*. If *no*, explain.

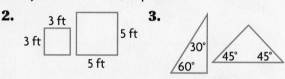

- **Make scale drawings.** (pages 236–238)

Scale: 1 in. = 2.5 mi

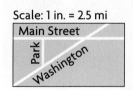

Main Street: 7.5 mi

$7.5 \div 2.5 = 3$ *Divide by 2.5.*

Main Street would be 3 in. on the scale drawing.

The scale of a scale drawing is $\frac{3}{8}$ in. = 1 ft. Find the length of the measurement on the scale drawing.

4. 12 ft   5. 40 ft   6. 10 ft

If the scale is 1 cm = 20 m, find the length each measurement would be on a scale drawing.

7. 80 m   8. 125 m   9. 50 m

- **Recognize self-similarity.** (pages 239–240)

Since each smaller rectangle is similar to a larger rectangle, this figure shows self-similarity.

Tell whether the figure shows self-similarity. If it does, write the similarity ratio.

10. 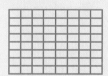   11.

- **Identify similar solid figures.** (pages 241–243)

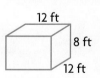

Corresponding angles are congruent.

$\frac{3}{12} = \frac{3}{12} = \frac{2}{8} = 0.25$

Ratios of corresponding sides are equal.

The solid figures are similar.

Write the ratios of corresponding sides as decimals. Then tell whether the objects in each pair are similar. Write *yes* or *no*.

12. 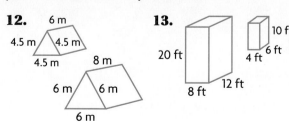   13.

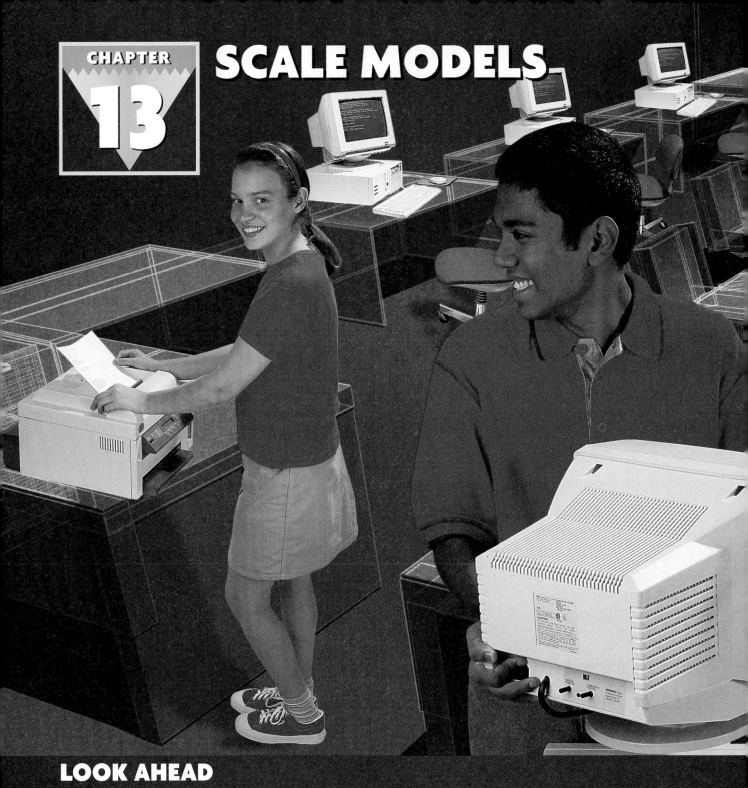

CHAPTER 13
SCALE MODELS

LOOK AHEAD

In this chapter you will solve problems that involve

- relating scale models, scale factors, and proportions
- making scale models with cubes and paper
- making scale models of triangular prisms and cylinders

Design Lab

Suppose your school is planning a new computer lab to house 30 computers and 12 printers in a room 50 ft × 30 ft. Draw a floor plan. Scale your model to fit an $8\frac{1}{2}$ × 11 in. sheet of paper.

YOU WILL NEED: ruler, scissors, glue or tape

ACTUAL DIMENSIONS

Lab	30 ft × 50 ft
Computer	20 in. wide × 28 in. deep
Printer	20 in. × 20 in.

Plan
- Work with a small group. Draw a floor plan of the computer lab. Include the computers and printers.

Act
- Decide on a scale factor. Convert all actual dimensions using the scale factor.
- Draw the floor plan. Cut out templates for the computers and printers.
- Put the templates on the floor plan.

Share
- Present your floor plan to the class.

DID YOU

- ✓ Decide on a scale factor?
- ✓ Convert actual dimensions?
- ✓ Complete the floor plan?
- ✓ Present your floor plan to the class?

COMPUTER LAB

WHAT YOU'LL LEARN
How scale factors relate scale models to objects

WHY LEARN THIS?
To understand how the size of a model you build is related to the size of the real object

WORD POWER
scale model

Scale Models and Scale Factors

A **scale model** is a proportional model of a solid, or three-dimensional, object. You may have seen scale models in hobby stores or toy stores. Some 3-D puzzles are scale models of real buildings.

A scale model can be the same size as the real object. However, like scale drawings, most scale models are either reductions or enlargements. For example, a 24-in. model of a human ear is an enlargement, but a 24-in. model of the adult human skeleton is a reduction.

To understand how a scale model is related to the real object, you need to know the scale factor. Recall that a scale factor is a ratio for pairs of corresponding sides of similar figures.

History Link

Dinosaurs roamed the Earth during most of the 180 million years of the Mesozoic era. If a time line has a scale of 1 cm = 10 million years, how long is the portion that shows the Mesozoic era?

EXAMPLE A hobby store has scale models of various dinosaurs. What scale factor relates a 20-in. scale model to an 80-ft apatosaurus?

Write the scale as a ratio.

$$20 \text{ in.}:80 \text{ ft} \qquad 20 \text{ in. to } 80 \text{ ft} \qquad \frac{20 \text{ in.}}{80 \text{ ft}}$$

$$\frac{20 \text{ in.}}{80 \text{ ft}} = \frac{1 \text{ in.}}{4 \text{ ft}} \qquad \textit{Write the ratio in simplest form.}$$

To find the scale factor, change one of the measurements of the ratio, if you need to, so that both use the same unit of measure.

$$\frac{1 \text{ in.}}{4 \text{ ft}} = \frac{1 \text{ in.}}{48 \text{ in.}} = \frac{1}{48} \qquad \textit{Change feet to inches.}$$
$$\textit{4} \times \textit{12 in.} = \textit{48 in.}$$

So, the scale factor relating the toy to the apatosaurus is $\frac{1}{48}$. One unit on the model represents 48 units on the apatosaurus.

• What if the model is 40 in. long? What scale factor relates the model to the 80-ft apatosaurus?

Copy and complete the table. Tell whether the scale model is *reduced, enlarged,* or the *same size* as the real object.

1.

Scale Factor	between 0 and $\frac{1}{1}$	$\frac{1}{1}$	greater than $\frac{1}{1}$
Scale Model	?	same size	?

2. Is the shape of a scale model different from the shape of the real object? Explain.

Change both measurements to inches, and write the ratio in simplest form.

3. 18 in.:5 ft   4. 36 in.:3 yd   5. 3 in.:10 yd   6. 10 ft:24 in.   7. 50 ft:1 in.

Write *enlarged* or *reduced* to describe the scale model made with the given scale.

1. 1 in.:18 in.   2. 1 yd:1 ft   3. 50 cm:1 cm   4. 1 in.:1 ft.

5. 25 in.:1 in.   6. 1 in.:3 ft   7. 100 m:1 cm   8. 6 in.:100 ft

Change both measurements to the same unit of measure, and find the scale factor.

9. 15-in. model of a 30-ft yacht

10. 24-in. model of a 66-ft rocket

11. 1-ft model of a 1-in. fossil

12. 6-in. model of a 6-ft sofa

13. 2-ft model of a 30-yd sports field

14. 4-ft model of a 6-yd whale

15. 24-in. model of the 1,250-ft Empire State Building

16. 4-in. model of a 1-cm computer chip (HINT: 1 cm ≈ 0.4 in.)

Problem-Solving Applications

17. A scientist wants to build a model, reduced 11,000,000 times, of the moon revolving around the Earth. Will the scale 48 ft:100,000 mi give the desired reduction? Explain. (HINT: 1 mi = 5,280 ft)

18. **CRITICAL THINKING** The museum was given a full-size scale model of the Skylab space station for public display. What scale factor was used?

19. Wally has an 18-in. model of a 42-ft dinosaur, the tyrannosaurus. What scale factor is used?

20. **WRITE ABOUT IT** Explain how you can tell whether a scale factor will make an enlarged scale model or reduced one.

WHAT YOU'LL LEARN
How to use scale
factors in proportions

WHY LEARN THIS?
To find the
measurements needed
for a scale model

ALGEBRA CONNECTION

Scale Models and Proportions

Scale models appear in many places. Some models are simple. Others are very detailed. In this lesson you will see different scale models of houses.

Each week Carlos and Samantha volunteer to read stories to a kindergarten class. For the story *Snow White and the Seven Dwarfs*, they want to make a simple scale model of the cottage for the children to paint and decorate.

After finding the plans for a real cottage shown below, Carlos and Samantha decide to use a scale of 2 in. to 3 ft.

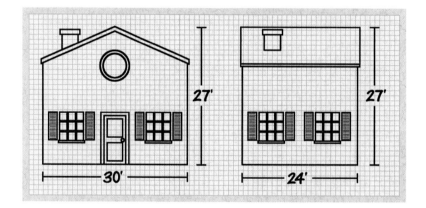

Talk About It

• What does a scale of 2 in. to 3 ft mean?

• What supplies will Samantha and Carlos need to make the scale model of the cottage?

What measurements should they use for the length, width, and height of their scale model?

To find the measurements for their scale model, follow these steps.

Step 1: Find the scale factor.

$$\frac{2 \text{ in.}}{3 \text{ ft}} = \frac{2 \text{ in.}}{36 \text{ in.}}, \text{ or } \frac{1 \text{ in.}}{18 \text{ in.}} \qquad \textit{Express both terms in the same unit.}$$

The scale factor is $\frac{1}{18}$.

Step 2: Write and solve a proportion for each dimension.

Let l = the length of the model in inches.

scale factor $\rightarrow \dfrac{1}{18} = \dfrac{l}{360} \leftarrow \dfrac{\text{length of scale model in inches}}{\text{length of real cottage in inches}}$

$18l = 1 \times 360$ *Find the cross products.*

$l = \dfrac{360}{18}$ *Solve.*

$l = 20$

The model will be 20 in. long.

Let w = the width of the model in inches.

scale factor $\rightarrow \dfrac{1}{18} = \dfrac{w}{288} \leftarrow \dfrac{\text{width of scale model in inches}}{\text{width of real cottage in inches}}$

$18w = 1 \times 288$ *Find the cross products.*

$w = \dfrac{288}{18}$ *Solve.*

$w = 16$

The model will be 16 in. wide.

Let h = the height of the model in inches.

scale factor $\rightarrow \dfrac{1}{18} = \dfrac{h}{324} \leftarrow \dfrac{\text{height of scale model in inches}}{\text{height of real cottage in inches}}$

$18h = 1 \times 324$ *Find the cross products.*

$h = \dfrac{324}{18}$ *Solve.*

$h = 18$

So, the scale model is 20 in. long, 16 in. wide, and 18 in. high.

—————————————————

Career Link

People in many different occupations need to know how to read blueprints and floor plans of buildings. What occupations can you think of in which people need to have that skill?

If you know the dimensions of an object and the scale factor, you can find the dimensions of a scale model.

EXAMPLE   At Tobu World Square, a theme park in Nikko, Japan, there are more than 100 scale models of world-famous landmarks $\frac{1}{25}$ the size of the originals. Using this scale factor, how high would a scale model of a 6-ft-tall person be?

Let h = the height of the scale model in inches.

scale factor $\rightarrow \dfrac{1}{25} = \dfrac{h}{72} \leftarrow \dfrac{\text{height of scale model in inches}}{\text{height of 6-ft person in inches}}$

$25h = 1 \times 72$ *Find the cross products.*

$h = \dfrac{72}{25}$ *Solve.*

$h = 2.88 \leftarrow$ Scale model would be 2.88 in. high,
              or about $2\frac{7}{8}$ in. high.

251

GUIDED PRACTICE

Regina bought a scale-model house for her N-gauge model railroad, whose scale factor is $\frac{1}{160}$. For Exercises 1–3, find the dimensions of a matching real house in inches and in feet and inches.

1. The scale model is $1\frac{1}{4}$ in. long and $1\frac{1}{2}$ in. wide. Find the full-size length and width.

2. At the highest point, the scale model measures 3 in. Find the full-size height.

3. The front door of the model is $\frac{1}{4}$ in. wide and $\frac{1}{2}$ in. high. Find the full-size width and height.

INDEPENDENT PRACTICE

Use the scale factor 12 in.:32 ft to find the unknown measurement.

1. model: _?_ in.
   actual: 64 ft

2. model: _?_ in.
   actual: 8 ft

3. model: _?_ in.
   actual: 10 ft

4. model: _?_ in.
   actual: 124 ft

5. model: 36 in.
   actual: _?_ ft

6. model: 12 in.
   actual: _?_ ft

7. model: 80 in.
   actual: _?_ ft

8. model: 2 in.
   actual: _?_ ft

Use the scale factor 14 in.:42 ft to find the unknown measurement.

9. model: _?_ in.
   actual: 84 ft

10. model: _?_ in.
    actual: 6 ft

11. model: 10 in.
    actual: _?_ ft

12. model: 14 in.
    actual: _?_ ft

13. model: _?_ in.
    actual: 126 ft

14. model: 4 in.
    actual: _?_ ft

Problem-Solving Applications

An artist made a small reproduction of a famous house. Her scale model has a width of 5 in., and the real house has a width of 25 ft.

15. Find the scale factor.

16. The height of the model is 6 in. Find the height of the real house in inches and feet.

17. The front door of the model is $1\frac{1}{4}$ in. high. Find the height of the real door in inches and in feet and inches.

18. A window of the model is 1 in. wide. Find the width of the real window in inches and in feet and inches.

19. ▬ **WRITE ABOUT IT** The scale factor for a model is $\frac{1}{48}$. If the real object is 40 ft high, how can you find the scale model's height in inches?

In **Mighty Math Cosmic Geometry** you can go to *Geo Academy* and visit *Similarity, Congruency, and Scale*. Share what you know about scale models!

MORE PRACTICE Lesson 13.2, page H63

Using Cubes to Model

Centimeter cubes can be used as building blocks for scale models of various solid figures, including larger cubes.

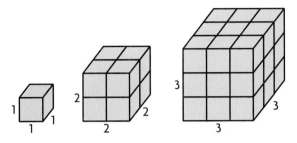

1-cm cube $1 \times 1 \times 1 = 1$ cube
Each edge is 1 cm.

2-cm cube $2 \times 2 \times 2 = 8$ cubes
Each edge is 2 cm.

3-cm cube $3 \times 3 \times 3 = 27$ cubes
Each edge is 3 cm.

The 2-cm and 3-cm cubes are enlarged scale models of the 1-cm cube. You can compare the linear dimensions, volumes, and related scale factors of the cubes. The volume of a 1-cm cube is 1 cm^3.

Model	Comparison with 1-cm Cube	Scale Factor
2-cm cube	Linear dimensions: 2 times as large, or 200%	$\frac{2}{1}$
	Volume: $2 \times 2 \times 2$, or 8 times as large	$\frac{8}{1}$
3-cm cube	Linear dimensions: 3 times as large, or 300%	$\frac{3}{1}$
	Volume: $3 \times 3 \times 3$, or 27 times as large	$\frac{27}{1}$

• **CRITICAL THINKING** For the 2-cm and the 3-cm cubes, how is the scale factor for volume related to the corresponding scale factor for dimensions?

• For a 4-cm cube, how are the scale factors for linear dimensions and volume related?

REMEMBER:
....
Linear dimensions are measurements of distances or of lengths, widths, and heights of objects. **See page H25.**

Volume is the number of cubic units needed to fill the space occupied by a solid figure. **See page H25.**

253

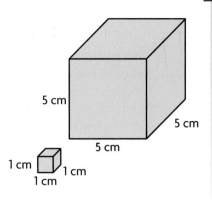

5 cm
5 cm
5 cm

1 cm
1 cm
1 cm

EXAMPLE Suppose a 5-cm cube is built from 125 small cubes, each 1 cm. How does a 1-cm cube compare with the 5-cm cube?

There are different ways to compare the similar cubes.

$$\frac{1\text{-cm cube}}{5\text{-cm cube}} = \frac{1}{5} \quad \textit{ratio of corresponding edges}$$

$$\frac{1\text{-cm cube}}{5\text{-cm cube}} = \frac{1}{125} \quad \textit{ratio of volumes}$$

The scale factors that relate the 1-cm cube to the 5-cm cube are $\frac{1}{5}$ for the linear dimensions and $\frac{1}{125}$ for the volumes.

- How do the linear dimensions and volume of a 1-cm cube compare with those of a 10-cm cube? with those of a 6-cm cube?

ACTIVITY

WHAT YOU'LL NEED: 1-cm cubes—110 for each group

Work with a group.

- Make a figure like the one shown at the left, using three 1-cm building blocks. Now build an enlarged scale model, using a scale factor of $\frac{2}{1}$ for the linear dimensions.

- How many cubes are in your enlargement?

- How do the linear dimensions and volume of the scale model compare with those of the original figure?

The figure shown at the left is a reduced scale model, built with four 1-cm building cubes and a linear scale factor of $\frac{1}{3}$.

- Use cubes to build the larger, original figure on which this figure was modeled.

- How many cubes are in the larger figure?

- How do the linear dimensions and volume of the figure you built compare with those of the scale model?

GUIDED PRACTICE

Find how many 1-cm cubes are needed to build the given figure. Then find the two scale factors that relate the linear dimensions and volume to those of a 1-cm cube.

1. 4-cm cube **2.** 6-cm cube **3.** 8-cm cube **4.** 10-cm cube

For each given cube, an enlarged scale model is built using a scale factor of $\frac{3}{1}$. Find the length of the model and the number of 1-cm cubes used to build it.

1. 2-cm cube   **2.** 3-cm cube   **3.** 4-cm cube   **4.** 5-cm cube

For each given cube, a reduced scale model is built using a scale factor of $\frac{1}{2}$. Find the length of the model and the number of 1-cm cubes used to build it.

5. 4-cm cube   **6.** 6-cm cube   **7.** 8-cm cube   **8.** 12-cm cube

A box measures 12 cm × 4 cm × 8 cm, and a scale model of it is built using the given scale factor. Find the dimensions of the model, and find the number of 1-cm cubes used to build it.

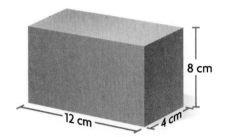

9. $\frac{1}{2}$ **10.** $\frac{1}{4}$ **11.** $\frac{3}{4}$

Problem-Solving Applications

12. CRITICAL THINKING Five 1-cm cubes are used to build a solid. How many cubes are used to build a scale model of the solid with a linear scale factor of 2 to 1? The arrangement of the cubes does not matter.

13. ✏️ **WRITE ABOUT IT** If the linear scale factor of a model is $\frac{1}{2}$, what is the relationship between the volumes of the original and the model?

Mixed Review

Find the perimeter of the regular polygon. The length of each side is given.

14. square, 4 m   **15.** triangle, 3 in.   **16.** pentagon, 2.4 in.   **17.** octagon, 3.5 m

Tell whether the figures in each pair are similar. If they are not, tell why.

18. 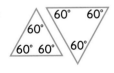   **19.** 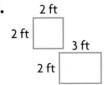   **20.**   **21.**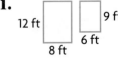

22. CUSTOMARY UNITS Mary bought 4 oz of chocolate stars, 5 oz of peanut clusters, and 11 oz of caramels. The candy cost $3.99 per pound. How much did she spend? (HINT: 16 oz = 1 lb)

23. CHOOSE A STRATEGY Ron saved $43 for a surfboard that costs $323. If he saves $35 a week, in how many weeks will he have enough money?

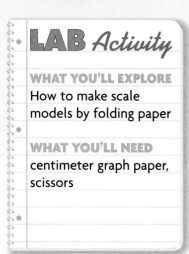

COOPERATIVE LEARNING

Making a Scale Model

LAB Activity

WHAT YOU'LL EXPLORE
How to make scale models by folding paper

WHAT YOU'LL NEED
centimeter graph paper, scissors

You can use different materials to make scale models of rectangular prisms. One of the easiest and least expensive ways is by folding strips of graph paper.

You can fold a 2-cm × 8-cm strip of paper into different models of open rectangular prisms. One way is to make a prism that is 2 cm × 3 cm × 1 cm, as shown.

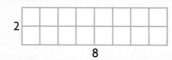

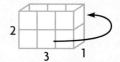

Explore

• Work with a partner to make a 2-cm × 2-cm × 2-cm open cube. Think about how big the paper strip must be and where the strip should be folded.

• Make an enlarged scale model in which each dimension of your first cube is doubled.

• Fold a third strip of centimeter graph paper to make a scale model that is larger than your second cube.

Think and Discuss

• What size of paper strip did you use for each cube?

• How did you fold each strip to make the cube?

• What scale factors relate the linear dimensions of each of your scale models to those of the 2-cm cube?

• How do the volumes of your scale models compare with the volume of the 2-cm cube?

Try This

• Use the paper-folding method to make a scale model of a cardboard carton that is 24 cm long, 16 cm wide, and 8 cm high. Use a linear scale factor of $\frac{1}{8}$.

• **CRITICAL THINKING** Make the largest possible open cube by using a strip of paper cut from one sheet of centimeter graph paper.

 *Technology* Link

E–Lab • Activity 13 Available on CD-ROM and the Internet at http://www.hbschool.com/elab

Scale Models of Other Solid Figures

WHAT YOU'LL LEARN
How to make scale models of pyramids and cylinders

WHY LEARN THIS?
To make models of larger and smaller objects

Scale models are not limited to rectangular prisms. You can make scale models of other solid figures, such as triangular prisms and cylinders. All scale models have corresponding dimensions proportional.

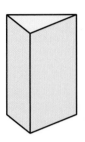   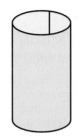

REMEMBER:

A triangular prism is a solid figure in which all five faces are polygons: two are congruent and parallel triangular bases, and three are parallelograms. **See page H23.**

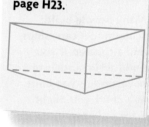

EXAMPLE   A stone monument is in the shape of a triangular prism. The sides of the triangular base are 3 ft, 4 ft, and 5 ft, and the height is 8 ft. For a 4-in.-high paper scale model of this monument, how long should the paper be? What will the widths of the faces be?

Follow these steps to find the widths of the faces of a 4-in.-high scale model.

Step 1: Find the scale factor.

$$\frac{4 \text{ in.}}{8 \text{ ft}} = \frac{4 \text{ in.}}{96 \text{ in.}}, \text{ or } \frac{1 \text{ in.}}{24 \text{ in.}}$$

The scale factor is $\frac{1}{24}$.

Step 2: Find the length the paper should be.

3 ft + 4 ft + 5 ft = 12 ft = 144 in.   *Find the actual perimeter.*

$\frac{1}{24} \times$ 144 in. = 6 in.   *Multiply by the scale factor.*

The length of the paper should be 6 in.

3 ft

4 ft

8 ft

5 ft

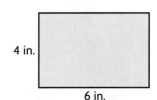

4 in.

6 in.

Step 3: Find the widths of the faces.

$\frac{1}{24} \times 36$ in. $= 1\frac{1}{2}$ in.

$\frac{1}{24} \times 48$ in. $= 2$ in.

Multiply the width of each side of the actual monument by the scale factor.

$\frac{1}{24} \times 60$ in. $= 2\frac{1}{2}$ in.

The widths of the faces of the scale model are $1\frac{1}{2}$ in., 2 in., and $2\frac{1}{2}$ in.

Cylinders

The following activity will help you learn more about making scale models of solid figures.

ACTIVITY

WHAT YOU'LL NEED: 4-in. $\times$ 6-in. index card, $8\frac{1}{2}$-in. $\times$ 11-in. sheet of paper, tape, customary ruler

- Tape the ends of an $8\frac{1}{2}$-in. $\times$ 11-in. sheet of paper together to make an open cylinder. Now make another cylinder the same way, using the 4-in. $\times$ 6-in. index card. Does the small cylinder appear to be a scale model of the large cylinder? Explain.

- Write ratios to compare the widths and lengths of the paper and the index card.

$$\frac{\text{width of paper}}{\text{width of index card}} \leftrightarrow \frac{?}{?} \qquad \frac{\text{length of paper}}{\text{length of index card}} \leftrightarrow \frac{?}{?}$$

- Can you make a proportion with your ratios? Explain.

- Do your findings about the ratios support your observation about whether the smaller cylinder is a scale model of the larger cylinder? Explain.

- Cut the index card so that it is about $5\frac{1}{8}$ in. long, and then make a new cylinder. Is the new cylinder reasonably close to being a scale model of the large cylinder? Explain.

GUIDED PRACTICE

A cylinder is 48 in. tall with a circumference of 108 in. An open scale model is made using the given height. Find the scale factor and the circumference of the model.

1. model height: 4 in.

2. model height: 8 in.

3. model height: 12 in.

teen times

Many people build scale-model cars, ships, and airplanes. If you build scale models or have models you built as a child, you might want to hang on to them. Some older scale models are worth many times their original cost.

INDEPENDENT PRACTICE

The sides of a triangular prism measure 2 ft, 3 ft, and 4 ft, and the height measures 12 ft. An open scale model is made using the given height. Find the dimensions of the paper and the widths of the faces.

1. model height: 12 in.   **2.** model height: 24 in.   **3.** model height: 6 in.

For Exercises 4–5, suppose you want to make a half-size open scale model of the solid figure at the right.

4. Find the size of the paper strip you would need.

5. What would be the widths of the faces? Where would the paper strip be folded?

6. Suppose you want the scale model to have a scale factor of $\frac{2}{1}$. Find the size of the paper strip.

7. Suppose you want the scale model to have a scale factor of $\frac{1}{4}$. Find the size of the paper strip.

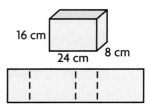

Problem-Solving Applications

8. The monument Square of the Five Towers, near Mexico City, is a group of five triangular prisms. The prisms range from 135 to 165 ft tall. Using a scale factor of $\frac{1}{60}$, find the heights, in inches, of the shortest and tallest prisms in a scale model.

9. The Pentagon in Washington, D.C., is a building shaped like a regular pentagonal prism. Its perimeter is about 1 mi. Using a scale factor of $\frac{1}{528}$, find the length, in inches, of each side of a scale model.

10. ✏️ **WRITE ABOUT IT** An architect is making a scale model of a high-rise building that is shaped like a rectangular prism. If the high-rise is 320 ft high, which scale factor—$\frac{1}{8}$, $\frac{1}{80}$, or $\frac{8}{1}$— would be the most appropriate for the model? Explain.

Mixed Review

Write = or ≠ .

11. $\frac{2}{3}$ ● $\frac{8}{12}$ **12.** $\frac{16}{20}$ ● $\frac{10}{15}$ **13.** $\frac{4}{9}$ ● $\frac{6}{18}$ **14.** $\frac{8}{10}$ ● $\frac{32}{40}$ **15.** $\frac{9}{27}$ ● $\frac{2}{6}$

Tell whether the rectangular prisms are similar. Write *yes* or *no*.

16. 5 m × 4 m × 10 m; 15 m × 12 m × 30 m   **17.** 2.5 m × 3.5 m × 8.5 m; 10 m × 14 m × 16 m

18. **RATIOS** A frost killed 14,000 acres out of 20,000 acres of vegetables. What percent of the crop was lost?

19. **NUMBER SENSE** The sum of 4 plus a number is equal to 6 minus the number. What is the number?

CULTURAL CONNECTION

CO OPERATIVE LEARNING

Roman Art to Scale

Anthony's grandfather used to be an architect in Rome. With his grandfather's help, Anthony will make a scale model of a Roman house to show what it looked like in 100 B.C. The Roman house measured 15 m × 25 m. The model will need to be 75 cm × 125 cm. What is the scale factor for the model?

Write ratios to compare the model to the house.

75 cm : 15 m   75 cm to 15 m $\frac{75 \text{ cm}}{15 \text{ m}}$

125 cm : 25 m   125 cm to 25 m $\frac{125 \text{ cm}}{25 \text{ m}}$

Write the ratio in simplest form.

$\frac{75 \text{ cm}}{15 \text{ m}} = \frac{5 \text{ cm}}{1 \text{ m}}$ $\frac{125 \text{ cm}}{25 \text{ m}} = \frac{5 \text{ cm}}{1 \text{ m}}$

Change meters to centimeters. $1 \times 100 \text{ cm} = 100 \text{ cm}$

$\frac{5 \text{ cm}}{1 \text{ m}} = \frac{5 \text{ cm}}{100 \text{ cm}} = \frac{1}{20}$

The scale factor for the model is $\frac{1}{20}$.

Work Together

1. Anthony made square floor tiles for the model house he and his grandfather are building. The length of the sides of the tiles is 2.5 cm. Using the scale factor $\frac{1}{20}$, what was the length of a tile in the Roman house?

2. There are two circular pillars, one on each side of the door that leads from the house to the garden. The actual pillars have a height of 4 m. The diameter of the pillars is 0.4 m. Use the scale factor for the house, 1 cm : 20 cm, to make a paper model of one of the pillars.

3. A statue of the Roman ruler Augustus is 6 ft tall. Anthony will use the scale of $\frac{3}{4}$ in. : 1 ft to make a model of the statue of Augustus. What will be the height of the model of the statue?

CULTURAL LINK

A Roman farm house or villa served as a retreat or summer home for city dwellers. Remains of garden spaces, swimming pools, and rooms for bathing have been uncovered. Elegant features such as designed floor tiles, atriums in the center of the house, and lavish wall decorations show the lifestyle of the Romans.

EXAMPLES

- **Use scale factors to relate scale models to objects.** (pages 248–249)

Find the scale factor relating a 36-in. model to the 984-ft Eiffel Tower.

$\dfrac{36 \text{ in.}}{984 \text{ ft}} = \dfrac{3 \text{ in.}}{82 \text{ ft}}$ *Write the scale as a ratio.*
Write in simplest form.

$\dfrac{3 \text{ in.}}{82 \text{ ft}} = \dfrac{3 \text{ in.}}{984 \text{ in.}} = \dfrac{1}{328}$ *Change to same unit of measure and simplify.*

- **Use proportions with scale factors.** (pages 250–252)

Use the scale factor of $\frac{1}{24}$ to find h.

$\dfrac{1}{24} = \dfrac{h}{96}$ ← height of scale model in inches / height of real object in inches

$24h = 1 \times 96$ *Find the cross products and solve.*

$h = 4$ *The height is 4 in.*

- **Make scale models from cubes.** (pages 253–255)

How many 1-cm cubes are needed to build a 4-cm cube? Compare these similar cubes.

$4 \times 4 \times 4 = 64$ cubes *Each edge is 4 cm.*

ratio of edges: *ratio of volumes:*

$\dfrac{1\text{-cm cube}}{4\text{-cm cube}} = \dfrac{1}{4}$ $\dfrac{1\text{-cm cube}}{4\text{-cm cube}} = \dfrac{1}{64}$

- **Make scale models of other solid figures.** (pages 257–259)

Find the length of the paper needed to make a 7-in.-high open scale model of a triangular prism. The sides of the base are 6 ft, 8 ft, and 10 ft, and the height is 14 ft.

$\dfrac{7 \text{ in.}}{14 \text{ ft}} = \dfrac{7 \text{ in.}}{168 \text{ in.}}$, or $\dfrac{1}{24}$ *Find the scale factor.*

$6 \text{ ft} + 8 \text{ ft} + 10 \text{ ft} = 24 \text{ ft}$ *Find the actual*
$= 288 \text{ in.}$ *perimeter.*

$\dfrac{1}{24} \times 288 \text{ in.} = 12 \text{ in.}$ *Multiply by the scale factor.*

EXERCISES

1. **VOCABULARY** A proportional model of a solid, or three-dimensional, object is called a ?.

Change to one unit of measure, and find the scale factor.

2. 6-ft statue to an 8-in. replica
3. 18-in. model to a 264-ft submarine

Use the scale factor of 18 in.:24 ft to find the unknown measurement.

4. model: ? in.   5. model: ? in.
   actual: 4 ft   actual: 18 ft

6. model: 6 in.   7. model: 9 in.
   actual: ? ft   actual: ? ft

For the given linear scale factor and the given cube, find the length of a scale model and the number of 1-cm cubes needed to build it.

8. scale factor: $\frac{1}{4}$ 9. scale factor: $\frac{1}{8}$
   4-cm cube   24-cm cube

10. scale factor: $\frac{4}{1}$ 11. scale factor: $\frac{5}{1}$
    2-cm cube   3-cm cube

The sides of the base of a triangular prism measure 3 ft, 4 ft, and 5 ft, and the height measures 8 ft. For an open scale model, find the dimensions of the paper and the widths of the sides.

12. model height: 8 in.
13. model height: 24 in.
14. model height: 32 in.
15. model height: 16 in.

PROPORTIONS, EQUATIONS, AND PERCENTS

LOOK AHEAD

In this chapter you will solve problems that involve

- finding a percent of a number
- finding a number when a percent of it is known

- finding the percent one number is of another
- estimating with percents

Team-Up Project

Patch by Patch

Quilt block patterns are composed of a balance of light, medium, and dark shades to create different effects. Analyze the Z block and ZZ block patterns. How does the percent of light, medium, and dark tones affect their overall design?

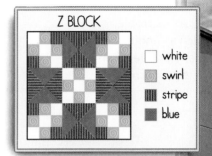

Z BLOCK
- white
- swirl
- stripe
- blue

Plan
- Work with a small group. Separate the Z block and ZZ block into nine patches each. Look at the patterns in each block. Then find the percent each pattern is of each block.

Act
- Write the fraction each pattern is of one Z block and one ZZ block.
- Write each fraction as a percent.
- Suppose a quilt is made up of five Z blocks and four ZZ blocks. Find the percent each pattern is of the whole quilt.

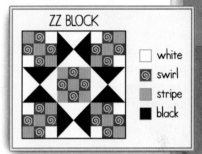

ZZ BLOCK
- white
- swirl
- stripe
- black

Share
- Compare your findings with another group. Discuss the effect a change in the tones of the patterns would have on each block's design.

DID YOU

- ☑ Write each pattern as a fraction?
- ☑ Write each fraction as a percent?
- ☑ Find the percent each pattern is of the whole quilt?

Finding a Percent of a Number

You can use two-color counters to model the percent of a number when working with *friendly* percents and numbers.

ACTIVITY

WHAT YOU'LL NEED: 20 two-color counters

Place 10 yellow counters in a row to represent 100%.

- How many counters would you turn over to make 10% red? 50% red? 30% red?

- Can you make 25% of the counters red? Explain.

Now place 20 yellow counters in two rows to represent 100%.

- How many counters would you turn over to make 50% red? 30% red?

- Can you make 25% of the counters red? Explain.

———————————————

Another way to find a percent of a number is to change the percent to a fraction or a decimal and then multiply.

EXAMPLE 1   Nick answered 85% of the 40 problems on his test correctly. How many problems did Nick answer correctly?

Change 85% to a fraction.   Change 85% to a decimal.

$85\% = \frac{85}{100} = \frac{17}{20}$ *Simplify.* $85\% = 0.85$

$\frac{17}{20} \cdot 40 = \frac{17}{20} \times \frac{40}{1}$ *Multiply.* $0.85 \times 40 = 34$ *Multiply.*

$\qquad\quad = \frac{17}{20} \times \frac{40}{1}$

$\qquad\quad = \frac{34}{1}$, or 34

So, Nick answered 34 problems correctly.

To find the percent of a number, you can also write and solve an equation or a proportion. Sometimes it is easier to solve the equation if you use a fraction instead of a decimal.

EXAMPLE 2 Of the 60 students who took the math test, $33\frac{1}{3}\%$ thought it was easy and $66\frac{2}{3}\%$ thought it was hard. How many students thought the test was easy?

Let n = the number of students who thought the test was easy.

Equation	**Proportion**

What is $33\frac{1}{3}\%$ of 60?
  ↓ ↓   ↓

$n = 33\frac{1}{3}\% \cdot 60$

$n = \frac{1}{3} \cdot 60$

$n = 20$

$33\frac{1}{3}$ is to 100 as what number is to 60?

$\dfrac{33\frac{1}{3}}{100} = \dfrac{n}{60}$ *Find cross products.*

$100 \cdot n = 60 \cdot 33\frac{1}{3}$

$100n = 2{,}000$ *Solve.*

$n = 20$

So, 20 students thought the test was easy.

• What fraction is equivalent to $66\frac{2}{3}\%$?

• Use an equation or a proportion to find the number of students who thought the test was hard.

Sometimes percents are greater than 100%. With a percent greater than 100%, a percent of a number will be greater than the original number.

EXAMPLE 3 Find 175% of 80, using an equation and a proportion.

Equation	**Proportion**

What is 175% of 80?

$n = 1.75 \times 80$ *Change percent to decimal.*
$n = 140$

175 is to 100 as what number is to 80?

$\dfrac{175}{100} = \dfrac{n}{80}$ *Find cross products.*

$100 \cdot n = 80 \cdot 175$

$100n = 14{,}000$ *Solve.*

$n = 140$

So, 175% of 80 is 140.

• What is 240% of 50?

Science Link

Geneticists, scientists who study inherited characteristics, often use percents when describing large populations. Suppose that in a cross between two hybrid tall plants, 25% of the offspring are short plants. How many short plants would you expect if the total number of offspring is 392?

Use a model or mental math to solve.

1. 25% of 80   **2.** 50% of 300   **3.** 80% of 250   **4.** 20% of 1,000

INDEPENDENT PRACTICE

Write an equation for the problem. Then solve.

1. Find 25% of 200.   **2.** Find 5% of 90.   **3.** Find $66\frac{2}{3}$% of 180.

Write a proportion for the problem. Then solve.

4. Find 7% of 400.   **5.** Find 75% of 360.   **6.** Find 125% of 56.

Find the percent of the number.

7. 150% of 900   **8.** 15% of 900   **9.** 1.5% of 900   **10.** 15% of 90

11. 80% of 65   **12.** 12% of 250   **13.** 225% of 84   **14.** 54% of 60

15. 2.5% of 120   **16.** 55.5% of 90   **17.** $33\frac{1}{3}$% of 51   **18.** $66\frac{2}{3}$% of 642

Problem-Solving Applications

19. There were 120 questions on the science test. Darla answered 87.5% of the questions correctly. How many questions did Darla answer correctly?

20. Krista's starting pay was $5.20 per hour. After six months she was given a 5% increase. How much per hour was Krista's raise?

21. Dean's automobile insurance premium will increase by 5% next year. If Dean's premium is $955 this year, by how much will it increase next year? What will the premium be next year?

22. ✏️ **WRITE ABOUT IT** Is 13.2 a reasonable answer for 150% of 88? Explain.

Mixed Review

Write the fraction as a percent.

23. $\frac{1}{4}$ **24.** $\frac{4}{5}$ **25.** $\frac{12}{15}$ **26.** $\frac{3}{8}$ **27.** $\frac{8}{5}$ **28.** $\frac{13}{4}$

Write *enlarged* or *reduced* to describe the scale model made with the given scale.

29. 1 in.:12 in.   **30.** 3 yd:1 ft   **31.** 4 m:2 cm   **32.** 1 mm:10 cm

33. **ESTIMATION** George ran the 100-yd dash. Each of his strides was about $3\frac{4}{5}$ ft. Estimate the number of strides he took.

34. **SEQUENCES** Find the next two terms of the sequence.

$^-$3, 9, $^-$27, 54

MORE PRACTICE Lesson 14.1, page H64

Finding the Percent One Number Is of Another

Sometimes you want to find what percent one number is of another number. When the numbers are friendly, you can use mental math.

There are 30 students enrolled in Mr. Perez's math class. He will postpone a chapter test if more than 25% of his class is absent. There were 6 students absent on test day. Did Mr. Perez postpone the test?

$$\frac{\text{students absent}}{\text{all students}} = \frac{6}{30} = \frac{1}{5} = 20\% \leftarrow \text{Think of the ratio as a percent.}$$

Since only 20% of the students were absent, Mr. Perez did not postpone the test.

• If there were 25 students in the class and 8 were absent, would Mr. Perez postpone the test? Explain.

When the numbers are not friendly, you can use an equation or a proportion to find what percent one number is of another.

EXAMPLE 1 The stem-and-leaf plot shows the scores for the 24 students who took the test. What percent of the students who took the test scored 90 or above?

Look at the plot. Seven of the students scored 90 or above.

Test Scores

Stem	Leaves
4	2
5	8
6	2 4 8
7	0 4 6 8 8
8	0 2 4 4 8 8 9
9	0 2 2 4 6
10	0 0

Equation

What percent of 24 is 7?

$$\begin{array}{ccc} \downarrow & \downarrow & \downarrow \\ n & \cdot\ 24 = & 7 \end{array}$$

$n \cdot 24 = 7$

$24n = 7$

$n = \dfrac{7}{24}$

$n \approx 0.2917$, or about 29%

Proportion

What number is to 100 as 7 is to 24?

$$\frac{n}{100} = \frac{7}{24}$$

$24 \cdot n = 100 \cdot 7$

$24n = 700$

$n \approx 29.17$, or about 29

$$\frac{29}{100} = 29\%$$

So, about 29% of the students scored 90 or above.

Sometimes one number is greater than 100% of another number.

EXAMPLE 2   Joan started a savings account last year with a deposit of $150. She now has $270 in the account. What percent of Joan's original deposit is the amount she now has in her account?

Equation	**Proportion**

Equation

What percent of 150 is 270?

$$n \cdot 150 = 270$$

$$150n = 270$$

$$n = \frac{270}{150}$$

$n = 1.8$, or 180%   *Change decimal to percent.*

Proportion

What number is to 100 as 270 is to 150?

$$\frac{n}{100} = \frac{270}{150}$$

$$150 \cdot n = 100 \cdot 270$$

$$150n = 27,000$$

$$n = 180$$

$$\frac{180}{100} = 180\%$$

So, $270 is 180% of $150.

• What percent of 16 is 40?

Talk About It   💡 CRITICAL THINKING

• When is a number greater than 100% of another number?

• When is a number less than 100% of another number?

• When is a number more than 200% of another number?

GUIDED PRACTICE

Tell whether the answer will be greater than or less than 100%.

1. What percent of 5 is 3?   **2.** What percent of 78 is 42?

3. What percent of 5 is 15?   **4.** What percent of 78 is 79?

5. 72 is what percent of 36?   **6.** 299 is what percent of 350?

Some percent problems are best solved with a calculator.

EXAMPLE 3   Cindy has a savings certificate that pays 5.877% interest per year. This year she earned $38.10 in interest. What was the value of the certificate?

38.10 .05877 | 648.28994 |

So, Cindy's certificate had a value of $648.29.

📟 **Calculator Activities, page H33**

Write an equation for the problem. Then solve.

1. What percent of 72 is 18?

2. 6 is what percent of 9?

3. What percent of 45 is 90?

4. 4 is what percent of 50?

Write a proportion for the problem. Then solve.

5. What percent of 36 is 18?

6. 16 is what percent of 40?

7. What percent of 25 is 40?

8. 2 is what percent of 16?

Solve by using any method.

9. What percent of 60 is 48?

10. 90 is what percent of 120?

11. What percent of 140 is 175?

12. 15 is what percent of 75?

13. 75 is what percent of 15?

14. What percent of 48 is 96?

15. 14 is what percent of 42?

16. What percent of 14 is 42?

17. What percent of 120 is 63?

18. 50 is what percent of 60?

19. What percent of 200 is 350?

20. 0.75 is what percent of 60?

Copy and complete.

21. Since 9 is 15% of 60,

18 is ___% of 60.

27 is ___% of 60.

90 is ___% of 60.

22. Since 8 is 5% of 160,

8 is ___% of 80.

8 is ___% of 40.

8 is ___% of 20.

23. Since 20 is 200% of 10,

20 is ___% of 20.

20 is ___% of 40.

20 is ___% of 80.

Problem-Solving Applications

For Problems 24–27, use the results of the achievement test that Kyle took.

24. Complete the last column to show the percent of the items that were correct on each section of Kyle's test.

25. How many items in all were on the test? How many were correct?

26. What percent of all the items on Kyle's test were correct?

27. ✏️ **WRITE ABOUT IT** Describe two ways to solve Problem 26.

ACHIEVEMENT TEST			
Section	Number Correct	Number of Items	Percent Correct
Reading	9	10	?
Vocabulary	12	16	?
Spelling	23	25	?
Math Computation	12	18	?
Math Reasoning	4	10	?

Modeling to Find a Number When a Percent of It Is Known

You can use decimal squares to model some percent problems.

Explore

27 is 30% of what number?

• Use a 1×10 decimal square. Represent 30%. Since $30\% = \frac{3}{10}$, shade 3 of the sections. The model shows that if 3 sections equal 27, then each 10% section represents 9.

• If 10% is 9, what is 100%? 27 is 30% of what number?

Think and Discuss

• To find 20% of what number is 70, how many sections of a 1×10 decimal square would you shade? What number would each 10% section represent?

• Describe how to use a decimal square to find a number when 40% of it is 80.

Try This

Use decimal squares to find the number.

15 is 20% of what number?   280 is 50% of what number?

16 is 80% of what number?   2.4 is 60% of what number?

Technology Link ▶
E–Lab • Activity 14 Available on CD-ROM and the Internet at http://www.hbschool.com/elab

Finding a Number When a Percent of It Is Known

WHAT YOU'LL LEARN
How to find a number when a percent of it is known

WHY LEARN THIS?
To solve problems such as finding the total earnings when you know the percent that is saved

In the third type of percent problem, you find a number when you know a percent of the number.

You can use mental math with a model to solve problems with friendly numbers.

EXAMPLE 1 On weekends Bradley works at the Pizza Palace. Each week he saves $15 from his earnings for his college fund. This represents 25% of his weekly earnings. How much money does Bradley earn each week?

25% → $15   50% → $30   100% → $60

If 25% is $15, then 50% is $30, and 100% is $60. So, Bradley earns $60 each week.

• One week Bradley worked more hours and saved $18 as 25% of his earnings. How much did Bradley earn that week?

You can use an equation or a proportion to solve problems with numbers that are not friendly.

EXAMPLE 2 Ashley spent 17% of the money in her savings account to buy a pair of in-line skates. The skates cost $89.59. How much did Ashley have in her account before she bought the skates?

Equation	**Proportion**

17% of what number is 89.59?
  ↓   ↓   ↓
17% × n = 89.59
$0.17 \times n = 89.59$
$0.17n = 89.59$
$\dfrac{0.17n}{0.17} = \dfrac{89.59}{0.17}$
$n = 527$

17 is to 100 as 89.59 is to what number?

$$\frac{17}{100} = \frac{89.59}{n}$$
$17 \times n = 89.59 \times 100$
$17n = 8{,}959$
$n = 527$

So, Ashley had $527 in her account before she bought the skates.

EXAMPLE 3 Jared shared $33\frac{1}{3}\%$ of his supply of bubble gum with his teammates. He gave out 17 pieces of bubble gum. How many pieces of bubble gum did he have left?

First find the amount of bubble gum Jared had before he shared with his teammates.

Equation	Proportion
$33\frac{1}{3}\%$ of what number is 17?	$33\frac{1}{3}$ is to 100 as 17 is to what number?

Equation

$$33\frac{1}{3}\% \text{ of what number is } 17?$$

$$\frac{1}{3} \cdot n = 17$$

$$\frac{1}{3}n = 17$$

$$\frac{1}{3}n \div \frac{1}{3} = 17 \div \frac{1}{3}$$

$$n = 17 \div \frac{1}{3}$$

$$n = 51$$

Proportion

$$33\frac{1}{3} \text{ is to } 100 \text{ as } 17 \text{ is to what number?}$$

$$\frac{33\frac{1}{3}}{100} = \frac{17}{n}$$

$$33\frac{1}{3} \cdot n = 17 \cdot 100$$

$$33\frac{1}{3}n = 1,700$$

$$33\frac{1}{3}n \div 33\frac{1}{3} = 1,700 \div 33\frac{1}{3}$$

$$n = 1,700 \div 33\frac{1}{3} = 51$$

So, Jared had 51 pieces of bubble gum before he shared.

Think: If Jared shared $33\frac{1}{3}\%$ of the gum, then he has $100\% - 33\frac{1}{3}\%$, or $66\frac{2}{3}\%$, left. So, he has $66\frac{2}{3}\%$ of 51 pieces of bubble gum left.

$$66\frac{2}{3}\% \times 51 = \frac{2}{3} \times 51 = 34$$

So, Jared had 34 pieces of bubble gum left.

• Note that $2 \times 17 = 34$. Explain.

GUIDED PRACTICE

Write an equation and a proportion for the problem.

1. 18% of what number is 30?   **2.** 30% of what number is 95?

3. 65% of what number is 82?   **4.** 4 is 45% of what number?

5. 56 is 75% of what number?   **6.** 124 is 5% of what number?

INDEPENDENT PRACTICE

Write an equation for the problem. Then solve.

1. 85% of what number is 68?   **2.** 77 is 25% of what number?

3. 56% of what number is 39.2?   **4.** 51 is 6% of what number?

Write a proportion for the problem. Then solve.

5. 10% of what number is 55?

6. 24 is 15% of what number?

7. 180% of what number is 6?

8. 14 is $33\frac{1}{3}$% of what number?

Solve.

9. 75% of what number is 66?

10. 74 is 37% of what number?

11. 15% of what number is 24?

12. 75.4 is 130% of what number?

13. 26.8 is 4% of what number?

14. 75% of what number is 75?

15. 372 is 93% of what number?

16. 7% of what number is 58.1?

17. 16% of what number is 0.32?

18. 6 is 250% of what number?

19. 1% of what number is 2,300?

20. 12.75 is 15% of what number?

In *Mighty Math Astro Algebra* you can go to *Cargo Bay* and complete *A Buying Frenzy* mission to find a number when the percent is known.

Copy and complete.

21. Since 1% of 600 is 6,
2% of ___ is 6.
4% of ___ is 6.
8% of ___ is 6.

22. Since 100% of 240 is 240,
50% of ___ is 240.
25% of ___ is 240.
10% of ___ is 240.

23. Since 5% of 80 is 4,
10% of ___ is 4.
20% of ___ is 4.
40% of ___ is 4.

Problem-Solving Applications

24. There were 352 students at Maple Middle School who bought a school lunch on Friday. This represents 55% percent of the students who were in school that day. How many students were in school on Friday?

25. During basketball practice Shawn made 32 free throws. He made $66\frac{2}{3}$% of the free throws he attempted. How many free throws did Shawn attempt during practice?

26. Mrs. Plocar earns $679.00 a week. She has budgeted 15% of her weekly earnings for food. Last week she went food shopping three times and spent $45.00, $27.50, and $42.50. Did Mrs. Plocar stay within her food budget last week? Explain.

27. ✏️ **WRITE ABOUT IT** Write a percent problem that you could solve by using this equation:

$$0.65 \times n = 300$$

ALGEBRA CONNECTION

Estimating with Percents

You have solved the three types of percent problems by using models with mental math, equations, and proportions.

Three Types of Percent Problems	
1. Finding a percent of a number	35% of 140 = n
2. Finding the percent one number is of another	n% of 140 = 49
3. Finding a number when a percent of it is known	35% of n = 49

Sometimes when you are working with percents, you do not need an exact answer. You may need only an estimate. There are several ways you can estimate with percents.

To estimate when finding a percent of a number, you can use multiples of 10%.

EXAMPLE 1 Ski jackets are on sale for 40% off the regular price, and goggles are on sale for 15% off the regular price. About how much will you save during the sale if you buy a jacket that has a regular price of $79 and goggles that have a regular price of $42?

Estimate: 40% of 79 is about what number?

Think: 40% is 4 × 10%.
  10% of 79 is about 8.

So, 40% of 79 is about 32.

Estimate: 15% of 42 is about what number?

Think: 10% of 42 is about 4.
  5% of 42 is about 2.

So, 15% is about 4 + 2, or 6.

So, you will save about $32 + $6, or about $38, if you buy both the jacket and the goggles on sale.

Talk About It 💡CRITICAL THINKING

• How would you use multiples of 10% to estimate a 15% tip for a meal that cost $58?

• How would you use multiples of 10% to estimate 28% of 610?

• If you know 10% of a number, how can you find 60% of the number? 35% of the number? 5% of the number?

Explain how you would use multiples of 10 to estimate the number. Then give the number.

1. 20% of 493   **2.** 15% of $162   **3.** 35% of 81 students

4. 60% of $1,475   **5.** 25% of 494 books   **6.** 55% of 810

7. 50% of 989   **8.** 35% of 198 cats   **9.** 1% of $20,500

10. 45% of 610   **11.** 5% of 306   **12.** 95% of $148

Another way to estimate with percents is to use compatible numbers and mental math. This technique can be used with all three types of percent problems.

EXAMPLE 2 Ski boots are on sale for 25% off the regular price. About how much will Neil pay for ski boots that had an original price of $158.99?

Estimate: 25% of 158.99 is about what number?

158.99 is about 160. $25\% = \frac{1}{4}$

$\frac{1}{4}$ of 160 = 40   *Find the discount.*

160 − 40 = 120   *Subtract the discount from the original price.*

Another Method There is another way to estimate how much Neil will pay for the ski boots. First, think of the original price of the boots as 100%.

original price − amount of discount = sale price

100%   −   25%   = 75%

The sale price is 75% of the original price.

$$75\% = \frac{3}{4}$$

$$\frac{3}{4} \times 160 = 120$$

So, Neil will pay about $120 for the ski boots.

• Which of these two methods do you prefer to use to estimate the price of Neil's boots? Explain your choice.

• Snow skis are 25% off. About what is the sale price of snow skis that had an original price of $195.99?

275

EXAMPLE 3 Amy saved $9.75 on the purchase of a pair of ski mittens that originally cost $31.99. About what percent of the original price did she save?

Estimate: About what percent of 31.99 is 9.75?

$\frac{9.75}{31.99}$ is about $\frac{1}{3}$,   or $\frac{9.75}{31.99}$ is about $\frac{3}{10}$.

$\frac{1}{3} = 33\frac{1}{3}\%$ $\frac{3}{10} = 30\%$

So, two different estimates for the amount Amy saved are $33\frac{1}{3}\%$ and 30%.

• Which ratios are nearly equivalent to these percents: 23%, 52%, 65%, 13%, 74%?

EXAMPLE 4 Everything on the bargain table is $66\frac{2}{3}\%$ off the original price. Bryan found a pair of ski pants on the bargain table with a sale price of $42.25. About what was the original price of the ski pants?

Think: If the pants are $66\frac{2}{3}\%$ off, they cost $33\frac{1}{3}\%$ of the original price.

Estimate: $33\frac{1}{3}\%$ of about what number is 42.25?

$33\frac{1}{3}\% = \frac{1}{3}$; 42.25 is about 40.

Think: $\frac{1}{3}$ of what number is 40?

$\frac{1}{3}$ of 120 is 40.

So, the original price of the ski pants was about $120.

Restaurants only have to pay servers about 40% of the minimum wage that workers are entitled to by law. The rest will come from tips. If the minimum wage is $5.15 per hour, a server needs to make about $25.00 in tips during an 8-hr day to earn an amount equal to the minimum wage.

INDEPENDENT PRACTICE

Choose the best estimate. Write *a, b,* or *c.*

1. 10% of 61.4
  a. 0.6
  b. 6
  c. 60

2. 50% of 29.85
  a. 3
  b. 12
  c. 15

3. $35\frac{1}{2}\%$ of 92
  a. 30
  b. 3
  c. 45

4. 75% of $238.99
  a. $150
  b. $180
  c. $230

5. 65% of $298.99
  a. $20
  b. $100
  c. $200

6. 105% of $776.50
  a. $80
  b. $900
  c. $800

Write the common, or friendly, ratio that is nearly equivalent to the percent.

7. 24%   **8.** 9.5%   **9.** 61%   **10.** 35%   **11.** 49%   **12.** 77%

Write the common, or friendly, percent that is nearly equivalent to the ratio.

13. $\frac{26}{51}$ **14.** $\frac{42}{160}$ **15.** $\frac{14}{18}$ **16.** $\frac{21}{99}$ **17.** $\frac{31}{90}$ **18.** $\frac{98}{101}$

Estimate the number.

19. 50% of 297 is about what number?

20. 25% of 1,925 is about what number?

21. About what number is 77% of 95?

22. About what number is 10.5% of 88?

Estimate the percent.

23. About what percent of 73 is 24?

24. About what percent of 42 is 31?

25. 88 is about what percent of 180?

26. 9.1 is about what percent of 21?

Estimate the number.

27. 48 is 20% of about what number?

28. 795 is 50% of about what number?

29. 61 is 74% of about what number?

30. 98 is 26% of about what number?

Problem-Solving Applications

31. Mr. Mills has spent $145.55 of the $300.00 he budgets for food each month. About what percent of his monthly allotment has he spent?

32. Yesterday 294 books were checked out of the library. This is only 42% of the number usually checked out in a day. About how many books are usually checked out in a day?

33. Of the 1,050 students at Longmeadow Middle School, 48% ride the bus to school. About how many students ride the bus to school?

34. **WRITE ABOUT IT** Explain how you can estimate 1%, 10%, and 100% of 3,051.

Mixed Review

Find the amount you would save if you bought the item at the sale price.

35. original price: $57; sale price: $49

36. original price: $89.99; sale price: $45.59

Use the scale of 2 in.: 5 ft to find the unknown measurement.

37. _?_ in. = 30 ft   **38.** _?_ in. = 85 ft   **39.** _?_ in. = 29 ft   **40.** _?_ in. = 124 ft

41. **AVERAGES** Sharon scored a 98, 89, and 92 on her first three tests. What must her scores average on the last two tests for an overall average of 95?

42. **NUMBER SENSE** The ages of Mike, Juan, and Anna are all prime numbers. The product of their ages is 1,001. What are their ages?

MATH FUN!

POPULAR LETTERS

PURPOSE To practice finding the percent one number is of another (pages 267–269)

YOU WILL NEED index cards, 26 letter cards with A–Z written on them

Work with a partner or a small group. Each player writes two topics such as sports or pizza on two different index cards. Put the topic cards and the letter cards in two different piles. Draw one topic card and write three sentences about that topic. Then, count the total number of letters in the sentences.

Next, draw a letter card. Count the number of times the letter appears in the sentences. Find the percent the drawn letter is of the total number of letters. The player with the greatest percent earns 1 point. The first player to reach 5 points is the winner.

HOME NOTE Challenge your family to a game of Popular Letters.

ESTIMATION GAME

PURPOSE To practice estimating with percents (pages 274–277)

YOU WILL NEED index cards, two sets of number cards each numbered 0–9

Work with a partner or a small group. Put the two sets of number cards in two different piles. Draw two cards from the first pile. This represents a percent. Draw three cards from the second pile. This represents a number.

Each player estimates the percent of the number.

EXAMPLE Draw 1: 0 and 8   Draw 2: 7, 8, and 2

Estimate 8% of 782.

Find the exact answer with a calculator. The player with the estimate closest to the actual number earns 5 points. The first player to reach 50 points is the winner.

PUZZLING PERCENTS

PURPOSE To practice solving percent problems (pages 262–279)

Solve the percent problems and match the letter with the answer to find the secret sentence.

A What number is 20% of 200?
F What percent of 175 is 7?
H 5% of what number is 3?
I 18% of 50 is what number?

M 7 is what percent of 140?
N 13 is 50% of what number?
S What number is 95% of 40?
T What percent of 500 is 5?
U 75% of what number is 9?

___ ___ ___ ___ ___ ___ ___ ___ ___!
5% 40 1% 60 9 38 4% 12 26

EXAMPLES

- **Find a percent of a number.** (pages 264–266)

What number is 35% of 60?

Equation

$n = 0.35 \times 60$

$n = 21$

Proportion

$\dfrac{35}{100} = \dfrac{n}{60}$

$100 \cdot n = 35 \cdot 60$

$100n = 2{,}100$

21 is 35% of 60. → $n = 21$

- **Find the percent one number is of another.**
  (pages 267–269)

What percent of 50 is 12.5?

Equation

$n \times 50 = 12.5$

$50n = 12.5$

$n = 0.25$

Proportion

$\dfrac{n}{100} = \dfrac{12.5}{50}$

$50 \cdot n = 12.5 \cdot 100$

$50n = 1{,}250$

$n = 25$

So, 12.5 is 25% of 50.

- **Find a number when you know a percent of it.**
  (pages 271–273)

150% of what number is 90?

Equation

$1.5 \times n = 90$

$1.5n = 90$

$n = 60$

Proportion

$\dfrac{150}{100} = \dfrac{90}{n}$

$150 \cdot n = 90 \cdot 100$

$150n = 9{,}000$

$n = 60$

So, 150% of 60 is 90.

- **Estimate with percents.** (pages 274–277)

24% of 238.99 is about what number?

24% is about 25%; 238.99 is about 240.

$25\% \text{ of } 240 = \dfrac{1}{4} \times 240 = 60$

So, 24% of 238.99 is about 60.

EXERCISES

Find the number.

1. What number is 25% of 180?
2. What number is 5% of 200?
3. What number is 120% of 950?
4. 12.5% of 64 is what number?
5. 0.5% of 350 is what number?

Find the percent.

6. What percent of 72 is 36?
7. What percent of 48 is 18?
8. What percent of 17 is 68?
9. 3 is what percent of 600?
10. 0.25 is what percent of 2?

Find the number.

11. 37% of what number is 74?
12. 180% of what number is 45?
13. 58% of what number is 145?
14. 34 is 100% of what number?
15. 1.14 is 0.6% of what number?
16. 0.8 is 200% of what number?

Estimate the percent or the number.

17. 48% of 159 is about what number?
18. About what percent of 148 is 51?
19. 15% of about what number is 61?
20. 75% of $39.99 is about what number?

LOOK AHEAD

In this chapter you will solve problems that involve

- modeling percents of increase and decrease
- determining commission and total pay

- finding the amount of tax due
- computing simple and compound interest

Team-Up Project

Disappearing Act

Scientists say the measure of how completely salt dissolves is solubility. Solubility is affected by temperature. Table salt is called sodium chloride, or NaCl. A salt substitute is potassium chloride, or KCl.

Plan
- Work with a small group. Find the percent of increase or decrease in the solubility of NaCl and KCl at each temperature compared to their solubility at room temperature.

Act
- Room temperature is 20°C. Find the difference in solubility at each temperature compared to room temperature.
- Use a calculator. Calculate the percent of increase or decrease in solubility for each temperature compared to room temperature.
- Record your results. Make a double-line graph.

Share
- Compare your results with another group.

SOLUBILITY CHART

TEMPERATURE (°C)	NaCl (grams that dissolved in 100g of water)	KCl (grams that dissolved in 100g of water)
0°	35.7	28.0
10°	35.7	31.2
20°	35.8	34.2
30°	36.1	37.0
50°	36.8	42.9
80°	38.0	51.2
100°	39.2	56.3

DID YOU

☑ Find the difference in solubility?

☑ Find the percent of increase or decrease?

☑ Make a double-line graph?

☑ Compare with another group?

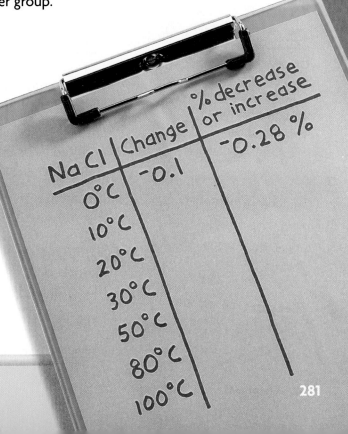

NaCl	Change	% decrease or increase
0°C	-0.1	-0.28 %
10°C		
20°C		
30°C		
50°C		
80°C		
100°C		

Percents of Increase and Decrease

WHAT YOU'LL LEARN
How to find the percent of increase or decrease

WHY LEARN THIS?
To determine how prices for some items change over time

WORD POWER
percent of increase
percent of decrease

How can you model percents of increase and decrease?

ACTIVITY

WHAT YOU'LL NEED: two 3-in. × 5-in. cards, scissors, ruler

• Shade one side of each card. Let the area of each card represent 100%.

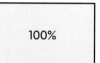

• Cut one card into 4 equal parts. What percent of the card is represented by each part?

• Use the shaded side of a whole card and 1 of the 4 equal shaded parts to model a **percent of increase** of 25%.

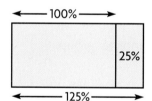

• Use the unshaded side of a whole card and 3 of the 4 equal shaded parts to model a **percent of decrease** of 25%.

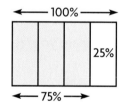

• How would you use the cards to model a percent of increase of 50%? a percent of decrease of 50%?

• Into how many equal pieces would you cut a card if you wanted to use it to show a decrease of 20%? How many of your equal pieces would you use to show a decrease of 20%?

You can use percents of increase and decrease when you shop to help you see the change in price.

REMEMBER:

One way to write a ratio as a percent is to write an equivalent ratio that has 100 as the second term.

$$\frac{1}{5} = \frac{1 \times 20}{5 \times 20} = \frac{20}{100} = 20\%$$

Another Method Write and solve a proportion.

$$\frac{0.31}{1.55} = \frac{n}{100}$$

$$1.55n = 0.31 \times 100$$

$$1.55n = 31$$

$$n = 20, \text{ or } 20\%.$$

See pages H16 and H18.

EXAMPLE 1   Lorin works in a store that is having a special on Nike® sneakers. Nike sneakers with an original cost of $100 now sell for $70. Find the percent of decrease in the price.

$100 - 70 = 30$ *Find the amount of decrease.*

$$\frac{\text{amount of decrease}}{\text{original amount}} = \frac{30}{100} = 30\% \leftarrow \text{The percent of decrease is 30\%.}$$

EXAMPLE 2 During the sale the average number of pairs of Nike® sneakers sold per day increased from 40 to 68. Find the percent of increase.

$68 - 40 = 28$ *Find the amount of increase.*

$\dfrac{\text{amount of increase}}{\text{original amount}} = \dfrac{28}{40}$ *Write a ratio comparing the amount of increase with the original amount.*

$\dfrac{28}{40} = \dfrac{7}{10} = \dfrac{70}{100} = 70\%$ *Write the ratio as a percent.*

So, the percent of increase is 70%.

• Is a change from an average sale of 68 pairs of sneakers to an average sale of 40 pairs a 70% decrease? Explain.

GUIDED PRACTICE

Write *I* or *D* to tell if there is an increase or a decrease. Then write the amount of the increase or decrease.

1. 40 to 55   **2.** 85 to 30   **3.** $55 to $90

4. 100 to 45   **5.** $35 to $65   **6.** 87 to 97

Find the percent of increase or decrease.

7. 30 to 45   **8.** $90 to $72   **9.** $72 to $90

Using Percents of Increase and Decrease

You can use the percent of increase or decrease to find the new price or the original price of an item.

EXAMPLE 3 A year ago, T.J. bought a new computer for $1,800. Since then, there has been a 35% decrease in the price. What is the new price of the computer?

Think: To find the new price, you need to know the amount of decrease. Let n = the amount of decrease.

35% of 1,800 is what number?

$0.35 \times 1,800 = n$ *Use an equation, and write the percent as a decimal.*

$\qquad\quad 630 = n$

amount of decrease: $630

$\$1,800 - \$630 = \$1,170$ *Subtract the amount of decrease from the original price.*

So, the new price of the computer is $1,170.

Consumer Link

Most sports-shoe companies pay athletes to endorse their products. Some fans see the endorsements and buy the shoes, often at higher prices than shoes without endorsements. Suppose plain basketball shoes cost $85 and similar shoes that an NBA star endorses cost $102. What is the percent of increase?

REMEMBER:
....
You can use an equation or a proportion to find the percent of a number. **See page H19.**

EXAMPLE 4   The Sportstore marked down the price of all its in-line skates by 15%. What was the original price for a pair of skates that is now selling for $136?

Think: Because the skates were marked down 15%, they now cost 85% of the original price. Let n = the original price.

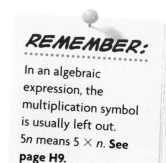

Use an equation.

85% of what number is 136?

$0.85n = 136$

$\dfrac{0.85n}{0.85} = \dfrac{136}{0.85}$

$n = 160$

Use a proportion.

$\dfrac{85}{100} = \dfrac{136}{n}$

$85n = 136 \cdot 100$

$85n = 13{,}600$

$n = 160$

So, the original price for the skates was $160.

• What was the amount of decrease?

• A different pair of in-line skates is now selling for $119. What was the original price for this pair of skates?

Talk About It 💡 CRITICAL THINKING

• How can you use a percent to represent a new cost that is half the original cost?

• Is it possible to have a percent of increase of more than 100%? Explain.

• Is it possible to have a percent of decrease of more than 100%? Explain.

INDEPENDENT PRACTICE

Find the amount of increase or decrease.

1. original price: $200
new price: $250

2. original cost: $16
new cost: $12

3. original sales: $8,000
new sales: $9,600

4. original earnings: $1,050
new earnings: $1,155

5. original savings: $1,000
new savings: $500

6. original amount: 500
new amount: 1,000

Find the percent of increase or decrease to the nearest percent.

7. original amount: 125
new amount: 160

8. original sales: $45
new sales: $55

9. original cost: $8.80
new cost: $17.60

10. original price: $62.50
new price: $22.50

11. original cost: $6.29
new cost: $5.99

12. original amount: 800
new amount: 716

Find the missing number.

13. original price: $500
new price: __?__
20% increase

14. original amount: 140
new amount: __?__
50% increase

15. original cost: $88
new cost: __?__
50% decrease

16. original amount: __?__
new amount: 230
15% increase

17. original sales: __?__
new sales: $273
30% decrease

18. original price: __?__
new price: $4.20
5% increase

19. original amount: $2,000
new amount: __?__
100% decrease

20. original sales: __?__
new sales: $29,700
1% decrease

21. original cost: $15,000
new cost: __?__
5% decrease

Problem-Solving Applications

22. When the game Candy Land® was introduced in 1949, it sold for $0.95. Today the game sells for $5.99. What is the percent of increase in the price?

23. The game Monopoly® sold for $2.50 when it was introduced in 1935. Today the game sells for $10.99. What is the percent of increase?

24. When the Etch-A-Sketch® toy was introduced in 1960, it sold for $3.98. Since then, there has been a 176% increase in its price. What is the current price?

25. Today you can buy a Slinky® for $1.99. This represents a 99% increase in price since 1945. How much did the Slinky sell for in 1945?

26. When Game Boy® was introduced, it sold for $99. In 1996 you could buy a Game Boy for $54. What was the percent of decrease in the price?

27. During a sale the price of a computer game was decreased by 50%. By what percent must the sale price be increased to restore the original price?

28. ◖▬▶ **WRITE ABOUT IT** Use mental math to find the percent of increase from 80 to 100 and the percent of decrease from 100 to 80.

Mixed Review

Solve for *x*.

29. $20x = 8$

30. $0.25x = 15$

31. $6(3) + 2 = x$

32. $9 - 2(0.5) = x$

Find the percent.

33. 20% of 200

34. 35% of 150

35. 82% of 75

36. 40% of $49.95

37. **MENTAL MATH** Ms. Chen baked chocolate cakes for a cake sale. She put $\frac{1}{3}$ of a cake in the freezer. Of the remaining $\frac{2}{3}$, she gave away $\frac{1}{2}$. Then she put the rest of the cake in the freezer. How much of the cake was in the freezer?

38. **CONSUMER MATH** Tomatoes are packaged in two different ways at the store. A 2-lb package of tomatoes costs $1.55. A 5-lb package costs $3.75. Which package has the lower unit cost?

MORE PRACTICE Lesson 15.1, page H65

Commission

Some salespeople are paid a commission rather than a salary. What is a commission?

A **commission** is a fee paid to a person who makes a sale. The commission is usually a percent of the selling price. The percent is called the **commission rate**.

Karina Pearce works in an appliance store. She is paid a 5% commission rate on all appliances that she sells. What is her commission on the sale of a television set that costs $369?

commission = commission rate × total sales

To find the commission, you can write and solve an equation. Let c = the amount of commission.

5% × 369 = c	*Write an equation.*
0.05 × 369 = c	*Write the percent as a decimal.*
18.45 = c	*Solve for c.*

So, Karina Pearce's commission is $18.45.

• Suppose the commission rate is 8%. Find the commission on a $675 refrigerator.

Other salespeople are paid a commission plus a regular salary. Their total pay is a percent of the sales they make plus a salary.

total pay = commission + salary

EXAMPLE 1   Josh Lee earns a weekly salary of $300 and a 6% commission on his sales. Last week his sales totaled $3,500. What was his total pay?

Think: To find the total pay, p, write and solve an equation.

6% × 3,500 + 300 = p	*Write an equation.*
0.06 × 3,500 + 300 = p	*Write the percent as a decimal.*
210 + 300 = p	*Multiply to find the commission.*
510 = p	*Add to find the total pay.*

So, Josh Lee's total pay was $510.

Find the commission.

1. commission rate: 5%
   total sales: $200

2. commission rate: 6%
   total sales: $1,500

Find the total pay.

3. commission rate: 3%
   total sales: $1,800
   salary: $250

4. commission rate: 2%
   total sales: $25,000
   salary: $400

Finding the Commission Rate

You can use the commission and the selling price to find the commission rate.

EXAMPLE 2 The commission on the sale of a $1,150 video camera is $69. What is the commission rate?

Find what percent 69 is of 1,150. Let r = the commission rate.

$r \times 1,150 = 69$ *Use an* $\dfrac{69}{1,150} = \dfrac{r}{100}$ *Use a*

$\dfrac{r \times 1,150}{1,150} = \dfrac{69}{1,150}$ *equation.* $1,150r = 69 \times 100$ *proportion.*

$\qquad r = 0.06,$ or 6% $\quad 1,150r = 6,900$

$\qquad\qquad\qquad\qquad\qquad r = 6 \leftarrow \frac{6}{100} = 6\%$

So, the commission rate is 6%.

• What is the commission rate if the commission on the sale of a $950.00 video camera is $47.50?

You can find the selling price from the commission and the commission rate.

EXAMPLE 3 The commission rate is $3\frac{1}{2}$%, and the commission on a sale of software is $15.75. What is the selling price?

Think: $3\frac{1}{2}$% of what number is 15.75? Let s = the selling price.

Use an equation.   *Use a proportion.*

$0.035s = 15.75$ $\dfrac{3.5}{100} = \dfrac{15.75}{s}$

$\dfrac{0.035s}{0.035} = \dfrac{15.75}{0.035}$ $3.5s = 15.75 \cdot 100$

$\qquad s = 450$ $3.5s = 1,575$

$\qquad\qquad\qquad\qquad s = 450$

So, the selling price of the software is $450.00.

INDEPENDENT PRACTICE

Find the commission to the nearest cent.

1. total sales: $12,000
   commission rate: 2%

2. total sales: $375
   commission rate: 4%

3. total sales: $75.50
   commission rate: 3%

4. total sales: $900
   commission rate: 3.5%

5. total sales: $67.50
   commission rate: $10\frac{1}{2}$ %

6. total sales: $895.75
   commission rate: $4\frac{1}{4}$ %

Find the total pay. Round to the nearest cent when needed.

7. total sales: $350
   commission rate: 12%
   monthly salary: $175

8. total sales: $865.50
   commission rate: 5%
   monthly salary: $412

9. total sales: $7,525
   commission rate: 6%
   monthly salary: $125

10. total sales: $2,500
    commission rate: 5.5%
    monthly salary: $350

11. total sales: $1,985
    commission rate: $3\frac{1}{2}$%
    monthly salary: $535

12. total sales: $35,957.75
    commission rate: $2\frac{1}{2}$%
    monthly salary: $100

In **Mighty Math Astro Algebra** you can go to *Cargo Bay* and participate in *The Great Galactic Garage Sale* mission. Bring all you know about finding the percent of a number.

Find the missing number.

13. total sales: $5,000
    commission rate: _?_
    commission: $250

14. total sales: _?_
    commission rate: 6%
    commission: $12

15. total sales: $8,300
    commission rate: _?_
    commission: $581

16. total sales: _?_
    commission rate: 8%
    commission: $61.20

17. total sales: _?_
    commission rate: 6.5%
    commission: $380.25

18. total sales: $5,920
    commission rate: _?_
    commission: $207.20

Problem-Solving Applications

19. Rob earns a monthly salary of $250 plus a commission on his total sales. Last month his total sales were $6,500, and he earned a total of $510. What is his commission rate?

20. Heather works in a clothes shop that pays a commission of 5% and no salary. What will Heather's weekly sales have to be so that she will earn $375?

21. If you sell about $5,000 worth of CDs monthly, which plan is better? Why?

    Plan A: $200 monthly salary and
            2% commission
    Plan B: no salary and 8% commission

22. ✏ **WRITE ABOUT IT** Explain the difference between being paid a commission alone and being paid a salary plus commission.

Smith-Anderson Associates
Elizabeth Hardwick
Dec. 18, 1998
Salary: $1,692.31

Dean-Gallagher, Inc.
Matthew Johnson
June 26, 1998
Salary: $849.87
Total sales: 11,982.00
Commission: 599.10
Total: $1,448.9

MORE PRACTICE Lesson 15.2, page H66

Taxes

In most places people pay tax both on the money they spend and on the money they earn. A **sales tax** is the tax on the sale of an item or a service. It is usually a percent of the purchase price and is collected by the seller.

Nathan Jackson works at a music store. Most of the CDs are priced at $11.88 each. A customer buys 2 CDs. The state sales tax rate is 6%. To the nearest cent, how much should Nathan charge for sales tax?

Music Town	
2 CDs @	$11.88
subtotal	23.76
tax	1.43
total	$25.19
Thank you!	

$2 \cdot 11.88 = 23.76$ *Multiply to find the price for 2 CDs.*

$0.06 \cdot 23.76 = 1.4256$ *Multiply by 0.06 to find the sales tax.*

$1.4256 \approx 1.43$ *Round to the nearest hundredth.*

So, Nathan should charge the customer $1.43 for sales tax.

EXAMPLE 1   Find the amount of sales tax due on 3 jazz CDs at $11.88 each and 2 CDs on sale for $4.99 each. The sales tax rate is 6%.

$(3 \cdot 11.88) + (2 \cdot 4.99) = 45.62$ *Find the total price.*

$0.06 \cdot 45.62 = 2.7372$ *Find the sales tax on this total.*

$2.7372 \approx 2.74$ *Round to the nearest hundredth.*

So, the sales tax is $2.74.

You can also find the total cost (price plus sales tax).

EXAMPLE 2   Find the total cost of the CDs in Example 1.

One way to find the total cost of the CDs is to add the total price and the tax.

$$45.62 + (0.06 \cdot 45.62) = 48.3572$$

Another Method   You can also find the total cost of the CDs by first thinking of the total price for the 5 CDs as 100%. Then for the sales tax, add 6% to the 100%. The total cost for the 5 CDs is 106% of the total price.

$$106\% \times 45.62 = 1.06 \cdot 45.62 = 48.3572$$

So, rounded to the nearest cent, the total cost is $48.36.

WHAT YOU'LL LEARN
How to find the amount of sales tax and the percent of withholding tax

WHY LEARN THIS?
To know how taxes affect the money you spend and earn

WORD POWER
sales tax
withholding tax

Real-Life Link

In some areas, the state, the county, and the city each collect a sales tax. The total sales tax rate is the sum of the individual sales tax rates. Suppose a state collects a sales tax of 4%, the county collects a 2% sales tax, and the city a 1% sales tax. What is the total sales tax rate? What would be the total cost of a phone that is priced at $69.99?

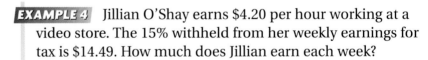

GUIDED PRACTICE

Find the amount of sales tax to the nearest cent.

1. 4% on $20   **2.** 5% on $20   **3.** 6% on $20

4. 8% on $26.98   **5.** 7% on $125.50   **6.** $5\frac{1}{2}$% on $45

Find the total cost to the nearest cent by using only one calculation.

7. 5% on $150   **8.** 7% on $12.50   **9.** $5\frac{1}{2}$% on $100

Do you earn more than $6,550 per year? If you do, you must pay income tax on your earnings greater than $6,550. Many small businesses don't withhold income tax from teens' pay because most teens don't earn more than $6,550. Most large businesses, however, withhold income tax from the pay of all employees. If tax is withheld wrongly from your pay, you can get a refund by filing a 1040EZ tax return.

A **withholding tax** is a deduction from a person's earnings as an advance payment on income tax.

EXAMPLE 3 Of the $37.80 Liu Chen earns each week, $5.67 is withheld for tax. What percent of Liu's earnings is withheld?

Think: What percent of $37.80 is $5.67? Find out by using an equation or a proportion. Let p = the percent that is withheld.

$p \cdot 37.80 = 5.67$ *Use an equation.*

$\dfrac{p \cdot 37.80}{37.80} = \dfrac{5.67}{37.80}$

$p = 0.15$

$0.15 = 15\%$

$\dfrac{p}{100} = \dfrac{5.67}{37.80}$ *Use a proportion.*

$37.80p = 5.67 \cdot 100$

$37.80p = 567$

$p = 15$

$\dfrac{15}{100} = 15\%$

So, 15% of Liu Chen's earnings is withheld for tax.

EXAMPLE 4 Jillian O'Shay earns $4.20 per hour working at a video store. The 15% withheld from her weekly earnings for tax is $14.49. How much does Jillian earn each week?

Think: 15% of what number is $14.49? Let e = the amount of Jillian's weekly earnings.

$0.15e = 14.49$ *Use an equation.*

$\dfrac{0.15e}{0.15} = \dfrac{14.49}{0.15}$

$e = 96.6$

$\dfrac{15}{100} = \dfrac{14.49}{e}$ *Use a proportion.*

$15e = 14.49 \cdot 100$

$15e = 1,449$

$e = 96.6$

So, Jillian O'Shay earns $96.60 each week.

• How would you find the number of hours Jillian works each week? How many hours does she work?

INDEPENDENT PRACTICE

Find the sales tax and the total cost to the nearest cent.

1.

New Jersey sales tax rate of 6%

2.

Indiana sales tax rate of 5%

3.

Colorado sales tax rate of 3%

4.

Nevada sales tax rate of 6.5%

5.

Virginia sales tax rate of 3.5%

6.

Texas sales tax rate of 6.25%

Copy and complete this table.

	Name	Percent Withheld for Tax	Amount Earned	Amount Withheld
7.	Martin Smith	15%	$375.50	?
8.	Maria Elena Gonzalez	15%	?	$35.20
9.	Thelma Rosser	?	$125.00	$18.75
10.	Jacob Greenberg	15%	?	$119.55

Problem-Solving Applications

For Problems 11–13, find the total cost of the purchase with a sales tax rate of 7%.

11. 4 yellow-dot specials

12. 2 red-dot specials and 1 yellow-dot special

13. 1 red-dot special and 3 green-dot specials

CD DEALS!
- RED-DOT SPECIAL $6.99
- YELLOW-DOT SPECIAL $8.99
- GREEN-DOT SPECIAL $12.99

14. Alex Bevins wants to buy a computer that is priced at $3,199.50. He can buy it in city A, which has a 7% sales tax, or in city B, which has a 5% sales tax. How much will he save if he buys it in city B?

15. ✏️ **WRITE ABOUT IT** Suppose you know the price and the sales tax rate. Explain two ways to find the total cost.

ALGEBRA CONNECTION
Simple Interest

If you borrow money from a bank, you pay interest to the bank for the use of the money. If you deposit money in a bank, the bank pays you interest for the use of your money. **Interest** is a fee paid for the use of money.

Matt James borrows $10,000 for 5 yr at a yearly interest rate of $4\frac{1}{2}\%$. How much total interest will he pay?

To find simple interest, I, use the formula $I = prt$.

$p =$ **principal**, the amount of money borrowed or invested
$r =$ **rate of interest**, the percent charged or earned
$t =$ **time** (in years) that the money is borrowed or invested

$I = prt$
$I = 10,000 \cdot 0.045 \cdot 5 \leftarrow p = 10,000; r = 4\frac{1}{2}\%,$ or $0.045; t = 5$
$I = 2,250$

So, Matt James will pay a total of $2,250 in interest.

You can find the total amount (principal + interest) that Matt James will pay in loan payments. To find the total amount, A, use the formula $A = p + I$.

EXAMPLE 1 What is the total amount that Matt James will pay?

$A = p + I$
$A = 10,000 + 2,250 \leftarrow p = 10,000; I = 2,250$
$A = 12,250$

So, the total amount that Matt James will pay is $12,250.

EXAMPLE 2 Mimi Frank deposited $2,600 in an account that has a 4% yearly interest rate. She earned $52 in interest. How long was the money invested?

$I = prt$
$52 = 2,600 \cdot 0.04 \cdot t \leftarrow I = 52; p = 2,600; r = 4\%,$ or 0.04
$52 = 104t$
$0.5 = t$

So, the money was invested for 0.5 yr, or 6 mo.

Find the interest and the total amount to the nearest cent.

1. $225 at 5% per year for 3 yr

2. $775 at 8% per year for 1 yr

3. $4,250 at 7% per year for $1\frac{1}{2}$ yr

4. $45.50 at $4\frac{1}{2}$ % per year for 2 yr

INDEPENDENT PRACTICE

Find the interest and the total amount to the nearest cent.

1. $397 at $5\frac{1}{2}$ % per year for 6 mo

2. $2,975 at $5\frac{1}{4}$ % per year for 5 yr

3. $4,000 at 6% per year for 10 yr

4. $585.50 at $7\frac{3}{4}$ % per year for 3 mo

Find the missing number.

5. interest = $90
   principal = __?__
   rate = 3% per year
   time = 6 yr

6. interest = $367.50
   principal = $1,500
   rate = __?__
   time = $3\frac{1}{2}$ yr

7. interest = $1,237.50
   principal = $45,000
   rate = $5\frac{1}{2}$ % per year
   time = __?__

Problem-Solving Applications

8. Sean King borrows $1,500 for 18 mo at 12% interest per year. How much interest will Sean King pay? What is the total amount he will pay?

9. At Thrift Bank, if you keep $675 in a savings account for 12 yr, your money will earn $486. What yearly interest rate will your money earn?

10. Deanna Morris borrowed $4,500 to buy a used car. The bank charged 12% interest per year. She paid $1,620 in interest. For what period of time did Deanna Morris borrow the money?

11. ✏️ **WRITE ABOUT IT** Which loan would cost the borrower less: $2,000 at 8% for 3 yr or $2,000 at 9.5% for 2 yr? How much less would that loan cost?

Mixed Review

Solve for x.

12. $\frac{3}{8} = \frac{x}{12}$

13. $\frac{2}{3} = \frac{x}{240}$

14. $\frac{3}{5} = \frac{x}{120}$

15. $\frac{2}{5} = \frac{x}{75}$

Solve.

16. 2 is 5% of what number?

17. 100 is 25% of what number?

18. **SPORTS** Throwing a discus is one of the competitions in the Olympic Games. A discus is circular with a radius of 11 cm. What is the area of the discus? What is the circumference? (Use 3.14 for π.)

19. **RATES** Taxi A charges $2.50 for the first mile and $0.75 for each additional mile. If taxi B has a flat rate of $1.00 a mile, which taxi has the better rate for a 10-mi ride? Explain.

ALGEBRA CONNECTION
Compound Interest

LAB Activity

WHAT YOU'LL EXPLORE

How to compute compound interest

WHAT YOU'LL NEED

graph paper, calculator or spreadsheet software

Banks often pay compound interest on money deposited. **Compound interest** is computed on both the principal and the interest previously earned. Each time the interest is computed, you earn a little more than you earned the time before.

This iteration diagram shows how compound interest is computed.

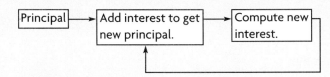

WORD POWER

compound interest
annually
semiannually
quarterly

ACTIVITY 1

Explore

• Make a table or use a spreadsheet to find the amount of money you will have if you deposit $100.00 in an account that pays 8% interest compounded annually. If interest is compounded **annually**, it is computed once a year. Continue the table to show the total amount at the end of year 10.

Year	Principal	Interest Rate	Compound Interest	Total Amount
1	$100.00	0.08	$8.00	$108.00
2	$108.00	0.08	$8.64	$116.64
3	$116.64	0.08	$9.33	$125.97
4	$125.97	0.08	$10.08	$136.05
5	$136.05	0.08	$10.88	$146.93

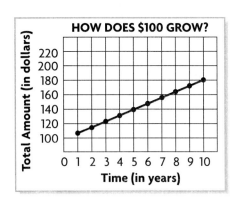

HOW DOES $100 GROW?

The graph shows the total amount you will have if you earn 8% simple interest on $100.00 for 10 years (year 1: $108, year 2: $116, and so on).

• Copy this graph. On your copy, show the total amounts you found for compound interest.

• Look at the graphs. How are simple interest and compound interest different?

Calculator Activities, page H39

Another Method You can compute compound interest by using the formula $A = p(1 + r)^n$ where $A = $ *amount* (new balance), $p = $ *principal* (amount deposited), $r = $ *rate* of interest per period, and $n = $ *number* of interest periods.

ACTIVITY 2

Explore

• Suppose you deposit $2,000 at 8% interest compounded annually. Use the formula and a calculator to compute the amount of money you will have after 15 yr.

$$A = p(1 + r)^n$$

$$A = 2,000(1 + 0.08)^{15} \leftarrow p = 2,000; r = 8\%, \text{ or } 0.08; n = 15$$

2,000 ⊠ 🄲 1 ⊞ 0.08 🄳 x^y 15 ⊟ $\boxed{6344.3382}$

So, you would have $6,344.3382, or $6,344.34.

With compound interest, the amount earned depends on how frequently the money is compounded. If interest is compounded **semiannually**, it is computed twice a year. If it is compounded **quarterly**, it is computed four times a year.

To find the rate of interest per period, divide the annual interest rate by the number of interest computations in one year. To find the number of interest periods, multiply the number of interest computations in one year times the number of years.

semiannually: $r = 8\% \div 2 = 4\%$, or $0.04; n = 30 \leftarrow 2 \times 15$

quarterly: $r = 8\% \div 4 = 2\%$, or $0.02; n = 60 \leftarrow 4 \times 15$

$A = p(1 + r)^n$

$A = 2,000(1 + 0.04)^{30}$

$A = \$6,486.80$

$A = p(1 + r)^n$

$A = 2,000(1 + 0.02)^{60}$

$A = \$6,562.06$

Think and Discuss 💡 CRITICAL THINKING

• How does the number of times the money is compounded in a year affect the money earned?

Try This

Suppose interest is compounded annually. Find the balance by using the method of your choice.

1. $60,000 at 12% for 2 yr

2. $500 at 7% for 4 yr

E–Lab • Activity 15 Available on CD-ROM and the Internet at http://www.hbschool.com/elab

CULTURAL CONNECTION

COOPERATIVE LEARNING

GREEK FESTIVALS

Folk dancing is an important part of Greek festivals. Sophia and Nicholas are members of a Greek dance group. They will perform at the Greek Festival in October. There are 10 members in their group. Last year there were only 8. What percent increase was there in the number of dancers?

Subtract to find the amount of increase.

$$10 - 8 = 2$$

Write the ratio of the amount of increase to the original amount. Rewrite the ratio as a percent.

$$\frac{\text{amount of increase}}{\text{original amount}} \rightarrow \frac{2}{8} = \frac{1}{4} = 25\%$$

The percent of increase in the number of dancers is 25%.

Work Together

1. Special events for visitors to the festival were printed on a schedule. Look at the schedule below. Find the total number of hours for each of the four different activities. What percent of the total time is allowed for each activity?

1:00 − 2:00	Greek Travel Videos	4:30 − 6:30	Greek Dancing
2:00 − 2:30	Greek Cooking	6:30 − 7:00	Greek Cooking
2:30 − 3:00	Group Performances	7:00 − 8:00	Greek Travel Videos
3:00 − 4:00	Greek Dancing	8:00 − 11:00	Greek Dancing
4:00 − 4:30	Group Performances		

2. Sophia made aprons as part of the dance costume. She spent $22 on fabric. The salesperson earned a 10% commission on the sale. What was the salesperson's commission from this sale?

3. Nicholas spent $8.56 at the festival for lunch. He bought dolmathes for $3.00, souvlakia for $2.50, fruit punch for $1.00, and baklava for $1.50. The total amount he spent included sales tax. What was the sales tax rate?

There are many Greek festivals in the United States sponsored by members of Greek organizations. Hundreds of visitors come to sample the Greek foods. During the festival, children and adults form lines for the sirtaki and other Greek folk dances. Whenever Greek families celebrate, there is singing, dancing, and bouzouki music. In the United States, Greek people share their traditions with other Americans during their festivals.

EXAMPLES

- **Find the percent of increase or decrease.**
  (pages 282–285)

  original price: $35   new price: $42

  Find the percent of increase.

  $$42 - 35 = 7$$ *Subtract to find the amount of increase.*

  $\dfrac{\text{amount of increase}}{\text{original amount}} = \dfrac{7}{35}$ *Compare increase with the original amount.*

  $\dfrac{7}{35} = \dfrac{1}{5} = 20\%$ ← percent of increase

- **Find the amount of commission and the total pay.** (pages 286–288)

  commission rate × total sales = commission
  commission + salary = total pay

  total sales: $2,500; commission rate: 5%;
  monthly salary: $300

  $0.05 \times 2,500 = 125$ ← Commission is $125.
  $125 + 300 = 425$ ← Total pay is $425.

- **Find the amount of sales tax and percent of withholding tax.** (pages 289–291)

  amount of sale: $12.50; sales tax rate: $6\frac{1}{2}\%$

  $0.065 \cdot 12.50 = 0.8125$ *Find the sales tax.*
  $\quad\quad 0.8125 \approx 0.81$ ← sales tax ≈ $0.81
  $12.50 + 0.81 = 13.31$ ← Total cost is $13.31.

- **Find simple interest and the total amount.**
  (pages 292–293)

  interest = principal × rate × time, or $I = prt$
  total amount = principal + interest, or $A = p + I$

  $$p = \$4,000 \quad r = 5\frac{1}{4}\% \quad t = 3\frac{1}{2}$$

  $4,000 \cdot 0.0525 \cdot 3.5 = 735$ *Find the interest.*
  $\quad\quad 4,000 + 735 = 4,735$ *Find total amount.*

  The interest is $735; total amount, $4,735.

EXERCISES

VOCABULARY

1. A change from 40 to 50 represents a percent of _?_ of 25%.
2. A change from 50 to 40 represents a percent of _?_ of 20%.

Find the amount of increase or decrease and the percent of increase or decrease.

3. original price: $60
   new price: $80

4. original price: $600
   new price: $360

5. total sales: $10,000; commission rate: 2%; monthly salary: $500
   Find the commission and total pay.
6. total sales: $350; commission: $14
   Find the commission rate.
7. commission: $601.25; commission rate: $3\frac{1}{4}\%$
   Find the total sales.

Find the sales tax and total cost.

8. 5% on $30
9. 7% on $6.95
10. 6% on $525
11. 10% on $15.95

Find the amount earned.

12. percent withheld: 15%
    amount withheld: $180

Find the interest and the total amount.

13. $6,500 at 4% for 2 yr
14. $475 at 12% for 6 mo
15. $2,000 at 8% for 20 yr

Find the time for the investment.

16. principal: $15,000
    rate: $8\frac{1}{4}\%$
    Interest: $618.75

17. principal: $1,200
    rate: $9\frac{1}{2}\%$
    Interest: $741

VOCABULARY CHECK

1. Figures that have the same shape but not necessarily the same size are __?__ . (page 232)

2. The common ratio of the pairs of corresponding sides of two similar figures is the __?__ . (page 233)

3. When small parts of a figure are scale drawings of the whole figure, the figure is __?__ . (page 239)

4. A fee paid to a person who makes a sale is a __?__ . (page 286)

EXAMPLES

- **Make scale drawings.** (pages 236–238)

Scale: 1 cm = 30 ft

Find how tall Building A would be in the scale drawing.

$120 \div 30 = 4$ ← Building A would be 4 cm tall.

- **Identify similar solid figures.** (pages 241–243)

Are the two solid figures similar?

Corresponding angles are congruent.

$\frac{3}{9} = \frac{1}{3} = \frac{2}{6} = 0.\overline{3}$, or $\frac{9}{3} = \frac{3}{1} = \frac{6}{2} = 3$

Ratios of corresponding sides are equal.

So, the figures are similar.

- **Make scale models of other solid figures.** (pages 257–259)

Find the length of paper to make a 6-in.-high open scale model of a triangular prism. The sides of the base are 12 ft, 16 ft, and 20 ft, and the height is 24 ft.

$\frac{6 \text{ in.}}{24 \text{ ft}} = \frac{6 \text{ in.}}{288 \text{ in.}}$, or $\frac{1}{48}$ *Find the scale factor.*

$12 + 16 + 20 = 48$ ft $= 576$ in. ← perimeter

$\frac{1}{48} \times 576$ in. $= 12$ in. ← length of paper: 12 in.

EXERCISES

The scale of a scale drawing is $\frac{1}{2}$ in. = 15 yd. Find the length of the measurement on the scale drawing.

5. 30 yd   **6.** 135 yd

7. 210 yd   **8.** 75 yd

Write the ratios of corresponding sides as decimals. Then tell whether the objects in each pair are similar. Write *yes* or *no*.

9.
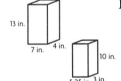

10.

The sides of a triangular prism measure 6 ft, 8 ft, and 10 ft, and the height measures 16 ft. Find the length of the paper needed to make an open scale model with the given height.

11. model height: 6 in.

12. model height: 12 in.

13. model height: 20 in.

14. model height: 10 in.

- **Find the percent one number is of another.**
  (pages 267–269)

What percent of 84 is 63?

$n \times 84 = 63$ *equation* $\quad \dfrac{n}{100} = \dfrac{63}{84}$ *proportion*

$84n = 63 \qquad\qquad 84n = 63 \times 100$

$\quad\; n = 0.75 \qquad\quad 84n = 6{,}300$

So, 75% of 84 is 63. $\qquad\quad n = 0.75$

Find the percent.

15. What percent of 56 is 14?

16. 0.8 is what percent of 1.25?

17. What percent of 40 is 110?

18. 84.6 is what percent of 235?

- **Find a number when you know a percent of it.**
  (pages 271–273)

40% of what number is 80?

$0.4 \times n = 80$ *equation* $\quad \dfrac{40}{100} = \dfrac{80}{\text{n}}$ *proportion*

$0.4n = 80 \qquad\qquad 40n = 80 \times 100$

$\quad\; n = 200 \qquad\qquad 40n = 8{,}000$

So, 40% of 200 is 80. $\qquad\quad n = 200$

Find the number.

19. 15% of what number is 84?

20. 150% of what number is 60?

21. 92 is 80% of what number?

- **Find the amount of sales tax, total cost, and percent of withholding tax.** (pages 289–291)

The 20% withheld from monthly earnings for tax is $90.68. How much is earned monthly?

$0.2e = \$90.68$ *Use an equation or a proportion.*

$\dfrac{0.2e}{0.2} = \dfrac{90.68}{0.2}$

$e = 453.40 \leftarrow \$453.40$ is earned monthly.

Find the amount earned.

22. percent withheld: 18%
    amount withheld: $239.40

23. percent withheld: 14%
    amount withheld: $119.91

Find the total cost with the given sales tax.

24. 9% on $23.00   **25.** 4% on $358.25

- **Find simple interest and the total amount.**
  (pages 292–293)

interest = principal × rate × time

$\quad ? \qquad\quad \$650 \qquad 6\% \qquad 2\ yr$

$I = 650 \times 0.06 \times 2$ *Find simple interest.*

$I = 78 \leftarrow$ Interest is $78.00

Find the simple interest.

26. *principal* = $6,4000
    rate = 7%
    time = 6 mo

PROBLEM SOLVING

27. Alice rented three videos for $2.99 each and a VCR for $6.99. The sales tax rate was 5%. What was the total cost?
(pages 289–291)

28. Ricardo borrowed $3,500 for 30 months at 11.5% interest per year. What is the total amount that he had to pay back?
(pages 292–293)

➡ Write About It

1. The actual measurements of a room are shown at the right. How long is each side on the scale drawing that uses a scale of $\frac{1}{2}$ in. = 12 ft.?
(pages 236–238)

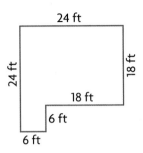

2. Use 1-cm cubes to show an enlarged scale model, using a scale factor of $\frac{3}{1}$. How many centimeter cubes are needed? (pages 253–255)

3. Write the steps you would use to find what percent of 360 is 270. (pages 267–269)

4. Explain the steps needed to solve the problem. (pages 286–288)

Andrew earns a weekly salary of $400 and a 4% commission. What was his total pay for sales of $4,000?

✔ Performance Assessment

Choose a strategy and solve. Explain your method.

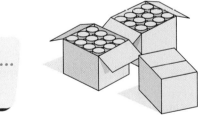

Problem-Solving Strategies
- **Find a Pattern**   • **Act It Out**   • **Write an Equation**
- **Make a Model**   • **Make a Table**   • **Draw a Diagram**

5. Paul's shadow is 4 ft long. The shadow of an oak tree is 24 ft long. If Paul is 6 ft tall, how tall is the tree? (pages 232–234)

6. Ralph is constructing a scale model of a toy building that measures 18 in. × 6 in. × 12 in. Find the dimensions of the model, and find the number of 1-in. cubes needed to build it if the scale factor is $\frac{1}{3}$. (pages 253–255)

7. A class collected 450 canned goods for a food bank. To increase that amount by 8%, how many more cans must they collect? (pages 264–266)

8. Pam earns $6.00 an hour plus commission on her total sales. She works 80 hr, sells $700 of goods, and makes $515. How much commission does she earn? What is her rate of commission? (pages 286–288)

CUMULATIVE REVIEW

Solve the problem. Then write the letter of the correct answer.

1. Estimate what percent 118 is of 301.
(pages 49–51)
   A. about 10%   **B.** about 25%
   C. about 40%   **D.** about 50%

2. Find the quotient. $^-10 \div 5$
(pages 66–68)
   A. $^-50$ **B.** $^-2$
   C. 2   **D.** 50

3. It cost the Lee family $34.00 for Internet use in November. The monthly fee is $20.00 for 20 hr plus $1.75 for each additional hour. How many hours did they use the Internet in November? (pages 126–127)
   A. 8 hr   **B.** 19 hr
   C. 28 hr   **D.** 34 hr

4. Which linear equation is represented by the graph below? (pages 160–163)

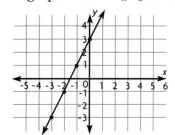

   A. $y = 2x + 3$ **B.** $y = 2x - 3$
   C. $y = 3x + 2$ **D.** $y = 3x - 2$

5. Which phrase describes an Archimedean spiral? (pages 184–186)
   A. a spiral with loops not evenly spaced
   B. a spiral with loops evenly spaced
   C. equal angles of intersection
   D. a curve in space that circles an axis

6. Find the next three terms in the sequence.
$^-48, 24, ^-12, 6, \ldots$ (pages 212–213)
   A. $0, ^-6, 12$ **B.** $3, ^-2, 1$
   C. $^-3, 1.5, ^-0.75$ **D.** $^-6, 12, ^-24$

7. The scale of a scale drawing is 1 in. = 20 ft. Find the actual measurement.
scale drawing: 9.25 in. (pages 236–238)
   A. 29.25 ft   **B.** 92.5 ft
   C. 120 ft   **D.** 185 ft

8. A candy box measures 4 in. × 6 in. × 1.5 in. A similar box measures 10 in. × 15 in. × 3.75 in. Find the ratio of the corresponding sides. (pages 241–243)
   A. 0.4 or 2.5   **B.** 0.6 or 6
   C. 2 or 2.25   **D.** 4.5 or 9

9. Aaron made a scale model of a skyscraper for class. His scale model has a height of 18 in. The real skyscraper has a height of 144 ft. What is the scale factor?
(pages 248–249)
   A. $\dfrac{1}{144}$ **B.** $\dfrac{1}{96}$
   C. $\dfrac{1}{18}$ **D.** $\dfrac{1}{8}$

10. Find the percent of the number.
165% of 80 (pages 264–266)
   A. 52   **B.** 132
   C. 185   **D.** 245

11. Ed bought a baseball card in 1994 for $3.00. Since then, the value of the card has increased 85%. What is the card worth today? (pages 282–285)
   A. $2.55   **B.** $3.55
   C. $5.55   **D.** $25.50

12. National Bank offers a simple interest rate of 8% per year. Nina puts $500 in her savings account. What will her account be worth in 15 years? (pages 292–293)
   A. $600   **B.** $1,100
   C. $3,000   **D.** $6,500

CHAPTER 16

COLLECTING DATA AND PREDICTING

LOOK AHEAD

In this chapter you will solve problems that involve

- sampling and making predictions about populations
- making appropriate displays of data

- interpolation and extrapolation of data
- predicting growth trends

Bean There, Done That

In a box of 200 candy bars, between 20 and 110 wrappers will be marked "Instant Winner." Some people will win a radio and some will win a watch. Design a data sample to predict how many will win radios and how many will win watches.

Plan
- Work with a small group. Create a simulation by marking lima beans. Trade with another group and predict the number of radio and watch winners.

Act
- Decide how many radios and watches will be won. The total number should be between 20 and 110.
- In a bag of 200 lima beans, mark each bean that represents a radio with an *X* and each bean that represents a watch with an *O*.
- Trade bags with another group. Use proportions to predict the number of radio and watch winners.

Share
- Share your results with the other group. See how close you came to the actual numbers.

DID YOU

☑ Decide the number of radio and watch winners?

☑ Mark the lima beans?

☑ Trade with another group?

☑ Predict the number of winners?

Because teens spend a lot of money on clothes, store managers want to know what teens like. Many department stores have teen advisory boards and do surveys to find out what clothes teens will buy.

ALGEBRA CONNECTION
Predicting with Samples

A survey is used to gather information about a group. For example, consumers are surveyed when companies test new products. In what type of surveys have you participated?

When a group is large, it is too expensive to include each member in the survey. So, a part of the group, called a **sample**, is selected to represent the whole group, called the **population**.

To be unbiased, the sample must represent the entire population. One way to get an unbiased sample is to randomly select participants. This means that everyone in the population has an equal chance of being chosen.

The table shows how a sample of students could be biased.

SAMPLING METHOD	HOW IT IS BIASED
A. Select one student at random from each bus.	**A.** Some students may not ride a bus to school.
B. Select an equal number of boys and girls from each grade.	**B.** There may be more sixth graders, or more girls than boys.

• **CRITICAL THINKING**   How would you select an unbiased sample for this survey?

You can use the results from an unbiased sample to make predictions about the total population.

EXAMPLE   There are 1,528 students at your school. In a survey, 44 of 50 students said they will buy pencils at the school store. Use the survey results to predict about how many students will buy pencils at the school store.

Use a proportion. Let n represent the predicted number.

$$\text{sample} \rightarrow \frac{44}{50} = \frac{n}{1,528} \leftarrow \text{population} \qquad \textit{Find cross products.}$$

$$50n = 44 \times 1,528 \qquad \textit{Solve.}$$

$$n = \frac{67,232}{50}$$

$$n = 1,344.64$$

So, the predicted number is about 1,345 students.

GUIDED PRACTICE

A marketing company specializing in pets does a survey to find out what brand of dog food is purchased most frequently. Tell whether the given sample is biased. If it is, tell why.

1. a random survey of 100 pet store customers

2. a random survey of 100 pet store customers that own dogs

3. a random survey of 100 pet store customers that own big dogs

4. a random survey of 100 pet store customers that shop on Saturdays

Suppose people have 3,652 licensed dogs in your city. Use the unbiased survey results to predict about how many dog owners in your city will buy each brand next week.

5. Of 100 owners, 36 use Brand XYZ.

6. Of 100 owners, 42 use Brand ABC.

INDEPENDENT PRACTICE

The Color Institute does a survey of U.S. teens aged 13–15 to find out what colors are their favorites. Tell whether the given sample is biased. If it is, tell why.

1. a random survey of 250 teens living in the Midwest

2. a random survey of 250 teens

3. a random survey of 250 teens aged 13–15

4. a random survey of 250 teen boys

There are 1,540 students at your school. Use the unbiased survey results to make an estimate about the school population.

5. Of 200 students, 50 like to study in the kitchen.

6. Of 200 students, 66 like to study in the bedroom.

7. Of 200 students, 40 like to study in the dining room.

8. Of 200 students, 44 like to study in the family room.

Problem-Solving Applications

9. For an advertising campaign, you need to survey people to find out why they like to visit the San Diego Zoo. How can you select an unbiased sample for this survey?

10. You will run a school radio station. Suppose 125 out of 300 students you surveyed prefer jazz music. How much time should you devote to jazz if you are on the air 10 hr each day?

11.  **WRITE ABOUT IT** Explain why it is important to use an unbiased sample to make predictions. Give an example.

PROBLEM-SOLVING STRATEGY
Solving a Simpler Problem

Problem Solving
- **Understand**
- **Plan**
- **Solve**
- **Look Back**

Science Link

NASA scientists use computers to record the location of manatees. Suppose 12 manatees are in a given location. If this is about 10% of the manatee population, about how many are in the population?

306 **Chapter 16**

Sometimes you can use a simpler situation to make estimates about a population.

Marine biologists are monitoring a group of manatees. How can you help them find the size of the area's manatee population?

✓ **UNDERSTAND**   What are you asked to find?

What facts are given?

✓ **PLAN**   What strategy will you use?

It would be very costly and almost impossible to count every manatee. So, you can solve a simpler problem by estimating the population from samples. A good sampling procedure to use with wildlife is capture-recapture.

✓ **SOLVE**   How will you solve the problem?

For a given period of time, capture all the manatees you find. Tag each with a marker, and then release them in the area. Suppose you capture, tag, and release 8 manatees.

On another day, during the same period of time and under similar conditions, collect a second sample. Count the marked and unmarked manatees. Suppose you count 4 unmarked and 3 marked manatees.

Substitute the data from the two samples into the following proportion. Let x represent the unknown manatee population of the area. Each ratio stands for marked to total manatees.

$$\frac{\text{number with marks}}{\text{total in second sample}} = \frac{\text{number in the first sample}}{\text{population}}$$

$$\frac{3}{7} = \frac{8}{x} \qquad \textit{Find cross products.}$$

$$3x = 56 \qquad \textit{Solve.}$$

$$x = 18\frac{2}{3}$$

So, the estimated population of the area is about 19 manatees.

✓ **LOOK BACK**   Is this an exact count of manatees? Explain.

What if . . . you were asked to verify your estimate? How could you do this?

PRACTICE

Solve a simpler problem.

1. Zoologists are tracking polar bears living in the Arctic. The first week, they tagged 16 bears. The second week, they counted 7 tagged and 4 untagged bears. Estimate the polar bear population in this region.

2. To estimate the number of trout in a tank, the Forest Service caught and marked 121 trout. In a second sample, 15 marked and 90 unmarked trout were counted. Estimate the number of trout in the tank.

3. Charles needs to estimate the number of zebras in a game preserve. One week he tagged 14 zebras. A week later he counted 12 tagged and 4 untagged zebras. Estimate the number of zebras in the game preserve.

4. From a jar filled with jelly beans, you remove and mark 24 of the jelly beans. You return them to the jar and mix them with the unmarked jelly beans. You remove 22 jelly beans and find that 6 are marked. Estimate the number of jelly beans in the jar.

MIXED APPLICATIONS

CHOOSE

Choose a strategy and solve.

> ### Problem-Solving Strategies
> - **Solve a Simpler Problem**
> - **Guess and Check**
> - **Work Backward**
> - **Draw a Diagram**
> - **Find a Pattern**
> - **Write an Equation**

5. Scott uses the Internet to do research for his class papers. The rate for the first 20 hr each month is $19.50, and each additional hour is $0.70. This month's bill is $32.80. How many hours did Scott use the Internet?

6. A group of friends are in line to buy tickets to a concert. Al is 22 spaces behind Robin and 7 spaces behind Lee. Janet is 5 spaces ahead of Lee. How far behind Robin is Janet?

7. Juanita and Henry won a total of 9 blue ribbons in the county fair. Juanita won 3 more ribbons than Henry. How many ribbons did Henry win?

8. Joyce has $1.15 in dimes and quarters. She has fewer than 5 of each type of coin. Find the number of each type of coin she has.

9. To estimate expenses for the dance, Lori wants to predict the number of tickets that will be sold. There are 625 students in the school, and 7 of 10 students say they plan to go to the dance. Predict the total ticket sales.

10. **WRITE ABOUT IT** Write a problem similar to Problems 1–4. Exchange with a classmate and solve.

Displaying Data

When you display data you have collected, it is important to select an appropriate graph. You must consider both the type of data and the way you want to use the graph.

In an economics class, a survey about family budgets included the following question:

> Suppose your family budget is divided into these four categories:
>
> Bills 45%   Food 25%
>
> Savings x%   Fun y%
>
> How much would you budget for savings? Use integer values greater than 0 for x.

The histogram below shows one way to display the responses to this question.

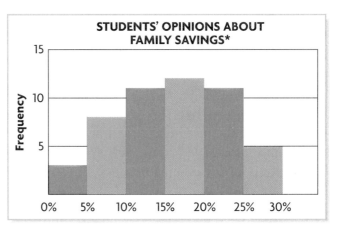

A value occurring on the edge of a bar is included in the bar on the left. For example, responses of 0%–5% are included in the first bar.

Responses to the question can vary from 0% to 30%. In the histogram, this range of responses is divided into six equal intervals. The height of a bar shows the number of students who responded in that interval.

• How many students said they would budget more than 10% but not more than 25% for savings?

• How many students said they would budget more than 5% but not more than 15% for savings?

EXAMPLE 1 Nancy organized the class responses to the survey question in the following table. How can she graph the data to compare the responses of the boys and girls?

PERCENT FOR SAVINGS

	0–5%	6–10%	11–15%	16–20%	21–25%	26–30%
Boys	1	5	6	6	5	2
Girls	2	3	5	6	6	3

REMEMBER:

Multiple-bar graphs and multiple-line graphs are useful for comparing similar sets of data. **See page H30.**

A **side-by-side histogram** is one way to organize, display, and compare two sets of similar data.

PERCENT FOR SAVINGS

Boys	Interval	Girls
	0–5%	
	6–10%	
	11–15%	
	16–20%	
	21–25%	
	26–30%	

6 5 4 3 2 1   **Frequency**   1 2 3 4 5 6

• Compare the displays of the girls' responses and the boys' responses. How are they similar? How are they different?

EXAMPLE 2 Saul's response to the survey question on page 308 was 20% for savings. He uses a circle graph and a stacked bar graph to show his family budget.

SAUL'S FAMILY BUDGET

Fun 10%
Bills 45%
Savings 20%
Food 25%

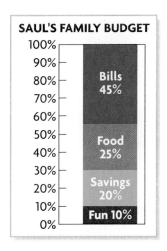

SAUL'S FAMILY BUDGET

Bills 45%
Food 25%
Savings 20%
Fun 10%

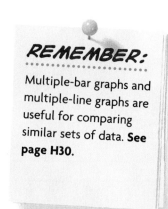

Technology Link

In **Data ToolKit** you can make a histogram, a circle graph, and a stacked bar graph.

• Which graph do you prefer for showing how the categories of the budget are related? Explain.

GUIDED PRACTICE

Use the following data from the Bureau of Labor Statistics.

PERCENT OF THE LABOR FORCE BY AGE IN YEARS					
	15–24	25–34	35–44	45–54	55 plus
1979	24	27	19	16	14
1992	15	28	27	18	12
2005	16	21	25	24	14

1. Make three stacked-bar graphs side by side, one for each year. Use the same scale for all the graphs.

2. Which bars represent the percent of the labor force between the ages of 25 and 34?

3. What do the three graphs show you about the data?

The line plot shows the heights of the children on Coach Connor's basketball team.

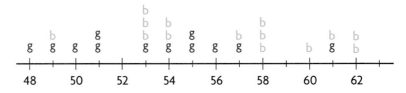

Coach Connor organized and recorded the data in this **back-to-back stem-and-leaf plot**.

Heights of Children (in inches)

Boys' Heights		Girls' Heights
Leaves	Stem	Leaves
9	4	8 9
8 8 8 7 4 4 3 3 3	5	0 1 1 3 4 5 5 6 7
2 2 1 0	6	1

5 | 3 represents 53 in.

Talk About It

• What does the line plot show you about the data?

• Look at the stem-and-leaf plot. Where is the one girl with a height of 53 in. recorded? Where are the two groups of three boys with the same height recorded?

• How are the stem-and-leaf plot and the line plot alike?

In **Data ToolKit** you can use spreadsheets to display data in various kinds of graphs. Record the set of data in Example 1 on page 309 and then display the data in various graphs.

INDEPENDENT PRACTICE

Lori conducted a survey to determine the number of students who prefer different beverages. For Exercises 1–2, use Lori's results in the table at the right.

STUDENT BEVERAGE PREFERENCES			
	Milkshakes	**Soft Drinks**	**Fruit Juices**
Girls	17	6	27
Boys	30	10	10

1. Select an appropriate graph to compare the results for the three beverages. Explain your choice. Then graph the results.

2. Make a multiple-bar graph to compare girls' and boys' responses. What does this graph show you?

Problem-Solving Applications

For Problems 3–9, use the test scores in the table at the right.

3. Make a circle graph to compare the four grades.

4. What other type of graph could you use? Explain.

5. What grade did most students receive?

6. Make a back-to-back stem-and-leaf plot to compare the girls' scores with the boys' scores.

7. Make a side-by-side histogram to compare the relationship of the girls' scores to the boys' scores.

8. Which of the graphs from Problems 6–7 do you prefer? Explain.

9. Would you use the circle graph, the back-to-back stem-and-leaf plot, or the side-by-side histogram to determine the number of A's? Explain.

10. ✏️ **WRITE ABOUT IT** Describe the difference between a side-by-side histogram and a back-to-back stem-and-leaf plot.

TEST SCORES		
Grades	**Girls**	**Boys**
A (90–99)	99 92 99 91	90 99 96
B (80–89)	89 88 82 84 86 81	87 88 88 85 83 80 87
C (70–79)	72	79 76
D (60–69)	67	69

Mixed Review

Find the missing number in each sequence.

11. 4, 8, 12, ?, 20
12. 1, 4, 7, ?, 13
13. 15, 13, 11, ?, 7
14. 12, 16, 14, 18, ?

Find the percent of increase or decrease.

15. original amount: 80 new amount: 20

16. original amount: 125 new amount: 225

17. original amount: 33 new amount: 99

18. **AVERAGES** Bill's average test score for the last five tests is 71. What score would he have to get on the sixth test to bring up his average to 75?

19. **MODELS** A model of a NASCAR race car is $14\frac{1}{4}$ in. long and $3\frac{3}{4}$ in. high. If the actual car is about 16 ft long, about how high is it?

ALGEBRA CONNECTION
Predicting with Graphs

Tables and graphs can help you see patterns in your data.

Suppose you have a part-time job that pays $4.50 per hour. You can make a table or graph to show the relationship between the number of hours worked and the amount you earn.

EARNINGS AT $4.50 PER HOUR	
Hours Worked	**Amount Earned**
x	*y*
0	$0.00
1	$4.50
2	$9.00
3	$13.50

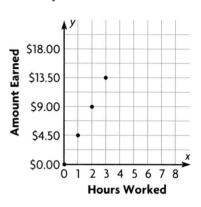

When you graph the data in the table, you see that the points for the ordered pairs (*x*,*y*) lie in a straight line. The graph shows a linear relationship.

The table contains only a few pairs of numbers. You can connect the points on the graph with a line to predict your earnings for hours of work that are not listed in the table.

EXAMPLE 1 Suppose you work for $2\frac{1}{2}$ hr and are paid $4.50 per hour. Use the graph to predict your earnings.

On the horizontal axis of the graph, locate $2\frac{1}{2}$.

Draw a vertical line segment from this point to the line of the graph.

From there, draw a horizontal line segment to the vertical axis. It intersects the axis halfway between $9.00 and $13.50.

So, if you work $2\frac{1}{2}$ hr, you will earn $11.25.

An **interpolation** is an estimate or a prediction of an unknown value between two known values. You can make a table and sketch a graph to interpolate, or use a calculator.

EXAMPLE 2 Find the value of $y = 3^x$ for $x = 1.5$.

One way to find $3^{1.5}$ is to make a table of values and use ordered pairs to sketch a graph.

Choose values for x, and compute the corresponding y-values.

Then plot points for these ordered pairs (x, y).

x	y
0	1
1	3
2	9
3	27

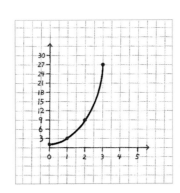

To interpolate, or estimate, the value of $3^{1.5}$, locate 1.5 on the horizontal axis and draw a vertical line segment to the line of the graph. From there, draw a horizontal line segment to the vertical axis. The segment intersects the axis at about 5.

So, the interpolated value of $3^{1.5}$ is about 5.

Another Method You can use the y^x key on a calculator to find the value of $3^{1.5}$.

3 y^x 1.5 = 5.196152423

So, the calculator value of $3^{1.5}$ is about 5.2.

- Use the graph to interpolate the value of $3^{2.5}$.

- Use a calculator to check your interpolated value.

GUIDED PRACTICE

1. Make a table of ordered pairs (x, y) for $y = 4^x$. Let $x = 0, 1, 2, 3$. Then graph the equation.

Use the graph you made in Exercise 1 to estimate the value of y.

2. $x = 1.5$ **3.** $x = 2.25$ **4.** $x = 2.75$

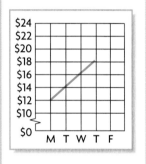
You can use graphs to identify patterns or trends in data. Then you can extend the pattern beyond the known values to predict unknown values. An **extrapolation** is an estimate or a prediction of an unknown value beyond known values.

EXAMPLE 3 Deana has kept this log of her salary. If the trend continues, when will she earn more than $18,000 per year?

Year	1993	1994	1995	1996	1997
Salary	$13,500	$14,000	$14,500	$15,000	$15,500

First, graph her data. The graph shows a linear pattern.

To extrapolate, or predict, when Deana will earn more than $18,000, extend the line of the graph until it intersects the horizontal grid line for $18,000.

At this intersection point, draw a vertical line segment to the horizontal axis.

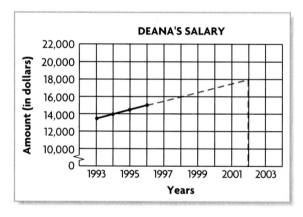

The segment intersects the horizontal axis at the year 2002.

So, if the trend continues, Deana will earn more than $18,000 after the year 2002.

Talk About It

- **CRITICAL THINKING** Look at the prediction in Example 3. What could happen to make this prediction inaccurate?

- If this trend continues, what do you predict Deana will earn in the year 2004?

- How are an interpolation and an extrapolation alike? How are they different?

INDEPENDENT PRACTICE

For Exercises 1–4, use the graph at the right.

1. Estimate the value of the investment in 1991.

2. Predict the value of the investment in 2000.

3. By how much did the investment grow from 1986 to 1996?

4. If this trend continues, when will the value of the initial investment reach about $6,000?

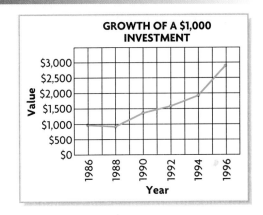

Problem-Solving Applications

For Problems 5–9, use the data at the right.

5. Display the data in a line graph.

6. Estimate the income in 1988.

7. What is the trend of the data?

8. Predict the income in 2010.

9. What might cause a decrease in future income?

QUICKER CORPORATION			
Year	Income (in millions)	Year	Income (in millions)
1975	$4	1990	$12
1980	$6	1995	$16
1985	$8	2000	$20

10. The record for the mile run at Johnson Middle School has been reduced by 5 sec each year for the last 5 years. Why will this trend not continue?

11. **WRITE ABOUT IT** Explain how interpolation and extrapolation can be misleading.

Mixed Review

Find the value.

12. $85 + 80 + 87$

13. $10 + 9 + 8 + 9.4$

14. $\frac{625}{25}$

15. $\frac{558}{6}$

Find the percent of the number.

16. 10% of $45

17. 6% of $88.95

18. 18% of $356

19. 1.5% of $678

20. **LOGICAL REASONING** Mrs. Hall spent $13.85 on gift certificates for hamburgers and fries. One hamburger costs $0.99 and one order of fries costs $0.79. How many of each type of gift certificate did she buy? How many of each type of gift certificate can she buy with $22.75?

21. **PREDICTION** Tom is running for class treasurer. He needs a minimum of 201 votes out of 400 votes to win. In an unbiased survey, 35 of 50 students said they would vote for him. What are his chances of winning?

ALGEBRA CONNECTION
Patterns and Graphs

One way to collect data for a graph is to use a model. In this activity you will build a model and make a graph to explore a relationship based on exponents.

Explore

• Work in a group. Cut the following lengths of string:
2 cm, 4 cm, 8 cm, 16 cm, 32 cm, 64 cm, 128 cm, and 256 cm.

• On paper at least 270 cm long, draw and label a horizontal axis and a vertical axis. The scales for the axes can be different. The *x*-axis should have equal intervals marked with the whole numbers 0–8 and should be labeled "String." The *y*-axis should have equal intervals marked from 0 to 256 and should be labeled "Length of String (in cm)."

• Tape or paste your eight strings in order, from the shortest to longest, vertically above the points marked 1–8 on the *x*-axis. The strings should be stretched tight and should be perpendicular to the *x*-axis and parallel to each other and to the *y*-axis.

• At the top of each string, mark a point with a marker or crayon. The point marks the height of the string above the *x*-axis. Connect these points to draw a graph.

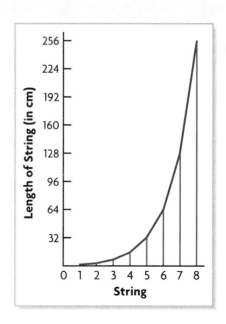

Think and Discuss

- What pattern do you see in the lengths of string?

- What pattern do you see in your graph?

x	y
1	2
2	4
3	8

- Organize all of the data from your model in a table. It should start like the one at the right.

- Use your table to write ordered pairs in the form (x,y) to represent the points on your graph. What pattern do you see that relates the values of x to the values of y in the ordered pairs? (HINT: How are the powers of 2 related to your data?)

- Using each ordered pair, verify that the equation $2^x = y$ is another way to represent the relationship you have described.

- Use the equation $2^x = y$ to predict the lengths of string you would need to extend your model for $x = 9$ and $x = 10$.

Try This

- On the x-axis of your model, locate the point that corresponds to $x = 2.5$. Draw a vertical line segment from this point to the line of your graph. Be careful to keep the segment parallel to the y-axis and the strings.

- Measure the length of this line segment to find the y-coordinate that corresponds to $x = 2.5$, and write the ordered pair (2.5, ?). Now substitute the x- and y-values of the ordered pair into the equation $2^x = y$.

- Compare this new equation with the equations $2^2 = 4$ and $2^3 = 8$. Does your value of y in $2^{2.5} = y$ make sense? Explain.

- Using the same procedure, draw a vertical line segment on your model at $x = 3.5$. Measure the segment's length to find the value of y when $x = 3.5$ in the equation $2^x = y$.

- Continue drawing new vertical line segments on your model and measuring them to find estimates of the following values of y.

  a. $y = 2^{0.5}$ **b.** $y = 2^{1.5}$

  c. $y = 2^{4.5}$ **d.** $y = 2^{5.5}$

  e. $y = 2^{6.5}$ **f.** $y = 2^{7.5}$

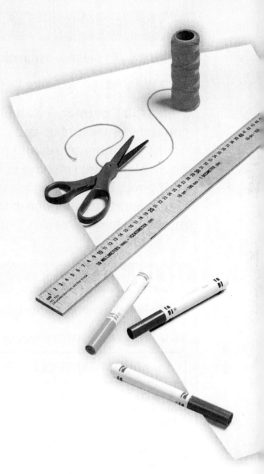

Technology Link

E–Lab • Activity 16 Available on CD-ROM
and the Internet at http://www.hbschool.com/elab

MATH FUN!

COIN TOSS

PURPOSE To practice predicting with samples (pages 304–305)

YOU WILL NEED masking tape, coin

Use masking tape to make a design on the floor like the one shown at the right. From a distance of 10 ft from the figure, try to toss the coin to earn the most possible points. Toss the coin 20 times and record the number of points earned each time. Predict how many times you would earn 5 points if you tossed the coin 100 times.

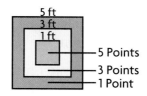

5 ft
3 ft
1 ft

— 5 Points
— 3 Points
— 1 Point

GONE FISHING

PURPOSE To practice estimating populations (pages 306–307)

YOU WILL NEED counters, bag

Work with a partner or a small group. Let the counters represent fish and the bag, a pond. Count a number of fish and put them in your pond. Make sure you have at least 50 fish in your pond. Exchange ponds with a partner. Estimate the number of fish in the pond by marking a handful of fish. Put the marked fish back in the pond. Take another sample and use a proportion to estimate the fish population. The player who comes closest to the actual population earns a point.

 HOME NOTE Teach your family to estimate the fish population by taking a sample.

RUN FOR IT

PURPOSE To practice displaying data (pages 308–311)

YOU WILL NEED large sheet of drawing paper

MAXIMUM SPEED OF ANIMALS			
Animal	**mph**	**Animal**	**mph**
Elephant	25	Greyhound	39
Squirrel	12	Lion	50
Cheetah	70	Cat	30
Human	28	Giraffe	32

Look at the chart on the left. Decide what type of graph would best display the data. Draw the graph on a large piece of drawing paper. Choose one of the animals and write a paragraph about it. Draw a picture of the animal to go with the paragraph. Share your poster with your classmates.

EXAMPLES

EXERCISES

• Use unbiased samples to predict.
(pages 304–305)

In an unbiased survey, 34 out of 50 students watch TV comedies. Predict how many students out of 600 watch comedies.

$\frac{34}{50} = \frac{n}{600}$ *Find cross products.*

$50n = 600 \times 34$ *Solve.*

$n = 408$

So, about 408 watch comedies.

There are 5,850 people over 18 in your community. Use the unbiased survey results to make an estimate about this population.

1. Of 250 people, 175 said they prefer shopping at Supermart.
2. Of 250 people, 5 said Supermart needs to improve its service.
3. Of 250 people, 30 said Supermart's prices are high.

• Solve a simpler problem. (pages 306–307)

PROBLEM-SOLVING TIP: For help in solving problems by solving a simpler problem, see pages 10 and 306.

4. In a certain area, a zoologist tagged 66 Key deer in one week. The next week, she counted 30 tagged and 47 untagged Key deer. Estimate the number of Key deer in the area.

• Display data in graphs. (pages 308–311)

WEEKLY LOWS IN JANUARY (IN °F)					
Detroit	16°	18°	19°	22°	26°
St. Louis	19°	22°	24°	24°	33°

A back-to-back stem-and-leaf plot can be used to compare the two sets of similar data.

For Problems 5–8, use the data at the left.

5. Make a back-to-back stem-and-leaf plot to show the relationship between the temperatures in Detroit and St. Louis.
6. What does the graph show you about the data?
7. Compare Detroit's temperatures with St. Louis's temperatures.

• Use graphs to make predictions.
(pages 312–315)

To estimate, or predict, the number of college students in 1979, you can use interpolation. See page 313.

College Students
(in thousands)

1964	3,500
1974	6,200
1984	7,500
1994	8,900

← *1979 is between 1974 and 1984.*

8. **VOCABULARY** An estimate or prediction of an unknown value beyond known values is ? .

For Exercises 9–11, use the data at the left.

9. Display the data in a line graph.
10. Estimate the number of college students who were enrolled in 1979.
11. Predict the number of college students who will be enrolled in 2004.

CHAPTER 17

STATISTICS: ANALYZING DATA

Rolf's Barking

Day	Minutes
1	7.2
2	9
3	3.8
4	6.8
5	10
6	
7	
8	

LOOK AHEAD

In this chapter you will solve problems that involve

- central tendency and variability of data
- box-and-whisker graphs, stem-and-leaf plots, and scatterplots
- analyzing misleading graphs

Team-Up Project

The Distracted Statistician

Clara collected data about her dog, Rolf. For 17 days, she put Rolf in the yard and timed how long it took him to bark. Just as she started to analyze the data, Rolf snatched it off her desk and ate it. Clara knows the mean of the data is between 6 and 7 minutes, and the mode is 3.8 minutes. What might Clara's data look like? What could the median of the data be?

Plan
- Work with a small group. Find 17 data points that agree with what Clara remembers about the data.

Act
- Make a table or graph to help choose data points.
- Fill in 17 data points. Adjust your data until you have the correct mean and mode.
- Find the median.

Share
- Trade data with another group. Do their data have the same mean and mode? Do their data have the same median?

DID YOU
- ✓ Make a table or graph?
- ✓ Adjust your data correctly?
- ✓ Find the median?
- ✓ Trade data with another group?

Central Tendency

WHAT YOU'LL LEARN
How to find measures
of central tendency
and determine which
is appropriate for a
given situation

WHY LEARN THIS?
To be able to describe
a set of data with a
single number

WORD POWER
central tendency

You can use three measures to summarize a set of data. They are the mean, the median, and the mode. Each of these three central values, or measures of **central tendency**, is a type of average. The most appropriate measure to use for a given situation depends on the distribution of the data.

EXAMPLE 1 Cassandra found this table in a 1995–1996 almanac. Which measure of central tendency should she use to describe the average population of these cities?

TEN LARGEST CITIES IN THE UNITED STATES			
City	Population (in millions)	City	Population (in millions)
Chicago	2.8	New York	7.3
Dallas	1.0	Philadelphia	1.6
Detroit	1.0	Phoenix	1.0
Houston	1.7	San Antonio	1.0
Los Angeles	3.5	San Diego	1.1

A line plot can help you locate the mode and the median.

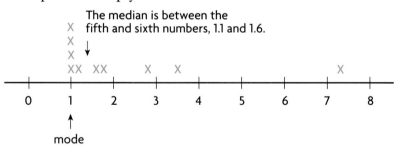

The median is between the fifth and sixth numbers, 1.1 and 1.6.

mode: 1.0   median: $\frac{1.1 + 1.6}{2} = 1.35$

mean: $\frac{2.8 + 1.0 + 1.0 + 1.7 + 3.5 + 7.3 + 1.6 + 1.0 + 1.0 + 1.1}{10} = 2.2$

The mode is the smallest population, so it is not a good measure of central tendency.

New York's population is much larger than the rest. This distorts the mean, so it is not a good measure of central tendency.

Most of the populations are clustered around the median. It is the best measure of central tendency for these populations.

REMEMBER:
....
The mode is the number or numbers that occur most frequently. The median is the middle number, or the sum of the 2 middle numbers divided by 2, when the numbers are arranged in order. The mean is the sum of the numbers divided by the number of addends. **See pages H29–30.**

Calculator Activities, page H37

EXAMPLE 2 Mrs. Hicks used a back-to-back stem-and-leaf plot to record the test scores of two classes. What measure of central tendency could she use to summarize and compare the classes?

First-Period Scores Leaves	Stem	Second-Period Scores Leaves
6 4 4	2	
	3	6 8
	4	6 6 6
6	5	8 8
8	6	2 6 6 8
8 8 8 6 6 4 4 0	7	0 2 6 6 8 8
8 6 4 4 2 2 0 0 0 0	8	0 4 4 6
2 0	9	2 2 8 8 8
	10	0

8 |6| 2 represents 68 in the first-period class and 62 in the second-period class.

First, find the measures of central tendency for each class.

first-period class: mean: 72.4; median: 78; mode: 80

second-period class: mean: 72.3; median: 76; modes: 46 and 98

Then, look at the distribution of the data to determine which measure best summarizes the scores for each class.

In the first-period class, three low scores distort the mean, so it is not a good measure of central tendency. The median and the mode are close to each other. Both are appropriate for this class.

In the second-period class, since the two modes, 46 and 98, are near the extremes of the data, they are not good measures of central tendency. The mean and the median are close to each other. Both are appropriate for this class.

To compare the two classes, Mrs. Hicks should use the same measure for each. The median is the best measure of central tendency for the data.

GUIDED PRACTICE

Tell which measure of central tendency was used. Write *mean*, *median*, or *mode*.

1. Half the students were at least 5 ft tall.

2. The average American household contains 2.63 people.

REMEMBER:
A stem-and-leaf plot is also called a stem-and-leaf display or diagram. It allows you to see how the data is distributed without losing the original data. **See page 310.**

Although New York, Chicago, Detroit, and Philadelphia are among the largest cities in the United States, their populations are getting smaller. On the other hand, Los Angeles, Phoenix, San Antonio, and San Diego are among the fastest-growing American cities.

Find the mean, median, and mode.

1. 7, 5, 4, 6, 8, 3, 5, 2, 5   **2.** $21, $34, $44, $36, $42, $29   **3.** 2.0, 4.4, 6.2, 3.2, 4.4, 6.2

For Exercises 4–6, use the table at the right.

4. What are the mean, median, and mode for the field-goal points Philip scored? for the free-throw points?

5. Find the mean, median, and mode for the total points Philip scored.

6. Which measures of central tendency best describe the total points Philip scored? Why?

Game	Field-Goal Points	Free-Throw Points	Total Points
1	6	2	8
2	8	0	8
3	12	8	20
4	8	7	15
5	2	2	4
6	12	6	18
7	12	0	12
8	10	3	13
9	6	5	11
10	4	4	8

PHILIP'S POINTS IN BASKETBALL

Write a set of data with at least five values and the given measures.

7. a mode of $8

8. a median of 5.5 mi

9. a mean of ⁻2°F

10. a mode of 5 and a mean of 10

11. a median of 4, a mean of 6, and a mode of 3

Problem-Solving Applications

12. Why is the median the best measure of central tendency for these salaries? $1,250, $425, $350, $375, $350, $410

13. Give the measure of central tendency that is best for these test scores. Explain. 95, 95, 90, 67, 66, 60, 55

14. The mean number of hours Joshua worked during the last 3 days is 12. He worked 10 hr on Monday and 11 hr on Tuesday. How many hours did he work on Wednesday?

15. On her last seven math quizzes, Tamika scored 86, 88, 92, 88, 30, 96, 84. Find the mean, median, and mode for her scores. Which measure is best? Why?

16. Jen caught five bass that measured 15 cm, 23 cm, 17.5 cm, 23 cm, and 18 cm. To make her fish seem as long as possible, should she use the mean, median, or mode? Why is this measure misleading?

17. ✏️ **WRITE ABOUT IT** Make a list of your test scores for one of your classes. Which measure of central tendency would you use to describe the data? Why?

MORE PRACTICE Lesson 17.1, page H68

Variability: The Spread of the Data

Sometimes values in a set of data are spread out. Other times they are clustered together. The spread of the values is called the **variability** of the data.

The distances of the 12 field goals Anne and Samantha kicked are shown. How can you show the variability of the data?

Anne: 43, 36, 25, 22, 34, 40, 18, 32, 43, 49, 29, 36

Samantha: 21, 51, 36, 38, 45, 52, 28, 16, 41, 33, 45, 26

Box-and-whisker graphs are good displays for data sets.

Order the data from least to greatest. Find the **second quartile**, which is the median; the **first quartile**, which is the median of the lower half of the data; and the **third quartile**, which is the median of the upper half of the data.

Anne: 18 22 25 29 32 34 36 36 40 43 43 49

	27		35		41.5	
↑	↑	↑	↑	↑		
lower extreme	first quartile	second quartile	third quartile	upper extreme		
↓	↓	↓	↓	↓		
	27		37		45	

Samantha: 16 21 26 28 33 36 38 41 45 45 51 52

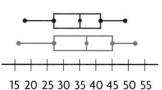

Draw a scale that includes all the distances for both kickers.

Draw boxes above the scale. The ends of each box are at the first and third quartiles. The line inside the box is at the median, or second quartile.

From each box, draw whiskers to the least value, or lower extreme, and to the greatest value, or upper extreme, in the data set.

- Whose data are in the top box? What is the range of the data shown in the top box? in the bottom box?

WHAT YOU'LL LEARN
How to show the variability of data by using a box-and-whisker graph and a stem-and-leaf plot

WHY LEARN THIS?
To visually compare how data are spread out or clustered together

WORD POWER
variability
box-and-whisker graphs
second quartile
first quartile
third quartile

REMEMBER:
The range is the difference between the greatest and least values. **See page H30.**

This box-and-whisker graph represents the number of points Brian scored in the last 10 basketball games.

2 4 6 8 10 12 14 16 18

1. What is the range of points?

2. What is the median score?

3. What determines the length of the box?

4. Why is one whisker longer than the other?

A back-to-back stem-and-leaf plot is useful when comparing two sets of data.

EXAMPLE Use a back-to-back stem-and-leaf plot to compare the spread of Hank's and Drew's field-goal distances.

Hank: 43, 36, 25, 22, 34, 40, 18, 32, 43, 49, 29, 36

Drew: 21, 51, 36, 38, 45, 52, 28, 16, 41, 33, 45, 26

In **Data ToolKit** you can make box-and-whisker graphs and stem-and-leaf plots.

Field-Goal Distances (in feet)

Hank		Drew
Leaves	Stem	Leaves
8	1	6
9 5 2	2	1 6 8
6 6 4 2	3	3 6 8
9 3 3 0	4	1 5 5
	5	1 2

range = 49 − 18
= 31

range = 52 − 16
= 36

0|4|1 represents a distance of 40 ft for Hank and 41 ft for Drew.

The stem-and-leaf plot shows that Drew kicked the longest and shortest distances and therefore had the greater range.

Talk About It

• How are a box-and-whisker graph and a stem-and-leaf plot alike?

• How does each show the variability of the data?

• Which display would you use if you wanted to show all the values in a set of data?

• **CRITICAL THINKING** What does a box-and-whisker graph tell you about data that measures of central tendency do not?

The temperatures in this table were recorded on a day in February.

1. Make a box-and-whisker graph for the high temperatures and a box-and-whisker graph for the low temperatures. Use one number line for both graphs.

2. Make a back-to-back stem-and-leaf plot to display this same data on the high and low temperatures.

Problem-Solving Applications

For Problems 3–7, use your box-and-whisker graph and stem-and-leaf plot of temperatures from Exercises 1 and 2.

3. What are the median high temperature and the median low temperature?

4. What are the range of high temperatures and the range of low temperatures?

5. Where are the high temperatures close to each other? How is this shown on the box-and-whisker graph?

6. How would you describe the spread of the low temperatures? Explain.

7. ✏️ **WRITE ABOUT IT** Find high and low temperatures for eight to ten other United States cities. Make a double box-and-whisker graph and a back-to-back stem-and-leaf plot for your data.

CITY	TEMPERATURE (°F)	
	High	**Low**
Atlanta, GA	65	48
Chicago, IL	42	32
Denver, CO	45	28
Fargo, ND	20	18
Los Angeles, CA	66	55
Memphis, TN	60	47
Miami, FL	76	54
New York, NY	47	37
Salt Lake City, UT	43	39
San Antonio, TX	83	58
Santa Fe, NM	52	28
Seattle, WA	44	38
Sioux Falls, SD	28	17
Washington, DC	49	36

Mixed Review

Graph the ordered pairs on a coordinate plane.

8. (3,0), (4,1), (5,2), (6,3), (4,1.5), (3.5,0.5), (5.5,3)

9. ($^-$1,0), (2,2), (4,5), (4,$^-$2), (3,1), (5,3), (4,$^-$0.5)

10. ($^-$1,6), (1,4), (2,3), (3,3), (1.5,3.5), (3,2.5), (0,5)

There are 852 students in the school. Use the unbiased survey results to make an estimate about the school population.

11. Of 50 students, 30 ride the bus to school.

12. Of 50 students, 11 walk to school.

13. **ESTIMATES** In the last 51 years, more than 3,030,000 miles of wire have been used to produce Slinky® spring toys. There is 80 ft of wire in each toy. Estimate the number of toys made.

14. **PERCENTS** In 1938, the federal minimum wage was $0.25 per hour. In 1997, it was $5.15. What was the percent of increase?

COOPERATIVE LEARNING

ALGEBRA CONNECTION

Drawing a Line to Show a Pattern

LAB Activity

WHAT YOU'LL EXPLORE
How to use a graph to see whether there is a pattern that relates two variables in a data set

WHAT YOU'LL NEED
graph paper, straw

To find a relationship between two variables, graph the data and then look for a pattern in the location of the data points.

Explore

- Work with a partner. Copy this table, and complete the row of ordered pairs (year, height). (HINT: Use last 2 digits of year.)

Olympic Records for Men's High Jump							
Year	1972	1976	1980	1984	1988	1992	1996
Height (inches)	88	89	93	93	94	92	94
Ordered Pair	?	?	?	?	?	?	?

- Graph the ordered pairs.
- Place the straw on the graph so that it follows the pattern formed by most of the data points.
- Draw a straight line on the graph in place of the straw.

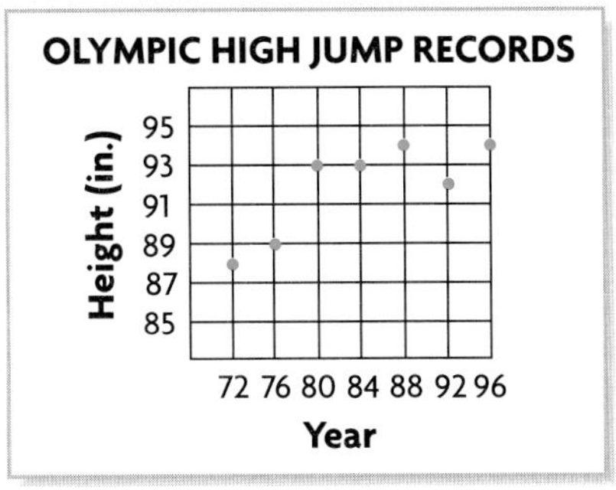

Think and Discuss

- Look at the line you drew. How many data points are on the line? above the line? below the line?

Try This

- Use the data in the table below to repeat what you did. Graph the ordered pairs and place a straw on the graph to follow the pattern of most of the points.

Olympic Records for Women's Freestyle Swimming							
Year	1972	1976	1980	1984	1988	1992	1996
Time (in seconds)	58.6	55.7	54.8	55.9	54.9	54.7	54.5

Technology Link
E-Lab • Activity 17 Available on CD-ROM and the Internet at http://www.hbschool.com/elab

Scatterplots

A graph that shows the relationship between variables in a data set is called a **scatterplot**. The straight line drawn to follow the pattern in the data is called a **line of best fit**. This line helps you interpret how the two variables are related, or correlated.

Ten students each did a different number of jumping jacks and then recorded their heart rate in the table.

• How is heart rate related to exercise?

Student	1	2	3	4	5	6	7	8	9	10
Jumping Jacks	0	5	10	15	20	25	30	35	40	45
Heart Rate	78	76	84	86	93	90	96	92	100	107

WORD POWER

scatterplot
line of best fit
positive correlation
negative
   correlation
no correlation

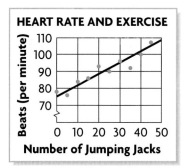

HEART RATE AND EXERCISE

As the exercise increases, the heart rate increases. A **positive correlation** exists when the values of both variables increase or decrease together.

The line of best fit slants upward.

This scatterplot shows how heart rate is related to rest time after exercise.

As the rest time after exercise increases, the heart rate decreases.

A **negative correlation** exists when the values of one variable increase as the values of the other variable decrease. The line of best fit slants downward.

This scatterplot shows how heart rate is related to month of birth.

When the data points are scattered, there is **no correlation** between the two variables.

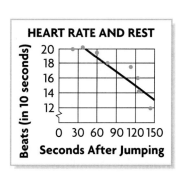

HEART RATE AND REST

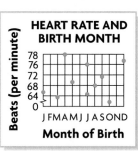

HEART RATE AND BIRTH MONTH

Technology Link

You can use **Data ToolKit** to make a scatterplot and draw a line of best fit.

329

For each graph, write *positive, negative,* or *no correlation* to describe the relationship. If appropriate, describe where a line of best fit would be drawn.

1.

2.

3.

INDEPENDENT PRACTICE

Draw a scatterplot for each set of data. If there is a correlation, draw a line of best fit.

1.

Team	A	B	C	D	E	F	G	H	I	J
Average Hits per Game	6.5	4.2	3.5	9.6	8.0	7.5	6.4	10.2	7.0	12.1
Games Won	8	3	5	16	14	12	9	12	6	15

2.

Team	A	B	C	D	E	F	G	H	I	J
Average Age of Players (in years)	8.0	12.5	9.5	12.0	8.5	10.0	11.5	9.0	8.5	13.5
Games Won	8	3	5	16	14	12	9	12	6	15

Problem-Solving Applications

For Problems 3–6, use the scatterplot at the right.

3. The population of Michigan is about 9,500,000. About how many square miles is Michigan?

4. The area of Minnesota is about 79,000 mi^2. About how many people live there?

5. The midwestern state with the greatest population is Illinois. About how many people live there?

6. The midwestern state with the least area is Indiana. About how many square miles is Indiana? About how many people live there?

7. ✏ **WRITE ABOUT IT** Describe the three different relationships that can be shown on a scatterplot.

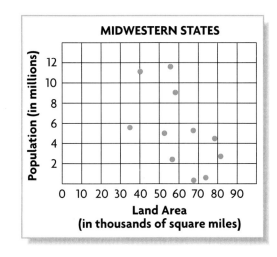

MIDWESTERN STATES

Population (in millions) vs Land Area (in thousands of square miles)

MORE PRACTICE Lesson 17.3, page H69

Misleading Graphs and Statistics

Sometimes statistics and graphs about data are used to show one point of view only. They are misleading because they distort the truth or do not give an accurate picture of the whole story.

EXAMPLE 1 What is misleading about this graph?

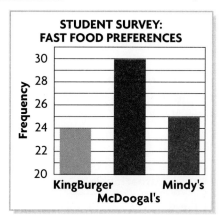

Notice that the scale does not start at 0. This makes the lengths of the bars look as if twice as many students preferred McDoogal's as Mindy's or KingBurger. In fact, only 5 fewer students preferred Mindy's and 6 fewer students preferred KingBurger.

• How could you more accurately display the data?

Computer graphics are used to make data displays more inviting. Be careful when looking at objects that are different sizes!

EXAMPLE 2 How is this graph misleading?

When you look at the graph, your impression might be that the population of Gotham City was greater in 1980 than it was in 1970, and greater yet in 1990.

When you study the graph you see that the population was 200,000 in 1970, in 1980, and in 1990.

The graph is misleading because the bars on the graph that represent the same value have different heights.

It is important that objects on a graph representing identical values be the same size.

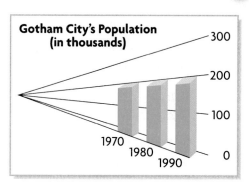

• How would you correct this graph so that it accurately displays the populations of Gotham City in 1970, 1980, and 1990?

331

GUIDED PRACTICE

1. What is misleading about this graph?

2. How would you change the graph to make it accurately display the data?

3. How can you change the graph to make it appear that sweets are the favorite?

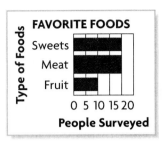

FAVORITE FOODS

Type of Foods: Sweets, Meat, Fruit

People Surveyed: 0 5 10 15 20

Statistics can be used to mislead you about situations.

EXAMPLE 3 Amber was told by an employment agency that the mean salary for the last five people placed in jobs was $38,000. How could this statistic be misleading?

Look at the following sets of salaries.

Situation 1	
Employee A	$35,000
Employee B	$35,000
Employee C	$42,000
Employee D	$40,000
Employee E	$38,000

Situation 2	
Employee A	$12,000
Employee B	$12,000
Employee C	$12,000
Employee D	$10,000
Employee E	$142,000

Both situations have a mean salary of $38,000. Because the mean can be distorted by extreme values, you should always be cautious when it is used to represent a given situation.

If Amber is thinking of salaries like those in Situation 1, she could be very disappointed if the agency's placements were at salaries like most of those listed in Situation 2.

Talk About It

- **CRITICAL THINKING** Look at the graphs in this lesson. Can a table or graph be correct but misleading? Explain.

- Does using a broken scale make a bar graph misleading? Explain.

For Exercises 1–4, use the graph of textbook sales.

1. What does the graph suggest about the sales?

2. How much did sales increase from the second period (1971–1975) to the third? from the fourth to the fifth?

3. Why is the graph misleading?

4. How would you correct the graph so that it more accurately shows the sales?

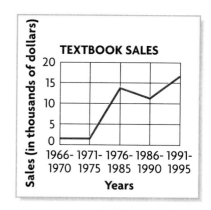

For Exercises 5–7, use the graph of manatee deaths.

5. What does the graph suggest about the numbers of deaths?

6. Estimate the ratio of 1992 deaths to 1993 deaths.

7. How would you correct the graph so that it shows the data more accurately?

Problem-Solving Applications

8. Use the data in the table to draw a misleading graph.

9. Use the same data to make a better graph.

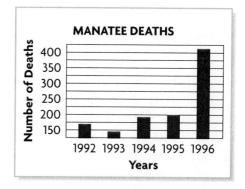

10. ✏️ **WRITE ABOUT IT** Describe two things that are sometimes done to make graphs or statistics misleading.

Mixed Review

Make a list of all the ways the set of items can be ordered.

Animal	Speed (in mph)
cheetah	70
antelope	61
lion	50
elk	45

11. boy, girl   12. dog, cat, bird   13. red, blue, green, pink

For Exercises 14–17, use the graph to estimate y.

14. $x = 0.5$ 15. $x = 1.5$

16. $x = 2.25$ 17. $x = 2.5$

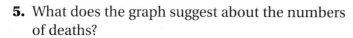

$y = 2^x + 1$

18. **ORDER** Five girls ran the 100-yd dash. Pat came in first. Mel came in last. Ann finished in front of Sue, and Gail finished just behind Sue. Who came in second?

19. **DECIMALS** Write a decimal that represents 25%.

CULTURAL CONNECTION

CHINESE NEW YEAR

The Chinese celebrate the New Year according to the lunar calendar. The celebration starts with the new moon on the first day of the new year and ends on the full moon 15 days later. On the 15th day of celebration is the Lantern Festival. Lanterns are made with red paper to symbolize joy and festivity. The dragon dance, lion dance, and stilt walkers help to create a festive atmosphere.

Liang and his classmates are raising money for a trip to Chinatown in San Francisco to take part in the Chinese New Year celebration. So far, 8 of Liang's friends have raised $29, $17, $15, $32, $24, $20, $8, and $23. What is the mean amount of money raised by Liang's friends?

$$\frac{29 + 17 + 15 + 32 + 24 + 20 + 8 + 23}{8} = 21$$

So, the mean amount raised is $21.

WORK TOGETHER

Day	Profit
1	$6
2	$5
3	$12
4	$18
5	$12
6	$21
7	$40

1. To earn money for the trip, Liang organized a school store to sell supplies. The profit of the first seven days is shown in the chart at the right. Find three measures of central tendency for the data.

2. Make a stem-and-leaf plot with the data in the chart. What is the range of the data?

3. Make a bar graph that is misleading using the data from Exercise 1. Exchange with a partner and tell what is misleading about your partner's bar graph.

4. Liang kept track of how many customers came to the store each day. Make a scatterplot with the data shown below.

Customers	2	3	7	8	3	9	12
Profit	$6	$5	$12	$18	$12	$21	$40

CULTURAL LINK

Chinatown in San Francisco is one of the world's largest Asian districts outside of Asia. This part of San Francisco resembles the culture and traditions of Hong Kong. The businesses in Chinatown have the signs outside their stores written in Chinese and English. Some of the best food in the world can be found in the restaurants of Chinatown.

EXAMPLES

- **Find central tendencies, and determine which is the appropriate measure.** (pages 322–324)

Find the best measure of central tendency:
90, 88, 45, 85, 90

ordered scores: 45, 85, 88, 90, 90
median: 88   mode: 90   mean: 79.6

The median is the best measure.

- **Show and describe the distribution of data.**
(pages 325–327)

Heights of Students (in cm)								
135	168	148	160	159	148	163	165	167

Draw a box-and-whisker graph.

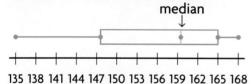

135 138 141 144 147 150 153 156 159 162 165 168

- **Draw and interpret the data in scatterplots.**
(pages 329–330)

Describe the relationship shown in this scatterplot.

positive correlation →

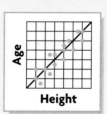

- **Identify and correct misleading statistics.**
(pages 331–333)

The graph is misleading. Begin the scale at 0, and show intervals of 10.

EXERCISES

Find the mean, median, and mode for each set of temperatures. Then tell which measures are appropriate for each set.

1. 65°, 85°, 87°, 89°, 87°
2. 72°, 65°, 68°, 72°, 62°, 66°
3. 28°, 37°, 29°, 32°, 45°, 47°, 22°

For Exercises 4–5, use the table below.

Temperatures (°F) in Centerville for 9 Days									
High	55	47	64	81	58	62	72	81	61
Low	39	27	44	51	41	39	55	65	40

4. Draw a box-and-whisker graph for each set of temperatures.
5. Draw a back-to-back stem-and-leaf plot for the temperatures.

For Exercises 6–8, use the table above.

6. Draw a scatterplot to show the relationship between the high and low temperatures.
7. Draw a line of best fit if appropriate.
8. Describe the relationship shown in the plot.

For Exercises 9–10, use the graph below.

9. What is misleading about this graph?
10. How would you improve the graph?

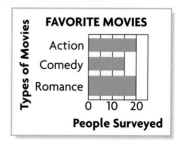

PROBABILITY

LOOK AHEAD

In this chapter you will solve problems that involve

- counting outcomes and finding probabilities of outcomes
- permutations and combinations
- independent and dependent events

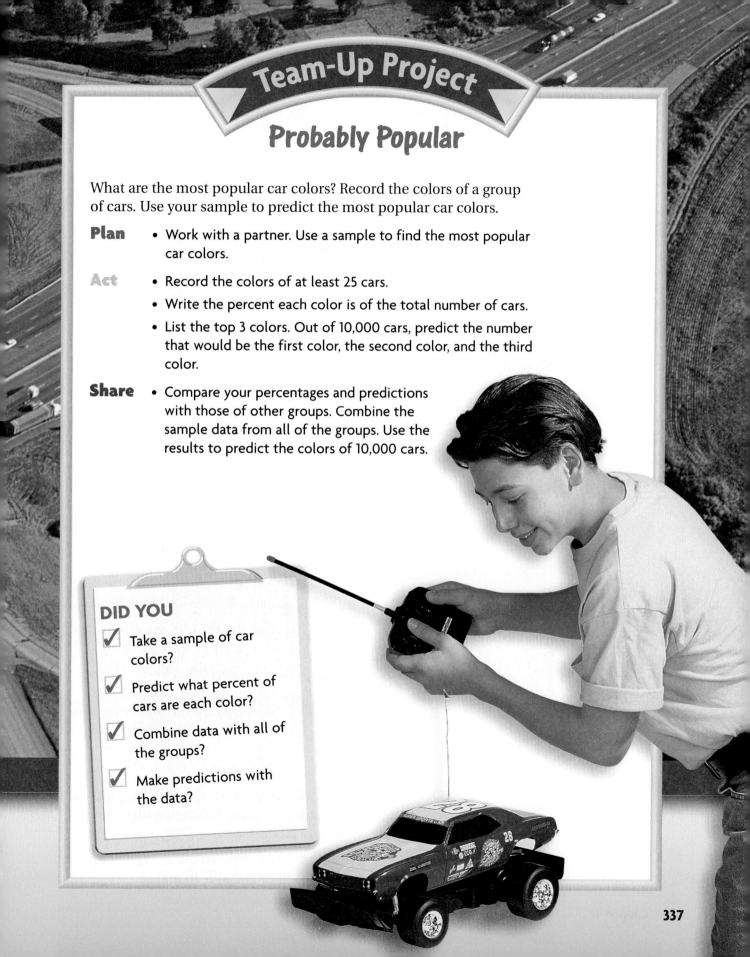

Team-Up Project

Probably Popular

What are the most popular car colors? Record the colors of a group of cars. Use your sample to predict the most popular car colors.

Plan
- Work with a partner. Use a sample to find the most popular car colors.

Act
- Record the colors of at least 25 cars.
- Write the percent each color is of the total number of cars.
- List the top 3 colors. Out of 10,000 cars, predict the number that would be the first color, the second color, and the third color.

Share
- Compare your percentages and predictions with those of other groups. Combine the sample data from all of the groups. Use the results to predict the colors of 10,000 cars.

DID YOU
- ✓ Take a sample of car colors?
- ✓ Predict what percent of cars are each color?
- ✓ Combine data with all of the groups?
- ✓ Make predictions with the data?

PROBLEM-SOLVING STRATEGY

Accounting for All Possibilities

WHAT YOU'LL LEARN
How to use a tree diagram to find all possible outcomes

WHY LEARN THIS?
To make a systematic list of all outcomes

WORD POWER
sample space
tree diagram

Problem Solving
• **Understand**
• **Plan**
• **Solve**
• **Look Back**

When there are a number of choices or several possible outcomes, how do you know when you've accounted for all of them?

Students at Jim's school wear school uniforms. Boys can choose from 3 different shirts and 4 different pants, all of which coordinate to make outfits. How many different outfits can Jim make?

✓ **UNDERSTAND**   What are you asked to find?

What facts are given?

✓ **PLAN**   What strategy will you use?

You can *make a list* to account for all possible outfits.

✓ **SOLVE**   How will you solve the problem?

TREE DIAGRAM		
Shirts	**Pants**	**Outcome**
S_1	P_1	S_1, P_1
	P_2	S_1, P_2
	P_3	S_1, P_3
	P_4	S_1, P_4
S_2	P_1	S_2, P_1
	P_2	S_2, P_2
	P_3	S_2, P_3
	P_4	S_2, P_4
S_3	P_1	S_3, P_1
	P_2	S_3, P_2
	P_3	S_3, P_3
	P_4	S_3, P_4

In this problem the set of all possible outfits is called the **sample space**. You can use a tree diagram to show a sample space. A **tree diagram** is a systematic list of all possible outcomes.

Call the shirts S_1, S_2, and S_3, and the pants P_1, P_2, P_3, and P_4.

Since each final branch of the tree diagram represents one outfit, count the branches to find the total number of outfits. There are 12 branches, so Jim can make 12 different outfits.

✓ **LOOK BACK**   Suppose the girls can choose from 4 tops and 3 skirts. How many different outfits can the girls make? Explain.

What if . . . the school adds a fourth shirt to the uniform choices for boys? How many outfits will Jim be able to make?

Solve by accounting for all possibilities.

1. The Deli Express prepares tuna, cheese, and egg salad sandwiches on rye and wheat bread. Draw a tree diagram to show the possible outcomes. How many different sandwiches are there?

2. Draw a tree diagram to show the possible outcomes of heads and tails if you toss a penny, a nickel, a dime, and a quarter. How many outcomes are possible?

3. The Beau's Chicken carry-out offers two choices of chicken: roasted and fried; three choices of side dishes: mashed potatoes, baked beans, and cole slaw; and two choices of dessert: apple pie and blueberry cobbler. Draw a tree diagram to show the possible outcomes. How many different meals are there?

4. You are buying a car. You have narrowed your choice to five exterior colors: red, silver, tan, white, and black; two interior colors: tan and black; and two kinds of upholstery: leather and fabric. Draw a tree diagram to show the possible outcomes. How many different car choices do you have?

MIXED APPLICATIONS

CHOOSE

Choose a strategy and solve.

Problem-Solving Strategies
- **Account for All Possibilities**
- **Find a Pattern**
- **Use a Formula**
- **Guess and Check**
- **Make a Model**
- **Write an Equation**

5. Katie has a 14-in. × 24-in. sheet of thin corkboard. She plans to construct an open box. Find the dimensions with the maximum volume.

6. Write an expression for the nth term in the sequence 21, 32, 43, 54, 65. Use the expression to find the 26th term.

7. A box measures 12 cm × 6 cm × 9 cm. How many 1-cm blocks would you need to build a scale model of the box, using a scale factor of $\frac{1}{3}$? What are the dimensions of the scale model?

8. Bob travels 10 days out of each month for his job. His employer pays him $0.32 for each mile. Last year, Bob was paid $1,798.40 for mileage. How many miles did he travel?

9. Marsha sold 184 decorated vests at the school craft fair. She sold 30% more hand-painted vests than crocheted vests. How many hand-painted vests did she sell?

10. At Pizza Pizzazz you have a choice of regular or Sicilian pizza and one topping: mushrooms, pepperoni, peppers, or onions. How many choices are there?

11. **WRITE ABOUT IT** Write a problem that you could solve by accounting for all possibilities. Exchange with a classmate and solve.

ALGEBRA CONNECTION

The Fundamental Counting Principle

WORD POWER

Fundamental Counting Principle

You can use tree diagrams and other methods to find all possible outcomes when more than one event occurs.

EXAMPLE 1 There are 3 ways to travel from Los Angeles to San Francisco and 2 ways to travel from San Francisco to Honolulu. In how many ways can a person travel from Los Angeles to Honolulu with a stopover in San Francisco?

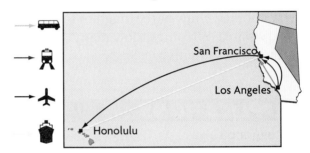

You can make an organized list to show all the ways. In each ordered pair, let the first letter represent the transportation from Los Angeles to San Francisco and the second letter represent from San Francisco to Honolulu. The letters *C, T, P,* and *S* represent travel by car, train, plane, and ship.

$$(C,P), (C,S) \qquad (T,P), (T,S) \qquad (P,P), (P,S)$$

So, there are 6 ways to go from Los Angeles to Honolulu with a stopover in San Francisco.

You can also use the Fundamental Counting Principle.

Fundamental Counting Principle   When one event can happen in *m* ways and a second event can happen in n ways, the two events can happen together in $m \times n$ different ways.

Consumer Link

Telephone area codes are three-digit numbers with 2 to 9 in the hundreds place. The tens digit and the units digit can be any number from 0 to 9. How many different area codes are possible?

EXAMPLE 2 The soup choices are chicken noodle, bean, tomato, and vegetable. The sandwich choices are cheese, ham, hot dog, tuna salad, turkey, and veggie burger. How many different soup-and-sandwich combinations can you choose from?

Use the Fundamental Counting Principle. Let *m* represent the number of soups, and let *n* represent the number of sandwiches.

$$m \times n = 4 \times 6 = 24 \leftarrow \textbf{24 different combinations}$$

So, there are 24 different soup-and-sandwich combinations.

GUIDED PRACTICE

Make an organized list to find the number of possible outcomes.

1. birds: parrot, cockatiel, parakeet
cages: round, square

2. bagels: sesame, sourdough, plain
spreads: plain, chives, veggie

3. colors: purple, fuchsia, teal, orange
sizes: small, medium, large, extra-large

4. destinations: Paris, London, Madrid
months: May, June, July, December

INDEPENDENT PRACTICE

Make an organized list to find the number of possible outcomes.

1. games: tennis, golf, basketball
times: morning, afternoon

2. flavors: vanilla, chocolate, strawberry
toppings: chocolate, caramel, fudge

Find the number of possible outcomes.

3. 3 concert dates, 2 show times on each

4. 6 movies, 4 showings of each

5. 5 tops, 3 pants, 2 jackets

6. 3 appetizers, 6 entrees, 4 desserts

Problem-Solving Applications

For Problems 7–8, use the chart at the right.

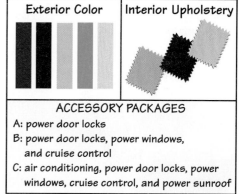

Exterior Color	Interior Upholstery

ACCESSORY PACKAGES
A: power door locks
B: power door locks, power windows,
  and cruise control
C: air conditioning, power door locks, power
  windows, cruise control, and power sunroof

7. Mr. Kelly is planning to buy a new car. The dealership gave him a brochure about the options. How many combinations are possible with a choice of one exterior color, one interior upholstery, and one accessory package?

8. Mr. Kelly decides he wants a red car. How many combinations are possible now?

9. You need to register for one course in each of six subject areas. The school offers 2 in math, 3 in foreign languages, 4 in science, 4 in English, 4 in physical education, and 5 electives. In how many ways can you register?

10. In the game Clue®, you need to solve a crime. On your suspect list are Mrs. White, Professor Green, Miss Scarlet, Mrs. Peacock, and Colonel Mustard. The crime took place in the conservatory, dining room, kitchen, library, study, or ballroom with a candlestick, lead pipe, revolver, wrench, rope, or knife. How many possible solutions are there to the crime?

11. ◁▭ **WRITE ABOUT IT** Explain the Fundamental Counting Principle in your own words.

ALGEBRA CONNECTION

Permutations and Combinations

WHAT YOU'LL LEARN
How to find the number of permutations and combinations

WHY LEARN THIS?
To find the number of arrangements of numbers, letters, or people and the number of different selections you can make from a set of objects

WORD POWER
factorial
permutation
combination

Suppose you're playing a word game. You need to rearrange the letters *H, I, M, E,* and *C* to form a word. In how many ways can the 5 letters be arranged?

It may surprise you to know there are 120 ways to arrange 5 different letters. However, they may not all form English words.

To see how to find the number of arrangements, you can use the Fundamental Counting Principle. Think about the number of choices you have for each of the 5 positions. Once you put a letter in one position, there are fewer choices for the next position.

choices for Position 1	remaining choices for Position 2	remaining choices for Position 3	remaining choices for Position 4	remaining choices for Position 5
↓	↓	↓	↓	↓
5 ×	4 ×	3 ×	2 ×	1 = 120

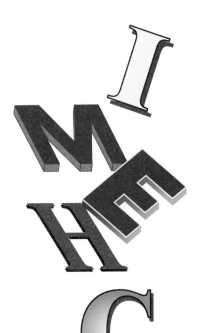

You can express the product $5 \times 4 \times 3 \times 2 \times 1$ with the factorial symbol. A **factorial** is the product of all the whole numbers, except zero, less than or equal to a number.

$$5 \times 4 \times 3 \times 2 \times 1 = 5! \quad \textit{\textbf{Read:} 5 factorial.}$$

• What does 6! mean? What is its value?

• What does 4! mean? How can you find its value?

There is a factorial key on many scientific calculators. Often you have to use the ⟨ 2nd ⟩ or SHIFT key first.

EXAMPLE 1 Find the value by using a calculator.

A. 8!   8 SHIFT *x!*   ⟨ 40'320. ⟩

B. $\dfrac{5!}{3!}$ 5 SHIFT *x!* ÷ 3 SHIFT *x!* =   ⟨ 20. ⟩

C. $\dfrac{12!}{(12-8)!}$ 12   SHIFT *x!*

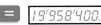 = ⟨ 19'958'400. ⟩

🖩 Calculator Activities, page H34

Permutations

An arrangement of things in a definite order is a **permutation**. Suppose you have 7 books to arrange on a bookshelf. There are $7! = 5,040$ possible arrangements, or permutations.

You can use symbols to represent permutations. The symbol $_7P_7$ represents the permutations of all 7 books on the bookshelf.

$$\underbrace{_7P_7 = 7 \times 6 \times 5 \times 4 \times 3 \times 2 \times 1}_{\text{7 factors}} = 5,040$$

number of books ↑ ↑
number of positions on shelf

Suppose you have 7 books, but there is room on the shelf for only 3 of them. How many permutations can you make of 7 books taken 3 at a time?

number of books

3 factors

$$_7P_3 = \frac{7!}{(7-3)!} = \frac{7!}{4!} = \frac{7 \times 6 \times 5 \times \overset{1}{\cancel{4}} \times \overset{1}{\cancel{3}} \times \overset{1}{\cancel{2}} \times 1}{\underset{1}{\cancel{4}} \times \underset{1}{\cancel{3}} \times \underset{1}{\cancel{2}} \times 1} = 7 \times 6 \times 5 = 210$$

↑
number of positions on shelf

So, there are 210 permutations of 7 books taken 3 at a time.

EXAMPLE 2 Only the runners who finish in first place and second place qualify for the finals. In how many ways can the first and second places be filled if there are 8 runners?

number of runners

2 factors

$$_8P_2 = \frac{8!}{(8-2)!} = \frac{8!}{6!} = \frac{8 \times 7 \times \overset{1}{\cancel{6}} \times \overset{1}{\cancel{5}} \times \overset{1}{\cancel{4}} \times \overset{1}{\cancel{3}} \times \overset{1}{\cancel{2}} \times 1}{\underset{1}{\cancel{6}} \times \underset{1}{\cancel{5}} \times \underset{1}{\cancel{4}} \times \underset{1}{\cancel{3}} \times \underset{1}{\cancel{2}} \times 1} = 8 \times 7 = 56$$

↑ number of first- or
second-place winners

So, there are 56 different ways.

GUIDED PRACTICE

Find the value.

1. $4!$ **2.** $6!$ **3.** $\dfrac{10!}{8!}$ **4.** $\dfrac{12!}{(9-2)!}$

Write the number of permutations as a factorial expression. Then find the value.

5. $_9P_9$ **6.** $_5P_3$ **7.** $_7P_2$ **8.** $_{10}P_3$

Combinations

Order is not always important when you are selecting items. A **combination** is a selection or arrangement in which the order does not matter.

EXAMPLE 3 Patrick likes sausage (S), pepperoni (P), mushrooms (M), and olives (O) on pizza. He can afford a pizza with only 2 toppings. In how many different ways can Patrick order a 2-topping pizza?

$$_4P_2 = \frac{4!}{(4-2)!} = \frac{4!}{2!} = \frac{4 \times 3 \times 2 \times 1}{2 \times 1} = 4 \times 3 = 12$$

The number of permutations of 4 toppings taken 2 at a time is 12.

However, when you list the permutations, you see duplications—a pizza with sausage and pepperoni is the same as a pizza with pepperoni and sausage.

S,P	S,M	S,O	P,M	P,O	M,O
P,S	M,S	O,S	M,P	O,P	O,M

So, there are only 6 different combinations. The number of combinations is the number of permutations divided by 2, the number of ways each 2-topping choice can be selected.

You can use permutations and factorials to find the number of combinations, when order is not important.

EXAMPLE 4 Diane received an ad to join a CD club. If she agrees to be a member, she can select 6 free CDs from a list of 40 CDs. In how many ways can Diane select the 6 CDs?

Since the order of the CDs is not important, Diane wants to know how many different combinations of 6 of the 40 CDs are possible.

number selected ↓
number of CDs ↓ $_{40}C_6 = \frac{_{40}P_6}{6!}$ ← number of permutations, n
← number of ways items can be selected, r

$$_{40}C_6 = \frac{_{40}P_6}{6!} = \frac{40!}{(40-6)!} \div 6! \qquad \textit{Substitute 40 for n and 6 for r.}$$

40 SHIFT x! ÷ 34 SHIFT x! ÷ 6 SHIFT x! =

$$\boxed{3'838'380.}$$

So, there are 3,838,380 combinations of 6 CDs that Diane can choose from the 40 CDs on the list.

Find the value.

1. 3!

2. 10!

3. $\dfrac{14!}{6!}$

4. $\dfrac{15!}{(12-3)!}$

5. $8! - 3!$

Find the number of permutations.

6. $_{11}P_{11}$

7. $_8P_4$

8. $_9P_6$

9. $_{20}P_2$

10. $_{50}P_5$

11. A softball coach chooses the first, second, and third batters for a team of 9 players.

12. Three-digit numbers are formed from the digits 5, 6, 7, and 8, with no digits repeated.

Find the number of combinations.

13. $_5C_2$

14. $_8C_6$

15. $_{12}C_2$

16. $_{10}C_5$

17. $_{15}C_{12}$

18. There are 6 players. How many possible teams of 3 can be formed?

19. How many possible pizzas can be made with 4 of 8 different toppings?

Problem-Solving Applications

For Problems 20–22, determine whether the solution represents *permutations* or *combinations.* Then solve.

20. In how many ways can a president and vice-president be chosen from a club with 16 members?

21. If 10 students go hiking in pairs, how many different pairs of students are possible?

22. After school, 4 friends play Monopoly®. Each player can choose one token to move around the board. The token choices are a wheelbarrow, thimble, hat, shoe, horse, iron, dog, or race car. How many combinations of player and token are possible?

23. ✏ **WRITE ABOUT IT** What is the difference between a combination and a permutation?

Mixed Review

Write in simplest form.

24. $\dfrac{4}{10}$

25. $\dfrac{8}{12}$

26. $\dfrac{9}{15}$

27. $\dfrac{15}{20}$

28. $\dfrac{21}{56}$

29. $\dfrac{24}{48}$

Find the mean, median, and mode.

30. 90, 92, 85, 82, 90

31. 55, 67, 45, 82, 47, 43

32. 35, 32, 33, 32, 38, 39

33. **SURVEY** There are 1,250 students in your school. Of 225 students, 135 said they like Chip's fast-food menu. Use the unbiased survey results to make an estimate about this population.

34. **PERCENT** To buy a condo, Lisa March borrows $65,000 for 15 years at a yearly simple interest rate of 7.5%. What is the total amount that Lisa will pay?

GEOMETRY CONNECTION
Finding Probability

In many sports the players toss a coin to see who goes first. When you toss a coin, the outcome cannot be predicted. Yet you feel that you have the same chance of getting heads as you have of getting tails.

The **mathematical probability** of an event is the number used to describe the chance that an event will occur.

To find the mathematical probability, P, of an event, E, you can use this ratio:

$$P(E) = \frac{\text{number of favorable outcomes}}{\text{number of possible outcomes}}$$

When you toss a coin, the number of possible outcomes is 2. The sample space is heads and tails. The probability of getting heads is:

$$P(\text{heads}) = \frac{1}{2} \begin{matrix} \leftarrow \text{ number of favorable outcomes} \\ \leftarrow \text{ number of possible outcomes} \end{matrix}$$

• What is the probability of getting tails?

Getting heads and getting tails on a coin are equally likely since they have an equal chance of happening. Some events are not equally likely.

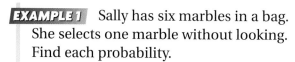

EXAMPLE 1 Sally has six marbles in a bag. She selects one marble without looking. Find each probability.

A. P(blue)   **B.** P(red or green)   **C.** P(purple)

$\frac{3}{6} = \frac{1}{2}$ $\frac{2}{6} = \frac{1}{3}$ $\frac{0}{6} = 0$

• You can express the probability of an event by using a decimal. What is P(blue) expressed as a decimal?

Talk About It   CRITICAL THINKING

• Are the colors equally likely to be selected? Explain.

• What is P(blue, red, yellow, or green)?

• Explain why P(purple) = 0.

• Can a probability ever be greater than 1? Explain.

EXAMPLE 2 Look at the spinner on the right. All the sections of the spinner are congruent. Find each probability.

A. P(red)

$$\frac{2}{8} = \frac{1}{4}$$

B. P(8)

$$\frac{1}{8}$$

C. P(red or 4)

$$\frac{3}{8}$$

• Are the colors equally likely to be selected? Explain.

GUIDED PRACTICE

A bag contains 4 blue marbles, 2 green marbles, 1 red marble, and 3 black marbles. You choose one marble without looking.

1. What is the sample space?

2. How many possible outcomes are there?

Find the probability.

3. P(blue)

4. P(green or red)

5. P(not green)

Odds

You can use odds to compare favorable outcomes with unfavorable outcomes. In Chapter 2 you saw that the odds in favor of an event can be found by using this ratio:

$$\text{odds in favor} = \frac{\text{number of favorable outcomes}}{\text{number of unfavorable outcomes}}$$

To find the odds against an event, you can use this ratio:

$$\text{odds against} = \frac{\text{number of unfavorable outcomes}}{\text{number of favorable outcomes}}$$

EXAMPLE 3 Suppose you are playing a game in which you roll a number cube labeled with the numbers 1, 2, 3, 4, 5, and 6. What are the odds against rolling a 2?

$$\text{odds against} = \frac{5}{1} \begin{array}{l} \leftarrow \text{ number of unfavorable outcomes} \\ \leftarrow \text{ number of favorable outcomes} \end{array}$$

So, the odds against your rolling a 2 in the game are 5 to 1.

Talk About It

• What are the odds in favor of rolling a 2?

• What is the probability of rolling a 2?

• How are odds and probability different?

A bag contains 4 clear marbles, 3 red marbles, 2 green marbles, and 3 blue marbles. You choose one marble without looking. Find the probability.

1. P(clear)   2. P(red or blue)

3. P(white)   4. P(not red)

You spin the pointer of a spinner whose sections are congruent. Find the probability.

5. P(1)   6. P(2 or 5)

7. P(not orange)   8. P(4 and blue)

9. P(1, 2, or 3)   10. P(4 or blue)

You roll a number cube numbered 1 to 6. Find the probability.

11. P(3)   12. P(2 or 4)

13. P(not 4)   14. P(even number)

15. P(number > 1)   16. P(multiple of 3)

 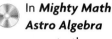

In **Mighty Math Astro Algebra** you can go to the Variablox Station and complete *A Chotchkee Holiday* mission, using what you know about using ratios to express probability.

Write *yes* or *no* to tell whether the given outcomes are equally likely. If not, explain.

17. You roll a number cube numbered 1 to 6 and get an even or odd number.

18. You toss a coin 2 times and you get 2 heads or 2 tails.

19. You spin the pointer of this spinner and it lands on red.

You roll a number cube numbered 1 to 6. Find the odds in favor of and the odds against each event.

20. rolling a 3   21. rolling an odd number   22. rolling a 1 or a 6

Problem-Solving Applications

23. Jill's little brother tore the labels off 6 cans of food. Now all the cans look alike. Jill knows that 2 cans contain beans, 3 contain corn, and 1 contains beets. She chooses one can. Find the probability of not choosing the can of beets.

24. A game company's catalogs have cosmic red, astro purple, hot pink, or neon orange covers. If you ask for a catalog, what is the probability of getting a hot pink one?

25. For a number cube numbered 1 to 6, $P(6) = \frac{1}{6}$. What is P(not 6)? Using words, write a ratio you can use to find P(not E).

26. ⬅ **WRITE ABOUT IT** Explain how to find the probability of a given event.

MORE PRACTICE Lesson 18.4, page H70

Relating Events

In this activity you will discover how an event may be affected by another event.

Explore

- Work with a partner. Write the numbers 1 to 5 on separate index cards. Place the cards in the box.

- Without looking, choose a card, replace it, and then choose another card.

- How many cards were in the box each time you made a choice? What was the probability of choosing any card for your first choice? your second choice?

- Without looking, choose a card, do not replace it, and then choose another card.

- How many cards were in the box each time you made a choice? What was the probability of choosing any card for your first choice? your second choice?

Think and Discuss 💡 CRITICAL THINKING

- When you chose a card, replaced it, and chose a second card, did your first choice have any effect on which card might be your second choice? Explain.

- When you chose a card, did not replace it, and chose a second card, did your first choice have any effect on which card might be your second choice? Explain.

- How did the probability of choosing a card change when you did not replace the first card? Why did it change?

Try This

- Choose 2 cards from the box, replace one card, and then choose another card. Does the first event have an effect on the second event?

- Spin the spinner, and then toss the coin. Does the first event have an effect on the second event?

LAB Activity

WHAT YOU'LL EXPLORE
How to tell whether one event affects another event

WHAT YOU'LL NEED
5 index cards, box, spinner, paper clip, coin

Technology Link ➤
E-Lab • Activity 18 Available on CD-ROM and the Internet at http://www.hbschool.com/elab

WHAT YOU'LL LEARN
How to find the probability of independent events and dependent events

WHY LEARN THIS?
To see how a decision you make or an event that occurs affects future events

WORD POWER
independent events
dependent events

Independent and Dependent Events

Kevin has a bag of colored cubes, shown on the right. If Sandra draws one cube out of the bag without looking, what is the probability that she will draw a red cube?

Before Sandra draws a second cube, she returns the first one to the bag. What is the probability that she will draw a red cube on the second draw?

There are 2 ways out of 12 to select a red cube on the first draw. If Sandra replaces the first cube she draws, there are still 2 ways out of 12 to draw a red cube. These two events are called **independent events** because the outcome of the first event does not affect the outcome of the second event.

You can find the probability of independent events by finding the product of their probabilities.

> **Probability of Two Independent Events** If A and B are independent events, then P(A and B) = P(A) × P(B).

Suppose Sandra draws a cube out of the bag, replaces it, and draws another cube. What is the probability that she will draw a red cube on the first draw and a red cube on the second draw?

first draw: $P(red) = \frac{2}{12}$, or $\frac{1}{6}$ *Find the probability.*

second draw: $P(red) = \frac{2}{12}$, or $\frac{1}{6}$ *Find the probability.*

$P(red \text{ and } red) = P(red) \times P(red)$

$$= \frac{1}{6} \times \frac{1}{6} = \frac{1}{36}$$ *Multiply the probabilities.*

So, the probability of drawing a red cube both times is $\frac{1}{36}$.

- What is the probability that Sandra will draw a blue cube and then a red cube?

- What is the probability that Sandra will draw a yellow cube and then a white cube?

History Link

Many ideas about probability were developed by a French mathematician, Blaise Pascal. Born in 1623, Pascal invented the first calculating machine in 1645. His work on probability may have been related to his interest in games. Suppose you roll a number cube numbered 1 to 6 and then roll it a second time. What is P(3 and 4)?

EXAMPLE 1 In a game, Leslie has to use two different spinners. What is the probability that the first pointer will land on red and the second pointer on 3 or 6?

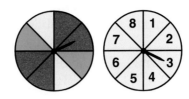

first spinner: $P(red) = \frac{4}{8}$, or $\frac{1}{2}$ *Find the probability.*

second spinner: $P(3 \text{ or } 6) = \frac{2}{8}$, or $\frac{1}{4}$ *Find the probability.*

$P(red \text{ and } 3 \text{ or } 6) = P(red) \times P(3 \text{ or } 6) = \frac{1}{2} \times \frac{1}{4} = \frac{1}{8}$ *Multiply.*

So, $P(red \text{ and } 3 \text{ or } 6)$ is $\frac{1}{8}$.

Talk About It

• Are the events of spinning two pointers independent events? Suppose Leslie had to spin just one of the pointers two times. Are the events independent? Explain.

• If you use the first spinner for two spins, what is P(red and red)? What is P(red and yellow)?

GUIDED PRACTICE

You toss a coin and then spin the pointer of this spinner. Find the probability.

1. P(tails and blue)   **2.** P(heads and blue)

3. P(heads and red)   **4.** P(tails and red or blue)

Nine cards labeled *T, E, N, N, E, S, S, E,* and *E* are in a box. One card is drawn from the box and replaced. Another card is drawn. Find the probability.

5. P(*T* and *E*)   **6.** P(*S* and *T* or *N*)   **7.** P(*T* and not *E*)

Dependent Events

In a game with 7 cards, Bryan must pick one of these cards without looking, keep it, and then pick a second card. He can win the game if he picks the 3 card and then the 5 card. What is the probability that Bryan will win the game?

Sometimes the outcome of one event affects the outcome of another. The chance of picking the 5 card depends on the card that was picked first. These events are called **dependent events**.

As with independent events, you can find the probability of dependent events by finding the product of their probabilities.

> **Probability of Two Dependent Events**   If A and B are dependent events, then P(A and B) = P(A) × P(B after A).

The first time Bryan picks a card, there are 7 cards. The second time, there are 6 cards.

$P(3) = \frac{1}{7}$ $P(5) = \frac{1}{6}$ ← One card was removed, so only 6 cards are left.

$P(3 \text{ and } 5) = \frac{1}{7} \times \frac{1}{6} = \frac{1}{42}$ *Multiply the probabilities.*

So, the probability that Bryan will win the game is $\frac{1}{42}$.

- Suppose the first card is replaced after it is drawn. What is P(3 and 5), and why is it different from the probability when the card is not replaced?

EXAMPLE 2   Julie, Scott, Bob, and Nanette are on the school dance committee. To find out who will be responsible for cleanup, they each write their names on slips of paper and drop them in a hat. Julie then draws one name, and then a second name without replacing the first. What is the probability that she will draw Nanette's name and then Scott's name?

$P(\text{Nanette}) = \frac{1}{4}$ $P(\text{Scott}) = \frac{1}{3}$ ← One name was removed, so only 3 names are left.

$P(\text{Nanette and Scott}) = \frac{1}{4} \times \frac{1}{3} = \frac{1}{12}$ *Multiply the probabilities.*

So, P(Nanette and Scott) is $\frac{1}{12}$.

- What is P(Scott and Nanette)? Does the order matter?

- What is P(Scott and Nanette and Julie)?

INDEPENDENT PRACTICE

Tell whether the events are *independent* or *dependent*.

1. Carl draws a cube from a box. Without replacing it, he draws a second cube.

2. Tasha tosses a nickel, rolls a number cube, and tosses a dime.

3. Scott draws a marble from a bag. He replaces it, and draws a second marble.

4. Matt draws one name from a hat. Without replacing it, he draws a second name. Then without replacing it, he draws a third name.

You use these two spinners. Find the probability.

5. P(blue and 2)   **6.** P(yellow and 5)   **7.** P(red and 1)

8. P(red and 1 or 3)   **9.** P(yellow and 2)   **10.** P(red and not 1)

11. P(blue and even number)   **12.** P(yellow and 2 or 3)

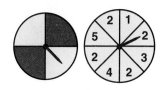

A box contains 5 red marbles, 3 blue marbles, and 7 white marbles. The marbles are selected at random, one at a time, and are not replaced. Find the probability.

13. P(red and blue)   **14.** P(white and red)   **15.** P(blue and white)

16. P(white and blue)   **17.** P(red and not red)   **18.** P(blue and not blue)

19. P(red and white and blue)   **20.** P(white and blue and blue)

Problem-Solving Applications

21. In the game Yahtzee®, you roll five number cubes. Yahtzee is five of one kind. On Ahmeena's first roll, she got 3 sixes. To get Yahtzee, she needs 2 more sixes. On her next roll, she rolls two cubes. Find the probability that she rolls 2 sixes.

22. Karen's mother brought home a bag of cookies from the bakery. The bag contains 5 chocolate chip, 3 peanut butter, 4 oatmeal, and 4 sugar cookies. What is the probability that Karen will pull out an oatmeal cookie and then Donald will pull out a sugar cookie?

23. In the game Scrabble®, there are 42 vowels, 56 consonants, and 2 blank letter tiles. You select one tile at random. Without replacing the tile, you select a second tile. Find P(vowel and blank).

24. ▬▷ **WRITE ABOUT IT** What is the difference between the probability of independent events and the probability of dependent events?

Mixed Review

Find the product.

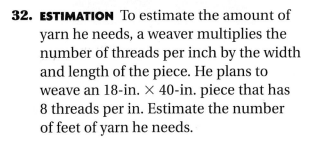

25. $\frac{1}{2} \times 50$ **26.** $\frac{3}{4} \times 80$ **27.** $\frac{5}{8} \cdot 40$ **28.** $0.4 \cdot 250$ **29.** $0.35 \cdot 125$

For Exercises 30–31, use the box-and-whisker graph at the right.

30. What is the range of the scores?

31. What is the median score?

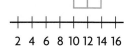

2 4 6 8 10 12 14 16

32. **ESTIMATION** To estimate the amount of yarn he needs, a weaver multiplies the number of threads per inch by the width and length of the piece. He plans to weave an 18-in. × 40-in. piece that has 8 threads per in. Estimate the number of feet of yarn he needs.

33. **PAYMENTS** The Smiths are buying a new car. They plan to make monthly car payments. They have two options: 36 monthly payments of $420 or 60 monthly payments of $268. With which option will they spend less money?

MATH FUN!

WORD SCRAMBLE

PURPOSE   To practice using permutations (pages 342–345)

Work with a partner or a small group. Unscramble the letters listed below and at the right to form words. You may want to use the permutations of the letters to find the words. The person who unscrambles all the words first is the winner.

1. tamh   **2.** itsl   **3.** rowk

4. htiw   **5.** orfm   **6.** aifr

7. mrte   **8.** sgmae   **9.** ziapz

 Make a list of your own words. Challenge your family to unscramble them within a certain time.

SPECTACULAR SPINNER

PURPOSE   To practice finding the probability of an event (pages 346–348)

YOU WILL NEED   8-section spinner, markers

Work with a partner or a small group. Shade an 8-section spinner like the one shown at the right. Find the probability of the pointer landing on each of the different colors. Make a game and game board based on your findings. Then play the game.

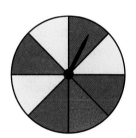

RIGHT OR LEFT

PURPOSE   To practice finding the probability of independent events (pages 350–353)

YOU WILL NEED   number cube numbered 1–6, counter

Make an enlarged version of the design shown at the right. Place a counter on the start square. The object is to move your counter to the red 3 or the blue 3. You can move your marker one square to the right by rolling an even number and one square to the left by rolling an odd number.
Find the probability of moving to the red 3 in 3 rolls P(odd and odd and odd) and to the blue 3 in 3 rolls. Then, see how many rolls it takes.

EXAMPLES

- **Solve problems by accounting for all possibilities.** (pages 338–339)

PROBLEM-SOLVING TIP: For help in solving problems by accounting for all possibilities, see pages 7 and 338.

- **Use multiplication to find the number of possible outcomes.** (pages 340–341)

Find the number of possible outcomes:
    8 movies, 3 showings of each

$8 \times 3 = 24 \leftarrow$ 24 different outcomes

- **Find the number of permutations and combinations.** (pages 342–345)

In how many orders can speeches be given if there are 6 students but only 2 speeches?

$_6P_2 = \dfrac{6!}{(6-2)!}$ *Find the number of permutations.*

$\dfrac{6!}{(6-2)!} = \dfrac{6!}{4!} = \dfrac{6 \times 5 \times \overset{1}{\cancel{4}} \times \overset{1}{\cancel{3}} \times \overset{1}{\cancel{2}} \times 1}{\underset{1}{\cancel{4}} \times \underset{1}{\cancel{3}} \times \underset{1}{\cancel{2}} \times 1}$ *Find the value.*

$= 6 \times 5 = 30 \leftarrow$ 30 different orders

- **Find the mathematical probability of an event.** (pages 346–348)

You roll a number cube numbered 1 to 6. Find P(4).

$P(4) = \dfrac{1}{6} \begin{array}{l} \leftarrow \text{ number of favorable outcomes} \\ \leftarrow \text{ number of possible outcomes} \end{array}$

- **Find the probability of independent and dependent events.** (pages 350–353)

You toss a coin and then roll a number cube numbered 1 to 6. Find P(heads and 6).

$P(A \text{ and } B) = P(A) \times P(B)$
$P(\text{heads and } 6) = P(\text{heads}) \times P(6)$

$= \dfrac{1}{2} \times \dfrac{1}{6} = \dfrac{1}{12} \leftarrow$ probability: $\dfrac{1}{12}$

EXERCISES

1. Cindy's Sweet Shop offers vanilla, strawberry, chocolate, and butter pecan ice cream in sugar and waffle cones. Draw a tree diagram to show the possible outcomes.

Find the number of possible outcomes.

2. 6 golf courses, 4 tee times
3. 5 sizes, 6 colors, 3 skirt lengths
4. 3 fruits, 4 muffins, 5 cereals
5. 4 appetizers, 6 entrees, 6 desserts

---

6. **VOCABULARY** An arrangement of things in a definite order is a $\underline{\ ?\ }$.

Find the number of permutations or combinations.

7. $_3P_3$ 8. $_7P_1$ 9. $_{10}P_4$
10. $_4C_2$ 11. $_8C_3$ 12. $_{11}C_5$

Tell whether *permutations* or *combinations* are described. Then find the number.

13. 5 players, teams of 3
14. 6 books to be arranged on a shelf

You roll a number cube numbered 1 to 6. Find the probability.

15. P(5)   16. P(not 1)
17. P(1 or 5)   18. P(odd number)

Six cards labeled *E, V, E, N, T,* and *S* are in a jar. Tell whether the events are independent or dependent. Then find the probability.

19. selecting *E* and then *V* without replacing the first card
20. selecting *E* and then *N* with replacement of the first card

EXPERIMENTS WITH PROBABILITY

LOOK AHEAD

In this chapter you will solve problems that involve

- finding experimental, mathematical, and geometric probabilities
- conducting a simulation

Team-Up Project

What are the Chances?

Experiments with probability can be useful to help predict many things such as the number of winners in a contest. Perform the probability experiment below.

YOU WILL NEED: bag, blank tiles, marker

Plan
- Make a number tile for each positive integer 1–100.

Act
- Predict the chances of randomly drawing a tile that is a multiple of 3 from the 100 tiles. Write it down.
- Put the tiles in a bag. Randomly draw 20 tiles. Record how many are multiples of 3.
- Compare your prediction to the results.
- Repeat for multiples of 2, 5, 7 and 10. Each time use a random sample of 20 tiles.

Share
- Make a larger sample by combining your samples with those of another group. Compare your predictions to the results for each multiple.

DID YOU
- ✓ Predict the chances of drawing a multiple of 3?
- ✓ Compare your prediction to the results?
- ✓ Combine samples with another group?

357

Experimental Probability

In the video game Tetris, seven shapes, each a different color, fall randomly from the top of the screen. The player rotates and moves the pieces, trying to position them so that they will leave no gaps as they fall into place.

Three players had these results.

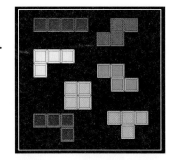

  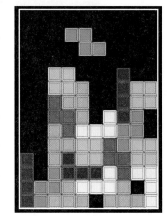

Experimental probabilities are based on the results of an experiment.

EXAMPLE 1 Use the players' results to find for each color the experimental probability that it will appear next.

Find the number of shapes of each color on the three screens.

Color	Magenta	Light blue	Dark blue	Yellow	Gray	Green	Red
Times Appeared (Total of 50)	4	8	5	6	10	9	8

Use the number of shapes of each color and the total number of shapes to write a ratio and a percent for the experimental probability.

magenta: $\frac{4}{50}$, or 8%; light blue: $\frac{8}{50}$, or 16%; dark blue: $\frac{5}{50}$, or 10%; yellow: $\frac{6}{50}$, or 12%; gray: $\frac{10}{50}$, or 20%; green: $\frac{9}{50}$, or 18%; red: $\frac{8}{50}$, or 16%

REMEMBER:

Probability is a number used to describe the chance that an event will occur.

$P(E) =$ $\frac{\text{number of favorable outcomes}}{\text{number of possible outcomes}}$

See page H32.

1. The colors of the next 50 shapes that appear in a Tetris game are shown in the table below. Find the experimental probability for each color as a ratio and as a percent.

Color	Magenta	Light blue	Dark blue	Yellow	Gray	Green	Red
Times Appeared	8	7	7	8	6	5	9

2. Combine the data from Example 1 on page 358 and the data in the table above. Find the experimental probability of each color's appearing, using the combined data. Write the probabilities as ratios and as percents.

3. If each color is equally likely to appear, what is the mathematical probability of each color's appearing?

4. Are the experimental probabilities based on 50 shapes or those based on 100 shapes closer to the mathematical probabilities? Explain.

You can use experimental probabilities to predict.

EXAMPLE 2 The table shows the number of hits and the number of walks Tyler has had in his last 150 times at bat. How many hits can Tyler expect to get in his next 50 times at bat?

	At Bats	Hits	Walks
Tyler's Record	150	45	30

Find the probability of Tyler's getting a hit his next time at bat.

$$P(\text{hit}) = \frac{\text{number of hits}}{\text{number of times at bat}} = \frac{45}{150} = \frac{3}{10}, \text{ or } 30\%$$

Use the probability to determine how many hits Tyler can expect to get during his next 50 times at bat.

hits expected = times at bat × probability
= 50 × 0.30
= 15

So, Tyler can expect to get 15 hits in his next 50 times at bat.

• What is the probability of Tyler's getting a walk his next time at bat? How many walks can Tyler expect to get in his next 50 times at bat?

teen times

The first commercial video game, Pong, was developed in 1972. Since then video games have gone from little blips of light bouncing around TV screens to incredibly realistic simulations that can make you feel as if you're really flying combat jets or saving Earth from invading aliens instead of sitting at a computer.

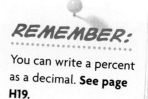

REMEMBER:

You can write a percent as a decimal. **See page H19.**

30% = 0.30

INDEPENDENT PRACTICE

The batting results for one team during a softball game are shown in the table. Find the experimental probability for each.

Result	No.
Singles	13
Doubles	10
Triples	3
Home runs	2
Walks	4
Outs	18
Total	50

1. A batter hits a single.

2. A batter hits a double.

3. A batter hits a triple.

4. A batter hits a home run.

5. A batter gets a walk.

6. A batter makes an out.

7. If each result were equally likely to happen, what is the mathematical probability for each result?

There are 5 different colors of candy in a candy bin. Rachel took a sample from the bin and counted the colors. Her results appear in the table at the right.

Color	No.
Yellow	24
Green	27
Orange	18
Purple	21
Red	30
Total	120

8. Find the experimental probability of choosing a red piece of candy.

9. Find the experimental probability of choosing an orange piece of candy.

10. Find the experimental probability of choosing a yellow or purple piece of candy.

11. Suppose someone scoops 200 pieces out of the bin. How many of them would you expect to be green?

12. If the bin contains 1,500 pieces of candy, how many of them can you expect to be orange?

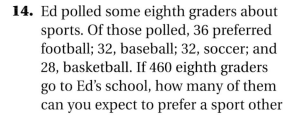

Problem-Solving Applications

13. While recording data about traffic at an intersection, Randy noted that 65 cars, 40 trucks, 30 minivans, and 15 motorcycles had passed by. What is the experimental probability that the next vehicle that passes through the intersection will be a minivan?

14. Ed polled some eighth graders about sports. Of those polled, 36 preferred football; 32, baseball; 32, soccer; and 28, basketball. If 460 eighth graders go to Ed's school, how many of them can you expect to prefer a sport other than soccer?

15. Sheila made number tiles for the integers 1–20. She placed the tiles facedown and asked a classmate to pick a tile. What are the chances of picking a number that is a multiple of 5? a multiple of 4? a multiple of 3? a multiple of 2?

16. ✏️ **WRITE ABOUT IT** Write a paragraph at least five sentences long about your favorite food. Find the number of each of the different vowels in your paragraph. Use those numbers to write a problem about experimental probability. Exchange with a partner and solve.

MORE PRACTICE Lesson 19.1, page H71

Random Numbers

To generate a list of random numbers from 0 to 9, you could repeatedly use a spinner.

Or you could use a calculator that generates random numbers. On one graphing calculator, this key sequence will generate a random list of numbers from 0 to 9.

Press **MATH** ▶ to display the **MATH NUM** menu.

```
MATH NUM HYP PRB
1:round(
2:iPart
3:fPart
4:int
5:min(
6:max(
```

Press **4** to select **int**. Press ▬ **(** ▬ .

```
int (■
```

Press **MATH** ▶ to display the **MATH PRB** menu.

```
MATH NUM HYP PRB
1:rand
2:nPr
3:nCr
4:!
```

Press **1** to select **rand**. Press ▬ **×** **10** ▬ **)** to generate random numbers from 0 to 9.

```
int (rand*10)
```

Repeatedly press **ENTER** to generate random numbers.

```
int (rand*10)
               6
               4
               0
               9
               8
               6
```

Explore

- Use a spinner to generate a list of 30 random numbers from 0 to 9.

- Use a calculator to generate a list of 30 random numbers from 0 to 9.

Think and Discuss

- How could you use the spinner above to generate a sequence of two-digit numbers?

- How would you change the calculator key sequence listed above to generate random numbers from 0 to 99?

Try This

- Use two different techniques to generate 50 random numbers from 0 to 99. Which of your ways takes less time?

Technology Link ▶
E–Lab • Activity 19 Available on CD-ROM and the Internet at http://www.hbschool.com/elab

PROBLEM-SOLVING STRATEGY
Acting It Out Using Random Numbers

WHAT YOU'LL LEARN
How to use random numbers to act out a probability experiment

WHY LEARN THIS?
To model situations

Problem Solving
• **Understand**
• **Plan**
• **Solve**
• **Look Back**

The local middle school mascot is the wildcat. The cafeteria is sponsoring a contest. On the bottom of each lunch tray is one letter from the word *wildcats*. Equal numbers of letters in *wildcats* are randomly placed on the lunch trays. The first student to collect all letters will win free lunches for one week. About how many lunches would you have to buy to get all the needed letters?

✓ **UNDERSTAND**   What are you asked to find?

What facts are given?

✓ **PLAN**   How can you solve the problem?

You can do an experiment, or *act it out*, using random numbers to represent the eight letters.

✓ **SOLVE**   The table shows 50 random numbers from 1 to 8.

7	1	8	2	6	6	3	6	1	6
8	1	6	6	1	5	5	7	3	4
5	6	2	5	2	3	3	2	2	4
5	7	2	2	6	2	8	1	6	8
4	5	7	7	8	6	1	1	2	5

Choose any starting point in the table, and count the numbers you pass before you have found all the numbers 1–8. Do this twice, and find the average of the results.

Trial 1: 8, 2, 6, 6, 3, 6, 1, 6, 8, 1, 6, 6, 1, 5, 5, 7, 3, 4 ← **18 lunches**   *Start with 8 in the third column. Read across each row, left to right.*

Trial 2: 7, 8, 5, 5, 4, 1, 1, 6, 7, 5, 8, 6, 2, 2, 7, 2, 6, 5, 2, 7, 6, 1, 2, 6, 8, 6, 5, 3 ← **28 lunches**   *Start with 7 in the first column. Read down each column, left to right.*

$\frac{18 + 28}{2} = 23$ lunches   *Find the average of the two trials.*

So, on average you would need to buy about 23 lunches.

✓ **LOOK BACK**   Can you read the table in a different way?

What if . . . you needed 9 random numbers? How would the table change?

Calculator Activities, page H35

PRACTICE

A computer-generated list of random numbers 1–6 is shown at the right. Use it to find experimental probabilities for Exercises 1–3. Select any row and column as a starting point.

6	1	3	4	3	2	4
4	6	6	3	6	6	1
6	5	1	4	3	4	3
4	2	1	4	1	3	6
2	2	4	4	1	2	2
2	2	6	2	3	1	1
4	4	1	4	5	5	2

1. A number cube has the numbers 1–6 marked on its sides. Estimate how many times you will have to roll the cube before you get the numbers 1–6.

2. At a local fast-food restaurant, 4 of every 6 customers order fries. Let the numbers 1–4 represent people who order fries. Estimate the number of people you will have to randomly survey before you find four who ordered fries.

3. Pearl's Pizza is holding a contest. To win, you must collect 6 different puzzle pieces. An equal number of puzzle pieces are divided randomly among the pizza boxes. Estimate the number of pizzas you must buy to win the contest.

MIXED APPLICATIONS

CHOOSE

Choose a strategy and solve.

> **Problem-Solving Strategies**
> ....
> • **Act It Out**   • **Work Backward** • **Solve a Simpler Problem**
> • **Draw a Diagram** • **Find a Pattern** • **Write an Equation**

4. An equal number of blue, black, green, purple, white, and red marbles are placed in a bag. Mike randomly picks 30 marbles out of the bag. Estimate how many will be red. Let the number 6 represent a red marble. Use the first 30 numbers from the random-number table above.

5. Jorge left his home and walked 10 blocks north, 6 blocks east, and 7 blocks south. He then walked 4 blocks west and 3 blocks south. How far west must Jorge walk to get back to his home?

6. A publicity poster is to be placed every 15 yd around the rectangular playing area at a football game. The playing area has dimensions 165 yd × 90 yd. How many posters are needed?

7. At the start of the school year, Jeremy bought $17.42 worth of supplies. He bought 6 notebooks for $5.79, 3 packs of paper for $6.32, and pens at $0.59 each. How many pens did he buy?

8. Five captains from one football team and four from the other team meet at mid-field and shake hands, with opponents and with their own teammates. Find the total number of handshakes.

9. An inchworm climbs up a branch 5 in. each day and slides back 4 in. each night. If the branch is 30 in. long, how many days will it take the inchworm to reach the end of the branch?

REMEMBER:

A simulation is a model of an experiment that would be too difficult or time-consuming to actually perform. **See page 304.**

Science Link

Biologists often study small areas as representatives of much larger areas. Suppose there are 50 prairie dogs in a 100 hectare prairie-study area. Predict the number of prairie dogs in 1 million hectares of prairie.

ALGEBRA CONNECTION

Using Proportions in a Simulation

One way conservationists estimate wildlife populations is to conduct a simulation. A given number of animals are captured, banded or tagged with an identifying label, and released back into their natural habitat. After a period of time, animals of the same type are captured, and a count is taken of those wearing bands.

EXAMPLE 1 In a region along the Mississippi River, 100 eagles, 100 mallard ducks, and 100 cranes were banded last summer. The graph at the right shows the numbers of banded and unbanded birds found during a recapture effort. About how many eagles live in this region?

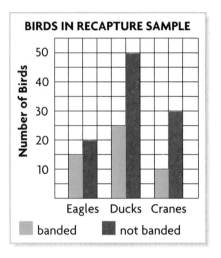

BIRDS IN RECAPTURE SAMPLE

Use this proportion.

$$\frac{\text{banded eagles in recapture}}{\text{total eagles in recapture}} = \frac{\text{original number banded}}{\text{total eagles in region}}$$

Let e represent the total number of eagles in the region.

$\frac{15}{35} = \frac{100}{e}$ *Write a proportion.*

$15e = 3{,}500$ *Find cross products.*

$e \approx 233$ *Solve for e.*

So, about 233 eagles live in the region.

Talk About It

- How do you know that the total number of eagles captured in the sample was 35?

- What proportion would you use to find out how many ducks live in the region?

- 💡**CRITICAL THINKING** What could you do to increase the chances that your estimate of the eagles in the region is accurate?

EXAMPLE 2 Without looking in the bag, how can Ashley estimate the number of red marbles in this bag of 150 marbles?

She can conduct an experiment to determine experimental probabilities and then use those probabilities to estimate the number of each color.

For the experiment, she draws a marble from the bag, records the color, and then puts the marble back in the bag. She does this 25 times.

She uses this proportion to predict the number of red marbles in the bag.

$$\frac{\text{red marbles in sample}}{\text{total marbles in sample}} = \frac{\text{red marbles in bag}}{\text{total marbles in bag}}$$

red ||||||||||||

blue ||||

green |||||||

Let r represent the number of red marbles in the bag.

$\dfrac{13}{25} = \dfrac{r}{150}$ *Write a proportion.*

$25r = 1{,}950$ *Find cross products.*

$r = 78$ *Solve for r.*

So, Ashley predicts that about 78 marbles are red.

• If Ashley continues to draw marbles from the bag, will the experimental probabilities change?

• Based on the experiment, how many blue marbles are in the bag? How many green marbles?

GUIDED PRACTICE

Write the proportion you would use to solve the problem.

1. In a particular region, 50 deer were caught, tagged, and released. Later, 30 were caught and 21 of them had tags. Estimate the deer population.

2. A conservationist caught 80 geese and found 32 of them to be banded. Originally, 40 geese had been caught, banded, and released. Estimate the goose population.

3. Greg randomly drew 30 game chips out of a bag of 400 and found 9 to be red. Estimate how many of the 400 are red.

4. In a pond, 65 catfish were caught, tagged, and released. A few weeks later, 40 catfish were caught and 8 of them had tags. Estimate the population of catfish in the pond.

INDEPENDENT PRACTICE

Use a proportion to estimate the population.

1. A ranger caught, banded, and released 200 deer in a forest. Six weeks later, 80 were caught and 17 of them had tags. Estimate the deer population in the forest.

2. Near a lake, 60 ducks were caught and 48 of them had bands. A few weeks earlier, 120 had been caught, banded, and released. Estimate the population of ducks near the lake.

3. In an area of southern Florida, 40 manatees were caught and 18 of them had tags. Originally, 70 had been caught, tagged, and released. Estimate the manatee population in the area.

4. Andre has a collection of 1,215 baseball cards from the 1970's and 1980's. He randomly chooses 50 cards and finds 17 to be from the 1970's. Estimate the number of baseball cards he has from the 1970's.

In **Mighty Math Astro Algebra**, you can go to the *Cargo Bay*. Then you can use what you know about solving proportions to complete *The Ruler of the Chotchkees* mission.

Problem-Solving Applications

5. The lake at a mountain resort is restocked with trout if the trout population falls below 800. Before the fishing season, owners of the resort catch, tag, and release 200 trout. A week later, they catch 110 trout and find 11 to be tagged. Does the lake need to be restocked with trout? Explain.

6. Bob's Bottles produces 60,000 bottles every week. If more than 1,000 bottles are defective in a week, the bottle machine must be shut down for repair. After a week of production, Bob randomly selects 125 bottles and finds 5 to be defective. Should he shut down the bottle machine? Explain.

7. **WRITE ABOUT IT** A box of cereal has red, yellow, and orange pieces. There are 2,512 pieces in the box. Explain how to estimate how many pieces are red.

Mixed Review

Write each fraction as a percent.

8. $\frac{17}{100}$

9. $\frac{17}{50}$

10. $\frac{17}{25}$

11. $\frac{3}{8}$

12. $\frac{80}{256}$

Find the value.

13. $4!$

14. $8!$

15. $\frac{8!}{4!}$

16. $\frac{12!}{10!}$

17. $\frac{10!}{(9-7)!}$

18. **NUMBER SENSE** The difference of two numbers is 71. Their sum is 227. What are the numbers?

19. **FRACTIONS** Will a nail $\frac{5}{8}$ in. long go through a board $\frac{11}{16}$ in. thick?

MORE PRACTICE Lesson 19.3, page H72

Geometric Probability

Geometric probability is the probability that a random point is located in a particular part, or subregion, of a larger region.

Use this ratio to calculate geometric probability:

$$\frac{\text{area of subregion}}{\text{area of larger region}}$$

WHAT YOU'LL LEARN
How to find or estimate probabilities based on geometric relationships

WHY LEARN THIS?
To find the probability that an object will land in a certain region

EXAMPLE 1 What is the probability that a point randomly placed on this figure is in region *A*? in region *B*?

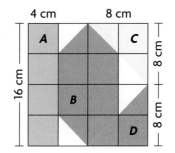

First, use the formulas for the areas of rectangles and triangles to find the area of the whole region and the areas of regions A and B.

The area of the whole region is 16 cm × 16 cm, or 256 cm².

The area of region *A* is 4 cm × 16 cm, or 64 cm².

The area of region *B* is 8 cm × 8 cm + 4 × $\frac{1}{2}$(4 cm × 4 cm), or 96 cm².

Then, write a ratio to find each probability.

$\dfrac{\text{area of region } A}{\text{area of whole region}} \rightarrow \dfrac{64}{256} = \dfrac{1}{4}$, or 25%

$\dfrac{\text{area of region } B}{\text{area of whole region}} \rightarrow \dfrac{96}{256} = \dfrac{3}{8}$, or 37.5%

So, the probability that the point is in region *A* is $\frac{1}{4}$, or 25%, and the probability that the point is in region *B* is $\frac{3}{8}$, or 37.5%.

- What is the probability that a point randomly placed on the figure is in region *C*?

> **REMEMBER:**
> The formula for the area of a rectangle is $A = lw$.
>
> The formula for the area of a triangle is $A = \frac{1}{2}bh$.
>
> **See pages H25 and 209.**

Talk About It 💡 CRITICAL THINKING

- Explain how you would find the probability that the point is in region *C* or region *D*. Then find the probability.

- Explain how you would find the probability that the point is not in region *C* or region *D*. Then find the probability.

- Explain how you would find the probability that the point is in region A, region B, region C, or region D. Find the probability.

EXAMPLE 2 A helicopter drops a box of supplies onto this field in an isolated community. If the box lands in a random location on the field, what is the probability that the supplies will land in the swamp?

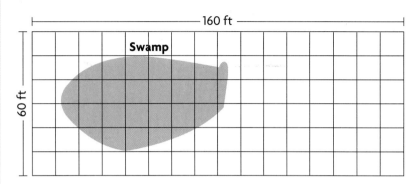

Estimate the area covered by the swamp. Then use that estimated area and the area of the whole region to calculate the probability.

$$\frac{\text{estimated area of swamp}}{\text{area of field}} \rightarrow \frac{2,100}{9,600} = \frac{7}{32}, \text{ or about } 22\%$$

- How would you find the probability that the supplies will land in a dry place? Find the probability.

GUIDED PRACTICE

An object falls somewhere on the target. Find the geometric probability that a randomly dropped object will land in a shaded region.

1.
2 2 2
2 [ ][ ][ ] 2
2 [ ][ ][ ] 2
2 2 2

2.
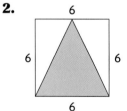
6
6   6
6

3.
2 2 2
2 [ ][ ][ ] 2
2 [ ][ ][ ] 2
2 2 2

INDEPENDENT PRACTICE

An object falls somewhere on the target. Use the figure at the right to find the geometric probability that a randomly dropped object will fall in the given region.

1. *A*

2. *B*

3. *C*

4. *D*

5. *A* or *B*

6. *C* or *D*

7. *A, B,* or *C*

8. *B, C,* or *D*

9. white regions

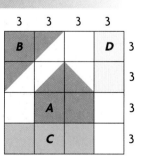

Problem-Solving Applications

This map shows a lake and a cow pasture on a large area of land. Supplies are being dropped in this area and will land at a random location. Use the map for Problems 10–13.

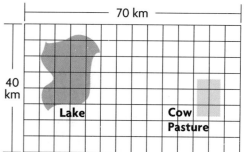

10. Estimate the probability that the supplies will land in the lake.

11. Estimate the probability that the supplies will land in the cow pasture.

12. Estimate the probability that the supplies will land in the lake or cow pasture.

13. Estimate the probability that the supplies will not land in the lake or cow pasture.

14. An open hole in a rectangular section of a street is shown at the right. What is the geometric probability that a ball dropped in this section of the street will fall into the hole? What is the geometric probability that it will not fall into the hole? Use 3.14 for π.

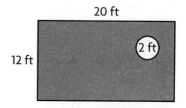

15. Carla's round sink is in a corner, on a triangular counter as shown at the right. When getting ready to do the dishes, Carla took off her ring and dropped it. What is the geometric probability that her ring fell into the sink? Use 3.14 for π.

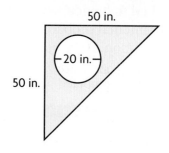

16. ✏️ **WRITE ABOUT IT** Draw a picture of a dartboard. Write a problem involving geometric probability. Exchange with a partner and solve.

Mixed Review

Trace the angle, and use a protractor to find the measure.

17.   **18.**   **19.**   **20.**

A bag contains 8 red chips, 4 blue chips, 3 green chips, and 5 yellow chips. You choose one chip without looking. Find the probability.

21. P(red)   **22.** P(blue)   **23.** P(blue or green)   **24.** P(yellow or red)

25. CONSUMER MATH Ricky bought a new coat for 75% off. He paid $50 for the coat. How much did he save?

26. NUMBER SENSE In 6 years, Brian will be 4 times as old as he was 6 years ago. How old is he now?

CULTURAL CONNECTION

Scottish Highland Games

Scotland is a country in Europe located north of England. The Highland Games have long been a tradition of Scotland. People compete in events such as foot races, dancing, playing bagpipes, putting the stone, and caber tossing. The caber is a long wooden pole that can weigh close to 200 lb. Competitors lift the caber and toss it. The toss is scored on accuracy. All competitors in the Highland Games wear a traditional Scottish kilt. The Highland Games are so popular, they are held all over the world.

Amy is competing in a Highland Games competition for Scottish dancing in California. In her last five competitions, Amy has finished first once, second three times, and fifth once. Find the experimental probability that Amy will finish second in this competition. Write your answer as a ratio and percent.

$$\frac{\text{times in second place}}{\text{total times competed}} = \frac{3}{5}, \text{ or } 60\%$$

WORK TOGETHER

1. Amy's uncle is participating in the caber toss. He practiced the week before the event by tossing the caber 50 times. He had a successful toss 15 times. How many successful tosses can he expect to have out of 10 tosses he will make during the competition?

2. At the games, some of the 600 programs were randomly marked with a Scottish flag. Anyone with a marked program won a souvenir. Amy randomly surveyed 30 people and found 6 of their programs were marked. Estimate the number of people who won a souvenir.

3. In the putting-the-stone competition, Amy's brother putted the stone in the area shown on the grid at the right. Find the geometric probability that the stone landed in the blue area. Each square on the grid represents 2 yd^2.

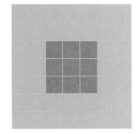

CULTURAL LINK

Another popular sport in Scotland is golf. It is believed that the game of golf was invented in Scotland in the 14th or 15th century. It became so popular that a law was passed banning the sport. People were expected to practice archery to defend their territory instead of hitting a ball with a club. The law was ignored and golf's popularity continued to grow.

EXAMPLES

- **Find the experimental probability of an event.**
  (pages 358–360)

  Jim got 22 hits in 80 times at bat. Predict how many hits he will get in his next 100 times at bat.

  experimental probability: $\frac{22}{80} = \frac{11}{40} = 27.5\%$

  $100 \times 0.275 = 27.5$, or about 28 hits

- **Use the strategy** *act it out* **to solve problems.**
  (pages 362–363)

  PROBLEM-SOLVING TIP: For help in solving a problem by acting it out, see pages 3, 362.

1	4	4	2	2	2	4	5
2	1	4	4	3	3	2	3
5	1	3	4	5	3	4	1
4	3	2	2	4	5	5	3
4	2	4	4	4	4	2	5

- **Use a proportion to estimate a population.**
  (pages 364–366)

  A bag contains 400 blue, green, and red marbles. Forty are randomly drawn, and 14 of them are red. Estimate the total number of red marbles.

  $\frac{14}{40} = \frac{x}{400}$ *Use a proportion.*

  $40x = 5,600$ *Find cross products.*

  $x = 140$ ← There are about 140 red marbles.

- **Find the geometric probability.** (pages 367–369)

  A yard whose area is 400 m^2 has a pool in it whose area is 50 m^2. Find the geometric probability that a ball randomly thrown into the yard will land in the pool.

  $\frac{50}{400} = \frac{1}{8}$, or 12.5%

EXERCISES

In a football game, Bob completes 8 out of 10 passes. Find the experimental probability of each event.

1. Bob completes his next pass.
2. Bob does not complete his next pass.
3. How many completed passes can Bob expect during his next 40 tries?

Use the random-number table at the left.

4. A bag holds equal numbers of marbles of 5 different colors. Estimate how many times you will have to draw a marble from the bag to get all 5 colors.
5. Two of every 5 bags of chips contain a coupon for free chip dip. Let 1 and 2 represent bags with coupons in them. Estimate how many bags you would have to buy to get 2 coupons.

Use a proportion to simulate the population.

6. A conservationist catches, bands, and releases 150 cranes. A few weeks later, 50 are caught and 19 of them have bands. Estimate the population of cranes.
7. From a bag of 500, 25 game chips are randomly drawn. Of these, 17 are red. Estimate the total number of red chips.

Find the geometric probability that a randomly dropped object will fall in the given region.

8. *A*   9. *B*
10. *C*   11. *D*
12. *A, B,* or *C*

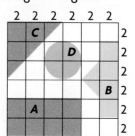

VOCABULARY CHECK

1. The spread of the values in a set of data is called the __?__ of the data. (page 325)

2. The number used to describe the chance that an event will occur is the mathematical __?__ of an event. (page 346)

EXAMPLES

- **Use unbiased samples to predict.**
  (pages 304–305)

  There are 800 students in your school. In an unbiased survey, 70 out of 100 students say their favorite lunch is pizza. Predict how many students in the school prefer pizza.

  $\dfrac{70}{100} = \dfrac{n}{800}$ *Write a proportion.*

  $100n = 800 \times 70$ *Solve.*

  $n = 560$ So, about 560 students prefer pizza.

- **Use graphs to make predictions.** (pages 312–315)
  Predict the July attendance in the year 2000.

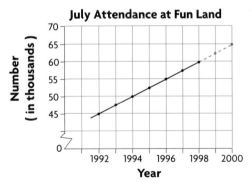

July Attendance at Fun Land

- **Use multiplication to find the number of possible outcomes.** (pages 340–341)

  Find the number of possible outcomes:
  3 drink sizes, 5 soda flavors
  $m \times n$ = number of different outcomes
  $3 \times 5 = 15$ 15 different outcomes

EXERCISES

There are 1,500 people who work in a theme park. Use the unbiased survey results to make an estimate about this population.

3. Of 200 people, 140 said they prefer working the day shift.

4. Of 200 people, 50 said they prefer working indoors.

For Exercises 5–8, use the graph at the left.

5. Estimate the number of people who visited Fun Land in July of 1993.

6. What is the trend in the data?

7. Predict the number of people who will visit Fun Land in July 2002.

8. Predict the number of people who will visit Fun Land in July 2003.

Find the number of possible outcomes.

9. 8 buses, 4 departure times each

10. 4 salespeople, 24 customers

11. 6 pizzas, 3 sizes, 8 toppings

- **Find the number of permutations or combinations.** (pages 342–345)

In how many combinations can a student choose 4 classes from a list of 6?

$_6C_4 = {_6P_4} \div 4!$

$= \dfrac{6!}{(6-4)!} \div 4! \leftarrow {_6P_4} = \dfrac{6!}{(6-4)!}$

$= \dfrac{6!}{2!} \div 4! \qquad \downarrow Expand\ factorials.$

$= \dfrac{6 \times 5 \times 4 \times 3 \times 2 \times 1}{2 \times 1} \div (4 \times 3 \times 2 \times 1)$

$360 \div 24 = 15 \quad$ 15 combinations

Find the number of combinations and permutations.

12. $_3P_2$ **13.** $_9P_3$ **14.** $_{11}P_4$

15. $_6C_2$ **16.** $_7C_2$ **17.** $_{10}C_8$

Tell whether *permutations* or *combinations* are described. Then find the number.

18. 4 out of 6 people sitting in a row of 4 chairs

- **Find the experimental probability of an event.** (pages 358–360)

Of the 25 hr Sal spent working on the computer, 18 were spent on the Internet. Predict how many of his next 50 hr on the computer will be on the Internet.

experimental probability: $\dfrac{18}{25} = 72\%$

$50 \times 0.72 = 36 \leftarrow$ 36 hr on the Internet

Ed correctly answers 5 out of 8 questions.

19. Find the experimental probability that Ed incorrectly answers the next question.

20. How many questions can Ed expect to answer correctly out of the next 32 questions?

- **Find the geometric probability.** (pages 367–369)

Find the geometric probability a randomly thrown object will land on region 3. Each square is 5 cm × 5 cm.

$A = 400\ cm^2$

$\dfrac{\text{area of region 3}}{\text{area of whole region}} = \dfrac{25}{400}$

$= \dfrac{1}{16}, \text{ or } 6.25\%$

The probability is $\dfrac{1}{16}$, or 6.25%.

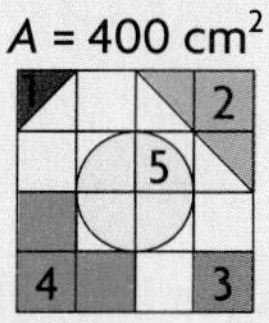

Find the probability that a randomly thrown object will land on the figure at the left in the given region.

21. region 2

22. region 4

23. region 1

24. region 5 $(A = \pi r^2)$

PROBLEM SOLVING

Solve. Explain your method.

25. Teams are being formed for a basketball game. From 10 students, how many possible teams of 5 players can be formed? (pages 342–345)

26. A game has 24 cards, 4 with pictures and 20 with numbers on them. Chen picks the top 2 cards. What is the probability that both are picture cards? (pages 350–353)

WHAT DID I LEARN?

Write About It

1. Use the information in the table to make two stacked-bar graphs.
(pages 308–311)

Population of State Capitals			
	Austin, TX	**Columbus, OH**	**Albany, NY**
1980	345,890	565,021	101,727
1990	456,648	632,945	100,031

2. Show how you would use a stem-and-leaf plot to compare the spread of Doreen's test scores this quarter with the spread of her test scores last quarter. Explain. (pages 325–327)

Quarter 1	81, 89, 86, 92, 99, 88, 77, 83, 95, 95
Quarter 2	74, 87, 89, 83, 88, 99, 99, 96, 85, 89

3. In how many ways can the letters FOUR be arranged? Explain.
(pages 342–345)

4. How can you find the geometric probability that a randomly dropped object would land in the shaded region. Find the probability. (pages 367–369)

✔ Performance Assessment

Choose a strategy and solve. Explain your method.

Problem-Solving Strategies

- Solve a Simpler Problem
- Make a List
- Make a Model
- Make a Graph
- Write an Equation
- Guess and

5. Scientists want to estimate the number of deer in a park. One week they captured and tagged 6 deer. The next week they captured 12 deer, 4 of which were tagged. Estimate the number of deer in the park.
(pages 306–307)

6. Is there a relationship between the two sets of data? What is it? Draw a scatterplot and the line of best fit. (pages 329–330)

	A	B	C	D	E	F	G	H	I	J
Ages in years	10	12	14	16	18	20	22	24	26	28
Push-ups	5	10	16	20	26	30	34	38	44	52

7. A shop offers 3 kinds of coffee, 4 kinds of bagels, and 5 kinds of cheese spreads. How many combinations are possible?
(pages 342–345)

8. Ms. Wu randomly selects 1 of 6 flavors of tea each day. Use the table on page 363 to estimate the number of days it will take to select all 6 flavors. (pages 362–363)

CUMULATIVE REVIEW

Solve the problem. Then write the letter of the correct answer.

1. What is 25,000,000 written in scientific notation? (pages 20–23)

    A. 2.5×10^{-8} **B.** 2.5×10^{-7}
    C. 2.5×10^{7} **D.** 2.5×10^{8}

2. Solve for x. $3x - 2 = \frac{1}{2}(4 - 2x)$
(pages 139–141)

    A. $x = 1$ **B.** $x = 2$
    C. $x = 3$ **D.** $x = 4$

3. Ben earns $5.25 an hour. He saves 20% of his earnings. Find the amount Ben saves in a week if he works a 20-hr, 25-hr, and 30-hr week. (pages 205–207)

    A. $2.10, $2.63, $3.15
    B. $21.00, $26.25, $31.50
    C. $85.00, $111.25, $137.50
    D. $105.00, $131.25, $157.50

4. Find the 15th term of the arithmetic sequence.   42, 48, 54, 60, . . . (pages 214–216)

    A. 66   **B.** 75
    C. 126   **D.** 138

5. Find the scale factor.
5-ft-long model of a 35-yd-long parking lot
(pages 248–249)

    A. $\frac{1}{35}$ **B.** $\frac{1}{21}$ **C.** $\frac{1}{5}$ **D.** 5

6. What percent of 125 is 300? (pages 267–269)

    A. 24%   **B.** 42%
    C. 240%   **D.** 300%

7. Bea earns $400 a month plus a 3% commission on her sales. Last month she earned a total of $544. What did her sales total? (pages 286–288)

    A. $144   **B.** $480
    C. $1,480   **D.** $4,800

8. There are 1,230 students in your school. In a survey, 38 of 60 students said they prefer basketball to soccer. Predict about how many students in your school prefer basketball to soccer. (pages 304–305)

    A. about 451   **B.** about 644
    C. about 779   **D.** about 923

9. Find the mean of the temperatures in the table. (pages 322–324)

65°	72°	58°	71°	64°	60°	65°	71°	68°	66°

    A. 64°   **B.** 66°
    C. 68°   **D.** 71°

10. At the deli, you have your choice of one of 3 meats, white or wheat bread, and one of 5 dressings. How many different sandwiches could you order?
(pages 340–341)

    A. 10 sandwiches   **B.** 15 sandwiches
    C. 20 sandwiches   **D.** 30 sandwiches

11. You roll a cube numbered 1 to 6. What is the probability of rolling an odd number?
(pages 346–348)

    A. $\frac{1}{6}$ **B.** $\frac{1}{3}$ **C.** $\frac{1}{2}$ **D.** $\frac{2}{3}$

CONSTRUCTING AND DRAWING

LOOK AHEAD

In this chapter you will solve problems that involve

- constructing parallel and perpendicular lines
- bisecting line segments and angles
- constructing similar triangles

Team-Up Project

Finding Your Way

Two hundred years ago, a sailor might have used a compass with a star design pointing to North, South, East, West, and points between these such as Northeast or Southwest. You can construct a compass rose using a ruler and compass.

YOU WILL NEED: compass, ruler

Plan • Work with a partner. Construct a compass rose.

Act • Draw a circle with a 4 cm radius. Use a ruler to draw the East and West segment. Open your compass 7 cm. Put the compass point on West and East to draw arcs to find North and South. Draw the North and South segment with a ruler. Label all directions.

• Open your compass 4 cm. Put the compass point on North, South, East, and West to draw the arcs to find Northeast, Southeast, Southwest, and Northwest. Use a ruler to draw the segments. Label all directions.

• Divide your compass rose into as many equal parts as you wish, labeling each direction.

Share • Share your compass rose with the class.

HOW TO CONSTRUCT A COMPASS ROSE

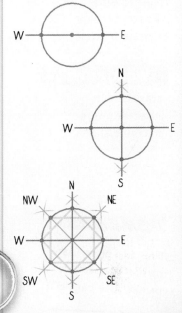

DID YOU
- ☑ Construct a compass rose?
- ☑ Label all directions?
- ☑ Share your compass rose with the class?

Parallel and Perpendicular Lines

REMEMBER:

Lines in a plane that do not intersect are parallel. **See page H21.**

$\overleftrightarrow{AB} \parallel \overleftrightarrow{CD}$

$\overleftrightarrow{AB}$ is parallel to $\overleftrightarrow{CD}$.

Two angles whose measures have a sum of 180° are supplementary angles. **See page H20.**

Civil engineers often use parallel and perpendicular lines when they design layouts for town streets.

On this map Washington Street and Lincoln Street appear to be parallel. Skyway Boulevard intersects both of these streets. When two parallel lines are cut by a third line, a **transversal**, four pairs of corresponding angles are formed.

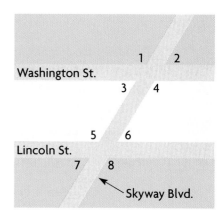

The pairs of corresponding angles on the map are angles 1 and 5, angles 2 and 6, angles 3 and 7, and angles 4 and 8.

ACTIVITY 1

WHAT YOU'LL NEED: graph paper, protractor, straightedge

- Draw a pair of parallel lines. Then draw a transversal and label the angles as shown.

- Measure the eight angles. Copy and complete this table to show the measures.

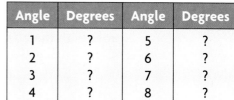

- Describe the patterns you see in the measures of corresponding angles.

Angle	Degrees	Angle	Degrees
1	?	5	?
2	?	6	?
3	?	7	?
4	?	8	?

- Explain how you can find the measures of angles 2 through 8 if you know that the measure of angle 1 is 110°.

The angles in the yellow area on the map are on the inner sides of two lines cut by a transversal and are called **interior angles**. The angles in the green areas are on the outer sides of two lines cut by a transversal and are **exterior angles**. Angles 3 and 6 and angles 4 and 5 are alternate interior angles. The alternate exterior angles are angles 1 and 8 and angles 2 and 7.

- How are the measures of interior and exterior angles related?

You can use a compass and a straightedge to construct a line parallel to another line.

EXAMPLE 1 Construct a line parallel to $\overleftrightarrow{YZ}$.

Step 1	Step 2	Step 3
Choose any point P above $\overleftrightarrow{YZ}$. Draw a line through point P that intersects $\overleftrightarrow{YZ}$. Label the point of intersection W.	*Construct an angle congruent to $\angle PWZ$ at point P. Label the point Q.*	*Draw $\overrightarrow{PQ}$. $\overrightarrow{PQ}$ is a line parallel to $\overleftrightarrow{YZ}$. $\overrightarrow{PQ} \parallel \overleftrightarrow{YZ}$*
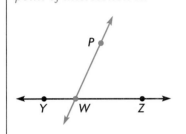	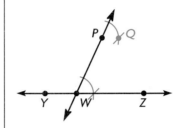	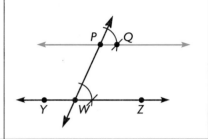

• How are the angle you constructed and $\angle PWZ$ related?

GUIDED PRACTICE

For Exercises 1–9, use the figure at the right.
Find the measure of the given angle.

1. $\angle 2$ **2.** $\angle 3$

3. $\angle 5$ **4.** $\angle 8$

Name the corresponding angle.

5. $\angle 4$ **6.** $\angle 6$ **7.** $\angle 3$ **8.** $\angle 5$

9. Explain how you found $\angle 5$.

ACTIVITY 2

WHAT YOU'LL NEED: tracing paper, straightedge

• Use a straightedge to draw $\overleftrightarrow{AB}$ on tracing paper. Place a point, *P*, above the line and a point, *Q*, on the line.

• How could you fold the paper so that the fold line is perpendicular to $\overleftrightarrow{AB}$ and goes through point *P*?

• What is the measure of each angle formed by the intersection of perpendicular lines?

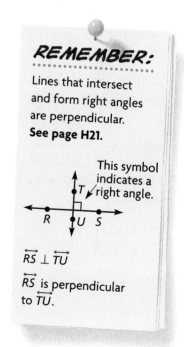

REMEMBER:
....
Lines that intersect and form right angles are perpendicular.
See page H21.

This symbol indicates a right angle.

$\overleftrightarrow{RS} \perp \overleftrightarrow{TU}$

$\overleftrightarrow{RS}$ is perpendicular to $\overleftrightarrow{TU}$.

You can use a compass and a straightedge to construct a perpendicular line through a point.

EXAMPLE 2 Construct a line perpendicular to $\overleftrightarrow{AB}$ through a point P.

Step 1	Step 2	Step 3
Place the compass point on point P. Draw an arc that intersects $\overleftrightarrow{AB}$ as shown. Label C and D.	*Using the same compass opening, draw intersecting arcs from points C and D.*	*Draw $\overleftrightarrow{PE}$. $\overleftrightarrow{PE}$ goes through P and is perpendicular to $\overleftrightarrow{AB}$. $\overleftrightarrow{PE} \perp \overleftrightarrow{AB}$.*
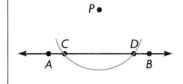	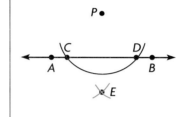	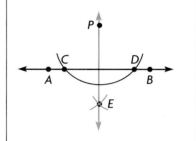

Talk About It

- How can you construct a line perpendicular to $\overleftrightarrow{ST}$ through point R? (HINT: First, place the compass point on point R and draw two arcs.)

- If 90° angles are formed when two parallel lines are cut by a transversal, how is the transversal related to the parallel lines?

INDEPENDENT PRACTICE

For Exercises 1–9, use the figure at the right. Find the measure of the given angle.

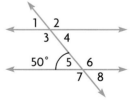

1. ∠1

2. ∠2

3. ∠3

4. ∠4

5. ∠6

6. ∠7

7. Name the four pairs of corresponding angles.

8. Name the alternate interior angles.

9. Name the alternate exterior angles.

Tell whether the lines appear to be *parallel* or *perpendicular*.

10.

11.

12.

13.

Trace $\overleftrightarrow{ST}$ and P as shown for each.

14. Construct a line through point P and parallel to $\overleftrightarrow{ST}$.

15. Construct a line through point P and perpendicular to $\overleftrightarrow{ST}$.

16. Construct a line through point P and perpendicular to $\overleftrightarrow{ST}$.

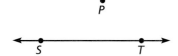

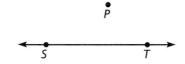

Problem-Solving Applications

17. Copy $\overleftrightarrow{AB}$, C, and R. Construct $\overleftrightarrow{CD} \perp \overleftrightarrow{AB}$. Then construct $\overleftrightarrow{RT} \perp \overleftrightarrow{CD}$. What is the relationship between $\overleftrightarrow{AB}$ and $\overleftrightarrow{RT}$?

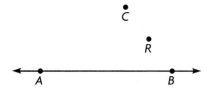

18. The city planners are proposing a new street. It will be perpendicular to First Street and go through point A. Make a map they can show to the city council.

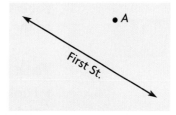

19. In Exercise 18, how many streets through point A can be perpendicular to First Street?

20. ▬▶ **WRITE ABOUT IT** Explain how you can check your construction of two parallel lines and of two perpendicular lines.

Mixed Review

Use a protractor to draw each angle.

21. m$\angle ABC = 50°$

22. m$\angle DEF = 80°$

23. m$\angle GHI = 120°$

A football quarterback completes 16 out of 20 passes. Use this information to find the experimental probability.

24. completing the next pass

25. not completing the next pass

26. **COMPARISON** The Library Parking Garage charges $4 for the first hour and $1 for each additional hour. The City Parking Garage charges $3 per hour. Which parking garage would be the better buy for 1 hr? for 2 hr? How much more does it cost for 5 hr in the City Parking Garage than in the Library Parking Garage?

27. **MEASUREMENT** Beth has 17 links in her 20-cm-long bracelet. If she removes one link, what will be the new length of her bracelet?

WHAT YOU'LL LEARN
How to bisect line
segments and angles

WHY LEARN THIS?
To be able to
construct angles that
are 45° and to bisect
line segments for
drawings and diagrams

WORD POWER
bisect

Bisecting Line Segments and Angles

To **bisect** is to divide into two congruent parts. Midpoints of line segments and bisectors of angles can be found by paper folding.

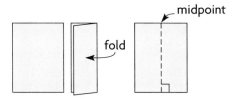

midpoint

fold

Use the top edge of a sheet of paper as the segment. Fold so the endpoints are together.

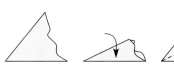

Cut an angle from paper. Fold at the vertex so the two sides are together.

Talk About It

- Look at the construction at the right. Point *X* is the midpoint of segment *RS*. Describe how a compass and a straightedge were used to find point *X*.

- What do you know about the lengths of segments *RX* and *XS*?

- How can you use a compass and a straightedge to find the midpoint of segment *AB*?

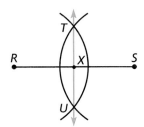

$$\overline{RX} \cong \overline{XS}$$
$$\overline{RS} \perp \overline{TU}$$

EXAMPLE   Construct the bisector of ∠*GKH*.

Step 1	Step 2	Step 3
Draw ∠K. Place the point of the compass at point K and draw an arc through the sides of ∠K.	*With the same compass opening, draw intersecting arcs from points G and H.*	*Draw $\overrightarrow{KF}$. $\overrightarrow{KF}$ is the bisector of ∠K.* *∠GKF ≅ ∠FKH*

Trace the figure. Then bisect it.

1.
R ———————————— U

2.
P
          Q

3.

A
B C

4.

D
E F

5.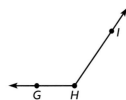

I
G H

INDEPENDENT PRACTICE

Draw the figures by using a ruler and a protractor. Then construct the bisector of each by using a compass and a straightedge.

1. a 5-in. line segment

2. an 84° angle

3. a 110° angle

4. a 4-in. line segment

5. a 90° angle

6. a 6-in. line segment

7. an 8-in. line segment

8. a 160° angle

Problem-Solving Applications

9. Diane has a 9-in. × 16-in. sheet of paper. Explain how she can divide it into four congruent sections without using a ruler. A 16-in. edge of the sheet should be used as a line segment.

10. Draw any line segment. Then use a compass and a straightedge to divide it into four congruent parts. Explain the steps of your construction.

11. Paul is bisecting $\overline{AB}$. He places the point of the compass on point A, opens the compass, and draws an arc that intersects $\overline{AB}$. He places the point of the compass on point B, opens the compass, and draws another arc that intersects $\overline{AB}$. Paul realizes that the arcs do not intersect each other. What is his mistake?

12. Ben created a compass rose with a compass and a ruler. First he drew a 3-in. square. Next he bisected each angle of the square. Then he labeled each bisector with a direction. Make your own compass rose by completing the steps used by Ben.

13. ✎ **WRITE ABOUT IT** How are the steps of bisecting an angle similar to the steps of bisecting a line segment?

REMEMBER:
. . . .
In congruent figures, corresponding sides are congruent and corresponding angles are congruent. **See pages 44 and 232.**

$\triangle ABC \cong \triangle DEF$

$\overline{AB} \cong \overline{DE}$ $\angle A \cong \angle D$

$\overline{BC} \cong \overline{EF}$ $\angle B \cong \angle E$

$\overline{CA} \cong \overline{FD}$ $\angle C \cong \angle F$

Constructing Congruent Triangles

You can make sure that two triangles are congruent.

ACTIVITY

WHAT YOU'LL NEED: three 4-in. × 6-in. index cards, ruler, protractor, scissors, compass

Along one of the longer edges of each card, mark a 5-in. segment as shown.

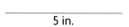

On Card 1

- Draw a 37° angle at one endpoint of the 5-in. segment. Mark a 4-in. segment along the ray you drew.

- Connect the endpoints of the segments. Cut out the triangle.

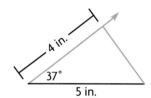

On Card 2

- Draw a 37° angle at one endpoint of the 5-in. segment. Draw a 53° angle at the other endpoint.

- Extend the rays until they intersect to form the other two sides of the triangle. Cut out the triangle.

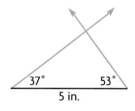

On Card 3

- With a compass, swing a 4-in. radius from one endpoint of the 5-in. segment. Swing a 3-in. radius from the other endpoint.

- Connect the endpoints of the 5-in. segment with the intersection point of the arcs. Cut out the triangle.

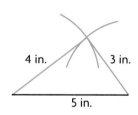

Talk About It    CRITICAL THINKING

- Are the three triangles congruent? Explain.

- Which three corresponding parts did you use to draw each triangle?

To determine whether two triangles are congruent, you need only three corresponding congruent parts and these rules.

If this is true, triangles are congruent.	Name of Rule	Example
Two sides and the included angle of one triangle match two sides and the included angle of another triangle.	Side-Angle-Side (SAS)	
Two angles and the included side of one triangle match two angles and the included side of another triangle.	Angle-Side-Angle (ASA)	
Three sides of one triangle match three sides of another triangle.	Side-Side-Side (SSS)	

You can use the rules for congruence of two triangles, along with a straightedge and a compass, to construct congruent triangles.

EXAMPLE 1 Using the SAS rule, construct a triangle congruent to △ABC.

Think: Use these parts: $\overline{AB}$, ∠A, and $\overline{AC}$.

Step 1	Step 2	Step 3	Step 4
Construct $\overline{PR} \cong \overline{AB}$.	Construct ∠P ≅ ∠A.	Construct $\overline{PT} \cong \overline{AC}$.	Draw $\overline{TR}$. △PRT ≅ △ABC
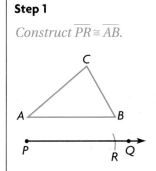	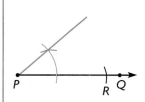	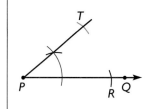	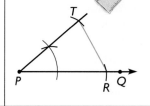

EXAMPLE 2 Using the ASA rule, construct a triangle congruent to △JKL.

Think: Use these parts: ∠J, $\overline{JK}$, and ∠K.

Step 1	Step 2	Step 3	Step 4
Construct $\overline{AB} \cong \overline{JK}$.	Construct ∠A ≅ ∠J.	Construct ∠B ≅ ∠K.	Label C. △ABC ≅ △JKL
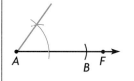	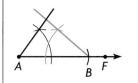	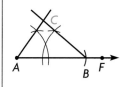	

The straightedge, compass, protractor, and triangle help you draw basic elements—line segments, circles, and angles. Elements like these are combined in complicated ways with powerful computers and CAD (computer-aided design) software. The basic elements can be duplicated, moved, rotated, or scaled almost instantly. Suppose a designer needs to duplicate a triangle 100 times for bridge supports. What is the smallest group of features the designer might need to specify for all these congruent triangles?

EXAMPLE 3 Using the SSS rule, construct a triangle congruent to △*JKL*.

Think: The corresponding sides must have the same length.

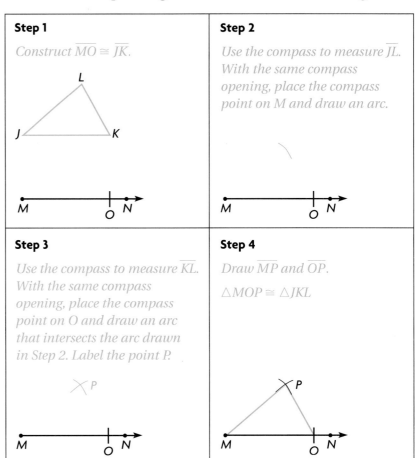

Step 1	Step 2
Construct $\overline{MO} \cong \overline{JK}$.	Use the compass to measure $\overline{JL}$. With the same compass opening, place the compass point on M and draw an arc.

Step 3	Step 4
Use the compass to measure $\overline{KL}$. With the same compass opening, place the compass point on O and draw an arc that intersects the arc drawn in Step 2. Label the point P.	Draw $\overline{MP}$ and $\overline{OP}$. $\triangle MOP \cong \triangle JKL$

• Why is the choice of angles and sides important when using the ASA rule or the SAS rule?

GUIDED PRACTICE

Determine whether the triangles are congruent by *SSS*, *SAS*, or *ASA*.

1.  **2.**  **3.**

4. Construct a congruent triangle. Use the ASA rule.

INDEPENDENT PRACTICE

Use the marked sides and angles to determine whether the triangles are congruent. Write *yes*, *no*, or *not necessarily*. Then explain.

1.

2.

3.

Use the indicated rule to construct a triangle congruent to the given triangle.

4. ASA

5. SAS

6. SSS

Problem-Solving Applications

7. In the figure two homes are located at points *B* and *C* on either side of a lake. The distances *PB*, *PC*, *PA*, *PD*, and *AD* and the measure of angle *BPC* are shown. Find *BC*, the distance between the homes. Give the reason for your answer.

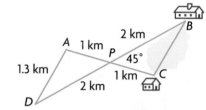

8. A builder wants to verify that triangular roof supports are exactly the same. Does he need to measure all six corresponding parts? Explain.

9. ✏️ **WRITE ABOUT IT** Explain how you can use the SSS, SAS, and ASA rules to help you construct congruent triangles.

Mixed Review

Solve each proportion for *x*.

10. $\frac{x}{10} = \frac{11}{22}$

11. $\frac{9}{27} = \frac{3}{x}$

12. $\frac{4}{x} = \frac{12}{36}$

13. $\frac{8}{12} = \frac{x}{21}$

Use the figure at the right to find the probability.

14. A point randomly placed is in Region *A*.

15. A point randomly placed is in Region *B*.

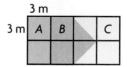

16. **AVERAGES** Sonya is studying to be a court reporter. Her goal is to average 225 recorded words a minute. If she records 1,140 words in 5 min, has she reached her goal? Explain.

17. **RATES** Morgan's taxi ride to the airport cost $53.00. If the first $\frac{1}{8}$ mi cost $1.60 and each additional $\frac{1}{8}$ mi cost $0.20, how many miles did Morgan travel to the airport?

MORE PRACTICE Lesson 20.3, page H73

Making Similar Triangles

Congruent figures have the same size and shape. Similar figures have the same shape but not necessarily the same size.

Explore

Work with a partner to make similar triangles.

- Cut four right triangles, each with 3-in., 4-in., and 5-in. sides, from index cards.

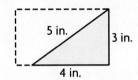

- Make perpendicular cuts through three of the triangles to make triangles with the dimensions shown. Label each vertex and side.

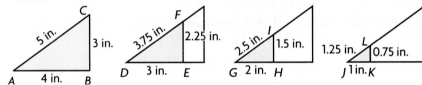

Think and Discuss

- Find the ratios of corresponding sides of △*ABC* and △*DEF*. How are the ratios related? Are the two triangles similar?

- Compare the ratios of corresponding sides of △*DEF* and △*GHI* and of △*GHI* and △*JKL*. Are all four triangles similar?

- How do the perimeters of the four triangles compare? How do the areas compare?

Try This

- Cut two congruent right triangles from one index card. Label the vertices of each triangle *A*, *B*, and *C*.

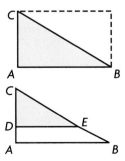

- In one triangle, make a cut parallel to $\overline{AB}$ to make a smaller triangle. Label the smaller triangle *CDE*.

- Measure and record the lengths of the sides of the triangles.

- Compare the ratios of corresponding sides of the triangles. Are the triangles similar?

Technology **Link**

E–Lab • Activity 20 Available on CD-ROM and the Internet at http://www.hbschool.com/elab

Constructing Similar Triangles

These letters were printed on a personal computer in the same style but different point sizes. The letters are similar but not congruent.

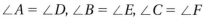

48 point   36 point   24 point   12 point

Similarity is used to compare or construct geometric figures.

> If triangles are similar, then corresponding angles are congruent and corresponding sides are proportional.

$\triangle ABC$ and $\triangle DEF$ are similar.

So, their angles are congruent.
$\angle A = \angle D$, $\angle B = \angle E$, $\angle C = \angle F$

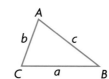

Their sides are proportional.
$$\frac{a}{d} = \frac{b}{e} = \frac{c}{f}$$

- **CRITICAL THINKING**   If two triangles are congruent, how do you know they are also similar? If two triangles are similar and congruent, what is the ratio of corresponding sides?

EXAMPLE   Construct $\triangle DEF$ similar to $\triangle ABC$ so that $\overline{EF}$ has a length of 5 in.

Write and solve proportions to find the lengths DE and DF.

$$\frac{4}{5} = \frac{6}{DE} \qquad \frac{4}{5} = \frac{3}{DF}$$
$4(DE) = 5 \times 6 \qquad 4(DF) = 5 \times 3$
$4(DE) = 30 \qquad 4(DF) = 15$
$DE = 7\frac{1}{2} \qquad DF = 3\frac{3}{4}$

Draw a 5-in. segment, and label the endpoints E and F.

Swing a $7\frac{1}{2}$-in. arc from E and a $3\frac{3}{4}$-in. arc from F. The point where the arcs intersect is vertex D. Draw $\overline{DE}$ and $\overline{DF}$.

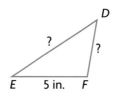
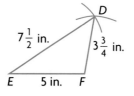

WHAT YOU'LL LEARN
How to identify and construct similar triangles

WHY LEARN THIS?
To be able to draw maps and make scale models of real-world objects

Computer Link

If you write reports or letters with a personal computer that has a word processing program, you can change the size of the type. Type size is measured in units called points (pt). Using 12-pt type, you can get about 6 lines of type per inch. About how many lines fit on a standard 8.5-in. × 11-in. piece of paper, with a 1-in. margin at the top and bottom of the page?

389

Triangle *RST* was constructed to be similar to △*JKL*. Angles *R*, *S*, and *T* correspond to angles *J*, *K*, and *L*.

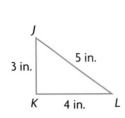
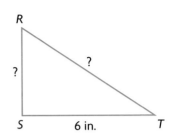

1. What is the ratio of the corresponding sides of the triangles?

2. What is the length of $\overline{RT}$?

3. What can be said about the angles of the two triangles?

Construct △*ABC* similar to △*DEF*. Make $\overline{AB}$ correspond to $\overline{DE}$, and use the given length of $\overline{AB}$. △*DEF* is not drawn to scale.

1. *AB* = 2 in.   2. *AB* = 4 cm   3. *AB* = 7.5 cm   4. *AB* = 3 in.

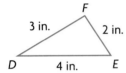
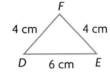
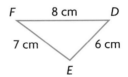
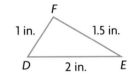

Draw a triangle with the given angle measures. Then construct a triangle similar to but not congruent to the first triangle.

5. 30°, 60°, 90°   6. 45°, 45°, 90°   7. 45°, 55°, 80°   8. 20°, 30°, 130°

Problem-Solving Applications

9. In △*ABC*, *AB* = 5 in., *BC* = 12 in., and *CA* = 13 in. In △*DEF*, *DE* = 7.5 in. If △*ABC* is similar to △*DEF*, what is the ratio of the perimeters?

10. Triangle *XYZ* has a 30° angle and an 80° angle. Triangle *RST* has a 70° angle and an 80° angle. Explain why △*XYZ* is similar to △*RST*.

11. Mr. Woods has a triangular garden with sides 3 ft, 4 ft, and 5 ft long. He will enlarge the garden by making each side 1.5 times as long. Will the new triangle be similar? Explain.

12. Construct two triangles whose corresponding sides have the ratio of 3 to 4. Are the triangles similar? Explain.

13. The drawing at the right shows the shape Mr. Waldron wants his garage roof to be. Trace the drawing of the roof only. Construct a model that is twice the size.

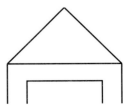

14. ⬤▶ **WRITE ABOUT IT** Describe the steps you take to construct a triangle similar to a given triangle.

Constructing Other Triangles

Two 3-in. straws, joined by a twist tie, can be used to represent two sides of an isosceles triangle. If one side is held in a horizontal position, the other side can be moved. Imagine a third side, $\overline{BC}$, forming a changing $\triangle ABC$.

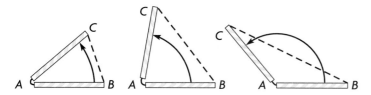

Talk About It

• How does the length of $\overline{BC}$ change?

• Will the length of $\overline{BC}$ ever be equal to or greater than 6 in.? Explain.

• What range of measures of $\angle A$ will make triangle $\triangle ABC$ acute? obtuse? What measure will make $\triangle ABC$ equilateral? right?

These two special properties hold for all triangles:

The sum of the lengths of two sides of a triangle is greater than the length of the third side.	The sum of the measures of the three angles of a triangle is 180°.

You can draw and measure triangles with a ruler and a protractor.

EXAMPLE 1 Draw an isosceles triangle with a 40° $\angle A$ between two 3-in. sides, $\overline{AB}$ and $\overline{AC}$.

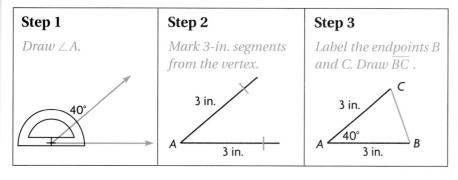

Step 1	**Step 2**	**Step 3**
Draw $\angle A$.	*Mark 3-in. segments from the vertex.*	*Label the endpoints B and C. Draw $\overline{BC}$.*

WHAT YOU'LL LEARN
How to draw and construct isosceles, equilateral, and right triangles

WHY LEARN THIS?
To be able to make figures with given measures for drawings and diagrams

REMEMBER:
....
An isosceles triangle is a triangle with two congruent sides. A scalene triangle is a triangle with no congruent sides.
See page H22.

391

GUIDED PRACTICE

Draw an isosceles triangle with the given dimensions.

1. a 60° angle between two 2-in. sides

2. a 120° angle between two 4-in. sides

3. a 45° angle between two 3-cm sides

4. a 70° angle between two 1.75-in. sides

5. a 30° angle between two 3-in. sides

6. a 50° angle between two 5-cm sides

You can construct equilateral and right triangles using only a compass and a straightedge.

REMEMBER:

An equilateral triangle is a triangle with three congruent sides. **See page H22.**

EXAMPLE 2 Construct an equilateral triangle.

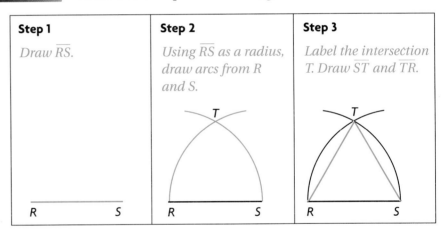

Step 1	**Step 2**	**Step 3**
Draw $\overline{RS}$.	*Using $\overline{RS}$ as a radius, draw arcs from R and S.*	*Label the intersection T. Draw $\overline{ST}$ and $\overline{TR}$.*

• How do you know △*RST* is an equilateral triangle?

EXAMPLE 3 Construct a right triangle.

Step 1	**Step 2**	**Step 3**
Mark any point P on a segment. Draw arcs of equal radii on both sides of P. Label A and B.	*Open the compass wider than AP. Swing arcs of equal radii from A and B. Draw $\overline{QP}$.*	*Draw $\overline{QB}$. △QPB is a right triangle.*

INDEPENDENT PRACTICE

Draw a triangle with these dimensions.

1. a 50° angle between two 3-in. sides

2. a 40° angle between 3-in. and 2-in. sides

3. a 60° angle between two 6-cm sides

Use the triangles drawn in Exercises 1–3.

4. Measure the third side of each triangle. Does every pair of sides in each triangle have combined lengths greater than that of the remaining side?

5. Classify each triangle as scalene, isosceles, or equilateral.

Use a ruler and a protractor to draw a triangle with these dimensions.

6. a 2-in. side between two 70° angles

7. a 4-cm side between 120° and 20° angles

8. a 3-cm side between 40° and 50° angles

Use the triangles drawn in Exercises 6–8.

9. Measure the third angle of each triangle. Do the measures of the three angles add up to 180°?

10. Classify each triangle as acute, right, or obtuse.

In *Mighty Math Cosmic Geometry* you can go to *Geo Movies* and have fun using what you know about constructing triangles.

Construct the figure.

11. an equilateral triangle with sides the same length as the given segment

$$\overline{A \qquad\qquad B}$$

12. an isosceles triangle with equal sides the same length as the given segment

$$\overline{C \qquad\qquad D}$$

Problem-Solving Applications

Construct each figure. Think about the measures of the angles of right and equilateral triangles.

13. a 90° angle

14. a 60° angle

15. a 120° angle

16. a 150° angle

17. a square

18. a rectangle

19. Construct a scalene, an isosceles, and an equilateral triangle. Construct the bisector of each angle in each triangle. Describe any similarities you discover.

20. ✏️ **WRITE ABOUT IT** Explain why you cannot construct a triangle with sides 4 cm, 6 cm, and 12 cm long.

MORE PRACTICE Lesson 20.5, page H74

MATH FUN!

HOME RUN STRATEGY

PURPOSE To practice bisecting angles (pages 382–383)

YOU WILL NEED compass, straightedge

The bases are loaded. It's your turn to bat. You decide the best strategy is to hit the ball exactly between two players. Four possible hits are between the third baseman and the short stop, the short stop and the pitcher, the pitcher and the second baseman, and the second baseman and the first baseman.

Copy the diagram. Bisect the four angles for a home run.

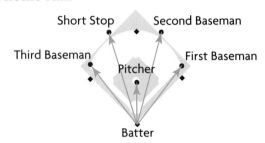

TRIANGLE PICS

PURPOSE To practice identifying congruent triangles (pages 384–385)

YOU WILL NEED 18 toothpicks

Make the figure with toothpicks or any moveable short straight lines of the same length. Then complete these puzzles.

1. Remove 4 toothpicks to leave exactly 4 congruent equilateral triangles.

2. Remove 5 toothpicks to leave exactly 5 congruent triangles.

 Challenge your family to solve these puzzles.

GO FOR THE GOLD

PURPOSE To practice constructing triangles (pages 389–393)

YOU WILL NEED compass, ruler

If you start with measurements that are Fibonacci numbers for 3 sides of a triangle, you can construct a golden triangle. Construct △ABC with a base of 5 in. Make the other 2 sides each 8-in. Swing an arc from B equal to $\overline{AB}$. Mark the point where it crosses $\overline{AC}$, as D. Draw a line from B to D.

Swing an arc from A equal to $\overline{AD}$. Mark the point where it crosses $\overline{BD}$, as E. Draw a line from A to E.

Measure the sides of your new triangles. Are these measures Fibonacci numbers? Did you construct a golden triangle?

394   Math Fun!

EXAMPLES

EXERCISES

- **Construct parallel and perpendicular lines.**
  (pages 378–381)

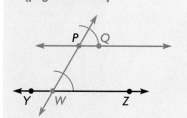

Use a compass and a straightedge to construct a line parallel to $\overleftrightarrow{YZ}$ at point P.

1. **VOCABULARY** Angles on the outer sides of two lines cut by a _?_ are called exterior angles.

Construct the following.

2. $\overleftrightarrow{PQ} \parallel \overleftrightarrow{AB}$

3. $\overleftrightarrow{PQ} \perp \overleftrightarrow{AB}$

- **Bisect line segments and angles.**
  (pages 382–383)

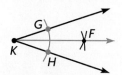

Use a compass and a straightedge to construct the bisector ∠K.

4. **VOCABULARY** When an angle or a line segment is divided into two congruent parts, it is _?_ .

Draw the figure, and then bisect it.

5. a 2-in. line segment
6. a 160° angle
7. a 3-in. line segment
8. a 45° angle

- **Identify and construct congruent triangles.**
  (pages 384–387)

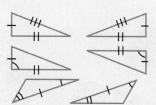

Side-Side-Side (SSS)

Side-Angle-Side (ASA)

Angle-Side-Angle (ASA)

Determine whether the triangles are congruent by *SSS*, *SAS*, or *ASA*.

9.

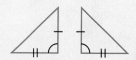

10. Construct a congruent triangle.

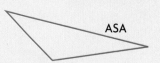

ASA

- **Identify and construct similar triangles.**
  (pages 389–390)

$\triangle ABC$ is similar to $\triangle DEF$. Find length $\overline{DE}$.

$$\frac{5}{2.5} = \frac{3}{DE}$$
$$5DE = 7.5$$
$$DE = 1.5$$

$\triangle XYZ$ was constructed to be similar to $\triangle RST$. Find the unknown lengths in centimeters.

11.

- **Draw and construct isosceles, equilateral, and right triangles.** (pages 391–393)

For help on drawing and constructing isosceles, equilateral, and right triangles, see page 391.

Construct the figure.

12. an equilateral triangle with sides the same length as *AB*

CHAPTER 21

TRANSFORMATIONS

LOOK AHEAD

In this chapter you will solve problems that involve

- recognizing and drawing transformations of plane figures and solid figures
- drawing tessellations that include dilations
- recognizing and drawing dilations on the coordinate plane

Team-Up Project

Animated Artists

Animation artists use geometric transformations to invent special effects. You can simulate how they work on a computer by using a combination of flips, slides, and turns to animate a design.

Plan
- Work with a partner to make a flip book that shows animated effects.

Act
- Choose a drawing.
- Transform it at least five times using a combination of rotations, reflections and translations.
- Combine your transformations into a flip book to generate special effects.

Share
- Share your animated art with the class.

DID YOU
- ✓ Choose a drawing?
- ✓ Transform it five times?
- ✓ Make a flip book?

REMEMBER:

A transformation is
a movement of a
geometric figure. **See
page H23.**

Constellations are
groups of stars that
have been given the
names of images. Ursa
Major—the "big bear"
—can be seen from
the Earth's Northern
Hemisphere. Find out
why it cannot be seen
from the Southern
Hemisphere.

ALGEBRA CONNECTION

Transformations of Plane Figures

A prominent feature of the
northern sky at night is the Big
Dipper. Its seven stars are part
of the constellation Ursa Major.

If you watch the Big Dipper, it
appears to rotate around the
Polaris, the North Star.

In this activity you will see how the movement of the Big Dipper
around the North Pole illustrates a rotation. A movement of a
plane figure about a point in a plane is called a rotation or a
turn transformation.

ACTIVITY

WHAT YOU'LL NEED: tracing paper, ruler

• Trace the Big Dipper near
the bottom of a sheet of
tracing paper.

• Using the distance between
stars *A* and *B* as 1 unit, mark
a point 5 units up from *B*
along ray *AB*. This point is
the approximate location of
Polaris. Label the point.

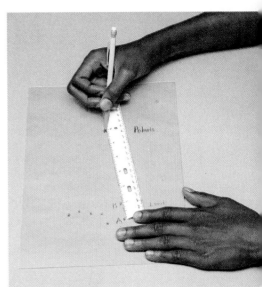

• Place your pencil point on
Polaris, and rotate the Big
Dipper around Polaris by
turning your paper
clockwise about the
pivot point.

• In 24 hours the Big Dipper makes one complete 360° rotation.
How many degrees does the Big Dipper rotate between 9 P.M.
and 3 A.M.? between 9 P.M. and 9 A.M.? between 9 A.M. and 10 A.M.?

• How long does it take for the Big Dipper to rotate 60°?
120°? 30°?

A figure in a new position and location is the result of a rotation. The figure in its new position and location is called the **image**.

EXAMPLE 1 The vertices of △*ABC* are *A*(2,1), *B*(7,3), and *C*(5,4). Graph △*ABC*. Then graph the image of △*ABC* after a 90° counterclockwise rotation about the origin.

To locate the image, trace the figure, place your pencil point on (0,0), and rotate the tracing 90° counterclockwise about (0,0).

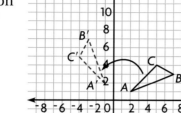

△ABC → △A′B′C′

$A(2,1) \rightarrow A'(^-1,2)$

$B(7,3) \rightarrow B'(^-3,7)$

$C(5,4) \rightarrow C'(^-4,5)$

- Compare the *x*- and *y*-coordinates of the original figure and the image. How are they related?

- Rotate △*ABC* 90° clockwise about (0,0). Name the coordinates of △*A′B′C′*. Explain how the coordinates of the original figure and the image are related.

- Now rotate △*ABC* 180° clockwise about (0,0). Name the coordinates of △*A′B′C′*. Explain how the coordinates of the original figure and the image are related.

A movement in which all points of a plane figure move the same distance is a translation, or slide transformation.

EXAMPLE 2 The vertices of △*EFG* are *E*(2,12), *F*(2,6), *G*(0,6). Graph △*EFG*. Then graph the image of the triangle after a translation 6 units to the right and 8 units down.

To find the vertices of the image, add 6 to each *x*-coordinate and ⁻8 to each *y*-coordinate of the original figure.

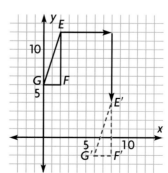

△EFG   △E′F′G′

$E(2,12) \rightarrow E'(2 + 6, 12 + {}^-8) \rightarrow E'(8,4)$

$F(2,6) \rightarrow F'(2 + 6, 6 + {}^-8) \rightarrow F'(8,^-2)$

$G(0,6) \rightarrow G'(0 + 6, 6 + {}^-8) \rightarrow G'(6,^-2)$

- Translate △*EFG* 1 unit to the left and 2 units up. What are the coordinates of △*E′F′G′*?

 Calculator Activities, page H40

REMEMBER:

You read *A′B′C′* as "A prime, B prime, C prime."

Add a positive value when you move to the right or up. Add a negative value when you move to the left or down. **See page H29.**

Art Link

When a cartoon character is animated, its position is translated. This is done through a series of drawings called cels. If each second of cartoon animation requires the drawing of 30 cels, how many cels are needed for a 75-min feature cartoon?

A movement of a plane figure in which all points of the figure are flipped about a line to form a mirror image is a reflection, or flip transformation.

EXAMPLE 3 The vertices of trapezoid *HIJK* are *H*(6,2), *I*(2,2), *J*(2,7), *K*(3,7). Graph trapezoid *HIJK*. Then graph the image of the trapezoid after a reflection about the *y*-axis.

To find the vertices of the image, count the units each vertex of the original figure is from the *y*-axis, and graph the corresponding point on the opposite side of the *y*-axis.

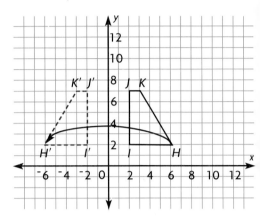

HIJK	*H'I'J'K'*
H(6,2)	→ *H'*(⁻6,2)
I(2,2)	→ *I'*(⁻2,2)
J(2,7)	→ *J'*(⁻2,7)
K(3,7)	→ *K'*(⁻3,7)

• How are the coordinates of the figure and the image related?

• Reflect trapezoid *HIJK* over the *x*-axis. What are the coordinates of trapezoid *H'I'J'K'*? How are the coordinates of the figure and the image related?

• **CRITICAL THINKING** In rotations, translations, and reflections, how are the original figure and the image alike? How are they different?

GUIDED PRACTICE

Identify the type of transformation. Write *rotation, translation,* or *reflection.*

1.
2.
3.

Copy △*ABC* on a coordinate plane. Graph the given transformation.

4. Rotate △*ABC* 90° clockwise about (0,0).

5. Translate △*ABC* 1 unit right and 3 units up.

6. Reflect △*ABC* over the *x*-axis.

Graph △ABC and △A'B'C'. Then tell whether the transformation is a *rotation, translation,* or *reflection.*

1. A(⁻1,⁻2)   A'(1,2)
   B(⁻4,⁻3)   B'(4,3)
   C(⁻4,⁻8)   C'(4,8)

2. A(1,3)   A'(⁻1,3)
   B(5,5)   B'(⁻5,5)
   C(5,3)   C'(⁻5,3)

Copy quadrilateral *ABCD* on a coordinate plane. Then draw the rotation. Rotate about the point (0,0).

3. Rotate 180° clockwise.

4. Rotate 90° counterclockwise.

5. Rotate 270° counterclockwise.

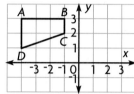

Graph the figure on a coordinate plane.
Then draw the reflection about the given axis.

6. *x*-axis
   A(⁻1,2)
   B(⁻5,2)
   C(⁻3,5)

7. *x*-axis
   A(2,⁻1)
   B(2,⁻4)
   C(5,⁻1)

8. *y*-axis
   A(2,2)
   B(2,5)
   C(5,2)

Problem-Solving Applications

For Problems 9–12, use the figure to create a border.

9. Copy the figure on a coordinate plane. Rotate 90° clockwise using (⁻5,5) as the point of rotation. Draw the rotation.

10. Translate the image 1 unit left. Draw the translation.

11. Draw the reflection of the figure and its image about the *y*-axis.

12. Draw the reflection of the figure and its three images about the *x*-axis.

13. Martha and Will created a map for a treasure hunt. At each point starting with (4,3), a clue will be given to find the next point. Follow their clues and write the coordinates of each point. Clue 1: Go 6 units west and 1 unit north. Clue 2: Go 3 units east and 7 units south. Clue 3: Go 4 units west to find the treasure.

14. ✏️ **WRITE ABOUT IT** Explain how to form a rotation, a translation, and a reflection of a figure.

🔘 In **Mighty Math Cosmic Geometry** you can enter *Amazing Angles* and use what you know about transforming plane figures to complete the *Transformations* mission.

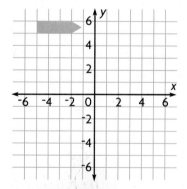

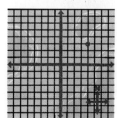

Transformations of Solid Figures

You perform transformations of solid figures when you rearrange a piece of furniture or load luggage into a car.

In this activity you will model the different ways a mattress can be placed on the springs of a bed.

ACTIVITY

WHAT YOU'LL NEED: index card, paper

• Trace the outline of the index card on the paper. The card represents the three-dimensional mattress, and the tracing represents the bed springs.

• Draw an arrow pointing to one end on one side of the card. Place the card in the outline in as many different positions as you can.

For a rectangular mattress, four positions are possible. Starting with a given position, the other three can be viewed as 180° rotations from the original about three different axes.

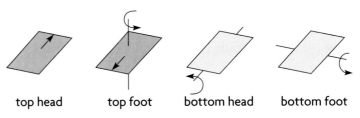

| top head | top foot | bottom head | bottom foot |

EXAMPLE How can you use a sequence of translations and rotations to move this dresser so it is in the corner of the room but against the adjacent wall?

There are two sequences of transformations that can be used.

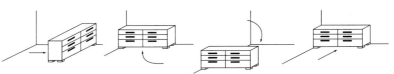

Translate dresser out from wall. Then rotate it 90° clockwise against other wall.

Rotate dresser 90° clockwise from wall. Then translate it against other wall.

Tell how many ways you can place the solid figure on the outline.

1.   **2.** 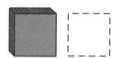 **3.**

Tell how many ways you can place the solid figure on the outline.

1. 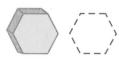 **2.**  **3.**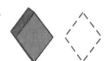

Name the transformation that will move the solid figure from Position 1 to Position 2. Write *translation, rotation,* or *reflection.*

4.

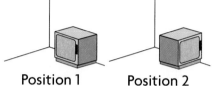

Position 1   Position 2

5.

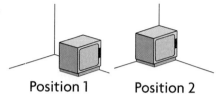

Position 1   Position 2

6.

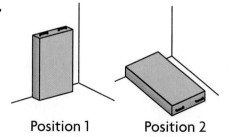

Position 1   Position 2

7.

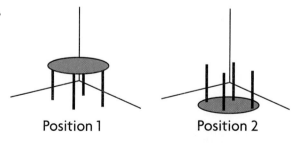

Position 1   Position 2

Problem-Solving Applications

8. Eight boxes of the same size are stacked in a corner as shown. Describe the locations of the labeled boxes as translations of Box 1.

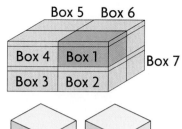

9. Suppose you have a cube and a box in which the cube fits perfectly. In how many different positions can the cube be placed in its box? (HINT: Each of the 6 faces of a cube has 4 edges.)

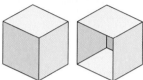

10. ✏ **WRITE ABOUT IT** Think of transformations of solid figures that happen in your everyday life. Give several examples.

ALGEBRA CONNECTION
Dilations

Translations, reflections, and rotations are transformations that don't change the size or shape of a figure. A **dilation** is a transformation that enlarges or reduces a figure. It doesn't change the shape of a figure, but it does change the size.

EXAMPLE 1 Enlarge $\triangle ABC$ to 150%. What are the coordinates of the image?

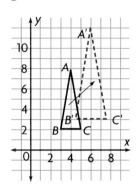

To enlarge the triangle to 150%, use a scale factor of 1.5.

To find the vertices of the image, multiply the coordinates of the original figure by 1.5.

$\triangle ABC$ $\qquad\qquad\qquad\qquad$ $\triangle A'B'C'$

$A(4,8) \rightarrow A'(4 \times 1.5, 8 \times 1.5) \rightarrow A'(6,12)$

$B(3,2) \rightarrow B'(3 \times 1.5, 2 \times 1.5) \rightarrow B'(4.5,3)$

$C(5,2) \rightarrow C'(5 \times 1.5, 2 \times 1.5) \rightarrow C'(7.5,3)$

Talk About It

• What do you think you will find if you measure and compare the corresponding angles of the two triangles?

• What do you think you will find if you measure and compare the lengths of the corresponding sides of the two triangles?

• Name the coordinates of the vertices of the image if the triangle is enlarged to 200%.

A dilation can be viewed as a projection from a point. In this lesson the origin is used as the point of projection.

• Copy the figures from Example 1, and draw a ray from the point of projection (0,0) through each vertex of the original figure.

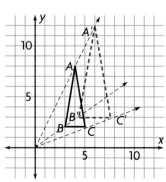

• How are these rays related to the vertices of the image?

You can check a dilation by making sure that corresponding vertices of the original figure and the image lie on the same ray.

EXAMPLE 2 Reduce △EFG to $66\frac{2}{3}$%. What are the coordinates of the image?

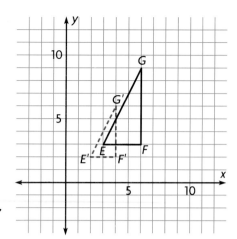

To reduce the triangle to $66\frac{2}{3}$%, use a scale factor of 2 to 3, or $\frac{2}{3}$.

To find the vertices of the image, multiply the coordinates of the original figure by $\frac{2}{3}$.

△EFG   △E'F'G'

$E(3,3) \rightarrow E'(3 \times \frac{2}{3}, 3 \times \frac{2}{3}) \rightarrow E'(2,2)$

$F(6,3) \rightarrow F'(6 \times \frac{2}{3}, 3 \times \frac{2}{3}) \rightarrow F'(4,2)$

$G(6,9) \rightarrow G'(6 \times \frac{2}{3}, 9 \times \frac{2}{3}) \rightarrow G'(4,6)$

Talk About It

• Why do you use a scale factor of $\frac{2}{3}$ to reduce the triangle in Example 2 to $66\frac{2}{3}$%?

• What scale factor would you use to reduce the triangle in Example 2 to 50%?

• What scale factor would you use to reduce a figure to 25%? to $33\frac{1}{3}$%?

GUIDED PRACTICE

Tell whether the image, shown in red, is an *enlargement* or a *reduction*.

1.   **2.** 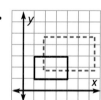   **3.**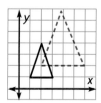

Find the scale factor.

4. Enlarge to 125%.   **5.** Enlarge to 300%.

6. Reduce to 75%.   **7.** Reduce to 25%.

8. Enlarge to 350%.   **9.** Reduce to 45%.

10. Reduce to 10%.   **11.** Enlarge to 500%.

Computer Link

Have you ever had a photo you wanted to "blow up"? In the past that meant having an enlargement printed from a negative. But photos can now be enlarged at home on personal computers. A digital photo can be scaled, or a printed photo can be scanned into the computer and then scaled. If you have a 3-in. × 5-in. photo and you want to enlarge it to about the size of an 8.5-in. × 14-in. sheet of paper, what scale factor can you use?

405

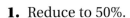

INDEPENDENT PRACTICE

Copy the figure on the right on a coordinate plane. Perform the given dilation from the origin. Give the coordinates of the image, and check it by drawing rays.

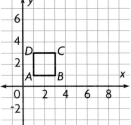

1. Reduce to 50%.

2. Enlarge to 150%.

3. Enlarge to 125%.

4. Reduce to 25%.

5. Reduce to 75%.

6. Enlarge to 200%.

7. Enlarge to 175%.

8. Reduce to 90%.

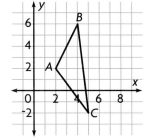

Find the coordinates of the image projected from the origin.

9. Reduce to $\frac{1}{3}$.
   A(3,3)
   B(3,6)
   C(6,3)

10. Reduce to 20%.
    A(5,5)
    B(10,5)
    C(10,15)
    D(5,15)

11. Enlarge to 400%.
    A(1,1)
    B(5,1)
    C(6,6)
    D(2,6)

12. Enlarge to 350%.
    A(4,2)
    B(8,4)
    C(6,6)

Problem-Solving Applications

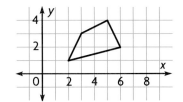

13. Fritz wants to enlarge the woodworking pattern shown at the right to 250%. Draw the image. Next he wants to reduce the original pattern to 50%. Draw the image.

14. Dee has a photograph that is 4-in. long and 5-in. wide. If she enlarges the width to 7 in., what should be the length? Draw the figure on a coordinate plane and use rays to find the answer.

15. ✏ **WRITE ABOUT IT** Explain how you can check the drawing of a dilation for accuracy.

Mixed Review

Start with the given number and multiply by $\frac{1}{2}$ three times.

16. 32

17. 100

18. $\frac{1}{10}$

19. 1

Construct the following.

20. $\overleftrightarrow{AB} \perp \overleftrightarrow{PQ}$

21. $\overleftrightarrow{CD} \parallel \overleftrightarrow{FG}$

22. **PROBABILITY** Earl bought 5 raffle tickets for a computer. If 750 tickets were sold, what is the probability that he will win?

23. **LENGTH** The perimeter of an equilateral triangle is 48 ft. What is the length of each side?

MORE PRACTICE Lesson 21.3, page H75

Combining Transformations

You can transform a geometric figure on a coordinate grid by combining rotations, translations, reflections, and dilations.

Explore

Work with a partner to show an image after two consecutive transformations.

- On graph paper, draw a triangle or a quadrilateral. Label the vertices.

- Select two transformations to perform on the figure. Draw the image after the second transformation.

- Record the transformations you used and the coordinates of the vertices after each move.

- Exchange graphs with another pair of students, and describe the transformations they used to create their second image.

Think and Discuss

- How can you tell if one of the moves was a dilation?

- 💡 **CRITICAL THINKING**   Is it possible for the original figure and the image to be congruent if both moves are dilations? Explain.

Try This

- Draw a figure with these vertices: $A(4,4)$, $B(6,6)$, $C(4,8)$, $D(0,4)$. Draw the image with these vertices: $A''(2,^-2)$, $B''(3,^-3)$, $C''(4,^-2)$, $D''(2,0)$.

- Describe two transformations that would change the original figure to the image.

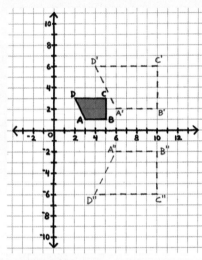

Transformations Used

1. dilation to enlarge to 200%
   A'(6,2), B'(10,2), C'(10,6), D'(4,6)

2. reflection about the x-axis
   A"(6,⁻2), B"(10,⁻2), C"(10,⁻6), D"(4,⁻6)

LAB *Activity*

WHAT YOU'LL EXPLORE
How to recognize and create images when two or more transformations are combined

WHAT YOU'LL NEED
graph paper, tracing paper, scissors

REMEMBER:
You can choose from these transformations:
   rotation
   translation
   reflection
   dilation to enlarge
   dilation to reduce
See page H23.

Shrinking and Expanding

REMEMBER:

A tessellation is a repeating pattern of plane figures that completely covers a plane with no gaps or overlapping. **See page 176.**

In a tessellation, shapes are arranged to cover a surface with no gaps or overlapping.

You have created tessellations with geometric figures that are the same size and shape.

In this lesson you will look at regions that are tessellated by using shapes that are repeatedly reduced.

A square region can be tessellated repeatedly using smaller and smaller squares, as shown below. The pieces in successive stages are reduction dilations with a scale factor of 1 to 2.

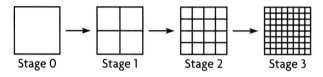

This iteration diagram shows the rule for creating the tessellation.

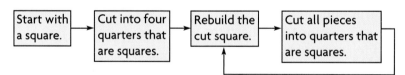

The table shows how the number and dimensions of the pieces change.

Stage	0	1	2	3
Number of pieces	1	4	16	64
Length of each piece	1	$\frac{1}{2}$	$\frac{1}{4}$	$\frac{1}{8}$
Area of each piece	1	$\frac{1}{4}$	$\frac{1}{16}$	$\frac{1}{64}$

• Look for patterns in the table. What pattern do you see in the number of pieces? in the length of each piece? in the area of each piece?

• Predict the number of pieces, the length of each piece, and the area of each piece in Stage 4.

ACTIVITY

WHAT YOU'LL NEED: an 8-in. paper square, scissors

- Follow this rule to build successive tessellation stages.

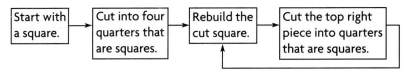

- Arrange the pieces, rebuilding stage after stage.

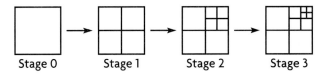

Stage 0   Stage 1   Stage 2   Stage 3

- How is the number of pieces at each stage related to the number of pieces at the previous stage?

Stage	0	1	2	3
Number of pieces	1	4	7	10

- What scale factor is used to reduce the length of the square from one stage to the next?

GUIDED PRACTICE

For Exercises 1–3, use the following reduction dilation.

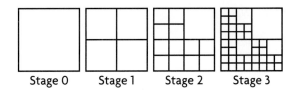

Stage 0   Stage 1   Stage 2   Stage 3

1. Copy and complete the table.

Stage	0	1	2	3	4
Number of pieces	1	4	?	?	?

2. What scale factor is used to reduce the length of the square from one stage to the next?

3. How is the number of pieces at each stage related to the number of pieces at the previous stage?

Wallpaper patterns often show tessellations, and so do gameboards, such as those for backgammon, checkers, and Parcheesi. Look for other examples of tessellations.

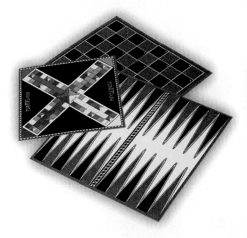

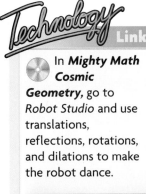

Special designs can also be created by using repeated sequences of dilations, translations, reflections, and rotations.

EXAMPLE 1 Describe this design of repeatedly reduced squares in terms of dilations, translations, reflections, and rotations.

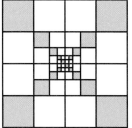

dilations and translations: The design is a sequence of squares that have been dilated by a scale factor of 1 to 2 from the four corners toward the center. The squares are translated from the corners toward the center.

reflections and rotations: The design can be reflected about the center vertical line or the center horizontal line. The design can be rotated 90° clockwise (or counterclockwise) about the center.

Some designs created by repeatedly reduced shapes are symmetrical.

A design has line symmetry if a line can separate the design into two parts, each of which is the mirror image of the other. A design has rotational symmetry if it looks exactly the same after it has been rotated less than 360° about a central point.

EXAMPLE 2 This hexagonal design is made from repeatedly reduced equilateral triangles. Describe this design in terms of line symmetry and rotational symmetry.

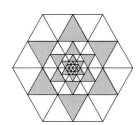

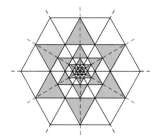

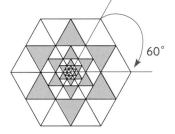

The design has six lines of symmetry. If you fold the design along any of the lines of symmetry, the two parts will match exactly.

The design has rotational symmetry. It looks the same after being rotated 60°, 120°, or 180° clockwise or counterclockwise.

• Does the design appear to shrink or expand?

INDEPENDENT PRACTICE

For Exercises 1–4, use the following reduction dilation.

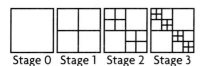

Stage 0 Stage 1 Stage 2 Stage 3

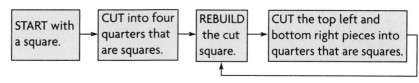

START with a square. → CUT into four quarters that are squares. → REBUILD the cut square. → CUT the top left and bottom right pieces into quarters that are squares.

1. Copy and complete the table.

Stage	0	1	2	3	4	5
Number of pieces	1	4	?	?	?	?

2. What scale factor is used to reduce the length of the square from one stage to the next?

3. How is the number of pieces at each stage related to the number of pieces at the previous stage?

4. What will be the number of pieces at Stage 6? at Stage 7?

Problem-Solving Applications

5. Describe this design in terms of line symmetry and rotational symmetry.

6. Describe this design in terms of line symmetry and rotational symmetry.

7. Describe the design at Stage 3 of Exercise 1 in terms of translations, reflections, and rotations.

8. ✏️ **WRITE ABOUT IT** Explain why the figure at Stage 3 of Exercise 1 is a tessellation.

Mixed Review

Solve.

9. What percent of 250 is 50?

10. What percent of 320 is 128?

Determine whether the triangles are congruent by *SSS*, *ASA*, or *SAS*.

11.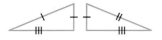

12.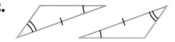

13.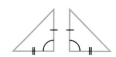

14. **OUTCOMES** Kelli has chosen a three-digit number. The hundreds digit can be any number 2 to 8. The tens and the units digits can be any number 1 to 9. How many possible numbers are there?

15. **PATTERNS** Esther has 12 pennies in a row. She replaces every other coin with a nickel. Then she replaces every third coin with a dime. Find the final value of the coins in the row.

CULTURAL CONNECTION

NATIVE AMERICAN ART

Native Americans often decorate their personal belongings with geometric shapes. Merle went to the Native American display at the Art Center. One of his favorite pieces was a round box made from birch tree bark and decorated with porcupine quills, like the box at the right. He sketched the pattern from the lid and rotated the design around the center point. What is the least number of degrees he can rotate the design so the pattern looks the same? Does the design have rotational or line symmetry? Explain your answer.

Work Together

1. Look at the designs on the Chippewa bag at the right. Describe the different patterns that you see. Make a copy of one of the diamond (parallelogram) designs and make a tessellation pattern.

2. Look at the wampum belt design below. What transformations do you see?

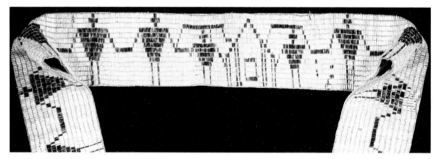

3. Draw one of the designs shown here on a coordinate plane. Dilate it one or more times.

CULTURAL LINK

The wampum belt shown at the left symbolizes peace between the original thirteen states and the six Iroquois Nations. It is the longest wampum belt known, and is referred to as the Washington Covenant Belt.

EXAMPLES

- **Identify and create transformations of plane figures.** (pages 398–401)

rotation	translation
90° clockwise	2 units up,
about the origin	2 units right

- **Identify and create transformations of solid figures.** (pages 402–403)

Tell how may ways a square mattress can be placed on the springs of a bed.

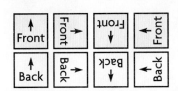

There are 8 different ways.

- **Identify and create dilations of plane figures.** (pages 404–406)

Enlarge △ABC to 200%.
Draw the dilation.

$A(1,1) \rightarrow A'(1 \times 2, 1 \times 2) \rightarrow A'(2,2)$ *Multiply*
$B(2,1) \rightarrow B'(2 \times 2, 1 \times 2) \rightarrow B'(4,2)$ *by a scale*
$C(2,3) \rightarrow C'(2 \times 2, 3 \times 2) \rightarrow C'(4,6)$ *factor of 2.*

- **Recognize and create tessellations by using dilations.** (pages 408–411)

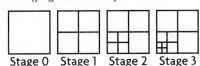

Stage	0	1	2	3
Number of pieces	1	4	7	10

scale factor: 1 to 2, or $\frac{1}{2}$

EXERCISES

Graph △ABC with vertices $A(2,^-2)$, $B(5,1)$, and $C(2,3)$ on a coordinate plane. Draw the transformation. Then give the new coordinates.

1. Rotate 270° counterclockwise about the origin.
2. Reflect about the *y*-axis.
3. Move 2 units right, 3 units down.
4. Rotate 90° counterclockwise about $C(2,3)$.

5. Tell how many ways you can place the solid figure on the outline.

Name the transformations that will move the bed from Position 1 to Position 2.

6.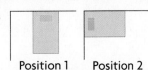

    Position 1   Position 2

7. **VOCABULARY** A transformation that enlarges or reduces a figure is a **?** .

Find the coordinates of the dilation.

8. Reduce to 40%.   9. Enlarge to 150%.
    $A(8,4)$ $A(1,^-1)$
    $B(12,5)$ $B(1,4)$
    $C(6,8)$ $C(6,3)$

10. Reduce to 50%.
    $A(2,4)$, $B(3,6)$, $C(7,5)$, $D(5,2)$

11. In the diagram at left, how is the number of pieces at each stage related to the number at the previous stage?
12. Predict the number of pieces at Stage 4.
13. Describe the design in terms of transformations.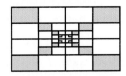

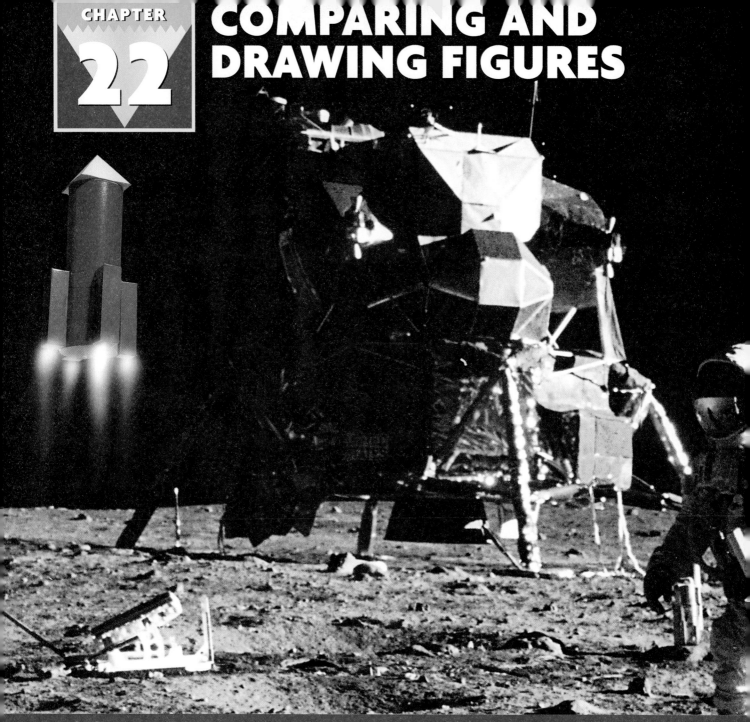

LOOK AHEAD

In this chapter you will solve problems that involve

- creating and comparing nets for polyhedrons
- drawing different views of solid figures

- drawing solid figures
- drawing solid figures in perspective

Team-Up Project

Special-Effects Space Ships

Special-effects artists make movies fun to watch. They make models of scary creatures, zooming space ships, and cozy homes. They start with simple models. Then they make detailed models so they look real.

YOU WILL NEED: graph paper, ruler, scissors, tape

Plan
- Work with a partner. Think of an idea for a space ship. Sketch it.

Act
- Sketch a design of your ship. Decide which geometric solids to use to build your model.
- Construct the model with paper shapes you have made from nets.
- Try to improve your design as you make the model.

Share
- Present your model to the class. Tell which solids you used to construct it.

GEOMETRIC SOLIDS

cube

rectangular prism

cylinder

triangular pyramid

square pyramid

cone

DID YOU

☑ Sketch a design of your ship?

☑ Use a variety of solid shapes?

☑ Try to improve your design?

☑ Present your model to the class?

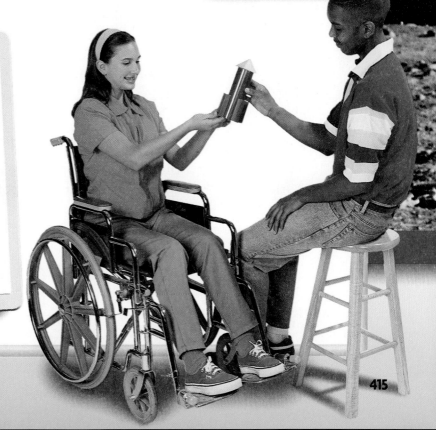

415

Nets for Solid Figures

A given polyhedron can be formed from a pattern called a net, an arrangement of faces that folds up to form the polyhedron.

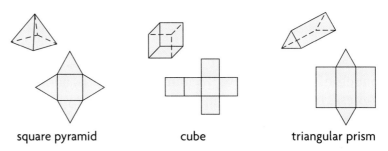

square pyramid   cube   triangular prism

Designers and architects often make three-dimensional models to help them visualize how finished objects will look.

A model can be made by cutting faces from paper, taping them together to form a net, and then folding up the net.

Here is one way the six faces of a model can be arranged to form a net. When the net is folded up, it forms a 2-in. × 4-in. × 3-in. rectangular prism.

2 in. 3 in.

4 in.

Talk About It

• What are the dimensions of the six rectangles that form the faces of the prism?

• What are the overall length and width of this arrangement?

The prism can be placed in many different positions. These figures show six different positions of this one prism.

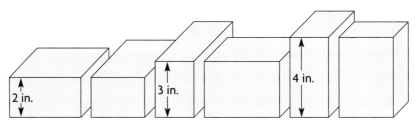

2 in.

3 in.

4 in.

• 💡 **CRITICAL THINKING** How do these figures differ?

In this activity you will make other nets for the model.

WHAT YOU'LL NEED: three 4-in. × 6-in. index cards, ruler, removable tape, scissors, pencil

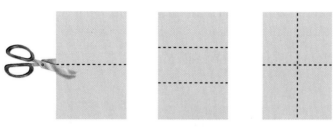

- Cut the index cards into rectangles with the dimensions shown. Use two rectangles of each size for this activity.

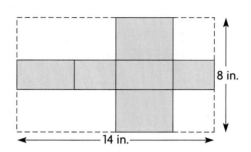

- Arrange the six pieces like this to form a net.

- Tape the pieces together, and fold up the net to form the model.

- The overall dimensions of this arrangement are 14 in. × 8 in. What is the area of the 14-in. × 8-in. rectangle? What is the area of the net?

- If this net is cut from a 14-in. × 8-in. sheet of paper, what percent of the total area is used for the net?

- Arrange the pieces like this. Try to visualize this pattern folded. Will it form the polyhedron?

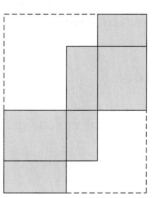

- Tape the pieces together and check your answer.

- What are the overall dimensions of this net? What percent of the area of the large rectangular region is used for the net?

- Rearrange the six rectangles to form other nets for the same model. Draw a diagram for each net you form.

- Find the overall dimensions of the large rectangular region for each of your nets. What are the overall dimensions of the region with the least area?

417

GUIDED PRACTICE

For Exercises 1–3, use the net at the right.

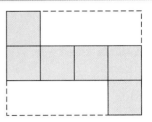

1. Each face is 4 in. × 4 in. Find the overall dimensions of this arrangement.

2. Find the area of the rectangle with the overall dimensions of the net. Then find the area of the net.

3. What percent of the rectangle's area is the net's area?

INDEPENDENT PRACTICE

Tell whether the pattern can be folded up to form a closed polyhedron. If it cannot, rearrange the faces to form a net.

1.    2.

For Exercises 3–6, use the net at the right.

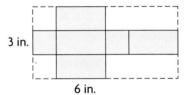

3 in.   6 in.

3. Find the overall dimensions of the net.

4. Find the area of the rectangle with the overall dimensions of the net. Find the area of the net.

5. What percent of the rectangle's area is the net's area?

6. Copy the faces, and then rearrange them to form other nets for the same solid. Use your nets to find the overall dimensions of the rectangle with the least area.

Problem-Solving Applications

7. A movie-set designer needs to make a 2-ft. × 3-ft. × 4-ft. prism for a space tower. The designer wants to find the overall dimensions of the net with the least area. What are they? What is the area? Draw the net.

8. How many nets for 4-in. cubic boxes can be cut out of a 28-in. × 24-in. cardboard sheet? Use translations, reflections, or rotations to arrange the nets side by side without any overlapping faces. What percent of the sheet is used for the boxes?

9. ◀▭▷ **WRITE ABOUT IT** Explain how to find the percent that compares a net's area with the area of the rectangle having the net's overall dimensions.

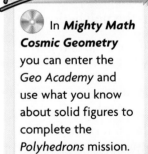

In **Mighty Math Cosmic Geometry** you can enter the *Geo Academy* and use what you know about solid figures to complete the *Polyhedrons* mission.

MORE PRACTICE Lesson 22.1, page H75

Drawing Diagrams to Show Different Views

Architectural plans for a building often include drawings of all vertical sides of the building. These drawings, called elevations, help people visualize how the building will look.

Tyler designed a new library. He used cubes to make a model of the library. Each cube represents one floor of one section of the building.

In his report, Tyler has described in words what the building would look like from the top, the front, the right side, and the left side. What else can he include in his report to help people visualize the building from different viewpoints?

☑ **UNDERSTAND**   What are you asked to do?

☑ **PLAN**   What facts are given?

What strategy will you use?

☑ **SOLVE**   Draw a front elevation, side elevations, and a back elevation.

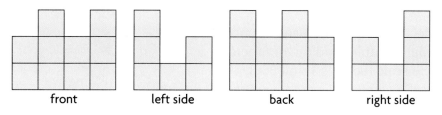

| front | left side | back | right side |

☑ **LOOK BACK**   How can you be sure that the elevations match the model?

What if . . . the model had one more floor in each section? How would the diagrams change?

PRACTICE

Use the strategy *draw a diagram* to solve.

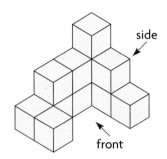

1. Lori made this model of her county's courthouse. Draw a front elevation, side elevations, and a back elevation that she can use in a report.

2. Compare your front and back elevations of Lori's model. What relationships do you see between them?

3. The solid shown at the right is made up of 16 cubes. Draw a set of building plans for the model. The set includes a top view, a front elevation, and a side elevation. How many squares are in the top view? in the front elevation? in the side elevation?

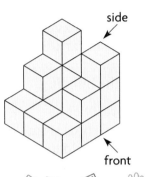

4. Use the model in Exercise 3. What is the greatest number of cubes that you can add without changing the front and top views? What is the greatest number of cubes that you can remove without changing the front and top views?

MIXED APPLICATIONS

CHOOSE

Choose a strategy and solve.

Problem-Solving Strategies
- Draw a Diagram
- Act It Out
- Use a Formula
- Work Backward
- Make a Model
- Write an Equation

5. Before Bill can go to the movies at 7:30 P.M., he must complete a report. He needs to spend 3 hr on research, 2 hr writing, 30 min proofing, and 15 min typing. What is the latest time he should begin his report?

6. Adam and Jessie collect comic books. Adam has 14 fewer than 2 times the number Jessie has. Adam has 40 comic books. How many does Jessie have?

7. Draw the top view of this model of a new post office. The length of each cube in the model is 1 unit. Find the perimeter of the base in units. The model's scale factor is 1 unit:35 ft. Find the perimeter of the post office in feet.

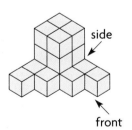

8. ✏️ **WRITE ABOUT IT** Draw a set of plans for a building made up of cubes. Include a top view, a front elevation, and a side elevation. Exchange with a classmate. Use cubes to make a model of your classmate's building. Compare the models and the plans.

MORE PRACTICE Lesson 22.2, page H76

Drawing Three-Dimensional Figures

Joanne is a drafter. She is using a computer program to make a technical drawing of a car CD player.

- How is this computer drawing different from an elevation?

- A drawing that shows more than one face of a three-dimensional object can be more useful than an elevation. In what way?

You can use isometric dot paper or graph paper to sketch a figure showing all the faces of a three-dimensional object.

EXAMPLE 1 Sketch a rectangular prism that is 4 units long, 2 units deep, and 3 units high.

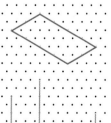

On dot paper, lightly draw the edges of the bottom face, the 2-unit × 4-unit base of the prism.

For the lateral faces, lightly draw vertical line segments 3 units long from the vertices of the base.

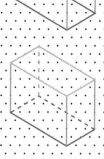

Lightly draw the top face.

Darken the lines. Use solid lines for the edges that are visible. Use dashed lines for the edges that are hidden.

- How many edges are visible? How many edges are hidden?

- Make a sketch of this prism by using the 3-unit × 4-unit face as the base.

EXAMPLE 2 Sketch a rectangular pyramid with a 4-unit × 2-unit base and a 5-unit height.

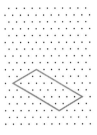

Draw the edges of the base.

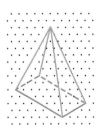

Locate the point for the top vertex 5 units above the center of the base.

Draw edges for the lateral faces. Use solid lines and dashed lines to show the edges.

- How would you change your drawing to show a pyramid whose height is greater? whose height is less?

- Draw a pyramid with a 2-unit square base and a height of 4 units.

Talk About It

- Which edges of a rectangular prism are parallel?

- Copy the drawing of the prism in Example 1. Label the vertices *A* through *H*, and then list the parallel edges.

- Are edges that are parallel on a prism also parallel on the drawing of the prism? Explain.

- Now look at the drawing of the rectangular pyramid above. Are edges that are parallel on the rectangular pyramid also parallel on the drawing? Explain.

GUIDED PRACTICE

1. Using dot paper, sketch a cube with sides 3 units long.

2. How many edges are visible in your sketch? How many edges are hidden?

3. How many faces are visible in your sketch? How many faces are hidden?

4. Draw a rectangular prism so that the height is greater than the length or width.

Using isometric dot paper, sketch the figure.

1. a rectangular pyramid that is 3 units high and has a 2-unit × 4-unit base

2. a rectangular prism that is 1 unit high and has a 3-unit × 4-unit base

Tell the dimensions of the base and the height. Name the edges that are parallel.

3.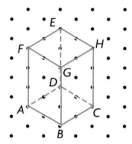

4.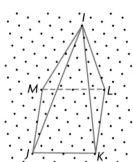

5.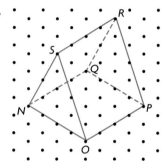

Problem-Solving Applications

For Problems 6–7, use isometric dot paper.

6. A designer needs to show her client a three-dimensional sketch of a package. Sketch a rectangular box that is 3 units long, 5 units high, and 1 unit deep.

7. A sculptor plans to use a rectangular pyramid for a monument. The base will be 2 units × 6 units. The height will be 7 units. Sketch this rectangular pyramid.

8. ✏️ **WRITE ABOUT IT** Describe the difference between a dot-paper drawing and elevation drawings of a three-dimensional object.

Mixed Review

Describe each polyhedron. Include the shapes of the bases and faces.

9. square prism

10. triangular prism

11. rectangular prism

Graph the quadrilateral *DEFG* with vertices *D*(2,2), *E*(2,3), *F*(4,4), and *G*(4,2) on a coordinate plane. Draw the transformation. Then give the new coordinates.

12. Rotate 90° clockwise about (2,2).

13. Move 3 units left, 4 units down.

14. **LOGICAL THINKING** Bert, Al, and Diane are on the yearbook staff. One is the editor, one is the photographer, and one is the manager. Diane's only exercise is running. Al and the photographer golf together. Al and the editor are cousins. Find each person's job.

15. **PERIMETER** A park's picnic pavilion is shaped like an octagonal prism. Each side is 40 ft. long. On holidays the roof's perimeter is decorated with lights. If there is a light every foot, how many lights are there in all?

Perspective Drawings

These two drawings show a cube. Are they different?

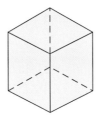

The second drawing shows the cube drawn in perspective. **Perspective** is a technique used to make three-dimensional objects appear to have depth and distance on a flat surface. It imitates the way we see things, making objects appear nearer or farther away.

EXAMPLE 1 Make a left-view, one-point perspective drawing of a rectangular prism.

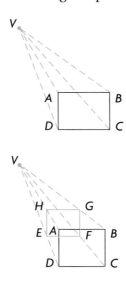

*Draw the front face. Label the vertices A through D. Mark a point, V, above the face and to its left, as shown. Draw a dashed line from each vertex to V. This point where the lines meet, V, is called a **vanishing point**.*

Choose a point, G, on $\overline{BV}$. Draw $\overline{GH}$ parallel to $\overline{AB}$. Draw $\overline{HE}$ parallel to $\overline{AD}$. Lightly draw $\overline{GF}$ parallel to $\overline{BC}$. Lightly draw $\overline{EF}$.

Darken the visible edges $\overline{ED}$, $\overline{AH}$, $\overline{GB}$. Show dashed segments for the hidden edges, $\overline{FE}$, $\overline{FG}$, $\overline{FC}$. Erase the vanishing point and all the segments that join it to the prism.

- In the perspective drawing of the prism, which edges are parallel?

- If you make a model of this prism, which edges will be parallel?

- Where do you place the vanishing point to draw a right view?

In one-point perspective, there is one vanishing point. You can also draw a figure in two-point perspective, by using two vanishing points.

In the drawing of the cube, shown below, *V* and *W* are the two vanishing points. They lie on a horizontal line called the **horizon line**. This line represents the viewer's eye level.

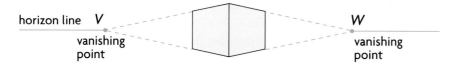

horizon line   V   W

vanishing point   vanishing point

By moving the horizon line, you can show different views of the cube.

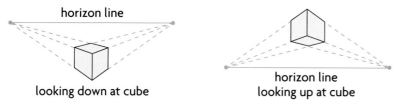

horizon line

looking down at cube

horizon line
looking up at cube

EXAMPLE 2   Make a two-point perspective drawing of a rectangular prism.

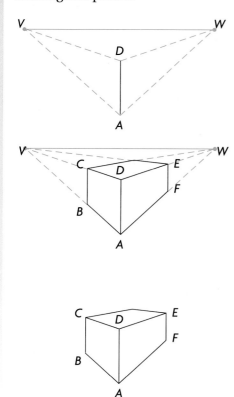

Draw the edge nearest the viewer. Label it $\overline{AD}$. Mark a vanishing point, V, above the edge and to its left, and a vanishing point, W, above the edge and to its right, as shown.

Draw dashed segments from point A to each vanishing point and from point D to each vanishing point.

Choose a point, B, on $\overline{AV}$ and a point, F, on $\overline{AW}$. Draw $\overline{BC}$ and $\overline{FE}$ parallel to $\overline{AD}$. Draw $\overline{CD}$ and $\overline{DE}$. Draw $\overline{EV}$ and $\overline{CW}$. Draw $\overline{BA}$ and $\overline{AF}$.

Erase the horizon lines, the vanishing points and all the segments that join them to the prism.

• Is the viewer looking down or looking up at the prism?

425

Draw each prism. Use one-point perspective.

1. a rectangular prism viewed from the right

2. a triangular prism viewed from the left

Draw each prism. Use two-point perspective.

1. a rectangular prism at the same level as the horizon line

2. a rectangular prism with the horizon line above it

Problem-Solving Applications

3. This building is drawn in two-point perspective. Copy the drawing and add a building with its lower front edge at line segment *AB*.

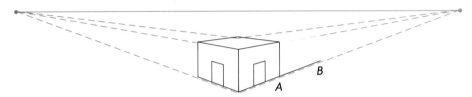

4. Draw a picture of a building at your school or in your home town. Use two-point perspective.

5. ✏️ **WRITE ABOUT IT** Describe the differences between a dot-paper drawing of a cube and a perspective drawing of a cube.

Mixed Review

Identify the situation that the graph represents. Write *a, b,* or *c.*

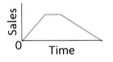

6. a. Sales decrease, then remain constant, then increase.
b. Sales increase, then remain constant, then decrease.
c. Sales remain constant, then decrease, then increase.

Find the coordinates of the dilation.

7. Enlarge to 300%. $A(2,2)$, $B(3,2)$, $C(3,4)$

8. Reduce to 75%. $A(4,^-4)$, $B(4,8)$, $C(12,3)$

9. **PAYMENTS** Mrs. George's medical bills totaled $1,456 last year. She paid $200 and 20% of the remaining bill. Her insurance company paid the rest. How much did Mrs. George pay? How much did the insurance company pay?

10. **PATTERNS** Betty has five piggy banks in a row. Each bank has 15 more coins than the previous one, and the banks hold a total of 650 coins. How many coins are in each bank?

Cross Sections of Solid Figures

Think of slicing a solid figure with a plane. The new face formed by the slicing is called a **cross section**. The shape of the cross section depends on the type of solid and the position of the plane.

cylinder

cross section formed by horizontal plane

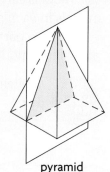

pyramid

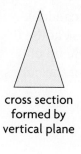

cross section formed by vertical plane

LAB *Activity*

WHAT YOU'LL EXPLORE
How to visualize the cross sections formed when a solid is sliced by a plane

WHAT YOU'LL NEED
paper, straightedge

WORD POWER
cross section

Explore

Work with a partner as you visualize and draw cross sections of solid figures sliced by planes.

• Visualize this cone being sliced by a horizontal plane. Draw the cross section.

• How will the cross section change if the cone is sliced by a horizontal plane closer to its vertex? closer to its base?

• Visualize the cone being sliced by a vertical plane through the vertex. Draw the cross section.

Think and Discuss 💡 CRITICAL THINKING

• How could you slice a cylinder with a plane so that the cross section is a circle? is not a circle?

• How could you slice a cone with a plane so that the cross section is neither a circle nor a triangle?

Try This

• Visualize different ways that a cube can be sliced by a plane to form each of these cross sections. Draw a diagram for each way.

   a. rectangle   b. trapezoid   c. triangle

Technology Link ▶

E–Lab • **Activity 22** Available on CD-ROM
and the Internet at http://www.hbschool.com/elab

MATH FUN!

3-D MYSTERY

PURPOSE To practice identifying different views of a solid figure (pages 419–420)

YOU WILL NEED 6 cubes

It's amazing how the same figure can look different from different views. Look at the 6 models below. Each model is made up of 6 cubes joined face-to-face. Some of the cubes are hidden from view.

The models can be grouped into 3 pairs. The models in each pair have the same shape. Work with a partner to find the matching pairs. Each model belongs to only one pair.

HOME NOTE Challenge your family to match each pair.

 A 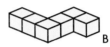 B 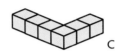 C D E F

FOOL THE EYE

PURPOSE To practice making isometric drawings (pages 421–423)

YOU WILL NEED 1-in. graph paper

Have you ever looked at your image in a distorting mirror? Some parts are enlarged, some are reduced, and others are distorted in other ways. Look at the distorted drawing. What solid figure do you see? First, copy the normal grid on graph paper. Then transfer the part of the outline in each square to the normal grid. What did you find?

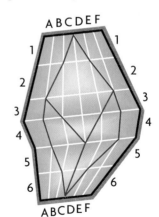

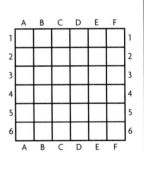

PUT IT IN PERSPECTIVE

PURPOSE To practice making perspective drawings (pages 424–426)

YOU WILL NEED colored pencils or pens

Suppose you invent a toy clay press. What would a big piece of brightly colored clay look like after being pushed through your press? Sketch or trace a front view of a fun shape a child would like such as a star or a heart. Then make a perspective drawing of the shape after it has been through your press.

EXAMPLES

EXERCISES

• **Create and compare different nets for a polyhedron.** (pages 416–418)

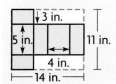

overall area: 154 in.²
area of net: 94 in.²
percent for net: 61%

overall area: 180 in.²
area of net: 94 in.²
percent for net: 52%

For Exercises 1–3, use the net below.

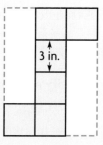

1. Find the overall dimensions of the net.
2. What percent of the total area is the net's area?
3. Copy the faces, and rearrange them for other nets of the same figure.

• **Solve problems by drawing diagrams to show different views.** (pages 419–420)

PROBLEM-SOLVING TIP: For help in solving problems by drawing diagrams, see pages 2 and 419.

4. Zoe made the model shown at the right. Draw a top view and front elevation.

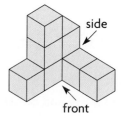

• **Draw three-dimensional figures on isometric dot paper.** (pages 421–423)

Sketch a rectangular prism on dot paper.

Draw the edges of the bottom face of the prism.

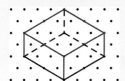

Draw vertical line segments from vertices of the base.
Draw the top face.

Using dot paper, sketch each figure.

5. a cube with sides 4 units long
6. a rectangular prism 6 units long, 3 units deep, and 2 units high
7. a square pyramid 4 units high with a 5-unit × 5-unit base
8. a triangular prism 3 units high with a 5-unit × 4-unit base

---

• **Draw three-dimensional figures in perspective.** (pages 424–426)

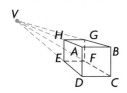

Draw the front face. Mark a vanishing point, V. Draw a dashed line from each vertex to V. Choose a point, G, on $\overline{BV}$.

Draw $\overline{GH}$ parallel to $\overline{AB}$, $\overline{HE}$ parallel to $\overline{AD}$, $\overline{GF}$ parallel to $\overline{BC}$. Draw $\overline{EF}$. Erase segments not on the prism.

9. **VOCABULARY** The technique used to make three-dimensional objects appear to have depth and distance on a flat surface is called ? .
10. Use one-point perspective to draw a rectangular prism viewed from below.
11. Use two-point perspective to draw a rectangular prism viewed from above.

VOCABULARY CHECK

1. To divide lines or angles into two congruent parts is to _?_. (page 382)

2. A transformation that enlarges or reduces a figure is a _?_. (page 404)

EXAMPLES

- **Identify and create transformations of solid figures.** (pages 402–403)

Tell how many ways the triangular prism with an equilateral triangle for a base can be placed on the outline.

The base can be placed on each vertex from the front, and from the back.
total = 6 ways

- **Identify and create dilations of plane figures.** (pages 404–406)

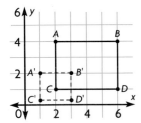

Reduce *ABCD* to 50%.

Draw the dilation, *A′B′C′D′*.

Multiply the original coordinates by 0.5.

- **Recognize and create tessellations by using dilations.** (pages 408–411)

Stage 0   Stage 1   Stage 2   Stage 3

Stage	0	1	2	3
Number of Pieces	1	4	10	22

The scale factor used to reduce the square is 1 to 2, or $\frac{1}{2}$.

EXERCISES

Tell how many ways you can place the solid figure on the outline.

3.

4.

Find the coordinates of the dilation.

5. Enlarge to 400%

  A(4,4)
  B(6,4)
  C(6,2)
  D(4,2)

6. Reduce to 20%

  A(⁻10,10)
  B(⁻3,10)
  C(⁻10,5)
  D(⁻3,5)

7. In the diagram at the left, how many pieces are in Stage 3?

8. What is the relation of the number of pieces from one stage to the next?

9. Predict the number of pieces you will add to Stage 3 to get to Stage 4.

10. Predict the number of pieces in Stage 5.

- **Create and compare different nets for a polyhedron.** (pages 416–418)

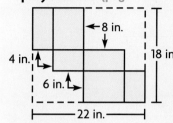

overall area: 396 in.^{2}

area of net: 208 in.^{2}

percent of overall area used for the net: about 50%

For Exercises 11–13, use the net below.

11. Find the overall area.
12. Find the area of the net.
13. What percent of the total area is the net's area?

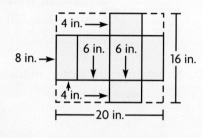

- **Draw three-dimensional figures on isometric dot paper.** (pages 421–423)

On dot paper, sketch a rectangular pyramid with a 3-unit × 2-unit base and a 3-unit height.

Draw the edges of the base.

Locate the top vertex 3 units above the center of the base.

Draw edges for the lateral faces.

Darken the lines: Use solid lines for visible edges. Use dashed lines for hidden edges.

Using dot paper, sketch each figure.

14. a cube with sides 5 units long

15. a rectangular prism with a 3-unit × 4-unit base and a 2-unit height

16. a rectangular pyramid 4 units high with a 6-unit × 5-unit base

17. Label the vertices of the rectangular prism in Exercise 15, and name the edges that are parallel.

PROBLEM SOLVING

Solve. Explain your method.

18. △*JKL* is similar to △*EFG*. In △*JKL*, *KL* = 15 in. and *JK* = 10 in. In △*EFG*, *FG* = 12 in. How long is *EF*? (pages 389–390)

20. Use the model of a building, at the right. Draw a front elevation. (pages 419–420)

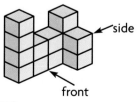

side

front

19. △*ABC* is drawn with the following coordinates: A(3,2), B(5,5), C(6,4). A new triangle, △*A′B′C′*, is drawn 150% larger than the original. What are the coordinates of △*A′B′C′*? (pages 404–406)

21. The length of each cube in the model at the left is 1 unit. Find the perimeter of the base in units. (pages 419–420)

👉 Write About It

1. Use a compass to bisect $\overline{AB}$.

A •———————• B   Explain your method.

(pages 382–383)

2. Show how you would reduce the triangle 50%. (pages 404–406)

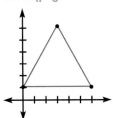

3. Draw a right view, one-point perspective of a cube. (pages 424–426)

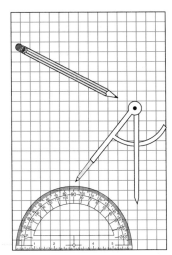

✔ Performance Assessment

Choose a strategy and solve. Explain your method.

Problem-Solving Strategies

- **Find a Pattern**
- **Make a Model**
- **Write an Equation**
- **Make a Table or Graph**
- **Act It Out**
- **Draw a Diagram**

4. Draw a triangle with sides of 12 units, 9 units, and 15 units on grid paper. Draw a second triangle with corresponding sides that has a ratio of 4 to 6 with the first triangle. Label all sides. Explain whether the two triangles are similar. (pages 389–390)

5. Sandy wants to enlarge this pattern 200% so she can use it as a screen saver on her computer. Copy the figure first and then enlarge the image on grid paper.

(pages 404–406)

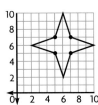

6. Here is the model of the new fitness center. Draw the elevations of all four sides of the building. (pages 419–420)

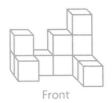

Front

CUMULATIVE REVIEW

Solve the problem. Then write the letter of the correct answer.

1. Erica had a piece of string that was $16\frac{1}{4}$ in. long. She cut it into 5 equal pieces. How long was each piece? **(pages 81–84)**

   A. $2\frac{3}{4}$ in.   **B.** $3\frac{1}{4}$ in.

   C. $3\frac{1}{2}$ in.   **D.** $3\frac{3}{4}$ in.

---

2. Solve. $\frac{y}{9} = {}^-3$ **(pages 119–121)**

   A. $y = {}^-27$ **B.** $y = {}^-3$
   C. $y = 3$ **D.** $y = 27$

---

3. Which pattern is converging? **(pages 188–191)**

   A. 1, 2, 4, 8, . . .   **B.** 5, 25, 125, 625, . . .
   C. 27, 9, 3, 1, . . .   **D.** 1, 10, 100, 1,000, . . .

---

4. The rectangles below are similar. Find the value for x. **(pages 232–234)**

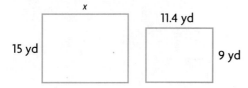

   A. 17.4 yd   **B.** 19 yd
   C. 20.4 yd   **D.** 21 yd

---

5. At the soccer game, 312 people, or 65% of the people who attended the game, were cheering. How many people attended the soccer game? **(pages 271–273)**

   A. 347 people   **B.** 377 people
   C. 420 people   **D.** 480 people

---

6. Find the number of permutations.
$_5P_3 = \dfrac{5!}{(5-3)!}$ **(pages 342–345)**

   A. 60   **B.** 120
   C. 5,040   **D.** 86,400

---

7. A recent survey of 110 students showed that 44 students preferred vanilla ice cream, 39 preferred chocolate, and 27 preferred strawberry. Out of 280 students, how many would you expect to prefer vanilla? **(pages 358–360)**

   A. 44 students   **B.** 112 students
   C. 220 students   **D.** 314 students

For Exercises 8–9, use the figure below.

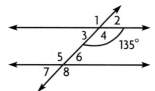

8. Find m $\angle 7$. **(pages 378–381)**

   A. 35°   **B.** 45°
   C. 90°   **D.** 135°

---

9. Which pair of angles are alternate exterior angles? **(pages 378–381)**

   A. $\angle 1$ and $\angle 6$ **B.** $\angle 4$ and $\angle 5$
   C. $\angle 3$ and $\angle 8$ **D.** $\angle 2$ and $\angle 7$

---

10. What percent of the total area is the area of the net? **(pages 416–418)**

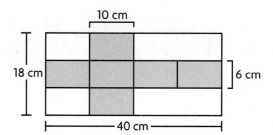

   A. 20%   **B.** 40%
   C. 50%   **D.** 60%

CHAPTER
23
SEEING RELATIONSHIPS

LOOK AHEAD

In this chapter you will solve problems that involve

- comparing and interpreting tables and graphs
- solving problems by making a table

- using scatterplots to see the relationship between two variables
- recognizing inverse variation

Goofy Graphs

People can use graphs in misleading ways. Suppose that you and your group are running a car wash business. Your task is to create a misleading graph that makes it look like your business is doing much better than it really is.

YOU WILL NEED: poster board, markers

Plan
- Work with a small group. Make up data about the profit of your business during the last 6 months. Use the data to make a misleading graph.

Act
- Make a table to organize the data about your profits.
- Fill the table with false data.
- Make a graph that looks realistic but is misleading. Be sure it looks as if your business is doing well.
- Draw your graph on poster board.

Share
- Present your graph to the class. Have them find what is misleading about your graph.

OUR PROFITS

Month	Profit
April	$200
May	$100
June	$225
July	$250
August	$50
September	$275

DID YOU

 Make a table to organize data?

 Fill the table with false data?

 Make a misleading graph?

 Present your graph to the class?

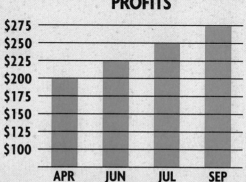

PROFITS

Tables and Graphs

WHAT YOU'LL LEARN
How to compare
tables and graphs

WHY LEARN THIS?
To recognize the
differences between
tables and graphs for
displaying information

The drama club sells candy from a candy machine during the school day. Once a day, a member of the club fills the candy machine. The machine holds 500 pieces of candy and takes one minute to fill. The table shows how many pieces of candy were in the machine each hour during a school day.

Pieces of Candy in Machine								
Time	8 A.M.	9	10	11	12 P.M.	1	2	3
Candy	115	85	24	425	352	312	201	25

• What two things are compared in the table?

• How many pieces of candy were purchased between 9:00 A.M. and 10:00 A.M.? between 10:00 A.M. and 11:00 A.M.?

• When was the candy machine filled?

Another way to display the information is to use a graph.

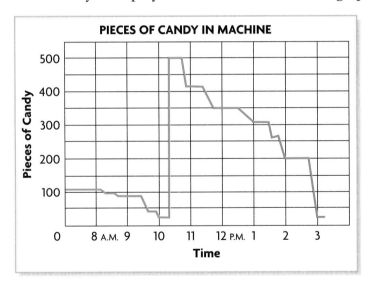

Talk About It

• What does the vertical line between 10:00 A.M. and 11:00 A.M. represent in the graph?

• Was the candy machine filled at a time closer to 10:00 A.M. or 11:00 A.M.? How can you tell?

• Was the candy purchased constantly? How can you tell?

You can compare the relationship between the dimensions and areas of geometric figures by using tables and graphs.

EXAMPLE Use the table and the graph to answer the questions about a rectangle with a perimeter of 18 ft.

RECTANGLE WITH A PERIMETER OF 18 FT

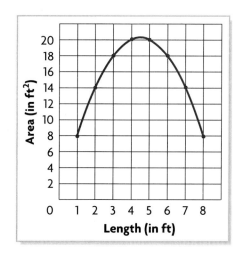

Length (in ft)	Width (in ft)	Area (in ft²)
1	8	8
2	7	14
3	6	18
4	5	20
5	4	20
6	3	18
7	2	14
8	1	8

Look at the table. At what length does the rectangle have the greatest area?

The greatest area is when the length is 4 ft or 5 ft.

Look at the graph. At what length does the rectangle have the greatest area?

The greatest area is when the length is about 4.5 ft.

- **CRITICAL THINKING** Can a rectangle with a length greater than or equal to 9 ft have a perimeter of 18 ft? Explain.

Business Link

Dog owners like to give their dogs plenty of room to run and exercise. Shirley wants to build a dog run. She has a choice of fencing an area that is 12.5 ft × 12.5 ft or an area that is 14 ft × 13 ft. Fencing material costs $12.50 per foot. How much would Shirley save on fencing material if she built the 12.5 ft × 12.5 ft dog run?

GUIDED PRACTICE

For Exercises 1–3, use the table and graph from the Example.

1. Look at the table. What are the possible lengths when the area of the rectangle is 12 ft²?

2. Look at the graph. What are the possible lengths when the area of the rectangle is 12 ft²?

3. Does the table or graph give a better description of the relationship between the area and length of the rectangle? Explain.

INDEPENDENT PRACTICE

This table and this graph relate a square's perimeter, *P* (in centimeters), and its area, *A* (in square centimeters).

1. Look at the table. What is the area when the perimeter is 10 cm?

2. Look at the graph. What is the area when the perimeter is 10 cm?

Problem-Solving Applications

This table and this graph show the performance of two race cars in a 140-mi race.

3. Look at the graph. Exactly how long did it take car A to go from 35 mi to 70 mi?

4. Look at the table. Exactly how long did it take car A to go from 35 mi to 70 mi?

5. Look at the table. What happened to car B between 35 mi and 70 mi?

6. Look at the graph. What happened to car B between 35 mi and 70 mi?

7. Does the table or the graph give better information about the race car performances? Explain.

8. Look at the graph. For which 10-min interval did car A travel fastest? Explain.

9. Look at the table or graph. Which car traveled at a constant speed at some time during the race? Explain.

10. ⬤▭▶ **WRITE ABOUT IT** Do you think a table or a graph gives more information? Explain.

PERIMETER AND AREA OF A SQUARE

P	A
4	1
8	4
12	9
16	16
20	25

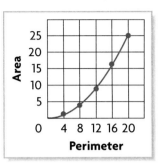

CAR TIMES (IN MIN)		
	A	B
35 mi	29	13
70 mi	45	39
105 mi	52	52
140 mi	61	73

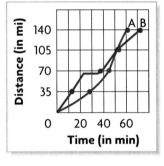

Mixed Review

11. Use the table at right to make a line graph.

12. Between which two years did rainfall increase the most?

13. Between which two years did rainfall decrease the most?

Total Rainfall	
1990	42 in.
1991	31 in.
1992	33 in.
1993	29 in.
1994	40 in.

Sketch a rectangular prism with the given dimensions.

14. 2 cm × 4 cm × 2 cm   **15.** 2 in. × 3 in. × 4 in.   **16.** 5 cm × 4 cm × 6 cm

17. **NUMBER SENSE** The product of two numbers is 150 and their sum is 25. What are the numbers?

18. **RATIOS** A model of a truck is 9 in. long and 5 in. high. The actual truck is 13.5 ft long. How high is it?

MORE PRACTICE Lesson 23.1, page H77

Interpreting Tables and Graphs

Lisa and Rodney are in charge of raising the flag to the top of the flagpole before school. Lisa raises the flag one day and Rodney raises it the next day. It takes both Lisa and Rodney 8 seconds to raise the flag. The flagpole is 16 ft high. Rodney raises the flag slowly at first and gradually speeds up. Lisa raises the flag at a constant rate.

TABLE A	
Height of Flag (in ft)	Time (in sec)
0.50	1
1.00	2
1.75	3
2.75	4
4.00	5
6.00	6
9.00	7
16.00	8

TABLE B	
Height of Flag (in ft)	Time (in sec)
2	1
4	2
6	3
8	4
10	5
12	6
14	7
16	8

- Which table represents the relationship between time and height when Lisa raises the flag? when Rodney raises the flag?

The graphs show the relationship between the height of the flag and the time it takes Lisa and Rodney to raise the flag.

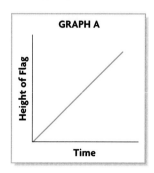

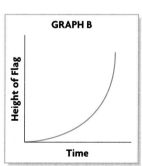

- Which graph represents the relationship between time and height when Lisa raises the flag? when Rodney raises the flag?

Science Link

Scientists use tables and graphs to compare two variables such as time and temperature. The graph below shows the relationship between time and temperature. Describe this relationship.

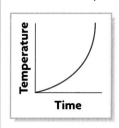

Talk About It

- How did you know which graph represented the relationship between time and height when Lisa raised the flag? when Rodney raised the flag?

EXAMPLE 1 Tell which of the three graphs corresponds to each situation below.

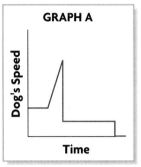

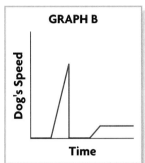

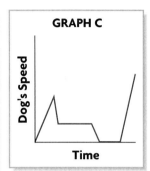

1. Dog sits inside munching on bone. Dog hears noise and runs to backyard. Dog sits at base of tree barking at squirrel. Dog trots back inside house.

2. Dog trots beside Jim, who is jogging. Dog chases cat. Jim calls to dog to stop and come back. Dog walks slowly back to Jim. Dog sits at Jim's side.

Graph A corresponds to situation 2. Graph B corresponds to situation 1.

EXAMPLE 2 Tell which of the three tables corresponds to each situation above. Each situation lasts 60 seconds.

TABLE A		TABLE B		TABLE C	
Time (in sec)	Speed (in mph)	Time (in sec)	Speed (in mph)	Time (in sec)	Speed (in mph)
10	12	12	0	11	8
35	5	22	18	20	18
39	0	23	0	21	5
51	0	40	0	55	0
60	15	60	4	60	0

Table B corresponds to situation 1. Table C corresponds to situation 2.

Match each graph to one of the given situations.

1. an oven at a constant temperature

2. a cool morning that warms up quickly and then slowly

3. the inside of a refrigerator whose door is left open and then closed

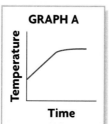
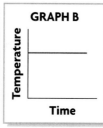
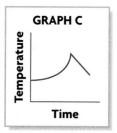

INDEPENDENT PRACTICE

In Exercises 1–4, Ben, Terrence, Sue, and Juan each go to school.
School begins at 7:20 A.M. Tell which table corresponds to each trip.

TABLE A	
Time	Distance to School
7:00 A.M.	1,600 yd
7:05 A.M.	1,200 yd
7:10 A.M.	800 yd
7:15 A.M.	400 yd
7:20 A.M.	0 yd

TABLE B	
Time	Distance to School
7:00 A.M.	1,900 yd
7:05 A.M.	1,400 yd
7:10 A.M.	1,400 yd
7:15 A.M.	1,400 yd
7:20 A.M.	0 yd

TABLE C	
Time	Distance to School
7:00 A.M.	1,450 yd
7:05 A.M.	1,450 yd
7:10 A.M.	1,450 yd
7:15 A.M.	800 yd
7:20 A.M.	300 yd

TABLE D	
Time	Distance to School
7:00 A.M.	1,360 yd
7:05 A.M.	1,200 yd
7:10 A.M.	1,200 yd
7:15 A.M.	700 yd
7:20 A.M.	0 yd

1. Ben wakes up late. He rushes out the door and jogs to school. He gets tired and slows down. He arrives late.

2. Terrence leaves his home and walks at a steady pace until he arrives at school.

3. Sue leaves her home and walks slowly. She stops to play with a dog. Then she realizes she may be late and walks quickly to school. She arrives on time.

4. Juan leaves his home and walks to his friend's house. He waits for his friend to get ready. His friend's mother gives them a ride to school in her car.

Problem-Solving Applications

5. Suppose Kim left for school and constantly increased her speed until she got to school. Sketch a graph relating time and her speed.

6. Suppose Kim lives 1,200 yd from school. Make a table relating time and distance to school if she constantly increased her speed until she got to school.

7. ✐ **WRITE ABOUT IT** Describe your trip to school today by relating time and speed. Then draw a graph to show the relationship.

Making a Graph

WHAT YOU'LL LEARN
How to make a graph
to help solve problems

WHY LEARN THIS?
So you can solve
problems that involve
two variables

Problem Solving
. . . .
• **Understand**
• **Plan**
• **Solve**
• **Look Back**

Science Link

Graphs and tables
can be used
for estimating
temperature
conditions on
mountains since
temperature drops
about 5°F for every
1,000 ft of elevation.
In Colorado the
temperature is 56°F
at Colorado Springs
(elevation 6,000 ft)
and 35°F at Cripple
Creek (elevation
10,000 ft). Estimate
the temperature at
the top of Pikes Peak
(elevation 14,000 ft).
Make a graph to help
you decide.

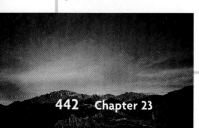

Sometimes making a graph will help you solve a problem.

Mike's Manufacturing plant drains its excess water into a storage tank. A cross-section of the tank is shown. When the drain hose is running at a constant rate, the deepest part of the tank fills in 30 min. The entire tank fills in 90 min. About how long will it take the water at the deep end to reach 9 ft?

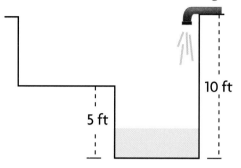

✓ **UNDERSTAND**   What are you asked to find?

What facts are given?

✓ **PLAN**   What strategy will you use?

You can *make a graph* to show the relationship between time and the depth of the water.

✓ **SOLVE**   How can you make a graph to solve this problem?

Let time be the horizontal axis and depth be the vertical axis of the graph. Graph (30,5) to show a depth of 5 ft in 30 min. Since the tank fills at a constant rate, draw a straight line from (0,0) to (30,5). Graph (90,10) to show a depth of 10 ft in 90 min. Draw a straight line from (30,5) to (90,10).

To find the time for 9 ft, draw a horizontal line from 9 ft until it intersects the graph. Then draw a vertical line from that point until it intersects the horizontal axis.

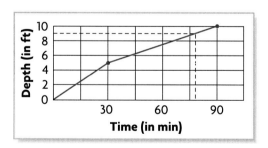

The water will be 9 ft deep in about 78 min.

✓ **LOOK BACK**   Is 78 min a reasonable answer? Explain.

What if . . . the tank took 120 minutes to fill? How would you change the graph?

Solve by *making a graph*.

1. At the local swim center, the lap pool is 6 ft deep and fills at a constant rate. It takes 12 min for the water depth to reach 2 ft and 24 min for the water depth to reach 4 ft. About how deep will the water be after 27 min?

2. The student enrollment in Green County Schools in 1985 was 15,491. In 1990 the enrollment was 19,648, and in 1995 the enrollment was 25,357. Estimate the student enrollment for 1988 and 1994.

3. Use this table to make a graph. Use the graph to predict the population of the United States for the year 2030.

United States Population (in millions)				
Year	1870	1910	1950	1990
Population	38.6	92.2	151.3	248.7

4. At the start of an experiment, the temperature of a liquid is 60°F. The temperature increases constantly for 10 min until it reaches 63°F. For the next 15 min, the temperature increases constantly until it reaches 70°F. Use a graph to estimate the temperature of the liquid 20 min into the experiment.

MIXED APPLICATIONS

CHOOSE

Choose a strategy and solve.

Problem-Solving Strategies
- Make a Graph
- Guess and Check
- Solve a Simpler Problem
- Find a Pattern
- Use a Formula
- Write an Equation

5. Jim starts jogging at a speed of 12 mph. His speed decreases constantly for 20 min until it is 6 mph. Estimate Jim's speed 15 min after he starts jogging.

6. The number of pairs of in-line skates sold at Super Sports Store over the past four months were 25, 31, 38, and 46. If this pattern continues, how many pairs will be sold this month?

7. Serena spent $4.28 on pencils and notebooks. Each pencil cost $0.07, and each notebook cost $0.43. How many pencils and how many notebooks did she buy?

8. On a long trip, Mr. Akin drove his truck on the freeway at a speed of 65 mph for $3\frac{1}{2}$ hr. How far did Mr. Akin drive?

9. Fred and his friend Jamie go out to lunch to celebrate their birthdays. The bill for the lunch is $16.93. How much money should they leave for the tip if they want it to be about 15% of the bill?

10. At Super Sports Store, the price of a baseball glove is 6 times the price of a baseball. The baseball glove costs $41.70. How much does the baseball cost?

Using Scatterplots

Ben is on the school basketball team. One night when the temperature was cool, he scored 21 points. This made him think that when the temperature was lower, he would score more points than when the temperature was higher. To test his theory, he made a scatterplot, using the points he scored in each game and the corresponding temperature during that game.

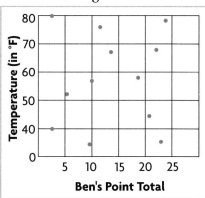

Talk About It

• Is there a relationship between the number of points scored and the temperature? Explain.

• If Ben's point total increased when the temperature was lower, how would the scatterplot look?

• If Ben's point total increased when the temperature was higher, how would the scatterplot look?

EXAMPLE 1 Use the table. Draw a scatterplot to see if there is a relationship between the number of hours Ben practices the week of a game and the number of points he scores.

Week	1	2	3	4	5	6	7	8	9	10	11	12
Hours	2	4	5	8	1	0	6	7	9	3	6	4
Points	5	10	14	23	3	2	18	22	24	9	21	12

The scatterplot shows a positive correlation between the practice hours and Ben's point total. So, there is a relationship.

• What happens to Ben's point total as the number of practice hours increases?

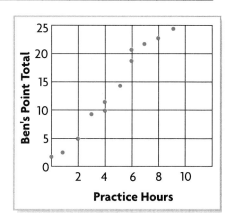

A city council surveys 12 cities to see if there is a relationship between the number of car accidents per year and the number of police officers in a city. The results are below.

Town	Car Accidents	Police Officers
A	5	15
B	12	11
C	38	7
D	65	4
E	8	10
F	24	8

Town	Car Accidents	Police Officers
G	47	5
H	5	18
I	29	6
J	35	7
K	59	3
L	44	4

EXAMPLE 2 Use a scatterplot to see if there is a relationship between the number of police officers employed and the number of car accidents. What should the city council do?

The scatterplot shows a negative correlation. The number of accidents decreases as the number of police officers increases. So, the city council should hire more police officers to reduce the number of car accidents.

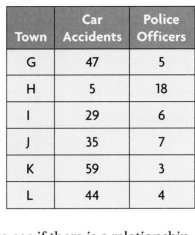

Technology Link

In *Data ToolKit* you can practice making scatterplots to see if there is a relationship between variables.

• **CRITICAL THINKING** The council cannot hire more officers. What else could be compared with car accidents?

GUIDED PRACTICE

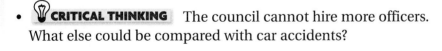

Describe the relationship shown in the scatterplot.

1.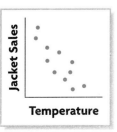

Jacket Sales / Temperature

2.

Test Scores / Study Time

3.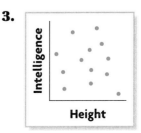

Intelligence / Height

445

The results of a survey about leisure time and ages are shown on the scatterplot. For Exercises 1–4, use the scatterplot.

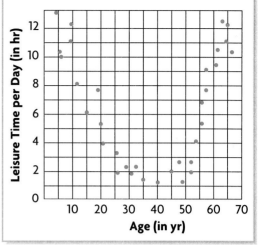

1. Is there a relationship between age and leisure time?

2. At what ages do people have the most leisure time?

3. At what ages do people have the least leisure time?

4. What reasons might there be for the differences in the amounts of leisure time?

For Exercises 5–6, use the table below.

5. Draw a scatterplot.

6. Is there a relationship between height and weight? If so, describe the relationship.

Height (in cm)	176	171	195	151	200	163	190
Weight (in kg)	79	61	91	44	97	53	85

Problem-Solving Applications

For Problems 7–8, use the scatterplot at the right.

7. According to the scatterplot, how might you reduce the number of your mistakes?

8. What kind of additional data would be needed for the scatterplot to show no relationship between practice and mistakes?

9. ✏️ **WRITE ABOUT IT** Describe an example of a relationship that is a positive correlation. Then draw a scatterplot for the data.

Mixed Review

Solve each equation for x when $y = 0$.

10. $2x + 2y = 12$ 11. $5x + 4y = 90$ 12. $3x = 48 + 19y$ 13. $4x = 3y - 12$

Sketch the rectangular pyramid described.

14. base 4 cm × 3 cm, height 5 cm   15. base 2 cm × 3 cm, height 6 cm

16. **NUMBER SENSE** When 3 friends divide 4 boxes of candy evenly, they each get 48 pieces of candy. How many pieces of candy are in each box?

17. **LOGICAL REASONING** It took Wanda 5 min to saw an oak board into 3 pieces. How long would it take her to saw a board into 9 pieces?

MORE PRACTICE Lesson 23.4, page H78

Direct Variation

When the values of two sets of data increase or decrease together at a constant rate, there is **direct variation** between the sets of data. The graph of the data is linear. You can use a graph to see if sets of data show direct variation.

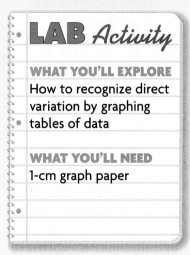

LAB *Activity*

WHAT YOU'LL EXPLORE
How to recognize direct variation by graphing tables of data

WHAT YOU'LL NEED
1-cm graph paper

Explore

- Use graph paper to make a graph for the data in each table.

Table A: Ken's Income							
Hours worked	1	2	3	4	5	6	7
Pay (in dollars)	5.75	11.50	17.25	23.00	28.75	34.50	40.25

Table B: Time and Speed Needed to Travel 300 mi							
Speed (in mph)	5	6	7.5	10	15	30	60
Time (in hr)	60	50	40	30	20	10	5

WORD POWER
direct variation

Think and Discuss

- Which graph shows direct variation? Explain. Which graph does not show direct variation? Explain.

Try This

- Make a graph of the data in each table. Tell which graph shows direct variation. Explain.

Table A: Triangle with Area of 48 cm^2							
Base (in cm)	2	4	6	8	12	16	24	48
Height (in cm)	48	24	16	12	8	6	4	2

Table B: Corn Chips Produced							
Number	36	108	84	120	72	144	60
Time (in min)	3	9	7	10	6	12	5

E–Lab • Activity 23 Available on CD-ROM and the Internet at http://www.hbschool.com/elab

CULTURAL CONNECTION

THE SWISS ALPS

Perhaps the most famous part of the Alps mountain system is the Swiss Alps. The Swiss Alps cover most of Switzerland. Thousands of tourists visit the Swiss Alps each year. During the winter, the Swiss ski on the Alps and during the summer they mountain-climb. There are many magnificent natural sights in the region, including waterfalls and the peaks of the Alps.

Elise and her family went to visit their relatives in Bern, Switzerland. While there, they went skiing. Which of the two graphs below shows the relationship between time and the distance Elise traveled on one of her ski runs?

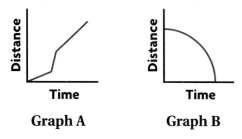

Graph A   **Graph B**

Graph A shows the relationship, since distance increases as time increases.

WORK TOGETHER

1. Elise begins to ski down a slope at a constant rate, stops and rests, skis down the rest of the slope at a constant rate, and then walks to the ski lodge. Which graph below corresponds to the time and Elise's speed?

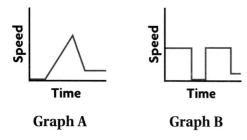

Graph A   **Graph B**

2. The scatterplot at the right shows the relationship between the altitude of the Alps and the temperature. Describe the relationship.

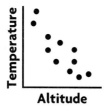

EXAMPLES

- **Compare tables and graphs.** (pages 436–438)

RUNNERS' TIMES (IN SEC)		
Distance	**Time**	
	A	**B**
100 m	11	12
200 m	22	24
300 m	33	51
400 m	56	64

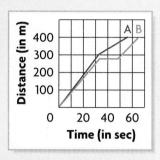

The distances for two runners are compared.

- **Interpret tables and graphs.** (pages 439–441)

Graph A shows a car at a constant rate.

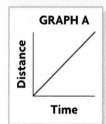
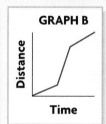
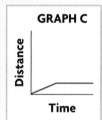

- **Use the strategy** *make a graph* **to solve problems.** (pages 442–443)

PROBLEM-SOLVING TIP: For help in solving problems by making a graph, see pages 9 and 442.

- **Use a scatterplot to see relationships.** (pages 444–446)

There is no relationship between weight and test scores.

EXERCISES

For Exercises 1–4, use the table and graph from the example.

1. Look at the table. What happened to runner B between 200 m and 300 m?
2. Look at the graph. What happened to runner B between 200 m and 300 m?
3. Look at the table. How much sooner did runner A finish than runner B?
4. Look at the graph. How much faster did runner A finish than runner B?

Use the graphs from the example to tell which graph corresponds to the given situations.

5. A person walks and then sits on a bench.
6. A person walks at a steady pace.
7. A person walks, then runs, then walks.
8. Describe another situation for Graph B.

9. In 1990 the attendance at home football games was 5,096. In 1995 the attendance was 8,150. Estimate the attendance for 1992.
10. At 5:00 A.M. the temperature was 50°F. At 10:00 A.M. the temperature was 59°F. Find what the temperature was at 6:30 A.M.

Use the scatterplot below.

11. Is there a relationship between comfort level and temperature? If so, describe it.

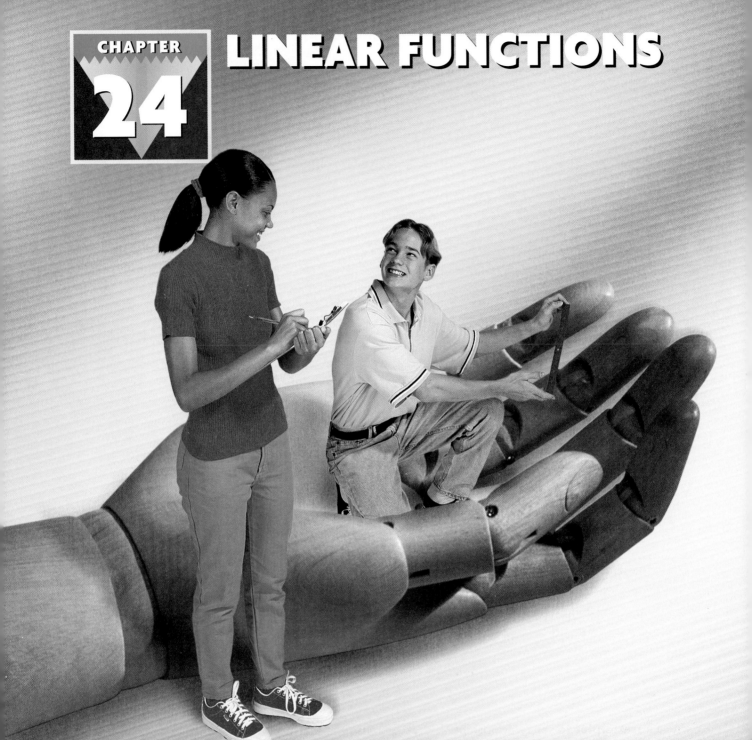

LOOK AHEAD

In this chapter you will solve problems that involve

- slope and systems of equations
- identifying relations and functions
- linear and nonlinear functions

Finger Joint Function

If you know the length of the second joint of a person's finger, can you estimate the length of the third joint?

YOU WILL NEED: ruler

Plan
- Work with a small group. Measure the lengths of second and third finger joints. Graph the results. Decide if the length of the third finger joint is a function of the length of the second.

Act
- Measure the length of your second and third finger joints.
- Graph your results.
- Write an equation to express the length of the third finger joint as a function of the length of the second.
- Measure a second finger joint. Use your equation to find the length of the third joint.

Share
- Compare results with another group.

DID YOU

- ✓ Measure finger joint lengths?
- ✓ Graph your measurements?
- ✓ Write an equation?
- ✓ Use your function to find joint lengths?

JOINT MEASUREMENTS

SECOND JOINT

THIRD JOINT

Finger	Second Joint	Third Joint
Index	34 mm	57 mm
Middle	39 mm	67 mm
Ring	36 mm	58 mm
Little	28 mm	46 mm

Slope of a Line

Recall that the graph of a linear equation is a straight line. The measure of the steepness of a line is called the **slope** of the line. You can use graph paper to find the slope.

Explore

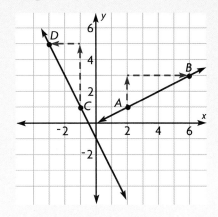

- In a coordinate plane, graph A(2,1). Then graph B(6,3). Draw a line through the points.

- From point A, move up until you are across from B. This move is the vertical change from point A to point B. How many vertical units did you move?

- Now move right until you reach point B. This move is the horizontal change from point A to point B. How many horizontal units did you move?

- What is the ratio of the vertical change to the horizontal change?

- What is the vertical change from C to D? What is the horizontal change from C to D? (HINT: Since you moved left in the coordinate plane, write this as a negative number.) What is the ratio of the vertical change to the horizontal change?

Think and Discuss   💡 CRITICAL THINKING

- You can find the slope of a line by forming the ratio of vertical change to horizontal change. You found this ratio for line AB and for line CD. For each line is the slope positive or negative?

- Look at line AB and line CD. How are the lines alike? different?

- A line that rises from left to right has a positive slope. What is the appearance of a line with a negative slope?

Try This

Graph the line containing the given points. Then find the slope.

1. (3,2), (⁻2,⁻1)   **2.** (4,⁻4), (⁻2,1)   **3.** (2,⁻3), (4,7)

Slopes and Intercepts

The slope of a line is the measure of the steepness of a line. To calculate slope, find the ratio of the vertical change to the horizontal change. This ratio can be positive or negative.

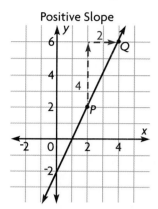

Positive Slope

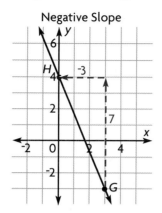

Negative Slope

The slope of line PQ is $\frac{4}{2}$, or 2.   The slope of line GH is $\frac{-7}{3}$.

You can find the slope of a line when you know the coordinates of two points on the line. To calculate the slope of the line, find the difference of the points' y-coordinates and the difference of the points' x-coordinates. Suppose the points are (3,1) and (⁻2,2).

$1 - 2 = {}^-1$ ← **vertical change**   *Subtract y-coordinates.*

$3 - {}^-2 = 5$ ← **horizontal change**   *Subtract x-coordinates.*

$\text{slope} = \dfrac{\text{vertical change}}{\text{horizontal change}} = \dfrac{^-1}{5}$ *Write the ratio.*

So, the slope of the line containing (3,1) and (⁻2,2) is $\frac{-1}{5}$.

- How would you find the slope of the line containing (2,⁻3) and (4,7)? What is the slope?

The **x-intercept** of a line is the x-coordinate of the point where the graph crosses the x-axis.
The **y-intercept** of a line is the y-coordinate of the point where the graph crosses the y-axis.

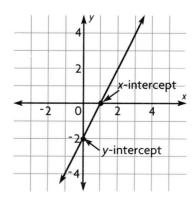

For the graph at the right, the x-intercept is 1. The y-coordinate of this point is 0. The y-intercept is ⁻2. At this point, the x-coordinate is 0.

Language Link

The verb *intercept* means "to seize or stop on the way, before arrival at the intended place." In football an interception is a pass that is caught by a defender before it reaches its intended receiver. How is an interception in a football game like the *x*-intercept?

453

REMEMBER:

The x-coordinate of a point on the y-axis is 0. The y-coordinate of a point on the x-axis is 0. **See page H29.**

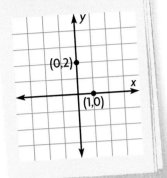

You can find the intercepts of a line and use them to draw the graph of the linear equation.

EXAMPLE 1   Find the x-intercept and the y-intercept of $2x + 3y = 6$. Use the intercepts to graph the equation.

To find the x-intercept, substitute 0 for y and solve for x.

$$2x + 3y = 6$$
$$2x + 3 \cdot 0 = 6$$
$$2x + 0 = 6$$
$$2x = 6$$
$$\frac{2x}{2} = \frac{6}{2}$$
$$x = 3$$

The x-intercept is 3.

To find the y-intercept, substitute 0 for x and solve for y.

$$2x + 3y = 6$$
$$2 \cdot 0 + 3y = 6$$
$$0 + 3y = 6$$
$$3y = 6$$
$$\frac{3y}{3} = \frac{6}{3}$$
$$y = 2$$

The y-intercept is 2.

So, the graph of $2x + 3y = 6$ contains the points (3,0) and (0,2). Plot these points, and draw a line through them.

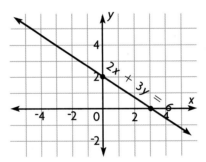

- What is the x-intercept of $4x + 2y = 6$? What is the y-intercept?

GUIDED PRACTICE

Find the slope of the line containing the given points.

1. (1,3), (2,4)   **2.** (3,6), (0,2)   **3.** (⁻1,2), (5,5)

4. (⁻1,⁻1), (⁻3,2)   **5.** (0,0), (6,⁻3)   **6.** (2,⁻5), (1,⁻2)

7. How do you find the x-intercept of a line?

8. How do you find the y-intercept of a line?

9. What is the same about every x-intercept? about every y-intercept?

Find the x-intercept and the y-intercept. Use the intercepts to graph the equation.

10. $2x + 3y = 12$ **11.** $3x - 2y = 6$ **12.** $3x - y = 1$

13. $5x + 3y = 15$ **14.** $6x - 3y = ⁻18$ **15.** $x + 2y = 4$

Calculator Activities, page H42

Slope-Intercept Form

Linear equations can be written in the form $y = mx + b$. This is called the **slope-intercept form** of an equation. The m is the slope, and the b is the y-intercept.

$$y = mx + b \leftarrow y\text{-intercept} \qquad y = {}^{-}2x + 4 \leftarrow y\text{-intercept}$$
$$\uparrow \qquad\qquad\qquad\qquad \uparrow$$
$$\text{slope} \qquad\qquad\qquad\quad \text{slope}$$

- Identify the slope and the y-intercept of the equation $y = 5x - 3$.

- What is the slope and the y-intercept of $y = {}^{-}4x + 2$?

You can quickly graph any linear equation written in the slope-intercept form.

EXAMPLE 2 Graph the linear equation $y = \frac{2}{3}x + 3$.

Think: Use the y-intercept as one point, and use the slope to find a second point on the graph. Then draw a line through the points.

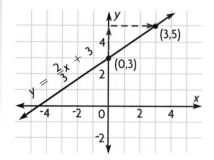

The y-intercept is 3, so graph point (0,3).

Since the slope is $\frac{2}{3}$, from (0,3) move 2 units up and 3 units to the right. Graph the second point (3,5).

Draw a line through the points. Label the line by writing the equation.

Talk About It

- When you use the slope to find a second point, does it matter whether you move vertically and then horizontally or horizontally and then vertically? Explain.

- How can you use the slope-intercept form to graph the equation $y = {}^{-}3x + 5$?

INDEPENDENT PRACTICE

Find the slope of the line containing the given points.

1. (1,2), (4,5)

2. (6,4), (1,3)

3. (3,1), (0,3)

4. (2,5), (6,2)

5. (4,3), (2,2)

6. ($^{-}$1,$^{-}$1), ($^{-}$3,2)

7. (0,0), (6,$^{-}$3)

8. (1,4), (6,6)

9. ($^{-}$2,$^{-}$3), (2,4)

10. (0,$^{-}$2), ($^{-}$6,3)

Find the *x*-intercept and the *y*-intercept. Use the intercepts to graph the equation.

11. $x + y = 5$ **12.** $3x - y = 3$ **13.** $x + 2y = 8$

14. $2x + 4y = 8$ **15.** $4x - 2y = 20$ **16.** $4x - 3y = 12$

17. $6x - y = 18$ **18.** $2x + y = 7$ **19.** $5x + 4y = 20$

20. $3x + 3y = 9$ **21.** $5x + 4y = {}^-20$ **22.** $3x - 9y = 27$

In **Mighty Math Astro Algebra,** you can report to the *Grapher.* Bring all you know about slope and intercepts so you can complete the *Join the Circuits* mission.

Find the slope and the *y*-intercept. Then graph the equation.

23. $y = \frac{1}{2}x + 5$ **24.** $y = \frac{3}{4}x + 4$ **25.** $y = \frac{{}^-1}{2}x + 4$

26. $y = \frac{3}{2}x - 6$ **27.** $y = \frac{5}{7}x - 3$ **28.** $5y - 2x = 15$

29. $4y - 8x = 8$ **30.** $2y - 6x = 14$ **31.** $2x + 5y = 10$

Problem-Solving Applications

For Problems 32–35, write the slope-intercept form for each equation described.

32. The slope is 5, and the *y*-intercept is 10.

33. The slope is $\frac{{}^-3}{4}$, and the *y*-intercept is $^-5$.

34. The slope is $\frac{1}{4}$, and the *y*-intercept is 0.

35. The slope is $^-3$, and the *y*-intercept is $^-4$.

36. It is important for the roof lines of houses to be steep enough to let the rain run off. Find the slope of the roof line.

37. ✏️ **WRITE ABOUT IT** Explain how a graph of an equation can show you whether the slope of a line is positive or negative.

Mixed Review

Tell whether the line contains the point. Write *yes* or *no*.

38. $y = x - 2$; (3,1) **39.** $y = x + 6$; (2,9) **40.** $y = x - 4.5$; (9,4) **41.** $y = x + 5$; ($^-5$,0)

42. $y = 7 + x$; (2,9) **43.** $y = 3x + 2$; (1,5) **44.** $y - 3x = 9$; (2,6) **45.** $2x + 2y = 8$; (0,2)

Find the mean, median, and mode.

46. 17, 18, 20, 21, 16 **47.** 14, 18, 15, 19, 24, 24 **48.** 27, 28, 23, 14, 23

49. **CURRENCY** Jeff is planning a trip to Japan. He wants to exchange U.S. dollars for Japanese currency before he leaves. If the current exchange rate is 106.77 yen per $1.00, how many yen will he receive for each $20.00 he exchanges?

50. **BUDGET** A children's store budgets 2% of sales for newspaper advertising. If sales totaled $2,920,000, how much will be budgeted for newspaper advertising?

MORE PRACTICE Lesson 24.1, page H78

Systems of Equations

Two or more linear equations graphed in the same coordinate plane form a **system of equations**. The equations $y = ^-x + 4$ and $y = x$ form a system of equations. You can use a geoboard and graph paper to find their solutions.

ACTIVITY

WHAT YOU'LL NEED: geoboard, rubber bands, graph paper

- Place two rubber bands on your geoboard to represent the x- and y-axes and Quadrant I in the coordinate plane.

- Copy and complete each table of values.

$y = ^-x + 4$

x	$^-x + 4$	y	Solutions
0	$^-0 + 4$	?	(0,?)
2	$^-2 + 4$	?	(2,?)
4	$^-4 + 4$	?	(4,?)

$y = x$

x	y	Solutions
0	?	(?,?)
3	?	(?,?)
4	?	(?,?)

- Model each equation by joining the points for the ordered pairs with a rubber band.

- On graph paper, make a diagram of your model.

Talk About It

- Describe the model of each equation.

- How are the models of the two equations related?

- How many solutions do the equations have in common? How do you know?

To solve a system of equations, graph the equations in the same coordinate plane. Sometimes the graphs of the equations intersect at a point. The coordinates of that point are the **solution of the system**.

- Look at the graph of the system of equations shown at the right. At what point do the graphs intersect?

- What is the solution of the system?

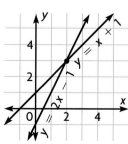

You can tell whether an ordered pair is a solution of a system of equations by substituting the coordinates of the ordered pair for the variables in each equation.

EXAMPLE 1   Is ($^-$1,4) a solution of the system of equations $y = x + 5$ and $y = ^-4x$?

Think: If the coordinates make both equations true, the ordered pair is a solution of the system of equations.

$y = x + 5$ *Substitute $^-$1 for*
$4 = ^-1 + 5$ *x and 4 for y.*
$4 = 4$ ✓

$y = ^-4x$ *Substitute $^-$1 for*
$4 = ^-4 \cdot ^-1$ *x and 4 for y.*
$4 = 4$ ✓

($^-$1,4) makes both equations true. So, ($^-$1,4) is a solution of the system of equations.

- How can you find out whether (0,2) is a solution of the system of equations $y = x + 2$ and $y = 5x - 3$?

You can solve some real-life problems by writing and graphing systems of equations.

EXAMPLE 2   Tremayne and Tomika run a total of 8 mi each day. Tomika runs 2 mi more than Tremayne. How many miles does each run?

Let x = the distance Tremayne runs.   *Choose the variables.*
Let y = the distance Tomika runs.

$x + y = 8$, or $y = 8 - x$ *Write two equations*
$y = x + 2$ *for the problem.*

Make a table of values for each equation.

x	$8 - x$	y	(x,y)
0	$8 - 0$	8	(0,8)
2	$8 - 2$	6	(2,6)
4	$8 - 4$	4	(4,4)

x	$x + 2$	y	(x,y)
0	$0 + 2$	2	(0,2)
2	$2 + 2$	4	(2,4)
4	$4 + 2$	6	(4,6)

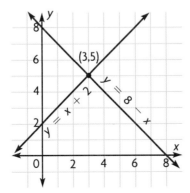

Graph both equations in the same coordinate plane. Label the point where the graphs of the equations intersect.

solution of the system: (3,5)

So, Tremayne runs 3 mi and Tomika runs 5 mi.

Tell whether the ordered pair is a solution of the system of equations. Write *yes* or *no*.

1. $y = 2x - 1$
$y = x + 1$
(2,3)

2. $y = 5x - 3$
$y = 3x + 1$
(2,7)

3. $y = 4x - 4$
$y = 2x$
(2,4)

4. $y = 2x + 1$
$y = 3x - 2$
(2,2)

5. $y = {}^-2x - 1$
$y = 2x + 1$
(0,1)

Copy and complete the tables of values. Graph the equations to solve the system.

6.

x	3x − 2	y	(x,y)
1	3 · 1 − 2	?	(1,?)
2	3 · 2 − 2	?	(2,?)
3	3 · 3 − 2	?	(3,?)

x	2x + 2	y	(x,y)
1	2 · 1 + 2	?	(1,?)
2	2 · 2 + 2	?	(2,?)
3	2 · 3 + 2	?	(3,?)

INDEPENDENT PRACTICE

Tell whether the ordered pair is a solution of the system of equations. Write *yes* or *no*.

1. $y = 3x - 4$
$y = 2x + 1$
(5,11)

2. $y = 4x + 1$
$y = 3x$
(⁻1,5)

3. $y = x - 3$
$y = 2x + 3$
(0,⁻3)

4. $y = {}^-3x + 1$
$y = 5x - 7$
(1,2)

5. $y = {}^-x - 1$
$y = 4x + 4$
(⁻1,0)

Solve the system of equations by graphing.

6. $y = x + 1$
$y = 2x - 1$

7. $y = {}^-3x + 2$
$y = 4x - 5$

8. $y = 5x - 3$
$y = 2x + 6$

9. $y = 4x - 3$
$y = 2x + 5$

10. $y = {}^-x - 2$
$y = 3x + 2$

11. $y = 3x - 6$
$y = x + 2$

12. $y = {}^-3x + 5$
$y = x - 3$

13. $y = 2x - 3$
$y = 4x - 3$

14. $y = {}^-2x + 5$
$y = x - 4$

15. $y = 2x - 2$
$y = 4x + 4$

Problem-Solving Applications

For Problems 16–18, write a system of equations for each problem. Solve by graphing.

16. Donna and Tony exercise a total of 15 hr each week. Tony exercises 3 hr more than Donna. How many hours does each exercise?

17. Jill and Brian both like to make pottery. They made 12 clay pots in all. Jill made 4 more than Brian. How many did each make?

18. John and Beth share a paper route. They deliver newspapers to 36 homes. John delivers twice as many papers as Beth. How many papers does each deliver?

19. ▭▷ **WRITE ABOUT IT** Describe how to solve a system of equations.

Relations and Functions

Sergej is a speed skater. He trains every day by skating at least 1,000 m. His trainer recorded Sergej's distance every 20 sec. How was the distance he skated related to the time elapsed?

Time, x	0	20	40	60	80	100
Distance, y	0	200	400	600	800	1,000

A **relation** is a set of ordered pairs. You can represent a relation with a table, a graph, or a rule.

- What are the ordered pairs of the relation?

- Write a rule to describe the relationship between the distance and the time.

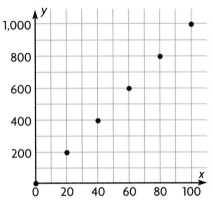

In a relation, the **domain** is the x-coordinates of the ordered pairs. The **range** is the y-coordinates. In the relation shown above, the domain is {0, 20, 40, 60, 80, 100} and the range is {0, 200, 400, 600, 800, 1,000}.

EXAMPLE 1   Give the domain and the range for the relation.

Amount of order, x	$10	$12	$16	$18	$27
Cost including shipping, y	$14	$16	$20	$22	$31

domain: {10, 12, 16, 18, 27}; range: {14, 16, 20, 22, 31}

A **function** is a relation in which no two ordered pairs have the same x-value.

This relation is a function:
(0,10), (1,2), (2,3)

Each of the ordered pairs has a different x-value.

This relation is not a function:
(1,1), (1,2), (2,3)

(1,1) and (1,2) have the same x-value.

- Is the relation in Example 1 a function? Explain.

You can describe a function by using function notation. Often you will see the function notation $f(x)$ instead of y. Read $f(x)$ as "f of x." The table and graph below show this notation.

Jake's Discount House					
Regular price, x	$5	$10	$15	$20	$25
Discount, $f(x)$	$1	$2	$3	$4	$5

$$f(x) = 0.20x$$

• What is the relationship between $f(x)$ and x?

GUIDED PRACTICE

Give the domain and the range for the relation.

1.

Hours, x	0	1	2	3	4	5
Wages in dollars, y	0	4.50	9.00	13.50	18.00	22.50

Write *yes* or *no* to tell whether the relation is a function.

2. {(1,2), (2,3), (3,4), (3,1)}   3. {(1,4), (⁻1,4), (2,8),(⁻2,8)}

4. {(0,2), (2,4), (2,6), (4,8)}   5. {(0,0), (1,3), (2,6), (3,9)}

You can determine whether a graph represents a function by using the **vertical line test**. If any vertical line intersects a graph at more than one point, the graph does not represent a function. Otherwise, the graph does represent a function.

EXAMPLE 2   Use the vertical line test to determine whether the graphs represent functions.

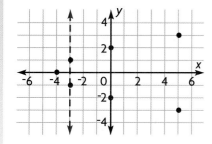

a vertical line with two intersections

So, the relation is *not* a function.

no vertical line with two or more intersections

So, the relation is a function.

Geography Link

Just like lines on a graph, streets and roads cross to form intersections. One of the world's most famous intersections is in New York City at 42nd Street and Broadway. This intersection is called Times Square. On New Year's Eve, many thousands of people from all parts of the world gather there to welcome the New Year. Identify an intersection in your hometown, and describe its importance.

461

Give the domain and the range for the relation.

1.

Height (in inches) for Boys				
Age (in years), x	1	4	8	14
Height, y	27	39	50	62

2.

Calories Used per Minute of Biking				
Weight, x	100	120	150	170
Calories, f(x)	5.4	6.5	8.1	9.2

Write *yes* or *no* to tell whether the relation is a function.

3. $\{(1,0), (2,2), (3,2), (4,3)\}$

4. $\{(1,2), (2,3), (4,4), (5,3)\}$

5. $\{(1,^-1), (3,3), (1,1), (4,4)\}$

6. $\{(2,^-5), (6,3), (2,1), (5,3)\}$

7. $\{(5,^-6), (4,2), (4,1), (6,8)\}$

8. $\{(2,2), (^-2,6), (6,4), (8,5)\}$

9. $\{(4,^-4), (3,4), (2,0), (0,0)\}$

10. $\{(0,^-1), (1,1), (2,3), (3,4)\}$

11. $\{(0,3), (3,6), (2,0), (3,4)\}$

12. $\{(^-4,6), (0,1), (4,^-4), (7,^-8)\}$

13. $\{(2,1), (^-1,3), (^-1,4), (^-4,5)\}$

14. $\{(^-6,3), (0,2), (6,1), (6,5)\}$

Use the vertical line test to determine whether the graph shown by the set of points is a function. Write *yes* or *no*.

15.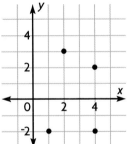

16.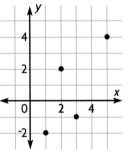

17.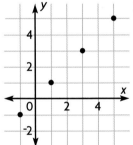

18.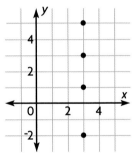

Problem-Solving Applications

For Problems 19–20, write a word rule for each relation.

19.

Sweater Prices (in dollars)				
Original price, x	30	40	55	75
Sales price, f(x)	20	30	45	65

20.

Wages of Employees				
Hours, x	20	25	35	40
Wages, f(x)	$120	$150	$210	$240

21. Jody sees three sweaters that she would like to buy. Their original prices are $45, $55, and $85. Use the word rule from Problem 19 to find the sale price of each sweater.

22. Bill's father gets paid every 2 weeks. He works 37.5 hr each week. Use the word rule from Problem 20 to find his wages for 2 weeks.

23. ✏️ **WRITE ABOUT IT** Explain the difference between a relation and a function.

MORE PRACTICE Lesson 24.3, page H79

Linear Functions

During a recent snowstorm, the snow accumulated at the rate of 3 in. per hour.

Number of hours, x	0	1	2	3
Amount of snow, $f(x)$	0	3	6	9

You can write the values of x and $f(x)$ from the table of values as ordered pairs, using x as the first coordinate and $f(x)$ as the second coordinate.

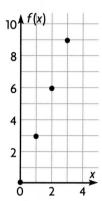

The graph of these ordered pairs is shown at the left. The relationship between x and $f(x)$ can be expressed by writing an equation. This type of equation is often called a function rule.

$f(x) = 3x \leftarrow$ **Read as "f of x equals 3 times x."**

• What pattern is suggested by these four points?

A function whose graph is a straight line is called a **linear function**. $f(x) = 3x$ is a linear function. The domain is the set of whole numbers. Unless stated otherwise, both the domain and range for a linear equation are the set of real numbers.

EXAMPLE 1 Use the table of values, and graph the function $f(x) = 2x - 2$.

x	0	1	2	3
$f(x)$	$^-2$	0	2	4

Identify the set of ordered pairs. $\{(0,^-2), (1,0), (2,2), (3,4), (4,6)\}$

Graph the ordered pairs. The domain is real numbers, so connect the points with a line.

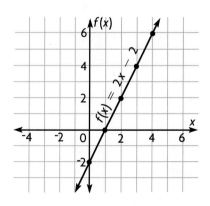

• Look at the table of values. How does increasing the value of the domain by 1 affect the value of the range?

• Suppose the value of the domain is 4. What is the value of the range?

WHAT YOU'LL LEARN
How to represent linear functions by using a table of values, ordered pairs, an equation, and a graph

WHY LEARN THIS?
To solve real-life problems such as finding total earnings

WORD POWER
linear function

REMEMBER:
Any equation whose graph is a straight line is a linear equation. You can graph a linear equation by using at least two ordered pairs. **See page 160.**

A domain and a range have a linear relationship if this is true: all increases by a fixed amount in the value of the domain variable result in changes by a fixed amount in the value of the range variable.

EXAMPLE 2 Li works at an animal shelter and earns $5 per hour. The function rule $f(x) = 5x$ gives the total earnings as a function of the number of hours worked. Is this relationship a linear function?

Number of hours, x	0	1	2	3	4
Total earnings, $f(x)$	$0	$5	$10	$15	$20

Think: Find the differences between the values of the domain and the differences between the values of the range.

differences of values of the domain:

$$
\begin{array}{l}
0 \\
1 \\
2 \\
3 \\
4
\end{array}
\begin{array}{l}
> 1 \\
> 1 \\
> 1 \\
> 1
\end{array}
$$

differences of values of the range:

$$
\begin{array}{l}
0 \\
5 \\
10 \\
15 \\
20
\end{array}
\begin{array}{l}
> 5 \\
> 5 \\
> 5 \\
> 5
\end{array}
$$

Increases of 1 in the value of the domain result in changes of +5 in the value of the range. So, $f(x) = 5x$ is a linear function.

• How can you graph the linear function $f(x) = 5x$?

• Predict the appearance of the graph of $f(x) = 5x$.

You can write a function rule for a linear function by using the graph to find the slope and the y-intercept.

EXAMPLE 3 Write a function rule for this graph.

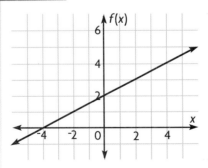

The y-intercept is 2.
Find the slope by using the points (4,4) and (2,3).

slope $= \frac{4-3}{4-2} = \frac{1}{2}$

Substitute the slope and the y-intercept in the slope-intercept form $y = mx + b$.

The equation is $y = \frac{1}{2}x + 2$.

So, the function rule is $f(x) = \frac{1}{2}x + 2$.

• What other points could you use to find the slope?

Social Studies Link

Animal protection agencies, such as the Humane Society, depend mostly on volunteers. Suppose one volunteer can care for 20 animals. How many volunteers would be needed to care for 240 animals?

GUIDED PRACTICE

Complete the table of values, write the ordered pairs, and graph the
linear function.

1.

x	0	1	2	3
$f(x)$	3	4	5	?

2.

x	0	2	4	6
$f(x)$	⁻4	⁻2	0	?

3.

x	⁻1	0	1	2
$f(x)$	⁻3	0	3	?

4.

x	0	1	2	3
$f(x)$	0	4	8	?

5.

x	0	2	4	6
$f(x)$	1	5	9	?

6.

x	⁻1	0	1	2
$f(x)$	2	0	⁻2	?

INDEPENDENT PRACTICE

Write *yes* or *no* to tell whether the relationship is a linear function.

1.

x	0	1	2	3
$f(x)$	0	4	8	12

2.

x	⁻1	0	1	2
$f(x)$	⁻2	1	4	7

3.

x	0	2	4	6
$f(x)$	1	3	6	10

For each graph, identify the slope and the y-intercept. Then write
a function rule for the linear function.

4. 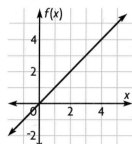 **5.** 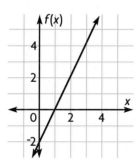 **6.** 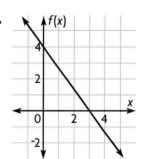 **7.**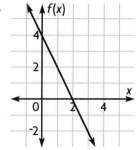

Problem-Solving Applications

8. Every T-shirt in the store is marked down $5 for inventory clearance. Write a function rule for the clearance price of each T-shirt. Graph the function. If the original price of a T-shirt is $13.99, what is the clearance price?

9. Craig pet-sits for his neighbors. Craig earns $4 each time he walks the neighbors' dog for an hour. Write a function rule for his total earnings. Graph the function. How much will he earn if he walks the dog a total of 7 hr?

10. Ana is selling calendars for the Humane Society. Each calendar costs $6. Write a function rule for the total possible earnings from the sale of the calendars. Graph the function to find out how much Ana will earn if she sells 5 calendars.

11. ✏️ **WRITE ABOUT IT** Explain how you can determine whether a relationship is a linear function.

Nonlinear Functions

WHAT YOU'LL LEARN
How to represent nonlinear functions by using a table of values, ordered pairs, and a graph

WHY LEARN THIS?
To solve real-life problems such as finding how quickly gossip can spread

WORD POWER
nonlinear function

Not all functions are linear. Many have graphs that are not straight lines. A function whose graph is not a straight line is called a **nonlinear function**. The graphs of many nonlinear functions are curves.

ACTIVITY

• Play gossip. At Step 1, appoint a leader to tell two students a secret message. At Step 2, each student who just received the message should tell two others. How many students are told the message at Step 2?

• At Step 3, each of the students who just received the message should tell two others. How many students are told the message at Step 3?

• At Step 4 how many students would receive the message? How many steps would be necessary for every student in your class to receive the message?

You can represent the relationship between the step, x, and the number of students told the message, $f(x)$, with a tree diagram, a table of values, a set of ordered pairs, and a graph.

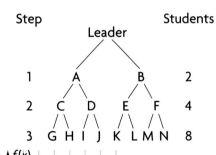

Number of step, x	1	2	3
Number of students, $f(x)$	2	4	8

• Write a set of ordered pairs that represents the relationship between x and $f(x)$.

You can graph the set of ordered pairs.

$f(x) = 2^x$

Talk About It

• Look at the graph shown at the left. What pattern is suggested by the three points?

• Does this graph represent a linear function or a nonlinear function? Explain.

• The rule for this function is $f(x) = 2^x$. How many people would be told the message at Step 5? at Step 6? at Step 10?

• **CRITICAL THINKING** Can there be values between the ordered pairs? Explain.

Many other real-life situations can be represented by nonlinear functions.

EXAMPLE 1 Wendy makes cube-shaped food containers and records the lengths and the volumes. Let x = the length of an edge and $f(x)$ = the volume. Make a table of values and a graph for $f(x) = x^3$. Let the domain = {0, 1, 2, 3}.

Length of an edge, x	0	1	2	3
Volume, $f(x)$	0	1	8	27

Make a table of values.

{(0,0), (1,1), (2,8), (3,27)}

Identify the ordered pairs.

Graph the ordered pairs.

Connect the points with a smooth curve.

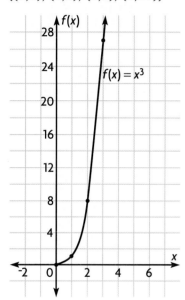

REMEMBER:

Volume is the number of cubic units needed to fill the space occupied by a solid figure. The formula for the volume of a cube is $V = e^3$. See page H25.

- What is the volume of a cube with a length of 4 cm? of 5 cm? of 6 cm?

- What is the volume of a cube with a length of 2.5 m?

In this lesson and in Chapter 8, you explored these equations for nonlinear functions: $f(x) = x^3$, $y = x^2$, and $y = 3x^2$.

- How are the exponents of the variables alike in these equations?

Whenever the equation of a function has a variable with an exponent other than 1, the function is nonlinear.

You can classify a function as linear or nonlinear by looking at the exponent of the variable in the equation.

EXAMPLE 2 Is $f(x) = x^2 + 1$ a linear or a nonlinear function?

Think: Is the exponent of the variable 1? Is it other than 1?

The exponent of the variable is 2. So, the function is nonlinear.

- Is $f(x) = 4x - 1$ a linear or a nonlinear function? Explain.

Art Link

Pablo Picasso, possibly the best-known painter of the twentieth century, developed a style of art called Cubism. Cubism emphasizes the flat, two-dimensional surface of a figure and does not show the three-dimensional appearance of an object. In a Cubist painting, a cube would appear to be what two-dimensional figure?

GUIDED PRACTICE

Write the ordered pairs, and graph the function. Tell whether the graph shows a *linear* or a *nonlinear* function.

1.
x	0	1	2	3
f(x)	⁻1	1	7	17

2.
x	0	1	2	3
f(x)	⁻5	⁻4	3	22

Tell whether the equation is that of a *linear* or a *nonlinear* function.

3. $f(x) = x + 3$

4. $f(x) = x^4$

5. $f(x) = {}^-3x$

6. $f(x) = 5x + 7$

7. $f(x) = 2x^2$

8. $f(x) = x^3 - 5$

9. $f(x) = 10x - 2$

10. $f(x) = {}^-x^4$

11. $f(x) = {}^-7x^2 + 3$

Technology **Link**

In *Data ToolKit* you can graph linear and nonlinear functions.

The graphs of some nonlinear functions form special curves.

EXAMPLE 3 Graph the nonlinear function $f(x) = \frac{1}{x}$.

x	⁻3	⁻2	⁻1	$\frac{-1}{2}$	$\frac{1}{2}$	1	2	3
f(x)	$\frac{-1}{3}$	$\frac{-1}{2}$	⁻1	⁻2	2	1	$\frac{1}{2}$	$\frac{1}{3}$

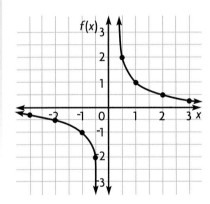

Identify and graph the ordered pairs: $\{(^-3, \frac{-1}{3}), (^-2, \frac{-1}{2}), (^-1, ^-1), (\frac{-1}{2}, ^-2), (\frac{1}{2}, 2), (1,1), (2,\frac{1}{2}), (3,\frac{1}{3})\}.$ *Then connect the points with smooth curves.*

• What is the shape of the graph?

• Suppose the value of the domain is 4. What is the value of the range?

REMEMBER:

$1 \div 3 = \frac{1}{3}$

$1 \div \frac{1}{2} = \frac{1}{1} \times \frac{2}{1} = 2$

$1 \div \frac{1}{3} = \frac{1}{1} \times \frac{3}{1} = 3$

See page 37.

INDEPENDENT PRACTICE

Write the ordered pairs, and graph the function. Tell whether the graph shows a *linear* or a *nonlinear* function.

1.
x	0	1	2	3
f(x)	⁻3	⁻1	1	3

2.
x	0	1	2	3
f(x)	1	3	9	19

3.
x	0	1	2	3
f(x)	⁻2	⁻1	6	25

4.
x	0	1	2	3
f(x)	6	7	8	9

5.
x	0	1	2	3
f(x)	0	1	8	9

6.
x	0	1	2	3
f(x)	⁻1	2	5	8

Write *linear* or *nonlinear* to describe the function.

7. $f(x) = x^2 + 3$ **8.** $f(x) = 7x + 2$ **9.** $f(x) = 2x - 8$ **10.** $f(x) = 2x^5 - 10$

11. $f(x) = 2 - 4x$ **12.** $f(x) = {}^-5x^3$ **13.** $f(x) = \frac{1}{x} + 10$ **14.** $f(x) = 8x - 1$

Write five ordered pairs for each nonlinear function.
Let $x = {}^-2, 0, 1, 2,$ and 3. Then graph.

15. $f(x) = x^2 - 1$ **16.** $f(x) = 2x^3$ **17.** $f(x) = 2x^2 - 10$ **18.** $f(x) = x^2 + 4$

Problem-Solving Applications

For Problems 19–22, use the graph of the nonlinear function
shown at the right.

19. The cost of first-class postage is related to the weight of a
letter. The graph shows the cost of the postage as a function,
$f(x)$, of the weight in ounces, x. What is the cost of the
postage for a letter that weighs 2 oz? $3\frac{1}{2}$ oz? (HINT: An open
circle means that the value is not a solution. A closed
circle means that the value is a solution.)

20. Name two different weights that cost $0.78.

21. Why is the function graphed only in Quadrant I?

22. This type of nonlinear function is called a step function. Why
do you think it has this name?

23. ✏️ **WRITE ABOUT IT** What two methods can you use to tell
whether a function is linear or nonlinear?

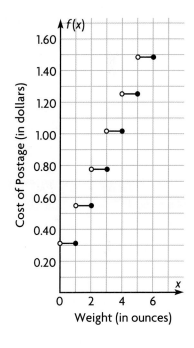

Mixed Review

Find the value of the expression for $x = {}^-2$ and $x = 2$.

24. $x^2 + 2x + 1$ **25.** $x^2 + 4x + 3$ **26.** $x^2 + x - 2$ **27.** $x^2 - x - 6$ **28.** $x^2 - 4$

Write *positive*, *negative*, or *no correlation* to describe the
relationship between the sets of data.

29. outside temperature and
air conditioning use

30. pages read in book and
pages left to read

31. weight and first digit in
phone number

32. **PARTY PLANNING** Of the 25 students in the
class, 17 like everything on their pizza, 8
like just cheese. Rachel plans to serve 3
pieces per student. If a large pizza is cut
into 12 pieces, how many pizzas should
she order in all? How many should be
cheese pizzas, without other toppings?

33. **HISTORY** In the 1932 presidential
election, the popular vote totaled
39,744,313. Franklin D. Roosevelt
received 57% of the popular vote.
Herbert Hoover received 40%.
How many votes did each receive?

MATH FUN!

SAFE LANDINGS

PURPOSE To practice finding the slope (pages 452–456)

Work with a partner. Find the slope and draw a picture for each landing. Imagine how each passenger would feel about the landing experience. Then rate the pilot's landing as Poor or Excellent.

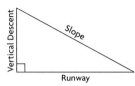

Pilot	Vertical	Runway	Slope
A	1.5 m	6 m	
B	1.5 m	2 m	

MAP IT OUT

PURPOSE To practice solving a system of equations (pages 457–459)

YOU WILL NEED coordinate plane, a map of your city

You are lost. You can't find the new sports stadium, so you ask for directions. The person you ask says to go straight on "$y = 3x$" until you meet "$y = 4 - x$." Draw the path you are to take on a coordinate grid. You start at (0,0) and see the y-axis in front of you. Then graph the second equation to find the exact location of the sports stadium.

HOME NOTE Work with your family to locate your house on a city map. How close would $y = 3x$ be to your house if the y-axis points roughly north and your school is at (0,0)?

PENNY PARADOX

PURPOSE To practice graphing nonlinear equations (pages 466–469)

Suppose you start with a penny, and ask for 2 pennies from a classmate, 4 pennies from a second classmate, 8 pennies from a third classmate, and so on from all your classmates. Could you become rich? Make a table to find out. Write the ordered pairs and graph the function that describes this pattern.

How many pennies would your tenth classmate give you? your twentieth classmate? After you collect from the twentieth classmate, how many total pennies would you have?

CHAPTER 24 REVIEW

EXAMPLES

- **Use slope and intercepts to graph a linear equation.** (pages 453–456)

$$y = \frac{-1}{2}x + 1 \qquad y = mx + b \leftarrow \text{y-intercept: 1}$$

slope: $\frac{-1}{2}$

- **Solve a system of equations.** (pages 457–459)

Solve the system $y = 2x$ and $y = x + 1$.

Graph both equations in the same coordinate plane. The point where the graphs intersect is the solution of the system.

The solution of the system is (1,2).

- **Represent relations and functions.** (pages 460–462)

domain: {1, 2, 2, 4}   range: {8, 16, 24, 32}
ordered pairs: {(1,8), (2,16), (2,24), (4,32)}
This relation is not a function since (2,16) and (2,24) have the same *x*-value.

- **Represent linear functions.** (pages 463–465)

Graph $f(x) = 4x - 2$.

Make a table of values, and identify the set of ordered pairs. Graph ordered pairs. Connect points with a line.

For help, see pages 463–464.

- **Represent nonlinear functions.** (pages 466–469)

$f(x) = x^2 - 1$

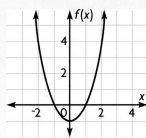

A function that has a variable with an exponent other than 1 is nonlinear.

EXERCISES

Find the slope and the *y*-intercept. Then graph the equation.

1. $y = 4x - 5$ 2. $y = 6x + 6$
3. $y = \frac{-2}{7}x + 2$ 4. $y = \frac{1}{2}x + 2$

Solve the system of equations by graphing.

5. $y = 3x + 1$ 6. $y = 4x + 1$
   $y = 2x + 1$ $y = 3x - 2$
7. $y = 2x - 1$ 8. $y = 5x$
   $y = x - 1$ $y = 3x - 2$
9. $y = x - 3$ 10. $y = x$
   $y = 3x + 1$ $y = 4x - 3$

Write *yes* or *no* to tell if the relation is a function.

11. {(1,⁻4), (2,⁻4), (3,⁻4), (4,⁻4)}
12. {(3,14), (12,⁻8), (3,⁻14), (10,⁻12)}
13. {(1.5,⁻6), (4,⁻3), (6,5.5), (3,⁻10.5)}

Make a table of values for each function. Let $x = 0, 1,$ and 2. Then write the ordered pairs and graph the function.

14. $f(x) = 3x - 3$ 15. $f(x) = 3x + 5$
16. $f(x) = 0.5x - 4$ 17. $f(x) = 2x + 3$

Write *linear* or *nonlinear* to describe the function.

18. $f(x) = 2x - 7$ 19. $f(x) = x^3 - 8$
20. $f(x) = 2x^2 + 3$ 21. $f(x) = 8x + 4$
22. $f(x) = 5x^2 - 1$ 23. $f(x) = 9x^4 + 3$
24. $f(x) = 3x^5 - 9$ 25. $f(x) = x - 49$

CHAPTER 25 POLYNOMIALS

LOOK AHEAD

In this chapter you will solve problems that involve

- modeling polynomials
- evaluating and simplifying polynomials
- adding and subtracting polynomials

Team-Up Project

Stamps Old and New

Postal rates have changed throughout the years, but they are always a function of the weight of the letter.

Plan
- Work with a small group. Calculate the cost to mail a 1 oz, 3 oz, 5 oz, and 11 oz letter in the years shown. Write an equation to find the cost of a first class letter of any weight mailed in those years.

Act
- Make a table. Record the cost to mail a letter of each weight for each year.
- Graph your results.
- Write an equation to find the cost of any first class letter mailed in each year. Let x represent the weight of the letter and let y represent the cost.
- Display your results.

Share
- Compare results with another group.

Weight	Year		
	1928	1986	1996
first ounce	2¢	22¢	32¢
each additional ounce or fraction of an ounce	2¢	17¢	23¢

First Class Postal Rates

DID YOU
- ✓ Make a table and record the data?
- ✓ Graph your results?
- ✓ Write an equation to find the cost?
- ✓ Compare results with another group?

Modeling Monomials

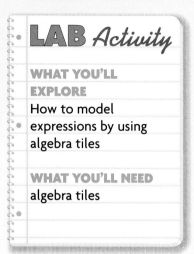

In this lab you will use algebra tiles to model expressions called monomials. A **monomial** is an expression that is a number, a variable, or the product of a number and one or more variables.

monomials: 4, $2x$, $^-3x^2$, ^-9xy

Explore

• Let one yellow square represent 1. Use yellow squares to model the number 4.

• Let one small red square represent $^-1$. Model $^-3$. How many small red squares did you use?

• Let one green rectangle represent x. Use green rectangles to model $2x$. Let one red rectangle represent ^-x. Model ^-5x.

• Let one large blue square represent x^2. Model $2x^2$.

• Let one large red square represent $^-x^2$. How would you model $^-3x^2$?

1 · ⁻1
x
^-x
x^2
$^-x^2$

Think and Discuss

• Look at the algebra tile that represents 1 and $^-1$. Which side represents 1? Which side represents $^-1$?

• Which side of the rectangular tile represents x? ^-x? Which side of the large square tile represents x^2? $^-x^2$?

• How is the color of an algebra tile related to the sign of the monomial it represents?

• **CRITICAL THINKING** Compare the length of the algebra tile that represents x with the length of the tile representing x^2. Did you expect this result? Explain.

Try This

Model the monomial with algebra tiles or a drawing.

1. 9   **2.** $^-5$ **3.** $6x$

4. $3x$ **5.** $2x^2$ **6.** $^-4x^2$

Technology Link
E-Lab • Activity 25 Available on CD-ROM and the Internet at http://www.hbschool.com/elab

Polynomials

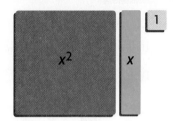

Monomials, such as 7, 9x, and $^-4x^2$, are terms that can be used to form expressions called polynomials. A **polynomial** is a monomial or the sum of two or more monomials. Polynomials are classified by the number of terms.

WHAT YOU'LL LEARN
How to model, classify, and evaluate polynomials

WHY LEARN THIS?
To speak, write, and understand the language of algebra

WORD POWER
polynomial

Type of Polynomial	Number of Terms	Example
monomial	1	$10y^4$
binomial	2	$3a^2 + 8$
trinomial	3	$a^2 - 4a + 3$

• What type of polynomial is $b^3 + 8$? Explain.

You can use algebra tiles to model polynomials.

ACTIVITY

WHAT YOU'LL NEED: algebra tiles

• Model the polynomial $3x^2 + 5x + 6$. How many large blue squares did you use? green rectangles? small yellow squares?

• Identify the polynomial represented by the model at the right.

In a polynomial written with a subtraction symbol, the term after the symbol is considered as the opposite and is added.

$$x^2 - 5x - 4 \qquad \rightarrow \qquad x^2 + {}^-5x + {}^-4$$

This model shows the polynomial $x^2 - 5x - 4$:

• Identify the terms of $x^2 - 5x - 4$.

x^2 x 1

REMEMBER:

A term is a real number, a variable, or the product of real numbers and variables. Each of the following is a term:
8, $^-3.5$, x^2, and ^-3c.
See page 105.

To subtract an integer, add its opposite.
$10 - {}^-4 = 10 + 4 = 14$
See page 59.

You can evaluate a polynomial by substituting values for the variables and finding the value of the numerical expression.

EXAMPLE 1   Evaluate $5x^2 - 8x - 2$ for $x = {}^-3$.

$5x^2 - 8x - 2$ *Write the expression.*

$5({}^-3)^2 - 8({}^-3) - 2$ *Substitute ${}^-3$ for x.*

$5(9) - 8({}^-3) - 2$ *Use the order of operations.*

$45 - ({}^-24) - 2$

67

• Evaluate $3y^2 - 6y + 7$ for $y = {}^-1$.

You can evaluate polynomials that involve two or more different variables using pencil and paper or a calculator.

EXAMPLE 2   Evaluate $4x^3 + 3y^2 - 9$ for $x = {}^-5$ and $y = 2$.

$4x^3 + 3y^2 - 9$ *Write the expression.*

$4({}^-5)^3 + 3(2)^2 - 9$ *Substitute ${}^-5$ for x and 2 for y.*

• How do you know that the cube of ${}^-5$ is negative?

GUIDED PRACTICE

Model the polynomial with algebra tiles or a drawing.

1. $x - 7$ **2.** $2x^2$ **3.** ${}^-x^2 + 3x$ **4.** $4x^2 - 6x + 5$

Classify the polynomial by writing *monomial, binomial,* or *trinomial.*

5. $x + 27$ **6.** ${}^-9x^3$ **7.** ${}^-5x^2 + x - 10$

8. 68 **9.** $a^2 + 7$ **10.** $6k^4 + k - 2$

Identify the terms of the polynomial.

11. $3y - 1$ **12.** ${}^-c^3 - 2c + 15$ **13.** $6n^2 - 7n - 9$

14. $x^2 + 9$ **15.** $d^4 + 5d - 10$ **16.** $9y^3 - 6y + 4$

Evaluate the polynomial for $x = {}^-2$.

17. $5x - 21$ **18.** $3x^3 - 8x$ **19.** ${}^-9x^2 + 6x + 4$

REMEMBER:

The sign of the square of a negative integer is positive.

$({}^-4)^2 = {}^-4 \cdot {}^-4 = 16$

See page H10.

Language Link

How is a polynomial related to polyester and rap music? Each is named or described by a word beginning with the prefix *poly*, which means "much, many, more than one." Polyester is a fabric made of several kinds of plastics. Rap music uses polyrhythm—strongly contrasting rhythms in simultaneous voice parts. Why is *polynomial* an appropriate name for the expressions in this lesson?

Calculator Activities, page H39

INDEPENDENT PRACTICE

Classify the polynomial by writing *monomial*, *binomial*, or *trinomial*.

1. $x^2 + 3$ **2.** $a^2 + 6a + 9$ **3.** $2k^2 - 18$ **4.** $8y^3$ **5.** $x^4 - x - 12$

Identify the terms of the polynomial.

6. $x^2 + x - 12$ **7.** $8y^3 - 15$ **8.** $^-s^2 + 18$ **9.** $5k^2 - 6k - 9$ **10.** $x^2 + 6x + 12$

Evaluate the polynomial for $x = 3$.

11. $7x^2$ **12.** $x^2 - 4$ **13.** $2x^2 - 2x$ **14.** $^-x^2 - 4x - 4$ **15.** $x^2 + 6x$

16. $x^2 - x - 12$ **17.** $x^2 - 3x + 2$ **18.** $2x^2 + 2x - 8$ **19.** $^-x^4 + 4$ **20.** $x^3 - x + 2$

Evaluate the polynomial for $x = 2$ and $y = ^-3$.

21. $x^2 - y^2$ **22.** $3x^2 + y^2$ **23.** $y^2 - x + 2$ **24.** $x^3 + y - 4$ **25.** $^-x^2 - y^2 - 2$

Problem-Solving Applications

26. Jill needs to purchase molding to make a picture frame. Suppose the width, w, is 11 in. and the height, h, is 16 in. Evaluate $2w + 2h$ to find the total length of molding she needs.

27. The postal rate for a first-class letter can be expressed by the polynomial $0.32 + 0.23(x - 1)$ where x is the weight in ounces. Find the cost for a 5-oz letter.

28. Write a trinomial. Then model the expression with algebra tiles or a drawing.

29. ✏ **WRITE ABOUT IT** Explain how you would evaluate the expression $4x^2 - 2x + 1$ for $x = ^-4$.

Mixed Review

Find the value.

30. $11 + 6$ **31.** $11 - 6$ **32.** $11 - ^-6$ **33.** $^-11 + ^-6$ **34.** $11 + ^-6$ **35.** $^-11 - ^-6$

Find the x-intercept and the y-intercept. Use the intercepts to graph the equation.

36. $4x - y = 8$ **37.** $3y - 2x = 12$ **38.** $5y + 3x = 15$ **39.** $^-3x - y = 9$

40. **COMPARE AND ORDER** Final standings in the middle school art show were based on the average of three judges' scores for the entrant's use of color, use of medium, and creativity. Ann received scores of 88, 74, 83. Tyrone received scores of 75, 87, 90. Ron received scores of 90, 82, 82. Who came in first? second? third?

41. **INEQUALITIES** Sonya is saving her baby-sitting money to buy a skateboard. She would like to save at least $126 in the next 3 months. How much should she save each month to reach her goal? Write an inequality and solve.

WHAT YOU'LL LEARN
How to simplify
polynomials

WHY LEARN THIS?
To solve real-life
problems

WORD POWER

simplify a
polynomial
standard form

REMEMBER:

Like terms are terms
that have the same
variables and the
same powers of
these variables. In the
expression $n^3 + 6n - 2n^3$, the like terms are n^3
and $-2n^3$. **See page 105.**

What is 4-H? 4-H is a
youth program that
encourages learning,
leadership, and good
citizenship. The name
4-H stands for *head,
heart, hands, health.*

Simplifying Polynomials

The members of the Southside 4-H Club
delivered 4 boxes of holiday favors to the residents
of a nursing home. The members of the Eastside
4-H Club delivered 5 boxes of holiday favors.

You can use a polynomial to represent the number of holiday
favors. Let x represent the number in each box. So, $4x + 5x$
represents the total number of favors.

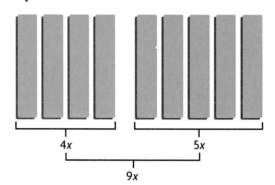

*Use algebra tiles to
model $4x + 5x$.*

The polynomial $4x + 5x$ contains two like terms. You can simplify
a polynomial that contains like terms. To **simplify a polynomial**
means to combine (add or subtract) like terms. A polynomial is
in simplest form when it has no like terms.

simplest form	not simplest form
$7x - 3x^2$	$x + 3x$

You can represent like terms of a polynomial with algebra tiles
of the same shape and size. Then you can use the tiles to simplify
the polynomial.

ACTIVITY

WHAT YOU'LL NEED: algebra tiles

• Model $x^2 - x^2 + 3x - 5 + 8x - 2$. Rearrange the tiles so that
like terms are side by side. Identify the like terms.

• Combine like terms. What is the result of combining x^2 and
$-x^2$? Explain.

• What is the result of combining $3x$ and $8x$? -5 and -2?

• What tiles remain? Write the polynomial in simplest form.

You can also simplify a polynomial without using algebra tiles.

EXAMPLE 1 Simplify. $n^2 + 4n - 9n + 7 - 5$

$n^2 + 4n - 9n + 7 - 5$ *Collect like terms by using the*

$n^2 + (4n - 9n) + (7 - 5)$ *Associative Property.*

$n^2 + (^-5n) + 2$ *Combine like terms.*

$n^2 - 5n + 2$

GUIDED PRACTICE

Identify the like terms. If there are no like terms, write *none*.

1. $4, ^-9n, 6n^2, 3n$ **2.** $3x^4, ^-5x^2, 3x$ **3.** $4k^2, 9, ^-12k^2, k$

Write *yes* or *no* to tell whether the polynomial is in simplest form.

4. $10x^3 + 8$ **5.** $^-7y^2 + 6 - 4$ **6.** $^-2c + 7c^3 + c^2$

Simplify the polynomial by combining like terms.

7. $^-7b^2 - 2b + 4b^2$ **8.** $2y^3 - 6y + 9 - y$ **9.** $6 - 5k^2 - 8$

A polynomial is written in **standard form** when its terms are arranged so that the exponents of a variable decrease from left to right.

$$3h^4 + 2h^3 - 4h^2 + 6h + 5 \quad \leftarrow \text{standard form}$$

Think of each term as a product of a number and a power of h. The exponent of h is understood to be 1. The number 5 is the product of itself and h^0.

$$(3 \cdot h^4) + (2 \cdot h^3) + (^-4 \cdot h^2) + (6 \cdot h^1) + (5 \cdot h^0) \quad \leftarrow \text{exponents:}$$
$$4, 3, 2, 1, 0$$

- Rewrite $^-2h^2 - 9h + 3h^3 + 1 + 4h^4$ in standard form.

You can simplify and write a polynomial in standard form.

EXAMPLE 2 Simplify the polynomial, and write the result in standard form. $3 + 5x^4 + x^2 - 4x^2 - 6 + 2x^3$

$3 + 5x^4 + x^2 - 4x^2 - 6 + 2x^3$ *Combine like terms by using*

$5x^4 + (x^2 - 4x^2) + (^-6 + 3) + 2x^3$ *the Commutative and*

$5x^4 - 3x^2 - 3 + 2x^3$ *Associative Properties.*

$5x^4 + 2x^3 - 3x^2 - 3$ *Rearrange by exponents.*

REMEMBER:

Any number to the first power equals that number. Any number (except zero) to the zero power equals 1.

$5^1 = 5 \quad x^1 = x$

$5^0 = 1 \quad x^0 = 1$

See page H10.

INDEPENDENT PRACTICE

Identify the like terms. If there are no like terms, write *none*.

1. $3, x^2, x, 2x^2$ **2.** $a^3, 2a^2, 5$ **3.** $3k^2, k, {}^-2k$

4. $6, y^2, y, 2$ **5.** $4, y^3, y^2, {}^-5$ **6.** $c^4, c^2, c, 8$

Write *yes* or *no* to tell whether the polynomial is in simplest form. If the answer is no, simplify by combining like terms.

7. $4x^2 + x - 3x^2$ **8.** $5x^3 + 2x^2 + 5$ **9.** $3k^4 + k + k^2 - 5$

10. $1 + y^2 + y + y + 2$ **11.** $5x^2 + 6x$ **12.** $3a^3 + a^3 - 2$

13. $2y^3 + y^2 + y + 2$ **14.** $3 - y^2 + y + 2y^2$ **15.** $5 + k^2 - 5k^2 + k$

Write *yes* or *no* to tell whether the polynomial is written in standard form. If the answer is no, rewrite it in standard form.

16. $2x^2 + 4x - 8$ **17.** $b^3 + b^2 - b - 3$ **18.** $3 + x^3 + 2x + x^2$

19. $y^2 + 4y + 12$ **20.** $5x + 9 - x^2$ **21.** $y^2 + 2y^4 + 5 - y$

22. $7y^3 + 4y^2 + y$ **23.** $12 - x + 4x^2$ **24.** $n^5 - 5n^3 + 3n - 1$

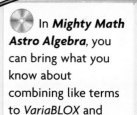

In *Mighty Math Astro Algebra*, you can bring what you know about combining like terms to *VariaBLOX* and embark on the *Disk Trouble II* mission.

Simplify the polynomial, and write the result in standard form.

25. $3k^4 - k^2 + k^5 - 5 + k$ **26.** $2x^2 + 3x - 3x^2 + 2x^4 - 9$ **27.** $2 + y^2 + 3y + 6y + 3 + y^2$

28. $y^2 + 2y - 9y + 8 - 3y^2$ **29.** $x^2 + 3x^5 - 3x + 4x^4 - x$ **30.** $t^4 - 5t + t^2 + 7 + 3t - 4$

31. $t^3 + 4t + t^3 - 12 - t - 4$ **32.** $2k^4 - k + k^2 - 5 + k - 2$ **33.** $x^2 + 3x^2 + 4x + 4x^3 - x$

34. $4 + 2x^3 + x + x^3 + 1$ **35.** $3y^4 - y^2 - 5 + 6y^4 + 3$ **36.** $12 - a^2 + 5a^2 + 4a + 6a$

Problem-Solving Applications

37. The length, width, and perimeter of a rectangular garden can be expressed by the polynomials $4x + 2$, x^2, and $4x + 2 + x^2 + 4x + 2 + x^2$. Simplify the polynomial for the perimeter, and write the result in standard form.

38. The Bartons bought a triangular building lot. The perimeter can be expressed as $x^3 + 2 + x + 20 + x + 20$. Simplify the polynomial, and write the result in standard form.

39. Abe is making a large mat for a picture that is 5 in. by 8 in. Write polynomials in simplest form to represent the length and the width of the mat.

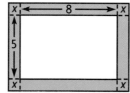

40. ✏️ **WRITE ABOUT IT** Explain the difference between writing a polynomial in simplest form and writing it in standard form.

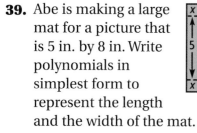

MORE PRACTICE Lesson 25.2, page H80

Adding Polynomials

Finding the sum of two or more polynomials is similar to combining like terms. You can use algebra tiles. When you combine, or add, an equal number of positive and negative tiles of the same kind, the sum is zero.

ACTIVITY

WHAT YOU'LL NEED: algebra tiles

Work together to model $(x^2 - 10x - 4) + (^-3x^2 + 6x + 9)$.

- Model $x^2 - 10x - 4$ and $^-3x^2 + 6x + 9$.

- Group like tiles. Which tiles did you group?

- Find the sum of the large square tiles. How many pairs of positive and negative tiles did you form and remove? What tiles remained? Write the monomial that represents this sum.

- Find the sum of the rectangular tiles. How many pairs of positive and negative tiles did you form and remove? What tiles remained? What monomial represents this sum?

- Find the sum of the small square tiles. How many pairs of positive and negative tiles did you form and remove? What tiles remained? What monomial represents this sum?

- What is $(x^2 - 10x - 4) + (^-3x^2 + 6x + 9)$? In what order should the terms appear?

You can also calculate the sum of polynomials by using what you know about combining like terms.

WHAT YOU'LL LEARN
How to add polynomials

WHY LEARN THIS?
To represent and solve real-life problems such as finding the perimeter of a park

REMEMBER:

The sum of a number and its opposite is zero.

$^-8 + 8 = 0$

$a + {}^-a = 0$

See page 56.

The coefficient is the numerical factor of an algebraic term. In the term ^-4t, $^-4$ is the coefficient.

See page 100.

 **EXAMPLE 1**   Find the sum. $(3y^2 - 9y + 6) + (^-5y^2 + 4y - 2)$

$\quad\downarrow\qquad\downarrow\qquad\downarrow$

$\;\;3y^2 - 9y + 6$ *Line up like terms.*

$\dfrac{^-5y^2 + 4y - 2}{^-2y^2 - 5y + 4}$ *Add the coefficients of like terms, and add the numerical terms.*

-  **CRITICAL THINKING**   Why is it important to line up like terms?

- Find the sum by using mental math.
  $(6d^2 + 3d) + (^-2d^2 + 8d)$

Do you have a park near your hometown? Is a national park nearby? The United States has set aside more land for national parks (81 million acres) than any other country. Suppose $x = 10$. Write a polynomial to represent the number of millions of acres of land occupied by national parks.

To find the sum of two polynomials with different numbers of terms, line up like terms and leave a space where there is no like term.

EXAMPLE 2   Find the sum. $(\overline{}3a^2 - 9a - 2) + (5a^2 - 6)$

$$
\begin{array}{ll}
\overline{}3a^2 - 9a - 2 & \textit{Line up like terms.} \\
\underline{5a^2 - 6} & \textit{Leave a space for the missing term.} \\
2a^2 - 9a - 8 & \textit{Add the coefficients of like terms,} \\
& \textit{and add the numerical terms.}
\end{array}
$$

You can represent and solve some real-life problems by adding polynomials.

EXAMPLE 3   The Town of Beaumont plans to enclose a small triangular park with fencing. What is the perimeter of the park? Express it as a polynomial. Suppose $n = 10$. How many feet of fencing are needed?

Beaumont Park

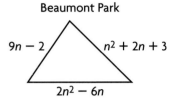

Think: Find the perimeter by adding the lengths of the sides.

$$
\begin{array}{ll}
n^2 + 2n + 3 & \textit{Line up like terms.} \\
2n^2 - 6n & \textit{Leave a space for each missing term.} \\
\underline{ 9n - 2} & \\
3n^2 + 5n + 1 & \textit{Add the coefficients of like terms, and} \\
& \textit{add the numerical terms.}
\end{array}
$$

$3n^2 + 5n + 1 \leftarrow$ perimeter

$3(10)^2 + 5 \cdot 10 + 1$ *Evaluate the polynomial for $n = 10$.*

$3(100) + 50 + 1$

$351 \leftarrow$ perimeter in feet

So, the perimeter is $3n^2 + 5n + 1$, and 351 ft of fencing are needed.

• How can you find the length of each side in feet?

GUIDED PRACTICE

Find the sum by using algebra tiles or making a drawing.

1. $(3x^2 + 2x) + (x^2 + 4x)$ **2.** $(x^2 - 6x + 4) + (\overline{}2x^2 + 2x + 8)$

Find the sum.

3. $(2c^2 - 4c - 3) + (3c^2 + 8c)$ **4.** $(5t^2 - 2t + 4) + (\overline{}3t^2 + 6t - 7)$

Find the sum by using algebra tiles or making a drawing.

1. $(4x + 2) + (3x + 5)$ **2.** $(5x^2 + 6) + (^-3x^2 + 2)$ **3.** $(x^2 - 2x + 4) + (2x^2 + x)$

4. $(4x^2 - 4x + 6) + (2x^2 + 3x - 5)$ **5.** $(^-3x^2 + 2x + 7) + (4x^2 + 2x - 9)$

Find the sum.

6. $(3x + 7) + (6x - 10)$ **7.** $(^-3b^2 + 7b) + (3b^2 + 3b)$ **8.** $(6x^2 - x) + (2x^2 - 5x + 1)$

9. $(2x^2 - 3) + (5x - 9)$ **10.** $(8x^2 - x + 5) + (3x^2 + 8)$ **11.** $(b^2 + b) + (2b^2 - 4b - 1)$

12. $(10x^2 - 2x - 3) + (4x^2 + 6x - 17)$ **13.** $(4y^2 - 5y + 12) + (3y^2 - 6y - 18)$

14. $(4a^2 + 3a + 9) + (6a^2 + 3a + 12)$ **15.** $(2x^2 + 10x - 4) + (^-4x^2 + 6x - 22)$

Problem-Solving Applications

16. To advertise his new store, Carlos wants to string lights around the perimeter of the building. The length and width in feet can be expressed by the polynomials $x^2 + 4x + 4$ and $10x + 3$. Express the perimeter as a polynomial. If $x = 10$, how many feet of lights are needed?

17. The polynomial $5n^2 + 10n$ represents the amount of money in dollars that Erica has saved, and the polynomial $20n + 5$ represents the amount Paco has saved. What polynomial represents the amount they have saved in all? If $n = 5$, how much have they saved in all?

18. Joan sold muffins at a craft show. The polynomial $3k^2 - 9$ represents the amount of her expenses, and the polynomial $2k^2 + 17$ represents the amount of her profit. What polynomial represents the amount she earned?

19. The corner was torn from Tim's math homework paper. All that remained of Exercise 1 was the sum $3x^2 + 8x$ and the binomial $^-4x^2 + 5x$. Find the binomial that must be added to $^-4x^2 + 5x$ to give the sum $3x^2 + 8x$.

20. ✏️ **WRITE ABOUT IT** How is adding polynomials like adding integers?

Mixed Review

Write an addition problem for each subtraction problem.

21. $12 - ^-3$ **22.** $18 - 5$ **23.** $^-8 - ^-12$ **24.** $^-10 - 15$ **25.** $11 - ^-5$

Write *linear* or *nonlinear* to describe the function.

26. $f(x) = 5x^2 - 1$ **27.** $f(x) = x^2 + x + 1$ **28.** $f(x) = 6x - 14$ **29.** $f(x) = ^-2x + 6$

30. **PERCENTS** Pearls with an estimated value of $500 sold at an auction for $211,500. What was the percent of increase?

31. **NUMBER SENSE** The sum of three consecutive numbers is 165. Find the numbers.

Subtracting Polynomials

REMEMBER:

Sometimes it is easier to add the opposite of a number instead of subtracting a number. **See page 60.**

How is subtracting polynomials similar to adding them? You added polynomials by adding like monomials. To subtract polynomials, find the differences of like monomials.

ACTIVITY

WHAT YOU'LL NEED: algebra tiles

Work together to model $(4x^2 + 5x + 6) - (3x^2 + 2x + 4)$.

• Model $4x^2 + 5x + 6$. What algebra tiles did you use?

• Subtract $3x^2 + 2x + 4$ from the model by removing tiles that represent $3x^2$, $2x$, and 4. What tiles did you remove for $3x^2$? for $2x$? for 4?

• What tiles remain? What is $(4x^2 + 5x + 6) - (3x^2 + 2x + 4)$?

You can also subtract a polynomial by adding its opposite.

EXAMPLE 1 Find the difference.

$$(3x^2 + 7x + 6) - (6x^2 - 2x + 8)$$

Think: Subtract by adding the opposite.

polynomial: $6x^2 - 2x + 8$ **opposite:** $^-6x^2 + 2x - 8$

$$
\begin{array}{l}
3x^2 + 7x + 6 \\
-(6x^2 - 2x + 8)
\end{array}
\rightarrow
\begin{array}{l}
3x^2 + 7x + 6 \\
+(^-6x^2 + 2x - 8) \\
\hline
^-3x^2 + 9x - 2
\end{array}
$$

Line up like terms. Rewrite to add the opposite. Add like terms.

• What is the opposite of $12d^2 + 4d - 5$?

You can represent some real-life problems by subtracting polynomials.

EXAMPLE 2 Last week Ruki earned $x^2 - 5$ by selling ice cream cones at an arts and crafts show. Her expenses were $x^2 - 2x + 3$. What polynomial represents the profit she made?

Think: To find profit, subtract expenses from sales.

$$
\begin{array}{l}
x^2 \qquad - 5 \\
-(x^2 - 2x + 3)
\end{array}
\rightarrow
\begin{array}{l}
x^2 \qquad - 5 \\
+(^-x^2 + 2x - 3) \\
\hline
2x - 8
\end{array}
$$

Line up like terms. Rewrite to add the opposite. Add like terms.

So, Ruki made a profit of $2x - 8$.

Consumer Link

Do you like ice cream cones? An ice cream shop serves 500,000 ice cream cones every year. Write a monomial for the total amount of ice cream served. Let x = the amount per cone.

Model the subtraction with algebra tiles or a drawing.

1. $(5x + 5) - (3x + 2)$ **2.** $(3x^2 + 4x + 8) - (x^2 + x + 4)$ **3.** $(2x^2 + 2x + 4) - (2x^2 + x)$

Write the opposite of the polynomial.

4. $4x^2 + 6x + 12$ **5.** $6a^2 - 2a + 3$ **6.** $^-5y^2 + 8y - 9$ **7.** $^-2x^2 - x - 5$

Subtract by adding the opposite.

8. $(6y - 5) - (y - 2)$ **9.** $(3x^2 + 5x - 3) - (^-4x^2 + x + 3)$ **10.** $(3b^2 + 2b + 6) - (2b^2 + 3b)$

Write the opposite of the polynomial.

1. $^-3x^2 - 7x$ **2.** $^-5y^2 + 4y - 2$ **3.** $2x^2 - 4x + 7$ **4.** $6b^2 + 3b + 12$

5. $^-2a^2 + 3a - 10$ **6.** $9x^2 - 5x - 12$ **7.** $^-8y^2 + y + 9$ **8.** $3x^2 - 5x + 4$

Find the difference.

9. $(8x^2 + 3) - (5x^2 + 5)$ **10.** $(^-3b^2 + 7b) - (4b^2 + 7b)$ **11.** $(x^2 - 5x + 1) - (5x^2 - 3x)$

12. $(4m^2 - 5) - (m^2 + 4)$ **13.** $(5c^2 - 3c + 8) - (7c^2 + 2)$ **14.** $(3k^2 + 6k) - (7k^2 - 2k)$

15. $(4x^2 - 3) - (5x - 2)$ **16.** $(3x^2 - 2x + 3) - (6x^2 + 5)$ **17.** $(2b^2 - 4b - 5) - (b^2 + 4b)$

18. $(8x^2 - 2x - 5) - (4x^2 + 6x - 12)$ **19.** $(2y^2 - 7y - 12) - (6y^2 - 6y - 4)$

20. $(7a^2 + 3a + 12) - (6a^2 + 5a + 9)$ **21.** $(3x^2 + 12x - 12) - (^-5x^2 + 6x - 10)$

Problem-Solving Applications

22. Lea is putting a work island in the kitchen and is replacing the floor tiles not covered by the island. The binomial $6x^2 + 10x$ represents the original area of the floor in ft^2, and $3x^2 - 10$, the area of the island in ft^2. Subtract to find the area needing new tiles. If $x = 3$, what is the area needing new tiles?

23. Jerry sold balloons at the state fair. If $10s^2 + 50s$ represents the amount of his sales in dollars and $s^2 + 5s$ represents his expenses, what binomial represents his profit? If $s = 1.20$, what was the amount of his profit?

24. A factory produces $10g^2 + 4g - 2$ glasses a day, but $g^2 - 12$ glasses have flaws and cannot be sold. What polynomial represents the number of glasses that can be sold? Suppose $g = 30$. How many glasses can be sold?

25. 🖉 **WRITE ABOUT IT** What is the result of subtracting a negative monomial from itself? Give an example.

COOPERATIVE LEARNING

Polynomials From Guatemala

Most of Guatemala's manufactured products are consumer goods, such as processed foods and beverages, clothing, and textiles. Alicia helped her mother unpack boxes shipped from Guatemala for their import store. There were 2 boxes with long skirts woven with Mayan patterns and 3 boxes with blouses. Each box had the same number of items inside. Write a polynomial that shows the number of items received. Let x = the number of items in each box and y = the total number of items. Simplify the polynomial.

$2x + 3x = y \rightarrow 5x = y$

Let $x = 12$. Solve the equation for y.

Work Together

1. Alicia keeps a record of the skirts and blouses sold. The same number of items were sold each day for the first 3 days. On the fourth day, four times as many items were sold than on the third day. On the fifth day, the same number of items were sold as on the first day. Two skirts were sold on the sixth day. Let b represent the number of items sold on each of the first 3 days. Write an equation to show the number of blouses and skirts sold during the six days. Simplify the equation. Let $b = 4$. Solve the equation.

2. More skirts and blouses sold in the first two weeks of the month than in the last two weeks. Alicia wrote this polynomial expression to find the difference between sales during the first two weeks and the last two weeks: $(34 + c^3) - (3c + c + 2)$. Let c equal 2. Evaluate the expression.

3. There were several items left at the end of the month. The price of each was $4x - 2$. The items were put on sale. The sale price was $(4x - 2) - (x - 5)$. Write an expression with polynomials to show the difference between the regular price and the sale price. Then let $x = \$10$ and solve the equation.

CULTURAL LINK

About one-half of the people of Guatemala are Amerindian. Many follow centuries-old Mayan traditions. The people in many villages wear clothing made from hand-woven cloth patterned with bright colors. You can tell which village a person is from by the color and style of their clothing.

EXAMPLES

- **Model, classify, and evaluate polynomials.**
  (pages 475–477)

Evaluate $3x^3 + 5x - 4$ for $x = {}^-2$.

$3({}^-2)^3 + 5({}^-2) - 4$ *Substitute $^-2$ for x.*

$3({}^-8) + 5({}^-2) - 4$ *Use the order of operations.*

${}^-24 + ({}^-10) - 4$

${}^-38$

- **Simplify polynomials.** (pages 478–480)

Simplify the polynomial, and write the result in standard form.

$5x^2 - 3 + x^3 + 4x^2 - 3x + 10$

$(5x^2 + 4x^2) + ({}^-3 + 10) + x^3 - 3x$ *Combine like terms.*

$9x^2 + 7 + x^3 - 3x$

$x^3 + 9x^2 - 3x + 7$ *Rearrange the terms in order by exponents.*

- **Add polynomials.** (pages 481–483)

Find the sum.

$({}^-4y^2 + 3y - 3) + (5y^2 + 1)$

$\begin{array}{r} {}^-4y^2 + 3y - 3 \\ 5y^2 + 1 \\ \hline y^2 + 3y - 2 \end{array}$

Line up like terms.
Leave space for missing term.
Add the coefficients of like terms and add the numerical terms.

- **Subtract polynomials.** (pages 484–485)

Find the difference.

$(3x^2 - 2x - 8) - (2x^2 + 4x - 6)$

$\begin{array}{r} 3x^2 - 2x - 8 \\ -(2x^2 + 4x - 6) \\ \hline \end{array}$ *Line up like terms.*

$\begin{array}{r} 3x^2 - 2x - 8 \\ +({}^-2x^2 - 4x + 6) \\ \hline x^2 - 6x - 2 \end{array}$

Rewrite to add the opposite.
Add like terms.

EXERCISES

1. **VOCABULARY** A _?_ is a monomial or the sum of two or more monomials.

Evaluate the polynomial for $x = {}^-4$.

2. $6x + 28$ 3. $4x^3$ 4. ${}^-2x^2 + 1$

5. $3x^2 + 4x - 10$ 6. $5x^2 - 2x + 3$

7. $x^3 - 3x^2 + 4x$ 8. ${}^-x^2 + 8x - 2$

Simplify the polynomial, and write the result in standard form.

9. $6x^2 + 3x^3 + 4x^2 + 5 + 4x + 10 - 2x^3$

10. ${}^-3a^3 + 6a + 7a^5 - 3a + 5 - 2a^5 - 6$

11. $3x^2 - 3x^3 - 4x^3 + 6x^5 - 3x + 10 - 2x^5$

12. $12 + 2x^2 + 4x^2 - 6x^3 + 6x^4 - 5x - 5$

Find the sum.

13. $(5b^2 + 3b + 4) + (6b^2 - 5)$

14. $(8x^2 - 4x + 3) + (2x^2 - 6x + 8)$

15. $(2y^2 - 3y + 7) + (6y^2 - 8y - 9)$

16. $(4x^2 - 3x - 7) + (3x + 12)$

Write the opposite of the polynomial.

17. $3x^2 + 4x - 6$ 18. ${}^-7x^2 + 3x + 5$

Find the difference.

19. $(6x^2 - 5x) - (4x^2 - 3x - 4)$

20. $(3y^2 + 5y - 8) - (7y^2 + 4y - 4)$

21. $(4a^2 + 2a + 14) - (3a^2 + 6a + 11)$

22. $(5x^2 - 4x + 6) - (5x - 2)$

VOCABULARY CHECK

1. The x-coordinate of the point where a graph crosses the x-axis is the ? .
(page 453)

2. A relation in which no two ordered pairs have the same x-value is a ? .
(page 460)

3. A function whose graph is a straight line is called a ? function. (page 463)

4. The sum of two or more monomials is a ? . (page 475)

EXAMPLES

- **Use a scatterplot to see relationships.**
  (pages 444–446)

Describe the relationship in the scatterplot.

As family size increases, car size increases.

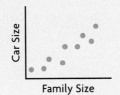

- **Use slope and intercepts to graph a linear equation.** (pages 453–456)

Find the slope and the y-intercept.

$y = \frac{3}{4}x - 4$ $y = mx + b \leftarrow y\text{-intercept}$
$\qquad\qquad\qquad\uparrow$
$\qquad\qquad\quad$ slope

slope: $\frac{3}{4}$; y-intercept: $^-4$

- **Represent linear functions.** (pages 463–465)

Graph $f(x) = 2x + 1$.

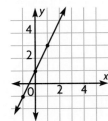

Complete a table of values, and identify the set of ordered pairs.

Graph the ordered pairs.

Connect the points with a line.

EXERCISES

5. Look at the scatterplot below. Is there a relationship between indoor sports and temperature? If so, describe it.

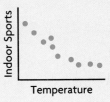

Find the slope and the y-intercept. Then graph the equation.

6. $y = ^-5x + 3$ **7.** $y = 2x + 4$

8. $y = \frac{^-1}{2}x + 1$ **9.** $y = 6x - \frac{1}{2}$

Make a table of values for each function. Let $x = 0, 1,$ and 2. Then write the ordered pairs and graph the function.

10. $f(x) = 2x$ **11.** $f(x) = 4x + 3$

12. $f(x) = 2x - 1$ **13.** $f(x) = ^-3x + 1$

- **Simplify polynomials.** (pages 478-480)

Simplify the polynomial, and write the result in standard form.

Combine like terms.

$4x + 6x^3 - 5x^2 + 8 - x^3 + 2x^2 - 3x$
$(4x - 3x) + (6x^3 - x^3) + (^-5x^2 + 2x^2) + 8$
$x + 5x^3 - 3x^2 + 8$ *Rearrange the terms*
$5x^3 - 3x^2 + x + 8$ *in order by exponents.*

Simplify the polynomial, and write the result in standard form.

14. $14 - 7x^2 + 3x + 6x^3 - 4x + 4x^2 - 10$

15. $^-12a^2 - 5a - 9 + 2a^3 - 6a^2 + 3a^3 + 8a$

16. $7z - 11z^5 + 1 - 3z^2 + 9z^5 + 4z^4 - 8 + z^2$

- **Subtract polynomials.** (pages 484–485)

Find the difference.

$(5x^2 + 7x - 3) - (8x^2 + 2x - 6)$

$5x^2 + 7x - 3$ *Line up like terms.*
$\underline{- (8x^2 + 2x - 6)}$

$5x^2 + 7x - 3$ *Rewrite to add the opposite.*
$\underline{+ (^-8x^2 - 2x + 6)}$ *Add like terms.*
$^-3x^2 + 5x + 3$

Find the difference.

17. $(8w^2 - w - 5) - (7w^2 - 6w - 6)$

18. $(4x^2 + 6) - (2x^2 + 3x - 5)$

19. $(3y^2 - 8y + 4) - (9y^2 - 9y + 1)$

20. $(a^2 + 5a - 2) - (^-3a^2 + 10)$

PROBLEM SOLVING

Solve. Explain your method.

21. A car uses 3 gal of gas to go 96 mi and 5 gal of gas to go 160 mi. If the car holds 13 gal of gas, how far can it go on one tank of gas? (pages 442–443)

22. Together Wade and Noel work 20 hr a week on the school newspaper. This week Wade worked 2.5 hr more than Noel. How many hours did each person work? (pages 457–459)

23. Find the binomial that is added to $8x^2 - 3x + 4$ to give the sum $^-2x^2 - x + 3$. (pages 481–483)

24. Ellen's weekly salary is represented by $15x^2 + 20x$, and her expenses are $5x^2 + 5x$. What binomial represents the difference? If $x = \$3$, what is the difference each week? (pages 484–485)

✏️ Write About It

1. Is this scatterplot an example of positive correlation? Why or why not? (pages 444–446)

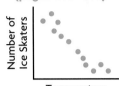

2. Solve the system of equations by graphing. Explain your method. (pages 457–459)

$y = 2x$
$y = 3x + 2$

3. Explain how you would find the sum of the polynomials. (pages 481–483)

$(4y^2 - 3y + 8) + (^-2y^2 + 5y - 3)$

✔️ Performance Assessment

Choose a strategy and solve. Explain your method.

Problem-Solving Strategies
- **Find a Pattern**   • **Act It Out**   • **Make a Model**
- **Make a Graph**   • **Write an Equation**

4. At the beginning of an experiment, the temperature of a liquid is 100°F. It increases at a constant rate of 15° per min. What will the temperature be after 5 min? When will the temperature reach the boiling point of 212°F? (pages 442–443)

5. Dion and Robert did a total of 24 push-ups. Dion did 3 times as many as Robert. How many push-ups did each boy do? Write a system of equations and solve by graphing. (pages 457–459)

6. The polynomial $3d + 10$ represents the amount of money raised by the seventh-grade class at the school fair. The amount raised by the eighth-grade class is represented by $6d + 5$. If $d = \$50$, how much was raised by the two classes? Explain your reasoning. (pages 481–483)

CUMULATIVE REVIEW

Solve the problem. Then write the letter of the correct answer.

1. What is 2^{-4} written as a fraction?
(pages 69–71)

A. $^-16$ B. $^-8$
C. $\dfrac{1}{16}$ D. $\dfrac{1}{8}$

2. Which inequality is represented by the graph below? (pages 164–166)

A. $y \geq 4 - 2x$
B. $y < 4 - 2x$
C. $y \leq 4 - 2x$
D. $y > 4 - 2x$

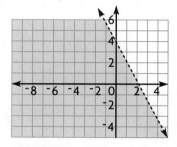

3. Convert from gallons to liters. (pages 196–198)

1 gal $\approx$ 3.79 L
5 gal $\approx$ ▦ L

A. 1.21 L   B. 1.32 L
C. 15.95 L   D. 18.95 L

4. A monument in town is a triangular prism 55 ft tall. Using a scale factor of $\dfrac{1}{30}$, find the height, in inches, of a scale model.
(pages 257–259)

A. 2 in.   B. 6 in.
C. 22 in.   D. 30 in.

5. A jar of pennies has 32 marked pennies in it. Josh reaches in and takes out 28 pennies, of which 10 are marked. Estimate the total number of pennies in the jar.
(pages 306–307)

A. 30 pennies   B. 40 pennies
C. 70 pennies   D. 90 pennies

6. A bag is tossed onto the area shown below. What is the geometric probability that the bag lands in section B? (pages 367–369)

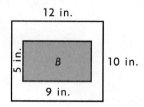

A. 30%   B. 37.5%
C. 50%   D. 62.5%

7. What is the slope of the line containing the points $(3,7)$ and $(5,3)$? (pages 453–456)

A. $^-2$ B. $-\dfrac{1}{2}$
C. $\dfrac{1}{2}$ D. 2

8. Which relationship below is NOT a linear function? (pages 466–469)

A.

x	0	1	2
$f(x)$	0	3	6

B.

x	1	2	3
$f(x)$	1	$\frac{1}{2}$	$\frac{1}{3}$

C.

x	1	3	5
$f(x)$	5	15	25

D.

x	-2	0	2
$f(x)$	$^-3$	0	3

9. Evaluate $3x^2 - 2x + 6$ for $x = 4$.
(pages 475–477)

A. 22   B. 46
C. 62   D. 142

10. Find the sum. $(^-4x^2 + 5x + 6) + (6x^2 - x)$
(pages 481–483)

A. $(2x^2 + 4x + 6)$ B. $(2x^2 - 5x - 5)$
C. $(2x^2 - 4x + 6)$ D. $(10x^2 - 4x + 6)$

MEASURING ONE, TWO, AND THREE DIMENSIONS

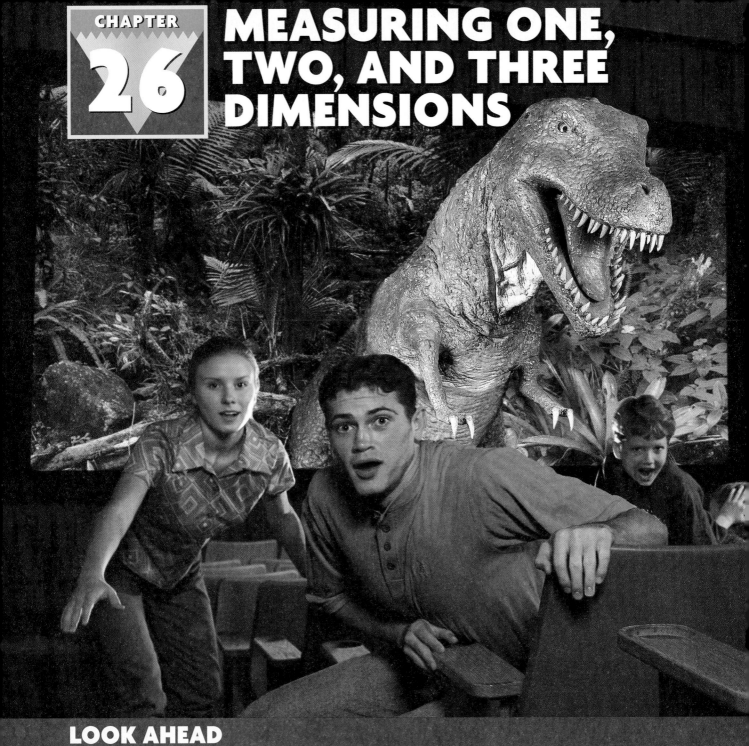

LOOK AHEAD

In this chapter you will solve problems that involve

- drawing and traveling networks
- finding the perimeter and area of two-dimensional figures
- finding the surface area and volume of three-dimensional figures

Collectible Containers

What is your favorite movie? What product can you invent that will go with the movie? Your product needs a container. Sketch your product. Build a custom-fit container for it.

YOU WILL NEED: construction paper, ruler, scissors, tape, colored markers

Plan
- Work with a partner. Think of a movie-related souvenir. Design and build a container for it. Use at least two of these shapes for the container: cube, rectangular prism, cylinder, cone, pyramid.

Act
- Brainstorm product ideas. Pick one idea and sketch it.
- Sketch a container for your souvenir.
- Build a prototype container. Decorate the label with the name of the souvenir, name of the movie, and volume of the container.

Share
- Display your container in a class gift shop with all the other containers.

DID YOU

- ☑ Make a sketch of your souvenir?
- ☑ Make a sketch of your container?
- ☑ Build a container?
- ☑ Display your container?

ALGEBRA CONNECTION
Networks

An Orlando trucking company makes shipments to Miami, Jacksonville, and Tallahassee. Goods from Orlando are delivered to each of the other cities before the truck returns to Orlando. What is the shortest round-trip route?

You can draw a network to show the distances between cities. A **network** is a figure made up of vertices and edges that shows how objects are connected. A **vertex** is a point that represents an object. An **edge** is a connection between vertices. Networks are not always drawn to scale.

In the network below, the vertices identify the cities. The edges are marked with the driving distances in miles.

J—Jacksonville   O—Orlando
M—Miami   T—Tallahassee

• What is the driving distance from Orlando to Miami?

Use the network to find the shortest route.

Find all possible routes.	Find distance in miles for each route.
OJMTO	107 + 369 + 556 + 325 = 1,357
OMJTO	236 + 369 + 176 + 325 = 1,106
OJTMO	107 + 176 + 556 + 236 = 1,075
OTJMO	325 + 176 + 369 + 236 = 1,106
OMTJO	236 + 556 + 176 + 107 = 1,075
OTMJO	325 + 556 + 369 + 107 = 1,357

The two shortest routes, *OJTMO* and *OMTJO*, are 1,075 mi each.

GUIDED PRACTICE

1. Each vertex represents a city. Starting at A, find all possible round-trip routes that include all the cities.

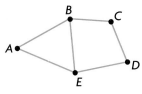

2. Find the distance in miles for each round-trip route.

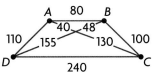

You can solve some problems by drawing a network.

EXAMPLE 1 Cindy Howard starts in Raleigh, makes sales calls in each of the four cities shown on the map, and returns to Raleigh. Draw a network that shows the shortest route.

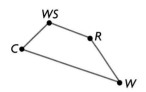

Draw and label 4 vertices to identify the 4 cities.

Connect the vertices with edges.

Route: R–W–C–WS–R   *Describe the route.*

• Draw networks for other possible routes.

Now see how the numbers of vertices and edges are related.

ACTIVITY

• Draw networks with 2, 3, 4, and 5 vertices. Connect every vertex with every other vertex once. Then find the number of edges in each network. Record your data by copying and completing the table.

Number of Vertices	2	3	4	5
Number of Edges	?	?	?	?

• **CRITICAL THINKING** The formula $e = \frac{v^2 - v}{2}$ describes the relationship between the number of vertices, v, and the number of possible edges, e, in a network. How can you use this formula to find the number of possible edges in a network with 10 vertices?

You can use what you know about vertices and edges to find the number of possible connections in a network.

EXAMPLE 2 An airline serves six different cities. How many different direct connections are possible between the cities?

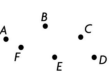

$$e = \frac{v^2 - v}{2}$$

Use the formula for the number of edges in the network.

$$e = \frac{6^2 - 6}{2}$$

Substitute 6 for v.

$$e = \frac{30}{2} = 15 \leftarrow \textbf{15 edges}$$

Find the value.

So, there are 15 different direct connections.

Starting at *A*, find all possible routes that include each vertex. Find the distance in miles for each.

1.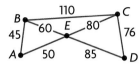

2.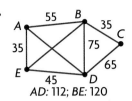

AD: 112; BE: 120

3.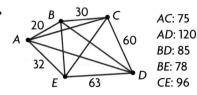

AC: 75
AD: 120
BD: 85
BE: 78
CE: 96

Find the number of different direct connections possible for the given number of locations.

4. 6 cities   **5.** 7 bus stops   **6.** 8 airports   **7.** 9 capitals   **8.** 10 islands

Problem-Solving Applications

9. An airline serves seven cities. Draw a network showing the direct route between the two cities in every possible pair. How many different direct routes are possible? How many routes can you find that connect two cities but stop at one other city on the way?

10. Debbie has 5 min between classes. She drew the network at the right to show the time in seconds it takes to walk between stops. Starting from Room A, find the shortest travel time for going to the school office, her locker, the school store, and finally to Room B in one trip. What is the route?

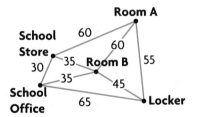

11. ✏️ **WRITE ABOUT IT** In your own words, explain what a network is. Then give an example of how a network helps you solve a real-life problem.

Mixed Review

Round to the nearest tenth.

12. 37.82   **13.** 8.46   **14.** 9.322   **15.** 18.68   **16.** 7.384

Simplify the polynomial, and write the result in standard form.

17. $5x^2 + 3x + 4x^2 - x + 2 + 4x$

18. $3b^2 - 4b^2 + 7b^3 - b - 5 - 4b^3$

19. **PRISMS** Mr. Peters makes stained-glass jewelry boxes in a hexagonal-prism shape. How many pieces of glass does he need to make 12 boxes?

20. **SPEED** Carly's family is driving 560 mi to a theme park. If they travel at an average of 65 mph, about how long will it take them to reach their destination?

MORE PRACTICE Lesson 26.1, page H81

Network Traveling

Some networks can be traveled without lifting a pencil off the paper and without retracing a line. Others cannot.

The number of vertices is important in deciding whether a network can be traveled. There are two types of vertices: odd and even. An **odd vertex** has an odd number of lines coming from it. An **even vertex** has an even number of lines.

odd vertices:    even vertices:

LAB Activity

WHAT YOU'LL EXPLORE
How to decide whether a network can be traveled

WHAT YOU'LL NEED
tracing paper

Explore

• Trace each of the networks. Then try to travel each network without lifting your pencil or retracing a line.

A   B   C   D   E

WORD POWER
odd vertex
even vertex

• Copy and complete the table. Look for patterns.

Network	Number of Even Vertices	Number of Odd Vertices	Can It Be Traveled?
A	6	0	?
B	?	?	?
C	?	?	?
D	?	?	?
E	?	?	?

Think and Discuss

• How many odd vertices are in the networks you traveled?

Try This

Write *yes* or *no* to tell whether you can travel the network.

1.   2.

Technology Link
E–Lab • Activity 26 Available on CD-ROM
and the Internet at http://www.hbschool.com/elab

Measuring Length

WHAT YOU'LL LEARN
How to determine the accuracy of a measurement and how to find perimeter and circumference

WHY LEARN THIS?
To compare the accuracy of measurements and to solve real-life problems involving measurement of length

WORD POWER
accuracy
significant digits

Carla and Kareem just completed a CD cabinet for a class project. Carla measures the width of the CD cabinet with a ruler that has marks every centimeter. Kareem uses a ruler that shows centimeters and millimeters. They report different measurements: 26 cm and 26.0 cm. Are these measurements equally accurate?

The **accuracy** of a measurement is shown by the number of significant digits. **Significant digits** tell the number of measured units.

You can compare the accuracy of two measurements by comparing the numbers of significant digits.

EXAMPLE 1 Are the measurements 26 cm and 26.0 cm equally accurate? If not, which is more accurate?

Think: A measurement with a greater number of significant digits is more accurate than one with fewer significant digits.

26 cm	measurement	26.0 cm
1 cm	unit of measure	0.1 cm
2, 6	significant digits	2, 6, 0
2	number of significant digits	3

$2 < 3$ *Compare numbers of significant digits.*

So, the two measurements are not equally accurate. The measurement 26.0 cm has more significant digits, so it is more accurate.

Measurement	Unit	Number of Units	Significant Digits	Number of Significant Digits
120.1 m	0.1 m	1,201	1, 2, 0, 1	4
120 m	1 m	120	1, 2, 0	3
1.2 m	0.1 m	12	1, 2	2
0.048 cm	0.001 cm	48	4, 8	2
3.06 cm	0.01 cm	306	3, 0, 6	3

GUIDED PRACTICE

Find the number of significant digits in each measurement based on the given unit of measure.

1. measurement: 36.1 cm; unit: 0.1 cm

2. measurement: 0.04 cm; unit: 0.01 cm

3. measurement: 8,000 cm; unit: 1 cm

4. measurement: 780 cm; unit: 10 cm

Tell which of the two measurements is more accurate.

5. measurement: 178.7 km; unit: 0.1 km
measurement: 178.70 km; unit: 0.01 km

6. measurement: 340 cm; unit: 10 cm
measurement: 340.0 cm; unit: 0.1 cm

In calculations with measurements, sometimes the answer is expressed with the same number of significant digits as in the measurement that has the fewest significant digits.

EXAMPLE 2 Find the perimeter of this polygon. Express the answer with the appropriate number of significant digits.

Think: 5.8 m, with 2 significant digits, has the fewest significant digits. Write the perimeter with 2 significant digits.

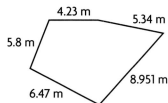

4.23 [+] 5.34 [+] 8.951 [+]   *Add the measures of all sides.*

6.47 [+] 5.8 [=] | 30.791 |

30.791 ≈ 31   **The perimeter is 31 m.**

Consider the accuracy of measurements when you find the circumference of a circle, using the formula $C = \pi d$ or $C = 2\pi r$.

EXAMPLE 3 Find the circumference of a circle with a diameter of 125 ft. Use $\pi = 3.14$.

Think: Both 125 and 3.14 have 3 significant digits.

$C = \pi d$

$C = 3.14 \cdot 125$ *Substitute 125 for d.*

$C = 392.5 \approx 393$ *Round to 3 significant digits.*

So, the circumference is 393 ft.

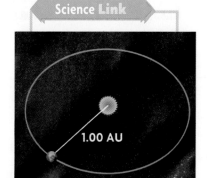

1.00 AU

What unit of measure would you choose for the vast distances of the solar system? Would meters be useful? Astronomers use astronomical units (AU). An AU is the average distance from the Earth to the sun (1.00 AU). Mars is about 1.52 AU from the sun, and Venus is about 0.72 AU from the sun. How many significant digits does each of these measures have?

REMEMBER:

Perimeter is the distance around a polygon. **See page H25.**

Circumference is the distance around a circle. **See page H25.**

499

Find the number of significant digits in each measurement, based on the given unit of measure.

1. measurement: 2,337.9 cm; unit: 0.1 cm

2. measurement: 0.67 cm; unit: 0.01 cm

3. measurement: 700 cm; unit: 1 cm

4. measurement: 700.0 m; unit: 0.1m

Tell which of the two measurements is more accurate.

5. measurement: 558.34 m; unit: 0.01 m
   measurement: 558.3 m; unit: 0.1 m

6. measurement: 33 cm; unit: 1 cm
   measurement: 33.1 cm; unit: 0.1 cm

7. measurement: 0.0345 m; unit: 0.0001 m
   measurement: 0.034 m; unit: 0.001 m

8. measurement: 45.75 m; unit: 0.01 m
   measurement: 45.7 m; unit: 0.1 m

Find the perimeter. Express the answer with the appropriate number of significant digits.

9.
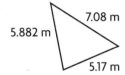
7.08 m
5.882 m
5.17 m

10.
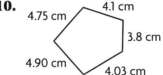
4.1 cm
4.75 cm
3.8 cm
4.90 cm
4.03 cm

11.
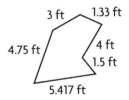
3 ft
1.33 ft
4.75 ft
4 ft
1.5 ft
5.417 ft

Find the circumference. Express the answer with the appropriate number of significant digits. Use $\pi = 3.14$.

12. diameter = 5 m

13. diameter = 42 m

14. radius = 4.20 in.

15. radius = 12 in.

Problem-Solving Applications

16. Jerry and Diane made a round basket. Jerry measures the diameter of the base as 30 cm, using a ruler that has marks every centimeter. Diane uses a ruler that is divided into centimeters and millimeters and measures the diameter as 30.2 cm. Find the circumference by using each diameter. Whose measurement is more accurate? Use $\pi = 3.14$.

17. Kaley found that the perimeter of this sandbox is 23.4 ft. What is the appropriate number of significant digits for the perimeter? Express the perimeter with that number of significant digits.
    4.25 ft
    6.4 ft
    6.75 ft
    6.0 ft

18. 💡 **CRITICAL THINKING** Samantha added the two measurements of her movie poster, 30.7 cm and 46.1 cm. She wrote the sum as 77 cm. Was she right? Explain.

19. ◖▶ **WRITE ABOUT IT** The zero in 230 m with a unit measure of 1 m is a significant digit. The zeros in 0.023 m with a unit measure of 0.001 m are not significant digits. Explain.

MORE PRACTICE Lesson 26.2, page H81

Use a Formula to Find the Area

WHAT YOU'LL LEARN
How to use formulas to find the area of composite figures

WHY LEARN THIS?
To solve real-life area problems

The PTA of Superior Middle School plans to sod an irregular section in front of the school. Evergreen Landscape Service charges $3 per square yard to do this work. What is the area of the section? What will be the total cost?

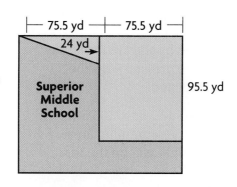

Problem Solving
• **Understand**
• **Plan**
• **Solve**
• **Look Back**

☑ **UNDERSTAND** What are you asked to find?

What facts are given?

☑ **PLAN** What strategy will you use?

You can *use a formula* to find the area of each part of the irregular section: a rectangle and a triangle.

☑ **SOLVE** How will you solve the problem?

Find the area of the rectangle.

$A = lw \leftarrow l = 95.5, w = 75.5$
$A = 95.5 \times 75.5$
$A = 7,210.25$

Find the area of the triangle.

$A = \frac{1}{2} bh$

$A = \frac{1}{2} \times 24 \times 75.5 = 906$

Find the total area.

$A = 7,210.25 + 906$
$A = 8,116.25 \leftarrow$ The total area is 8,116.25 yd^2.

Find the total cost.

total area $\times$ $3 = total cost
$8,116.25 \times 3 = 24,348.75 \leftarrow$ The total cost is $24,348.75.

☑ **LOOK BACK** Does $24,348.75 seem to be a reasonable answer? Explain.

What if . . . Evergreen Landscape computes the total area by using the rules of significant digits? How does the price change?

REMEMBER:

Area is the number of square units needed to cover a region. **See page H25.**

The formula for the area of a rectangle is $A = lw$. **See page H87.**

The formula for the area of a triangle is $A = \frac{1}{2}bh$. **See page H87.**

PRACTICE

Use a formula to solve. Use π = 3.14.

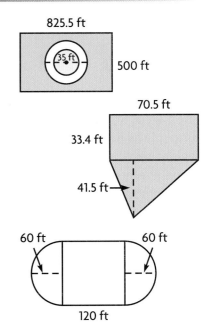

825.5 ft

35 ft

500 ft

70.5 ft

33.4 ft

41.5 ft—

60 ft   60 ft

120 ft

1. A circular fountain was installed in a city park. Find the park area that is outside the fountain and its surrounding sidewalk. Express the area with the appropriate number of significant digits.

2. The irregularly shaped lot purchased by the Jacobs family is shown at the right. Find its area, expressed with the appropriate number of significant digits.

3. On their lot, the Jacobs plan to build a 15-ft × 30.75-ft two-story house. They want to sod the remaining area. If the sod costs $3 per square foot, what will be the total cost of the sod?

4. The architect for the Springs Mall designed the stores around an atrium made up of a square and two congruent half circles. The imported tile for the atrium costs $9 per square foot. Find the area of the atrium. Then find the total cost of the tile.

MIXED APPLICATIONS

CHOOSE

Choose a strategy and solve.

Problem-Solving Strategies
• **Use a Formula** • **Account for All Possibilities** • **Make a Model**
• **Act It Out**   • **Draw a Diagram**   • **Write an Equation**

5. Jim Weber works for the Frame Shop. He is making a frame for an oil painting that is 60 in. high and 70.5 in. wide. The width of the framing boards is 4.75 in. What will be the size of the framed painting?

6. Lauren Kendrick hit a strong downdraft while flying a hang glider. This caused her to drop from an altitude of 10,000 ft to 6,800 ft in 5 min. What was the average change in altitude per minute?

7. Mr. and Mrs. Rossi work at a construction site outside of town. They drive a total of 3.5 hr each day to and from work. Going to work, they drive 45 mph. Returning home, they drive 30 mph. How many hours do they drive each way?

8. The band director is dividing some of the band members into trios for state competition. There are 9 pianists, 6 drummers, and 3 trumpeters. How many different ways can they be grouped?

9. ✏️ **WRITE ABOUT IT** Write a problem that can be solved with the strategy *use a formula*. Exchange with a classmate and solve.

MORE PRACTICE Lesson 26.3, page H82

ALGEBRA CONNECTION

Volumes of Solids

How is the volume of a prism related to the volume of a cylinder?

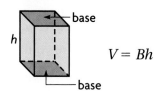

$V = Bh$

The volume of both a prism and a cylinder is $V = Bh$, where B is the area of the base and h is the height of the prism or cylinder. The formula for B varies according to the shape of the base.

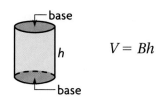

$V = Bh$

- How would you find the area of the base of the prism shown above? the area of the base of the cylinder?

If you know the radius and the height, you can find the volume of any cylinder.

EXAMPLE 1 Find the volume of the cylindrical storage tank. Use $\pi = 3.14$.

$V = Bh \leftarrow B = \pi r^2$

$V = \pi r^2 h$

$V \approx 3.14 \times 17^2 \times 16.5$ *Substitute 3.14 for π, 17 for r, and*

$V \approx 14{,}973.09$ *16.5 for h.*

$V \approx 14{,}973.09 \approx 15{,}000$ *Express the volume with 2 significant digits, since 17 has 2 significant digits.*

So, the volume is about 15,000 m³.

If you know B and h, you can find the volume of a prism.

EXAMPLE 2 Find the volume of the triangular prism.

Think: Use the formula $A = \frac{1}{2}bh$ to find the area of the base of the prism.

$V = Bh \leftarrow$ The area of the base is $\frac{1}{2} \times 16 \times 13.9$.

$V = (\frac{1}{2} \times 16 \times 13.9) \times 5$

$V = 556 \approx 600$ The volume is about 600 in³.

WHAT YOU'LL LEARN

How to find the volumes of solids

WHY LEARN THIS?

To solve real-life problems involving the volumes of solids

REMEMBER:

Volume is the number of cubic units needed to fill the space occupied by a solid figure. **See page H25.**
The formula for the area of a circle is $A = \pi r^2$. **See page 205.**

Real-Life Link

Grain is stored in cylindrical structures called silos. What is the volume of a silo with a diameter of 20 ft and a height of 30 ft?

A pyramid has $\frac{1}{3}$ the volume of a prism with the same base and height. A cone has $\frac{1}{3}$ the volume of a cylinder with the same base and height. You can use the formula $V = \frac{1}{3}Bh$ to find the volume of a pyramid or a cone.

EXAMPLE 3 Find the volume of the pyramid.

$V = \frac{1}{3}Bh \leftarrow$ Replace B with lw.

$V = \frac{1}{3} \times (6.5 \times 8.2) \times 10$

$V = 177.6666667 \approx 180$ *Express with 2 significant digits.*

So, the volume is about 180 m³.

• How can you find the volume of the cone shown at the right?

GUIDED PRACTICE

Find the volume. Use $\pi = 3.14$.

1.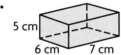

2.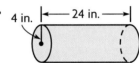

3.

4.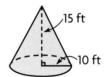

Volume of a Sphere

Use the formula $V = \frac{4}{3}\pi r^3$ to find the volume of a sphere.

EXAMPLE 4 Find the volume of a spherical water tank with a radius of 12 m. Use $\pi = 3.14$.

$V = \frac{4}{3}\pi r^3$

$V \approx \frac{4}{3} \times 3.14 \times 12^3$ *Substitute 3.14 for π and 12 for r.*

$V \approx 7{,}234.56 \approx 7{,}200$ *Express with 2 significant digits.*

So, the volume of the water tank is about 7,200 m³.

• Suppose the radius is 15 m. What is the volume?

• How would you find the volume of a sphere with a diameter of 20m?

INDEPENDENT PRACTICE

Find the volume of the cylinder or prism. Use π = 3.14.

1.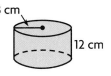
8 cm

12 cm

2.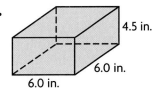
4.5 in.

6.0 in.

6.0 in.

Find the volume of the pyramid or cone. Use π = 3.14.

3.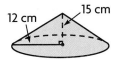
12 cm   15 cm

4.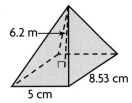
6.2 m

8.53 cm

5 cm

Find the volume of the sphere. Use π = 3.14.

5.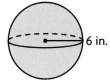
6 in.

6.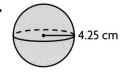
4.25 cm

Technology Link

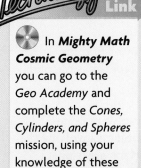

In *Mighty Math Cosmic Geometry* you can go to the *Geo Academy* and complete the *Cones, Cylinders, and Spheres* mission, using your knowledge of these solid figures.

Problem-Solving Applications

7. A paper drinking cup shaped like a cone has a 10-cm height and an 8-cm diameter. What is the volume of the cup? Use π = 3.14.

8. Ty and Vinnie built a recycling bin. The bin is a rectangular prism with a base 12 ft long × 6 ft wide. The volume of their bin is 576 ft³. What is the height?

9. A packaging company is developing a new line of sports-themed boxes. A basketball with a 29-cm diameter fits very tightly inside a cube-shaped box. What is the volume of the basketball? In the box, what is the volume that is not taken up by the basketball? Use π = 3.14.

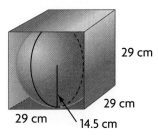
29 cm

29 cm

29 cm   14.5 cm

10. The Crispy Cereal Company is designing a cylindrical cereal container with a diameter of 12.5 cm and a height of 33 cm. What is the volume?

11. Citrus County built a new water tank that looks like an orange. It is a sphere with a diameter of 20.00 m. What is the volume of the water tank? Use π = 3.14.

12. ✏️ **WRITE ABOUT IT** How is the formula for the volume of a cylinder or prism similar to the formula for the volume of a cone or pyramid? How are they different?

ALGEBRA CONNECTION

Surface Area

WHAT YOU'LL LEARN
How to find the
surface areas of solids

WHY LEARN THIS?
To solve real-life
problems involving the
surface areas of
prisms, pyramids,
cylinders, and cones

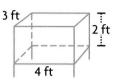

Rose Hill Middle School students are
constructing a cage for their school
mascot, a rabbit named Rusty. How much
wire mesh is needed to cover all sides of
the assembled frame?

The enclosed portion of the cage is a rectangular prism. To find
the amount of wire mesh, find the surface area of the rectangular
prism. The **surface area** of a solid is the sum of the areas of all
the surfaces of the solid.

WORD POWER

surface area
lateral surface
slant height

RUSTY
Rose Hill Middle School
Mascot

A: left side
B: bottom
C: right side
D: top
E: back
F: front

	E 2 x 4		
A 2 x 3	B 3 x 4	C 2 x 3	D 3 x 4
	F 2 x 4		

surface area = S = area A + area B + area C + area D +
      area E + area F

area A = area C; area A + area C = 2(2 × 3) = 12
area B = area D; area B + area D = 2(3 × 4) = 24
area E = area F; area E + area F = 2(2 × 4) = 16
S = 12 + 24 + 16 = 52 ≈ 50   *Use 1 significant digit since each*
                                measure has 1 significant digit.

Surface area is about 50 ft², so about 50 ft² of wire mesh is needed.

You can also find the surface area of a pyramid. Use formulas to
find the total area of the faces.

REMEMBER:
. . . .
A face is a flat surface
of a polyhedron. **See
page 180.**

EXAMPLE 1 Find the
surface area of the
square pyramid.

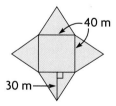

$S = 4(\frac{1}{2}bh) + s^2 \leftarrow s =$ **area of 4 triangular faces +
                            area of 1 square face**

$S = 4(\frac{1}{2} \times 40 \times 30) + (40)^2 \leftarrow b = 40, h = 30,$ **and** $s = 40$

$S = 4(600) + 1,600$ *Find the sum.*

$S = 4,000 \leftarrow$ *Think of the answer in terms of 2 significant digits.*

So, the surface area is about 4,000 m².

Identify the polygons that form the faces of the figure. Then find the area of each face.

1.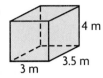
4 m
3.5 m
3 m

2.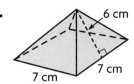
6 cm
7 cm
7 cm

Find the surface area of the figure.

3.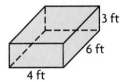
3 ft
6 ft
4 ft

4.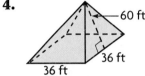
60 ft
36 ft
36 ft

Surface Areas of Cylinders and Cones

You can use formulas to find the surface area of a cylinder or a cone. The surface area of a cylinder or a cone is the sum of the areas of the bases or base and of the curved surface.

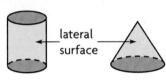
lateral surface

The curved surface of a cylinder or a cone is called the **lateral surface**.

To find the surface area of a cylinder, add the areas of the two bases (circles) and the area of the lateral surface (rectangle).

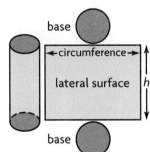
base
circumference
lateral surface   h
base

$S = 2(\text{area of circle}) + \text{area of rectangle}$

$\text{area of rectangle} = \text{circumference} \times \text{height, or } 2\pi r \cdot h$

$S = 2(\pi r^2) + (2\pi r \cdot h)$

EXAMPLE 2 Find the surface area.

Think: $h = 15$, $r = 5$, $\pi = 3.14$

$S = 2(\pi r^2) + (2\pi r \cdot h)$

$S \approx 2(3.14 \times 5^2) + (2 \times 3.14 \times 5 \times 15)$

$S \approx 2(78.5) + (471)$

$S \approx 157 + 471$

$S \approx 628 \approx 600$ The surface area is about 600 cm².

5 cm.
15 cm.

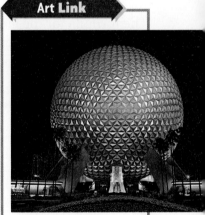

A cone consists of a base and a lateral surface.

- What is the shape of the base of a cone?

The **slant height** is the distance from the base of the cone to its vertex, measured along the lateral surface.

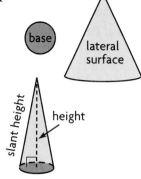

Talk About It

- 💡 **CRITICAL THINKING** Think about the height of a cone and the slant height of a cone. How are they different?

- The surface area of a cone consists of what two parts?

The formula for the area of the lateral surface of a cone is $A = \pi rs$, where r is the radius and s is the slant height.

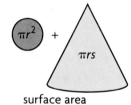

To find the surface area, S, of a cone, add the area of the base (circle) and the area of the lateral surface (πrs).

$S = $ area of circle + area of lateral surface

$S = \pi r^2 + \pi rs$

EXAMPLE 3 Find the surface area.

$S = \pi r^2 + \pi rs \leftarrow s = 5, r = 2.4$

$S \approx 3.14 \times (2.4)^2 + 3.14 \times 2.4 \times 5$

$S \approx 18.0864 + 37.68$

$S \approx 55.7664 \approx 60$ *Express with 1 significant digit.*

So, the surface area is about 60 m².

Geography Link

The largest cone in the world is Mauna Loa, an active volcano on the island of Hawaii. Mauna Loa has a height of about 4.17 km above sea level, a slant height of about 57.8 km, and a radius that averages about 57.5 km. What is the area of the lateral surface of this massive cone?

surface area

INDEPENDENT PRACTICE

Find the area of each surface of the figure. Use $\pi = 3.14$.

1.
10 cm
6 cm
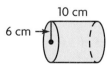

2.
3 in. $s = 5$ in.

3.
5.0 in.
7.0 in.
4.0 in.
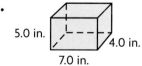

Find the surface area of the prism or pyramid.

4. 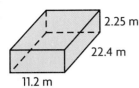 2.25 m

22.4 m

11.2 m

5. 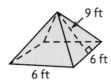 9 ft

6 ft

6 ft

6. 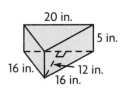 20 in.

5 in.

16 in. 12 in.

16 in.

Find the surface area of the cylinder or cone. Use π = 3.14.

7. 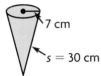 7 cm

s = 30 cm

8.  12.6 m

20.6 m

9.  3 in. s = 5 in.

Problem-Solving Applications

10. Jerome is wrapping the game Pente® for his sister's birthday gift. Pente® comes in a cylindrical canister that has a height of 18.0 in. and a diameter of 2.625 in. Will 175 in.² of gift wrap be enough to cover the cylinder? Explain.

11. Tina Lambert makes boxes from sheets of tin. The boxes are rectangular prisms measuring 4 in. × 6 in. × 6 in. What is the surface area of each? If tin costs 7¢ per square inch, what is the cost of the tin for one box?

12. A skylight is shaped like a square pyramid. Each skylight panel has a 4.0-m base. The slant height is 2.0 m, and the base of the pyramid is open. The installation cost is $5.25 per square meter. What is the cost to install 4 skylights?

13. ◖▬▶ **WRITE ABOUT IT** Explain how surface area is different from volume.

Mixed Review

Find the perimeter and the area of a rectangle with the given dimensions.

14. 5 in. × 12 in.   **15.** 9 m × 8 m   **16.** 12 ft × 12 ft   **17.** 11 ft × 13 ft

Find the sum or difference.

18. $(4a^2 + 3a - 1) + (3a^2 + 2a + 4)$ **19.** $(8a^2 - 5a + 3) - (2a^2 - 2a + 2)$

20. $(8x^2 - 4x) + (3x^2 - 6)$ **21.** $(4x^2 + 4x) - (2x^2 + 3x - 10)$

22. **SCHEDULING** Caro wants the cast of the school play ready 10 min before curtain call. They need 100 min for putting on makeup, 20 min for putting on costumes, and 30 min for a cast meeting. If the play starts at 8 P.M., at what time should the actors arrive?

23. **SPEED** Two race cars are clocked from the same time and place. One car makes a lap every 60 sec, and the other car makes a lap every 40 sec. At these rates, how long will it take the faster car to gain a lap on the slower car?

MATH FUN!

PLACES TO GO, SIGHTS TO SEE

PURPOSE To practice using a network (pages 494–496)

YOU WILL NEED atlas of the world

List three cities on other continents you would like to visit. Find about how far each city is from each other city, and how far each city is from your home city. Plan a trip. Start in your home city, fly to the other three cities, and fly home again. Draw a network that shows the trip. Find all the possible round-trip routes that include all the cities.

What is the shortest distance you could fly to stop in all the cities and come home again?

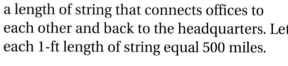

HUMAN NETWORK

PURPOSE To practice identifying networks that can be traveled without retracing (page 497)

YOU WILL NEED atlas of the United States, string, scissors, ruler

Work in small groups. Suppose your school is the headquarters of a company. One player works in the headquarters and the remaining players work in regional offices in different cities. Arrange yourselves into a human network that shows how each office is connected. Starting at the headquarters, cut a length of string that connects offices to each other and back to the headquarters. Let each 1-ft length of string equal 500 miles.

Can this network be traveled without retracing? To find out, challenge a classmate to walk the network without retracing steps.

AREA CONSTRUCTIONS

PURPOSE To practice finding the surface area of a solid (pages 506–509)

YOU WILL NEED small can, centimeter graph paper, ruler, tape, scissors

Work with a partner. Make a cylinder by wrapping a piece of graph paper around the can, cut it to fit, and tape it to the can. Trace the bases of the can on the graph paper, cut them out and tape them to the ends of the can. Then find the surface area.

Wrap a small box you find at home in graph paper. Be careful to line up your grid lines. Find the surface area.

EXAMPLES

- **Use networks to find all possible routes, the shortest route, and the number of connections.** (pages 494–496)

How many different direct connections are possible between 5 cities?

$e = \dfrac{v^2 - v}{2}$ *Find e, the number of edges.*

$e = \dfrac{5^2 - 5}{2}$ *Substitute 5 for v, the number of vertices.*

$e = \dfrac{20}{2} = 10$ ← **10 different direct connections**

EXERCISES

1. **VOCABULARY** A figure made up of vertices and edges that gives information about how objects are connected is a __?__ .

2. Find the shortest round-trip route starting with *A*. Find the distance in miles.

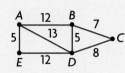

Find the number of different direct connections for the given number of locations.

3. 12 airports   4. 11 bus stops

- **Find the accuracy of a measurement, and find perimeter and circumference.** (pages 498–500)

Find the circumference.

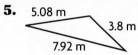

$C = \pi d$ ← $\pi = 3.14$
$C = 3.14 \times 12.0$
$C = 37.68 \approx 37.7$ ← **3 significant digits**

So, the circumference is about 37.7 ft.

Find the perimeter or circumference. Express the answer with the appropriate number of significant digits. Use $\pi = 3.14$.

5.

6.

- **Use formulas to find the area of composite figures.** (pages 501–502)

PROBLEM-SOLVING TIP: For help in solving problems by using a formula, see pages 11 and 501.

7. If sod costs $0.35 per square foot, what is the total cost of resodding the lawn?

- **Find the volumes of solids.** (pages 503–505)

$V = \dfrac{4}{3}\pi r^3$ ← $\pi = 3.14, r = 8$

$V \approx \dfrac{4}{3} \times 3.14 \times 8^3$

$V \approx 2{,}143.573333 \approx 2{,}000$ ← **volume ≈ 2,000 in.³**

Find the volume. Use $\pi = 3.14$.

8.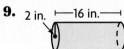

9.

- **Find the surface areas of solids.** (pages 506–509)

$S = \pi r^2 + \pi r s$ ← $\pi = 3.14$
$S \approx 3.14 \times (6)^2 + 3.14 \times 6 \times 10$
$S \approx 113.04 + 188.4$
$S \approx 301.44 \approx 300$ ← **surface area**
         ≈ 300 m²

Find the surface area. Use $\pi = 3.14$.

10.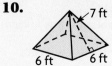

11.

27

CHANGES IN TWO AND THREE DIMENSIONS

LOOK AHEAD

In this chapter you will solve problems that involve

- maximum and minimum perimeters and areas
- doubling and halving dimensions
- maximum and minimum volumes

Stocking Up

The numbers show the number of items that can be stacked high (H), wide (W), and deep (D) in each location. Find out how many more can be displayed on an end aisle.

Plan
- Work with a partner. Study the stacking chart. Find out how much more room there is on an end aisle than on a home row.

Act
- Study the home row numbers. Calculate how many items are displayed.
- Study the end aisle numbers for the same product. Find the number of items displayed.
- Make a bar graph that compares the home row and end aisle data. How many more items can you display on an end aisle?

Share
- Compare your results with another group.

Product	Home Row H × W × D	End Aisle H × W × D
Soccer Balls	2 × 4 × 2	4 × 5 × 3
In-Line Skates	8 × 3 × 1	12 × 2 × 2
Bicycle Helmets	4 × 6 × 2	8 × 4 × 3
Ice Chests	3 × 2 × 1	4 × 2 × 3

DID YOU
- ✓ Find the number of items displayed on the rows?
- ✓ Make a bar graph?
- ✓ Compare results with another group?

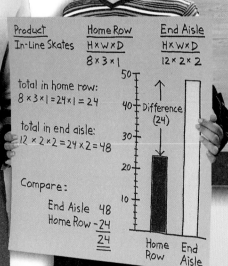

513

Maximum and Minimum Perimeter and Area

REMEMBER:

You can find the perimeter and area of a rectangle by using these formulas. **See page H25.**

$P = 2l + 2w$
$= (2 \times 12) + (2 \times 5)$
$= 24 + 10$
$= 34$

$A = lw$
$= 12 \times 5$
$= 60$

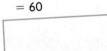

Jonathan is building a rectangular patio. He has 24 stone rectangles, each 2 ft × 3 ft. To make models of these 24 stones, he first cuts six 4-in. × 6-in. index cards in half lengthwise. Then he cuts each half in half crosswise.

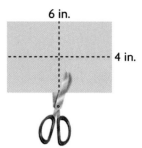

EXAMPLE 1 Find the length, width, perimeter, and area of the patio when the stones are in the arrangement shown below.

$8 \times 2 \text{ ft} = 16 \text{ ft} \leftarrow \text{length}$

$3 \times 3 \text{ ft} = 9 \text{ ft} \leftarrow \text{width}$

$P = 2(l + w)$ *Replace l with 16 and w with 9.*
$\quad = 2(16 + 9)$

$\quad = 2(25) = 50 \leftarrow \text{perimeter}$

$A = lw$

$\quad = 16 \times 9 = 144 \leftarrow \text{area}$

So, the length is 16 ft, the width is 9 ft, the perimeter is 50 ft, and the area is 144 ft^2.

EXAMPLE 2 What are the dimensions of some other rectangular arrangements of the same 24 stones?

You can use the cards to find other ways to arrange the 24 stones.

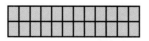

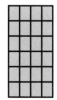

So, the dimensions of some other arrangements are 6 ft × 24 ft, 12 ft × 12 ft, and 18 ft × 8 ft.

• What is the area of each? Which arrangement has the least perimeter?

EXAMPLE 3 Jonathan used the cards to model this square arrangement of the 24 stones for the patio. What are some other rectangles with the same perimeter but not necessarily the same number of stones?

First, find the perimeter.

$P = 2(l + w)$ *Replace l with 12 and w with 12.*

$= 2(12 + 12)$

$= 2(24)$

$= 48$

So, the perimeter is 48 ft.

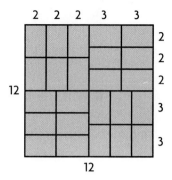

Other rectangles with the same perimeter include those with these dimensions:

8 ft × 16 ft $P = 2(8 + 16) = 2(24) = 48$
6 ft × 18 ft $P = 2(6 + 18) = 2(24) = 48$
4 ft × 20 ft $P = 2(4 + 20) = 2(24) = 48$

- Which of these rectangles with a perimeter of 48 ft has the greatest area?

- **CRITICAL THINKING** Which of these rectangles can be built without cutting any of the 2-ft × 3-ft pieces of stone?

The square has special properties for perimeter and area.

For a given area, the square is the rectangle with the minimum perimeter.	For a given perimeter, the square is the rectangle with the maximum area.

Sports Link

An American football field is 100 yd long and $53\frac{1}{3}$ yd wide. Each end zone is 10 yd deep. A Canadian football field is 110 yd long and 65 yd wide. Each end zone is 25 yd deep. Suppose an American team runs 9 laps around its field to warm up, and a Canadian team runs 7 laps around its field to warm up. Which team runs farther? How much farther?

GUIDED PRACTICE

Find the length, width, perimeter, and area of the arrangement of tiles. Measurements are in feet.

1.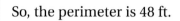
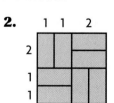

2.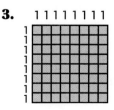

3.

4. Find the dimensions of four other rectangular arrangements that can be made from the tiles in Exercise 3.

515

INDEPENDENT PRACTICE

The rectangles in Exercises 1–5 all have the same perimeter. Find the area of each.

1. 10 ft × 2 ft **2.** 9 ft × 3 ft **3.** 8 ft × 4 ft **4.** 6 ft × 6 ft **5.** 3 ft × 9 ft

The rectangles in Exercises 6–10 all have the same area. Find the perimeter.

6. 18 ft × 2 ft **7.** 12 ft × 3 ft **8.** 6 ft × 6 ft **9.** 4 ft × 9 ft **10.** 3 ft × 12 ft

The area of a rectangle is given. Find the dimensions with the least perimeter.

11. 16 in.^{2} **12.** 49 m^2 **13.** 25 cm^2 **14.** 81 in.^{2} **15.** 100 in.^{2}

The perimeter of a rectangle is given. Find the dimensions of the rectangle with the greatest possible area.

16. 28 ft **17.** 36 cm **18.** 24 m **19.** 40 ft **20.** 50 ft

Problem-Solving Applications

21. Raphael has 20 in. of framing for his next painting. Find the whole-number dimensions of the rectangles he can make. Which dimensions give him the maximum area?

22. Bryan has 96 ft of fencing for a new playground. He wants to enclose as large a rectangular area as possible. What size rectangle should he make? What is the area of this rectangle?

23. Draw a graph showing the area, A, on the y-axis and the length, l, on the x-axis for each set of dimensions you found in Problem 21.

24. ➡ **WRITE ABOUT IT** Use the graph in Problem 23. As the length of a rectangle with a fixed perimeter increases, what happens to the area?

Mixed Review

Find the product or quotient.

25. 350 × 2 **26.** 460 × 2 **27.** 460 ÷ 2 **28.** 350 ÷ 2

Find the greatest possible error for each measurement.

29. 7 cm **30.** 10 yd **31.** 8 in. **32.** $3\frac{1}{4}$ mi **33.** 0.63 cm

34. **CIRCLE** Hanna wants 12 stars evenly spaced around a circle. Find the number of degrees between the center of one star and the center of the next. Suppose she wants to place 18 stars. Find the number of degrees between centers of stars.

35. **AREA** Lea has a square piece of construction paper. Each side measures 30 in. Find the approximate area of the largest circle Lea can cut out of the construction paper. (Use 3.14 for π.)

MORE PRACTICE Lesson 27.1, page H83

Doubling and Halving in Two Dimensions

When you change a plane figure by doubling or halving the width and length, how do the perimeter and area change?

ACTIVITY

Use the following information to explore the effects on a rectangle when you double its dimensions.

Property is often described by its width on the street and its depth. The shaded area in the diagram is the lot where Lorin lives. It is 50 ft wide and 150 ft deep. The three vacant lots for sale next to that lot have the same dimensions.

- Find the width and depth of each combination of adjacent lots.

  a. lots 9001 and 9002

  b. lots 9002 and 9004

  c. lots 9001, 9002, 9003, and 9004

- What if Lorin's family bought lot 9004? What would the area of the family's property be? the perimeter?

- Suppose lot 9001 were added to lot 9002. What would the width be? Express the combined area as a percent of the area of the single lot. Express the new perimeter as a percent of the old.

- To double both width and depth, all three vacant lots would need to be purchased. How would the area change? the perimeter?

- Describe the effect on the area of a rectangle caused by doubling

  a. the length or the width.
  b. both the length and the width.

- The length, l, and width, w, of a rectangle are doubled. Write a formula for the new perimeter and a formula for the new area.

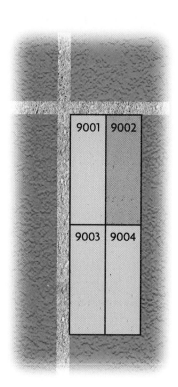

▶ Real-Life Link ▶

Many teens mow lawns in the summer to earn money. Most charge by the hour or by the size of the lawn. Suppose the average lawn in your neighborhood is 75 ft × 75 ft, and you charge $20 to mow it. How much should you charge Mr. Smith, whose corner lot is 150 ft × 150 ft?

Career Link

As you pass a construction area, you may notice people taking measurements with a marked pole and a transit, which looks like a telescope. They are surveying, or measuring, the site for the location of certain points, lines, and angles. Why is a construction site surveyed before a building, road, or bridge is actually built?

This table and the graphs below show how the perimeter of a 50-ft × 150-ft rectangular lot changes as the width repeatedly doubles while the length is fixed at 150 ft.

Length (in feet)	150	150	150	150
Width (in feet)	50	100	200	400
Perimeter (in feet)	400	500	700	1,100
Area (in square feet)	7,500	15,000	30,000	60,000

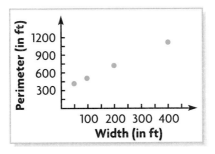

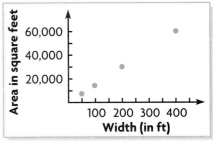

- What pattern do you see?

EXAMPLE How do the perimeter and area of a 50-ft × 150-ft rectangle change as the width is repeatedly halved?

Use this table to see how the perimeter and area change when the length is fixed at 150 ft.

Length	150	150	150	150
Width	50	25	12.5	6.25
Perimeter	400	350	325	312.5
Area	7,500	3,750	1,875	937.5

As the width is repeatedly halved, the perimeter converges towards 0. The area is repeatedly halved and converges towards 0.

GUIDED PRACTICE

1. Use the data in the Example above to graph how the perimeter of a rectangle changes when the width is repeatedly halved. Describe the changes you notice.

2. How do you think the perimeter and area of a rectangle change when both the length and width are doubled?

Copy and complete the table, showing the changing perimeter and area as the length of a rectangle is repeatedly doubled.

	Length (in feet)	125	250	500	1,000
	Width (in feet)	30	30	30	30
1.	Perimeter (in feet)	?	?	?	?
2.	Area (in square feet)	?	?	?	?

Find the perimeter and area of the figure. Then double the dimensions, and find the new perimeter and area.

3. 6 yd / 6 yd

4.  9 ft / 18 ft

5. 12.8 cm, 10 cm, 8 cm

6. 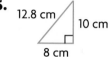 4 ft, 10 ft, 8 ft, 6 ft

Find the perimeter and area of each figure. Then halve the dimensions, and find the new perimeter and area.

7. 10 ft / 6 ft

8. 5 yd / 5 yd

9. 4.5 ft / 6 ft

10. 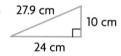 27.9 cm, 10 cm, 24 cm

Problem-Solving Applications

11. COINS Kevin has a total of $10.15. There are 5 more nickels than dimes and 3 times as many quarters as dimes. How many of each coin does Kevin have?

12. PERCENT Suppose a serving of food has 200 calories and 5 grams of fat. Each gram of fat has 9 calories. What percent of the calories are in the fat?

Mixed Review

Find the product.

13. $10 \times 12 \times 4$

14. $16 \times 7 \times 22$

15. $32 \times 21 \times 8$

16. $3.5 \times 5 \times 11$

Find the surface area of each rectangular prism.

17. 7 in. $\times$ 7 in. $\times$ 7 in.

18. 3 cm $\times$ 2 cm $\times$ 4 cm

19. 5 cm $\times$ 5 cm $\times$ 20 cm

20. David has two 20-in. $\times$ 30-in. posters. He wants to place them on his wall. How much area will they cover? Suppose he places a 24-in. $\times$ 36-in. poster on his wall. How much total area will the posters cover?

21. ✏️ **WRITE ABOUT IT** The length, p, and width, s, of a rectangle are halved. Write a formula for the new perimeter, P, and for the new area, A.

PROBLEM-SOLVING STRATEGY
Making a Model to Find Maximum Volume

You have a 9-in. × 12-in. sheet of paper and want to make an open box with the maximum volume. You use whole-number dimensions. What are the dimensions of the box?

✓ **UNDERSTAND** What are you asked to find?

What facts are given?

✓ **PLAN** What strategy will you use? You can *make a model* to find the dimensions of the box.

✓ **SOLVE** How will you solve the problem?

Make four boxes with depths of 1 in., 2 in., 3 in., and 4 in. Use the following procedure for each box.

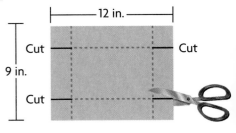

Step 1: Draw four lines parallel to the edges of the paper. Make their distance from the edges equal to the depth of the box.

Step 2: Make four cuts on the lines as shown. Fold in on the four lines.

Step 3: Make the corners even, and fasten them with paper clips.

Give the dimensions and compute the volume of each box.

Dimensions	Volume
10 in. × 7 in. × 1 in.	70 in.³
8 in. × 5 in. × 2 in.	80 in.³

Dimensions	Volume
6 in. × 3 in. × 3 in.	54 in.³
4 in. × 1 in. × 4 in.	16 in.³

So, the dimensions of the box with the maximum volume are 8 in. × 5 in. × 2 in.

✓ **LOOK BACK** Is the solution reasonable? Explain.

What if . . . the depth were $2\frac{1}{2}$ in.? What would the dimensions and volume be?

PRACTICE

Use the strategy *make a model* to solve.

1. Ed has an 11-in. × 17-in. piece of paper. He wants to make an open box with whole-number dimensions and the maximum volume. What are the dimensions and volume of this box?

2. Teri has an 8-in. × 10-in. piece of paper. She wants to make an open box with the maximum volume. Find the whole-number dimensions and volume of this box.

3. Sally has a piece of glass that is 20 in. × 28 in. She plans to cut it to make the sides and bottom of a fish tank. What are the dimensions of the tank with the maximum volume? What are the whole-number dimensions of each side and of the bottom?

4. Suppose a fruit packer has a piece of cardboard that is 36 in. × 36 in. He wants to construct an open packing box with the maximum volume to hold his fruit. What are the whole-number dimensions and volume of this box?

MIXED APPLICATIONS

CHOOSE

Choose a strategy and solve.

Problem-Solving Strategies

- **Make a Model**
- **Solve a Simpler Problem**
- **Work Backward**
- **Use a Formula**
- **Write an Equation**
- **Account for All Possibilities**

5. Kyle has a 20-in. × 30-in. piece of poster board. He wants to construct an open box with the maximum volume. Find the whole-number dimensions and volume of this box.

6. Joy and Paul passed out 133 flyers. Joy passed out 5 fewer flyers than twice the number that Paul did. How many flyers did Paul pass out?

7. Bert is laying 4-in. square tiles in his kitchen. His kitchen is 8 ft × 10 ft. How many tiles will he need?

8. Alice, Li, and Beth are standing in line at the ticket counter. In how many different orders can they be standing?

9. From a large jar, you scoop out and mark 36 marbles. You return them to the jar and mix them with the unmarked marbles. In a new scoopful, you find 8 marked marbles and 16 unmarked marbles. Use a proportion to predict the number of marbles in the jar.

10. After stop 4, there are 17 riders on the city bus. At stop 2, 5 riders got off, and 3 got on; at stop 3, 6 got off, and 2 got on; at stop 4, 2 got off, and 10 got on. How many riders got on at the first stop?

11. **WRITE ABOUT IT** Write a problem that you could solve by making a model. Exchange with a classmate and solve.

Exploring Changes in Prisms

In this activity you will make models of rectangular prisms from cards and from halves of cards.

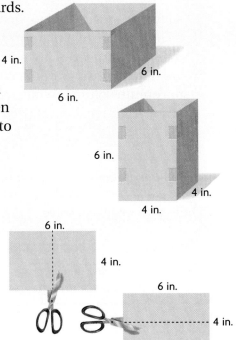

Explore

- Work with a partner to tape together four cards to make an open prism with no bases. Then tape together four more cards to make a different open prism.

- Cut four cards in half to form 4-in. × 3-in. rectangles. Tape the halves together to make open prisms with no bases.

- Cut four cards in half to form 2-in. × 6-in. rectangles. Tape the halves together to make open prisms with no bases.

Think and Discuss

- Compare the two prisms made from the 4-in. × 6-in. cards. Are the volumes the same? Explain.

- What are the dimensions of the prisms made from the 4-in. × 3-in. rectangles? from the 2-in. × 6-in. rectangles?

- Compare the prisms made from the halves of index cards. Are the volumes all the same? Explain.

Try This

- Repeat this activity with 3-in. × 5-in. index cards.

- Do you see the same relationships when you compare the results from the 4-in. × 6-in. prisms with those from the 3-in. × 5-in. prisms? Explain.

Technology Link
E-Lab • Activity 27 Available on CD-ROM and the Internet at http://www.hbschool.com/elab

Doubling and Halving in Three Dimensions

When you double the amount of each ingredient in a cake recipe, you will have twice the volume of batter. Does that mean you must also double each dimension of the baking pan?

EXAMPLE 1 A recipe calls for a 10-in. × 5-in. × 3-in. baking pan. When you double the recipe, could you double just one dimension of the pan?

3 in.

10 in.   5 in.

Original Dimensions	Double the Length	Double the Width	Double the Height
$V = lwh$	$V = (2l)wh$	$V = l(2w)h$	$V = lw(2h)$
$= 10 \times 5 \times 3$	$= 20 \times 5 \times 3$	$= 10 \times 10 \times 3$	$= 10 \times 5 \times 6$
$= 150$	$= 300$	$= 300$	$= 300$

The original pan has a volume of 150 in.^{3} You can double the volume to 300 in.^{3} by doubling any one of the dimensions.

• How did the volume change when a dimension was halved?

EXAMPLE 2 Another recipe calls for a round pan with a 9-in. diameter and a 1.5-in. height. Does doubling the height of the pan have the same effect on the volume as doubling the radius?

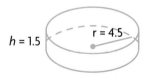

$h = 1.5$ $r = 4.5$

Original Dimensions	Double the Height	Double the Radius
$V = \pi r^2 h$	$V = \pi r^2(2h)$	$V = \pi(2r)^2 h$
$= \pi(4.5)^2(1.5)$	$= \pi(4.5)^2(3)$	$= \pi(9)^2(1.5)$
$= \pi(30.375)$	$= \pi(60.75)$	$= \pi(121.5)$
≈ 95.4	≈ 190.8	≈ 381.6

Doubling the height doubles the volume, but doubling the radius quadruples the volume.

• **CRITICAL THINKING** Explain why doubling the radius has a greater effect on the volume than doubling the height.

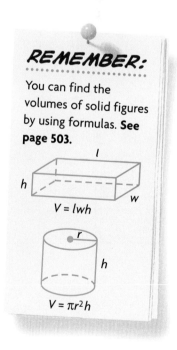

$V = lwh$

$V = \pi r^2 h$

523

Copy and complete the table to find the volume of the prism.

		Original	Double the Length	Double the Width	Double the Height
1.	Dimensions (in inches)	20 × 8 × 4	? × 8 × 4	20 × ? × 4	20 × 8 × ?
2.	Volume (in cubic inches)	?	?	?	?

ACTIVITY

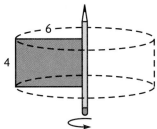

WHAT YOU'LL NEED: 4-in. × 6-in. index cards, scissors, tape, pencil

This activity will help you see the effects of halving the radius and the height of a cylinder.

- Tape the shorter edge of a 4-in. × 6-in. index card to a pencil as shown. Spin the pencil with your fingers so that the card traces a cylindrical figure. Use the formula $V = \pi r^2 h$ to find the volume of that cylinder in terms of π.

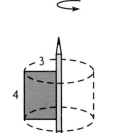

- Halve the radius by cutting the card in half. Spin the pencil again to see the solid. Then compute the new volume, again in terms of π.

- How does the volume of this new cylinder compare with the volume of the cylinder with the 4-in. height and 6-in. radius?

- What would the volume be, in terms of π, if you kept the original radius of 6 in. but halved the height so that it was 2 in.? How does this volume compare with the original volume?

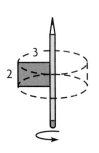

- This time, halve both the original radius and the original height so that the radius is 3 in. and the height is 2 in. Compute the volume in terms of π.

Talk About It

- What is the effect on the volume when you halve the height of a cylinder?

- What is the effect on the volume when you halve the radius of a cylinder?

- What is the effect on the volume when you halve the radius and the height of a cylinder?

INDEPENDENT PRACTICE

Find the volume of each figure. Then halve the height of each, and find the new volume. Use 3.14 for π.

1.
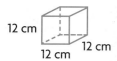
12 cm
12 cm
12 cm

2.

13 cm
r = 18 cm

3.

8 in.
6 in.

4.
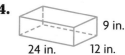
9 in.
24 in.
12 in.

Find the volume of each figure. Then double each dimension, and find the new volume. Use 3.14 for π.

5.
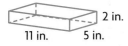
2 in.
11 in.
5 in.

6.

6 cm
6 cm
2 cm

7.

3 in.
9 in.

8.

18 in.
5 in.

Find the volume of each figure. Then halve each dimension, and find the new volume. Use 3.14 for π. Round answers to the nearest hundredth.

9.
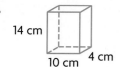
14 cm
10 cm
4 cm

10.
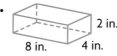
2 in.
8 in.
4 in.

11.

6 cm
3 cm

12.
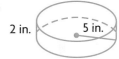
2 in.
5 in.

Problem-Solving Applications

13. A rectangular pan measures 13 in. × 9½ in. × 2 in. How does the volume change when you double the length and halve the depth?

14. A square pan has 8-in. sides and is 2 in. deep. How does the volume change when you halve the sides and double the depth?

15. Fine Foods is launching a new line of frozen gourmet foods. The original box, which contained 8 servings, was 8 in. × 2 in. × 2 in. The new package holds 1 serving and has the same shape as the original box. Find the dimensions of the new box.

16. ✏️ **WRITE ABOUT IT** The E-Z-Ship Packing Company offers several sizes of boxes. The smallest box is 8 in. × 10 in. × 12 in. and the largest box is 16 in. × 20 in. × 24 in. Is the volume of the largest box double, quadruple or 8 times the volume of the smallest box?

In *Mighty Math Cosmic Geometry* you can go to *Amazing Angles* to practice finding the volume of solid figures in which the dimensions have been doubled or halved.

CULTURAL CONNECTION

AUSTRALIAN WOOL

Australia is the world's leader in the production of wool. There are over 50,000 commercial wool growers. They own about 123 million sheep. Almost all of the wool produced in Australia is exported to other countries. The wool industry creates many jobs throughout the country and earns the Australian economy billions of dollars. One of the many jobs created is that of a sheep-shearer. A sheep-shearer removes the wool from a sheep with a tool called a shear. Many people who visit Australia watch sheep-shearing demonstrations.

Lyle is writing a report on Australia. He made a scale drawing of a pen that holds sheep. The drawing of the pen measures 12 in. $\times$ 8 in. It is too large for his paper so he decreases both dimensions by half. Find the area of the new drawing.

The original area is 96 in.^{2} Since both dimensions are decreased by half, the area is $\frac{1}{4}$ of 96 in.^{2}, or 24 in.^{2}

WORK TOGETHER

1. Suppose there is 116 yd of fencing available to make a pen to hold sheep before they are sheared. What are the dimensions of the rectangular pen that would hold the most sheep?

2. Lyle is making a model of the Australian desert as part of his report. He starts with a piece of plywood that is 18 in. $\times$ 18 in. What whole-number dimensions of the box will hold the maximum amount of sand?

3. In his report, Lyle included Ayers Rock, which is a large freestanding rock formation in central Australia. It is about 0.4 km high, 2 km long, and 1.5 km wide. What would the measurements be of a rock with half the volume of Ayers Rock?

4. Lyle read about a sheep farmer who patrolled the perimeter of his 225 mi^2 of land. What is the least amount of distance the farmer would have to patrol?

> ### CULTURAL LINK
>
> One of the most popular sports in Australia is Australian-rules football. The game was invented in Australia. It has rules similar to soccer, rugby, and American football. Thousands of fans fill large stadiums to cheer on their favorite teams. This sport is played mainly during the winter months.

EXAMPLES

EXERCISES

- **Relate the perimeter and area of a rectangle.**
  (pages 514–516)

For a rectangle with a perimeter of 16 in., you can have these areas:

$A = 4 \times 4 = 16$ ← greatest area
$A = 3 \times 5 = 15$
$A = 2 \times 6 = 12$
$A = 1 \times 7 = 7$

The area of a rectangle is given. Find the dimensions with the least perimeter.

1. 9 ft^2 **2.** 144 cm^2

The perimeter of a rectangle is given. Find the dimensions with the greatest possible area.

3. 8 in.   **4.** 20 yd
5. 32 ft   **6.** 44 m

- **Relate doubled or halved linear dimensions to change in the perimeter and area.**
  (pages 517–519)

Length	220	440	880
Width	100	100	100
Perimeter	640	1,080	1,960
Area	22,000	44,000	88,000

As the length doubles, the area doubles.

Double the dimensions and then find the perimeter and area of each figure.

7. ▭ 12 in.   **8.** ◹ 20 m / 12 m
      14 in.   16 m

Halve the dimensions and then find the perimeter and area of each figure.

9. ▭ 8 in.   **10.** ◹ 30 m / 18 m
      20 in.   24 m

- **Solve problems by using the strategy *make a model* to find the maximum volume.**
  (pages 520–521)

PROBLEM-SOLVING TIP: For help in solving problems by making a model, see pages 4 and 520.

11. Jack has an 8-in. × 8-in. sheet of origami paper. He wants to make an open box with whole-number dimensions and the maximum volume. What are the dimensions and volume of this box?

12. Lula has an 8-in. × 14-in. sheet of paper. She wants to make an open box with the maximum volume. Find the whole-number dimensions and volume.

- **Relate doubled or halved length, width, or height to changes in the volume of solid figures.** (pages 523–525)

The volume is 48 in.^{3}

If you double the height, the volume is 96 in.^{3}

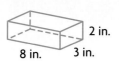
2 in. / 8 in. / 3 in.

Find the volume of each figure. Then double the height and find the new volume.

13. 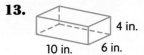 4 in. / 10 in. / 6 in.

14. 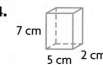 7 cm / 5 cm / 2 cm

15. A round pan has a 10-in. diameter and is 5 in. high. What is the volume if you double the diameter? Use 3.14 for π.

CHAPTER 28
INDIRECT MEASUREMENT

LOOK AHEAD

In this chapter you will solve problems that involve

- measuring with shadows and similar figures
- finding distances with the Pythagorean Property
- using trigonometric ratios

Westward Whoa!

The Overland Trail was an important route for settlers, but it was not always over land. With no bridges on the trail, settlers often had to cross dangerous rivers during their journey. You can use similar triangles to find the distances that wagons had to travel to cross rivers along the Overland Trail.

Plan
- Work with a small group. Set up pairs of similar triangles using the 30 yd × 50 yd reference triangle as one ratio. Calculate each crossing distance by solving the equivalent ratio.

Act
- Set up the similar triangles and equivalent ratios.
- Calculate the distance across each river.
- Draw a diagram that shows each river crossing.

Share
- Display your diagrams and discuss results.

	River Width	Measure along the bank of the river
Vermilion	n	83.3 yards
Platte	x	2,200 yards
Laramie	y	55.5 yards
Little Sandy	z	22.2 yards

DID YOU

☑ Use similar triangles and ratios?

☑ Find the river widths?

☑ Draw each river crossing?

☑ Display your diagrams?

Laramie Creek:

Far Bank (Fort Laramie and Beyond)

y ←— Laramie Creek —→

←— 50yd —→

←— 55.5yd —→ Reference Triangle 30yd

Near Bank

Equivalent Ratios $\dfrac{30}{50} = \dfrac{y}{55.5}$

Measuring with Shadows

WHAT YOU'LL LEARN

How to measure a height indirectly

WHY LEARN THIS?

To measure tall objects such as trees or buildings

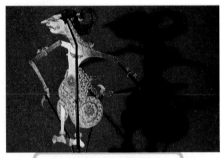

On most evenings in the island country of Indonesia, crowds of people, including many teenagers, gather in front of huge white screens to watch *wayang kulit*. But *wayang kulit* aren't movies, as you might think. They're dramatic shadow-puppet plays, which have been part of Indonesian culture for hundreds of years.

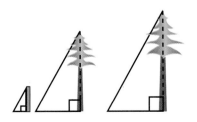

One of the simplest methods of indirect measurement uses similar triangles and shadows.

Suppose a 6-ft fence post casts an 8-ft shadow at the same time that a flagpole casts a 26-ft shadow. About how high is the flagpole?

The rays of the sun are parallel. So, the triangles formed by the post and pole and their shadows are similar. This means the corresponding sides are proportional.

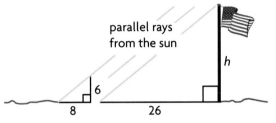

parallel rays from the sun

Let h represent the approximate height of the flagpole.

$$\frac{h}{6} = \frac{26}{8}$$ *Find the cross products.*

$$8h = 6 \times 26$$ *Solve the equation.*

$$8h = 156$$

$$h = 19\frac{1}{2}$$ ← The flagpole is about $19\frac{1}{2}$ ft high.

EXAMPLE Two trees cast shadows of 27 ft and 33 ft while a 4-ft post casts a shadow of 3 ft. What is the approximate difference in the heights of the trees?

The three similar triangles have corresponding sides that are proportional. Let s represent the height of the shorter tree and t represent that of the taller tree.

$$\frac{s}{4} = \frac{27}{3}$$ *Write the ratio in simplest form.* $$\frac{t}{4} = \frac{33}{3}$$

$$\frac{s}{4} = \frac{9}{1}$$ *Find the cross products.* $$\frac{t}{4} = \frac{11}{1}$$

$$1s = 4 \times 9$$ *Solve the equation.* $$1t = 4 \times 11$$

$$s = 36$$ $$t = 44$$

Since 44 ft − 36 ft = 8 ft, there is about an 8-ft difference in the heights of the trees.

• What if the shorter tree casts a 21-ft shadow? What would be the approximate difference in the heights of the trees?

A 5-ft tall person casts a 6-ft shadow. Find the approximate height of each object that casts the given shadow at about the same time.

1. 12 ft   **2.** 30 ft   **3.** 24 ft   **4.** 78 ft

A 6-ft-tall person casts a 4-ft shadow. Find the approximate height of each object that casts the given shadow at about the same time.

1. 28 ft   **2.** 32 ft   **3.** 18 ft   **4.** 92 ft   **5.** 136 ft

Problem-Solving Applications

6. At the Washington Monument, Mrs. Briggs asked her students to find the monument's height by measuring its shadow and their own shadow. Find the approximate height by using the similar triangles shown.

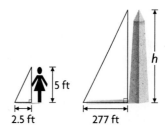

5 ft
h
2.5 ft   277 ft

7. At the Kennedy Space Center, the Saturn rocket casts a shadow of 181.5 ft and the Mercury rocket casts a shadow of 41.5 ft. A 3-ft sign casts a 1.5-ft shadow. What is the approximate height of each rocket?

8. Rynn is 1.5 m tall. On a sunny day, she casts a shadow of 1.2 m on her boat deck. Her mainsail casts a shadow of 15.2 m, and her secondary sail casts a shadow of 9 m. What is the approximate difference in the heights of the sails?

9. Louisa is 48 in. tall. Her father is 72 in. tall. Louisa's shadow is 32 in. long. About how long is her father's shadow?

10. ✏️ **WRITE ABOUT IT** Explain how you can measure the height of a tall object indirectly by using its shadow.

Mixed Review

Find the square root.

11. $\sqrt{9}$ **12.** $\sqrt{144}$ **13.** $\sqrt{196}$ **14.** $\sqrt{400}$ **15.** $\sqrt{0.64}$

The perimeter of a rectangle is given. Find the dimensions of the rectangle with the greatest possible area.

16. 20 ft   **17.** 36 yd   **18.** 60 mi   **19.** 100 in.   **20.** 440 m

21. **FRACTIONS** Of the 4,140 books in the middle school library, $\frac{5}{12}$ are fiction, $\frac{1}{4}$ are nonfiction, and $\frac{1}{3}$ are reference. How many of each type are there?

22. **ALGEBRA** Todd's and Carol's classes collected 348 cans of food. Carol's class collected 3 times as many as Todd's class. How many cans did each class collect?

ALGEBRA CONNECTION

The Pythagorean Property

WHAT YOU'LL LEARN
How the Pythagorean Property relates the sides of any right triangle to one another

WHY LEARN THIS?
To find unknown lengths when you cannot measure them directly

WORD POWER

leg
hypotenuse
Pythagorean
  Property

REMEMBER:

An isosceles right triangle has two congruent sides and a right angle. **See page H22.**

Right triangles have some very special relationships that other triangles do not have. The following activity will help you see a relationship among the lengths of the sides of right triangles.

Each of the two shorter sides of a right triangle is a **leg**. The longest side, opposite the right angle, is the **hypotenuse**.

ACTIVITY

WHAT YOU'LL NEED: crayons or markers, graph paper, and a ruler

• Copy the drawing of the isosceles right triangle and three squares, shown at the right.

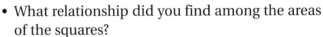

• Cut apart the two red squares of your drawing, and fit the pieces on top of the blue square.

• What relationship did you find among the areas of the squares?

• Try another isosceles right triangle. Is the relationship also true for it?

• Now make a graph-paper diagram like the one shown at the right.

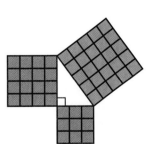

• What relationship is there between the areas of the red squares and the area of the blue square?

• Use graph paper to cut out three squares with sides that are 3 units, 4 units, and 6 units. Fit the squares together to form a triangle as shown at the right.

• 💡**CRITICAL THINKING** Is the same relationship between the areas of the red squares and the area of the blue square true for this triangle? Explain.

Your results in this activity show that in right triangles, a special relationship exists among the three sides. This relationship is called the **Pythagorean Property**.

PYTHAGOREAN PROPERTY

In any right triangle, the sum of the squares of the two legs is equal to the square of the hypotenuse.

$$a^2 + b^2 = c^2$$

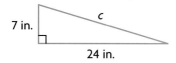

History Link

PYTHAGORAS PHILOSOPHE
Grec. Chap. 25.

EXAMPLE 1 A right triangle has legs measuring 7 in. and 24 in. What is the length of the hypotenuse?

You can use the Pythagorean Property.

$a^2 + b^2 = c^2$ *Write the property.*

$7^2 + 24^2 = c^2$ *Substitute 7 for a and 24 for b.*

$49 + 576 = c^2$ *Square the length of each leg.*

$625 = c^2$ *Since c^2 is 625, c is the square root of 625.*

$\sqrt{625} = c$ *Find the square root of 625.*

$25 = c$

So, the length of the hypotenuse of the right triangle is 25 in.

• What if the legs were 14 in. and 48 in.? What would be the length of the hypotenuse?

Pythagoras of Samos was the ancient Greek mathematician after whom the Pythagorean Property is named. He thought that everything in the universe could be explained by using counting numbers. He often represented number sequences as sets of objects arranged in geometric shapes. One such sequence is the triangular numbers 1, 3, 6, 10, 15, . . . What are the next two numbers in this sequence?

EXAMPLE 2 The hypotenuse of a right triangle is 17 cm long, and one leg is 8 cm long. How long is the other leg?

You can use a calculator and the Pythagorean Property to find the length of the other leg.

$a^2 + b^2 = c^2$ *Write the property.*

$8^2 + b^2 = 17^2$ *Substitute 8 for a and 17 for c.*

$b^2 = 17^2 - 8^2$

So, the other leg is 15 cm long.

• What if one leg is 24 cm and the hypotenuse is 51 cm? How long is the other leg?

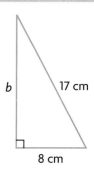

533

Find the unknown length.

1. ? 6 m 8 m

2. ? 5 m 12 m

3. 15 m 17 m ?

INDEPENDENT PRACTICE

Find the unknown length.

1. ? 3 m 4 m

2. 15 ft ? 20 ft

3. 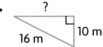 12 m ? 9 m

4. 20 ft 12 ft ?

Find the unknown length to the nearest tenth.

5. 4 m ? 4 m

6. ? 8 ft 10 ft

7. ? 16 m 10 m

8. 9 ft ? 7 ft

9. ? 12 ft 14 ft

10. ? 7 cm 4 cm

11. 18 ft ? 16 ft

12. 17 m ? 17 m

Problem-Solving Applications

13. Bill can cross the Wekiva River from point *C* to point *B*, a distance of 112 yd. What is the distance from point *A* to *B*?

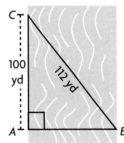

14. ✏️ **WRITE ABOUT IT** Suppose you know the lengths of two sides of a right triangle. Explain how to find the length of the third side.

Mixed Review

Find the value.

15. $1,000 \times 1,000$

16. $25,000 \times 25,000$

17. $\sqrt{40,000}$

18. $\sqrt{122,500}$

Halve the dimensions of each rectangle. Then, find the new perimeter and area.

19. 4 cm × 8 cm

20. 12 cm × 36 cm

21. 24 ft × 50 ft

22. $6\frac{1}{2}$ in. × $10\frac{1}{2}$ in.

23. **NUMBER SENSE** If *n* is an even number, is each expression odd or even?
  a. $n + 5$ **b.** $3n$ **c.** $3n + 1$

24. **MONEY** Alice has $3.20 in nickels and dimes. She has 4 more nickels than dimes. How many of each does she have?

MORE PRACTICE Lesson 28.2, page H84

ALGEBRA CONNECTION

Using the Pythagorean Property

The Pythagorean Property can be used to find distances without measuring them directly.

EXAMPLE 1 The direct air distance from Chicago to Denver is 920 mi. It is 580 mi from Chicago to Birmingham. How far is it from Denver to Birmingham?

Since the segments from Chicago to Denver and Chicago to Birmingham form a right angle, connect the three points to form a right triangle. Label the legs a and b and the hypotenuse c.

$$a^2 + b^2 = c^2 \quad \text{\textit{Write the Pythagorean Property.}}$$

$$920^2 + 580^2 = c^2 \quad \text{\textit{Substitute 920 for a and 580 for b.}}$$

$$846{,}400 + 336{,}400 = c^2 \quad \text{\textit{Square each leg.}}$$

$$1{,}182{,}800 = c^2 \quad \text{\textit{Since c^2 is 1,182,800, c is the square}}$$

$$\sqrt{1{,}182{,}800} = c \quad \text{\textit{root of 1,182,800.}}$$

$$1{,}090 \approx c \;\leftarrow\; \textbf{The distance is about 1,090 mi.}$$

EXAMPLE 2 Merritt is buying a board to use as a diagonal brace on a rectangular gate. The gate is 36 in. wide and 42 in. high. What should be the length of the board?

Since the diagonal brace is the hypotenuse of a right triangle, you can use the Pythagorean Property. Let c = the length of the board.

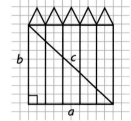

$$c^2 = a^2 + b^2 \quad \text{\textit{Write the property.}}$$
$$c^2 = 36^2 + 42^2 \quad \text{\textit{Substitute 36 for a}}$$
$$\text{\textit{and 42 for b.}}$$
$$c^2 = 1{,}296 + 1{,}764 \quad \text{\textit{Square each leg.}}$$
$$c^2 = 3{,}060 \quad \text{\textit{Since c^2 is 3,060, c is the square root of 3,060.}}$$
$$c = \sqrt{3{,}060}$$
$$c \approx 55.3 \;\leftarrow\; \textbf{The board should be about } 55\tfrac{1}{4} \textbf{ in. long.}$$

WHAT YOU'LL LEARN
How to solve problems by using the Pythagorean Property

WHY LEARN THIS?
To compute many unknown lengths, such as distances between cities on a map

Geography Link

Nevada is shaped like a rectangle in the north and like a triangle in the south. South Lake Tahoe is near the most western point where the rectangle and triangle meet. South Lake Tahoe is about 230 mi from the Oregon border and about 350 mi from the Utah border. About how far is South Lake Tahoe from the point where the borders of Nevada, Idaho, and Utah meet?

Find the unknown length.

1. 150 mi, c, 200 mi

2. c, 340 mi, 816 mi

3. 256 mi, c, 480 mi

4. 432 mi, 720 mi, b

Find the unknown length to the nearest tenth.

1. 175 mi, c, 115 mi

2. 42 m, 16 m, a

3. a, 425 km, 400 km

4. 2.5 mi, c, 4.0 mi

Solve. Round to the nearest tenth.

5. How far is the sailboat from the lighthouse?

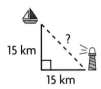

15 km, ?, 15 km

6. How high is the Ferris wheel?

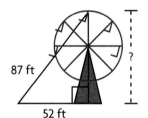

87 ft, ?, 52 ft

7. What is the distance across the lake?

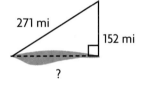

271 mi, 152 mi, ?

Problem-Solving Applications

8. The state of Colorado is basically rectangular in shape. Its greatest distance from east to west is 387 mi. Its greatest distance from north to south is 276 mi. Find the approximate distance between opposite corners of the state, to the nearest mile.

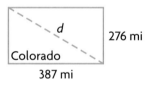

d, 276 mi, Colorado, 387 mi

9. If you drove 165 mi south from Cleveland and then 145 mi west, you would be in Cincinnati. Suppose a new highway is built, connecting them in a straight line. Find how long the highway would be, to the nearest tenth mile. Draw a picture, and then solve.

10. Jane walked 0.8 mi east on 42nd Street. John left from the same point as Jane. He walked 1.5 mi north on 7th Avenue. How far apart are they now? Draw a picture, and then solve.

11. ✏ **WRITE ABOUT IT** Use this map to write a problem of your own that can be solved with the Pythagorean Property. Exchange problems with a classmate. Solve.

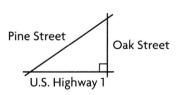

Pine Street, Oak Street, U.S. Highway 1

MORE PRACTICE Lesson 28.3, page H85

Trigonometric Ratios

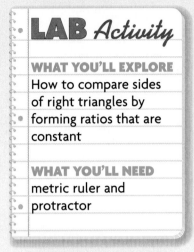

Y̶ou will measure the sides and angles of two right triangles.

Explore

- Measure the sides and angles of △ *ABC* and △ *RST*. Record your results in a table.

- Use your data for each triangle to write all possible ratios that compare the lengths of the sides. For example, in △ *ABC* one ratio is $\frac{AC}{BC} = \frac{27 \text{ mm}}{32 \text{ mm}}$.

- Use a calculator to change each ratio to decimal form. Record your results.

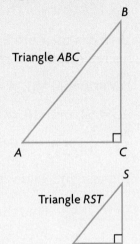

Triangle *ABC*

Triangle *RST*

LAB *Activity*

WHAT YOU'LL EXPLORE
How to compare sides of right triangles by forming ratios that are constant

WHAT YOU'LL NEED
metric ruler and protractor

WORD POWER
trigonometric ratio
trig ratio

Think and Discuss 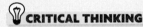 💡 CRITICAL THINKING

- Compare the ratios of △ *ABC* with those of △ *RST*. What conclusions can you draw?

- In △ *ABC*, look at ∠ *A*. Side *AC* is called the side adjacent to ∠ *A*, or next to it. Which side is opposite ∠ *A*? Which side is the hypotenuse?

Some special ratios, called **trigonometric ratios**, compare the lengths of the sides of a right triangle. These are called **trig ratios**.

$$\tan A \text{ (tangent of } \angle A) = \frac{\text{length of opposite side}}{\text{length of adjacent side}} = \frac{BC}{AC}$$

$$\sin A \text{ (sine of } \angle A) = \frac{\text{length of opposite side}}{\text{length of hypotenuse}} = \frac{BC}{AB}$$

$$\cos A \text{ (cosine of } \angle A) = \frac{\text{length of adjacent side}}{\text{length of hypotenuse}} = \frac{AC}{AB}$$

- Use △ *ABC* above to the right to write the trig ratios for ∠ *B*.
  HINT: The side opposite ∠ *B* is segment *AC*.

$$\tan B = \frac{?}{?} \qquad \sin B = \frac{?}{?} \qquad \cos B = \frac{?}{?}$$

Try This

- Draw a right triangle *PQR* with ∠ *R* as the right angle. Write the trig ratios for ∠ *P* and ∠ *Q*.

 Link ▶

E–Lab • Activity 28 Available on CD-ROM
and the Internet at http://www.hbschool.com/elab

ALGEBRA CONNECTION

Using Trigonometric Ratios

You can measure the angles and sides of $\triangle ABC$ and find decimal values for ratios of the sides.

For example, m$\angle A$ = 50°, BC = 64 mm,

AC = 54 mm, AB = 84 mm, and

$\frac{AC}{AB} = \frac{54}{84}$, or about 0.65.

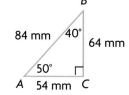

You can find values for the trig ratios of $\angle A$ and $\angle B$.

EXAMPLE 1   Find the cosine of 50°.

$\cos A = \frac{AC}{AB}$ *Write the trig ratio.*

$\cos 50° = \frac{54}{84}$ *Substitute 50° for A and $\frac{54}{84}$ for $\frac{AC}{AB}$.*

$\cos 50° \approx 0.64$ The cosine of 50° is $\frac{54}{84}$, or about 0.64.

Another way to find the values of trigonometric ratios is to use a scientific calculator.

EXAMPLE 2   Use a calculator to find tan 50°, sin 50°, and cos 50°.

50 [TAN] | 1.191753593 | *tan 50° ≈ 1.19*

50 [SIN] | 0.766044443 | *sin 50° ≈ 0.77*

50 [COS] | 0.64278761 | *cos 50° ≈ 0.64*

You can use the values of trig ratios to find heights that you cannot measure directly.

EXAMPLE 3   Find the unknown height of the tower, to the nearest meter. Let x represent the unknown height. You know that x is the length of the *side opposite the 60° angle.* You also know that 14 m is the length of the *side adjacent to the 60° angle.*
The tangent compares the opposite side to the adjacent side.

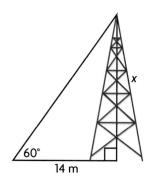

$\tan 60° = \frac{x}{14}$ *Write the trig ratio.*

$1.73 \approx \frac{x}{14}$ *Use a calculator to find the value of tan 60°.*

$14 \times 1.73 \approx x$ *Solve the equation.*

$24.22 \approx x \leftarrow$ The height of the tower is about 24 m.

 Calculator Activities, page H38

GUIDED PRACTICE

Find the trigonometric ratio to the nearest hundredth.

1. cos *A*
2. cos *B*
3. sin *A*
4. sin *B*
5. tan *A*
6. tan *B*

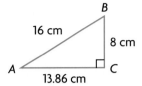

INDEPENDENT PRACTICE

Use a calculator or the table on page H88 to find the trigonometric ratio to the nearest hundredth.

1. cos 55°
2. tan 45°
3. tan 75°
4. sin 25°

Use trigonometric ratios to find the unknown length, *x*, to the nearest tenth.

5.
6.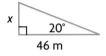
7.

8.
9.
10.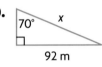

11.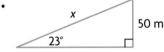
12.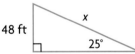

Problem-Solving Applications

13. A tree casts a shadow that is 40 ft long when the sun's rays make a 42° angle with the ground. Find the height of the tree, to the nearest foot.

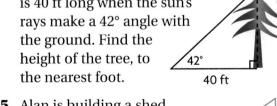

14. Sue is flying a kite. She has 120 ft of string. The string makes a 70° angle with the ground. To the nearest foot, how high from the ground is the kite?

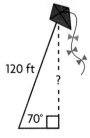

15. Alan is building a shed. He wants the pitch of the roof to be 36°. Find how high from the ground the roof will be, to the nearest foot.

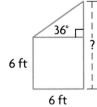

16. **WRITE ABOUT IT** If the length of each side of a right triangle is doubled, does tan *A* change? Explain.

MATH FUN!

MIRROR, MIRROR ON THE GROUND

PURPOSE To practice measuring with similar figures (pages 530–531)

YOU WILL NEED mirror, tape measure or yardstick

Place a mirror on a level spot near an object. Back up until you can see the top of the object in the mirror. The angles are equal because light reflects off a mirror at the same angle at which it hits. Now, apply

what you know about similar triangles to estimate the object's height.

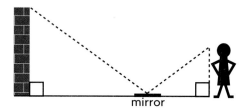

PROVE IT!

PURPOSE To practice using the Pythagorean Property (pages 532–534)

Bhaskara, an Indian mathematician who lived about 1200 A.D., wrote the shortest known proof of the Pythagorean Property. His proof was an unlabeled drawing like the one shown and one word: BEHOLD. The diagram represents c^2. Trace the diagram, cut it apart, and label the sides of each piece. Rearrange the pieces to prove that $a^2 + b^2 = c^2$.

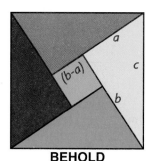

BEHOLD

ALL TIED UP IN KNOTS

PURPOSE To practice solving problems using the Pythagorean Property (pages 535–536)

YOU WILL NEED 16-ft. piece of string

In ancient Egypt, farmers marked off right-angled corners of their fields using long ropes tied with equally spaced knots. Tie a knot every foot in a piece of string. Use the Pythagorean Property to help you make a right triangle out of the string. A knot will be placed at every vertex. What is the

length of each side? These numbers are called a Pythagorean triple.

Challenge a member of your family to figure out how to form a right triangle out of the string.

EXAMPLES

EXERCISES

• **Measure heights indirectly with shadows.**
(pages 530–531)

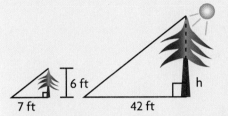

Find the height of the tree.

$$\frac{h}{6} = \frac{42}{7} \quad \textit{Find the cross products.}$$

$7h = 252$ *Solve.*

$h = 36 \leftarrow$ The tree is 36 ft tall.

A 4-m-tall object casts a 5-m shadow. Find the height of each object that casts the given shadow.

1. 35 m   **2.** 60 m

3. 24 m   **4.** 42 m

5. Ryan is 6 ft tall. He casts a shadow of 3 ft. The Vehicle Assembly Building casts a shadow of 276 ft. How tall is the Vehicle Assembly Building?

• **Use the Pythagorean Property to solve problems relating the sides of any right triangle to one another.** (pages 532–536)

Find the length of the hypotenuse of the right triangle.

$a^2 + b^2 = c^2$ *Write the Pythagorean Property.*

$6^2 + 8^2 = c^2$ *Substitute the known values.*

$36 + 64 = c^2$ *Square the length of each leg.*

$\sqrt{100} = c$ *Find the square root.*

$10 = c \leftarrow$ The length is 10 m.

6. VOCABULARY The longest side of a right triangle is the _?_ .

Find the unknown length to the nearest tenth.

7.   14 cm   ?   48 cm   **8.**   24 cm   ?   10 cm

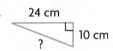

9.   ?   13 m   10 m   **10.**   ?   371 mi   1,272 mi

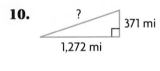

11.   65 mi   ?   65 mi   **12.**   526 mi   334 mi   ?

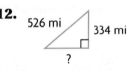

• **Use trigonometric ratios to solve problems.**
(pages 538–539)

Find the unknown length, x.

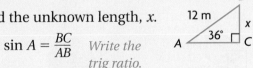

$\sin A = \frac{BC}{AB}$ *Write the trig ratio.*

$\sin 36° = \frac{x}{12}$ *Substitute the values.*

$0.59 \approx \frac{x}{12}$ *Find the value of sin 36°.*

$12 \times 0.59 \approx x$ *Solve.*

$7.08 \approx x \leftarrow$ The length is about 7.1 m.

13. VOCABULARY In a right triangle, the _?_ is the ratio of the length of the side opposite the angle to the length of the side adjacent to the angle.

Use trigonometric ratios to find the unknown length, x, to the nearest tenth.

14.   25°   x   32 m   **15.**   x   54°   10 ft

VOCABULARY CHECK

1. A figure made up of vertices and edges that shows how objects are connected is a __?__. (page 494)

2. The sum of the areas of all the surfaces of a solid is the __?__. (page 506)

3. In a right triangle, the longest side, opposite the right angle, is the __?__. (page 532)

EXAMPLES

- **Use networks to find all possible routes, the shortest route, and the number of connections.** (pages 494-496)

How many different direct connections are possible between 8 cities?

$e = \dfrac{v^2 - v}{2}$ *Write the formula.*

$e = \dfrac{8^2 - 8}{2}$ *Substitute 8 (cities) for v (vertices).*

$e = \dfrac{56}{2} = 28$ *Find e, the number of edges.*

So, there are 28 different direct connections.

EXERCISES

4. Starting at *A*, find the shortest round-trip route that includes each vertex.

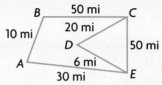

Find the number of different direct connections possible for the given number of locations.

5. 5 houses   6. 12 stores

7. 20 mailboxes   8. 15 offices

- **Find the volumes of solids.** (pages 503–505)

Cone:

$V = \dfrac{1}{3}\pi r^2 h$ $\leftarrow \pi = 3.14$

$V \approx \dfrac{1}{3} \times 3.14 \times 5^2 \times 8$

$V \approx 209.3333 \approx 200$ $\leftarrow$ 1 significant digit

So, the volume is about 200 in.^{3}

Find the volume. Use $\pi = 3.14$.

9. $V = Bh$ 10. $V = \pi r^2 h$

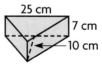   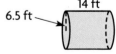

11. $V = lwh$ 12. $V = \dfrac{4}{3}\pi r^3$

- **Use the Pythagorean Property to solve problems relating the sides of any right triangle to one another.** (pages 532–536)

Find the length of the hypotenuse of the right triangle.

C ⎦ 8 m
15 m

$a^2 + b^2 = c^2$ *Write the Pythagorean Property.*

$8^2 + 15^2 = c^2$ *Replace a with 8 and b with 15.*

$64 + 225 = c^2$ *Square the length of each leg.*

$289 = c^2$

$\sqrt{289} = c^2$ *Find the square root.*

$17 = c$ ←The length is 17 m.

Find the unknown length to the nearest tenth.

13.
12 m   ?   16 m

14.
24 in.   18 in.   ?

15.
28 cm   ?   21 cm

16.
?   60 ft   80 ft

17.
?   90 cm   72 cm

18.
75 cm   ?   45 cm

- **Use trigonometric ratios to solve problems.**
(pages 538–539)

Find the unknown length x.

$\tan A = \dfrac{BC}{AC}$ *Write the trig ratio.*

$\tan 42° = \dfrac{x}{15}$ *Substitute the values.*

$0.90 \approx \dfrac{x}{15}$ *Use the trigonometric ratio table to find the value of tan 42°.*

$15 \times 0.90 \approx x$ *Solve.*

$13.5 \approx x$ ←The length is about 13.5 in.

Use trigonometric ratios to find the unknown length, x, to the nearest tenth.

19.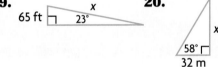
65 ft   23° x

20.
x 58°   32 m

21.
18 mi   38° x

22.
48 cm   71° x

PROBLEM SOLVING

Solve. Explain your method.

23. A square piece of grazing land, 150 ft on each side, has a circular water hole with a diameter of 60 ft in the center. How much land is available for grazing?
(pages 501–502)

24. A 12-ft pole casts a 16-ft shadow at the same time a tree casts a 48-ft shadow. How tall is the tree? (pages 530–531)

✏ Write About It

1. Find the surface area of the soda can. Explain your method. (pages 506–509)

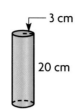

3 cm

20 cm

2. I have 24 square tables that I want to arrange. Draw an arrangement that would give the least perimeter using all 24 tables. (pages 514–516)

3. Find the unknown length. Explain your method. (pages 535–536)

9 cm

?

12 cm

✔ Performance Assessment

Choose a strategy and solve. Explain your method.

Problem-Solving Strategies
- Find a Pattern
- Write an Equation
- Make a Table
- Make a Model
- Act it Out
- Draw a Diagram

4. A groundskeeper wants to determine how much grass seed to buy for a new city park. The rectangular park is 700 yd by 500 yd, and it has three circular ponds that are each 20 yd in diameter. What is the land area of the park? (pages 501–502)

5. DeJuan has a 20-in. × 30-in. piece of poster board. He wants to construct an open box with the maximum volume. Find the whole-number dimensions and volume of the box. (pages 520–521)

6. A basketball court is 94 ft long and 50 ft wide. To the nearest foot, what is the distance from one corner to the opposite corner? (pages 535–536)

Solve the problem. Then write the letter of the correct answer.

1. Which pair of ratios forms a proportion? (pages 44–46)

A. $\frac{3}{8}, \frac{9}{32}$ **B.** $\frac{14}{20}, \frac{70}{80}$

C. $\frac{28}{63}, \frac{4}{9}$ **D.** $\frac{8}{88}, \frac{3}{36}$

2. Solve the inequality. $^-3x \geq 18$ (pages 144–147)

A. $x \geq {}^-6$ **B.** $x \leq {}^-6$
C. $x \geq 6$ **D.** $x \leq 6$

3. Find the 8th term of the geometric sequence. 3, 12, 48, 192, . . . (pages 217–219)

A. 284   **B.** 768
C. 12,288   **D.** 49,152

4. Of the $240.00 Shane earned last week, $28.80 was withheld for tax. What percent of Shane's earnings was withheld? (pages 289–291)

A. 8%   **B.** 12%
C. 15%   **D.** 18%

5. Find the mode of the data in the table. (pages 322–324)

17	35	24	6	21	14	17	10

A. 17   **B.** 18
C. 21   **D.** 24

6. Find the difference. (pages 484–485)
$(5y^3 - 2y^2 + 4y - 1) - (3y^3 - 2y^2 - 10)$

A. $8y^3 + 4y^2 + 4y + 11$
B. $2y^3 - 4y^2 + 4y - 9$
C. $2y^3 - 4y - 9$
D. $2y^3 + 4y + 9$

7. $\triangle QRS$ is similar to $\triangle XYZ$. QS corresponds to XZ and is 8 cm in length. What is the length of RS? (pages 389–390)

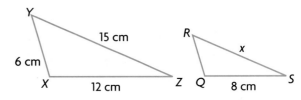

A. 4 cm   **B.** 10 cm
C. 16 cm   **D.** 30 cm

8. Find the volume to 1 significant digit. Use the formula $V = \frac{4}{3}\pi r^3$. Use $\pi = 3.14$. (pages 503–505)

A. 500 ft^3
B. 700 ft^3
C. 900 ft^3
D. $1{,}100 \text{ ft}^3$

9. A rectangular prism is 12 in. long, 10 in. wide, and 4 in. high. How does the volume change when you double the length and width and halve the height? (pages 523–525)

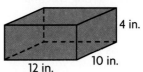

A. halves   **B.** doubles
C. quadruples   **D.** remains same

10. Use the Pythagorean Property, $a^2 + b^2 = c^2$. Find the length of the hypotenuse. (pages 535–536)

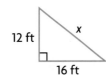

A. 8 ft
B. 20 ft
C. 25 ft
D. 28 ft

STUDENT HANDBOOK

1 PRIME AND COMPOSITE NUMBERS

A **prime number** has exactly two factors, 1 and the number itself.

A **composite number** has more than two factors.

Primes
↓

2	Factors are 1 and 2.
11	Factors are 1 and 11.
23	Factors are 1 and 23.
47	Factors are 1 and 47.

Composites
↓

4	Factors are 1, 2, and 4.
12	Factors are 1, 2, 3, 4, 6, and 12.
25	Factors are 1, 5, and 25.
63	Factors are 1, 3, 7, 9, and 63.

Examples   Determine whether the number is prime or composite.

A. 17

factors
1, 17 → prime

B. 16

factors
1, 2, 4, 16 → composite

C. 51

factors
1, 3, 17, 51 → composite

PRACTICE   Write *P* or *C* to tell whether the number is prime or composite.

1. 5   **2.** 14   **3.** 18   **4.** 2   **5.** 23   **6.** 27

7. 13   **8.** 39   **9.** 72   **10.** 49   **11.** 9   **12.** 89

2 DIVISIBILITY RULES

A number is divisible by another number when the division results in a remainder of 0. You can determine divisibility by some numbers with divisibility rules.

A number is divisible by		Divisible	Not Divisible
2	if the last digit is an even number.	11,994	2,175
3	if the sum of the digits is divisible by 3.	216	79
4	if the last two digits form a number divisible by 4.	1,024	621
5	if the last digit is 0 or 5.	15,195	10,007
6	if the number is divisible by 2 and 3.	1,332	44
9	if the sum of the digits is divisible by 9.	144	33
10	if the last digit is 0.	2,790	9,325

PRACTICE   Determine whether each number is divisible by 2, 3, 4, 5, 6, 9, or 10.

1. 56   **2.** 200   **3.** 75   **4.** 324   **5.** 42   **6.** 812

7. 784   **8.** 501   **9.** 2,345   **10.** 555,555   **11.** 3,009   **12.** 2,001

3 FACTORS AND MULTIPLES

When two numbers are multiplied to form a third, the two numbers are said to be **factors** of the third number. **Multiples** of a number can be found by multiplying the number by 1, 2, 3, 4, and so on.

Examples

A. List all the factors of 48.

$$1 \times 48 = 48$$
$$2 \times 24 = 48$$
$$3 \times 16 = 48$$
$$4 \times 12 = 48$$
$$6 \times 8 \ = 48$$

So, the factors of 48 are 1, 2, 3, 4, 6, 8, 12, 16, 24, and 48.

B. Find the first five multiples of 3.

$$3 \times 1 = 3$$
$$3 \times 2 = 6$$
$$3 \times 3 = 9$$
$$3 \times 4 = 12$$
$$3 \times 5 = 15$$

So, the first five multiples of 3 are 3, 6, 9, 12, and 15.

PRACTICE   List all the factors of the number.

1. 8   **2.** 20   **3.** 9   **4.** 51   **5.** 16   **6.** 27

Write the first five multiples of the number.

7. 9   **8.** 10   **9.** 20   **10.** 15   **11.** 7   **12.** 18

4 PRIME FACTORIZATION

A composite number can be expressed as a product of prime numbers. This is the **prime factorization** of the number. To find the prime factorization of a number, you can use a factor tree.

Example   Find the prime factorization of 24 by using a factor tree.

24	24	24
2×12	3×8	4×6
$2 \times 3 \times 4$	$3 \times 2 \times 4$	$2 \times 2 \times 2 \times 3$
$2 \times 3 \times 2 \times 2$	$3 \times 2 \times 2 \times 2$	
all primes	all primes	all primes

The prime factorization of 24 is $2 \times 2 \times 2 \times 3$, or $2^3 \times 3$.

PRACTICE   Find the prime factorization by using a factor tree.

1. 25   **2.** 16   **3.** 56   **4.** 18   **5.** 72   **6.** 40

5 GREATEST COMMON FACTOR

The **greatest common factor** (*GCF*) of two whole numbers is the greatest factor the numbers have in common.

Example Find the *GCF* of 24 and 32.

Method 1	**Method 2**
List all the factors for both numbers. *Find all the common factors.*	*Find the prime factorizations.* *Then find the common prime factors.*
24: 1, 2, 3, 4, 6, 8, 12, 24 32: 1, 2, 4, 8, 16, 32	24: 2 × 2 × 2 × 3 32: 2 × 2 × 2 × 2 × 2
The common factors are 1, 2, 4, and 8.	The common prime factors are 2, 2, and 2. The product of these is the *GCF*.
So, the *GCF* is 8.	So, the *GCF* is 2 × 2 × 2 = 8.

PRACTICE Find the *GCF* of each pair of numbers by either method.

1. 9, 15 **2.** 25, 75 **3.** 18, 30 **4.** 4, 10 **5.** 12, 17 **6.** 30, 96

7. 54, 72 **8.** 15, 20 **9.** 40, 60 **10.** 40, 50 **11.** 14, 21 **12.** 14, 28

6 LEAST COMMON MULTIPLE

The **least common multiple** (*LCM*) of two numbers is the smallest common multiple the numbers share.

Example Find the least common multiple of 8 and 10.

Method 1
List multiples of both numbers.

 8: 8, 16, 24, 32, 40, 48, 56, 64, 72, 80
10: 10, 20, 30, 40, 50, 60, 70, 80, 90

The smallest common multiple is 40.

So, the *LCM* is 40.

Method 2
Find the prime factorizations.

 8: 2 × 2 × 2
10: 2 × 5

The *LCM* is found by finding a product of factors.

2 × 2 × 2 × 5 = 40.   So, the *LCM* is 40.

PRACTICE Find the *LCM* of each pair of numbers by either method.

1. 2, 4 **2.** 3, 15 **3.** 10, 25 **4.** 10, 15 **5.** 3, 7 **6.** 18, 27

7. 12, 21 **8.** 9, 21 **9.** 24, 30 **10.** 9, 18 **11.** 16, 24 **12.** 8, 36

7 PLACE VALUE

A place-value chart can help you read and write numbers. The number 345,012,678,912.5784 (three hundred forty-five billion, twelve million, six hundred seventy-eight thousand, nine hundred twelve and five thousand seven hundred eighty-four ten-thousandths) is shown.

Billions	Millions	Thousands	Ones	Tenths	Hundredths	Thousandths	Ten-Thousandths
345,	012,	678,	912 .	5	7	8	4

Example   Name the place value of the digit.

A. the 7 in the thousands period
    7 → *ten-thousands place*

B. the 0 in the millions period
    0 → *hundred-millions place*

C. the 5 in the billions period
    5 → *one billion, or billions place*

D. all digits to the right of the decimal point
    5 → *tenths*, 7 → *hundredths*,
    8 → *thousandths*, 4 → *ten-thousandths*

PRACTICE   Name the place value of the underlined digit.

1. 123,456,789,123.0594

2. 123,456,789,123.0594

3. 123,456,789,123.0594

4. 123,456,789,123.0594

5. 123,456,789,123.0594

6. 123,456,789,123.0594

8 RULES FOR ROUNDING

To round to a certain place, follow these steps.

1. Locate the digit in that place, and consider the next digit to the right.

2. If the digit to the right is 5 or greater, round up. If the digit to the right is 4 or less, round down.

3. Change each digit to the right of the rounding place to zero.

Examples

A. Round 125,439.378 to the nearest thousand.
Locate digit.
    ↓
125,439.378
    ↑
The digit to the right is less than 5, so the digit in the rounding location stays the same.
    ↓
125,000 ← *Each digit to the right becomes zero.*

B. Round 125,439.378 to the nearest tenth.
Locate digit.
        ↓
125,439.378
        ↑
The digit to the right is greater than 5, so the digit in the rounding location increases by 1.
        ↓
125,439.400 ← *Each digit to the right*
125,439.4   *becomes zero.*

PRACTICE   Round 259,345.278 to the place indicated.

1. hundred thousand

2. ten thousand

3. thousand

4. hundred

9 COMPATIBLE NUMBERS

Compatible numbers divide without a remainder, are close to the actual numbers, and are easy to compute mentally. Use compatible numbers to estimate quotients.

Examples

A. Use compatible numbers to estimate the quotient. $6,134 \div 35$.

$6,134 \div 35$
$6,000 \div 30 = 200 \leftarrow$ *estimate*
$\uparrow \qquad \uparrow$
compatible numbers

B. Use compatible numbers to estimate the quotient. $647 \div 7$.

$647 \div 7$
$630 \div 7 = 90 \leftarrow$ *estimate*
$\uparrow \quad \uparrow$
compatible numbers

PRACTICE Estimate the quotient by using compatible numbers.

1. $345 \div 5$ **2.** $5,474 \div 23$ **3.** $46,170 \div 18$ **4.** $749 \div 7$ **5.** $861 \div 41$

6. $1,225 \div 2$ **7.** $968 \div 47$ **8.** $3,456 \div 432$ **9.** $5,765 \div 26$ **10.** $25,012 \div 64$

10 ADDING AND SUBTRACTING DECIMALS

When adding and subtracting decimals, you must remember to line up the decimal points vertically. You may add zeros to the right of the decimal point as place holders. Adding zeros to the right of the last digit after the decimal point doesn't change the value of the number.

Examples

A. Find the sum. $3.54 + 1.7 + 22 + 13.409$

$$
\begin{array}{r}
3.540 \\
1.700 \\
22.000 \\
+\ 13.409 \\
\hline
40.649
\end{array}
$$

B. Find the difference. $636.2 - 28.538$

$$
\begin{array}{r}
636.200 \\
-28.538 \\
\hline
607.662
\end{array}
$$

PRACTICE Find the sum or difference.

1. $0.687 + 0.9 + 27.25$ **2.** $87.34 - 6.8$ **3.** $65 + 0.0004 + 2.57$

4. $17 - 0.095$ **5.** $263.7 - 102.08$ **6.** $27 + 3.24 + 0.256 + 0.3689$

7. $24 - 0.0008$ **8.** $379.2 - 268.7$ **9.** $689.2 - 163.7$

10. $3.9 + 2.79 + 0.0005$ **11.** $46 + 10.8 + 6.73$ **12.** $96.674 - 78.51$

11 MULTIPLYING AND DIVIDING DECIMALS BY POWERS OF 10

Notice the pattern below.

$0.24 \times 10 = 2.4$ $10 = 10^1$
$0.24 \times 100 = 24$ $100 = 10^2$
$0.24 \times 1{,}000 = 240$ $1{,}000 = 10^3$
$0.24 \times 10{,}000 = 2{,}400$ $10{,}000 = 10^4$

*Think: When multiplying decimals by powers of 10, move the decimal point one place to the **right** for each power of 10, or for each zero.*

Notice the pattern below.

$0.24 \div 10 = 0.024$
$0.24 \div 100 = 0.0024$
$0.24 \div 1{,}000 = 0.00024$
$0.24 \div 10{,}000 = 0.000024$

*Think: When dividing decimals by powers of 10, move the decimal point one place to the **left** for each power of 10, or for each zero.*

PRACTICE   Find the product or quotient.

1. 10×9.26
2. 0.642×100
3. $10^3 \times 84.2$
4. 0.44×10^4
5. $69.7 \times 1{,}000$

6. $11.32 \div 10$
7. $1.276 \div 1{,}000$
8. $536.5 \div 10^2$
9. $5.92 \div 10^3$
10. $25 \div 10{,}000$

11. 6.78×10^5
12. $3.05 \div 10^3$
13. 78.12×10^4
14. 6.519×10^2
15. $3.7 \div 10^5$

12 MULTIPLYING DECIMALS

When multiplying decimals, multiply as you would with whole numbers. The sum of the number of decimal places in the factors equals the number of decimal places in the product.

Examples   Find the product.

A. 81.2×6.547

```
      6.547  ← 3 decimal places
   ×  81.2   ← 1 decimal place
    13094
    65470
 + 5237600
   531.6164  ← 4 decimal places
```

B. 0.376×0.12

```
      0.376  ← 3 decimal places
   ×  0.12   ← 2 decimal places
       752
 +    3760
   0.04512  ← 5 decimal places
```

PRACTICE   Find the product.

1. 6.8×3.4
2. 2.56×4.6
3. 6.787×7.6
4. 0.98×4.6
5. 0.97×0.76

6. 0.5×3.761
7. 42×17.654
8. 7.005×32.1
9. 9.76×16.254
10. 296.5×2.4

11. 7.7×6.5
12. 8.92×2.8
13. 6.001×27.4
14. 0.87×3.2
15. 0.03×0.204

16. 98.6×4.9
17. 0.002×8.1
18. 3.65×4.2
19. 0.004×8.6
20. 0.982×1.63

13 DIVIDING DECIMALS

When dividing with decimals, set up the division as you would with whole numbers. Pay attention to the decimal places, as shown below.

Examples

A. Find the quotient. $89.6 \div 16$

Place decimal point.
↓

$$
\begin{array}{r}
5.6 \\
16\overline{)89.6} \\
-80 \\
\hline
96 \\
-96 \\
\hline
0
\end{array}
$$

B. Find the quotient. $3.4 \div 4$

Place decimal point.
↓

$$
\begin{array}{r}
0.85 \\
4\overline{)3.40} \quad \leftarrow \textit{Insert zeros if necessary.} \\
-32 \\
\hline
20 \\
-20 \\
\hline
0
\end{array}
$$

PRACTICE Find the quotient.

1. $242.76 \div 68$ **2.** $40.5 \div 18$ **3.** $121.03 \div 98$ **4.** $3.6 \div 4$ **5.** $1.58 \div 5$

6. $0.2835 \div 2.7$ **7.** $8.1 \div 0.09$ **8.** $0.42 \div 0.28$ **9.** $15.12 \div 0.063$ **10.** $480.48 \div 7.7$

14 WRITING DECIMALS AS FRACTIONS

Using place value, you can write decimals as fractions.

Examples

A. Write 0.35 as a fraction in simplest form.

The last digit is in the hundredths place.
↓

$$0.35 = \frac{35}{100} = \frac{7}{20} \leftarrow \textit{simplest form}$$
↑

The denominator is the same as the place value of the last digit.

B. Write 0.018 as a fraction in simplest form.

The last digit is in the thousandths place.
↓

$$0.018 = \frac{18}{1,000} = \frac{9}{500} \leftarrow \textit{simplest form}$$
↑

The denominator is the same as the place value of the last digit.

PRACTICE Write as a fraction in simplest form.

1. 0.5   **2.** 0.09   **3.** 0.10   **4.** 0.15   **5.** 0.25   **6.** 0.025

7. 0.8   **8.** 0.04   **9.** 0.01   **10.** 0.046   **11.** 0.75   **12.** 0.87

13. 0.02   **14.** 0.98   **15.** 0.07   **16.** 0.62   **17.** 0.037   **18.** 0.095

15 WAYS TO SHOW MULTIPLICATION

Multiplication can be shown in several ways.

7×8 $7 \cdot 8$ $7(8)$ $(7)(8)$

When a variable is used in an expression with multiplication, the multiplication sign is usually omitted. An expression such as $5 \times n$ is written as $5n$.

PRACTICE   Write the expression in two other ways.

1. 4×8 **2.** 9×10 **3.** 3×15 **4.** 2×11 **5.** $(9)(2)(5)$

6. $3 \times b$ **7.** $7 \cdot n$ **8.** $5(k)$ **9.** $2 \times a \times b$ **10.** $4(c)$

11. $7 \cdot y$ **12.** $(3)(b)(f)$ **13.** $6 \cdot k$ **14.** $5(c)(d)$ **15.** $(a)(d)$

16 TERMINATING AND REPEATING DECIMALS

You can change a fraction to a decimal by dividing the numerator by the denominator. When the division produces a remainder of zero, the resulting decimal is said to be **terminating**. When the remainder repeats over and over, the resulting decimal is said to be **repeating**.

Example   Write $\frac{4}{5}$ and $\frac{2}{3}$ as decimals. Are the decimals terminating or repeating?

$$\frac{4}{5} = 4 \div 5 \quad \begin{array}{r} 0.8 \\ 5\overline{)4.0} \\ -4\,0 \\ \hline 0 \end{array} \rightarrow \frac{4}{5} = 0.8$$

$$\frac{2}{3} = 2 \div 3 \quad \begin{array}{r} .666 \\ 3\overline{)2.000} \\ -18 \\ \hline 20 \end{array} \rightarrow \frac{2}{3} = 0.666\ldots$$

→ This pattern will repeat.

The number 0.8 is a terminating decimal.

The number 0.666... is a repeating decimal. It can also be written as $0.\overline{6}$. The bar is placed over the digit or digits that repeat.

PRACTICE   Write as a decimal. Is the decimal terminating or repeating? Write *T* or *R*.

1. $\frac{1}{5}$ **2.** $\frac{1}{3}$ **3.** $\frac{3}{11}$ **4.** $\frac{3}{8}$ **5.** $\frac{7}{9}$ **6.** $\frac{7}{15}$

7. $\frac{3}{4}$ **8.** $\frac{5}{6}$ **9.** $\frac{4}{11}$ **10.** $\frac{5}{10}$ **11.** $\frac{1}{9}$ **12.** $\frac{11}{12}$

13. $\frac{5}{9}$ **14.** $\frac{8}{11}$ **15.** $\frac{7}{8}$ **16.** $\frac{23}{25}$ **17.** $\frac{3}{20}$ **18.** $\frac{3}{11}$

19. $\frac{5}{8}$ **20.** $\frac{7}{12}$ **21.** $\frac{199}{200}$ **22.** $\frac{7}{16}$ **23.** $\frac{47}{50}$ **24.** $\frac{7}{45}$

17 EXPONENTS

Exponents are used to represent repeated multiplication of the same number.

Examples

A. Write $7 \times 7 \times 7 \times 7 \times 7$ by using an exponent.

$$7 \times 7 \times 7 \times 7 \times 7 = 7^5 \leftarrow exponent$$

$\uparrow$ factors $\qquad \uparrow$ base

The exponent equals the number of times the base is used as a factor.

B. Find the values of 3^6, 3^0, and 3^1.

$$3^6 = 3 \times 3 \times 3 \times 3 \times 3 \times 3 = 729$$

Any number (except zero) $n^0 = 1$, and any number $n^1 = n$.

$$3^0 = 1 \qquad 3^1 = 3$$

PRACTICE Write by using an exponent.

1. $4 \times 4 \times 4 \times 4 \times 4$ **2.** $2 \times 2 \times 2 \times 2 \times 2 \times 2$ **3.** $8 \times 8 \times 8$ **4.** $14 \times 14 \times 14 \times 14$

Find the value.

5. 2^6 **6.** 4^3 **7.** 3^4 **8.** 5^3 **9.** 248^0 **10.** 15^1

18 SQUARES AND SQUARE ROOTS

To find the square of a number, multiply the number by itself. The square root of a number is one of the two identical factors of the number. The symbol for n squared is n^2. The symbol for the positive square root of n is $\sqrt{n}$.

Examples

Find the square.

A. 5

$$5^2 = 5 \times 5 = 25$$

B. 2.7

$$2.7^2 = 2.7 \times 2.7 = 7.29$$

Find the square root .

A. 25

Since $5 \times 5 = 25$, $\sqrt{25} = 5$.

NOTE: Although $^-5 \times {}^-5 = 25$, $\sqrt{n}$ stands for the positive square root of n. Therefore, $\sqrt{25} \neq {}^-5$.

B. $\sqrt{7.29}$

Since $2.7 \times 2.7 = 7.29$, $\sqrt{7.29} = 2.7$.

PRACTICE Find the square or square root. Use a calculator if necessary.

1. 7^2 **2.** 10^2 **3.** 9^2 **4.** 15^2 **5.** 3.9^2 **6.** 6.25^2

7. $\sqrt{49}$ **8.** $\sqrt{100}$ **9.** $\sqrt{81}$ **10.** $\sqrt{225}$ **11.** $\sqrt{15.21}$ **12.** $\sqrt{39.0625}$

19 ORDER OF OPERATIONS ON A CALCULATOR

Scientific calculators use an algebraic operating system (AOS), which automatically follows the order of operations. A calculator without AOS will operate from left to right.

Example   Determine if your calculator uses an AOS. Use your calculator to find the value of $6 + 8 \div 2$.

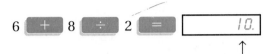

result for calculator with an AOS

result for calculator without an AOS

If your calculator does not have an AOS, you can follow the order of operations using the memory keys as shown below.

6 **M+** 8 **÷** 2 **M+** **MRC** $\boxed{10.}$

PRACTICE   Use a calculator to find the value.

1. $45 - 15 \div 3$ **2.** $51 + 48 \div 8$ **3.** $10 \div 2 + 8 \times 2$ **4.** $4 \times 12 - 4 + 8 \div 2$

5. $3^2 - 10 \div 2 + 4 \times 2$ **6.** $4 \div 2 + 8 \times 2^3 - 4$ **7.** $3 + 7 \times 5 - 1$ **8.** $30 + 22 \div 11 - 7 - 3^2$

20 PROPERTIES

The following are basic properties of addition and multiplication.

ADDITION

Commutative: $a + b = b + a$

Associative: $(a + b) + c = a + (b + c)$

Identity Property of Zero:
$a + 0 = a$ and $0 + a = a$

MULTIPLICATION

Commutative: $a \times b = b \times a$

Associative: $(a \times b) \times c = a \times (b \times c)$

Identity Property of One:
$a \times 1 = a$ and $1 \times a = a$

Property of Zero: $a \times 0 = 0$ and $0 \times a = 0$

Distributive: $a \times (b + c) = a \times b + a \times c$

PRACTICE   Name the property shown.

1. $4 + 0 = 4$ **2.** $(6 + 3) + 1 = 6 + (3 + 1)$ **3.** $7 \times 51 = 51 \times 7$

4. $5 \times 456 = 456 \times 5$ **5.** $17 \times (1 + 3) = 17 \times 1 + 17 \times 3$ **6.** $1 \times 5 = 5$

7. $(8 \times 2) \times 5 = 8 \times (2 \times 5)$ **8.** $72 + 1{,}234 = 1{,}234 + 72$ **9.** $0 \times 12 = 0$

10. $15.7 \times 1.3 = 1.3 \times 15.7$ **11.** $8.2 + (9.3 + 7) = (8.2 + 9.3) + 7$ **12.** $85.98 \times 0 \times 6.3$

21 EQUIVALENT FRACTIONS

Equivalent fractions are fractions that name the same amount.

Examples

A. Write two equivalent fractions for $\frac{15}{30}$.

Method 1 *Multiply both numerator and the denominator by a whole number.*

$$\frac{15 \times 2}{30 \times 2} = \frac{30}{60}$$

Method 2 *Divide by a common factor of the numerator and denominator.*

$$\frac{15 \div 5}{30 \div 5} = \frac{1}{2}$$

The fractions $\frac{30}{60}$ and $\frac{1}{2}$ are equivalent to $\frac{15}{30}$.

B. Are $\frac{4}{6}$ and $\frac{12}{18}$ equivalent?

Method 1 *Write the fractions in simplest form and compare.*

$$\frac{4 \div 2}{6 \div 2} = \frac{2}{3} \qquad \frac{12 \div 6}{18 \div 6} = \frac{2}{3}$$

The fractions are equivalent.

Method 2 *Cross multiply and compare.*

$4 \times 18 = 72 \quad \frac{4}{6} \diagup\diagdown = \diagdown\diagup \frac{12}{18} \quad 6 \times 12 = 72$

The fractions are equivalent since the cross products both equal 72.

PRACTICE Tell whether the fractions are equivalent. Write *yes* or *no*. Then, write two equivalent fractions for each.

1. $\frac{15}{30}, \frac{1}{2}$
2. $\frac{3}{18}, \frac{1}{3}$
3. $\frac{3}{4}, \frac{9}{12}$
4. $\frac{1}{2}, \frac{5}{10}$
5. $\frac{4}{16}, \frac{12}{18}$
6. $\frac{12}{21}, \frac{4}{7}$

22 SIMPLEST FORM OF FRACTIONS

A fraction is in **simplest form** when the numerator and denominator have no common factor other than 1.

Example Find the simplest form of $\frac{32}{40}$.

Method 1

Divide the numerator and denominator by common factors until the only common factor is 1.

$$\frac{32 \div 2}{40 \div 2} = \frac{16}{20} \qquad \frac{16 \div 4}{20 \div 4} = \frac{4}{5}$$

The simplest form of $\frac{32}{40}$ is $\frac{4}{5}$.

Method 2

Find the GCF of 32 and 40. Divide both the numerator and the denominator by the GCF.

$$\frac{32 \div 8}{40 \div 8} = \frac{4}{5} \leftarrow \text{GCF: 8}$$

The simplest form of $\frac{32}{40}$ is $\frac{4}{5}$.

PRACTICE Write in simplest form.

1. $\frac{20}{24}$
2. $\frac{4}{12}$
3. $\frac{14}{49}$
4. $\frac{60}{72}$
5. $\frac{40}{75}$
6. $\frac{12}{12}$

7. $\frac{35}{50}$
8. $\frac{32}{48}$
9. $\frac{3}{81}$
10. $\frac{56}{72}$
11. $\frac{12}{144}$
12. $\frac{50}{225}$

23 MIXED NUMBERS AND FRACTIONS

Mixed numbers can be written as fractions greater than 1, and fractions greater than 1 can be written as mixed numbers.

Examples

A. Write $\frac{23}{5}$ as a mixed number.

$$\frac{23}{5} \rightarrow \text{\textit{Divide the numerator}}$$
$$\text{\textit{by the denominator.}}$$

$$\begin{array}{r} 4 \\ 5\overline{)23} \\ -20 \\ \hline 3 \end{array} \rightarrow 4\frac{3}{5} \leftarrow \text{\textit{Write the remainder}}$$
$$\text{\textit{as the numerator}}$$
$$\text{\textit{of a fraction.}}$$

B. Write $6\frac{2}{7}$ as a fraction.

Multiply the denominator by the whole number.   *Add the product to the numerator.*

$$\downarrow \qquad\qquad \downarrow$$
$$6\frac{2}{7} \rightarrow 7 \times 6 = 42 \rightarrow 42 + 2 = 44$$

Write the sum over $\rightarrow \frac{44}{7}$
the denominator.

PRACTICE Write each mixed number as a fraction. Write each fraction as a mixed number.

1. $\frac{22}{5}$ **2.** $9\frac{1}{7}$ **3.** $\frac{41}{8}$ **4.** $5\frac{7}{9}$ **5.** $\frac{7}{3}$ **6.** $4\frac{9}{11}$

7. $\frac{47}{16}$ **8.** $3\frac{3}{8}$ **9.** $\frac{31}{9}$ **10.** $8\frac{2}{3}$ **11.** $\frac{33}{5}$ **12.** $12\frac{1}{9}$

24 BENCHMARK FRACTIONS AND DECIMALS

Some fractions and decimals are common. You can mentally convert between their fraction and decimal forms.

$$\frac{1}{2} = 0.5 \qquad \frac{1}{4} = 0.25 \qquad \frac{3}{4} = 0.75 \qquad \frac{1}{5} = 0.2 \qquad \frac{2}{5} = 0.4 \qquad \frac{3}{5} = 0.6 \qquad \frac{4}{5} = 0.8$$

Examples

A. Write $4\frac{1}{2}$ as a decimal.

Since $\frac{1}{2} = 0.5$, add 0.5 to 4. ·

$$4 + 0.5 = 4.5$$

B. Write 3.25 as a mixed number.

Since $0.25 = \frac{1}{4}$, add $\frac{1}{4}$ to 3.

$$3 + \frac{1}{4} = 3\frac{1}{4}$$

PRACTICE Write the mixed number as a decimal.

1. $4\frac{1}{4}$ **2.** $3\frac{3}{5}$ **3.** $7\frac{3}{4}$ **4.** $9\frac{1}{5}$

Write the decimal as a mixed number.

5. 1.8   **6.** 5.5   **7.** 2.4   **8.** 6.75

25 WRITING FRACTIONS AS DECIMALS

Two methods of changing fractions to decimals are shown below.

Examples

Method 1

If the denominator is a factor of 10 or 100, multiply to make the denominator 10 or 100.

A. $\dfrac{3}{5} \times \dfrac{2}{2} = \dfrac{6}{10} = 0.6$

B. $\dfrac{43}{50} \times \dfrac{2}{2} = \dfrac{86}{100} = 0.86$

C. $\dfrac{12}{25} \times \dfrac{4}{4} = \dfrac{48}{100} = 0.48$

Method 2

If the denominator is not a factor of 10 or 100, divide the numerator by the denominator.

A. $\dfrac{5}{8} = 5 \div 8 = 0.625$

B. $\dfrac{6}{11} = 6 \div 11 = 0.\overline{54}$

NOTE: Method 2 will work for any fraction.

PRACTICE Write each fraction as a decimal.

1. $\dfrac{1}{4}$ **2.** $\dfrac{1}{8}$ **3.** $\dfrac{17}{50}$ **4.** $\dfrac{7}{20}$ **5.** $\dfrac{2}{9}$ **6.** $\dfrac{4}{11}$

26 ADDING AND SUBTRACTING FRACTIONS

When you add or subtract fractions, the fractions must have the same denominator.

Examples

A. $\dfrac{1}{12} + \dfrac{3}{8}$

B. $\dfrac{3}{4} - \dfrac{1}{12}$

STEP 1 *Use the LCD to rename the fractions.*

$$\begin{array}{l} \dfrac{1}{12} \quad = \dfrac{1 \times 2}{12 \times 2} \quad = \dfrac{2}{24} \\[2mm] +\dfrac{3}{8} \quad = \dfrac{3 \times 3}{8 \times 3} \quad = \dfrac{9}{24} \end{array} \leftarrow \text{LCD: 24}$$

STEP 1 *Use the LCD to rename the fractions.*

$$\begin{array}{l} \dfrac{3}{4} \quad = \dfrac{3 \times 3}{4 \times 3} \quad = \dfrac{9}{12} \\[2mm] -\dfrac{1}{12} \quad = \dfrac{1 \times 1}{12 \times 1} \quad = \dfrac{1}{12} \end{array} \leftarrow \text{LCD: 12}$$

STEP 2 *Add. Write in simplest form.*

$$\dfrac{2}{24} + \dfrac{9}{24} = \dfrac{11}{24}$$

STEP 2 *Subtract. Write in simplest form.*

$$\dfrac{9}{12} - \dfrac{1}{12} = \dfrac{8}{12} = \dfrac{8 \div 4}{12 \div 4} = \dfrac{2}{3}$$

PRACTICE Add or subtract. Write the answer in simplest form.

1. $\dfrac{3}{4} + \dfrac{1}{6}$ **2.** $\dfrac{5}{6} + \dfrac{2}{3}$ **3.** $\dfrac{1}{2} + \dfrac{2}{5}$ **4.** $\dfrac{7}{9} - \dfrac{1}{3}$ **5.** $\dfrac{2}{3} - \dfrac{2}{5}$ **6.** $\dfrac{7}{8} - \dfrac{5}{6}$

7. $\dfrac{3}{4} + \dfrac{5}{9}$ **8.** $\dfrac{7}{8} + \dfrac{3}{5}$ **9.** $\dfrac{6}{7} + \dfrac{1}{8}$ **10.** $\dfrac{8}{9} - \dfrac{1}{2}$ **11.** $\dfrac{5}{8} - \dfrac{1}{3}$ **12.** $\dfrac{2}{3} - \dfrac{4}{7}$

27 MULTIPLYING FRACTIONS

When multiplying fractions, multiply numerator by numerator and denominator by denominator. Simplify the product if possible.

Examples

A. $\dfrac{5}{6} \times \dfrac{2}{3}$

$\dfrac{5}{6} \times \dfrac{2}{3} = \dfrac{5 \times 2}{6 \times 3}$ ← *Multiply.*

$\qquad = \dfrac{10}{18}$ ← *Write in simplest form.*

$\qquad = \dfrac{5}{9}$

B. $4\dfrac{2}{3} \times 2\dfrac{1}{4}$

Write as fractions.
$\qquad\downarrow\qquad\downarrow$

$4\dfrac{2}{3} \times 2\dfrac{1}{4} = \dfrac{14}{3} \times \dfrac{9}{4} = \dfrac{14 \times 9}{3 \times 4}$ ← *Multiply.*

$\qquad = \dfrac{126}{12}$ ← *Write in simplest form.*

$\qquad = \dfrac{21}{2}$, or $10\dfrac{1}{2}$

PRACTICE Multiply. Write the product in simplest form.

1. $\dfrac{4}{9} \times \dfrac{7}{12}$ **2.** $\dfrac{1}{6} \times \dfrac{2}{3}$ **3.** $\dfrac{3}{8} \times \dfrac{4}{7}$ **4.** $6\dfrac{1}{4} \times 5\dfrac{3}{5}$ **5.** $3\dfrac{1}{3} \times 2\dfrac{1}{7}$ **6.** $4\dfrac{2}{5} \times 10$

7. $\dfrac{4}{5} \times \dfrac{7}{8}$ **8.** $\dfrac{1}{5} \times \dfrac{3}{4}$ **9.** $1\dfrac{4}{5} \times 3\dfrac{1}{4}$ **10.** $1\dfrac{1}{2} \times 2\dfrac{1}{4}$ **11.** $\dfrac{7}{8} \times 4\dfrac{2}{3}$ **12.** $1\dfrac{2}{3} \times 5\dfrac{1}{2}$

28 DIVIDING FRACTIONS

Two numbers whose product is 1 are called reciprocals: $\dfrac{3}{2} \times \dfrac{2}{3} = \dfrac{6}{6} = 1$. When dividing fractions, use the reciprocal of the divisor to write a multiplication problem.

Examples

A. $\dfrac{5}{6} \div \dfrac{2}{3}$

$\dfrac{5}{6} \div \dfrac{2}{3} = \dfrac{5}{6} \times \dfrac{3}{2}$ ← *Use reciprocal of divisor.*

$\qquad = \dfrac{5 \times 3}{6 \times 2} = \dfrac{15}{12}$ ← *Multiply.*

$\qquad = \dfrac{5}{4}$, or $1\dfrac{1}{4}$ ← *Write in simplest form.*

B. $4\dfrac{2}{3} \div 2\dfrac{1}{4}$

Write as fractions.
$\qquad\downarrow\qquad\downarrow$

$4\dfrac{2}{3} \div 2\dfrac{1}{4} = \dfrac{14}{3} \div \dfrac{9}{4}$

$\qquad = \dfrac{14}{3} \times \dfrac{4}{9}$ ← *Use reciprocal of divisor.*

$\qquad = \dfrac{56}{27}$, or $2\dfrac{2}{27}$

PRACTICE Divide. Write the quotient in simplest form.

1. $\dfrac{3}{4} \div \dfrac{1}{3}$ **2.** $\dfrac{1}{10} \div \dfrac{5}{6}$ **3.** $\dfrac{2}{5} \div \dfrac{1}{6}$ **4.** $1\dfrac{1}{6} \div 5\dfrac{1}{4}$ **5.** $4\dfrac{2}{4} \div 2\dfrac{2}{6}$ **6.** $5\dfrac{2}{3} \div 12$

7. $\dfrac{3}{4} \div \dfrac{1}{5}$ **8.** $\dfrac{7}{9} \div \dfrac{2}{7}$ **9.** $9\dfrac{1}{4} \div \dfrac{1}{8}$ **10.** $4\dfrac{5}{6} \div 5\dfrac{2}{3}$ **11.** $12\dfrac{3}{4} \div 3$ **12.** $4 \div \dfrac{2}{9}$

29 EQUIVALENT RATIOS

You can find an **equivalent ratio** by multiplying or dividing the ratio by a common factor.

Examples

A. Find two equivalent ratios for 5:15.

Multiply.   *Divide.*

$$\frac{5}{15} = \frac{5 \times 2}{15 \times 2} = \frac{10}{30} \qquad \frac{5}{15} = \frac{5 \div 5}{15 \div 5} = \frac{1}{3}$$

$$\frac{5}{15} = \frac{10}{30} = \frac{1}{3}, \text{ or } 5:15 = 10:30 = 1:3$$

B. Tell whether the ratios $\frac{27}{63}$ and $\frac{9}{21}$ are equivalent.

$$\frac{27}{63} = \frac{27 \div 9}{63 \div 9} = \frac{3}{7} \qquad \frac{9}{21} = \frac{9 \div 3}{21 \div 3} = \frac{3}{7}$$

$\frac{27}{63}$ is equivalent to $\frac{9}{21}$ since both equal $\frac{3}{7}$.

PRACTICE   Find two equivalent ratios for the given ratio.

1. 2:3   **2.** 6:11   **3.** 12:16   **4.** 6 to 8   **5.** 7 to 14   **6.** 10 to 12

Tell whether the ratios are equivalent. Write *yes* or *no*.

7. $\frac{2}{1}; \frac{8}{4}$ **8.** $\frac{2}{5}; \frac{6}{12}$ **9.** $\frac{2}{6}; \frac{7}{21}$ **10.** $\frac{8}{10}; \frac{16}{25}$ **11.** $\frac{20}{45}; \frac{12}{27}$ **12.** $\frac{18}{48}; \frac{12}{32}$

30 PROPORTIONS

A **proportion** is an equation that shows that two ratios are equal. Two ratios are equal if they can be simplified to the same ratio or if their cross products are equal.

Examples   Determine whether the ratios form a proportion.

Method 1
Write the ratios in simplest form.

Ratios: $\frac{6}{8}, \frac{9}{12}$

$$\frac{6}{8} = \frac{6 \div 2}{8 \div 2} = \frac{3}{4} \qquad \frac{9}{12} = \frac{9 \div 3}{12 \div 3} = \frac{3}{4}$$

Since both ratios equal $\frac{3}{4}$, they form a proportion.

Method 2
Find the cross products.

Ratios: $\frac{4}{6}, \frac{5}{10}$

$$\frac{4}{6} \stackrel{?}{=} \frac{5}{10}$$

$$4 \times 10 \neq 6 \times 5$$

$$40 \neq 30 \qquad \frac{4}{6} \neq \frac{5}{10} \text{ The ratios do not form a proportion.}$$

PRACTICE   Tell whether the ratios form a proportion. Write *yes* or *no*.

1. 5:6, 11:18   **2.** 8:6, 4:5   **3.** 9:4, 27:12   **4.** 4:10, 2:5   **5.** 6:9, 10:15

6. 15:8, 30:15   **7.** 5:8, 15:32   **8.** 18:4, 9:2   **9.** 22:4, 44:12   **10.** 18:6, 6:3

31 SOLVING A PROPORTION

To solve a proportion, write the cross products and solve
the resulting equation.

Example Solve $\frac{6}{8} = \frac{n}{12}$.

STEP 1 *Write the cross products.*

$$\frac{6}{8} = \frac{n}{12}$$

$$6 \times 12 = 8 \times n$$

$$72 = 8n$$

STEP 2 *Solve the equation.*

$$72 = 8n$$

$$\frac{72}{8} = \frac{8n}{8}$$

$$9 = n$$

So, $\frac{6}{8} = \frac{9}{12}$.

PRACTICE Solve the proportion.

1. $\frac{9}{15} = \frac{a}{10}$ **2.** $\frac{3}{9} = \frac{b}{21}$ **3.** $\frac{t}{12} = \frac{12}{9}$ **4.** $\frac{20}{15} = \frac{16}{x}$ **5.** $\frac{12}{d} = \frac{4}{14}$ **6.** $\frac{a}{6} = \frac{2}{3}$

7. $\frac{7}{6} = \frac{c}{12}$ **8.** $\frac{1}{10} = \frac{19}{a}$ **9.** $\frac{m}{5} = \frac{42}{35}$ **10.** $\frac{4}{5} = \frac{y}{1.25}$ **11.** $\frac{b}{10} = \frac{27}{90}$ **12.** $\frac{4}{1} = \frac{0.56}{d}$

32 REPRESENTING PERCENT

Percent means "per hundred." Percents can be represented on
a 10×10 grid.

Examples

A. Represent 75% on the grid.

Shade 75 squares to represent 75 out of 100,
or 75%.

B. Represent 9% on the grid.

Shade 9 squares to represent 9 out of 100
or 9%.

PRACTICE Represent each percent on a 10×10 grid.

1. 12%   **2.** 92%   **3.** 24%   **4.** 47%   **5.** 76%   **6.** 39%

7. 50%   **8.** 66%   **9.** 83%   **10.** 19%   **11.** 7%   **12.** 0.5%

13. 98%   **14.** 26%   **15.** 67%   **16.** 1.5%   **17.** 12.5%   **18.** 8.5%

33 WRITING DECIMALS AS PERCENTS

Percent means "per hundred." For example, 27% is 27 per hundred or $\frac{27}{100}$.

Examples Write 0.27, 0.78, and 0.05 as percents.

$$0.27 = \frac{27}{100} = 27\% \qquad 0.78 = \frac{78}{100} = 78\% \qquad 0.05 = \frac{5}{100} = 5\%$$
$$\downarrow \qquad\qquad\qquad \downarrow \qquad\qquad\qquad \downarrow$$
$$0.27 = 27\% \qquad\qquad 0.78 = 78\% \qquad\qquad 0.05 = 5\%$$

Think: To change a decimal to a percent, move the decimal point two places to the right and add the percent symbol. This will work for any decimal number.

Examples Write 1.25, 0.056, and 0.4 as percents.

$$1.25 = 125\% \qquad\qquad 0.056 = 5.6\% \qquad\qquad 0.40 = 40\%$$

PRACTICE Write each decimal as a percent.

1. 0.37 **2.** 0.21 **3.** 0.03 **4.** 0.7 **5.** 2.44 **6.** 1.45

7. 0.245 **8.** 0.507 **9.** 0.8 **10.** 0.75 **11.** 0.007 **12.** 9.456

34 CHANGING FRACTIONS TO PERCENTS

You can write fractions as percents by first writing them as equivalent decimals and then writing the equivalent decimals as percents.

Examples

A. Write $\frac{1}{4}$ as a percent.

STEP 1 *Write $\frac{1}{4}$ as a decimal.*

$$\frac{1}{4} = \frac{1 \times 25}{4 \times 25} = \frac{25}{100} = 0.25$$

STEP 2 *Write 0.25 as a percent.*

$$0.25 = 25\%$$

$$\frac{1}{4} = 25\%$$

B. Write $2\frac{1}{3}$ as a percent.

STEP 1 *Write $2\frac{1}{3}$ as a decimal.*

$$2\frac{1}{3} = \frac{7}{3} = 7 \div 3 = 2.\overline{3}$$

STEP 2 *Write $2.\overline{3}$ as a percent.*

$$2.\overline{3} = 233.\overline{3}\%, \text{ or } 233\tfrac{1}{3}\%$$

$$2\frac{1}{3} = 233.\overline{3}\%, \text{ or } 233\tfrac{1}{3}\%$$

PRACTICE Write each fraction or mixed number as a percent.

1. $\frac{3}{4}$ **2.** $\frac{7}{20}$ **3.** $\frac{3}{10}$ **4.** $\frac{5}{8}$ **5.** $\frac{2}{3}$ **6.** $\frac{7}{11}$

7. $\frac{5}{6}$ **8.** $\frac{5}{9}$ **9.** $\frac{1}{2}$ **10.** $3\frac{1}{4}$ **11.** $5\frac{3}{4}$ **12.** $4\frac{5}{11}$

35 WRITING PERCENTS AS FRACTIONS AND DECIMALS

Recall that percent means "per hundred."

Examples

A. Write 75%, 0.06%, and 125% as fractions. Write the fractions in simplest form.

$$75\% = \frac{75}{100} = \frac{75 \div 25}{100 \div 25} = \frac{3}{4}$$

$$0.06\% = \frac{0.06}{100} = \frac{0.06 \times 100}{100 \times 100} = \frac{6}{10,000}$$

$$= \frac{6 \div 2}{10,000 \div 2} = \frac{3}{5,000}$$

$$125\% = \frac{125}{100} = \frac{125 \div 25}{100 \div 25} = \frac{5}{4} = 1\frac{1}{4}$$

B. Write 75%, 0.06%, and 125% as decimals. Look for a pattern.

$$75\% = \frac{75}{100} = 75 \div 100 = 0.75$$

$$0.06\% = \frac{0.06}{100} = 0.06 \div 100 = 0.0006$$

$$125\% = \frac{125}{100} = 125 \div 100 = 1.25$$

Think: To change a percent to a decimal, move the decimal point two places to the left.

PRACTICE Write each percent as a fraction and decimal. Write fractions in simplest form.

1. 36% **2.** 79% **3.** 136% **4.** 159% **5.** 0.07% **6.** 0.18%

7. 89% **8.** 175% **9.** 1% **10.** 650% **11.** 193% **12.** 0.5%

36 PERCENT OF A NUMBER

You can find the percent of a number by multiplying the number by the fraction or decimal equivalent of the percent.

Example What is 30% of 75?

Method 1

STEP 1 *Write the percent as a fraction.*

$$30\% = \frac{30}{100} = \frac{3}{10}$$

STEP 2 *Multiply by the fraction.*

$$\frac{3}{10} \times 75 = \frac{225}{10} = 22\frac{1}{2}$$

So, 30% of 75 = $22\frac{1}{2}$.

Method 2

STEP 1 *Write the percent as a decimal.*

$$30\% = 0.30 = 0.3$$

STEP 2 *Multiply by the decimal.*

$$0.3 \times 75 = 22.5$$

So, 30% of 75 = 22.5.

PRACTICE Find the percent of the number by either method.

1. 30% of 60 **2.** 50% of 40 **3.** 40% of 100 **4.** 25% of 44 **5.** 12% of 65

6. 10% of 94 **7.** 85% of 70 **8.** 98% of 40 **9.** 5% of 250 **10.** 6% of 890

37 IDENTIFYING POINTS, PLANES, LINES, RAYS, AND SEGMENTS

Definition	Example	Symbol/Read
A **point** is an exact location.	• *A*	none/point *A*
A **plane** is a set of points extending forever in all directions on the same surface.	*P*	none/plane *P*
A **ray** has one endpoint and extends forever in one direction.	*X* *Y*	$\overrightarrow{XY}$/ray *XY*
A **line** is a set of points in a straight path extending forever in two directions.	*X* *Y*	$\overleftrightarrow{XY}$/line *XY*
A **line segment** is part of a line or ray and consists of two endpoints and all points between those endpoints.	*X* *Y*	$\overline{XY}$/line segment *XY*

PRACTICE

1. Name four points.

2. Name a plane.

3. Name five rays.

4. Name four line segments.

5. Name a line.

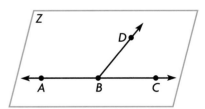

38 TYPES OF ANGLES

A circle is divided into 360 sections, each one of which is a degree. The degree is also the unit of measure for angles.

∠*COD* is **acute** since it measures between 0° and 90°.

∠*AOE* is **obtuse** since it measures between 90° and 180°.

∠*AOD* is **straight** since its measure is 180°.

∠*AOB* is **right** since its measure is 90°.

∠*BOC* and ∠*COD* are **complementary** since their measures sum to 90°.

∠*AOE* and ∠*EOD* are **supplementary** since their measures sum to 180°.

PRACTICE Tell if the angle is *acute, obtuse, straight,* or *right*.

1. ∠*YOZ* **2.** ∠*ZOV* **3.** ∠*WOZ* **4.** ∠*XOY*

Tell if the pair of angles are *complementary* or *supplementary*.

5. ∠*WOX* and ∠*XOY* **6.** ∠*WOV* and ∠*VOZ*

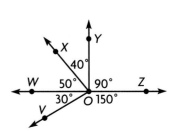

39 MEASURING ANGLES

You can use a protractor to measure angles. To measure an angle, place the base of the protractor on one of the rays of the angle and center it on the vertex. Look at the protractor scale that has zero on the first ray. Read the scale where the second ray crosses it. Extend the rays if necessary.

Examples

A. Measure $\angle ABC$.

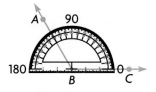

The measure of $\angle ABC$, or m$\angle ABC = 120°$.

B. Measure $\angle XYZ$.

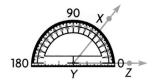

The measure of $\angle XYZ$, or m$\angle XYZ = 50°$.

PRACTICE Measure each of the following angles by using a protractor.

1.   **2.** **3.**   **4.**   **5.** **6.**

40 PERPENDICULAR AND PARALLEL LINES

Two lines in the same plane that do not intersect are **parallel**. Two lines in the same plane that intersect and form four right angles are **perpendicular**.

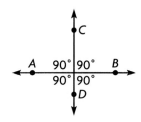

$\overleftrightarrow{AB}$ is perpendicular to $\overleftrightarrow{CD}$, or $\overleftrightarrow{AB} \perp \overleftrightarrow{CD}$.

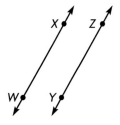

$\overleftrightarrow{WX}$ is parallel to $\overleftrightarrow{YZ}$, or $\overleftrightarrow{WX} \parallel \overleftrightarrow{YZ}$.

PRACTICE

1. Trace $\overleftrightarrow{AB}$. Draw $\overleftrightarrow{AB} \perp \overleftrightarrow{CD}$.

2. Trace $\overleftrightarrow{AB}$. Draw $\overleftrightarrow{AB} \parallel \overleftrightarrow{CD}$.

Tell if the lines are *parallel*, *perpendicular*, or *neither*.

3.   **4.**  **5.**   **6.**

41 TYPES OF POLYGONS

A **polygon** is a closed plane figure with at least three sides. Polygons are classified by number of sides and angles.

triangle	quadrilateral	pentagon	hexagon	octagon
3 sides, 3 angles	4 sides, 4 angles	5 sides, 5 angles	6 sides, 6 angles	8 sides, 8 angles

parallelogram	rectangle	rhombus	square	trapezoid
opposite sides parallel and congruent	parallelogram with 4 right angles	parallelogram with 4 congruent sides	rectangle with 4 congruent sides	quadrilateral with exactly 2 parallel sides

PRACTICE Name the polygon.

1.   2.  3.   4.   5.

42 TYPES OF TRIANGLES

Triangles are classified by the lengths of their sides and the measures of their angles.

acute triangle	obtuse triangle	right triangle
70° 60° 50°	30° 40° 110°	50° 90° 40°
all angles < 90°	one angle > 90°	one angle = 90°

scalene triangle	equilateral triangle	isosceles triangle
6 m 5 m 7 m	4 cm 4 cm 4 cm	8 ft 8 ft 5 ft
All sides have different lengths.	All sides have the same length.	Two sides have the same length.

PRACTICE Classify the triangles by using the given information.

1. 7 m 7 m 7 m 2. 50° 40° 90° 3. 65° 60° 55° 4. 5 ft 4 ft 5 ft 5. 6 m 4 m 5.5 m 6. 95° 50° 35°

43 TYPES OF SOLID FIGURES

Five basic types of solid figures are shown below.

rectangular prism	square pyramid	cylinder	cone	sphere
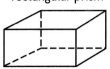				
The base is a rectangle.	The base is a square.	The base is a circle.	The base is a circle.	

PRACTICE Name the figure.

1.   2.   3.   4.   5.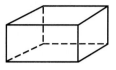

44 TRANSFORMATIONS

Three types of transformations are shown below.

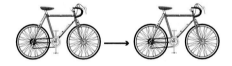   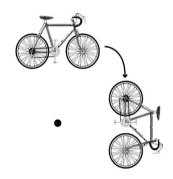

A **translation** occurs when a figure slides along a straight line.

A **reflection** occurs when a figure is flipped over a line.

A **rotation** occurs when a figure is turned around a point.

PRACTICE Identify the transformation as a *translation, reflection,* or *rotation.*

1.   2.   3.

4.   5.   6.

45 CONSTRUCTING LINE SEGMENTS AND ANGLES

Example 1 Construct a segment congruent to $\overline{CD}$.

STEP 1	STEP 2	STEP 3

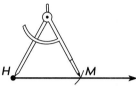

Draw a ray that is longer than $\overline{CD}$. Label the endpoint H.

Place the compass point on point C. Open the compass to the length of $\overline{CD}$.

Use the same opening. Put the compass point on H. Draw an arc that intersects the ray. Label the intersection point M.

$\overline{HM} \cong \overline{CD}$ NOTE: $\cong$ means "is congruent to."

Example 2 Construct an angle congruent to $\angle ABC$.

STEP 1	STEP 2	STEP 3

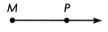

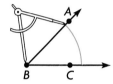

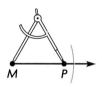

Draw $\overrightarrow{MP}$.

Draw an arc that intersects both rays of $\angle ABC$.

Use the same compass opening to draw an arc through $\overrightarrow{MP}$.

STEP 4	STEP 5	STEP 6

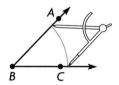

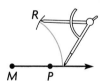

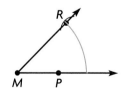

Use the compass to measure the arc in $\angle ABC$.

Use the same compass opening. Place the compass point on $\overrightarrow{MP}$ as shown, and draw an arc to locate point R.

Draw $\overrightarrow{MR}$.

$\angle PMR \cong \angle ABC$

PRACTICE Trace the figure. Construct a figure congruent to the given figure.

1.
R ●━━━━━● S

2.

3.

4.

46 PERIMETER AND CIRCUMFERENCE

The distance around a polygon is called **perimeter**. The distance around a circle is called **circumference**.

Examples

A. Find the perimeter.

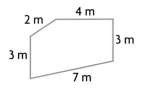

$P = a + b + c + d + e$
$P = 3 + 2 + 4 + 3 + 7$
$P = 19 \leftarrow 19$ m

B. Find the circumference. Use 3.14 for π.

$C = \pi d$
$C = 3.14 \times 10$
$C = 31.4 \leftarrow 31.4$ ft

C. Find the circumference. Use 3.14 for π.

$C = 2\pi r$
$C = 2 \times 3.14 \times 3$
$C = 18.84 \leftarrow 18.84$ m

PRACTICE   Find the perimeter or circumference. Use 3.14 for π.

1.
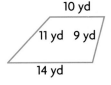

2.
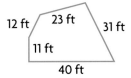

3.

4.

47 AREA AND VOLUME

Area is the number of square units needed to cover a given surface.
Volume is the number of cubic units needed to occupy a given space.

Examples

A. Find the area of the rectangle.

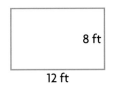

$A = lw$
$A = 8 \times 6$
$A = 48 \leftarrow 48$ ft^2

B. Find the volume of the rectangular prism.

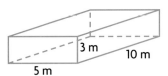

$V = lwh$
$V = 5 \times 10 \times 3$
$A = 150 \leftarrow 150$ m^3

PRACTICE   Find the area or volume.

1.
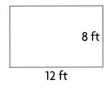

2.
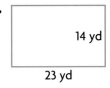

3.
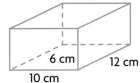

4.

48 PRECISION AND GREATEST POSSIBLE ERROR

When you measure something, the smaller the unit of measurement, the greater the **precision** of the measurement. The **greatest possible error** of any measurement is $\frac{1}{2}$, or 0.5, of the smallest unit used in the measurement. This is written as ±0.5 unit.

Examples

A. Which is more precise?

292 cm or 3 m

292 cm is more precise since its unit of measurement, 1 cm, is smaller than 1 m.

B. Find the greatest possible error for a measurement of 2.4 cm.

The unit of measurement is 0.1 cm.

$$0.5 \times 0.1 = 0.05$$

So, the greatest possible error is ± 0.05 cm.

PRACTICE Tell which is more precise.

1. 40 cm or 412 mm   **2.** 3.2 ft or 1 yd   **3.** 7 ft or 87 in.   **4.** 3,116 m or 3 km

Find the greatest possible error of the measurement.

5. 5 ft   **6.** 22 mm   **7.** 12.5 mi   **8.** 49.9 m

49 COMPARING AND ORDERING INTEGERS

A number line is helpful when comparing and ordering integers.

Examples

A. Use < or > to compare.

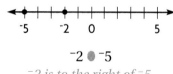

⁻2 ● ⁻5

⁻2 is to the right of ⁻5.

⁻2 > ⁻5

B. Write 2, ⁻4, and ⁻1 in order from least to greatest. Use < .

⁻4 is to the left of ⁻1, which is to the left of 2.

⁻4 < ⁻1 < 2

PRACTICE Use < or > to compare.

1. ⁻3 ● ⁻1   **2.** ⁻4 ● ⁻9   **3.** ⁻7 ● 4   **4.** ⁻8 ● ⁻9

Write in order from least to greatest. Use < .

5. 3, ⁻3, ⁻4   **6.** ⁻2, ⁻1, ⁻6   **7.** ⁻7, 0, ⁻2   **8.** ⁻1, ⁻2, ⁻3

50 ABSOLUTE VALUE AND OPPOSITES

The **absolute value** of a number is the distance the number is from zero on a number line. The symbol for absolute value is $| \ |$. Integers that are the same distance from 0 and are on opposite sides of 0 are called **opposites**.

Examples

A. Find $|^-5|$ and $|3|$.

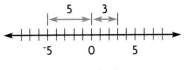

$|^-5| = 5 \qquad |3| = 3$

B. Name the opposite of 24.

The opposite of 24 is $^-24$.

C. Name the opposite of $^-8$.

The opposite of $^-8$ is 8.

PRACTICE Find the absolute value.

1. $|^-6|$ **2.** $|^-12|$ **3.** $|2.5|$ **4.** $|18|$ **5.** $|^-120|$ **6.** $|^-4.4|$

Name the opposite.

7. 13   **8.** 9   **9.** $^-28$ **10.** $^-54$ **11.** 85   **12.** 1

51 ADDING INTEGERS

When adding integers, consider the absolute values of the addends.

Examples

A. Find the sum. $^-4 + ^-1$

STEP 1 *When the signs of the integers are the same, add the absolute values of the integers.*

$$|^-4| + |^-1| = 4 + 1 = 5$$

STEP 2 *Use the sign of the addends.*

$$^-4 + ^-1 = ^-5$$

B. Find the sum. $7 + ^-3$

STEP 1 *When the signs of the integers are different, find the difference of their absolute values.*

$$|7| - |^-3| = 7 - 3 = 4$$

STEP 2 *Use the sign of the addend with the greater absolute value.*

$$|7| > |^-3| \rightarrow 7 + ^-3 = 4$$

PRACTICE Find the sum.

1. $5 + 8$ **2.** $^-8 + ^-9$ **3.** $^-6 + 8$ **4.** $^-12 + ^-2$ **5.** $8 + ^-19$ **6.** $^-1 + ^-24$

7. $^-3 + 14$ **8.** $34 + ^-19$ **9.** $^-53 + ^-14$ **10.** $^-83 + 59$ **11.** $^-42 + ^-15$ **12.** $27 + ^-73$

52 SUBTRACTING INTEGERS

To subtract an integer, add its opposite. Then use the rules for addition of integers to complete the problem.

Examples

A. $^-3 - 8$

STEP 1 *Rewrite the sentence as an addition problem.*

$$^-3 - 8 = {}^-3 + {}^-8$$

STEP 2 *Use the rules of addition to complete the problem.*

$$^-3 + {}^-8 \rightarrow |^-3| + |^-8| = 3 + 8 = 11$$
$$\downarrow$$

Both addends are negative. $\rightarrow {}^-3 - 8 = {}^-11$

B. $^-6 - {}^-4$

STEP 1 *Rewrite the sentence as an addition problem.*

$$^-6 - {}^-4 = {}^-6 + {}^+4 = {}^-6 + 4$$

STEP 2 *Use the rules of addition to complete the problem.*

$$^-6 + 4 \rightarrow |^-6| - |4| = 6 - 4 = 2$$
$$|^-6| > |4| \rightarrow {}^-6 - {}^-4 = {}^-2$$

PRACTICE Find the difference.

1. $^-4 - 9$ **2.** $12 - 28$ **3.** $^-10 - {}^-18$ **4.** $11 - {}^-11$ **5.** $^-6 - 2$ **6.** $^-10 - 12$

53 MULTIPLYING AND DIVIDING INTEGERS

Patterns like these show the rules for multiplying and dividing integers.

$2 \times 3 = 6$	$2 \times {}^-3 = {}^-6$	$6 \div 3 = 2$	$^-6 \div 3 = {}^-2$
$1 \times 3 = 3$	$1 \times {}^-3 = {}^-3$	$3 \div 3 = 1$	$3 \div {}^-3 = {}^-1$
$0 \times 3 = 0$	$0 \times {}^-3 = 0$	$0 \div 3 = 0$	$0 \div {}^-3 = 0$
$^-1 \times 3 = {}^-3$	$^-1 \times {}^-3 = 3$	$^-3 \div 3 = {}^-1$	$^-3 \div {}^-3 = 1$
$^-2 \times 3 = {}^-6$	$^-2 \times {}^-3 = 6$	$^-6 \div 3 = {}^-2$	$^-6 \div {}^-3 = 2$

Rules for Multiplication of Integers

When the signs of the factors are the same, the product is positive.

When the signs of the factors are different, the product is negative.

Rules for Division of Integers

When the signs of the dividend and divisor are the same, the quotient is positive.

When the signs of the dividend and divisor are different, the quotient is negative.

PRACTICE Find the product or quotient.

1. $^-3 \times 5$ **2.** $8 \times {}^-2$ **3.** $^-9 \times {}^-7$ **4.** 6×5 **5.** $^-12 \times 4$ **6.** $6 \times {}^-11$

7. $^-20 \div 5$ **8.** $8 \div {}^-2$ **9.** $^-12 \div {}^-3$ **10.** $25 \div 5$ **11.** $^-12 \div 4$ **12.** $77 \div {}^-11$

54 THE COORDINATE PLANE

A **coordinate plane** is formed with two perpendicular lines called **axes**. The horizontal axis is called the **x-axis**, and the vertical axis is called the **y-axis**. The axes intersect at a point called the **origin** and divide the coordinate plane into four parts called **quadrants**.

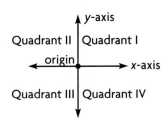

To locate or graph a point on a coordinate plane, you use an **ordered pair** of numbers (x,y). The **x-coordinate** tells the direction and number of spaces to move right or left. The **y-coordinate** tells the direction and number of spaces to move up or down.

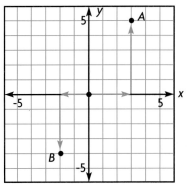

Example Graph and label the points $A(3,5)$ and $B(^-2,^-4)$.

For each point, start at the origin and move the direction and distance indicated by the x-coordinate and y-coordinate.

PRACTICE Draw a coordinate plane. Graph and label the point.

1. $A(2,3)$ **2.** $B(5,^-2)$ **3.** $C(^-4,5)$ **4.** $D(^-3,^-2)$ **5.** $E(^-2,1)$ **6.** $F(4,4)$

55 MEAN AND MEDIAN

The **mean** is the average of a set of numbers. To find the mean, add the numbers and divide the sum by the number of addends.

The **median** is the middle number of a set of numbers in numerical order. If there are two middle numbers, the median is the mean of those two numbers.

Examples

A. Find the mean of 36, 74, 43, 36, and 41.

STEP 1 *Find the sum of the numbers.*

$$36 + 74 + 43 + 36 + 41 = 230$$

STEP 2 *Divide the sum by the number of addends.*

$$230 \div 5 = 46$$

So, the mean is 46.

B. Find the median: 10, 6, 42, 18, 33, 64.

STEP 1 *Put numbers in numerical order.*

$$6, 10, 18, 33, 42, 64$$

STEP 2 *There are two middle numbers, 18 and 33. Their mean is the median.*

$$\frac{18 + 33}{2} = 25.5 \rightarrow 25.5 \text{ is the median.}$$

PRACTICE Find the mean and the median.

1. 32, 87, 45, 63, 73   **2.** 17, 44, 33, 10   **3.** 6, 52, 41, 21, 36, 48   **4.** 126, 99, 234.3

5. 56, 81, 75, 29   **6.** 26, 15, 83, 57, 91   **7.** 94, 106, 195, 132   **8.** 1.9, 8.5, 7.4, 5.6, 6.7

56 MODE AND RANGE

The **mode** of a set of numbers is the most commonly occurring number in the set. There may be more than one mode, or there may be no mode at all. The **range** is the distance between extremes in a set of numbers. You can find the range by finding the difference between the greatest number and the least number.

Examples Find the mode and range of the set of numbers.

A. 4, 25, 72, 4, 36, 4, 2, 25, 25, 98

Mode: Since both 4 and 25 occur three times, 4 and 25 are the modes.

Range: Greatest: 98   Least: 2

$98 - 2 = 96 \rightarrow 96$ is the range.

B. 4, 25, 72, 36, 41, ⁻2, 98

Mode: Since no number in the set occurs more than once, there is no mode.

Range: Greatest: 98   Least: ⁻2

$98 - {^-2} = 100 \rightarrow 100$ is the range.

PRACTICE Find the mode and the range.

1. 2, 1, 2, 5, 7, 9

2. 42, 8, 54, 192, 8, 0, 44, 16

3. ⁻12, 44, 324, 17, 41

4. 0, 77, 125, 77, 2, 2, 3, 5, 3

5. ⁻5, 0, 15, 25, ⁻5, ⁻23, 1

6. 297, 7, 12, 18, 5, 21, 17

57 MULTIPLE-BAR AND MULTIPLE-LINE GRAPHS

A multiple-bar graph and a multiple-line graph are shown below.

PRACTICE Use the bar graph for Exercises 1–3 and the line graph for Exercises 4–6.

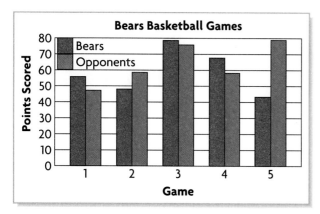

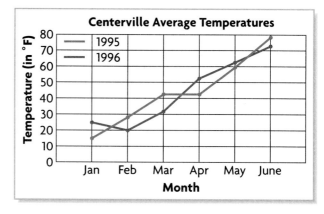

1. What do the vertical and horizontal scales show?

2. What is the interval of the vertical scale?

3. Did the Bears win more games than they lost?

4. What does the graph compare?

5. Which year had a lower average temperature in April?

6. For what month and year was the temperature the highest?

58 MAKING CIRCLE GRAPHS

A circle consists of 360°. To make a circle graph, you divide the 360° according to the data.

Example   Use the data from the table to make a circle graph.

Lunch Preferences	
Pizza	25%
Burger	35%
Sandwich	40%

STEP 1 *Multiply each percent by 360°.*

$25\% = 0.25, 0.25 \times 360° = 90°$

$35\% = 0.35, 0.35 \times 360° = 126°$

$40\% = 0.40, 0.40 \times 360° = 144°$

STEP 2 *Use a compass to draw a circle. Draw a radius.*

STEP 3 *Use a protractor to draw the first angle.*

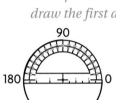

STEP 4 *Repeat Step 3 for the other angles.*

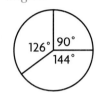

STEP 5 *Title and label the graph.*
LUNCH PREFERENCES

PRACTICE   At Oceanview Middle School, 20% of the students ride a bike to school, 65% ride the bus, and 15% ride in a car. Make a circle graph of the data.

59 SAMPLE SPACE

A set of all possible combinations of choices or all possible outcomes is called a **sample space**. You can show a sample space with a tree diagram or a list.

Example   For dinner, each person may select one meat and one vegetable from the choices below. What are the different combinations of meats and vegetables?

CHOICES

Meat	Vegetable
chicken	corn
beef	beans
	yams
	carrots

TREE DIAGRAM

chicken — corn
chicken — beans
chicken — yams
chicken — carrots
beef — corn
beef — beans
beef — yams
beef — carrots

LIST

chicken and corn
chicken and beans
chicken and yams
chicken and carrots
beef and corn
beef and beans
beef and yams
beef and carrots

The sample space is shown in the tree diagram and in the list.

PRACTICE   You can wear white or black shorts with a red, blue, green, or yellow shirt. Use a list or tree diagram to show the different combinations of shorts and shirts.

60 SIMPLE PROBABILITY

The number used to describe the chance of something happening is called the mathematical probability or simple probability of that event. The probability is found by dividing the number of favorable outcomes by the number of possible outcomes, or

$$P = \frac{\text{favorable outcomes}}{\text{possible outcomes}}.$$

Example   A total of 12 cubes of equal size are put in a bag: 1 cube is green, 2 are yellow, 6 are red, and 3 are blue. What is the probability that a blue cube will be randomly drawn from the bag?

$$P = \frac{\text{favorable outcomes}}{\text{possible outcomes}} = \frac{3 \text{ blue cubes}}{12 \text{ cubes in all}} = \frac{3}{12} = \frac{1}{4} \leftarrow simplified$$

Therefore, the probability that a blue chip will be drawn is $\frac{1}{4}$.

PRACTICE   A total of 20 candy bars of equal size are placed in a box. 5 are chocolate, 3 are caramel, 8 are peanut, 2 are mint, 1 is coconut, and 1 is vanilla. Find the probability of the following being randomly selected from the box.

1. chocolate   **2.** caramel   **3.** peanut   **4.** mint

5. vanilla   **6.** peanut or mint   **7.** peanut or vanilla   **8.** chocolate or mint

CALCULATOR *Activities*

ROUNDING THE BASES
Round a Decimal Number to a Given Place

What is Cecil's batting average to the nearest thousandth?

MIDDLETON YANKEES
APRIL BATTING STATISTICS

Player	AB	H	2B	3B	HR	RBI	BB
Cecil	23	9	2	0	0	2	2
Derek	20	5	0	0	0	1	4
Bernie	24	4	0	0	1	4	3

Find out by dividing Cecil's number of hits (*H*) by the number of times he was at bat (*AB*). Then round the quotient to the thousandths place. Or you can use a calculator key to automatically round your answer.

Using the Calculator

Use the following keys on the *Casio fx-65* to find the answer.

[FIX] 3 9 [÷] 23 [=] | 0.391 |

Use the following keys on the *TI Explorer Plus* to find the answer.

[2nd] [FIX] 3 9 [÷] 23 [=] | 0.391 |

So, Cecil's batting average to the nearest thousandth is 0.391.

PRACTICE

Use your calculator.

1. Calculate Derek's and Bernie's batting averages to the nearest thousandth.

Find the quotient or product. Round to the nearest thousandth.

2. $58.007 \div 5.1$ **3.** $464.999 \div 55.1$ **4.** $490.0 \div 0.99$

5. 4.39×1.89 **6.** 5.89×8.12 **7.** 17.98×2.59

8. $27.5 \div 2.8$ **9.** $698.37 \div 3.2$ **10.** 78.6×3.91

SQUADS, TEAMS, AND GROUPS
Solve Permutation and Combination Problems

Coach Donna needs to figure out how many different 5-player basketball squads she can form with the 12 girls on the Hurricanes' team. You can use your calculator to help her.

Using the Calculator

Use the following keys on the *TI Explorer Plus* to find the number of different 5-player combinations from the team.

12 (2nd) (nCr) 5 (=) [*792*]

With each squad of 5 players, how many ways can Coach Donna arrange the players? The number of possible arrangements of 5 players for 5 positions is $5 \cdot 4 \cdot 3 \cdot 2 \cdot 1$, or 5!. Use your calculator to show 5!.

5 (2nd) (x!) [*120*]

The Hurricanes play in a league with 7 other teams. In how many ways might the first-, second-, and third-place trophies be awarded among the 8 teams?

Use the following keys on the *TI Explorer Plus* to find the answer.

8 (2nd) (nPr) 3 (=) [*336*]

Use the following keys on the *Casio fx-65* to find the answer.

8 SHIFT nPr 3 [*336*]

PRACTICE
Solve. Use your calculator.

1. $_8C_5$ **2.** $_{12}C_6$ **3.** $_{15}C_3$ **4.** $_6P_2$ **5.** $_9P_3$ **6.** $_{13}P_3$

7. Find the number of ways 8 swimmers can place first, second, third, and fourth.

8. There are 15 students in Heidi's Spanish class. In how many ways can 4 students be chosen to win a trip for 4?

9. There are 10 pizza toppings. How many pizzas with 3 different toppings can be made?

10. In how many ways can a baseball coach arrange 9 players on a team with 9 positions?

WHO SHALL IT BE?
Simulate Probability Experiments

One thousand students attended the King Middle School Art Show. Each student received a ticket with a number between 0 and 0.999. The art committee gave a watercolor kit to 5 students chosen at random. How did the committee decide which students would receive the watercolor kits?

Using the Calculator

Use the following keys for the random-number generator on the *Casio fx-65*. Enter this key sequence 5 times:

Use the following keys for the random-number generator on the *TI Explorer Plus*. Enter this key sequence 5 times:

Students holding tickets with the generated random numbers would receive the watercolor kits. Of the first 100 students, 10 became the judges. The art committee gave each of the first 100 students a ticket with a number between 1 and 100. How did the committee decide which students would become the judges?

You can enter the following key sequence 10 times on the *TI Explorer Plus*:

Students holding tickets with the generated random numbers would become judges.

PRACTICE
Use your calculator.

1. Generate 5 more random numbers between 0 and 0.999. Did you repeat any of the random numbers you generated earlier?

2. A survey of 25% of a class of 32 students is to be conducted. Assign a number from 1 to 32 to each student. Use your calculator to randomly choose students.

3. Kathryn plans to choose 30% of her 50 employees to attend a meeting. Assign a number from 1 to 50 to each employee. Use your calculator to randomly choose employees.

STEP BY STEP
Number Patterns and Iterations

You can use your calculator to solve algebraic expressions when the value of the unknown varies. For the table shown at the right you can use your calculator to find the value of $5x + 3$ when $x = 2$.

x	$5x + 3$
1	8
2	

REMEMBER:

An iteration is the repeated application of a mathematical procedure, in which each step is applied to the output of the preceding step.

Using the Calculator

Use the following keys on the *Casio fx-65*:

$\boxed{\times}$ 5 [SHIFT] [SET 1] [AC] $\boxed{+}$ 3 [SHIFT] [SET 2] [AC]

2 [F1] [F2] $\boxed{ 13}$

To clear the calculator's function memory, press

[AC] [SHIFT] [F1] .

Use the following keys on the *TI Explorer Plus*:

$\boxed{\times}$ 5 [OP1] $\boxed{+}$ 3 [OP2] [CE/C]

2 [OP1] [OP2] $\boxed{ 13}$

When $x = 2$, $5x + 3 = 13$.

PRACTICE

Copy and complete each table. Use your calculator to help you.

1.

p	$2p + 36$
2	40
5	
9	
15	
45	

2.

r	$4r - 3$
2	5
10	
12	
15	
20	

3.

k	$\frac{k}{2} - 4$
2	$^-3$
6	
10	
24	
48	

I MEAN IT!

Analyze Data: Mean and Sum

Every week, the secretary of the student council counted how many people came to the meetings. This is what he found:

Week	1	2	3	4	5	6	7	8	9	10	11
Number of People	35	41	41	42	37	33	31	47	42	45	46

You can find the mean and sum of data with your calculator.

Using the Calculator

Use the following keys on the *Casio fx-65* to find the mean and sum of the data:

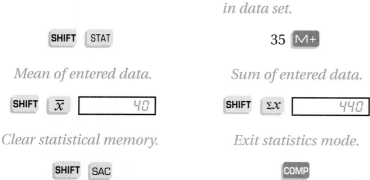

Enter statistics mode.

SHIFT STAT

Repeat for each number in data set.

35 M+

Mean of entered data.

SHIFT $\bar{x}$ [40]

Sum of entered data.

SHIFT Σx [440]

Clear statistical memory.

SHIFT SAC

Exit statistics mode.

COMP

Use the following keys on the *TI Explorer Plus* to find the mean and sum of the data:

Repeat these 2 keys after each number in data set.

35 2nd $\Sigma+$

Mean of entered data.

2nd $\bar{x}$ [40]

Sum of entered data.

 2nd Σx

Exit statistics mode.

ON/AC

PRACTICE

Find the mean and sum of the data sets. Use your calculator.

1. 45, 48, 47, 46, 41, 40, 43, 57, 61, 35, 39, 45, 47, 46, 41, 40, 43, 45, 46, 40

2. 168, 174, 195, 200, 156, 174, 168, 152, 132, 189, 195, 156, 185, 180, 182, 165

3. 23, 29, 31, 23, 22, 35, 39, 28, 26, 20, 25, 28, 33, 37, 36, 29, 35, 38, 30, 34

4. 50, 66, 59, 57, 62, 64, 67, 59, 60, 63, 56, 52, 55, 53, 59, 56, 61, 62, 64, 57, 58, 68

THE RIGHT TRIANGLE STUFF
Find Trigonometric Values

You can find the trigonometric ratios of the angles in triangles by using your calculator.

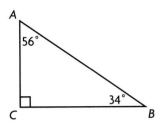

Use Your Calculator

Use the following keys on the *Casio fx-65* to find sin ∠A, cos ∠A, and tan ∠A. Round the answer to the nearest ten-thousandth.

Sin ∠A

56 [sin] [0.829037572]

Cos ∠A

56 [cos] [0.559192903]

Tan ∠A

56 [tan] [1.482560969]

You can use the same key sequences on the *TI Explorer Plus* to find sin ∠A, cos ∠A, and tan ∠A.

So, sin ∠A = 0.8290, cos ∠A = 0.5592, and tan ∠A = 1.4826

PRACTICE

Use your calculator to find the trigonometric values. Round the answer to the nearest ten-thousandth.

1. sin 6°   **2.** cos 37°   **3.** tan 78°   **4.** sin 89°   **5.** cos 63°   **6.** tan 21°

Solve. Use your calculator to find the trigonometric values. Round the answer to the nearest ten-thousandth.

7. $\sin 20° = \dfrac{x}{12}$ **8.** $\cos 32° = \dfrac{x}{29}$ **9.** $\tan 82° = \dfrac{x}{7}$ **10.** $\sin 6° = \dfrac{x}{4}$

11. $\cos 25° = \dfrac{x}{50}$ **12.** $\sin 14° = \dfrac{x}{42}$ **13.** $\tan 71° = \dfrac{x}{5}$ **14.** $\cos 19° = \dfrac{x}{31}$

EXPONENTIAL EXCLAMATIONS
Exponents and Roots

You can use your calculator to solve problems involving exponents and roots.

Find the value of 5^4 and $\sqrt[4]{81}$.

Using the Calculator

Use the following keys on the *Casio fx-65* to find the value of 5^4.

5  4 = | 625 |

Use the following keys on the *TI Explorer Plus* to find the value of 5^4.

5 [y^x] 4 [=] | 625 |

Use the following keys on the *Casio fx-65* to find the value of $\sqrt[4]{81}$.

81 [SHIFT] [$x^{1/y}$] 4 = | 3 |

Use the following keys on the *TI Explorer Plus* to find the value of $\sqrt[4]{81}$.

81 [2nd] [$\sqrt[x]{y}$] 4 [=] | 3 |

PRACTICE
Find the value. Use your calculator.

1. 6^5	**2.** 3^7	**3.** 9^5	**4.** $\sqrt[7]{128}$	**5.** $\sqrt[5]{1,024}$	**6.** $\sqrt[3]{343}$
7. 17^3	**8.** 8^5	**9.** 4^7	**10.** $\sqrt[3]{1,331}$	**11.** $\sqrt[4]{1,296}$	**12.** $\sqrt[8]{6,561}$
13. $\sqrt[6]{4,096}$	**14.** $\sqrt[5]{3,125}$	**15.** 29^3	**16.** 151^2	**17.** 19^3	**18.** $\sqrt[10]{1,024}$

PICTURE PERFECT
Showing Figures on the Coordinate Plane

Draw a triangle with vertices (⁻8, ⁻4), (1, 7), and (6, ⁻5).

Using the Calculator

Use the *TI-82 Graphing Calculator* to draw a triangle.

Clear the memory and brighten the screen.
Hold *until the display reappears.*

`2nd` `MEM` 3 2

`2nd` `▲` `ENTER`

`CLEAR`

Done

Ready to draw a line segment.

`CLEAR` `2nd` `DRAW` 2

Line (

REMEMBER:
When writing ordered pairs, the *x*-value is written first and the *y*-value is written second. When graphing a point written as an ordered pair, the *x*-value represents the horizontal movement and the *y*-value represents the vertical movement.

Enter ordered pairs for the line segment from (⁻8,⁻4) *to* (1,7).

 8 `,` 4 `,` 1 `,` 7

`)` `ENTER`

Line (−8, −4, 1, 7)

Use arrow key to move cursor. Use delete key as needed. Enter ordered pairs for the line segment from (1,7) *to* (6,⁻5).

`CLEAR` `2nd` `ENTRY`

Line (−8, −4, 1, 7)
Line (−8, −4, 1, 7)

Line (−8, −4, 1, 7)
Line (1, 7, 6, −5)

Now enter ordered pairs for the line segment from (6,⁻5) *to* (⁻8,⁻4) *as you did before.*

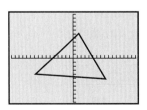

Line (−8, −4, 1, 7)
Line (1, 7, 6, −5)
Line (1, 7, 6, −5)

Line (−8, −4, 1, 7)
Line (1, 7, 6, −5)
Line (6, −5, −8, −4)

PRACTICE

Use your calculator to draw a triangle with the given vertices.

1. (1,9), (2,1), (7,8)   **2.** (−2,3), (4,3), (4,−8)   **3.** (0,0), (−5,−7), (7,−9)

A MODEL DECISION
Graphing Linear Equations

George can mail his package through the Fireball company, which charges a flat fee of $2.89 plus $0.59 per pound. His other choice is Firsthand Delivery, which charges a flat fee of $0.25 and $1.80 per pound. For how many pounds will sending a package cost the same?

Using the Calculator

Use the following keys to graph the equations $y = 0.59x + 2.89$ and $y = 1.80x + 0.25$ on the *TI-82 Graphing Calculator*.

Enter both equations on the equation screen.

`Y=` `CLEAR` 0.59 `X,T,θ` `+` 2.89

`ENTER`

`Y=` 1.80 `X,T,θ` `+` 0.25 `ENTER`

```
Y₁🔲0.59X+2.89
Y₂🔲1.80X+0.25■
Y₃=
Y₄=
Y₅=
Y₆=
Y₇=
Y₈=
```

Graph the equations.

`GRAPH`

Use the trace cursor to find where the graphs intersect.

`TRACE` ▶

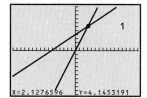

Since *x* represents pounds, the cost will be the same when the package weighs about 2 lb.

PRACTICE

Use your calculator. Graph both equations on the same graph. Use the trace key to find the *x* and *y* values where they intersect. Round to the nearest tenth.

1. $y = 2x + 7$
$y = {}^{-}4x + 7$

2. $y = 1.5x - 4$
$y = 0.75x + 1$

3. $y = 2.42x + 5$
$y = {}^{-}1.2x - 4$

4. $y = x + 3$
$y = {}^{-}2x + 4$

5. $y = 2.5x + 2$
$y = 4x - 1$

6. $y = 7.9x - 2$
$y = {}^{-}1.8x + 3$

THAT'S THE POINT
Explore x- and y-Intercepts

Luís is making alphabet blocks to sell at the Service Club Fair. He bought all the materials he needed for $7.00. Luís will sell the sets for $2.60 each. He writes the equation $y = 2.6x - 7$ to figure his profit where y is the profit and x is the number of sets sold. How much money is lost if he does not sell any sets? What is the least number of sets he must sell to make a profit?

If you graph the equation, the y-intercept is the money lost if no sets are sold. The x-intercept is where the profit begins.

Using the Calculator

Use the following keys to graph the equation $y = 2.6x - 7$ on the *TI-82 Graphing Calculator.* Enter the equation on the equation screen.

Graph the equation.

| Y= | 2.6 | X,T,θ | — | 7 | GRAPH |

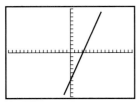

Since $y = -7$, the money lost is $7.00 if no sets are sold.

Use the right arrow key to move the cross hairs until they are on the point where the graph crosses the x-axis.

| TRACE | ▶ |

Use the trace cursor to find where the graph intersects the y-axis.

| TRACE |

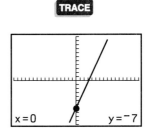

x = 0   y = −7

y = 0
x = 2.5531915

Since $x \approx 2.6$ and he can't sell part of a set, Luís must sell at least 3 sets to make a profit.

PRACTICE

Graph the equation. Use your calculator to find the x and y intercepts. Round to the nearest tenth.

1. $y = 2x + 7$ **2.** $y = 5x - 4$ **3.** $y = {}^-3x + 2.5$ **4.** $y = {}^-3x - 8.25$

5. $y = {}^-2x - 5$ **6.** $y = 4.8x + 1$ **7.** $y = {}^-2x + 3$ **8.** $y = {}^-5x - 4.5$

PUT YOUR SHADES ON
Graphing Inequalities

You can graph inequalities using the *TI-82 Graphing Calculator*.

Graph $y \geq 2x - 5$.

Using the Calculator

Enter the equation $y = 2x - 5$ as shown on page H41.

Graph the equation.

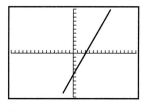

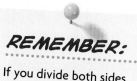
Choose a test point and decide which side of the line to shade. Prepare the calculator to shade the graph.

Shade (■

To graph $y \geq 2x - 5$, enter $2x - 5$ since you want to shade above the line $y = 2x - 5$. Then enter 10 since you want to shade below $y = 10$ on the calculator screen. Then enter 2 for the calculator's resolution. Shade the graph.

Shade (2x − 5, 10, 2)

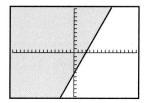

2 [X,T,θ] [−] 5 [,] 10 [,] 2 [ENTER]

Clear the graph.

To graph $y \leq 2x - 5$, enter the equation $y = 2x - 5$. Go to the shade screen. First enter ⁻10 since you want to shade above $y = ⁻10$ on the calculator screen. Then enter $2x - 5$ since you want to shade below the line $y = 2x - 5$. Then enter 2 for the calculator's resolution. Shade the graph.

Shade (−10, 2x − 5, 2)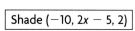

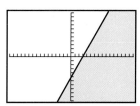

PRACTICE

Graph the inequality. Use your calculator.

1. $y \geq 4x - 5$ **2.** $y \geq 3x + 2$ **3.** $y \leq 2x - 1$ **4.** $⁻2y \geq ⁻2x - 6$

5. $y \leq ⁻2x + 1$ **6.** $y \geq ⁻1.5x - 1$ **7.** $y \geq 4x - 3$ **8.** $5y \leq ⁻6x + 3$

GROW SOME WHISKERS
Box-and-Whisker Graphs

You can draw a box-and-whisker graph using a *TI-82 Graphing Calculator.*

Use the following data to draw a box-and-whisker graph.

17, 28, 19, 24, 25, 17, 25, 28, 22, 25, 24, 26

Using the Calculator

Clear the memory and brighten the screen as shown on page H40.

STAT 1

Enter the data from the list above. Press **ENTER** *after each entry until all data items have been entered.*

L1	L2	L3
25		
28		
22		
25		
24		
26		

L1(13)=

Get to the graph menu.

 2nd **QUIT** **2nd** **STAT PLOT** 1

```
Plot1
On  Off
Type: ～ ⟋ ⊡ ⊡⊡
Xlist: L1 L2L3L4L5L6
Ylist: L1 L2 L3L4L5L6
Mark: ▫  +  ·
```

Select the box-and-whisker graph.

ENTER **▼** **▶** **▶** **ENTER**

Display the box-and-whisker graph.

2nd **QUIT** **ZOOM** 9

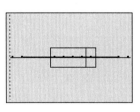

Use the left and right arrow keys to find the median, quartile values, and extremes.

 TRACE

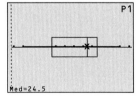

Med=24.5

PRACTICE

Draw a box-and-whisker graph with the data. Find the median, extreme values, and the upper and lower quartiles of the data. Use your calculator.

1. 1, 10, 8, 8, 0, 7, 2, 6, 1, 3, 6, 7, 7, 8, 10, 8

2. 8, 11, 10, 3, 2, 21, 13, 22, 20, 9, 8

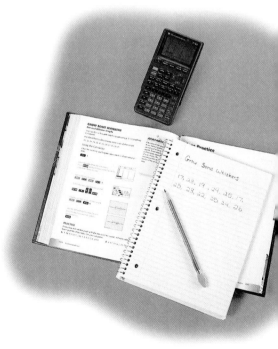

More Practice

CHAPTER 1

Lesson 1.1

Classify each number as a counting number, whole number, integer, or rational number.

1. $^-8$ **2.** 4.6 **3.** 258 **4.** $\frac{^-2}{3}$ **5.** 500

6. 0 **7.** $^-5.7$ **8.** $\frac{5}{8}$ **9.** $\sqrt{100}$ **10.** $^-\sqrt{81}$

Lesson 1.2

Write in exponent form.

1. $7 \times 7 \times 7 \times 7$ **2.** $4.3 \times 4.3 \times 4.3$ **3.** 5 **4.** $\frac{2}{3} \times \frac{2}{3}$

Find the value.

5. 4^2 **6.** 15^0 **7.** 7^3

8. $(1.3)^2$ **9.** 9^1 **10.** $\left(\frac{1}{4}\right)^3$

Write the prime factorization, using exponents.

11. 9 **12.** 54 **13.** 65

14. 26 **15.** 120 **16.** 900

Write in scientific notation.

17. 527 **18.** $67,465$

19. $2,345,600,000,000$ **20.** $35,692,300$

Write in standard form.

21. 9.343×10^6 **22.** 5.7395×10^9 **23.** 6.0845×10^7

Lesson 1.3

Write the product as one power.

1. $5^4 \cdot 5^3$ **2.** $3^3 \cdot 3^5$ **3.** $13^2 \cdot 13^5$

Write the quotient as one power.

4. $3^6 \div 3^1$ **5.** $5^9 \div 5^4$ **6.** $15^3 \div 15^3$

Write the product or quotient as one power.

7. $3^6 \cdot 3^4$ **8.** $9^7 \div 9^2$ **9.** $13^5 \times 13^2$ **10.** $5^{19} \div 5^8$

Lesson 1.4

Find the square.

1. 4^2 **2.** $(^-3)^2$ **3.** 10^2

4. $(^-7)^2$ **5.** 13^2 **6.** $(^-1.2)^2$

7. $(^-0.5)^2$ **8.** $\left(\frac{2}{3}\right)^2$ **9.** $\left(\frac{-5}{4}\right)^2$

Find the square root.

10. $\sqrt{9}$ **11.** $^-\sqrt{49}$ **12.** $\sqrt{225}$

13. $^-\sqrt{144}$ **14.** $^-\sqrt{36}$ **15.** $\sqrt{81}$

16. $^-\sqrt{64}$ **17.** $\sqrt{0.04}$ **18.** $^-\sqrt{\frac{4}{25}}$

Name the two integers the square root is between.

19. $\sqrt{15}$ **20.** $\sqrt{38}$ **21.** $\sqrt{79}$ **22.** $\sqrt{107}$ **23.** $\sqrt{175}$

24. $\sqrt{145}$ **25.** $\sqrt{110}$ **26.** $\sqrt{27}$ **27.** $\sqrt{89}$ **28.** $\sqrt{200}$

Lesson 1.5

Write an *R* or an *I* to classify the real number as rational or irrational.

1. $\frac{12}{15}$ **2.** $^-\sqrt{19}$ **3.** $\sqrt{157}$

Find the value to the nearest hundredth.

4. $\sqrt{0.16}$ **5.** $^-\sqrt{3}$ **6.** $^-\sqrt{5}$ **7.** $\sqrt{1.69}$ **8.** $^-\sqrt{0.0144}$

CHAPTER 2

Lesson 2.1

Jason earned money from cutting grass in his neighborhood. He plans to spend $50 of it on others. Listed below are the amounts he is giving to others. Copy and complete the table.

			Fraction	Decimal	Percent
1.	Jason's younger sister	$5			
2.	Toys for hospitalized children	$12			
3.	Food bank for the poor	$10			
4.	Gift for mother	$5			
5.	Gift for father	$5			
6.	Homeless shelter	$13			

7. Make a circle graph to display the data from Exercises 1–6.

Lesson 2.2

Find an equivalent fraction that has 100 as its denominator. Then write the percent.

1. $\frac{1}{5}$ **2.** $\frac{3}{5}$ **3.** $\frac{7}{20}$ **4.** $\frac{1}{2}$ **5.** $\frac{9}{20}$ **6.** $\frac{7}{10}$

7. $\frac{9}{25}$ **8.** $\frac{11}{50}$ **9.** $\frac{2}{100}$ **10.** $\frac{24}{25}$ **11.** $\frac{4}{400}$ **12.** $\frac{58}{200}$

Lesson 2.3

Write the ratio as a fraction in simplest form.

1. 5 to 45 **2.** 3 to 162 **3.** 16:48 **4.** 8 out of 100 **5.** 14:343

Decide whether the ratios form a proportion. Write = or ≠.

6. $\frac{5}{11}$ ▦ $\frac{12}{55}$ **7.** $\frac{5}{77}$ ▦ $\frac{5}{7}$ **8.** $\frac{10}{15}$ ▦ $\frac{14}{21}$ **9.** $\frac{9}{12}$ ▦ $\frac{27}{30}$ **10.** $\frac{4}{7}$ ▦ $\frac{60}{108}$

11. $\frac{120}{270}$ ▦ $\frac{4}{9}$ **12.** $\frac{14}{56}$ ▦ $\frac{2}{7}$ **13.** $\frac{2}{5}$ ▦ $\frac{32}{80}$ **14.** $\frac{5}{8}$ ▦ $\frac{150}{240}$ **15.** $\frac{26}{35}$ ▦ $\frac{13}{15}$

Copy and complete the ratio table.

16.

First term	3	?	7	9	?	13
Second term	6	10	?	18	?	26

17.

Sales (in units)	1,000	?	3,000	4,000	5,000	6,000
Profit (in dollars)	80	160	?	300	?	?

Lesson 2.4

1. The vet charges $9.86 for 10 pounds of cat food. The grocery store charges $4.95 for 5 pounds of the same cat food. Which charges less per pound?

2. A store offers two sizes for bags of potatoes. They sell a 20 pound bag for $5.25 and a 10 pound bag for $2.75. Which is the better deal?

Find the unit rate.

3. $99.75 for 21 hr of work

4. $11.97 for 3 lb of fish

5. 1500 calories for 6 servings of pie

6. 176 mi for 11 gal of gasoline

Lesson 2.5

Use mental math and compatible numbers to estimate an equivalent ratio.
Then write your ratio in simplest form.

1. $\frac{92}{372}$ 2. $\frac{12}{142}$ 3. $\frac{210}{325}$

4. $\frac{73}{418}$ 5. $\frac{76}{139}$ 6. $\frac{31}{618}$

Estimate the percent.

7. $\frac{62}{157}$ 8. $\frac{53}{248}$ 9. 47:109   10. 77 of 490   11. 136 of 149

12. 58:86   13. 24 of 110   14. 135 of 178   15. 42:97   16. 86 of 10,400

CHAPTER 3

Lesson 3.1

Find the sum.

1. $^-3 + 5$ 2. $^-1 + 5$ 3. $^-2 + {}^-6$ 4. $^-2 + 7$

5. $4 + {}^-9$ 6. $2 + {}^-5$ 7. $^-3 + {}^-3$ 8. $^-4 + 8$

9. $3 + {}^-9$ 10. $8 + {}^-2$ 11. $3 + {}^-1$ 12. $^-5 + 9$

13. $^-6 + {}^-9$ 14. $^-9 + {}^-6$ 15. $^-19 + 14$ 16. $^-44 + 12$

17. $8 + {}^-7$ 18. $^-10 + 14$ 19. $^-18 + {}^-9$ 20. $27 + {}^-39$

21. $^-10 + {}^-24$ 22. $54 + {}^-48$ 23. $^-191 + {}^-39$ 24. $^-87 + 56$

Lesson 3.2

Write an addition equation for each subtraction equation.

1. $6 - 9 = {}^-3$ 2. $15 - {}^-4 = 19$ 3. $7 - {}^-18 = 25$ 4. $^-7 - {}^-9 = 2$

5. $7 - 25 = {}^-18$ 6. $3 - {}^-14 = 17$ 7. $^-16 - 3 = {}^-19$ 8. $^-6 - {}^-1 = {}^-5$

Find the difference.

9. $5 - {}^-1$ 10. $9 - 17$ 11. $12 - {}^-5$ 12. $^-6 - 5$

13. $7 - {}^-8$ 14. $^-20 - 20$ 15. $^-45 - {}^-10$ 16. $^-130 - 220$

17. $6 - 7$ 18. $^-144 - {}^-144$ 19. $144 - {}^-144$ 20. $^-144 - 144$

21. $^-97 - 63$ 22. $152 - {}^-25$ 23. $^-197 - {}^-48$ 24. $^-82 - 82$

25. $517 - 63$ 26. $^-517 - 63$ 27. $517 - {}^-63$ 28. $^-517 - {}^-63$

Lesson 3.3

Find and extend a pattern to complete.

1. $^-3 \times {}^-5 = 15$
$^-3 \times {}^-4 = 12$
$^-3 \times {}^-3 = 9$
$^-3 \times {}^-2 = \blacksquare$
$^-3 \times {}^-1 = \blacksquare$
$^-3 \times 0 = \blacksquare$

2. $^-5 \times {}^-3 = 15$
$^-5 \times {}^-2 = 10$
$^-5 \times {}^-1 = 5$
$^-5 \times 0 = \blacksquare$
$^-5 \times 1 = \blacksquare$
$^-5 \times 2 = \blacksquare$

3. $^-2 \times 2 = {}^-4$
$^-2 \times 1 = {}^-2$
$^-2 \times 0 = 0$
$^-2 \times {}^-1 = \blacksquare$
$^-2 \times {}^-2 = \blacksquare$
$^-2 \times {}^-3 = \blacksquare$

4.

$^-2$	$^-1$	0	1	2	3
$^-6$	$^-3$	0			

5.

$^-3$	$^-2$	$^-1$	0	1	2
6	4	2			

Lesson 3.4

Tell whether the product or quotient is *positive* or *negative*.

1. $^-3 \times {}^-7$ **2.** $8 \times {}^-2$ **3.** $^-52 \div {}^-2$ **4.** $^-7 \times 5$

Find the product or quotient.

5. $60 \div 15$ **6.** $^-63 \div 21$ **7.** $^-4 \times {}^-12$ **8.** $^-16 \div {}^-4$

Find the value.

9. $(^-5 \times {}^-4) + 5$ **10.** $(4 \times 3) + 16 \div 2$ **11.** $5 \times {}^-3 + {}^-5$

12. $(2 - 5) - (^-3)^2 + 4$ **13.** $(8 - 3)^2 - 4 \times 7$ **14.** $(6 + 2.5) + 18 \div 9 - 2^2$

Lesson 3.5

Write as a fraction.

1. 4^{-3} **2.** 3^{-2} **3.** 2^{-7} **4.** 10^{-3}

5. 3^{-1} **6.** 4^{-2} **7.** 7^{-2} **8.** 10^{-5}

Write in scientific notation.

9. 0.00021 **10.** 0.00000102 **11.** 0.000000000438 **12.** 0.0050001

Write in standard form.

13. 1.6×10^{-7} **14.** 2.1×10^{-5} **15.** 9.126×10^{-6} **16.** 8.08×10^{-8}

17. 8.6×10^{-4} **18.** 6.359×10^{-3} **19.** 3.726×10^{-6} **20.** 9.051×10^{-8}

CHAPTER 4

Lesson 4.1

Tell whether the sum will be *positive* or *negative*.

1. $17.3 + {}^-9.2$ **2.** $7.2 + {}^-12$ **3.** $\frac{{}^-5}{7} + \frac{2}{7}$

4. $4 + \frac{{}^-1}{3}$ **5.** $2.6 + {}^-2.4$ **6.** ${}^-39.5 + 39.3$

Write the sum in simplest form.

7. ${}^-4.7 + {}^-3$ **8.** ${}^-2.6 + 2.6$ **9.** $2.4 + {}^-7.3$ **10.** ${}^-3 + 7.7$ **11.** $0.75 + {}^-0.25$

Write the sum in simplest form.

12. $\frac{{}^-3}{7} + \frac{5}{7}$ **13.** $\frac{{}^-4}{9} + \frac{1}{3}$ **14.** $\frac{{}^-3}{16} + \frac{5}{4}$

15. ${}^-2 + \frac{5}{7}$ **16.** $0.7 - 0.4$ **17.** ${}^-12.8 + 8.6$

18. $0.45 + {}^-0.15$ **19.** $18 + {}^-13.2$ **20.** ${}^-49.7 + {}^-2.9$

Lesson 4.2

Find the difference. Write it in simplest form.

1. ${}^-5.7 - {}^-3.2$ **2.** ${}^-4.2 - {}^-3.6$ **3.** $4.6 - {}^-3.5$ **4.** $15.2 - {}^-3.1$ **5.** ${}^-3.12 - {}^-6.32$

6. ${}^-9.2 - 3.7$ **7.** $8.6 - {}^-8.2$ **8.** ${}^-3.2 - {}^-18.7$ **9.** ${}^-25.6 - {}^-6.8$ **10.** $0.48 - {}^-5.14$

11. ${}^-24.3 - {}^-7.4$ **12.** $84.1 - {}^-9.6$ **13.** ${}^-6.3 - 52$ **14.** $71.1 - {}^-0.83$ **15.** ${}^-61.4 - {}^-3.1$

16. $93.7 - {}^-5.2$ **17.** ${}^-151.4 - 6.3$ **18.** ${}^-7.8 - {}^-5.1$ **19.** ${}^-59.3 - 17.5$ **20.** $98.7 - {}^-23.6$

Lesson 4.3

Tell whether the product or quotient will be *positive* or *negative*.

1. $3.6 \times {}^-4.2$ **2.** ${}^-4.1 \times 3.8$ **3.** ${}^-3.1 \times 0.2$ **4.** ${}^-4.9 \times {}^-0.31$

5. $\frac{{}^-1}{2} \times 0.3$ **6.** $4 \div \frac{{}^-1}{3}$ **7.** ${}^-0.3 \div 2$ **8.** ${}^-5 \div {}^-4.5$

9. $7.3 \div 4.2$ **10.** $0.4 \div 8$ **11.** $0.3 \div {}^-2$ **12.** ${}^-0.6 \div {}^-0.05$

Find the product or quotient. Write it in simplest form.

13. $3\frac{1}{2} \times 2$ **14.** $7 \times {}^-2.6$ **15.** $6.76 \div {}^-2.6$

16. ${}^-3 \div 2\frac{1}{4}$ **17.** $4.809 \div 2.1$ **18.** $2\frac{1}{3} \times {}^-6\frac{1}{2}$

19. ${}^-6.3 \times {}^-8.2$ **20.** $\frac{1}{2} \div \frac{{}^-3}{4}$ **21.** $7 \times {}^-0.4$

Lesson 4.4

Tell what you would do first to find the value of each expression.

1. $12.6 \times {}^{-}3.2 + 8 + {}^{-}3.1$ **2.** $2.1 + 6.3 \times 4.1 - 3.6$

3. $12.6 \times 3.1 \times {}^{-}4.1 \times {}^{-}3.6$ **4.** $({}^{-}2.1 + 6) \div (5 - 3.1)$

Find the value.

5. $1.8 \times (3.2 + {}^{-}6)$ **6.** $5 + 5.1 \times {}^{-}3.02$ **7.** $6.03 \times {}^{-}1.4 + 2$

8. $5.01^2 - 6.2 + 4$ **9.** ${}^{-}8.67 \times {}^{-}0.5 + 3$ **10.** $(10.8)^2 - 3.7 + 9.2$

CHAPTER 5

Lesson 5.1

Write *expression, equation,* or *inequality* for each.

1. $7 + 8 = 15$ **2.** $v + 17$ **3.** $19 + 7 \geq 20$ **4.** $y - 7 < 40$ **5.** 7×40

Use the expression to write an equation.

6. $118 - 6$ **7.** $42 + 4$ **8.** $91 - 11$ **9.** 5×7 **10.** $70 \div 7$

11. $2x + 3$ **12.** $9 - 2y$ **13.** $6t \div 2$ **14.** $12 - 3w$ **15.** $5 + 5p$

Use the expression to write an inequality.

16. $25 \div 5$ **17.** $4x + 10$ **18.** $13 + 9$ **19.** $2x$ **20.** $10g + 3$

Lesson 5.2

Evaluate the expression.

1. $2 + 7 \times 4 - 2$ **2.** $(7 + 2) \times 3 + 7$ **3.** $12 - 2^3 \times 5 + 8$

4. $\frac{1}{3} \times 9 - 2$ **5.** $2 + 6 \times 8 - 9$ **6.** $(2 + 9) \times 4 + 8$

Write *yes or no* to tell whether the expressions are equivalent.

7. $27 \div 3 + 5; 7 \times 2$ **8.** $64 \div 4 + 10; 62 - 10$ **9.** $(5 + 4) \div 3; 5 + 4 \div 3$

Write the variable and the coefficient of each expression.

10. $2.3y$ **11.** $7t^2$ **12.** $\frac{1}{3}j$ **13.** $\frac{d}{5}$ **14.** ${}^{-}47c$

15. $4x^3$ **16.** $\frac{5}{7}y$ **17.** $6.7c$ **18.** ${}^{-}3.6b$ **19.** $\frac{4}{5}d^7$

Lesson 5.3

Write an algebraic expression for the word expression.

1. the number of hours, h, increased by 3

2. the quotient of the number of days, d, and 7

3. the number of students, s, decreased by 4

4. the sum of 12 high notes and the total number of low notes, l

5. three times the amount saved last year, s

6. four less than the number of oboes, n

7. the number of eggs, e, divided by 12

8. \$3 off the cost of the paint, p

Lesson 5.4

Write the like terms.

1. $5a$, $6a$, 3, $2c$

2. $2x$, $3x$, 5, y

3. ^-3c, 8, $1.6c$, c

4. $\frac{x}{2}$, y, $2x$, 5

5. ^-4y, 3, $5.6y$, j

6. $3x$, $2y$, ^-5z, 1.6

7. $\frac{b}{7}$, $4b$, $3b$, $^-5$

8. $2a$, ^-6b, $8b$, $3a$, 7

Simplify by combining like terms.

9. $6 + b + 3b + ^-6 + 3b$

10. $2x + ^-3 + ^-3x + ^-7 + ^-5x$

11. $^-7 + 2x + ^-x + 2x + 8$

12. $1.3h + ^-3 + ^-h + 1.4h$

13. $3(x + 2) + ^-4$

14. $^-3 + 2(n + 4) + 3n$

CHAPTER 6

Lesson 6.1

Write an algebraic equation that represents the word sentence.

1. 75 decreased by a number, n, is 50.

2. 30 decreased by a number, x, is 20.

3. the sum of a number, n, and 12 is 200.

4. the sum of a number, m, and 7 is 12.

5. 5 times a number, m, equals 120.

6. 3 times a number, n, equals 33.

7. the quotient of 24 and a number, n, equals 6.

8. the quotient of 12 and a number, p, equals 2.

Choose the equation that represents the word problem.

9. Lee has saved \$20. He wants to save a total of \$37 by the end of the year. How much more does Lee need to save?
a. $s + 20 = 37$ **b.** $s - 20 = 37$

10. Sam measured today's wind speed at 23 kph. Yesterday he measured the wind speed at 16 kph. How much faster was the wind speed today than yesterday?
a. $16 - s = 23$ **b.** $16 + s = 23$

Lesson 6.2

Determine which value is a solution of the given equation.

1. $x - 3 = 8$
$x = 10, 11,$ or 12

2. $k - 16 = 51$
$k = 67, 68,$ or 69

3. $b + 5 = 21$
$b = 16, 17,$ or 18

4. $a + 15 = 41$
$a = 25$ or 26

5. $c + 5.41 = 8.01$
$c = 2.5, 2.6,$ or 2.7

6. $3k + 8 = 20$
$k = 3, 4,$ or 5

7. $3m = {}^-4.8$
$m = {}^-1.6, {}^-1.7,$ or ${}^-1.8$

8. ${}^-2.7q + 3 = 0.03$
$q = 1, 1.1,$ or 1.2

9. $a - 22 = {}^-14$
$a = 7, 8,$ or 9

10. $b - 18 = 13$
$b = 29, 30,$ or 31

11. $c + 8 = 19$
$c = 11, 12,$ or 13

12. $d + 12 = 53$
$d = 40, 41,$ or 42

Solve the equation and check the solution.

13. $x + 8 = 10$

14. $9 + z = 11$

15. $m - 12 = {}^-6$

16. $n - 17 = {}^-8$

17. $h + 56 = 31$

18. $w + \frac{3}{4} = \frac{1}{4}$

19. $m - 3.98 = 1.7$

20. $k - 14 = {}^-6$

21. $y + 5.9 = 21.7$

22. $a - \frac{2}{5} = \frac{1}{5}$

23. ${}^-17 + p = 6$

24. $t + 21 = {}^-528$

Lesson 6.3

Solve and check.

1. $8x = 48$

2. $\frac{x}{12} = 3$

3. $735 = 21b$

4. $\frac{y}{37} = 15y$

5. $22y = 176$

6. $9 = \frac{s}{1.6}$

7. $27.6 = 4.6e$

8. $\frac{z}{8.3} = 5$

9. $2.3m = 20.7$

10. $5.7p = 36.48$

11. $\frac{b}{1.87} = 7.1$

12. $\frac{a}{46} = {}^-261$

Lesson 6.4

Solve and check.

1. $2x + 9 = 21$

2. $9y + 6 = 42$

3. $8z - 4 = 20$

4. $7w - 12 = 30$

5. ${}^-6v - 9 = {}^-57$

6. ${}^-9u + 14 = 50$

7. $9t - 8 = {}^-35$

8. ${}^-4s - 16 = 20$

9. $\frac{a}{2} - 8 = 12$

10. $7 + \frac{b}{3} = 19$

11. $\frac{x}{5} - 16 = 20$

12. $6 - \frac{p}{2} = 8$

One mistake was made in solving each equation. Describe the mistake and find the solution.

13. $3x - 2 = 6$
$3x = 4$
$x = \frac{4}{3}$

14. $\frac{n}{4} + 6 = {}^-3$
$\frac{n}{4} = {}^-9$
$n = \frac{{}^-9}{4}$

15. $6a - 5 = 7$
$6a = {}^-2$
$a = \frac{{}^-1}{3}$

16. $5k + 1 = {}^-4$
$5k = {}^-5$
$k = {}^-25$

Lesson 6.5

1. On your journey to Mars, your spacecraft traveled six million miles more the second day than it traveled the first day. On the third day it doubled its distance from earth, reaching a distance of 30 million miles from earth. How many miles did you travel each day?

2. There were 13 riders on a bus after the third stop. At each stop, riders got off and on as follows: Stop 1—10 off, 15 on; Stop 2—8 off, 20 on; Stop 3—18 off, 3 on. How many riders were on the bus before the first stop?

CHAPTER 7

Lesson 7.1

Identify the like terms. Then solve and check.

1. $2y + 6y + 7 = 23$
2. $8 + 6x - 3x = 29$
3. $12 = 14x - 7x - 9$
4. $42 = 8a - 2a + 6$
5. $4 = {}^-4b - 2b + 22$
6. $2x + 31 + 3x = {}^-19$
7. $4c + 6 + 3c = 27$
8. $8d + 2d - 18 = 32$
9. $3x + 12 - x = 12$

Use the Distributive Property to solve. Then check.

10. $3(x - 2) + 5x = 10$
11. $4y + 3(y - 2) = 22$
12. $\frac{1}{2}(z + 2) - z = \frac{{}^-1}{2}$
13. $3y + 2(y + 4) = {}^-7$
14. $2y + 2(y + 4) = 12$
15. $3c + 2(2c - 3) = 1$
16. $4d + 3(3d + 1) = 42$
17. $2(x - 4) + x = 7$
18. $\frac{1}{3}(w + 1) + 2w = 12$
19. $13 = 3(d + 5) - 4d$
20. $y + 4(y - 3) = {}^-22$
21. $d + 2(3d - 1) = 33$
22. $5(x - 1) + 2x = 16$
23. $18 = 4(d - 3) + 6d$
24. $\frac{1}{4}(b + 2) + 3b = 7$

Lesson 7.2

Use the strategy *write an equation* to solve.

1. Sharon needs to fence in a rectangular garden. She has 40 ft of fencing. She wants the length of the space to be 1 foot less than twice its width. Find the length and width of the garden.

2. Lauren and Jeff were reviewing a school play. Jeff gave the play a score of 2 points less than twice the score Lauren gave to the play. Together, their scores added up to 76. What were the scores they gave the play?

Lesson 7.3

Tell which side of the equation has the term with the greater coefficient.

1. $3x + 1 = 5x + 3$ **2.** $5a - 3 = 2a + 21$ **3.** $2b + 12 = 5b + 1$

4. $20y - 10 = 3y - 800$ **5.** $6y - 3 = 8 + 2y$ **6.** $10 + y = 2y - 12$

Tell what you would add to or subtract from each side of the equation to collect like variable terms on one side.

7. $3y + 3 = 6y - 6$ **8.** $n + 7 = 8n - 7$ **9.** $12m - 6 = 8m + 18$

10. $5 - 2x = 7x - 4$ **11.** $8 - 3x = 9x - 4$ **12.** $12y + 3 = y + 19$

13. $2x - 7 = 2 - x$ **14.** $2y - 6 = 9 - 3y$ **15.** $9d - 1 = 2d + 20$

Solve and check.

16. $2n + 18 = 4n$ **17.** $4m - 16 = 5m$ **18.** $2p - 14 = 9p$

19. $16 - 2q = 6q$ **20.** $24 - 3s = s$ **21.** $18 - 6t = 3t$

22. $2n + 2 = 2(n + 1)$ **23.** $p - 22 = 3(2p - 4)$ **24.** $t - 19 = {}^-2(t + 5)$

Lesson 7.4

Tell whether the value is a *solution* or *not a solution* of the inequality.

1. $y + 2 \geq 4; y = 5$ **2.** $8 \leq 4p - 3; p = 1$ **3.** $5 \geq 5x + 2; x = 1$

4. $x + 2 > 3; x = 5$ **5.** ${}^-3 < 2n; n = 1$ **6.** $m - 7 \leq 3; m = 10$

Graph the inequality on a number line.

7. $x < 3$ **8.** $5 \leq p$ **9.** $8 > y$ **10.** $k > 4$ **11.** ${}^-2 \leq n$

Lesson 7.5

Write *yes* or *no* to tell whether the inequality symbol would be reversed in the solution.

1. $-3x > 4$ **2.** $2x < {}^-20$ **3.** $7p \geq 21$ **4.** ${}^-2x + 1 \leq 17$

In the correct order, name the operations you would use to solve the inequality.

5. $8x + 6 > 70$ **6.** $\frac{x}{2} + 4 \leq 3$ **7.** $3y - 3 \leq 3$

Solve and graph.

8. $a + 2 > 8$ **9.** $x + 4 < {}^-8$ **10.** $b - 3.8 \leq 1.6$ **11.** $\frac{k}{3} \geq 4$

12. $y - 3.6 \geq 9$ **13.** $3x \leq 300$ **14.** ${}^-20y \leq 80$ **15.** $\frac{{}^-b}{3} \geq 5$

CHAPTER 8

Lesson 8.1

Copy and complete the table of values.

	$y = 3 + x$			
	x	$3 + x$	y	(x,y)
1.	4	$3 + 4$	?	?
2.	$^-4$	$3 - 4$	?	?
3.	6	$3 + 6$	?	?
4.	2.5	$3 + 2.5$	?	?

	$y = 5x - 2$			
	x	$5x - 2$	y	(x,y)
5.	2	$10 - 2$	?	?
6.	4	$20 - 2$	?	?
7.	7	$35 - 2$	?	?
8.	$^-2$	$^-10 - 2$	?	?

Write *yes* or *no* to tell whether the ordered pair is a solution of the equation $y = 7 - 2x$.

9. $(^-2,11)$ **10.** $(1,5)$ **11.** $(^-2,10)$ **12.** $(2,^-3)$ **13.** $(5,^-3)$

Write *yes* or *no* to tell whether the ordered pair is a solution of the equation $y = 2x + 5$.

14. $(0,5)$ **15.** $(^-3,^-1)$ **16.** $(0,3)$ **17.** $(4,11)$ **18.** $(5,15)$

Rewrite the equation to express y in terms of x.

19. $y + 2x = 10$ **20.** $y - 3x = 1$ **21.** $y - 2x = 7$ **22.** $y + 3x = 3$

23. $2y - 2x = 6$ **24.** $3y - 9x = 36$ **25.** $5y + 15x = 5$ **26.** $2y + 7x = 1$

Make a table of values to find three solutions of the equation. Let $x = {}^-3, 0, 3$.

27. $y + 2x = 10$ **28.** $y - 2x = 6$ **29.** $y - x = 8$ **30.** $y + \frac{x}{3} = 9$

Lesson 8.2

Use the strategy *guess* and *check* to solve.

1. Sharon bought 10 plants for her garden, for a cost of $3.52. The gladiolas cost 59¢; mums cost 25¢. How many of each did she buy?

2. Samantha bought 12 CDs for a total of $149.88. Some of them sold for $11.99; the rest sold for $12.99. How many of each did she buy?

Lesson 8.3

Draw a coordinate plane. Graph and label these points.

1. $(5,0)$ **2.** $(^-5,5)$ **3.** $(2,^-2)$ **4.** $(3,3)$ **5.** $(0,^-1)$

6. $(2,5)$ **7.** $(0,3)$ **8.** $(5,^-2)$ **9.** $(^-4,0)$ **10.** $(^-2,6)$

Lesson 8.4

Write *yes* or *no* to tell whether the ordered pair is a solution of $y = 2 + 4x$.

1. (2,10)   **2.** (¯2,¯6)   **3.** (3,15)   **4.** (¯4,¯16)   **5.** (3,19)   **6.** (0,2)

Match the graph with the set of ordered pairs.

7. (¯1,4) (0,4) (1,4)   **8.** (¯1,¯3) (0,0) (1,3)   **9.** (¯1,¯1) (0,0) (1,1)

a. 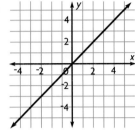   **b.** 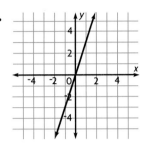   **c.**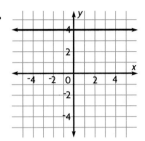

Match the graph with the equation.

10. $x + y = 2$ **11.** $2x + y = 4$ **12.** $4x + 2y = 0$

a. 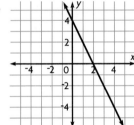   **b.** 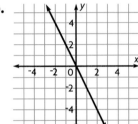   **c.**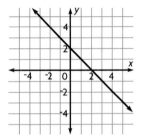

Lesson 8.5

Graph the inequality $y \leq x + 3$. Write *yes* or *no* to tell whether the ordered pair is a solution of the inequality.

1. (1,2)   **2.** (5,10)   **3.** (2,¯1)   **4.** (2,5)   **5.** (4,12)

6. (5,12)   **7.** (3,10)   **8.** (¯2,3)   **9.** (¯7,¯1)   **10.** (¯3,¯2)

CHAPTER 9

Lesson 9.1

Trace each figure, and see if you can use it as a basic unit for constructing a tessellation pattern of at least two rows. Write *yes* or *no* to tell whether the figure forms a tessellation.

1.   **2.**   **3.**

4.   **5.**   **6.**

Lesson 9.2

Match the named polyhedron to the net shown.

1.

2.

3.

4.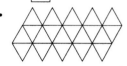

5.

6.

7.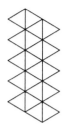

8.

9.

A. tetrahedron   **B.** cube   **C.** octahedron   **D.** dodecahedron   **E.** icosahedron

Complete the table below.

		Vertices (v)	Faces (f)	Edges (e)
10.	Tetrahedron	?	?	?
11.	Cube	?	?	?
12.	Octahedron	?	?	?
13.	Dodecahedron	?	?	?

Lesson 9.3

Write *Archimedean spiral*, *equiangular spiral*, or *helix* to classify each pattern.

1.

2.

3.

Lesson 9.4

Write *diverging* or *converging* to describe the pattern, and give the ratio.

1. 2, 6, 18, 54, ...

2. 64, 16, 4, 1, ...

3. 100, 20, 4, 0.8, ...

4. 5, 10, 20, 40, ...

5. 1, 6, 36, 216, ...

6. 0.8, 4, 20, 100, ...

CHAPTER 10

Lesson 10.1

Convert the given measurement.

1. 12 kg = ▦ lb
2. 110 lb = ▦ kg
3. 36 lb = ▦ kg
4. 42 kg = ▦ lb

5. 25 yd = ▦ ft
6. 135 ft = ▦ yd
7. 45 ft = ▦ in.
8. 83 in. = ▦ ft

9. 26 mi = ▦ ft
10. 132 ft = ▦ mi
11. 306 in. = ▦ yd
12. 47 yd = ▦ in.

13. 70 cm = ▦ in.
14. 76 in. = ▦ cm
15. 6 gal = ▦ L
16. 14 L = ▦ gal

Lesson 10.2

Predict whether each fraction is equivalent to a terminating or a repeating decimal. Then write each fraction as a decimal.

1. $\frac{3}{16}$
2. $\frac{7}{20}$
3. $\frac{5}{8}$
4. $\frac{3}{12}$

5. $\frac{1}{6}$
6. $\frac{11}{12}$
7. $\frac{5}{3}$
8. $\frac{9}{5}$

9. $\frac{11}{3}$
10. $\frac{14}{6}$
11. $\frac{7}{16}$
12. $\frac{11}{20}$

13. $\frac{3}{8}$
14. $\frac{14}{12}$
15. $\frac{7}{6}$
16. $\frac{19}{12}$

17. $\frac{8}{3}$
18. $\frac{11}{5}$
19. $\frac{7}{3}$
20. $\frac{11}{6}$

Write the equivalent fraction or mixed number in simplest form.

21. 1.75
22. 0.1875
23. 3.125
24. 4.375

25. 0.3125
26. 3.40
27. 0.65
28. $0.\overline{3}$

29. $3.\overline{3}$
30. $0.\overline{7}$
31. $0.\overline{5}$
32. $0.\overline{27}$

33. $0.\overline{63}$
34. $2.\overline{2}$
35. $1.\overline{27}$
36. 3.50

37. 0.5625
38. 2.625
39. 1.875
40. 1.125

Lesson 10.3

Tell whether each is divisible by 2, 3, or 6.

1. 140 batteries
2. $535.74
3. $220,000.50
4. 189 pans
5. $105.00

Tell whether each is divisible by 4 or 8.

6. $68.80
7. $21.69
8. 1572
9. 224 flowers
10. 876 pencils

Tell whether each is divisible by 5, 9, or 10.

11. 210 quarters
12. $15.75
13. 315
14. 3,510 books
15. 1,800 birds

Lesson 10.4

For Exercise 1, copy and complete the table.

A sales group pays a daily food allowance plus mileage for business trips. Use the formula Expenses = $72.00 + 0.28 m and a calculator. Round to the nearest cent.

1.

	Trip 1	Trip 2	Trip 3	Trip 4	Trip 5
Miles (m)	82	130	241	320	418
Expenses	?	?	?	?	?

2. What are the expenses for a 500-mile business trip?

CHAPTER 11

Lesson 11.1

1. Write the first four terms in an arithmetic sequence that begins with 1.5 and has a common difference of 2.5.

2. Write the first four terms of a geometric sequence that begins with ⁻8 and has a common ratio of ⁻0.5.

3. The fifth term of a geometric sequence is 80. The common ratio is ⁻2. What are the first four terms of the sequence?

4. Is the sequence 500, 250, 125, … arithmetic, geometric, or neither? Explain.

5. The fifth term of a geometric sequence is $\frac{5}{16}$. The common ratio is $\frac{1}{2}$. What are the first four terms of the sequence?

6. Is the sequence ⁻8, ⁻3, 2, 7, … arithmetic, geometric, or neither? Explain.

Lesson 11.2

Write an expression for the nth term of the sequence. Find the 25th term.

1. Start with 2.5 ⟶ Add 3

2. Start with ⁻1.3 ⟶ Subtract 1.1

3. Start with 3 ⟶ Add 2

4. Start with 8.1 ⟶ Subtract 0.3

Draw an interation diagram for the described sequence. Name the first five terms of the sequence.

5. Sequence starts with 8. Common difference is 3.

6. Sequence starts with 7. Common difference is 2.

Lesson 11.3

Write the first four terms of the sequence described by the iteration diagram. Draw the sequence on a number line. Write *converge* or *diverge* to describe it.

1. Start with 1,000 → Divide by 10

2. Start with 4 → Multiply by 5

Write an algebraic expression for the *n*th term.

3. Start with 3 → Multiply by $\frac{1}{3}$

4. Start with 1 → Multiply by $\frac{1}{4}$

Name the common ratio for the geometric sequence. Then draw an iteration diagram for the sequence.

5. 54, 18, 6, 2, …

6. $\frac{1}{4}, \frac{3}{4}, \frac{9}{4}, \frac{27}{4}, …$

7. 48, 24, 12, 6, …

Lesson 11.4

1. Find the first 20 terms of the Fibonacci sequence.

Multiply the first and last terms. Then tell whether this product is 1 more or 1 less than the product of the two middle terms.

2. 987, 1597, 2584, 4181

3. 1597, 2584, 4181, 6765

4. 4181, 6765, 10946, 17711

5. 21, 34, 55, 89

6. 13, 21, 34, 55

7. 144, 233, 377, 610

CHAPTER 12

Lesson 12.1

Tell whether the figures in each pair are similar. Write *yes* or *no*.

1. 21 cm, 11 cm, 6 cm, 12 cm

2. 10.5 m, 7 m, 7.5 m, 5 m

3. 12 in., 18 in., 24 in., 36 in.

The figures in each pair are similar. Find the scale factor. Then solve for *x*.

4. 18 ft, 15 ft, *x*, 5 ft

5. 12 ft, 18 ft, *x*, 6 ft

6. 9 ft, 5 ft, *x*, 15 ft

7. 26 m, 20 m, *x*, 6 m

Lesson 12.2

The scale of a scale drawing is $\frac{1}{2}$ in. = 8 ft. Find the actual measurement.

1. 4 in.　　**2.** 6 in.　　**3.** 1.5 in.　　**4.** 8 in.　　**5.** 9.5 in.　　**6.** 10.25 in.

The scale of a scale drawing is 1 in. = 15 ft. Find the actual measurement.

7. 4 in.　　**8.** 6 in.　　**9.** 1.5 in.　　**10.** 8 in.　　**11.** 9.5 in.　　**12.** 10.25 in.

The scale is 1 in. = 18 mi. Find the length each distance would be on
a scale drawing.

13. 54 mi　　**14.** 72 mi　　**15.** 126 mi　　**16.** 9.0 mi　　**17.** 11.7 mi　　**18.** 184.5 mi

Use the given scale to make a scale drawing.

19. square with an 18 in. side; scale 1 in. = 6 in.　　**20.** square with a 24 in. side; scale 1 in. = 4 in.

21. rectangle 10 ft × 50 ft; scale $\frac{1}{2}$ in. = 5 ft.　　**22.** rectangle 8 ft × 32 ft; scale 1 in. = 4 ft.

Lesson 12.3

Tell whether the figures show self-similarity. Write *yes* or *no*.

1. 　　**2.** 　　**3.**

4. 　　**5.** 　　**6.**

Lesson 12.4

Tell whether the objects in each pair are *similar, congruent, both* or *neither.*

1. 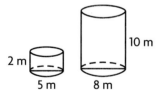　　**2.** 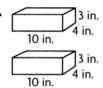　　**3.**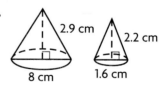

The objects in each pair are similar. Find the ratios of corresponding sides.
Write each as a decimal.

4. 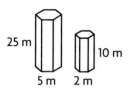　　**5.** 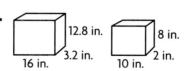　　**6.**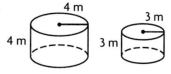

CHAPTER 13

Lesson 13.1

Write enlarged or reduced to describe the scale model made with the given scale.

1. 30 in. : 1 in.   **2.** 1 in. : 4 ft   **3.** 50 m : 1 cm   **4.** 6 in. : 200 ft

5. 1 in. : 8 in.   **6.** 1 yd : 1 in.   **7.** 25 cm : 1 cm   **8.** 1 in. : 20 in.

Change both measurements to the same unit of measure, and find the scale factor.

9. 8 in. model of a 30 ft object   **10.** 20 in. model of a 40 ft object

11. 2 ft model of a 1 in. object   **12.** 4 in. model of a 6 ft object

13. 2 ft model of a 20 yd object   **14.** 2 ft model of an 8 yd object

15. 20 in. model of a 1,200 ft object   **16.** 3 in. model of a 1 cm object
(HINT: 1 cm ≈ 0.4 in.)

Lesson 13.2

Use the scale factor 10 in.: 30 ft to find the unknown measurement.

1. model: 24 in.   **2.** model: 3 in.   **3.** model: 1 in.   **4.** model: 2 in.
   actual: _?_ ft   actual: _?_ ft   actual: _?_ ft   actual: _?_ ft

5. model: _?_ in.   **6.** model: _?_ in.   **7.** model: _?_ in.   **8.** model: _?_ in.
   actual: 72 ft   actual: 18 ft   actual: 144 ft   actual: 36 ft

Use the scale factor 11 in.: 40 ft to find the unknown measurement.

9. model: _?_ in.   **10.** model: _?_ in.   **11.** model: 10 in.   **12.** model: 14 in.
   actual: 84 ft   actual: 6 ft   actual: _?_ ft   actual: _?_ ft

Lesson 13.3

For each cube with the given length, an enlarged scale model is built using a scale factor of $\frac{4}{1}$. Find the length of the model and the number of centimeter cubes used to build it.

1. 2 cm   **2.** 3 cm   **3.** 4 cm   **4.** 5 cm

For the cube with the given length, a reduced scale model is built using a scale factor of $\frac{1}{3}$. Find the length of the model and the number of centimeter cubes used to build it.

5. 3 cm   **6.** 6 cm   **7.** 9 cm   **8.** 18 cm

Lesson 13.4

A cylinder is 32 in. tall with a circumference of 72 in. An open scale model is made using the given height. Find the scale factor and the circumference of the model.

1. model height: 8 in.   **2.** model height: 12 in.   **3.** model height: 16 in .

CHAPTER 14

Lesson 14.1

Write an equation for the problem. Then solve.

1. Find 30% of 150.   **2.** Find 7% of 80.   **3.** Find 33% of 210.

4. Find 45% of 200.   **5.** Find 11% of 90.   **6.** Find 62.5% of 160.

Write a proportion for the problem. Then solve.

7. Find 4% of 300.   **8.** Find 35% of 280.   **9.** Find 130% of 60.

10. Find 12% of 400.   **11.** Find 40% of 310.   **12.** Find 125% of 80.

Find the percent of the number.

13. 130% of 800   **14.** 65% of 90   **15.** 1.5% of 200   **16.** $33\frac{1}{3}$% of 195

17. 70% of 120   **18.** 5.5% of 200   **19.** 3% of 150   **20.** 65% of 100

Lesson 14.2

Write an equation for the problem. Then solve.

1. What percent of 67.5 is 135?   **2.** 12 is what percent of 18?   **3.** What percent of 36 is 9?

Write a proportion for the problem. Then solve.

4. What percent of 25 is 80?   **5.** 8 is what percent of 20?

Solve by using any method.

6. What percent of 30 is 24?   **7.** 270 is what percent of 360?

8. What percent of 70 is 175?   **9.** 30 is what percent of 75?

10. 48 is what percent of 200?   **11.** What percent of 24 is 96?

12. 8 is what percent of 4?   **13.** What percent of 84 is 14?

Lesson 14.3

Write an equation for the problem. Then solve.

1. 75% of what number is 90?

2. 154 is 25% of what number?

Write a proportion for the problem. Then solve.

3. 10% of what number is 22?

4. 48 is 15% of what number?

Solve.

5. 75% of what number is 132?

6. 148 is 37% of what number?

7. 30% of what number is 48?

8. 116 is 200% of what number?

Lesson 14.4

Write the common ratio that is nearly equivalent to the percent.

1. 76%   **2.** 52%   **3.** 34%   **4.** 59%   **5.** 10.3%   **6.** 26%

Write the common percent that is nearly equivalent to the ratio.

7. $\frac{20}{101}$ **8.** $\frac{32}{89}$ **9.** $\frac{97}{102}$ **10.** $\frac{27}{53}$ **11.** $\frac{40}{158}$ **12.** $\frac{13}{17}$

Estimate the number.

13. 40% of 301 is about what number?

14. 24% of 1,987 is about what number?

Estimate the percent.

15. About what percent of 151 is 48?

16. About what percent of 83 is 58?

CHAPTER 15
Lesson 15.1

Find the amount of increase or decrease.

1. original price: $200
new price: $260

2. original savings: $1,000
new savings: $625

3. original amount: 450
new amount: 975

Find the percent of increase or decrease to the nearest percent.

4. original amount: 125
new amount: 175

5. original cost: $7.10
new cost: $5.40

6. original amount: 700
new amount: 680

7. original price: $48
new price: $52

8. original cost: $1,000
new cost: $600

9. original amount: 8
new amount: 64

Lesson 15.2

Find the commission to the nearest cent.

1. total sales: $12,000
   commission rate: 7%

2. total sales: $800
   commission rate: 3.5%

3. total sales: $450
   commission rate: $4\frac{1}{4}\%$

Find the total pay. Round to the nearest cent when needed.

4. total sales: $500
   commission rate: 12%
   monthly salary: $225

5. total sales: $3,500
   commission rate: 5.5%
   monthly salary: $450

6. total sales: $42,500
   commission rate: $2\frac{1}{2}\%$
   monthly salary: $250

Find the missing number.

7. total sales: $6,000
   commission rate: _?_
   commission: $180

8. total sales: _?_
   commission rate: 6%
   commission: $24

9. total sales: $5,600
   commission rate: _?_
   commission: $336

Lesson 15.3

Copy and complete this table.

	Name	Percent Withheld for Tax	Amount Earned	Amount Withheld
1.	Martin Cooper	12%	$325.25	?
2.	Maria Rodrigues	12%	?	$33.66
3.	Mariam Stuart	?	$420.00	$50.40
4.	Alex Timor	12%	?	$97.44

Lesson 15.4

Find the interest and the total amount to the nearest cent.

1. principal = $430
   rate = 6%
   time = 6 mo

2. principal = $3,000
   rate = 4%
   time = 2 yr

3. principal = $5,500
   rate = 7%
   time = 3 mo

4. principal = $510
   rate = 5%
   time = 2 yr

5. principal = $6,500
   rate = 3.5%
   time = 3 yr

6. principal = $2,000
   rate = 9%
   time = 6 mo

Find the missing number.

7. Interest = $40
   principal = _?_
   rate = 4%
   time = 5 yr

8. Interest = $200
   principal = $2,000
   rate = 5%
   time = _?_

9. Interest = $175
   principal = $5,000
   rate = _?_
   time = 6 mo

CHAPTER 16

Lesson 16.1

You conduct a survey of U.S. teens aged 13–15 to find out what songs are their favorites. Tell whether the given samples are biased. If it is, tell why.

1. a random survey of 1,000 teens living on the West Coast

2. a random survey of 200 teens aged 13–15

3. a random survey of 250 teens aged 11–15

4. a random survey of 500 Latino teens

There are 2,400 students at your school. Use the unbiased survey results to make an estimate about the school population.

5. Of 400 students, 70 like to study in the kitchen

6. Of 400 students, 123 like to study in the dining room

7. Of 400 students, 87 like to study in the bedroom

8. Of 400 students, 157 like to study in the family room

Lesson 16.2

Solve a simpler problem.

1. Suppose you have a jar filled with marbles. You pull out and mark 18. After you return them to the jar and mix them with all the unmarked marbles, you take out another handful. In the new handful of 28 marbles, you find 9 marked marbles. Estimate the number of marbles in the jar.

2. Suppose you have a jar filled with marbles. You pull out and mark 12. After you return them to the jar and mix them with all the unmarked marbles, you take out another handful. In the new handful of 15 marbles, you find 5 marked marbles. Estimate the number of marbles in the jar.

Lesson 16.3

Sam conducted a survey to determine the number of students who prefer different kinds of fruit. For Exercises 1–2, use Sam's results in the table.

STUDENT FRUIT PREFERENCES			
	Orange	Cantaloupe	Peach
Girls	14	8	28
Boys	26	8	16

1. Select an appropriate graph to compare the results for the three beverages. Explain you choice. Then graph the results.

2. Make a multiple-bar graph to compare girls' and boys' responses. What does this graph show you?

Lesson 16.4

For Exercises 1–4, use the graph at the right.

1. Estimate the value of the investment in 1991.

2. Estimate the value of the investment in 1994.

3. By how much did the investment grow or shrink from 1986 to 1996?

4. By how much did the investment grow or shrink from 1990 to 1994?

CHAPTER 17

Lesson 17.1

Find the mean, median, and mode.

1. 10, 6, 8, 3, 13, 8, 9, 7   2. $24, $19, $17, $13, $18, $20   3. 4.3, 3.1, 2.1, 4.1, 1.9, 2.1, 2.1, 5.1

Write a set of data with at least five values and the given measures.

4. a mode of $85   5. a median of 18°F   6. a mean of 14°C

7. Why is the median the best measure of central tendency for these salaries? $2,400, $800, $680, $695, $680, $790

8. Which measure of central tendency is best for these values? Explain. 110, 120, 132, 134, 180, 190, 190

Lesson 17.2

The temperatures in this table were recorded during the first two weeks of September.

1. Make a box-and-whisker graph for the high temperatures and a box-and-whisker graph for the low temperatures. Use one number line for both graphs.

2. Make a back-to-back stem-and-leaf plot to display this same data on the high and low temperatures.

Use your box-and-whisker graph and stem-and-leaf plot from Exercises 1 and 2.

3. What are the range of high temperatures and the range of low temperatures?

4. What is the median high temperature? the median low temperature?

TEMPERATURE (°F)		
Date	High	Low
September 1	50	35
2	55	36
3	60	42
4	61	41
5	61	37
6	72	50
7	73	52
8	72	50
9	79	54
10	70	53
11	68	50
12	52	36
13	51	38
14	68	50

Lesson 17.3

For each graph, write *positive*, *negative*, or *no correlation* to describe the relationship.

1.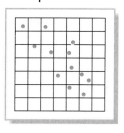

2.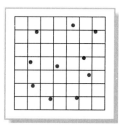

3.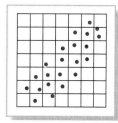

4.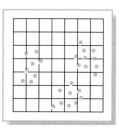

5.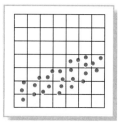

6.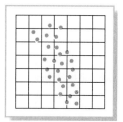

Lesson 17.4

For Exercises 1–4, use the graph of T-shirt sales.

1. What does the graph suggest about the sales?

2. How much did sales increase from the second period (1971–1975) to the third? from the fourth to the fifth?

3. Why is the graph misleading?

4. How would you correct the graph so that it more accurately shows the sales?

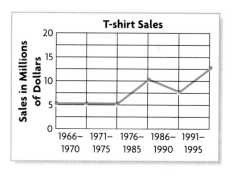

CHAPTER 18

Solve by accounting for all possibilities.

1. Draw a tree diagram to show the possible outcomes of heads and tails if you toss a quarter and a dime. How many outcomes are possible?

2. Draw a tree diagram to show the possible outcomes of heads and tails if you toss a penny, two nickels, and two dimes. How many outcomes are possible?

3. Draw a tree diagram to show possible outcomes, or outfits, of 4 different shirts and 5 different pants.

Lesson 18.2

Make an organized list to find the number of possible outcomes.

1. games: baseball, golf, racquetball
times: afternoon, evening

2. flavors: vanilla, butterscotch, blueberry
toppings: chocolate, marshmallow

Find the number of possible outcomes.

3. 2 concert dates, 3 show times on each

4. 3 appetizers, 5 entrees, 3 desserts

Lesson 18.3

Find the value.

1. $5!$ **2.** $9!$ **3.** $\frac{13!}{1!}$ **4.** $\frac{12!}{(12-5)!}$ **5.** $7! - 2!$

Find the number of permutations.

6. $_{11}P_8$ **7.** $_9P_3$ **8.** $_7P_2$ **9.** $_{18}P_5$ **10.** $_{40}P_4$

Find the number of combinations.

11. $_6C_2$ **12.** $_7C_5$ **13.** $_{10}C_4$ **14.** $_{11}C_3$ **15.** $_{14}C_{11}$

Lesson 18.4

A bag contains 3 peanuts, 4 almonds, 2 cashews, and 5 hazelnuts. You choose
one nut without looking. Find the probability.

1. P(peanut)   **2.** P(almond or cashew)   **3.** P(hazelnut)   **4.** P(not almond)

You spin the pointer of a spinner with 8 congruent sections numbered 1–8. Find the probability.

5. P(2)   **6.** P(3 or 6)   **7.** P(even)   **8.** P(3 or even)   **9.** P(1, 2, or 4)   **10.** P(not 4)

You roll a number cube numbered 1 to 6. Find the probability.

11. P(2)   **12.** P(3 or 5)   **13.** P(number < 4)   **14.** P(number > 6)

Write yes or *no* to tell whether the given outcomes are equally likely.
If no, explain.

15. You roll a number cube numbered 1 to 6
and get 3 or 4.

16. You toss a coin 3 times and you get
3 heads or 3 tails.

17. You roll a number cube numbered 1 to 6
and get an even number or an odd
number.

18. You toss a number cube and get a prime
number or a composite number.

Lesson 18.5

Tell whether the events are *independent* or *dependent*.

1. Carl draws a marble from a bag. Without replacing it, he draws a second marble.

2. Tasha tosses a cowrie shell, rolls a number cube, and tosses another cowrie shell.

A box contains 2 red marbles, 8 blue marbles, and 5 white marbles.
The marbles are selected at random, one at a time, and are not replaced.
Find the probability.

3. P(white and blue)

4. P(red and not red)

5. P(blue and not blue)

6. P(red and blue)

7. P(white and red)

8. P(white and blue and blue)

CHAPTER 19
Lesson 19.1

There are 5 different colors of marbles in a box. Michael took a sample from the box and counted the colors. His results appear in the table at the right.

Color	No.
Yellow	47
Green	38
Orange	28
Purple	52
Red	35
Total	200

1. Find the experimental probability of choosing a red marble.

2. Find the experimental probability of choosing an orange marble.

3. Find the experimental probability of choosing a yellow or purple marble.

4. Suppose someone scoops 300 marbles out of the box. How many of them would you expect to be yellow?

Lesson 19.2

A computer-generated list of random numbers 1–6 is shown. Use it to find experimental probabilities for Exercises 1–2. Select any starting point.

1	6	5	4	2	3	4
1	5	6	3	6	6	1
6	6	1	4	5	4	3
2	2	1	4	1	3	6
4	2	2	4	1	2	2
2	6	2	2	3	1	1
4	4	1	4	5	5	2

1. A number cube has the numbers 1–6 marked on its sides. Estimate how many times you will have to roll the cube before you get the numbers 1–6.

2. Estimate how many times you will have to roll the cube before you get the numbers 1–4.

Lesson 19.3

Use a proportion to estimate the population.

1. Red, yellow, green, and blue marbles are in a bag of 200. Paul randomly draws 40 marbles out of the bag and finds 13 of them to be green. Estimate the number of green marbles in the bag.

2. Red, yellow, green, and blue marbles are in a bag of 700. Maria randomly draws 50 marbles out of the bag and finds 31 of them to be yellow. Estimate the number of yellow marbles in the bag.

Lesson 19.4

A randomly dropped object falls on the figure at the right. Use the figure to find the geometric probability that a randomly dropped object will fall in the given region.

1. A   **2.** B   **3.** C   **4.** D   **5.** A or B

6. A or C   **7.** A or D   **8.** B or C   **9.** B or D   **10.** C or D

11. not D   **12.** not C   **13.** not B   **14.** not A   **15.** not (A or B)

CHAPTER 20

Lesson 20.1

For Exercises 1–7, use the figure at the right. Find the measure of the given angle.

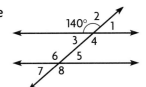

1. ∠1   **2.** ∠8   **3.** ∠3   **4.** ∠4

5. Name the four pairs of corresponding angles.

6. Name the alternate interior angles.

7. Name the alternate exterior angles.

Tell whether the lines appear to be *parallel, perpendicular,* or *neither*.

8.   **9.**   **10.**

Trace $\overleftrightarrow{ST}$ and P as shown for each.

11. Construct a line through point *P* and perpendicular to $\overleftrightarrow{ST}$.

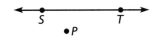

12. Construct a line through point *P* and parallel to $\overleftrightarrow{ST}$.

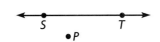

13. Construct a line through point *P* and perpendicular to $\overleftrightarrow{ST}$.

Lesson 20.2

Draw the figures by using a ruler and a protractor. Then construct the bisector of each by using a compass and a straightedge.

1. a 2 in. line segment

2. a 115° angle

3. a 70° angle

4. an 87° angle

5. a 7 in. line segment

6. a 9 in. line segment

7. a 30° angle

8. a 135° angle

9. a 140° angle

10. a 180° angle

11. a 5 in. line segment

12. an 8 in. line segment

Lesson 20.3

Determine whether the triangles are congruent. Write *yes, no,* or *not necessarily.* Then explain.

1.

2.

3.

4.

5.

6.

Use the indicated rule to construct a triangle congruent to the given triangle.

7. SAS

8. SSS

9. ASA

Lesson 20.4

Construct △*ABC* similar to △*DEF*. Make $\overline{AB}$ correspond to $\overline{DE}$, and use the given length of $\overline{AB}$. △*DEF* is not drawn to scale.

1. *AB* = 3 in.

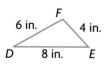

2. *AB* = 3 cm

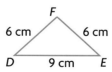

Draw a triangle with the given angle measures. Then construct a triangle similar to but not congruent to the first triangle.

3. 20°, 70°, 90°

4. 45°, 55°, 80°

5. 40°, 55°, 85°

6. 20°, 50°, 110°

7. 40°, 50°, 90°

8. 35°, 45°, 100°

9. 25°, 60°, 95°

10. 15°, 60°, 105°

Lesson 20.5

Draw a triangle with these dimensions.

1. a 30° angle between two 3 in. sides

2. a 80° angle between 3 cm and 4 cm sides

Use a ruler and a protractor to draw a triangle with these dimensions.

3. a 3 in. side between two 65° angles

4. a 4 cm side between 35° and 55° angles

Construct the figure.

5. an equilateral triangle with sides the same length as the given segment.

A ——————————————— B

6. an isosceles triangle with equal sides the same length as the given segment.

C ——————————— D

7. a right triangle with each side longer than 4 cm

CHAPTER 21

Lesson 21.1

Graph △ABC and △A'B'C'. Then tell whether the transformation is a *rotation, translation,* or *reflection.*

1. A(⁻2,⁻6)   A'(2,6)
B(⁻5,⁻1)   B'(5,1)
C(⁻3,4)   C'(3,⁻4)

2. A(1,4)   A'(⁻1,4)
A(4,6)   A'(⁻4,6)
A(6,2)   A'(⁻6,2)

3. A(1,3)   A'(4,3)
A(⁻3,4)   A'(0,4)
A(2,⁻4)   A'(5,⁻4)

Copy quadrilateral *ABCD* on a coordinate plane.
Rotate point *A* about the point (0,0). Draw the image.

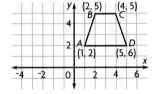

4. Rotate 180° clockwise.

5. Rotate 90° counterclockwise.

Lesson 21.2

Name the transformation that will move the solid figure from Position 1 to Position 2. Write *translation, rotation,* or *reflection.*

1.

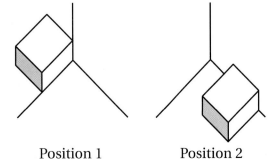

Position 1   Position 2

2.

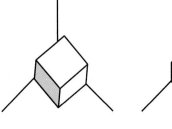
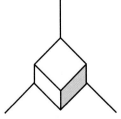

Position 1   Position 2

Lesson 21.3

Copy the figure on the right on a coordinate plane. Perform the given dilation. Give the coordinates of the image, and check it by drawing rays from the origin.

1. Reduce to 50%

2. Enlarge to 150%

3. Enlarge to 125%

4. Reduce to 25%

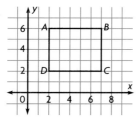

5. Reduce to 75%

6. Enlarge to 200%

7. Enlarge to 175%

8. Reduce to 90%

Lesson 21.4

For Exercises 1–3, use the following reduction dilation.

1. Copy and complete the table.

Stage	0	1	2	3	4	5
Number of pieces	1	3	?	?	?	?

2. What scale factor is used to reduce the square from one stage to the next?

3. Predict the number of pieces at Stage 6.

CHAPTER 22

Lesson 22.1

For Exercises 1–4, use the net at the right.

1. Find the overall dimensions of the net.

2. Find the area of the rectangle with the overall dimensions of the net. Then find the area of the net.

3. What percent of the rectangle's area is the net's area?

4. Copy the faces, and then rearrange them to form other nets of the same solid. Use your nets to find the overall dimensions of the rectangle with the least area.

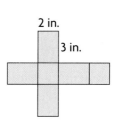

2 in.

3 in.

Lesson 22.2

Draw a front elevation, side elevations, and a back elevation of the model shown.

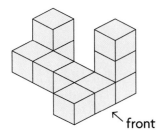

front

Lesson 22.3

Using isometric dot paper, sketch the figure.

1. a rectangular prism that is 3 units long, 2 units deep, and 2 units high.

2. a rectangular prism that is 2 units long, 4 units deep, and 6 units high.

3. a rectangular pyramid that is 5 units high and has a 4 unit × 4 unit base.

4. a rectangular pyramid that is 2 units high and has a 3 unit × 3 unit base.

5. a pentagonal prism that is 8 units high.

6. a pentagonal prism that is 7 units high.

7. a triangular prism that is 2 units high.

8. a triangular prism that is 5 units high.

9. a triangular pyramid that is 3 units high.

10. a square pyramid that is 2 units high and has a 4 unit × 4 unit base.

Lesson 22.4

Draw the given polygon. Then use one-point perspective to complete the drawing of a prism.

1. the vanishing point above and to the left

2. the vanishing point above and to the right

3. the vanishing point above and to the left

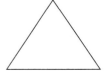

CHAPTER 23

Lesson 23.1

Use the graph at right to answer Exercises 1–3. This table and graph show the change in outdoor temperature one summer day.

Time	Temperature
8 A.M.	62°F
12 P.M.	78°F
4 P.M.	82°F
8 P.M.	80°F
12 A.M.	68°F

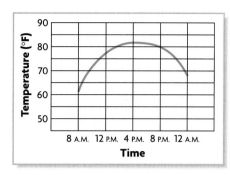

1. Look at the table. How long did it take the temperature to rise from 62°F to 82°F?

2. Look at the graph. How long did it take the temperature to rise from 62°F to 82°F?

3. Look at the graph and table. When is the maximum temperature reached? Which gives better information?

Lesson 23.2

Match each graph to one of the given situation.

1. an oven after it is turned off

2. a cool morning that warms up slowly and then quickly

3. a cyclist riding up a hill, then down

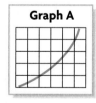

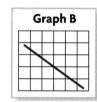

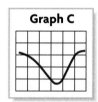

Lesson 23.3

Solve by *making a graph*.

1. The population of Hamford in 1970 was 24,241. In 1980 the population was 31,426, and in 1990 it increased to 36,021. Estimate the population in 1973 and 1987.

2. At 8 A.M., the outdoor temperature was 72°F. The temperature increased constantly to 84°F at 12 noon. Then, from noon until 4 P.M. the temperature increased constantly to 88°F. Use a graph to estimate the temperature at 11 A.M. and 1 P.M.

Lesson 23.4

Tell if the scatterplot shows a relationship between time and distance.

1.
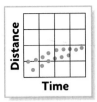

2.
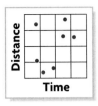

3.
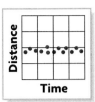

4.
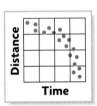

5.
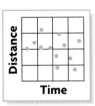

6.
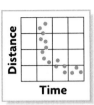

CHAPTER 24

Lesson 24.1

Find the slope of the line containing the given points.

1. $(^-1,^-1)$, $(^-5,2)$ **2.** $(0,0)$, $(6,3)$ **3.** $(1,4)$, $(6,8)$ **4.** $(^-2,^-3)$, $(4,4)$ **5.** $(0,^-2)$, $(^-8,3)$

Find the *x*-intercept and the *y*-intercept. Use the intercepts to graph the equation.

6. $x + y = 8$ **7.** $3x - y = 6$ **8.** $2x + 4y = 16$ **9.** $x + 2y = 4$ **10.** $2x - y = 10$

Find the slope and the *y*-intercept. Then graph the equation.

11. $y = \frac{1}{2}x + 6$ **12.** $y = \frac{1}{3}x + 4$ **13.** $y = \frac{1}{2}x + 7$ **14.** $y = \frac{1}{2}x - 7$ **15.** $y = \frac{1}{7}x + 3$

Write each equation in slope-intercept form.

16. $2x + y = 3$ **17.** $3x - 2y = 6$ **18.** $x - y = 5$ **19.** $4y - 12x = 14$

Lesson 24.2

Tell whether the ordered pair is a solution of the system of equations.
Write *yes* or *no*.

1. $3x + 2y = 1$
$3x - y = -2$
$(1,2)$

2. $x - 7 = ^-2$
$4x - 3y = ^-6$
$(0,3)$

3. $4x - 2y = 0$
$7x - 4y = 1$
$(^-1,^-2)$

4. $7x - y = 14$
$5x + y = 10$
$(0,2)$

Lesson 24.3

Give the domain and the range for the relation.

1.

x	y
1	18
2	26
3	19
4	18

2.

x	y
1	20
2	40
3	60
4	80

3.

x	y
1	50
2	20
3	$^-$10
4	$^-$40

Write *yes* or *no* to tell whether the relation is a function.

4. {(2,5), (1,5), (3,0), (2,4)} **5.** {(0,2), (2,0), (3,$^-$1), ($^-$1,3)} **6.** {(3,6), (1,8), ($^-$2,$^-$3), ($^-$2,0)}

Lesson 24.4

Complete the table of values, write the ordered pairs, and graph the function.

1.

x	f(x)
0	2
1	4
2	6
3	?

2.

x	f(x)
0	3
2	6
4	9
6	?

3.

x	f(x)
1	2
2	4
3	6
4	?

For each graph, identify the slope and the *y*-intercept. Then write a function rule for the linear function.

4.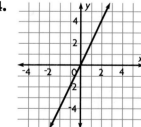

5.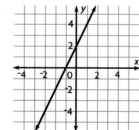

6.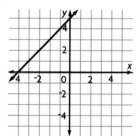

Lesson 24.5

Write three ordered pairs for each nonlinear function. Let $x = 0, 1, 2$.
Then graph.

1. $f(x) = 2x^2 + 1$ **2.** $f(x) = x^3 + 5$ **3.** $f(x) = x^2 - 7$ **4.** $f(x) = x^3 - 10$

5. $f(x) = 5x^2 - 2$ **6.** $f(x) = x^3 + 3$ **7.** $f(x) = {}^-2x^2 + 1$ **8.** $f(x) = 4x^2 - 7$

CHAPTER 25

Lesson 25.1

Classify the polynomial by writing *monomial*, *binomial*, or *trinomial*.

1. $x + 3$ **2.** $3x^2 - 5$ **3.** $2x^2 - 4x$ **4.** $3x^2 + 3x + 7$

Identify the terms of the polynomial.

5. $3x^2 - 2x - 8$ **6.** $5y^5 - 3y^2$ **7.** $^-8s^2 + 4$ **8.** $4k^2 + 2k + 1$

Evaluate the polynomial for $x = 1$.

9. $6x^2$ **10.** $2x^2 - 5$ **11.** $x^2 - 3x$ **12.** $^-2x^2 + 3x + 1$

Evaluate the polynomial for $x = ^-1$.

13. $3x^2$ **14.** $5x + 4$ **15.** $x^2 - x + 3$ **16.** $2x^2 + 2x + 1$

Lesson 25.2

Identify the like terms. If there are no like terms, write none.

1. $5, 3x^2, x, 2x^2$ **2.** $a^5, 3a^3, 7$ **3.** $3x^2, x, ^-5x$ **4.** $7, y^3, y, ^-5$

Write *yes* or *no* to tell whether the polynomial is in simplest form. If the answer is no, simplify by combining like terms.

5. $8x^2 + 2x - 3x^2$ **6.** $6y^3 + 3y^2 + 3$ **7.** $2k^4 + 2k - k^2 - 3$

8. $1 + p^2 + p + 2p + 4$ **9.** $3x^2 + 3x$ **10.** $5a^3 + 2a^3 - 21$

11. $4y^3 + y^2 - y - 3$ **12.** $5 - c^2 + 2c + 5c^2$ **13.** $7 - b^3 + b + 2b^3$

Write *yes* or *no* to tell whether the polynomial is written in standard form.

14. $3x^2 + 2x - 8$ **15.** $3y^2 - 5y^4 + 5 - 3y$ **16.** $1 + x^5 + 2x + 6$

17. $b^2 - 3b + 2$ **18.** $3b + 3 - b^2$ **19.** $c^3 + 2c^2 - c + 3$

20. $5y^3 + y^2 - y + 2$ **21.** $7 - k - 3k^2$ **22.** $3x^2 + x + 7$

Lesson 25.3

Find the sum.

1. $(4x^2 - 4x + 1) + (2x^2 + x - 5)$ **2.** $(^-3x^2 + 3x + 3) + (4x^2 + x - 5)$

3. $(4x + 2) + (2x + 3)$ **4.** $(3x^2 + 6) + (^-3x^2 - 2)$

5. $(x^2 - x + 5) + (3x^2 + x)$ **6.** $(x + 7) + (6x - 4)$

7. $(^-b^2 + b) + (b^2 + 3b)$ **8.** $(x^2 - x) + (2x^2 - 6x + 3)$

Lesson 25.4

Write the opposite of the polynomial.

1. $2x^2 - 3x$ **2.** $3y^2 + y - 4$ **3.** $3x^2 - 5x + 1$ **4.** $5b^2 - 2b + 10$

Find the difference.

5. $(2x^2 - 5) - (x^2 + 2)$ **6.** $(^-b^2 + 3b) - (2b^2 + 5)$ **7.** $(2x^2 - 2x + 5) - (5x + 8)$

8. $(3y^2 + 4) - (2y^2 + y + 1)$ **9.** $(^-c^2 + 6c) - (9c^2 + 7)$ **10.** $(4z^2 + 6z) - (^-3z^2 + 2z)$

CHAPTER 26

Lesson 26.1

Find the number of different direct connections possible for the given
number of locations.

1. 5 cities **2.** 8 bus stops **3.** 4 airports **4.** 10 capitals **5.** 12 islands

6. 3 libraries **7.** 7 cities **8.** 6 towns **9.** 12 schools **10.** 9 companies

Lesson 26.2

Find the number of significant digits in each measurement, based on the
given unit of measure.

1. measurement: 0.23 cm; unit: 0.01 cm **2.** measurement: 602.0 m; unit: 0.1m

3. measurement: 621 cm; unit 1 cm **4.** measurement: 1,216.4 cm; unit: 0.1 cm

Tell which of the two measurements is more accurate.

5. measurement: 41 cm; unit: 1 cm **6.** measurement: 41.82 m; unit: 0.01 m
measurement: 41.4 cm; unit 0.1 cm measurement: 41.8 m; unit: 0.1 m

7. measurement: 83 mi; unit: 1 mi **8.** measurement: 0.0127 m; unit: 0.0001 m
measurement: 83.0 mi; unit: 0.1 mi measurement: 0.012 m; unit: 0.001 m

Find the circumference. Express the answer with the appropriate number
of significant digits. Use $\pi = 3.14$.

9. diameter = 4 m **10.** diameter = 3.2 ft **11.** radius = 11 in. **12.** radius = 2.06 m

13. radius = 7.2 m **14.** diameter = 21 mi **15.** diameter = 72 in. **16.** diameter = 30.2 m

17. radius = 5.5 ft **18.** radius = 8 in. **19.** diameter = 29 m **20.** diameter = 48.6 cm

Lesson 26.3

Find the area of each shaded region. Use π = 3.14.

1.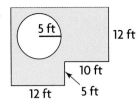

2.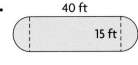

3.

Lesson 26.4

Find the volume of the cylinder or prism. Use π = 3.14.

1.

2.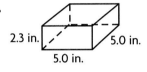

3.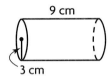

Find the volume of the prism or cone. Use π = 3.14.

4.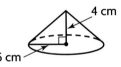

5.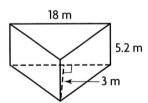

6.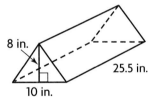

Find the volume of the sphere. Use π = 3.14.

7.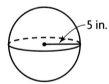

8.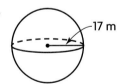

9.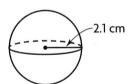

Lesson 26.5

Find the surface area of each figure. Use π = 3.14.

1.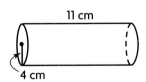

2.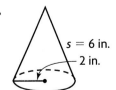

3.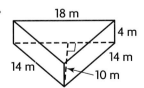

CHAPTER 27

Lesson 27.1

The rectangles in Exercises 1–5 all have the same perimeter. Find the area of each.

1. 8 ft × 7 ft   **2.** 9 ft × 6 ft   **3.** 10 ft × 5 ft   **4.** 11 ft × 4 ft   **5.** 12 ft × 3 ft

The rectangles in Exercises 6-10 all have the same area. Find the perimeter.

6. 8 ft × 6 ft   **7.** 12 ft × 4 ft   **8.** 24 ft × 2 ft   **9.** 16 ft × 3 ft   **10.** 24 ft × 2 ft

The area of a rectangle is given. Find the dimensions with the least perimeter.

11. 9 in.^2 **12.** 4 m^2 **13.** 36 cm^2 **14.** 64 in.^2 **15.** 121 in.^2

The perimeter of a rectangle is given. Find the dimensions of the rectangle with the greatest possible area.

16. 20 ft   **17.** 32 cm   **18.** 44 m   **19.** 48 ft   **20.** 60 ft

Lesson 27.2

Copy and complete the table, showing the changing perimeter and area as the dimensions of a rectangle are repeatedly doubled.

	Length (in feet)	20	40	80	160
	Width (in feet)	10	20	40	80
1.	Perimeter (in feet)	?	?	?	?
2.	Area (in square feet)	?	?	?	?

Find the perimeter and area of the figure. Then double the dimensions, and find the new perimeter and area.

3.
5 yd
5 yd

4.
8 ft
20 ft

5.
21 m
21 m

Lesson 27.3

Pierre has a 16 in. × 20 in. piece of paper. He wants to make an open box with whole number dimensions. Copy and complete the table.

Width	Length	Height	Volume
4 in.	8 in.	6 in.	?
6 in.	10 in.	?	?
8 in.	12 in.	?	?
10 in.	14 in.	?	?
12 in.	16 in.	?	?
14 in.	18 in.	?	?

1. What are the dimensions of the open box with maximum volume?

2. What are the dimensions of the open box with minimum volume?

Lesson 27.4

Find the volume of each figure. Then halve the height of each, and find the new volume. Use 3.14 for π.

1.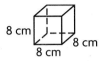
8 cm
8 cm
8 cm

2.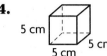
9 cm
8 cm

Find the volume of each figure. Then double each dimension, and find the new volume. Use 3.14 for π.

3.
2 in.
12 in.
4 in.

4.
5 cm
5 cm
5 cm

Find the volume of each figure. Then halve each dimension, and find the new volume.

5.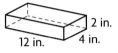
12 cm
4 cm
10 cm

6.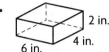
2 in.
6 in.
4 in.

7.
12 ft
5 ft

CHAPTER 28

Lesson 28.1

A 5-ft tall person casts a 2-ft shadow. Find the approximate height of each object that casts the shadow with the given length at about the same time.

1. 32 ft   **2.** 19 ft   **3.** 43 ft   **4.** 73 ft   **5.** 120 ft

6. 8 ft   **7.** 24 ft   **8.** 38 ft   **9.** 82 ft   **10.** 100 ft

Lesson 28.2

Find the unknown length.

1.
?
6 m
8 m

2.
7.5 ft
?
10 ft

3.
24 m
?
18 m

4.
10 ft
6 ft
?

Find the unknown length to the nearest tenth.

5.
5 m
?
5 m

6.
?
9 ft
11 ft

7.
9 m
17 m
?

8.
10 ft
?
7 ft

Lesson 28.3

Find the unknown length.

1.
126 mi, c, 168 mi

2. c, 80 mi, 192 mi

3. 504 mi, c, 945 mi

4. 243 mi, 405 mi, b

Find the unknown length to the nearest tenth.

5.
191 mi, 118 mi, c

6.
37 m, 12 m, a

7. a, 375 km, 300 km

8. 5.0 mi, c, 8.0 mi

Lesson 28.4

Use a calculator or the table on page H88 to find the trigonometric ratio to the nearest hundredth.

1. cos 53°   **2.** tan 42°   **3.** tan 81°   **4.** sin 36°   **5.** cos 41°   **6.** cos 82°

7. cos 21°   **8.** tan 54°   **9.** tan 10°   **10.** sin 8°   **11.** cos 72°   **12.** cos 18°

Use trigonometric ratios to find the unknown length, *x*, to the nearest tenth.

13. x, 45°, 41 cm

14. 402 m, 31°, x

15. x, 22°, 40 m

16. 12°, x, 52 m

17. 20 in., 45°, x

18. 22°, x, 28 ft

19. x, 20 m, 31°

20. x, 27 m, 42°

TABLE OF MEASURES

METRIC UNITS	CUSTOMARY UNITS

Length

METRIC UNITS	CUSTOMARY UNITS
1 millimeter (mm) = 0.001 meter (m)	1 foot (ft) = 12 inches (in.)
1 centimeter (cm) = 0.01 meter	1 yard (yd) = 36 inches
1 decimeter (dm) = 0.1 meter	1 yard = 3 feet
1 kilometer (km) = 1,000 meters	1 mile (mi) = 5,280 feet
	1 mile = 1,760 yards
	1 nautical mile = 6,076.115 feet

Capacity

METRIC UNITS	CUSTOMARY UNITS
1 milliliter (mL) = 0.001 liter (L)	1 teaspoon (tsp) = $\frac{1}{6}$ fluid ounce (fl oz)
1 centiliter (cL) = 0.01 liter	1 tablespoon (tbsp) = $\frac{1}{2}$ fluid ounce
1 deciliter (dL) = 0.1 liter	1 cup (c) = 8 fluid ounces
1 kiloliter (kL) = 1,000 liters	1 pint (pt) = 2 cups
	1 quart (qt) = 2 pints
	1 quart = 4 cups
	1 gallon (gal) = 4 quarts

Mass/Weight

METRIC UNITS	CUSTOMARY UNITS
1 milligram (mg) = 0.001 gram (g)	1 pound (lb) = 16 ounces (oz)
1 centigram (cg) = 0.01 gram	1 ton (T) = 2,000 pounds
1 decigram (dg) = 0.1 gram	
1 kilogram (kg) = 1,000 grams	
1 metric ton (t) = 1,000 kilograms	

Volume/Capacity/Mass for Water

1 cubic centimeter (cm^3) → 1 milliliter → 1 gram

1,000 cubic centimeters → 1 liter → 1 kilogram

TIME

1 minute (min) = 60 seconds (sec)	1 year (yr) = 12 months (mo)
1 hour (hr) = 60 minutes	1 year = 52 weeks
1 day = 24 hours	1 year = 365 days
1 week (wk) = 7 days	

FORMULAS

Perimeter

Polygon	$P =$ sum of the lengths of the sides
Rectangle	$P = 2(l + w)$

Circumference

Circle	$C = 2\pi r$, or $C = \pi d$

Area

Circle	$A = \pi r^2$	Parallelogram	$A = bh$
Rectangle	$A = lw$	Square	$A = s^2$
Triangle	$A = \frac{1}{2}bh$		

Trapezoid $A = \frac{1}{2}h(b_1 + b_2)$

Trigonometric Ratios

sine of $\angle A$ $\sin A = \dfrac{\text{length of side opposite } \angle A}{\text{length of hypotenuse}}$

cosine of $\angle A$ $\cos A = \dfrac{\text{length of side adjacent } \angle A}{\text{length of hypotenuse}}$

tangent of $\angle A$ $\tan A = \dfrac{\text{length of side opposite } \angle A}{\text{length of side adjacent } \angle A}$

Surface Area

Cone	$S = \pi r^2 + \pi rs$
Cylinder	$S = 2(\pi r^2) + (2\pi rh)$

Volume

Cone	$V = \frac{1}{3}Bh$, or $V = \frac{1}{3}\pi r^2 h$
Cube	$V = e^3$
Cylinder	$V = Bh$, or $V = \pi r^2 h$
Prism	$V = Bh$
Pyramid	$V = \frac{1}{3}Bh$ Sphere $V = \frac{4}{3}\pi r^3$

Other

Diameter	$d = 2r$
Pythagorean Property	$c^2 = a^2 + b^2$

Consumer

Distance traveled	$d = rt$
Interest (simple)	$I = prt$
Interest (compound)	$A = p(1 + r)^n$

SYMBOLS

$<$	is less than
$>$	is greater than
$\leq$	is less than or equal to
$\geq$	is greater than or equal to
$\neq$	is not equal to
2^3	the third power of 2
3^{-5}	the negative fifth power of 3
$0.\overline{16}$	repeating decimal 0.161616 . . .
7	positive 7
$^-7$	negative 7
$|^-4|$	absolute value of negative 4
$\sqrt{}$	positive square root
$^-\sqrt{}$	negative square root
(4,7)	the ordered pair 4,7
\$5/hr	the rate \$5 per hour
1:2	ratio of 1 to 2
%	percent
$\perp$	is perpendicular to

$\parallel$	is parallel to
$\cong$	is congruent to
$\sim$	is similar to
$\approx$	is approximately equal to
$\overleftrightarrow{AB}$	line AB
$\overrightarrow{AB}$	ray AB
$\overline{AB}$	line segment AB
$\angle ABC$	angle ABC
$m\angle A$	measure of $\angle A$
$\triangle ABC$	triangle ABC
$\overparen{AB}$	arc AB
$^\circ$	degree (angle or temperature)
π	pi (about 3.14 or $\frac{22}{7}$)
5!	factorial $5 \cdot 4 \cdot 3 \cdot 2 \cdot 1$
P(4)	the probability of the outcome 4
$_6P_4$	permutation $6 \cdot 5 \cdot 4 \cdot 3$
$_5C_3$	combination $\frac{5 \cdot 4 \cdot 3}{3 \cdot 2 \cdot 1}$

TRIGONOMETRIC RATIOS

Angle	Sin	Cos	Tan	Angle	Sin	Cos	Tan
1°	0.017	1.000	0.017	46°	0.719	0.695	1.036
2°	0.035	0.999	0.035	47°	0.731	0.682	1.072
3°	0.052	0.999	0.052	48°	0.743	0.669	1.111
4°	0.070	0.998	0.070	49°	0.755	0.656	1.150
5°	0.087	0.996	0.087	50°	0.766	0.643	1.192
6°	0.105	0.995	0.105	51°	0.777	0.629	1.235
7°	0.122	0.993	0.123	52°	0.788	0.616	1.280
8°	0.139	0.990	0.141	53°	0.799	0.602	1.327
9°	0.156	0.988	0.158	54°	0.809	0.588	1.376
10°	0.174	0.985	0.176	55°	0.819	0.574	1.428
11°	0.191	0.982	0.194	56°	0.829	0.559	1.483
12°	0.208	0.978	0.213	57°	0.839	0.545	1.540
13°	0.225	0.974	0.231	58°	0.848	0.530	1.600
14°	0.242	0.970	0.249	59°	0.857	0.515	1.664
15°	0.259	0.966	0.268	60°	0.866	0.500	1.732
16°	0.276	0.961	0.287	61°	0.875	0.485	1.804
17°	0.292	0.956	0.306	62°	0.883	0.469	1.881
18°	0.309	0.951	0.325	63°	0.891	0.454	1.963
19°	0.326	0.946	0.344	64°	0.899	0.438	2.050
20°	0.342	0.940	0.364	65°	0.906	0.423	2.145
21°	0.358	0.934	0.384	66°	0.914	0.407	2.246
22°	0.375	0.927	0.404	67°	0.921	0.391	2.356
23°	0.391	0.921	0.424	68°	0.927	0.375	2.475
24°	0.407	0.914	0.445	69°	0.934	0.358	2.605
25°	0.423	0.906	0.466	70°	0.940	0.342	2.747
26°	0.438	0.899	0.488	71°	0.946	0.326	2.904
27°	0.454	0.891	0.510	72°	0.951	0.309	3.078
28°	0.469	0.883	0.532	73°	0.956	0.292	3.271
29°	0.485	0.875	0.554	74°	0.961	0.276	3.487
30°	0.500	0.866	0.577	75°	0.966	0.259	3.732
31°	0.515	0.857	0.601	76°	0.970	0.242	4.011
32°	0.530	0.848	0.625	77°	0.974	0.225	4.331
33°	0.545	0.839	0.649	78°	0.978	0.208	4.705
34°	0.559	0.829	0.675	79°	0.982	0.191	5.145
35°	0.574	0.819	0.700	80°	0.985	0.174	5.671
36°	0.588	0.809	0.727	81°	0.988	0.156	6.314
37°	0.602	0.799	0.754	82°	0.990	0.139	7.115
38°	0.616	0.788	0.781	83°	0.993	0.122	8.144
39°	0.629	0.777	0.810	84°	0.995	0.105	9.514
40°	0.643	0.766	0.839	85°	0.996	0.087	11.430
41°	0.656	0.755	0.869	86°	0.998	0.070	14.301
42°	0.669	0.743	0.900	87°	0.999	0.052	19.081
43°	0.682	0.731	0.933	88°	0.999	0.035	28.636
44°	0.695	0.719	0.966	89°	1.000	0.017	57.290
45°	0.707	0.707	1.000				

GLOSSARY

absolute value The distance from a point on the number line to zero *(page 76)*

Addition Property of Opposites The property which states that the sum of a number and its opposite is zero *(page 77)*
Examples: $4 + {}^-4 = 0$
$a + {}^-a = 0$

algebraic equation An equation that contains one or more variables *(page 112)*

algebraic expression An expression that is written using one or more variables *(page 96)*
Examples: $x - 4$; $2a + 5$; $a + b$

algebraic inequality An inequality that contains a variable *(page 142)*

algebraic order of operations See *order of operations.*

alternate exterior angles A pair of angles on the outer sides of two lines cut by a transversal, but on opposite sides of the transversal *(page 378)*

alternate interior angles A pair of angles on the inner sides of two lines cut by a transversal, but on opposite sides of the transversal *(page 378)*

angle A geometric figure formed by two rays that have a common endpoint *(page 178)*

annually Once a year *(page 294)*

area The number of square units needed to cover a given surface *(page 501)*

Archimedean spiral A spiral in which the loops are evenly spaced; see *spiral. (page 184)*

arithmetic sequence An ordered list of numbers that has a common difference between consecutive terms. *(page 212)*
Example: 3, 7, 11, 15, . . .

Associative Property of Addition The property which states that for all real numbers a, b, and c, the sum is always the same, regardless of their grouping *(page H11)*

Associative Property of Multiplication The property which states that for all real numbers a, b, and c, the product is always the same, regardless of their grouping *(page H11)*

average See *mean.*

base The number that is used as a repeated factor *(page 20)*
Example: $6^3 = 6 \times 6 \times 6$
6 is the base; 3 is the exponent.

base A side of a polygon or a face of a solid figure by which the figure is measured or named *(page 503)*

basic unit The shape that is repeated in a tessellation *(page 176)*

biased sample A sample that does not fairly represent the population *(page 304)*

binomial The sum of two monomials *(page 475)*
Example: $3x + 5y$

bisect To divide into two congruent parts *(page 382)*

box-and-whisker graph An organization of data that shows how far apart and how evenly the data are distributed; includes the lower and upper extreme values of the data, the lower and upper quartiles of the data, and the median of the data *(page 325)*
Example:

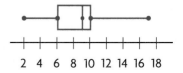

break A zigzag on a horizontal or vertical axis of a graph, indicating that the data do not include all of the values on the number line used *(page 314)*

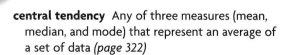

central tendency Any of three measures (mean, median, and mode) that represent an average of a set of data *(page 322)*

circumference The distance around a circle; $C = \pi d$ *(page 499)*

coefficient The number that is multiplied by the variable in an algebraic expression such as $5b$ *(page 100)*

combination An arrangement of items or events in which order does not matter *(page 344)*

combine like terms To add or subtract like terms *(page 106)*

commission A fee paid to a person for making a sale *(page 286)*

common difference The difference between any two successive terms in an arithmetic sequence *(page 212)*

common ratio The ratio used to multiply each term to produce the next term in a geometric sequence *(page 212)*

Commutative Property of Addition The property of addition that allows two or more addends to be added in any order without changing the sum *(page H11)*
Examples: $a + 4 = 4 + a$
$(2 + 5) + r = r + (2 + 5)$

Commutative Property of Multiplication The property of multiplication that allows two or more factors to be multiplied in any order without changing the product *(page H11)*
Examples: $3 \cdot a = a \cdot 3$
$4 \cdot 5 \cdot y = 5 \cdot 4 \cdot y$

complementary angles Two angles whose measures have a sum of 90° *(page H20)*

composite number A whole number that has more than two whole-number factors *(page 16)*

compound interest Interest computed on both the principal and the interest previously earned *(page 294)*

cone A solid figure with one vertex and one circular base *(page H23)*

congruent Having the same size and shape *(page 182)*

consecutive integers Integers that are next to one another in counting order *(page 187)*

converge To approach some fixed value *(page 189)*

coordinate plane A plane formed by two perpendicular number lines called axes; every point on the plane can be named by an ordered pair of numbers. *(page H29)*

coordinates The numbers of an ordered pair, (x,y) *(page H29)*

corresponding angles Angles that are in the same position and are formed by a transversal cutting two or more lines *(page 378)*

cosine (cos) In a right triangle, the ratio of the length of the side adjacent to an angle to the length of the hypotenuse *(page 537)*

cross section The figure formed by the intersection of a plane and a solid figure *(page 427)*
Example:

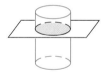

cube A square prism with six congruent square faces *(pages 28, 430)*

cube root One of the three equal factors of a number *(page 28)*

cylinder A solid figure with two parallel, congruent circular bases connected by a curved surface *(page H23)*

Density Property for Real Numbers The property which states that between any two real numbers, there is always another real number *(page 30)*

dependent events Events for which the outcome of one event is affected by the outcome of the other event *(page 351)*

diagonal A line segment that connects two non-adjacent vertices of a polygon *(page 185)*

diameter A chord that passes through the center of a circle *(page H87)*

dilation A transformation that enlarges or reduces a figure *(page 404)*
Example: The sides of the image are enlarged to 150%.

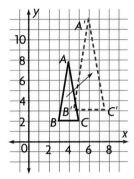

direct variation A relationship between two variables such that the data increase or decrease together at a constant rate *(page 447)*

Distributive Property of Multiplication over Addition The property which states that multiplying a sum by a number gives the same result as multiplying each addend by the number and then adding the products *(page H11)*
Examples: $3(4 + 5) = 3 \times 4 + 3 \times 5$
$3(a + b) = 3a + 3b$

diverge To get larger without bound *(page 189)*

domain The set of the first coordinates of the ordered pairs of a relation; see *range*. *(page 460)*
Example:
In the relation {(2,20), (3,30), (4,40), (5,50)}, the domain is {2, 3, 4, 5}.

E

edge The line segment along which two faces of a polyhedron intersect *(page 421)*

edge A connection between vertices in a network *(page 494)*

empirical probability See *experimental probability*.

enlargement An increase in size of all dimensions *(pages 236, 404)*

equation A mathematical sentence that uses an equals sign to show that two quantities are equal *(page 96)*

equiangular spiral A spiral in which the loops are not evenly spaced; see *spiral*. *(page 184)*

equilateral triangle A triangle with three congruent sides and three congruent angles *(page 392)*

equivalent Having the same value *(page 98)*

equivalent fractions Fractions that name the same number *(page H12)*

equivalent ratios Ratios that make the same comparison *(page H16)*

evaluate To find the value *(page 98)*

even vertex A vertex, in a network, that has an even number of lines coming from it *(page 497)*

experimental probability The ratio of the number of times the event occurs to the total number of trials or times the activity is performed *(page 358)*

exponent The number that indicates how many times the base is used as a factor; see *base*. *(page 20)*

exterior angles The angles on the outer sides of two lines cut by a transversal *(page 378)*
Example: Angles 1, 2, 7, and 8 are exterior angles.

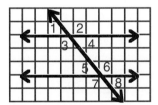

extrapolation An estimate or a prediction of an unknown value, based upon known values *(page 314)*

F

face A flat surface of a polyhedron *(page 506)*

factorial The product of all whole numbers, except zero, less than or equal to a number *(page 342)*
Example: $5! = 5 \times 4 \times 3 \times 2 \times 1$

Fibonacci sequence The infinite sequence of numbers formed by adding two successive numbers to get the next number *(page 220)*
Example: 1, 1, 2, 3, 5, 8, 13, 21, . . .

first quartile The median of the lower half of a set of data *(page 325)*

formula A rule that is expressed with symbols *(page 11)*
Example: $A = lw$

fractal A structure with repeating patterns containing shapes that are like the whole but of different sizes throughout *(page 188)*

function A relation in which no two ordered pairs have the same *x*-value *(page 460)*
Example:
function: {(1,5), (2,6), (3,7), (4,8)}
not a function: {(1,5), (1,6), (2,7), (3,8)}
1 is matched with both 5 and 6.

function table A table of ordered pairs that represent solutions of a function *(page 152)*

Fundamental Counting Principle The principle that all possible outcomes in a sample space can be found by finding the product of the number of ways each event can occur *(page 340)*

G

geometric probability The probability that a random point is located in a particular part, or subregion, of a larger region *(page 367)*

geometric sequence An ordered list of numbers that has a common ratio of consecutive terms *(page 212)*
Example: 2, 6, 18, 54, . . .

Golden Ratio The ratio that has a value of $\frac{1 + \sqrt{5}}{2}$ and a decimal value of about 1.61 *(page 50)*

Golden Rectangle A rectangle that has a length-to-width ratio of about 1.6 to 1 *(page 221)*

greatest common factor (GCF) The largest common factor of two or more given numbers *(page H4)*

H

greatest possible error (GPE) One half of the smallest unit used in a measurement *(page H26)*

height The distance from the vertex of a figure to its base, forming a right angle with the base *(page 503)*

helix A spiral-shaped curve in space that goes around an axis *(page 185)*

histogram A bar graph that shows the frequency of data within intervals *(page 308)*

horizon line A horizontal line that represents the viewer's eye level *(page 425)*

hypotenuse In a right triangle, the side opposite the right angle *(page 532)*
Example:

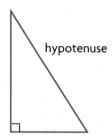

hypotenuse

I

Identity Property of One The property which states that multiplying a number by 1 does not change the number's value *(page H11)*
Examples: $6 \cdot 1 = 6$; $1 \cdot a = a$

Identity Property of Zero The property which states that adding zero to a number does not change the number's value *(page H11)*
Examples: $3 + 0 = 3$; $0 + y = y$

image The figure in a new position, location, or size that is the result of a transformation *(page 399)*

independent events Events for which the outcome of one event is not affected by the outcome of the other event *(page 350)*

inequality A mathematical sentence that shows that quantities are not equal, using $<$, $>$, $\leq$, $\geq$, or $\neq$ *(page 96)*

integers The set of whole numbers and their opposites *(page 17)*

intercept The place (or point) where a graph crosses the axis *(page 453)*
Example: The x-intercept is 1 and the y-intercept is ⁻2.

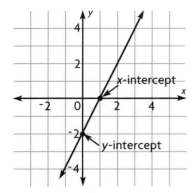

interest See *simple interest.*

interior angles Angles on the inner sides of two lines cut by a transversal *(page 378)*
Example: Angles 3, 4, 5, and 6 are interior angles.

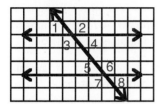

interpolation An estimated value between two known values *(page 313)*

intersecting lines Lines that cross at exactly one point *(page H21)*

intersecting planes Flat surfaces that intersect in a line, such as the sides of a box *(page 427)*
Example:

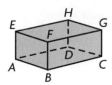

intersection The point at which two lines meet *(page 457)*

inverse operations Opposite operations that undo each other; addition and subtraction are inverse operations. *(pages 116, 119)*

irrational number A number that cannot be expressed as a repeating or terminating decimal *(page 29)*
Example: $\sqrt{2} \approx 1.414213562\ldots$

isosceles triangle A triangle with two congruent sides *(page 391)*

iteration The repetition of a process or set of instructions *(page 188)*
Example:

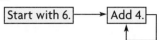

L

lateral surface The curved surface of a cylinder or a cone *(page 507)*

least common denominator (LCD) The smallest common multiple of two or more denominators *(page H14)*
Example: The LCD of $\frac{2}{3}$ and $\frac{4}{5}$ is 15.

least common multiple (LCM) The smallest number, other than zero, that is a multiple of two or more given numbers *(page H4)*
Example: The LCM of 8 and 10 is 40.

leg In a right triangle, either of the two sides that intersect to form the right angle; in an isosceles triangle, one of the two congruent sides *(page 532)*

like terms Expressions that have the same variables and the same powers of the variables *(page 105)*

line A set of points that extends without end in opposite directions *(page H20)*

linear equation An equation whose graph is a straight line *(page 160)*

linear function A function whose graph is a straight line *(page 463)*

line of best fit A straight line drawn through as much of the data as possible on a scatterplot *(pages 329, 444)*

line of symmetry A line that separates a figure into two congruent parts *(page 410)*

line plot A number line with marks or dots to show frequency *(page 310)*

line segment A part of a line that has two endpoints *(page H20)*

lower extreme The least number in a set of data *(page 325)*

mathematical probability The number used to describe the chance that an event will occur *(page 346)*

mean (average) The sum of a set of numbers divided by the number of addends *(page 322)*

measure of central tendency A measure used to describe data; the mean, median, and mode are measures of central tendency. *(page 322)*

median The middle number or the average of the two middle numbers in an ordered set of data *(page 322)*

midpoint The point that divides a line segment into two congruent line segments *(page 382)*

mode The number or numbers that occur most frequently in a set of data *(page 322)*

monomial An expression that is a number, a variable, or the product of a number and one or more variables *(page 474)*
Examples: 3x; 7; 5xy

multiple The product of any number and a whole number *(page H3)*

negative correlation A relation in which the values of one variable increase as the values of the other variable decrease *(page 329)*

negative exponent An exponent used to express a number less than 1 *(page 69)*
Examples: $4^{-2} = \frac{1}{16}$; $1.2 \times 10^{-3} = 0.0012$

net An arrangement of polygons that folds up to form a polyhedron *(pages 180, 416)*
Example: This net forms a tetrahedron.

network A figure made up of vertices and edges that show how objects are connected *(page 494)*

Example:

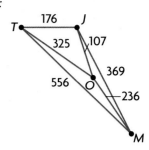

no correlation In a scatterplot, data points are scattered, and no pattern can be formed from the points. *(page 329)*

nonlinear function A function whose graph is not a straight line *(page 466)*

numerical expression An expression that includes numbers and at least one operation (addition, subtraction, multiplication, or division) *(page 96)*
Examples: 6 + 8.1   57 − 48   21.6 − 18.6

odd vertex A vertex, in a network, that has an odd number of lines coming from it *(page 497)*

odds A comparison of favorable outcomes and unfavorable outcomes *(page 347)*

opposites Two numbers represented by points on the number line that are the same distance from zero, but are on opposite sides of zero *(page H27)*

order of operations The correct order in which the operations are done within an expression *(page 67)*

ordered pair A pair of numbers that can be used to locate a point on the coordinate plane *(page H29)*

origin On a coordinate plane, the point where the x-axis and y-axis intersect; (0,0) *(page H29)*

parabola A U-shaped curve that opens upward or downward *(page 167)*

parallel lines Lines in a plane that do not intersect *(page 378)*

Pascal's triangle A triangular arrangement of numbers in which each row starts and ends with

1, and each other number is the sum of the two numbers above it *(page 204)*

percent The ratio of a number to 100; *percent* means "per hundred." *(page 41)*
Example: $25\% = \frac{25}{100}$

percent of decrease The percent that an original amount has decreased *(page 282)*

percent of increase The percent that an original amount has increased *(page 282)*

perfect square A number that has integers as its square roots *(page 26)*
Example: 16 is a perfect square.

perimeter The distance around a polygon *(pages 100, 514)*

permutation An arrangement of things in a definite order *(page 343)*

perpendicular bisector A line or line segment that intersects a given line segment at its midpoint and forms right angles *(page 382)*

perpendicular lines Lines that intersect to form right angles *(pages H21, 379)*

perspective A technique used to make 3-dimensional objects appear to have depth and distance on a flat surface *(page 424)*

pi (π) The ratio of the circumference of a circle to its diameter, having a value of approximately 3.14 or $\frac{22}{7}$ *(page 499)*

plane A set of points forming a flat surface that extends without end in all directions *(page H20)*

Platonic solids The five regular polyhedrons: tetrahedron, cube, octahedron, dodecahedron, and icosahedron *(page 180)*

point of intersection The point where two or more lines intersect *(page 457)*
Example:

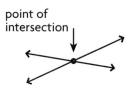

point of intersection

point of rotation A point around which a figure can be turned *(page 410)*

polygon A closed plane figure formed by three or more line segments *(page H22)*

polyhedron A solid figure in which all the surfaces, or faces, are polygons *(page 180)*

polynomial A monomial or the sum of two or more monomials *(page 475)*

population The total or entire group to be studied *(page 304)*

positive correlation A relation in which the values of two variables increase or decrease at the same time *(page 329)*

precision A property of measurement that is related to the unit of measure used; the smaller the unit of measure, the more precise the measurement. *(page H26)*
Example: 27 mm is more precise than 3 cm.

principal The amount of money borrowed or invested *(page 292)*

prism A polyhedron whose two bases are congruent polygons in parallel planes and whose lateral faces are parallelograms *(page H23)*

proportion An equation which states that two ratios are equivalent *(page 45)*
Example: $\frac{5}{10} = \frac{1}{2}$, or 5:10 = 1:2

pyramid A polyhedron, with one base that is a polygon, and with lateral faces that are triangles which share a common vertex *(page H23)*

Pythagorean Property In any right triangle, if a and b are the lengths of the legs and c is the length of the hypotenuse, then $a^2 + b^2 = c^2$. *(page 533)*
Example:

quadrant One of the four regions of the coordinate plane *(page H29)*

quadrilateral A four-sided polygon *(page H22)*

quarterly Four times a year *(page 295)*

radical An expression that has a root such as a square root or cube root; the expression $\sqrt{25}$ is a radical. *(page 26)*

radical symbol The symbol, $\sqrt{}$, used to represent the square root of a number *(page 26)* *Example:* $\sqrt{25}$ is read as "the square root of 25."

radicand The number under a radical symbol; in the expression $\sqrt{25}$, 25 is the radicand. *(page 26)*

radius A line segment with one endpoint at the center of the circle and the other endpoint on the circle *(page 205)*

random selection A selection made so that each person or item has an equal chance of being chosen *(pages 304–305)*

range The difference between the greatest number and the least number in a set of data *(page 325)*

range The set of the second coordinates of the ordered pairs of a relation; see *domain*. *(page 460)* *Example:* In the relation {(2,20), (3,30), (4,40), (5,50)}, the range is {20, 30, 40, 50}.

rate A ratio that compares quantities of different units, such as miles per hour, price per pound, students per class *(page 47)*

rate/distance Calculations based on the distance-rate-time formula, $d = rt$ *(page H87)*

ratio A comparison of two numbers *(pages 17, 44)* *Example:* 6 to 7, or 6:7, or $\frac{6}{7}$

rational number Any number that can be expressed as a ratio $\frac{a}{b}$, where a and b are integers and $b \neq 0$ *(page 17)*

ray A part of a line that has one endpoint and extends in one direction without end *(page H20)*

real numbers The set of numbers that includes all rational numbers and all irrational numbers *(page 29)*

reciprocal One of two numbers whose product is 1 *(page H15)*

Example: $\frac{2}{3} \times \frac{3}{2} = 1$
$\frac{3}{2}$ is the reciprocal of $\frac{2}{3}$.
$\frac{2}{3}$ is the reciprocal of $\frac{3}{2}$.

rectangle A parallelogram with four right angles *(page H22)*

rectangular prism A polyhedron whose bases are rectangles and whose other faces are parallelograms *(page H23)*

reflection (flip) The figure formed by flipping a geometric figure about a line to obtain a mirror image *(page H23)* *Example:*

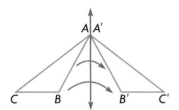

regular polygon A polygon in which all sides and all angles are congruent *(page H22)*

relation A set of ordered pairs *(page 460)*

repeating decimal A decimal in which one or more digits repeat indefinitely *(page 29)* *Examples:* 24.6666 . . . , or $24.\overline{6}$
5.272727 . . . , or $5.\overline{27}$

right angle An angle whose measure is 90° *(page H20)*

right circular cylinder A cylinder in which the bases are parallel circles perpendicular to the side of the cylinder *(pages 503, H23)*

right triangle A triangle containing exactly one right angle *(page H20)*

rotation (turn) A type of transformation, or movement, that results when a geometric figure is turned about a fixed point *(page H23)* *Example:*

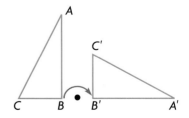

rotational symmetry A figure has rotational symmetry if it looks exactly the same after it has been rotated less than 360° about a central point. *(page 410)*

S

sales tax A tax on the sale of an item or a service *(page 289)*

sample A group of people or objects chosen from a larger group, or population *(page 304)*

sample space All possible outcomes in a given situation *(page 338)*
Example: The sample space for tossing 2 coins is (H, H), (H, T), (T, H), (T, T).

scale The ratio of the size of an object or the distance in a drawing to the actual size of the object or the actual distance *(page 236)*

scale drawing A drawing whose shape is the same as an actual object and whose size is determined by the scale *(page 236)*

scale factor The ratio for pairs of corresponding sides of similar figures *(page 189)*

scale model A proportional model of a solid, or three-dimensional object *(page 248)*

scalene triangle A triangle with no congruent sides *(page H22)*

scatterplot A graph made by plotting points on a coordinate plane *(page 329)*

scientific notation A method of expressing a number as the product of a number between 1 and 10, and a power of 10 *(page 21)*

second quartile The median of a set of data, that is the middle number, or the sum of the 2 middle numbers divided by 2, when the numbers are arranged in order *(page 325)*

self-similarity A figure has self-similarity if it contains a repeating pattern of smaller and smaller parts that are like the whole but different in size. *(page 239)*

semiannually Twice a year *(page 295)*

semiregular polyhedron A solid formed from patterns of more than one kind of regular polygon *(page 182)*

Example:

sequence An ordered list of numbers *(page 212)*

Sierpinski triangle A fractal pattern *(page 190)*

significant digits The number of digits used to express the accuracy of a measurement *(page 498)*

similar figures Figures with the same shape but not necessarily the same size *(page 232)*

similarity ratio See *scale factor.*

simple interest The amount obtained by multiplying the principal by the rate by the time; *I = prt (page 292)*

simplest form A fraction is in simplest form when the numerator and denominator have no common factors other than 1. *(page H12)*
Example: $\frac{6}{8}$ written in simplest form is $\frac{3}{4}$.

simplest form The form of an expression when all like terms are combined *(page 106)*

simplify To combine like terms *(pages 106, 478)*

simulation A model of an experiment that would be too difficult or too time-consuming to actually perform *(page 364)*

sine (sin) In a right triangle, the ratio of the length of the side opposite an angle to the length of the hypotenuse *(page 537)*

slant height The distance from the base of a cone to its vertex, measured along the lateral surface *(page 508)*
Example:

slope The measure of the steepness of a line; the ratio of vertical change to horizontal change:

$$\text{slope} = \frac{\text{vertical change}}{\text{horizontal change}} \text{ (pages 266, 452)}$$

slope-intercept form A linear equation written in the form $y = mx + b$ *(page 455)*

solid figure A three-dimensional figure *(page 180)*

solution The value or values that make an equation, an inequality, or a system of equations true *(pages 115, 142, 152, 457)*

sphere A solid figure with all points the same distance from the center *(page 504)*
Example:

spiral A curve traced by a point turning around and away from a fixed point *(page 184)*
Examples:

equiangular   Archimedean

spirolateral A geometric design generated from a sequence of numbers *(page 187)*

spreadsheet A computer program that organizes information in rows and columns and does calculations with numbers and formulas *(page 294)*

square A rectangle with four congruent sides *(page H22)*

square The product of a number and itself *(page 26)*
Example: 25 is the square of 5 because $5^2 = 5 \times 5$, or 25.

square root One of the two equal factors of a number *(page 26)*
Example: 6 is the square root of 36 because $6^2 = 36$.

squiggle See *break.*

standard form The form of a polynomial when its terms are arranged so that the exponents of a variable decrease from left to right *(page 479)*

stem-and-leaf plot A method of organizing intervals or groups of data *(page 323)*

substitute To replace a variable with a value *(page 115)*

supplementary angles Two angles whose measures have a sum of 180° *(page H20)*

surface area The sum of the areas of the faces, or surfaces, of a solid figure *(page 506)*

survey A method of gathering information about a population *(page 304)*

system of equations Two or more linear equations graphed in the same coordinate plane *(page 457)*
Example:

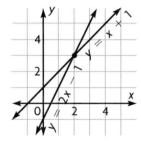

T

tangent (tan) In a right triangle, the ratio of the length of the side opposite an angle to the length of the side adjacent to the angle *(page 537)*

term A real number, a variable, or a product of real numbers and variables *(page 105)*

term A number in a sequence *(page 212)*

terminating decimal A decimal that ends; a decimal for which the division operation results in a remainder of zero *(page 29)*
Examples: $\frac{1}{2} = 0.5$ and $\frac{5}{8} = 0.625$

tessellation A repeating pattern of plane figures that completely covers a plane with no gaps and no overlaps *(page 176)*

theoretical probability See *mathematical probability.*

third quartile The median of the upper half of a set of data *(page 325)*

transformation A change in size, shape, or position of a geometric figure *(page H23)*

translation (slide) A movement of a geometric figure to a new position without turning or flipping it *(page H23)*
Example:

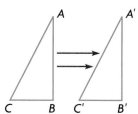

transversal A line that intersects two or more lines *(page 378)*
Example: Line *AB* is a transversal.

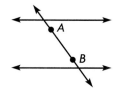

tree diagram A branching diagram that shows all possible outcomes *(page 338)*

trigonometric ratios (trig ratios) Ratios that compare the lengths of the sides of a right triangle. The common ratios are tangent, sine, and cosine. *(page 537)*

trinomial The sum of three monomials *(page 475)*
Example: $(3x + 5y + 7)$

unit price A price for one item *(page 47)*

unit rate A rate in which the second term is 1 *(page 47)*

upper extreme The greatest number in a set of data *(page 325)*

vanishing point In a perspective drawing, a point where lines running away from the viewer meet *(page 424)*

Example:

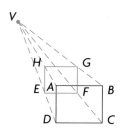

variability The spread of values in a set of data *(page 325)*

variable A letter used to represent one or more numbers in an expression, equation, or inequality *(page 96)*
Examples: $5a$; $2x = 8$; $3y + 4 \neq 10$

Venn diagram A diagram that is used to show relationships between sets *(page 16)*

vertex A point where two or more rays meet, where sides of a polygon meet, or where edges of a polyhedron meet *(page H20)*
Examples:

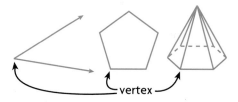

vertex

vertex In a network, a point that represents an object *(page 494)*

volume The number of cubic units needed to occupy a given space *(pages 28, 467, 503)*

withholding tax A deduction from a person's earnings as an advance payment on income tax *(page 290)*

x-axis The horizontal axis in a coordinate plane *(page H29)*

x-coordinate The first number in an ordered pair; tells whether to move right or left in the coordinate plane *(page H29)*

x-intercept The *x*-coordinate of the point where the graph of a line crosses the *x*-axis *(page 453)*

y-axis The vertical axis in a coordinate plane *(page H29)*

y-coordinate The second number in an ordered pair; tells whether to move up or down in the coordinate plane *(page H29)*

y-intercept The *y*-coordinate of the point where the graph of a line crosses the *y*-axis *(page 453)*

Answers to Selected Exercises

Chapter 1
Page 19
5. the even numbers (20, 22, 24, 26, 28, 30, 32, 34, 36, 38, 40) and the primes (23, 29, 31, 37)

7. R; R; C, W, I, R; W, I, R   **9.** true; $3 = \frac{3}{1}$

11. False; an integer such as $^{-}4$ is not a counting number   **13.** If the number can be written as a fraction in which the denominator is not equal to 0, then it is a rational number.   **15.** 64   **17.** 81   **19.** 39
21. 42   **23.** No, she needs $1.74 more.

Page 22
1. 6^2 **3.** 7^3 **5.** 4^1 **7.** 2^2 **9.** 6^5 **11.** 8
13. 1   **15.** 216   **17.** 32   **19.** 343   **21.** 625
23. 1.96   **25.** $\frac{1}{8}$ **27.** 5^2 **29.** 2×3^3
31. $2^3 \times 3$ **33.** $2^2 \times 17$ **35.** 3×5^2 **37.** $2^2 \times 11$ **39.** $5^2 \times 13$ **41.** $2^3 \times 3 \times 5$ **43.** 6.78×10^2 **45.** 9.87×10^8 **47.** 1.234×10^5
49. 1.0898×10^{11} **51.** 2.347809×10^{16}
53. 10,920   **55.** 92,000,000   **57.** 600,000,000
59. 12,785,550,000,000
61. 4,892,000,000,000   **63.** 8,978,500,000
65. 1,728 cm^3 **67.** 5.818429×10^9
69. $2^3 = 2 \times 2 \times 2 = 8; 3^2 = 3 \times 3 = 9$

Page 25
1. 3^{10} **3.** 7^6 **5.** 6^7 **7.** 9^8 **9.** 12^{11}
11. 6^3 **13.** 5^2 **15.** 4^4 **17.** 7^5 **19.** 12^7
21. 5^{10} **23.** 4^9 **25.** 3^2 **27.** 7^8 **29.** 10^{10}
31. 4^4 **33.** 6^5 **35.** 10^{17} **37.** 10^{11} grains of pollen   **39.** To find the product, add the exponents of the factors; to find the quotient, subtract the exponent of the divisor from the exponent of the dividend.

Page 27
1. 25   **3.** 36   **5.** 225   **7.** $\frac{1}{16}$ **9.** $\frac{4}{25}$
11. $^{-}6, 6$ **13.** $^{-}14, 14$ **15.** $^{-}20, 20$ **17.** $^{-}8$

19. 16   **21.** $^{-}30$ **23.** $^{-}0.3$ **25.** $^{-}\frac{5}{7}$ **27.** 5, 6
29. 10, 11   **31.** $^{-}7.07$ **33.** $^{-}6.71$
35. 11.66   **37.** 18 m   **39.** Squaring a number is the inverse of taking a square root.

Page 31
1. R   **3.** R   **5.** I   **7.** 2, 3   **9.** 3, 4   **11.** 0.8, 0.9   **13.** 11, 12   **15.** 0.6, 0.7   **17.** $^{-}0.8, ^{-}0.7$
19. 3.3   **21.** $^{-}2.8$ **23.** 0.6   **25.** No. As a decimal, it doesn't repeat or terminate.
27. The set of rational numbers and the set of irrational numbers are parts of the set of real numbers.   **29.** 0.1   **31.** 0.25
33. Associative Property of Addition
35. Distributive Property   **37.** 24 min; for 3 pieces, 2 cuts, and for 9 pieces, 8 cuts

Page 33
1. rational   **7.** 8.9896234×10^{21}
9. 162,345,000,000   **11.** 2,789,500,000
13. 10^3 **15.** 15^{14} **17.** 9^5 **19.** 5^6 **21.** $^{-}7$
23. $\frac{6}{7}$ **25.** 3, 4   **27.** 0.8, 0.9

Chapter 2
Page 39
11. Possible answers: $0.10, 10¢, $\frac{1}{10}$ of a dollar, 0.1 dollar   **13.** $6 + ^{-}7 = ^{-}1$
15. $^{-}5 + ^{-}2 = ^{-}7$ **17.** 27   **19.** 256
21. 32   **23.** 495,000,000

Page 46
1. $\frac{1}{8}$ **3.** $\frac{3}{8}$ **5.** $\frac{4}{103}$ **7.** $\frac{2}{9}$ **9.** $\frac{5}{8}$ **11.** $\neq$
13. $=$ **15.** $\neq$ **17.** $\neq$ **19.** $=$ **21.** 8, 12, 7, 35
23. 27 to 1, 27:1, or $\frac{27}{1}$ **25.** 1 to 3; 3 to 1

Page 48
1. $\frac{$0.20}{1 \text{ lb of bananas}}$ **3.** $\frac{22 \text{ mi}}{1 \text{ gal of gasoline}}$

5. 16 beats per measure of music   **7.** $13.125 per hr of work   **9.** $0.17 per min; $0.10 per min; the competitor   **11.** $0.20 per minute; $0.18 per minute: service B   **13.** $16.80   **15.** $8,567 per day   **17.** $3.49; $27.92

Page 51
1. $\frac{100}{400}; \frac{1}{4}$ **3.** $\frac{250}{500}; \frac{1}{2}$ **5.** $\frac{90}{120}; \frac{3}{4}$ **7.** about 50%
9. about 30%   **11.** about 100%   **13.** about 20%   **15.** about 60%   **17.** about 70%
19. about 10%   **21.** about 1%   **23.** about 70%   **25.** Yes; about 80% have the required income.   **27.** Possible answer: about 40%
29. 16   **31.** 145   **33.** 57   **35.** $^-3, 3$
37. $^-8, 8$ **39.** $^-9, 9$ **41.** 0.75 lb

Page 53
1. 0.75   **3.** 60%   **5.** 48%   **7.** 70%   **9.** 80%
11. 28%   **13.** proportion   **15.** ≠   **17.** =
19. 50 mi per hr   **21.** $1.35 for 1 gal of gasoline   **23.** about 50%   **25.** about 25%
27. about 100%

Chapter 3
Page 58
1. $^-1 + 3 = 2$ **3.** $^-3 + ^-3 = ^-6$
5. $^-2 + 6 = 4$ **7.** $^-2 + ^-2 = ^-4$
9. $2 + ^-6 = ^-4$ **11.** $^-3 + ^-2 = ^-5$
13. $3 + ^-2 = 1$ **15.** $^-5 + ^-4 = ^-9$ **17.** 4
19. 5   **21.** $^-3$ **23.** 0   **25.** $^-86$ **27.** 0
29. $^-49$ **31.** $^-65$ **33.** 17   **35.** $^-232$
37. 10°F   **39.** Subtract the absolute values. Then use the sign of the addend with the greater absolute value.   **41.** $6 + ^-2$ **43.** 0.3
45. 0.75   **47.** 0.455   **49.** $\frac{1}{2}$ or 0.5

Page 61
1. $7 + ^-8 = ^-1$ **3.** $8 + 10 = 18$
5. $9 + ^-14 = ^-5$ **7.** $^-10 + ^-2 = ^-12$
9. $^-15 + ^-11 = ^-26$ **11.** $12 + 8 = 20$ **13.** 5
15. 14   **17.** 12   **19.** $^-1$ **21.** $^-4$ **23.** $^-11$
25. 28   **27.** 95   **29.** 81   **31.** $^-193$ **33.** $^-10$
35. $^-322$ **37.** 942   **39.** 191   **41.** 660
43. 125   **45.** 37°   **47.** 1,812 ft

Page 68
1. negative   **3.** positive   **5.** negative   **7.** $^-4$
9. 3   **11.** 3   **13.** 6   **15.** $^-12$ **17.** 18
19. $^-45$ **21.** 16   **23.** $^-28$ **25.** $^-4$ **27.** 6
29. 8   **31.** $^-4$ **33.** $^-14$ **35.** $^-3$ **37.** $^-5$
39. $^-8$ **41.** 11   **43.** 48   **45.** $^-2$ **47.** 0
49. $^-180$ **51.** $^-1$ **53.** 32 days
55. $^-4 \times 8 = ^-32; ^-32$ m   **57.** With integers, you need to consider whether the answer is positive or negative. With whole numbers greater than zero, the answer is always positive.

Pages 70–71
1. $\frac{1}{100}$ **3.** $\frac{1}{36}$ **5.** $\frac{1}{100,000}$ **7.** $\frac{1}{8}$ **9.** $\frac{1}{25}$
11. $\frac{1}{256}$ **13.** 3.4×10^4 **15.** 5.9×10^{-7}
17. 6.8×10^{-5} **19.** 4.2×10^{-8}
21. 8.666×10^{-4} **23.** 8.79×10^{-7}
25. 3,500   **27.** 0.0445   **29.** 0.0053
31. 0.000079   **33.** 0.00029   **35.** 0.0000034
37. 1.06×10^{-8} cm   **39.** 1.0×10^{-6} **43.** $\frac{5}{12}$
45. $\frac{5}{9}$ **47.** 100%   **49.** 125%   **51.** 40%; 48%

Page 73
1. $^-4$ **3.** $^-9$ **5.** $^-4$ **7.** $^-1$ **9.** $^-10$
11. $^-6$ **13.** $^-3$ **15.** $^-2$ **17.** $^-4$ **19.** 26
21. $^-15$ **23.** 480 coats   **25.** $^-4$ **27.** 4
29. $^-9$ **31.** $^-3$ **33.** $\frac{1}{1,000}$ **35.** $\frac{1}{81}$ **37.** $\frac{1}{64}$
39. $\frac{1}{6}$ **41.** $\frac{1}{625}$

Chapter 4
Page 78
1. positive   **3.** negative   **5.** zero   **11.** $\frac{1}{2}$
13. $2\frac{1}{25}$ **15.** $^-1.6$ **17.** $\frac{-15}{26}$ **19.** $^-7\frac{2}{3}$
21. 0.3   **23.** $^-1.00$ **25.** $^-2.2$ **27.** $^-3.9$
29. $^-1.9$ **31.** No, he ran a total of only 14.7 mi.   **33.** 1,853.4 ft   **35.** $^-21$ **37.** $^-17$
39. $^-34$ **41.** 117   **43.** $^-60$ **45.** 2.63×10^8 words; 1.5×10^4 illustrations

Page 80
1. 15.5   **3.** 5.6   **5.** 11.44   **7.** 18.8   **9.** $^-17.6$
11. $^-24.7$ **13.** $^-64.5$ **15.** $^-89.5$ **17.** $^-2\frac{1}{4}$

19. $-11\frac{3}{10}$ **21.** $\frac{1}{7}$ **23.** $-18\frac{1}{2}$ **25.** $13\frac{7}{8}$

27. $-10\frac{5}{14}$ **29.** $7\frac{1}{3}$ **31.** 16.9°F **33.** $-$157.62

Page 84

1. negative **3.** negative **5.** negative
7. positive **9.** negative **11.** positive
13. 0.816 **15.** 8.019 **17.** $-16\frac{4}{5}$ **19.** $27\frac{1}{4}$

21. $-45\frac{1}{2}$ **23.** 5.6 **25.** -207 **27.** $1\frac{3}{4}$

29. $-2\frac{2}{3}$ **31.** $-2\frac{1}{91}$ **33.** -30 **35.** 3

37. -188.64 **39.** -53.06 **41.** 34.32

43. $-168\frac{3}{4}$ in.; The coastline is $168\frac{3}{4}$ in.

shorter. **45.** when the two rational numbers
are both negative **47.** 44 **49.** 7,260
51. 8.9×10^{-9} **53.** 7.8×10^{-10} **55.** $0.20
per oz; $0.15 per oz; the 24-oz box

Page 87

1. Subtract $11.1 - 6.4$. **3.** Divide $3.6 \div 2$.
5. Subtract $45.5 - 3.55$. **7.** -7.3 **9.** -18.7
11. $7\frac{7}{10}$ **13.** -6.64 **15.** 102.9

17. $6.5 - 9.6 + {}^-4 + (2.5 \times {}^-3.2); {}^-15.1$
19. $15 \times (3^2 + 45) = 810$ **21.** $-325,000 +$
$(10,800 \times 5) = {}^-271,000; \$271,000$

Page 89

1. $-1\frac{1}{3}$ **3.** 5.9 **5.** -17.58 **7.** $\frac{5}{9}$ **9.** $-14\frac{1}{2}$

11. 12.4 **13.** -71.8 **15.** $-12\frac{1}{10}$ **17.** 147.84

19. $-37\frac{7}{10}$ **21.** -52 **23.** $2\frac{15}{17}$ **25.** -218.45

27. 7.8 **29.** 45.198 **31.** $6\frac{1}{2}$ **33.** 0.86

35. $-5\frac{4}{15}$

Chapter 5

Page 97

1. equation **3.** inequality **5.** expression
7. equation **9.** expression **11.** expression
13. inequality **15.** equation **17.** $10s + 58$
19. 36×5 **21.** $>$ **23.** $=$ **25.** $<$ **27.** $>$
29. $=$ **31.** $52 + 6 = 58$ **33.** $12 \times 6 = 72$
35. $4y + 8 = 56$ **37.** $5s \div 3 = 5$

39. $7 + 7s = 28$ **41.** $4x - 3 < 36$ **43.** $6y \geq 6$
45. no; $12 + 15 \neq 28$ **47.** if there are 15 boys
and 16 girls: $15 + 16$ **49.** An equation has an
equals sign, and an expression does not.

Page 101

1. 15 **3.** -23 **5.** 79 **7.** 47.25 **9.** yes
11. no **13.** $s; 14$ **15.** $x; \frac{1}{3}$ **17.** $y; {}^-6.7$

19. 12 **21.** 20 **23.** -30 **25.** 10 **27.** 32 ft
29. Yes. Addition is commutative. **31.** four
times nine **33.** five minus four **35.** 1.3
37. 11.6 **39.** -20.8 **41.** 45.05 calories; 3.18
grams of sugar

Page 104

1. $n - 10$ **3.** $n \div 10$ **5.** $16d$ **7.** $d \div 30$
9. $s - 25$ **11.** $p \div 2$ **13.** $15 - f$ **15.** $2f$
23. $3.75t$ **25.** $\frac{c}{4}$

Page 107

1. $6 + 5b$ **3.** $2 + 2x$ **5.** $5x + 2$ **7.** $2s + 10$
9. $-9x + y + 6$ **11.** $9x + {}^-3y + {}^-5$
13. $2m + m + 5 + 4m + 2; 7m + 7; 28$ in.
15. Use the Distributive Property for $3(x + 4)$.
Then add like terms; $7x + 12$. **17.** Ten times
three equals thirty. **19.** Sixteen minus five
equals eleven. **21.** 5.75 **23.** -2 **25.** about
1.5 min; about 90 min, or 1.5 hr

Chapter 6

Page 114

1. $34 - n = 12$; *decreased by* **3.** $n + 5 = 300$;
sum **5.** a **7.** $d =$ Joey's deposit;
$\$120.23 + d = \$180.00$ **9.** $b =$ blue; $r =$ red;
$b = 3r$ **11.** Possible answer: 70 shirts were
sold, leaving 34 shirts in inventory. How
many shirts were in the original inventory?
13. 22 **15.** $12 + 6d$ or $6d + 12$ **17.** 8 in.
wide and 12 in. long

Page 118

1. 19 **3.** 8 **5.** 5.16 **7.** -1.2 **9.** $x = 5$
11. $m = 24$ **13.** $h = {}^-31$ **15.** $m = 10.53$
17. $y = 13.7$ **19.** $p = 21$ **21.** $k = {}^-5.4$
23. $c = {}^-1.1$ **25.** $m =$ the number of
markers Ned has; $m - 5 = 13$ **27.** $r =$ Rick's

batting average; $r + 0.024 = 0.315$
29. $x - 12.34 = 3.46; x = 15.80$
31. $m + 4.75 = 8.4; m = 3.65$

Page 121
1. $x = 4$ **3.** $b = 22$ **5.** $y = 9$ **7.** $d = 5$
9. $m = {}^-7$ **11.** $b = 25.116$ **13.** $t = {}^-27.93$
15. $x = {}^-4,347$ **17.** $x =$ Jerry's weekly
income; $\frac{x}{4} = 29$ **19.** Possible answer:
$18x = 72; x = 4$ in. **21.** $t - 26$ **23.** $10r + 4$
25. $16 + 16ab$ **27.** 6 in.

Page 125
1. $x = 5$ **3.** $z = 6$ **5.** $y = 5$ **7.** $d = 22$
9. $m = 4$ **11.** $k = 63$ **13.** $a = 13.5$
15. $m = {}^-1$ **17.** $p = 50$ **19.** $k = {}^-11$
21. $b = {}^-12$ **23.** $k = {}^-15$ **25.** $c = 1$
27. $b = 13$ **29.** added 4; $x = 2$ **31.** divided
by 2; $y = 20$ **33.** $0.15x + 29.99 = 35.54;$
$x = 37$ mi **35.** $\frac{x}{4} + 1,000 = 1,200; x = \$800$
37. $2d - 4 = 32;$ 18 mi

Page 129
1. $17 - n = 6$ **3.** $8 \div n = 2$ **5.** $x = 23$
7. $y = {}^-13$ **9.** $x = 11$ **11.** $b = 42.5$
13. $x = 2$ **15.** $z = {}^-2$ **17.** 9 prints

Chapter 7
Page 135
1. $3x, 2x$ and 5, 15; $x = 2$ **3.** $10a, 5a$ and 28,
2; $a = 6$ **5.** $x = 4$ **7.** $x = 3$ **9.** $x = 4$
11. $d = 6$ **13.** $c = {}^-2.5$ **15.** Jane; to check
the solution, substitute 5 for x. **17.** 8 yr
19. $5n = 55$ **21.** $n + 10 = 20$ **23.** $x = 3$
25. $x = 16$ **27.** $n = 4; 20$

Page 141
1. $n = 4$ **3.** $x = 3$ **5.** $n = 6$ **7.** $y = {}^-2$
9. $n = 20$ **11.** $x = 7$ **13.** $x = 1$ **15.** $n = 5$
17. $x = 3$ **19.** triangle at left: 6 m, 6 m, 5m;
triangle at right: 4 m, 7 m, 6 m **21.** 5 yr
23. Equations will vary.

Page 147
1. yes **3.** no **5.** yes **7.** addition and
multiplication **9.** addition and division

11. $z \le 11.9$ **13.** $k \ge 42$ **15.** $b > {}^-24$
17. $x < {}^-8$ **19.** $y \ge 3$ **21.** $b > {}^-28$
23. $x - 10 < 15, x < 25;$ less than \$25
25. when you multiply or divide by a negative
number **27.** $y = 3$ **29.** $y = 1$ **31.** $y = {}^-2$
33. $b = {}^-14$ **35.** 12 games

Page 149
1. $x = 1$ **3.** $b = 4$ **5.** $a = 2$ **7.** $x = 4$
9. $d = {}^-3$ **11.** $m = 5$ **13.** 22 newspapers
15. $y = {}^-3$ **17.** $b = {}^-5$ **19.** $x = {}^-2.5$
21. algebraic inequality

Chapter 8
Pages 154–155
1. 9, (4,9) **3.** 11, (6, 11) **5.** ${}^-4, (2, {}^-4)$
7. 11, (7, 11) **9.** yes **11.** no **13.** yes
15. no **17.** no **19.** $y = 15 - 3x$
21. $y = 5 + 10x$ **23.** $y = 3 + 2x$
25. $y = 3 - 4x$ **27.** $({}^-2, 25); (0, 17); (2, 9)$
29. $({}^-2, 3); (0, 9); (2, 15)$ **31.** $({}^-2, 0); (0, 6);$
$(2, 12)$ **33.** $({}^-2, 5); (0, 2); (2, {}^-1)$
35. $({}^-2, {}^-1); (0, 3); (2, 7)$ **37.** $({}^-2, 4); (0, 0);$
$(2, {}^-4)$ **39.** $y = x + 5;$ 10 hr **41.** $y = x + 9\frac{1}{2}$
45. $\ne$ **47.** $=$ **49.** $x = 17$ **51.** 494 people;
544 people

Pages 162–163
1. yes **3.** no **5.** no **7.** $({}^-1, {}^-4), (0, 0),$
$(1, 4)$ **9.** $({}^-1, {}^-9), (0, {}^-3), (1, 3)$ **11.** $({}^-1, {}^-6),$
$(0, {}^-2), (1, 2)$ **13.** $({}^-1, {}^-1), (0, 3), (1, 7)$
15. $({}^-1, 6), (0, 7), (1, 8)$ **17.** $({}^-1, {}^-0.5),$
$(0, 2.5), (1, 5.5)$ **29.** $y = 2x$ **31.** by graphing
the equation and verifying that the graph of
its solutions are points that lie in a straight
line **33.** $y \le 5$ **35.** $y > 25$ **37.** $p = 3$
39. $h = 0$ **41.** 15%

Page 166
1. no **3.** yes **5.** yes **7.** no **9.** yes
19. $\$15y$ **21.** yes; yes **23.** Possible
answers: (1, 1); (1, 2); (1, 3); (2, 1); (2, 2)
25. no; by replacing x and y with the values to
see if the inequality is true **27.** Possible
answer: $({}^-2, {}^-2)$

Page 169

1. ($^-$3, $^-$30), (0, 0), (2, 20)   3. ($^-$3, 16), (0, 10), (2, 6)   5. 6 of each type

Chapter 9

Pages 178–179

1. yes   3. no   5. yes   7. translation   11. A tessellation is an arrangement of plane figures that completely covers a plane with no gaps or overlapping.   15. ($^-$1, $^-$5), (0, 0), (1, 5)
17. ($^-$1, $^-$4), (0, $^-$3), (1, $^-$2)   19. Betty; Betty will spend $6,200 and Ed will spend $6,600.

Page 183

1. octahedron   3. dodecahedron
5. regular; 3 pentagons   13. All faces are polygons; regular polyhedron: one kind of polygon; semiregular polyhedron: more than one kind of polygon.

Page 186

1. helix   3. equiangular spiral
5. Archimedean spiral   7. equiangular spiral
9. For each turn of 45°, the point is one unit, or one circle, farther from the pole.

Page 191

1. diverging, 1 to 2   3. converging, 3 to 1
5. Length is half of previous length.   7. in top left, bottom left, and bottom right corners
9. 27; 81; 243; 3^n; $\frac{27}{64}$, $\frac{81}{256}$, $\frac{243}{1,024}$; $\left(\frac{3}{4}\right)^n$
11. converges; 4 to 3   13. 2,400   15. 375
21. about 266,800,150

Page 193

1. tessellation   3. translation   5. cube; square   7. equiangular spiral   9. scale factor   11. $\frac{64}{729}$, $\frac{256}{6,561}$, $\frac{1,024}{59,049}$

Chapter 10

Page 198

1. 37.4 lb   3. 17.1 kg   5. 108 ft   7. 1,260 in.
9. 221,760 ft   11. 8.75 yd   13. 38 in.
15. 15.16 L   17. >   19. >   21. >   23. >
25. about 379 km   27. 12 cans; 15 cans; 20 cans   29. Multiply the number of cm by the number of inches in 1 cm: 7 cm = 7 × 0.4 in. = 2.8 in.   31. 5   33. 8; 6; 12   35. 6; 8; 12
37. 432 ft^2; 168 ft

Page 201

1. T; 0.3125   3. T; 0.875   5. R; 0.8$\overline{3}$
7. T; 1.5   9. R; 3.$\overline{3}$ 11. 1$\frac{1}{4}$ 13. 4$\frac{1}{8}$ 15. $\frac{3}{16}$
17. $\frac{11}{20}$ 19. 4$\frac{2}{11}$ 21. $\frac{5}{9}$ 23. $\frac{3}{11}$ 25. $\frac{8}{11}$
27. 11 yd; 20.$\overline{3}$ yd; 26.$\overline{6}$ yd

Page 203

1. yes; no; no   3. yes; yes; yes   5. yes; yes; yes   7. no, no   9. yes; yes   11. no; no; no
13. yes; yes; no   15. yes; yes; yes   17. yes; no; yes   19. yes; yes; no

Page 207

1. $94.76, $113.00, $139.88, $172.20, $200.52
3. Pay = 10.25 × h − 6.28; $301.22; $378.10; $403.72   5. Problems will vary.   7. 20
9. 144 tiles   11. about 20%

Page 209

1. 3.75 ft   3. 45 ft   5. about 9 kg
7. about 35.2 in.   9. T; 0.5625   11. R; 0.916
13. $\frac{5}{16}$ 15. $\frac{4}{9}$ 17. yes; yes; no   19. yes; yes; no   21. yes; yes; no   23. yes; yes; no

Chapter 11

Page 213

1. arithmetic; 23, 26, 29   3. arithmetic; $^-$10, $^-$12, $^-$14   5. geometric; $^-$25.6, 102.4, $^-$409.6
7. arithmetic; 6$\frac{1}{3}$, 7$\frac{2}{3}$, 9   9. 2.5, 4.0, 5.5, 7.0
11. 3, $^-$6, 12, $^-$24   13. arithmetic
15. neither   17. 160 min, or 2 hr 40 min
19. $13,725; $10,294

Page 216

1. 3, 9, 15, 21, 27   3. 9.2, 5.2, 1.2, $^-$2.8, $^-$6.8
5. $^-$0.2, $^-$0.6, $^-$1.0   7. 10$\frac{1}{2}$, 12, 13$\frac{1}{2}$
9. 2 + 3(n − 1), or 3n − 1; 74
11. $^-$8 + 4(n − 1), or 4n − 12; 188   13. 8, 14, 20, 26   15. by writing the expression

$7 + 6(n - 1)$, or $6n + 1$, substituting the number of the term for n, and finding the value   **17.** 256   **19.** 0.0625   **21.** 6.5 ft
23. 143 lb   **25.** the case, at $3.91 per T–shirt

Page 219
1. 4   **3.** 5   **5.** $\frac{1}{2}$ **7.** diverge   **9.** diverge
11. converge   **13.** 24, 12, 6, 3; converge
15. $1 \times 7^{n-1}$, or 1×7^9; 40,353,607
17. $0.5 \times 4^{n-1}$, or 0.5×4^9; 131,072
19. $1 \times 3^{n-1}$, or 1×3^7; 2,187
21. $0.5 \times 4^{n-1}$, or 0.5×4^7; 8,192
23. $2 \times 2^{n-1}$, or 2×2^7; 256   **25.** 324
members; 972 members   **27.** $5.12;
$5,242.88

Page 222
1. 4,896; 1 more   **3.** 33,553; 1 more   **5.** 15th, 18th, 21st, and 24th terms   **7.** 16th, 20th, 24th, and 28th terms   **9.** yes   **11.** no
13. yes   **15.** 5 in. × 8 in.   **17.** $x = 1$
19. $x = 9$ **21.** T; 0.625   **23.** R; $0.8\overline{3}$
25. T; 0.45   **27.** 19°F

Page 225
1. arithmetic; 36, 44, 52   **3.** geometric; 16, 32, 64   **5.** 56, 66, 76   **7.** $3.5 + 2.5(n - 1)$, or $2.5n + 1$; 31   **9.** $2.2 + 1.2(n - 1)$, or $1.2n + 1$; 15.4   **11.** converge   **13.** $192 \times (0.5)^{n-1}$, or $192 \times (0.5)^7$; 1.5   **15.** 1.6 to 1   **17.** yes
19. no

Chapter 12
Page 234
1. yes   **3.** yes   **5.** $\frac{3}{4}$ or $\frac{4}{3}$; 13.5 ft   **7.** $\frac{3}{5}$ or $\frac{5}{3}$; 7.8 m   **9.** $A, C; \frac{1}{2}$ or 2   **11.** $\frac{1}{2.5}$ or 2.5; 7.5 in. × 12.5 in.   **13.** False; similar figures have the same shape but may have different sizes

Page 238
1. 60 ft   **3.** 20 ft   **5.** 130 ft   **7.** 2 in.
9. 6 in.   **11.** 9.5 in.   **17.** 45 in.; 30.77 in.
19. The first; in the first drawing, it took more inches to represent the actual dimensions.

21. $\frac{1}{16}$ **23.** $\frac{1}{10,000}$ **25.** geometric
27. neither   **29.** 15 and 16

Page 243
1. both   **3.** neither   **5.** about 0.67 or 1.5
7. Yes; all angles are congruent, and ratios of corresponding sides all equal 0.25 or 4.   **9.** 5
11. 1   **13.** 10.5   **19.** $264,000; $396,000

Page 245
1. scale factor or similarity ratio
3. No. The angles are not congruent.
5. 15 in.   **7.** 4 cm   **9.** 2.5 cm   **11.** no
13. All ratios are 0.5 or 2; yes.

Chapter 13
Page 249
1. reduced   **3.** enlarged   **5.** enlarged
7. enlarged   **9.** $\frac{1}{24}$ **11.** $\frac{12}{1}$, or 12   **13.** $\frac{1}{45}$
15. $\frac{1}{625}$ **17.** yes; $\frac{48}{5,280 \times 100,000} = \frac{1}{11,000,000}$

Page 252
1. 24 in.   **3.** $3\frac{3}{4}$ in.   **5.** 96 ft   **7.** $213\frac{1}{3}$ ft
9. 28 in.   **11.** 30 ft   **13.** 42 in.   **15.** $\frac{1}{60}$
17. 75 in.; 6 ft 3 in.

Page 255
1. 6 cm; 216 cubes   **3.** 12 cm; 1,728 cubes
5. 2 cm; 8 cubes   **7.** 4 cm; 64 cubes
9. $6 \times 2 \times 4$ cm; 48 cubes   **11.** $9 \times 3 \times 6$ cm; 162 cubes   **13.** The volume of the original is 8 times that of the model.   **15.** 9 in.
17. 28 m   **19.** No. Sides are not proportional.
21. yes   **23.** 8 weeks

Page 259
1. 9 in. × 12 in.; 2 in., 3 in., 4 in.   **3.** 4.5 in. × 6 in.; 1 in., 1.5 in., 2 in.   **5.** 4 cm, 12 cm, 4 cm, 12 cm; at 4 cm, 16 cm, and 20 cm   **7.** 4 cm × 16 cm   **9.** 24 in.   **11.** =   **13.** ≠   **15.** =
17. no   **19.** 1

Page 261
1. scale model   **3.** $\frac{1}{176}$ **5.** 13.5 in.   **7.** 12 ft

9. 3 cm; 27 cubes   **11.** 15 cm; 3,375 cubes
13. 24 in. $\times$ 36 in.; 9 in., 12 in., 15 in.
15. 16 in. $\times$ 24 in.; 6 in., 8 in., 10 in.

Chapter 14
Page 266
1. $n = 0.25 \times 200$; $n = 50$ **3.** $n = \frac{2}{3} \times 180$;
$n = 120$ **5.** $\frac{75}{100} = \frac{n}{360}$; $n = 270$ **7.** 1,350
9. 13.5   **11.** 52   **13.** 189   **15.** 3   **17.** 17
19. 105 questions   **21.** $47.75; $1,002.75
23. 25%   **25.** 80%   **27.** 160%
33. about 75 strides

Page 269
1. $72n = 18$; 25%   **3.** $45n = 90$; 200%
5. $\frac{n}{100} = \frac{18}{36}$; 50%   **7.** $\frac{n}{100} = \frac{40}{25}$; 160%   **9.** 80%
11. 125%   **13.** 500%   **15.** $33\frac{1}{3}$%   **17.** $52\frac{1}{2}$%
19. 175%   **21.** 30, 45, 150   **23.** 100, 50, 25
25. 79; 60   **27.** by writing an equation or a
proportion

Pages 272–273
1. $0.85n = 68$; 80   **3.** $0.56n = 39.2$; 70
5. $\frac{10}{100} = \frac{55}{n}$; 550   **7.** $\frac{180}{100} = \frac{6}{n}$; $3\frac{1}{3}$ **9.** 88
11. 160   **13.** 670   **15.** 400   **17.** 2
19. 230,000   **21.** 300, 150, 75   **23.** 40, 20, 10
25. 48 free throws   **27.** Possible answer: 65%
of what number is 300?

Pages 276–277
1. b   **3.** a   **5.** c   **7.** $\frac{1}{4}$ **9.** $\frac{3}{5}$ **11.** $\frac{1}{2}$
13. 50%   **15.** 75%   **17.** $33\frac{1}{3}$%
19. about 150   **21.** about 75   **23.** about
$33\frac{1}{3}$%   **25.** about 50%   **27.** about 250
29. about 80   **31.** about 50%   **33.** about 500
students   **35.** $8   **37.** 12   **39.** 11.6   **41.** 98

Page 279
1. 45   **3.** 1,140   **5.** 1.75   **7.** $37\frac{1}{2}$%
9. 0.5%   **11.** 200   **13.** 250   **15.** 190
17. about 80   **19.** about 400

Chapter 15
Pages 284–285
1. $50 increase   **3.** $1,600 increase
5. $500 decrease   **7.** 28% increase
9. 100% increase   **11.** 5% decrease
13. $600   **15.** $44   **17.** $390   **19.** 0
21. $14,250   **23.** 340%   **25.** $1.00
27. 100%   **29.** $x = 0.4$ **31.** $x = 20$ **33.** 40
35. 61.5   **37.** $\frac{2}{3}$ of the cake

Page 288
1. $240   **3.** $2.27   **5.** $7.09   **7.** $217
9. $576.50   **11.** $604.48   **13.** 5%   **15.** 7%
17. $5,850   **19.** 4%   **21.** Plan B; total pay
is $100 more.

Page 291
1. $15.66; $276.65   **3.** $38.97; $1,337.96
5. $3.45; $102.11   **7.** $56.33   **9.** 15%
11. $38.48   **13.** $49.18

Page 293
1. $10.92; $407.92   **3.** $2,400; $6,400
5. $500   **7.** 6 mo   **9.** 6%   **11.** the second
loan; $100 less   **13.** $x = 160$ **15.** $x = 30$
17. 400   **19.** Taxi A; $2.50 + 9(0.75) = 9.25$,
and $9.25 < 10.00$

Chapter 16
Page 305
1. Biased; it leaves out the other parts of the
country.   **3.** unbiased   **5.** about 385 in the
population   **7.** about 308 in the population
9. Randomly select visitors as they leave the
San Diego Zoo.

Page 311
11. 16   **13.** 9   **15.** 75% decrease   **17.** 200%
increase   **19.** about 4 ft

Page 315
1. about $1,500   **3.** about $1,750   **7.** an
increase over time   **9.** going out of business
11. They provide only estimates based on
trends, which may not be completely
accurate.   **13.** 36.4   **15.** 93   **17.** $5.34
19. $10.17   **21.** Good; based on the survey,
he should receive about 280 votes.

Page 319

1. about 4,095 people in the population
3. about 702 people in the population

Chapter 17

Page 324

1. 5; 5; 5   3. 4.4; 4.4; 4.4 and 6.2
5. 11.7; 11.5; 8   13. The mean, about 75; mode and median are extreme.
15. 80.6; 88; 88; median or mode because each is a middle value   17. Answers will vary.

Page 327

3. high: 48°F; low: 37.5°F   11. About 511 in the population ride the bus.   13. about 200,000,000 toys

Page 330

3. about 55,000 mi^2 5. about 12,000,000 people

Page 333

11. boy, girl; girl; boy   15. about 3.8
17. about 6.7   19. 0.25

Page 335

1. 82.6°; 87°; 87°; median or mode   3. 34.3°; 32°; no mode; mean or median

Chapter 18

Page 341

1. 6 outcomes   3. 6 outcomes   5. 30 outcomes   7. 45 combinations   9. 1,920 ways   11. The number of ways that two or more events can occur is the product of the numbers of ways that each of the events can occur separately.

Page 345

1. 6   3. 121,080,960   5. 40,314   7. 1,680
9. 380   11. 504 arrangements   13. 10
15. 66   17. 455   19. 70 pizzas
21. combinations; 45 pairs   23. In a combination the order of the items does not matter, and in a permutation the order does matter.   25. $\frac{2}{3}$ 27. $\frac{3}{4}$ 29. $\frac{1}{2}$ 31. 56.5; 51;

none   33. About 750 students like Chip's fast-food menu.

Page 348

1. $\frac{1}{3}$ 3. 0   5. $\frac{1}{8}$ 7. $\frac{6}{8} = \frac{3}{4}$ 9. $\frac{3}{8}$ 11. $\frac{1}{6}$
13. $\frac{5}{6}$ 15. $\frac{5}{6}$ 17. yes   19. No: There are more red sections than any other color.
21. $\frac{3}{3} = \frac{1}{1}; \frac{3}{3} = \frac{1}{1}$ 23. $\frac{5}{6}$

Pages 352–353

1. dependent   3. independent   5. $\frac{1}{8}$ 7. $\frac{1}{32}$
9. $\frac{1}{4}$ 11. $\frac{5}{32}$ 13. $\frac{1}{14}$ 15. $\frac{1}{10}$ 17. $\frac{5}{21}$
19. $\frac{1}{26}$ 21. P(6, 6) = $\frac{1}{6} \times \frac{1}{6} = \frac{1}{36}$
23. $\frac{42}{100} \times \frac{2}{99} = \frac{7}{825}$ 25. 25   27. 25   29. 43.75
31. 12   33. 36 monthly payments of $420

Page 355

3. 90 outcomes   5. 144 outcomes   7. 6
9. 5,040   11. 56   13. combinations; 10 teams   15. $\frac{1}{6}$ 17. $\frac{2}{6} = \frac{1}{3}$ 19. dependent; $\frac{1}{15}$

Chapter 19

Page 360

1. $\frac{13}{50}$, or 26%   3. $\frac{3}{50}$, or 6%   5. $\frac{2}{25}$, or 8%
7. $\frac{1}{6}$, or 16.7%   9. $\frac{3}{20}$, or 15%   11. 45 pieces
13. $\frac{1}{5}$, or 20%   15. $\frac{1}{5}, \frac{1}{4}, \frac{3}{10}, \frac{1}{2}$

Page 366

1. about 941 deer   3. about 156 manatees
5. No. The estimate is 2,000 trout.
7. Answers will vary.   9. 34%   11. 37.5%
13. 24   15. 1,680   17. 1,814,400   19. no

Pages 368–369

1. $\frac{3}{16}$, or 18.75%   3. $\frac{3}{16}$, or 18.75%   5. $\frac{5}{16}$, or 31.25%   7. $\frac{1}{2}$, or 50%   9. $\frac{3}{8}$, or 37.5%
11. about $\frac{4}{112}$, or 4%   13. about $\frac{96}{112}$, or 86%
15. $\frac{314}{1,250} = \frac{157}{625}$, or about 25%   17. 113°

19. 75° **21.** $\frac{8}{20} = \frac{2}{5}$ **23.** $\frac{7}{20}$ **25.** $150

Chapter 20

Pages 380–381
1. 50° **3.** 130° **5.** 130° **7.** ∠1 and ∠5, ∠3 and ∠7, ∠2 and ∠6, ∠4 and ∠8
9. ∠1 and ∠8, ∠2 and ∠7
11. perpendicular **13.** perpendicular
17. They are parallel. **19.** 1 street, or 2 streets if the street names change at the intersection **25.** $\frac{1}{5}$, or 20% **27.** 18.8 cm

Page 387
7. 1.3 km; by the SAS rule, $\triangle BPC$ and $\triangle APD$ are congruent. **11.** $x = 9$ **13.** $x = 14$
15. $\frac{3}{8}$, or 37.5% **17.** $32\frac{1}{4}$ mi

Page 390
9. 2 to 3 **11.** Yes. Corresponding sides will be proportional.

Page 393
5. scalene: 2; isosceles: 1; equilateral: 3
9. yes **19.** The bisectors in each triangle intersect at one point.

Page 395
1. transversal **11.** $\overline{XZ}$ is 7.5 cm; $\overline{YZ}$ is 6 cm

Chapter 21

Page 403
1. 12 ways **3.** 4 ways **5.** translation
7. reflection or rotation **9.** 24 positions

Page 406
9. $A'(1,1)$, $B'(1,2)$, $C'(2,1)$ **11.** $A'(4,4)$, $B'(20,4)$, $C'(24,24)$, $D'(8,24)$ **17.** 50, 25, 12.5
19. $\frac{1}{2}, \frac{1}{4}, \frac{1}{8}$ **23.** 16 ft

Page 411
3. Number is two times the previous number plus 2 **9.** 20% **11.** SSS **13.** SAS
15. $0.64

Page 413
1. $A'(^-2,^-2)$, $B'(1,^-5)$, $C'(3,^-2)$ **3.** $A'(4,^-5)$,

$B'(7,^-2)$, $C'(4,0)$ **5.** 4 ways **7.** dilation
9. $A'(1.5,^-1.5)$, $B'(1.5,6)$, $C'(9,4.5)$
11. number at previous stage plus 3

Chapter 22
Page 418
1. yes **3.** 9 in. × 18 in. **5.** about 56%
7. 8 ft. × 10 ft.; 80 ft.^{2}

Page 423
9. 4 parallelograms **11.** 4 parallelograms
13. $D'(^-1,^-2)$, $E'(^-1,^-1)$, $F'(1,0)$, $G'(1,^-2)$
15. 320 lights

Page 426
7. $A'(6,6)$, $B'(9,6)$, $C'(9,12)$
9. $451.20; $1,004.80

Page 429
1. 9 in. × 12 in. **9.** perspective

Chapter 23
Page 438
1. can't tell **3.** can't tell exactly **9.** B; the graph shows a straight line. **13.** 1990-1991
17. 10, 15

Page 441
1. Table C **3.** Table D

Page 443
5. about 7.5 mph **7.** 12 pencils, 8 notebooks or 55 pencils, 1 notebook **9.** about $2.55

Page 446
1. yes **3.** between 25 and 55 **7.** increase hours of practice **11.** $x = 18$ **13.** $x = ^-3$
17. 20 min

Page 449
1. Runner B slowed down. **3.** 8 sec sooner
5. Graph C **7.** Graph B **9.** about 6,500

Chapter 24
Pages 455–456
1. $\frac{3}{3}$, or 1 **3.** $\frac{^-2}{3}$ **5.** $\frac{1}{2}$ **7.** $\frac{^-1}{2}$ **9.** $\frac{7}{4}$
11. 5; 5 **13.** 8;4 **15.** 5; $^-$10 **17.** 3; $^-$18

19. 4; 5   **21.** ⁻4; ⁻5   **23.** $\frac{1}{2}$; 5   **25.** $\frac{-1}{2}$; 4

27. $\frac{5}{7}$; ⁻3   **29.** $y = 2x + 2$; 2; 2

31. $y = \frac{-2}{5}x + 2$; $\frac{-2}{5}$; 2   **33.** $y = \frac{-3}{4}x - 5$

35. $y = ^-3x - 4$ **39.** no   **41.** yes   **43.** yes
45. no   **47.** 19; 18.5; 24   **49.** 2,135.4 yen per
$20.00

Page 465
1. yes   **3.** no   **5.** 2; ⁻2; $f(x) = 2x - 2$
7. ⁻2; 4; $f(x) = ^-2x + 4$ **9.** $f(x) = 4x$; straight
line passes through (0,0) (1,4) (3,12); $28
11. It is if this is true: when domain values
increase by fixed amounts, the resulting range
values change by fixed amounts.

Pages 468–469
1. linear   **3.** nonlinear   **5.** nonlinear
7. nonlinear   **9.** linear   **11.** linear
13. nonlinear   **15.** {(⁻2,3), (0,⁻1), (1,0), (2,3),
(3,8)}   **17.** {(⁻2,⁻2), (0,⁻10), (1,⁻8), (2,⁻2),
(3,8)   **19.** $0.55; $1.01   **21.** Both the weight
and the cost are positive numbers.   **23.** Look
at the graph, and look at the exponent of the
variable in the equation.   **25.** ⁻1; 15
27. 0; ⁻4   **29.** positive   **31.** no correlation
33. Roosevelt: 22,654,258; Hoover: 15,897,725

Page 471
1. 4, ⁻5   **3.** $\frac{-2}{7}$, 2   **5.** (0,1)   **7.** (0,⁻1)

9. (⁻2,⁻5)   **11.** yes   **13.** yes   **15.** (0,5), (1,8),
(2,11)   **17.** (0,3), (1,5), (2,7)   **19.** nonlinear
21. linear   **23.** nonlinear   **25.** linear

Chapter 25
Page 477
1. binomial   **3.** binomial   **5.** trinomial
7. $8y^3$, ⁻15   **9.** $5k^2$, ⁻6k, ⁻9   **11.** 63   **13.** 12
15. 27   **17.** 2   **19.** ⁻77   **21.** ⁻5   **23.** 9
25. ⁻15   **27.** $1.24   **29.** Substitute ⁻4 for x.
Then use the order of operations.   **31.** 5
33. ⁻17   **35.** ⁻5   **37.** ⁻6; 4   **39.** ⁻3; ⁻9
41. $3m \geq 126$, $m \geq 42$; $42

Page 480
1. x^2, $2x^2$ **3.** k, ⁻2k   **5.** 4, ⁻5   **7.** no; $x^2 + x$

9. yes   **11.** yes   **13.** yes   **15.** no; $^-4k^2 +$
$k + 5$ **17.** yes   **19.** yes   **21.** no; $2y^4 + y^2 -$
$y + 5$ **23.** no; $4x^2 - x + 12$ **25.** $k^5 + 3k^4 -$
$k^2 + k - 5$ **27.** $2y^2 + 9y + 5$ **29.** $3x^5 +$
$4x^4 + x^2 - 4x$ **31.** $2t^3 + 3t - 16$ **33.** $4x^3 +$
$4x^2 + 3x$ **35.** $9y^4 - y^2 - 2$ **37.** $2x^2 + 8x +$
4   **39.** $2x + 8, 2x + 5$

Page 483
1. $7x + 7$ **3.** $3x^2 - x + 4$ **5.** $x^2 + 4x - 2$
7. $10b$ **9.** $2x^2 + 5x - 12$ **11.** $3b^2 - 3b - 1$
13. $7y^2 - 11y - 6$ **15.** $^-2x^2 + 16x - 26$
17. $5n^2 + 30n + 5$; $280   **19.** $7x^2 + 3x$
21. $12 + 3$ **23.** ⁻8 + 12   **25.** $11 + 5$
27. nonlinear   **29.** linear   **31.** 54, 55, 56

Page 485
1. $3x^2 + 7x$ **3.** $^-2x^2 + 4x - 7$ **5.** $2a^2 -$
$3a + 10$ **7.** $8y^2 - y - 9$ **9.** $3x^2 - 2$
11. $^-4x^2 - 2x + 1$ **13.** $^-2c^2 - 3c + 6$
15. $4x^2 - 5x - 1$ **17.** $b^2 - 8b - 5$
19. $^-4y^2 - y - 8$ **21.** $8x^2 + 6x - 2$
23. $9s + 45s$; $66.96   **25.** The answer is 0.
Possible example: $^-x^2 - ^-x^2 = ^-x^2 + x^2 = 0$

Page 487
1. polynomial   **3.** ⁻256   **5.** 22   **7.** ⁻128
9. $x^3 + 10x^2 + 4x + 15$ **11.** $4x^5 - 7x^3 +$
$3x^2 - 3x + 10$ **13.** $11b^2 + 3b - 1$
15. $8y^2 - 11y - 2$ **17.** $^-3x^2 - 4x + 6$
19. $2x^2 - 2x + 4$ **21.** $a^2 - 4a + 3$

Chapter 26
Page 496
5. 21 connections   **7.** 36 connections
9. 21 direct routes; 105 routes
11. A network is a figure made up of vertices
and edges; possible example: finding the
shortest route for running errands.   **13.** 8.5
15. 18.7   **17.** $9x^2 + 6x + 2$ **19.** 96 pieces

Page 500
1. 5   **3.** 3   **5.** 558.34 m   **7.** 0.0345 m
9. 18.1 m   **11.** 20 ft   **13.** 130 m   **15.** 75 in.
17. 2; 23 ft   **19.** The zero in 230 is not just a
place holder. The zeros in 0.023 are just place
holders.

Page 505

1. 2,411.52 cm^3 ≈ 2,000 cm^3 **3.** 2,260.8 cm^3 ≈ 2,300 cm^3 **5.** 904.32 in.^{3} ≈ 900 in.^{3}
7. 167.47 cm^3 ≈ 200 cm^3
9. 12,763.58 cm^3 ≈ 13,000 cm^3
11,625.42 cm^3 ≈ 12,000 cm^3
11. 4,186.6667 m^3 ≈ 4,190 m^3

Pages 508–509

1. two circles; 113.04 cm^2 ≈ 100 cm^2 each; lateral surface: 376.8 cm^2 ≈ 400 cm^2
3. rectangles: 28 in.^{2}; 28 in.^{2}; 35 in.^{2}; 35 in.^{2}; 20 in.^{2}; 20 in.^{2} **5.** 144 ft^2 ≈ 100 ft^2 **7.** 813.26 cm^2 ≈ 800 cm^2 **9.** 75.36 in.^{2} ≈ 80 in.^{2}
11. 168 in.^{2} ≈ 200 in.^{2}; $11.76   **13.** Surface area is the sum of the areas of all the surfaces of a solid figure. Volume is the number of cubic units that can fit inside a solid figure.
15. 34 m; 72 m^2 **17.** 48 ft; 143 ft^2
19. $6a^2 - 3a + 1$ **21.** $2x^2 + x + 10$
23. 120 sec, or 2 min

Page 511

1. network   **3.** 66 connections
5. 16.8 m ≈ 17 m   **7.** $3,696   **9.** 200.96 in.^{3} ≈ 200 in.^{3} **11.** 79.128 m^2 ≈ 79 m^2

Chapter 27
Page 516

1. 20 ft^2 **3.** 32 ft^2 **5.** 27 ft^2 **7.** 30 ft
9. 26 ft   **11.** 4 in. × 4 in.   **13.** 5 cm × 5 cm
15. 10 in. × 10 in.   **17.** 9 cm × 9 cm
19. 10 ft × 10 ft   **21.** Possible answers: 1 in. × 9 in., 2 in. × 8 in., 3 in. × 7 in., 4 in. × 6 in., 5 in. × 5 in., 6 in. × 4 in., 7 in. × 3 in., 8 in. × 2 in., 9 in. × 1 in.; 5 in. × 5 in.
25. 700   **27.** 230   **29.** 0.5 cm   **31.** $\frac{1}{2}$ in.
33. 0.005 cm   **35.** about 706.5 in.^{2}

Page 519

1. 310; 560; 1,060; 2,060   **3.** 24 yd, 36 yd^2; 48 yd, 144 yd^2 **5.** 30.8 cm; 40 cm^2; 61.6 cm, 160 cm^2 **7.** 32 ft, 60 ft^2; 16 ft, 15 ft^2 **9.** 21 ft, 27 ft^2; 10.5 ft, 6.75 ft^2 **11.** 11 dimes, 16 nickels, 33 quarters   **13.** 480   **15.** 5,376

17. 294 in.^{2} **19.** 450 cm^2 **21.** $P = p + s$; $A = \frac{1}{4}ps$

Page 525

1. 1,728 cm^3; 864 cm^3 **3.** about 904.32 in.^{3}; about 452.16 in.^{3} **5.** 110 in.^{3}; 880 in.^{3}
7. about 763.02 in.^{3}; about 6,104.16 in.^{3}
9. 560 cm^3; 70 cm^3 **11.** about 169.56 cm^3; about 21.20 cm^3 **13.** no change
15. 4 in. × 1 in. × 1 in.

Page 527

1. 3 ft × 3 ft   **3.** 2 in. × 2 in.   **5.** 8 ft × 8 ft
7. 104 in.; 672 in.^{2} **9.** 28 in.; 40 in.^{2}
11. 6 in. × 6 in. × 1 in.; 36 in.^{3} **13.** 240 in.^{3}; 480 in.^{3} **15.** 1,570 in.^{3}

Chapter 28
Page 531

1. about 42 ft   **3.** about 27 ft   **5.** about 204 ft   **7.** Saturn: about 363 ft; Mercury: about 83 ft   **9.** about 48 in. long   **11.** 3   **13.** 14
15. 0.8   **17.** 9 yd × 9 yd   **19.** 25 in. × 25 in.
21. 1,725 fiction; 1,035 nonfiction; 1,380 reference

Page 534

1. 5 m   **3.** 15 m   **5.** 5.7 m   **7.** 12.5 m
9. 18.4 ft   **11.** 8.2 ft   **13.** 50.4 yd
15. 1,000,000   **17.** 200   **19.** 2 cm × 4 cm; 12 cm; 8 cm^2 **21.** 12 ft × 25 ft; 74 ft; 300 ft^2
23. odd, even, odd

Page 536

1. 209.4 mi   **3.** 143.6 km   **5.** 21.2 km
7. 224.4 mi   **9.** 219.7 mi

Page 539

1. 0.57   **3.** 3.73   **5.** 25 cm   **7.** 29.4 ft
9. 66.6 cm   **11.** 127.9 m   **13.** 36 ft
15. 10 ft

Page 541

1. 28 m   **3.** 19.2 m   **5.** 552 ft   **7.** 50 cm
9. 8.3 m   **11.** 91.9 mi   **13.** tangent
15. 13.8 ft

INDEX

perimeter, 423
place value, 207
prediction, 315
prisms, 496
rates, 51, 107, 216, 293, 387
rational numbers, 222
ratios, 58, 147, 259, 438
scheduling, 509
sequences, 266
similar figures, 114
speed, 496, 509
sports, 147, 293
square roots, 191
surveys, 345
taxes, 19
weather, 179

Problem-solving strategies
Account for All Possibilities, 7, 338–339
Act It Out, 3, 362–363
Draw a Diagram, 2, 419–420
Find a Pattern, 8, 64–65
Guess and Check, 5, 156–157
Make a Model, 4, 520–521
Make a Table/Chart/Graph, 9, 442–443
Solve a Simpler Problem, 10, 306–307
Use a Formula, 11, 501–502
Work Backward, 6, 126–127
Write an Equation/Proportion, 12, 136–137

Problem-Solving Tips, 73, 129, 149, 169, 319, 355, 371, 429, 449, 511, 527

Products
cross, 45, 233, 241, 251
of powers, 24–25
See also Multiplication

Projects *See* Team-Up Projects

Properties
of addition, 106, H11
Associative, 106, H11
Commutative, 106, 132, 139, H11
Distributive, 106, 134, 139, 140, H11
Identity, H11
of multiplication, H11
of one, H11
of zero, H11

Proportions
and percent problems, 265–266, 267–269, 271–273
and ratios, 44–46, 282, H16
scale models, 250–252
similar figures, 232–234, 235, 241–243
and simulations, 364–366
solving, H17

Protractors, 378–381, 384–387, 391–393, 537, H21

Pyramids
shape of, 415, H23

square, 415, 416
surface area of, 506–509
volume of, 504–505

Pythagoras, 218, 533
Pythagorean Property, 532–534, 535–536, 540
Pythagorean triples, 540

Q

Quadrants, H29
Quadrilaterals
defined, H22
parallelograms, H22
rectangles, H22
rhombuses, H22
squares, H22
trapezoids, H22
Quartiles, 325–327
Quotients
of powers, 24–25
See also Division

R

Radical symbols, 26
Radius, H87
Random numbers, 361, 362–363
Ranges
of data, 325–327, H30
for relations, 460–462
Rates, 47–48, 52, 286, 292
Rational numbers
adding, 76–78, 88
defined, 17–19
dividing 83–84
in equations, 117–118, 140–141
in inequalities, 144–147
multiplying, 81–82
order of operations, 86–87, 88, 98
subtracting, 79–80, 88
writing, 29
Ratios
equivalent, 44–46, H16
estimating, 49–51
Golden, 50–51, 221–222
and percents, 41–43, 52, 282, 296
and proportions, 44–46, 282, H16
scales, 189–191, 233–234, 248–249, 260, 404–405
similarity, 233–234
simplest form, 44–46
slopes, 452, 453–456, 470
trigonometric, 537, 538–539, H38, H87, H88
Rays, H20

Real-Life Links
Business, 200, 212, 314, 368, 437
Career, 57, 99, 145, 251, 286, 386, 417, 518
Computer, 17, 178, 206, 233, 389, 405, 425, 495
Consumer, 41, 86, 106, 120, 283, 292, 340, 484
General, 124, 160, 289, 402, 455, 503, 517
Sports, 18, 45, 79, 102, 344, 458, 515
Real numbers, 29–31
Reasoning
See Logical Reasoning
Reciprocals, H15
Rectangles
area of, 501–502, H25, H87
defined, H22
Golden, 221–222, 223
squares, H22
Rectangular prisms, 415, 416, 421, 503–505, 506–509, 522, H23
Reflections, 397, 400–401, 402–403, 410–411, 412, H23
Regular polygons
equilateral triangles, H22
hexagons, 176, H22
octagons, H22
pentagons, 180, H22
perimeters of, 100, 515
squares, 180, H22
Regular polyhedrons
cube, 180–183
dodecahedron, 180–183
icosahedron, 180–183
octahedron, 180–183
tetrahedron, 180–183
Relations
domain, 460–462
functions, 460–462, 463–469
range, 460–462
vertical line test, 460–462
Repeating decimals, 29–31, 199–201, H9
Review
Chapter, 33, 53, 73, 89, 109, 129, 149, 169, 193, 209, 225, 245, 261, 279, 297, 319, 335, 355, 371, 395, 413, 429, 449, 471, 487, 511, 527, 541
Cumulative, 93, 173, 229, 301, 375, 433, 491, 545
Mixed, 19, 31, 39, 51, 58, 71, 78, 84, 101, 107, 114, 121, 135, 147, 155, 163, 179, 191, 198, 207, 216, 222, 238, 243, 255, 259, 266, 277, 285, 293, 311, 315, 327, 333, 345, 353, 366, 369, 381, 387, 406, 411, 423, 426, 438, 446, 456, 469, 477, 483, 496, 509, 516, 519, 531, 534
Study Guide & Review, 90, 170, 226, 298, 372, 430, 488, 542

maximum, 520–521, 526
of prisms, 503–505, 522, H25
of pyramids, 504–505
of spheres, 504–505

W

Weight, H86
What Did I Learn?, 92, 172, 228, 300, 374, 432, 490, 544
Whole numbers, 16–19
Withholding tax, 290–291
Word power
accuracy, 498
algebraic expression, 96
algebraic inequality, 142
annually, 294
Archimedean spiral, 184
arithmetic sequence, 212
back-to-back stem-and-leaf plot, 308
basic unit, 176
bisect, 382
box-and-whisker graph, 325
central tendency, 322
coefficient, 98
combination, 342
combine like terms, 106
commission, 286
commission rate, 286
common difference, 212
common ratio, 212
compound interest, 294
consecutive integers, 187
converge, 188
cross section, 427
Density Property, 29
dependent events, 350
dilation, 404
direct variation, 447
diverge, 188
domain, 460
edge, 494
equation, 96
equiangular spiral, 184
equivalent, 98
evaluate, 98
even vertex, 497
exterior angle, 378
extrapolation, 312
factorial, 342
Fibonacci sequence, 220
first quartile, 325
fractal, 188
function, 460
Fundamental Counting Principle, 340
geometric sequence, 212
Golden Ratio, 49, 220

Golden Rectangle, 220
graph of an equation, 160
helix, 184
horizon line, 424
hypotenuse, 532
image, 398
independent events, 350
inequality, 96
integers, 16
interest, 292
interior angle, 378
interpolation, 312
irrational number, 29
lateral surface, 506
leg, 532
like terms, 105
linear equation, 160
linear function, 463
line of best fit, 329
mathematical probability, 346
monomial, 474
negative correlation, 329
network, 494
no correlation, 329
nonlinear function, 466
numerical expression, 96
odds, 44
odd vertex, 497
parabola, 167
percent of decrease, 282
percent of increase, 282
perfect square, 26
permutation, 342
perspective, 424
Platonic solid, 180
polynomial, 475
population, 304
positive correlation, 329
principal, 292
proportion, 44
proportional, 232
Pythagorean Property, 532
quarterly, 294
range, 460
rate, 47
rate of interest, 292
rational number, 16
real numbers, 29
relation, 460
sales tax, 289
sample, 304
sample space, 338
scale drawing, 236
scale factor, 188
scale model, 248
scatterplot, 329
scientific notation, 20

second quartile, 325
self-similarity, 239
semiannually, 294
semiregular polyhedron, 180
side-by-side histogram, 308
Sierpinski triangle, 188
significant digits, 498
similar figures, 232
similarity ratio, 232
simplest form, 106
simplify, 106
simplify a polynomial, 478
slant height, 506
slope, 452
slope-intercept form, 453
solution, 115
solution of an equation with two variables, 152
solution of the system, 457
spiral, 184
spirolateral, 187
standard form, 478
substitute, 115
surface area, 506
system of equations, 457
term, 105, 212
tessellation, 176
third quartile, 325
time, 292
transversal, 378
tree diagram, 338
trigonometric ratio, 537
trig ratio, 537
two-step equation, 122
unit price, 47
unit rate, 47
vanishing point, 424
variability, 325
variable, 96
vertex, 494
vertical line test, 460
withholding tax, 289
x-intercept, 453
y-intercept, 453
Wright, Frank Lloyd, 419
Write About It, 19, 23, 25, 27, 31, 39, 43, 46, 48, 51, 58, 61, 65, 68, 71, 78, 80, 84, 87, 92, 97, 104, 107, 114, 118, 121, 125, 135, 137, 141, 143, 147, 155, 157, 159, 163, 166, 172, 179, 183, 186, 191, 198, 201, 203, 207, 213, 216, 219, 222, 228, 234, 238, 240, 243, 249, 252, 255, 259, 266, 269, 273, 277, 285, 288, 291, 293, 300, 305, 307, 311, 315, 324, 327, 330, 333, 339, 341, 345, 348, 353, 360, 366, 369, 374, 381, 383, 387, 390, 393, 401, 403, 406, 411, 418, 420, 423, 426, 432, 438, 441, 446, 456, 459, 462, 465,

469, 477, 480, 483, 485, 490, 496, 500,
502, 505, 509, 516, 519, 521, 525, 531, 534,
536, 539, 544

X

x-axis, H29
x-coordinate, 62, 158, H29
x-intercept, 453–456, H42

Y

Yards, 196–198, H86
y-axis, H29
y-coordinates, 62, 158, H29
y-intercept, 453–456, H42
Years, H86

Z

Zero
  as exponent, 20, 69, 479
  Property of, H11

http://www.hbschool.com

http://www.hbschool.com